OCT - - 2009

ESSENTIAL SOUTH

1st edition

Where to Stay and Eat
for All Budgets

Must-See Sights
and Local Secrets

Ratings You Can Trust

Fodor's Travel Publications   New York, Toronto, London, Sydney, Auckland
www.fodors.com

FODOR'S ESSENTIAL SOUTH

Editor: Salwa Jabado

Editorial Contributors: Rachel Klein, Jess Moss, Jennifer DePrima

Writers: Liz Biro, Carissa Bluestone, Michelle Delio, Mary Erskine, Paul A. Greenberg, Rena Havner Philips, Molly Jahncke, Alice Leccese Powers, Susan MacCallum-Whitcomb, Gary McKechnie, Amy McKeever, Amber Nimocks, Donna M. Owens, David Parker Jr., Kandace Power Graves, Michael Ream, Susan Reigler, Lan Sluder, Eileen Robinson Smith, Kerry Speckman, Sue Strachan, Christine Van Dusen, Ginger Warder

Production Editor: Jennifer DePrima

Maps & Illustrations: David Lindroth, Mark Stroud, *cartographers*; Bob Blake, Rebecca Baer, *map editors*; William Wu, *information graphics*

Design: Fabrizio La Rocca, *creative director*; Guido Caroti, Siobhan O'Hare, *art directors*; Tina Malaney, Chie Ushio, Ann McBride, Jessica Walsh, *designers*; Melanie Marin, *senior picture editor*

Cover Photo: (Cajun Crawfish): Terry Poche/Shutterstock. (Jockey, Kentucky Derby): Kanwarjit Singh Boparai/Shutterstock. (Gas lamp, Savannah): David Kay/Shutterstock. (Civil War cannon on Manassas battlefield, Virginia): J. Norman Reid/Shutterstock. (Natchez plantation, Mississippi): J C Hix/Shutterstock. (Cape Hatteras Lighthouse, Outer Banks, North Carolina): William Britten/iStockphoto. (Mint Julep): John Clines/Shutterstock. (Magnolia blossom): Jeremy Smith/Shutterstock

Production Manager: Amanda Bullock

1st edition

ISBN 978–1–4000–0339–6

ISSN 1946-3057

SPECIAL SALES

This book is available at special discounts for bulk purchases for sales promotions or premiums. Special editions, including personalized covers, excerpts of existing books, and corporate imprints, can be created in large quantities for special needs. For more information, write to Special Markets/Premium Sales, 1745 Broadway, MD 6-2, New York, New York 10019, or e-mail specialmarkets@randomhouse.com.

AN IMPORTANT TIP & AN INVITATION

Although all prices, opening times, and other details in this book are based on information supplied to us at press time, changes occur all the time in the travel world, and Fodor's cannot accept responsibility for facts that become outdated or for inadvertent errors or omissions. So **always confirm information when it matters**, especially if you're making a detour to visit a specific place. Your experiences—positive and negative—matter to us. If we have missed or misstated something, **please write to us**. We follow up on all suggestions. Contact the Essential South editor at editors@fodors.com or c/o Fodor's at 1745 Broadway, New York, NY 10019.

PRINTED IN THE UNITED STATES OF AMERICA

10 9 8 7 6 5 4 3 2 1

Be a Fodor's Correspondent

Your opinion matters. It matters to us. It matters to your fellow Fodor's travelers, too. And we'd like to hear it. In fact, we need to hear it.

When you share your experiences and opinions, you become an active member of the Fodor's community. That means we'll not only use your feedback to make our books better, but we'll publish your names and comments whenever possible. Throughout our guides, look for "Word of Mouth," excerpts of your unvarnished feedback.

Here's how you can help improve Fodor's for all of us.

Tell us when we're right. We rely on local writers to give you an insider's perspective. But our writers and staff editors—who are the best in the business—depend on you. Your positive feedback is a vote to renew our recommendations for the next edition.

Tell us when we're wrong. We're proud that we update most of our guides every year. But we're not perfect. Things change. Hotels cut services. Museums change hours. Charming cafés lose charm. If our writer didn't quite capture the essence of a place, tell us how you'd do it differently. If any of our descriptions are inaccurate or inadequate, we'll incorporate your changes in the next edition and will correct factual errors at fodors.com immediately.

Tell us what to include. You probably have had fantastic travel experiences that aren't yet in Fodor's. Why not share them with a community of like-minded travelers? Maybe you chanced upon a beach or bistro or B&B that you don't want to keep to yourself. Tell us why we should include it. And share your discoveries and experiences with everyone directly at fodors.com. Your input may lead us to add a new listing or highlight a place we cover with a "Highly Recommended" star or with our highest rating, "Fodor's Choice."

Give us your opinion instantly at our feedback center at www.fodors.com/feedback. You may also e-mail editors@fodors.com with the subject line "Essential South Editor." Or send your nominations, comments, and complaints by mail to Essential South Editor, Fodor's, 1745 Broadway, New York, NY 10019.

You and travelers like you are the heart of the Fodor's community. Make our community richer by sharing your experiences. Be a Fodor's correspondent.

Happy Traveling!

Tim Jarrell, Publisher

CONTENTS

ABOUT
THIS BOOK

Our Ratings

Sometimes you find terrific travel experiences and sometimes they just find you. But usually the burden is on you to select the right combination of experiences. That's where our ratings come in.

As travelers we've all discovered a place so wonderful that its worthiness is obvious. And sometimes that place is so unique that superlatives don't do it justice: you just have to be there to know. These sights, properties, and experiences get our highest rating, **Fodor's Choice**, indicated by orange stars throughout this book.

Black stars highlight sights and properties we deem **Highly Recommended**, places that our writers, editors, and readers praise again and again for consistency and excellence.

By default, there's another category: any place we include in this book is by definition worth your time, unless we say otherwise. And we will.

Disagree with any of our choices? Care to nominate a place or suggest that we rate one more highly? Visit our feedback center at www.fodors.com/feedback.

Budget Well

Hotel and restaurant price categories from ¢ to $$$$ are defined in the opening pages of each chapter. For attractions, we always give standard adult admission fees; reductions are usually available for children, students, and senior citizens. Want to pay with plastic? **AE, D, DC, MC, V** following restaurant and hotel listings indicate whether American Express, Discover, Diners Club, MasterCard, and Visa are accepted.

Restaurants

Unless we state otherwise, restaurants are open for lunch and dinner daily. We mention dress only when there's a specific requirement and reservations only when they're essential or not accepted—it's always best to book ahead.

Hotels

Hotels have private bath, phone, TV, and air-conditioning unless we specify otherwise. They may operate on the Continental Plan (CP, with a Continental breakfast), Breakfast Plan (BP, with a full breakfast), or Modified American Plan (MAP, with breakfast and dinner). We always list facilities but not whether you'll be charged an extra fee to use them, so when pricing accommodations, find out what's included.

Many Listings	
★	Fodor's Choice
★	Highly recommended
⊠	Physical address
⊹	Directions
⊕	Mailing address
☎	Telephone
⊟	Fax
⊕	On the Web
✎	E-mail
🖂	Admission fee
☉	Open/closed times
Ⓜ	Metro stations
⊟	Credit cards
Hotels & Restaurants	
🏨	Hotel
⇗	Number of rooms
⚖	Facilities
❑⊙❑	Meal plans
✗	Restaurant
⚖	Reservations
⤡	Smoking
ⓌⓎ	BYOB
✗🏨	Hotel with restaurant that warrants a visit
Outdoors	
𝚵	Golf
⚠	Camping
Other	
ⓒ	Family-friendly
⇨	See also
⊠	Branch address
☞	Take note

WHEN TO GO

Although the terrain is vast and conditions vary, spring is generally the most attractive time to visit this part of the United States. Throughout the South cherry blossoms are followed by azaleas, dogwoods, camellias, and apple blossoms from April into May, and temperatures remain pleasant. Summers are hot and humid in many areas, but local calendars are crowded with tempting festivals and sporting events. Fall can also be delightful, with flaming autumn foliage on display in the mountains; and winter, which is moderate for the most part, offers a welcome respite for Northern "snowbirds."

One caveat: given the number of high-profile tropical storms that have blown through the southernmost coastal regions in recent years, it's worth remembering that hurricane season officially begins June 1 and ends November 30. Severe storms can dampen your plans, disrupt public services, or worse. If you're advised about a Hurricane Watch before departing, consider postponing your trip.

Climate

In winter, temperatures generally average in the low 40s inland, in the 60s by the shore. Summer temperatures (modified by mountains in some destinations, by water in others), range from the high 70s to the mid-80s to the low 90s.

The following are average daily maximum and minimum temperatures for key Southern cities.

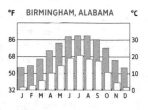

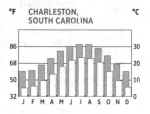

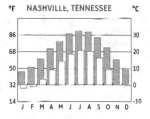

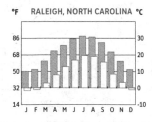

WHAT'S WHERE

The following numbers refer to chapters in the book.

1 Alabama. Within driving distance of cities like Birmingham, Montgomery, or Mobile, you can hike pine-green hills, play on beaches lapped by emerald-green water, and golf on the manicured greens of the Robert Trent Jones Trail. This state has an important past, too. Occupied by Native Americans for 8,000 years, it was the Cradle of the Confederacy during the Civil War and a hotbed of activity in the civil rights era.

2 Florida. You can hit the pause button in moss-draped Tallahassee and Panhandle towns like Apalachicola, where people still sip sweet tea on porch swings, or fast forward in Daytona Beach (site of the Daytona Speedway) and at the Space Coast (home to Kennedy Space Center). There is also ample opportunity for beach time, and top picks include Grayton and Cocoa beaches.

3 Georgia. Atlanta, having once burned, is now certifiably hot thanks to a vibrant arts scene and other New South amenities. Conversely, Savannah—which has America's largest preservation district—epitomizes the Old South. Underneath the latter lies a 100-mi coast where you can explore the Golden Isles (Jekyll, Sea, and St. Simons), as

well as the unspoiled expanses of Cumberland Island National Seashore, then veer inland to the swamps of Okefenokee National Wildlife Refuge.

4 Kentucky. Known for the "Greatest Two Minutes in Sports," the Bluegrass State is horse country through and through. Even if you're not visiting for the Kentucky Derby, there are plenty of spots to commune with the racehorses from Louisville to Lexington, never mind opportunities for sampling the world-famous bourbon and fine local cuisine.

5 Louisiana. Bewitching, beleaguered New Orleans understandably garners the lion's share of Louisiana tourists. A wealth of significant buildings and fine restaurants, fabulous nightlife, and lively events (Mardi Gras being the most notable) combine to create a city that feels both hip and historic. The surrounding territory has its own distinct appeal. North and west of New Orleans, the mansions of Plantation Country await. Due west, Cajun Country tempts visitors with crawfish, fais-do-do dances, and French fiddle music.

6 Mississippi. There is more to Mississippi than Civil War battlefields and partisan tales of ancestors fighting valiantly for the Confederacy.

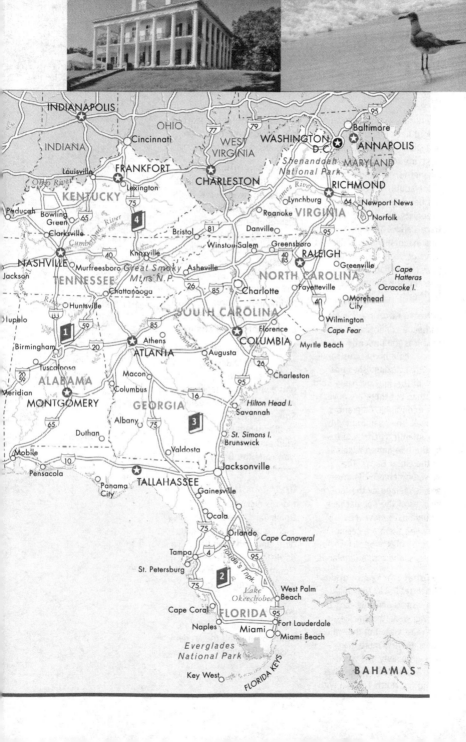

WHAT'S WHERE

The northern college town of Oxford lures literature lovers and Ole Miss alumni; to the west, the Mississippi Delta is a magnet for blues lovers; and, in the south, the Gulf Coast has beaches and casinos for hedonists. The scenic Natchez Trace Parkway, meanwhile, cuts diagonally across the heart of Dixie, passing Tupelo (Elvis's birthplace), Jackson (the capital), and antebellum Natchez.

7 North Carolina. Die-hard barbecue connoisseurs contend it is the preferred cut of pork (whole hog versus shoulder) that distinguishes one part of the Tar Heel State from another, but there are obvious geographic differences as well. The east, fronted by the Atlantic, is characterized by the tide-battered islands of the Outer Banks. The west, bordered by Tennessee, is marked by the forested inclines of the Appalachian Mountains. Sandwiched between them are cosmopolitan cities, world-class golf courses, and fertile farmlands.

8 Great Smoky Mountains National Park. Nine million visitors annually can't be wrong; while the Smokies is the most visited of the national parks, there is more than enough beauty and woodland in the 814 square miles along the North Carolina and Tennessee border for peaceful communion with nature or rambunctious family fun.

9 South Carolina. Anchored by Myrtle Beach in the north and Hilton Head in the south, the shore is punctuated by resorts offering everything from family entertainment to upscale golf-and-spa experiences. For a cultural fix, set your GPS for Charleston. This Lowcountry port has museums and galleries galore and hosts the Spoleto Festival USA, a preeminent annual arts event.

10 Tennessee. Tennessee promises a feast for the ears as well as the eyes. In Memphis you can tour legendary musical locales like Beale Street, Graceland, and Sun Studios, while Nashville counts the Country Music Hall of Fame and the Grand Ole Opry among its top attractions.

11 Virginia. No wonder Virginia is nicknamed the "Old Dominion." Centuries-old sites such as Jamestown, Williamsburg, and Yorktown lie within its Historic Triangle, as do Mount Vernon and Monticello (the homes of George Washington and Thomas Jefferson) and key Civil War sites including Richmond's Confederate White House and the Fredericksburg Battlefield.

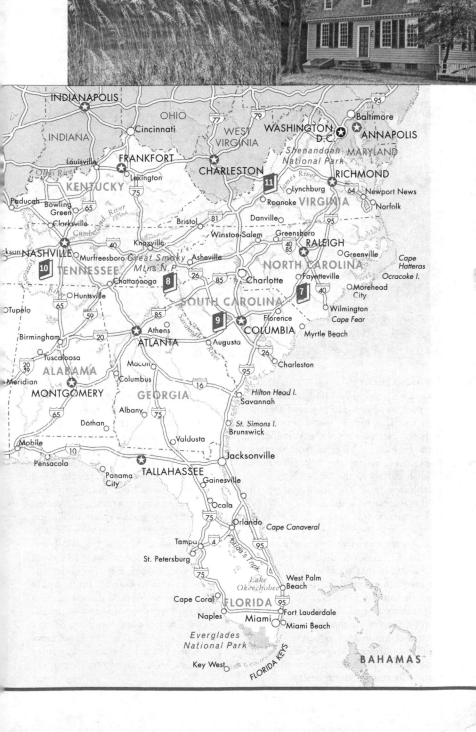

INDIANAPOLIS

INDIANA

OHIO

Cincinnati

WEST
VIRGINIA

WASHINGTON
D.C.

Baltimore

ANNAPOLIS

MARYLAND

Shenandoah
National Park

Louisville

FRANKFORT

CHARLESTON

RICHMOND

Newport News

Ohio River

Lexington

KENTUCKY

11

Lynchburg

Norfolk

64

Paducah

Bowling
Green

Roanoke

VIRGINIA

Bristol

Danville

Greensboro

Clarksville

Winston-Salem

RALEIGH

Greenville

Cape
Hatteras

NASHVILLE

Knoxville

Asheville

NORTH CAROLINA

Ocracoke I.

Murfreesboro

Great Smoky
Mtns. N.P.

10

TENNESSEE

Chattanooga

8

Charlotte

Fayetteville

Morehead
City

Huntsville

SOUTH CAROLINA

7

Wilmington

Tupelo

9

Florence

Cape Fear

Birmingham

COLUMBIA

Athens

Myrtle Beach

Tuscaloosa

ATLANTA

Augusta

ALABAMA

Macon

Charleston

MONTGOMERY

Columbus

GEORGIA

Hilton Head I.

Savannah

Albany

Dothan

St. Simons I.
Brunswick

Mobile

Valdosta

Pensacola

Jacksonville

Panama
City

TALLAHASSEE

Gainesville

Ocala

Orlando

Cape Canaveral

Tampa

St. Petersburg

FLORIDA

Lake
Okeechobee

West Palm
Beach

Cape Coral

Fort Lauderdale

Naples

Miami

Miami Beach

Everglades
National Park

Key West

FLORIDA KEYS

BAHAMAS

QUINTESSENTIAL SOUTH

American History

You don't need to feel passionate about the past to appreciate places where the course of U.S. history was determined—an inordinate number of them are located here. In eastern Virginia, for instance, Jamestown, where the first permanent English colony in the United States was established, and Yorktown, where the final major battle in the American War of Independence was fought, lie a mere 23 mi apart. Elsewhere in this region the density of sites means vacationers can tour plantation houses and designated heritage districts that stand as testimony to the antebellum era, then visit battlefields from the bloody Civil War that brought that age to an end. A century later, the South gave birth to the civil rights movement and landmarks associated with it stand proudly, too, from Martin Luther King Jr.'s crypt in Atlanta to the Rosa Parks Museum in Montgomery.

Down-Home Cooking

With classic dishes ranging from country ham and corn bread to grits and greens, good eats are a cornerstone of Southern culture. Yet precisely what you digest depends largely on where you are dining. Take seafood: although it is served virtually anywhere near water, the local specialty changes from place to place. Carolina cooks favor crabs and oysters; their Gulf Coast counterparts in Florida and Alabama never scrimp on shrimp. Catfish is king in Mississippi, and Louisianans go crazy for crawfish, be it in Cajun-style jambalaya or Creole étouffée. Even a staple—like that ubiquitous barbecued pork—can be dished up in a bewildering number of ways, with different cuts of meat and sauce ingredients used in different locales. The good news is that when you are on vacation, calories don't count, so feel free to try them all.

The South's distinctive culture may make it seem like a whole other world. But settling in isn't difficult. Sample a few local pleasures, and you'll be whistlin' Dixie in no time . . .

Memorable Music

If you've ever hummed along to "Sweet Home Alabama" and "The Tennessee Waltz" or had Georgia on your mind, you already know that the Southern states have an unforgettable soundtrack. What we do sometimes forget is how fertile a breeding ground they have been both for musicians and musical styles. Jazz was spawned in New Orleans, the city that gave us Louis Armstrong and Jelly Roll Morton. Memphis is heralded as the "Bastion of the Blues" and the "Birthplace of Rock 'n' Roll"; and country stalwarts such as the Grand Ole Opry and Ryman Auditorium solidify Nashville's reputation as Music City, U.S.A. Prefer the beat of a different drummer? Gospel, soul, ragtime, and bluegrass all emerged from Southern soil, too. Wherever you go in the region you're guaranteed to hear some toe-tapping, thigh-slapping, or soul-stirring tunes.

Fresh Air Activities

Name your sport, and you'll find places to pursue it in the South. Highly regarded courses, like the Robert Trent Jones Trail in Alabama or the courses on Hilton Head Island in South Carolina, collectively create a golfer's paradise. Rivers provide thrilling white-water rafting in North Carolina and excellent flat-water canoeing in every state. Needless to say, all that water holds challenges for anglers as well, especially in the rivers of Great Smoky Mountains National Park. The Appalachian and Blue Ridge mountains are laced with marked trails to help hikers get away from it all; and if beaches are your passion, you can pick between the bustling resorts of Myrtle Beach, Virginia Beach, and Mississippi's Gulf Coast, or opt for something quieter on the tony Golden Isles and windswept shores of Canaveral National Seashore.

IF YOU LIKE

Time Travel

Mississippi-born novelist William Faulkner wrote, "The past is never dead. It's not even past," and chances are you will agree with his assessment after spending time in some of the South's living history attractions. Colonial Williamsburg, the granddaddy of them all, is only the most famous.

■ At **Oconaluftee Indian Village** in Cherokee, North Carolina (near the entrance to Great Smoky Mountains National Park), native guides in period outfits erase the centuries by telling tales in a recreated council house, practicing age-old crafts like weaving and beading, and demonstrating traditional hunting methods. Nearby, the Museum of the Cherokee Indian recounts the tribe's 11,000-year legacy.

■ Experience a blast from the past at **Mission San Luis Archaeological and Historic Site** in Tallahassee, a national landmark that showcases Florida's earliest European settlers. Though the original was gutted by fire in 1704, the mission complex (now rebuilt on a working, 60-acre archaeological site and featuring costumed interpreters) details the daily lives of Spanish friars and the Apalachee Indians they sought to convert.

■ Part of Virginia's "Historic Triangle," **Colonial Williamsburg**, a restored 18th-century Colonial city, features some 300 acres that include 88 original structures and hundreds of other homes, shops, and public buildings where patriots laid the groundwork for the nation's founding. Nearly 1 million people visit annually for this well-created illusion of being back in time. Costumed interpreters and skilled craftspeople demonstrate, explain, and embody our nation's history.

Fun Food Festivals

The South boasts some unique cuisine, and it manifests itself not merely on restaurant tables but in an array of bake-offs, barbecues, and other food-oriented events. No matter which direction you turn, you'll likely stumble across something that provides a genuine taste of local culture.

■ Barbecue fans gather for three days every spring for Memphis's **World Championship Barbecue Cooking Contest,** part of the Memphis in May festival. Hundreds of grill-masters from around the country compete for bragging rights and cash prizes in three major categories: whole hog, shoulder, and ribs. Dubbed the "Super Bowl of Swine," winners of other sanctioned barbecue contents are guaranteed a booth to compete here.

■ Forrest Gump was right. There are lots of ways to prepare shrimp: you can barbecue it, boil it, broil it, bake it, sauté it . . . Or you can head for Alabama's **National Shrimp Festival**—held the second full weekend of October in Gulf Shores—and let someone else do the cooking. Shrimping is big business here, and 300,000 hungry festival-goers arrive annually to feast on the local haul.

■ The **Crawfish Festival,** which takes place the first full weekend in May, fittingly occurs in Breaux Bridge, Louisiana, the Crawfish Capital of the World. The festival draws more than 100,000 visitors to this little village on Bayou Teche. This is the place to hear Cajun and zydeco music, with over 30 bands playing during the three-day festival. Aside from sampling crawfish cooked every which way, there's a crawfish race, dance off, crawfish eating contest, and, of course, a Crawfish Queen.

Good Libations

Need something to wash down that fabulous food? Sipping a tall glass of sweet tea—a drink steeped in Southern tradition—is almost mandatory in this neck of the woods. Mountain Dew, mint juleps, and moonshine also have firm regional roots, as do these favorite beverages. Bottoms up!

■ Some go to Kentucky for its rolling hills, while others are more attracted by its stills' water—especially if it's limestone-filtered, then mixed with corn mash to produce "America's Native Spirit." More than 95 percent of the world's bourbon originates here, and tracking it down is a breeze on the **Bourbon Trail,** which links eight distilleries: Buffalo Trace, Four Roses, Heaven Hill, Jim Beam, Maker's Mark, Tom Moore, Wild Turkey, and Woodford Reserve.

■ Virginia has been fulfilling oenophiles' grape expectations for a surprisingly long time. It's believed wine was first made here by Jamestown settlers in 1609, and in the past few decades the industry has truly come into its own. Currently the Commonwealth has more than 130 **wineries,** many of which welcome visitors. When you're on the road, watch for a grape-cluster sign identifying one nearby.

■ As a shrine to the best-known brand on the planet, Atlanta's **World of Coca-Cola** redefines "pop culture" through themed art and artifacts. The museum also has 4-D films (3-D plus moving seats), a working bottling facility, and videos of classic ads, all of which prove how far Coke has come since 1886. Its global reach is evident in the Taste It! hall where you can try a worldwide range of products.

Blissful Beaches

We all picture the perfect beach differently. But as the Southern states (bounded by both the Atlantic and the Gulf of Mexico) lay claim to half the contiguous U.S. coastline, endless options are available. Whether you want to lounge, look, surf, or swim, there is a beach to suit your mood.

■ **Myrtle Beach,** the focal point of South Carolina's 60-mile-long Grand Strand, is a magnet for families and other fun seekers. Beyond the hard-packed sand and Atlantic surf, you'll discover a wide assortment of amusement parks, arcades, outlet malls, and other diversions. The combination gives the beach a carnivalesque atmosphere that pulls in almost 14 million visitors per year.

■ Although the Florida Panhandle has a surplus of Grade-A Gulf beaches, **Grayton Beach State Park,** about halfway between Panama City and Pensacola, may contain the pick of the lot. Named one of "America's Best" by Stephen Leatherman (aka Dr. Beach), the 2,133-acre park is blessed with white crushed-quartz sand and aqua-green water that is as clear as any in the Keys or the Bahamas.

■ Aiming to escape the crowds? Set course for **Cape Lookout National Seashore.** Accessible only by boat, its barrier islands are isolated enough to make Gilligan feel at home. One of North Carolina's most photogenic lighthouses (a diamond-patterned beauty) stands here, and the islands are otherwise undeveloped, so you relax in the shelter of dunes, not the shadow of high-rises.

Fast Livin'

Because denizens of the South are stereotypically known for their drawn-out drawl, it seems ironic that so many area attractions feed the need for speed. If you're pining for Talladega Nights, a Day at the Derby or even a trip "to infinity and beyond," you've come to the correct locale.

■ Florida's **Kennedy Space Center** has the right stuff for Buzz Aldrin and Buzz Lightyear fans alike. On-site you can witness a shuttle launch, admire aeronautic antiques ranging from Redstone rockets to an Apollo module, or take your own "giant leap" with the Astronaut Training Experience, half-day to two-day programs that culminate in a simulated mission. If you just can't get enough, visit the **United States Astronaut Hall of Fame,** which features more space memorabilia like the flag that made it to the moon and astronaut's personal stories.

■ Stock car enthusiasts take note. This region has a dozen NASCAR tracks, among them **Lowe's Motor Speedway,** in Charlotte, North Carolina, the heart of NASCAR Country. If you dream of putting the pedal to the metal yourself, many offer a Richard Petty Driving Experience that lets you slip into a driving suit, then into a Sprint Cup–style car.

■ Prefer real horsepower? Race to Louisville to see the world's fastest thoroughbreds run the **Kentucky Derby** on the first Saturday in May. Initiated in 1875, it is the longest continuously held sporting event in the United States—and the "Greatest Two Minutes in Sports." In case you can't make the date, the **Kentucky Derby Museum** has multimedia exhibits that capture the hoof-pounding action.

Glorious Golf

For anyone who believes a vacation *must* include golfing, one of the major advantages of a trip here is that the mild climate allows for four-season play. The scenery (imagine mountaintop and ocean-side holes) is as good as the weather, and the quality of the courses is beyond compare.

■ If you want a sense of how popular golf is in these parts, consider this. The **Robert Trent Jones Trail**—one of Alabama's foremost attractions—draws more than half a million players a year. The trail, consisting of 26 public courses in 11 locations, wends from Mobile to the state's northern reaches and has a total of 468 holes. Best of all, you can tee off for as little as $43.

■ In the shadow of the Harbor Town Lighthouse, Hilton Head Island's **Harbour Town Golf Links** is devilishly difficult. Although deceptively short by today's standards, South Carolina's top course leaves no room for error. A little ways away, Kiawah Island Golf Resort's **Ocean Course** offers views of the ocean from all 18 holes as it winds through salt marshes and seaside forests filled with wildlife, including the occasional alligator. This course has one of the most dramatic last holes in golf.

■ Georgia's **Augusta National** ranks among the world's leading clubs and is viewed as hallowed ground by golfers. The downside is you can't play it unless you are a member, nor can you watch its premier event—the **Masters Golf Tournament in April.** Clever souls can circumvent the exclusivity rule by applying for practice rounds tickets sold on a lottery basis.

The Great Outdoors

The South is notable for its varied landscape and rife with natural wonders, many of which are protected courtesy of federal or state law. The highest mountain peaks in the East plus thick forests, sublime waterways, pristine barrier islands, and primeval swamplands all wait to be explored.

■ If you go to your happy place wearing hiking boots, the **Appalachian Trail** is heaven. Stretching from Georgia to Maine, the original National Scenic Trail crosses 14 states (including Tennessee, North Carolina, and Virginia). While only the intrepid tackle all 2,175 mi, the Virginia portion of the trail—accounting for ¼ its total length—offers scenic options for day hikers.

■ With more than 9 million visitors a year, **Great Smoky Mountains National Park** is the most visited national park in the United States. Still, its half-million acres (divided between Tennessee and North Carolina) provide ample opportunities for communing quietly with nature. Go for a leisurely drive on Cades Cove Loop Road, one of the most scenic parts of the Smokies, and take in the views, historic buildings, and wildlife along the way. Or, if you're feeling more intrepid, hoof into the backcountry to view stunning mountain scenery and perhaps one of the park's 1,500 bears.

■ Few places are more evocative than the moss-draped South Carolina Lowcountry. Off the coast of **Georgetown**, a kayak is all you need to float past the ruins of rice plantations and slave cabins. Or, take a tour of the water and learn about the tidelands, hear ghost stories, and maybe even spot an alligator.

Heritage Lodgings

Evidence of the past is everywhere. So it seems natural that contemporary hotels would be complemented by historic alternatives. Inns, bed-and-breakfasts, and other vintage accommodations—some with sufficient character to qualify as destinations in their own right—invite you to turn back the clock.

■ You seldom actually get to *live* in a living history museum. For a truly time-warped night, book into one of the **Colonial Williamsburg Houses**. There are 26 on-site to choose from, among them Market Square Tavern, where Thomas Jefferson resided during his student days. All are authentically appointed (think fireplaces and canopy beds) but tricked out with modern bathrooms.

■ Treat yourself to Southern comfort at **Monmouth Plantation**, in Natchez, Mississippi, a National Historic Landmark. Built in 1818, this antique-laden Greek revival mansion combines antebellum elegance with up-to-date amenities like Jacuzzi tubs and Wi-Fi. Thanks to towering columns, broad verandas, and gracious gardens, it resembles the setting of *Gone With the Wind*.

■ The largest private home in the United States, **Biltmore Estate** is located just outside Asheville, North Carolina. The French Renaissance château was built in the 1890s. Its ornate 250 rooms are filled with exquisite art and antiques collected by the Vanderbilts. Many people who visit the Biltmore mansion long to stay overnight; the **Inn at Biltmore Estate** grants this wish with a posh hilltop property that mimics the look of Biltmore House and is located on the estate grounds.

GREAT ITINERARIES

As vacation lengths vary, we've designed the two multipart options below for maximum flexibility. Individual components can be covered in two to three days. If you're lucky enough to have time (and money) to spare, each can be combined to create a trip lasting a week to 10 days.

STEP BACK IN TIME WITH SOUTHERN HISTORY

It's possible to plan an entire Southern itinerary around the destinations you learned about in school. Simply pick a period and prepare for a magical history tour.

First Things First: The Colonial Era

For adults eager to brush up on the **colonial era** (or kids being introduced to it), eastern Virginia is just the ticket. Thirteen years before the Pilgrims set foot on Plymouth Rock, America's first permanent English settlement was established here at **Jamestown.** Today it is an active archaeological site that constitutes one point of **Virginia's Historic Triangle.** Nearby are convincing replicas of Jamestown's original fort and the shockingly small ships colonists arrived on in 1607, along with a native village like the one Pocahontas called home.

Colonial Williamsburg—the largest living history attraction in the world—is even more impressive. A recreation of Virginia's capital from 1699 to 1780, this 301-acre property is crammed with almost 600 restored or reconstructed buildings and populated by costumed interpreters who demonstrate old-time trades and act out historical vignettes. (You can even immerse yourself further in the scene by renting outfits for yourself and your children and sleeping on-site!) The result is an entertaining history lesson that is as easy

to digest as the traditional fare served in Colonial Williamsburg's taverns.

At the end of the 23-mi parkway that connects the Triangle sites sits **Yorktown Battlefield,** where, in 1781, the English lost the last major fight of the American Revolution and surrendered to General George Washington. Once you've seen the siege lines and checked out the visitor center exhibits (most notably, Washington's campaign tent), continue on to the **Yorktown Victory Center.** Located west of the battlefield, it has multimedia displays, museum-quality artifacts, and re-created outdoor environments that put the revolutionary events in context.

Let's Be Civil: The Civil War

Between 1861 and 1865 the **Civil War** ripped this region apart, changing it and the nation forever. More than 120 battles were fought in Virginia alone, and one way to appreciate their magnitude is to visit fiercely contested turf like that preserved at the **Fredericksburg/Spotsylvania National Military Park. Chickamauga, Shiloh, and Vicksburg** are other names that live on in history, and history can be relived there thanks to interpretative centers, guided

tours, and battle reenactments directed by the National Park Service.

Another way to approach the Civil War is to visit the spot where it began: **Charleston**. In December 1860, the Ordinance of Secession was signed here, making South Carolina the first state to leave the Union, and the first shot of the war was fired at **Fort Sumter** in Charleston Harbor four months later. Bone up on the backstory at the Fort Sumter Visitor Education Center on Liberty Square, then take a narrated boat trip to view the rebuilt fort and its on-site museum.

In the city, Museum Mile venues tackle the subject from different angles. The **Charleston Museum** offers an overview, while the **Old Slave Mart Museum** focuses on the slave trade. Mansions that human trafficking helped build line the route, providing a glimpse into antebellum life. For more on the antebellum South, head inland to **Drayton Hall**, the only Ashley River plantation not destroyed during Sherman's March. After touring the grand edifice, you can see a slave cemetery and participate in a docent-led program titled "Connections: From Africa to America."

Do the Rights Thing: Civil Rights

A century after the Civil War, the South was again engaged in a struggle over racial equality, one that ultimately paved the way for the first African-American president. To salute that achievement, begin at the **National Historic District in Atlanta** named for the undisputed leader of the civil rights movement: Martin Luther King Jr. Its key sites include an engaging visitor center, King's modest birthplace, and his final resting place, fronted by an eternal flame and fittingly inscribed with the words "Free at last, Free at last, Thank God Almighty, I'm Free at last."

Next drive 160 mi southwest to **Montgomery** (the capital of Alabama and onetime capital of the Confederacy), where King shares billing with Rosa Parks. The **Rosa Parks Library and Museum** is dedicated to the "Mother of the Civil Rights Movement" who kicked off an extraordinary chain reaction here by refusing to give up her bus seat in 1955. Dr. King is honored at the church he preached from (**Dexter Avenue King Memorial Baptist**) and the parsonage he lived in. Both are stops on a **civil rights audio tour.**

Turning west, follow the activists' footsteps in reverse on the **Selma to Montgomery National Historic Trail.** This 54-mi stretch of U.S. Highway 80 commemorates "foot soldiers" who participated in the pivotal Voting Rights March that King led in 1965. Can we still walk it? Yes we can, but driving these days is much more sensible. Plan to pause midway between the cities at the $10 million **Lowndes County Interpretive Center.** Opened in 2006, it chronicles the heroic events that finally allowed African-Americans in the South to exercise their franchise.

FACE THE MUSIC IN NASHVILLE, MEMPHIS, AND NEW ORLEANS

Many musical forms originated in the South, and tracing favorites back to their roots is a popular pastime. For the record, here are the top themed itineraries.

The Capital of Country: Nashville

For country music devotees, no destination looms larger than Nashville, Tennessee. Any proper pilgrimage here begins downtown at the **Country Music Hall of Fame and Museum**: a $37 million complex with state-of-the-art exhibits and

cases containing outrageous outfits, gold records, and vintage instruments. It also hosts live performances and serves as the starting point for tours to **RCA Studio B**, the oldest recording studio on **Music Row**. ■TIP→When strolling—or boot scootin'—to the latter, remember to look down at the stars lining Music Mile's Walk of Fame.

If Music Row is the nerve center of the country-and-western industry, historic **Ryman Auditorium** (just north of the Hall of Fame) is its heart. Fervent fans understandably approach the 2,000-seat venue with reverence. Built as a gospel tabernacle in 1892, it was home to the Grand Ole Opry from 1942 to 1974 and is still known as the "Mother Church of Country Music." Aspire to stardom yourself? Along with an up-close look at memorabilia, auditorium tours provide on-stage photo ops. You can even cut souvenir CDs in the Ryman Recording Booth.

Of course, no one can come to Nashville without visiting its *numero uno* attraction: the Grand Ole Opry's current site, about 10 mi northeast of town. **Opryland** offers its own tours and exhibits, but it's the legendary live shows that really pull in crowds, staged Friday and Saturday nights year-round with an additional show Tuesday nights from March to December. After applauding the Opry's established acts, be sure to check out up-and-comers in local haunts like the **Bluebird Café** and **Station Inn.**

A Musical Mélange: Memphis

For many people Memphis, Tennessee, means one thing: Elvis. Dedicated Presleyites happily hunker down at Graceland's Heartbreak Hotel and spend their vacation exploring the King's glitzy, garish suburban castle, **Graceland**. Elvis may have left the building, but his hip-

TIPS

■ Tickets for live broadcasts at the Grand Ole Opry go fast, so buy them online as early as possible: ⊕ www.opry.com has details.

■ If you have time left over in Memphis, get your licks in with a 45-minute tour of Gibson Guitar's Beale Street Showcase.

■ For the ultimate blues fix, follow Highway 61 (immortalized as the Blues Highway) from Memphis straight to New Orleans.

swiveling spirit is alive at the frozen-in-time landmark where he once lived and is now buried. Highlights of the 14-acre estate include the **Jungle Room** in all of its green-shag splendor; Elvis's **pink Cadillac,** parked for eternity at an adjacent car museum; and the sequined jumpsuits on display in **Sincerely Elvis.**

There is, however, much to see beyond the gates of Graceland. Eight miles north, **Sun Studio** (where Elvis, Carl Perkins, and Jerry Lee Lewis cut the first rock records) is well worth a tour. Opened in 1950, it's still a working studio used by such acts as Maroon 5. From there, continue to the **Stax Museum of American Soul Music,** which celebrates the evolution of Memphis Soul in the 1960s. Erected on the Stax studio's original McLemore Avenue site, it's packed with paraphernalia relating to Otis Redding, Isaac Hayes, and other oh-so-smooth singers.

To see how these different musical forms merged, head downtown to the Smithsonian-affiliated **Memphis Rock 'n' Soul Museum** (off Beale Street in the plaza of FedExForum), then pay tribute to the genre that first put this city on the musical map—the

blues. It arrived here via the Mississippi Delta at the turn of the 20th century, and current Beale Street must-sees include the **W. C. Handy Memphis Home and Museum,** dedicated to the "Father of the Blues," and **B.B. King's Restaurant and Blues Club.**

All that Jazz: New Orleans

The "Birthplace of Jazz" is a banner New Orleans wears proudly. Having spilled out of uptown dance halls in the early 1900s, jazz now resonates on every street. Nowhere, however, is the Big Easy's musical heritage more apparent than **Louis Armstrong Park.** Poised on the northern edge of the French Quarter, it contains a statue commemorating Satchmo and encompasses Congo Square, where slaves once gathered for rhythmic rituals, a precursor to jazz. The 31-acre green space is also the site of the **New Orleans Jazz National Historic Park.**

Though it already offers free programs and performances, this NPS park remains a work in progress. Late in 2009, a visitor center is slated to open in Perseverance Masonic Lodge (a temporary one is located at 916 N. Peters Street), and plans are underway for a jazz museum (a satellite of the park) in the Old U.S. Mint on Esplanade Street. So how should you occupy yourself while waiting for those to materialize? Do what the jazz greats did—improvise! Start by downloading a map at ⊕ *www.nps.gov/jazz/historyculture/places.htm* and take a DIY walking tour.

Visit the small **Backstreet Cultural Museum** on St. Claude Avenue to learn about jazz funerals and second-line traditions; then veer into the **French Quarter** to browse for hard-to-find recordings at the **Louisiana Music Factory.** Later catch some live acts at neighborhood clubs. In the French Quarter itself, **Preservation Hall** and the **Maple Leaf** are reliable bets. Alternately try the **Faubourg Marigny** neighborhood. If you stroll Frenchmen Street any evening, you'll hear jazz pouring from clubs such as the **Spotted Cat** and **Snug Harbor.**

ROAD TRIP THROUGH THE SOUTH

Jack Kerouac didn't take the interstate. OK, maybe *On the Road* predates the U.S. Interstate Highway System, but that's beside the point. Kerouac still wouldn't have ridden these fast-food outlet– and chain motel–crammed modern highways, even if he could have.

Four-lane interstates are a fine choice when you need to get from point A to point B pronto, but for unforgettable road trips, try to get off the beaten path and take a ramble down one of America's older highways. Sure, there are stoplights and stop signs on these classic roads—but that means you'll need to slow down enough to *see* the area you're driving through. Along the way you can experience some of the quirky local cultures, unique culinary traditions, and natural wonders that make this such a great country.

Every state boasts at least one distinctive road that tells a story about that place and its people. Most can be driven from start to finish in a day or two. (The Federal Highway Administration's National Scenic Byways Program has a great list at its Web site, ⊕ *www.byways.org.*) Other famous historic roads actually still cross broad swaths of the country and can take weeks to travel. Here are a few of our favorites for great road trips.

Blue Ridge Parkway

Connecting the Great Smoky Mountains in North Carolina and Shenandoah National Park in Virginia, the Blue Ridge Parkway is one of America's most scenic roadways. Relax and enjoy the view as it meanders 469 mi from the north near Waynesboro, Virginia, south to Cherokee, North Carolina. Even better, you won't get stuck behind an 18-wheeler; commercial vehicles are prohibited. If that weren't enough to help you relax, it's also free of billboards.

With elevations above 6,000 feet and more than 250 scenic overlooks, there are plenty of places to stop and experience the majesty of the mountains. Mile markers along the parkway identify points of interest, including Grandfather Mountain, famous for its Mile High Swinging Bridge, and Mt. Mitchell, the highest peak east of the Rockies.

The Great River Road

The 3,000-plus-mi Great River Road follows the Mississippi River from its start as a cold, tiny, crystal-clear stream in northern Minnesota to its warm, muddy merger with the Gulf of Mexico in Venice, Louisiana.

Created in 1938 from a jumble of local, state, and federal roads, it's a picturesque and varied journey (parts of the route comprise well-maintained dirt and gravel roads), passing through forests, prairies, swamps, tiny towns, and bustling cities. Travelers have many opportunities to experience America's own music (the blues, jazz, zydeco, and rock 'n' roll were all born along this highway) and sample unique regional tastes—barbecue in Memphis, tamales in the Delta, and Creole and Cajun cooking in Louisiana.

Highlights along the southern stretch of the Great River Road include Memphis (especially Sun Studio and Beale Street); the Mississippi Delta (especially Clarksville, Mississippi, for blues fans); Vicksburg, Mississippi (for antebellum architecture aficionados); and New Orleans.

If you're planning a trip along the Great River Road, check out ⊕*www.experiencemississippiriver.com* for more information.

U.S. Route 1

The northernmost part of what's now U.S. Route 1 dates back to at least 1636, when it took four days to make the 100-mi journey from Philadelphia to New York City. Today, this 2,425-mi circuit links Fort Kent, Maine, to Key West, Florida, and passes through a good chunk of U.S. history.

Route 1 has some spectacular scenery (even the Great Dismal Swamp in southeastern Virginia/northeastern North Carolina is startlingly charming), but it isn't always pretty, passing through plenty of urban blight and moldering towns that time forgot. That said, it's an endlessly fascinating highway—every bit of it has a story to tell.

The best sights along the southern portion include the Okefenokee Swamp (Georgia and Florida); the George Washington Masonic National Memorial in Alexandria, Virginia; and Old Town in St. Augustine, Florida.

7 MISTAKES NOT TO MAKE ON YOUR NEXT FAMILY ROAD TRIP

You've no doubt thought of everything. The enormous suitcase that brained you when it slid from the closet is now nestled in the trunk, well-packed with your family's wardrobe for the week. Your kids have enough snacks to forestall whining for days if necessary. You spent the morning neatly stapling computer-generated directions for each leg of your trip. And if you drive at high speeds—with the flow of traffic, of course—you'll make the eight-hour drive in excellent time. So what are you missing?

Well, for starters, you've already made several mistakes that could turn your family car trip into a disaster.

Mistake #1: Packing the wrong bag

When you're driving, there's no advantage to consolidating your family's clothes in that indestructible bag you use for flying. Think nylon or canvas duffel bags 24 to 30 inches long, one for each person's things. You'll be carting more bags around, but you'll be able to put your hands on everything more quickly. Plus, repacking the trunk will be easier, especially if you're fitting small bags around a stroller and all those jugs of laundry detergent you bought.

Mistake #2: Altering meal times

A common road-trip blunder is disrupting your family's normal meal schedule. If you don't hit the road until late morning, there's a temptation to drive through lunch and snack your way to dinner. You know your kids will have no restraint when it comes to snacks, and neither will you. Plus, if after hours of gorging you make a spontaneous lunch stop, you'll be wolfing down food while your kids complain about not being hungry. And if lunch is thrown off, you'll all be out of sync by dinner. By evening, your kids will be starving after both refusing to eat lunch and losing interest in the car snacks, and if it's later than you usually eat, dinner will be a miserable whinefest.

Solution: Keep it simple and eat all your meals at the usual times.

Mistake #3: Pacing the day badly

Nothing will sour a car trip faster than hitting the road at the wrong time. It's all too tempting to leave work at 4 or 5 PM on a Friday to get on the road for a weekend getaway. The good thing about this is that, regardless of their ages, your kids will immediately slide into comatose naps. The bad thing is that when you pull into your destination at 8 PM, they'll be up all night. A different tactic, hitting the road after 9 PM so that your kids fall asleep and stay asleep, works wonderfully, until you stop a few hours later. If they don't come to immediately, chances are they'll be wide awake by the time you've carried them inside.

Best bet: Sacrifice the evening escape and leave the following morning (or early enough the next afternoon so that a nap won't be disruptive). Ensure you're off the road for the day by dinnertime.

Mistake #4: Denying you could get lost

Computer-generated directions are nifty but accurate to a fault; one wrong turn, and they're next to useless. Bring a real road map and invest in a portable GPS device or request one for your rental ($10 or less daily fee; Hertz and Avis fleets are well-equipped with them). The first time a GPS generates an accurate course correction is the first time it pays for itself. Still, GPS isn't perfect. Like computer algorithms and your well-meaning friend's husband, they can overcomplicate

directions and, at times, fail to identify streets.

Pack the map no matter what.

Mistake #5: Driving like an idiot

We do stupid things on vacation that we don't do at home: skydiving, paying retail, eating organ meats we can't identify, and, curiously, driving more cavalierly than we normally do. This is a mistake no matter who's in the car, but the fact that the stakes are higher when you're driving with your family can't be overstated. One of the more perplexing things we do on the road is break traffic laws, making illegal turns or speeding because we're keeping up with the flow of traffic.

Sure, you can get away with it, and if you're a good driver you might rationalize the risk to your family. But don't underestimate the risk of being pulled over. Any leniency you might have been hoping for from that approaching highway patrolman will evaporate when he sees you have kids in the back.

Mistake #6: Not setting a budget for the little things

It's puzzling that many of us tirelessly research airfares, hotels, car rentals, and online coupon codes with the hope of saving a few dollars, yet when it comes to buying incidentals on the road, we're essentially careless. You wouldn't dream of giving your second-grader a $50 weekly allowance at home, but for a week on the road, if you dare consider the sum of a pack of sour candies here, a souvenir pen there, a keychain for her BFF, and the other little things for which you're constantly breaking $5 bills, giving each kid a $50 allowance with a "once you spend it it's gone" proviso can end up being a good deal.

A debit scenario works equally well for grown-ups.

Mistake #7: Forgetting that the journey is the destination

If your goal is to get from point A to point B as quickly as possible, you probably shouldn't be traveling by car. One of the benefits of road trips is that you can pull over at the farm rather than give the kids a blurry glimpse of a cow, eat the best steak and eggs of your life at that nondescript roadside diner, and take that throwaway snapshot by the guardrail that ends up being the quintessential photo of you and your daughter.

Hundreds of potentially undiscovered moments are around the next corner, which is why treating a drive as a means to an end rather than as part of your journey is the biggest mistake of all.

—*Paul Eisenberg*

TOP EXPERIENCES IN THE SOUTH

Travelers in our Forums share the destinations and experiences that make the South special to them. You can join the conversation and get advice for your trip at www.fodors.com.

Florida
"I live in Florida's panhandle and my favorite time to go to the beach is mid-September to late October. The crowds are gone, the air is a little cooler and less humid and the gulf is still plenty warm for swimming. If you want the most gorgeous beach (crystal clear water and snow white sand) check out the beaches of South Walton or Destin. If you want to take Fido along go to Cape San Blas or St. George Island." —sunshinesue

Georgia
"Islands along the Georgia coast are plentiful, and each is worthy of visiting—but don't try to see them all. When you reach Savannah, arm yourself ahead of time with tons of recommendations for that wonderful city." —Wayne

Louisiana
"We had a wonderful time in New Orleans. Go with an open mind. We enjoyed the southern hospitality that we don't have in cold old New England. Talk to the locals and listen to their stories. Feel the life that New Orleans history has imbedded into every nook and cranny. Grab a cold local beer, Abita, and a dozen oysters." —easygoer

Mississippi
"Absolutely take the Natchez Trace Parkway between Natchez and Nashville. You will not be sorry. It is a wonderful and educational drive. Allow time to really see and experience all this Trail has to offer. Take a picnic lunch and stop along the way." —cd

North Carolina
"I love Asheville. It's got a cool funky vibe to it, very artsy. There are some really great restaurants and shops and the location can't be beat. You can easily visit Lake Lure/Chimney Rock from Asheville as well." —tcreath

Great Smoky Mountains National Park
"In the Smokies, I would recommend doing the Roaring Fork Motor Trail and visiting Cades Cove, both of which can be seen from a vehicle, if people are not up to hiking/lots of walking. If it is a clear day, you might want to drive up to Clingman's Dome, the highest point in the Smokies." —BetsyinKY

South Carolina
"We all loved Charleston a lot. It's really one of the more walkable and charming cities in all of U.S.—no wonder we were told it's the #2 location wedding place in the U.S., only after Las Vegas." —rkkwan

Tennessee
"My son enjoyed Memphis and its festive atmosphere. There are a lot of outdoor concerts on Beale and the street is blocked off in the evenings. There is great BBQ to enjoy. I am not an Elvis Presley fan but the whole family enjoyed Graceland. The house, history, and car collection is fun." —annesherrod

Virginia
"I have 2 daughters aged 8 and 11 and we loved Williamsburg, Yorktown, and Jamestown. Loved the battle/weapons exhibition; the 11-year-old was able to be in the demonstration of the cannon shooting at Yorktown. They do an incredible job of bringing it all to life. The ships at Jamestown were a big hit too." —henny16

ON THE CALENDAR

	Southerners are justifiably famous for their hospitality. Experience it firsthand at one of these memorable annual events.
WINTER	
December	New Year's Eve revelers can have a ball almost anywhere thanks to assorted **First Night Events** and one-of-a-kind options like Atlanta's **Peach Drop.**
	Prefer pigskin to parties? Atlanta also hosts the **Chick-fil-A Bowl** (formerly the Peach Bowl), while Nashville is home to the **Music City Bowl.**
January	The year kicks off with two fierce college football competitions, the **Liberty Bowl** in Memphis and the **Sugar Bowl** in New Orleans.
	During **Martin Luther King Jr. Week,** Atlanta honors its native son with lectures, exhibits, rallies, and music.
	Daytona Beach revs up for **Speedweeks,** which begin with the Rolex 24-Hour Race and culminate in the fabled Daytona 500 in February.
Early February–Early March	Raucous, ritualistic **Mardi Gras** (aka "Fat Tuesday") is celebrated the day before Ash Wednesday and caps the post-Christmas Carnival Season. New Orleans hosts the biggest bash, but balls, parades, and parties are also held in Gulf Coast cities like Biloxi, Mobile, and Pensacola.
SPRING	
March	Savannah has one of America's oldest, largest **St. Patrick's Day Parades.** New Orleans has the most unusual: uptown, float riders toss Irish stew fixings instead of Mardi Gras beads.
	You don't need friends in high places to peek inside divine digs. Doors open at dozens of Mississippi mansions during Vicksburg's **Historic Home Tours** and Natchez's **Spring Pilgrimage.** South Carolina follows suit with Beaufort's **Spring Tour of Homes** and Charleston's **Festival of Houses & Gardens.**
April	Mark **Jazz Appreciation Month** by listening to America's indigenous musical form in New Orleans at the famed **New Orleans Jazz & Heritage Festival** and the **French Quarter Festival** (which boasts the world's largest jazz brunch).
	Flower aficionados can tiptoe through the tulips during the **Festival of Flowers** at North Carolina's Biltmore Estate; tour hundreds of grand Virginian gardens during **Historic Garden**

	Week; or go wild during the **Spring Wildflower Pilgrimage** in Great Smoky Mountains National Park.
	Something fishy is going on in Mississippi. Belzoni hosts the **World Catfish Festival,** and Biloxi spotlights "Cajun mudbugs" at the **Mississippi Coast Coliseum Crawfish Festival.**
SUMMER May	The month-long **Memphis in May** extravaganza includes the Beale Street Music Festival and World Championship Barbecue Cooking Contest.
	The **Gullah Festival** in Beaufort, South Carolina, highlights the arts, customs, and language of Lowcountry African-Americans.
	Starting in late May, **Spoleto Festival USA** brings world-class drama, dance, and music to Charleston, South Carolina. **Piccolo Spoleto** runs concurrently, giving regional performers a chance to shine.
June	The **American Dance Festival** returns to Durham, North Carolina, for six weeks of moving performances. To date it's presented more than 400 premieres.
	Nashville's **CMA Music Festival** (formerly Fan Fair) puts country fans close to stars at concerts, autograph sessions, and other noteworthy events.
	Rockers flock to Tennessee's **Bonnaroo** festival (Pearl Jam and Metallica are past headliners), while music lovers with eclectic tastes may prefer **Riverbend** in Chattanooga, where the lineup covers everything from metal to mountain strings.
July	New Orleans hosts the African-American-oriented **Essence Music Festival** the Fourth of July weekend. Free daytime empowerment seminars are followed by nighttime concerts by the hottest hip-hop and R&B acts.
	Angler alert! **Deep-Sea Fishing Rodeos** take place at Dauphin Island, Alabama, and Gulfport, Mississippi, the former billed as the largest saltwater fishing competition in the United States.
August	Fans of the King get all shook up when they converge on Memphis for **Elvis Week.** Tribute concerts and a candlelight vigil are on the agenda.

	Also running in August, the Shagadelic **Beach Music Festival** on Jekyll Island, Georgia, and **Mountain Dance and Folk Festival** (the nation's oldest folk fête) in Asheville, North Carolina.
FALL	
September	Everyone is in fine spirits when Bardstown celebrates its amber elixir at the **Kentucky Bourbon Festival.**
	Festivals Acadiens et Créoles in Lafayette honors Louisiana's French heritage through bayou food, catchy tunes, and cultural workshops.
October	October is **Wine Month** in Virginia, and corks pop statewide. Events include the **Virginia Wine Festival** in Leesburg, plus vino tours and tastings.
	Ready to get reel? **Film Festivals** occur in Charlottesville, Virginia, and New Orleans. Along with the screenings, expect panel discussions and popcorn.
	Motorcyclists arrive en masse for rallies, races, and demo rides at **Biketoberfest** in Daytona Beach.
November	Paging all bibliophiles! **Words and Music: A Literary Feast in New Orleans** offers seminars, readings, even writing classes.
November–December	The South unwraps Christmas in early November. Particularly "illuminating" events include **Charleston's Holiday Festival of Lights**; New Orleans's **Celebration in the Oaks**; **Stone Mountain Christmas** and **Savannah Southern Lights** in Georgia; the **Holiday Flotilla** in Wrightsville Beach, North Carolina; and **Winter Magic** in Gatlinburg, Tennessee.

Alabama

BIRMINGHAM, MONTGOMERY, MOBILE, AND THE GULF COAST

WORD OF MOUTH

"The art museum and botanical gardens [in Bir-
mingham] are great options. The Civil Rights Institute is a powerful experience. And if you like cars
and motorcycles, check out Barber Motorsports. It
is a little ways from downtown, but an amazing
collection."

—CarolWeaver

Updatd by
Rena Havner
Philips

If you believe its motto, then Alabama is a "state of surprises." Visitors marvel at its physical beauty: the rocky, wooded hills and vast caves of the northeast; the expansive lakes and broad rivers of the interior; and the white beaches of the Gulf Coast. Venturing off the interstate, you'll find something unexpected at almost every turn—a cascading waterfall or a showy stand of wildflowers, an archaeological excavation or a colonial fort, or perhaps one of Alabama's 13 covered bridges.

History and Southern tradition are around every bend of the road, whether you follow the path of Civil War soldiers or that of civil rights marchers. Many sections of the state have preserved the elegant antebellum homes so typical of the 19th century, yet the cities have an eye on the future. Huntsville hosts the high-tech U.S. Space and Rocket Center, where the Saturn rocket was designed. The new and progressive blend nicely with the old and historic—Montgomery's modern state government buildings stand just one block from the First White House of the Confederacy. Mobile celebrates the past with its oak-tree- and antebellum mansion–lined streets while looking forward to economic growth with the state's tallest skyscraper.

ORIENTATION AND PLANNING

GETTING ORIENTED

With the Appalachian Mountains stretching into the center of the state, Alabama has two different types of terrain. The northern part of the state is quite mountainous, and the southern part fairly flat and covered with extensive pine forests, while the southern edge of the state has beaches along the Gulf of Mexico. All are filled with outdoor recreational areas, historic sites, and plenty of chances to sample Southern tradition and culture. The small towns and back roads of Alabama are often a throwback to earlier, less hectic times.

Birmingham and North Alabama. Alabama's largest city grew up as an iron and steel manufacturing city, but now is better known for its banking and medical centers. The city is perhaps most famous for its role in the civil rights movement, with church bombings and visits from the Reverend Martin Luther King Jr.

Montgomery and Central Alabama. Alabama's capital city was the first capital of the Confederacy. It was home to country great Hank Williams Sr. and now hosts the renowned Alabama Shakespeare Festival.

1

TOP REASONS TO GO

Southern cooking: From fried chicken and collard greens to fresh Gulf Coast seafood, Alabama has an abundance of good, old-fashioned Southern cooking. The state also has more than its fair share of barbecue joints. You can try vinegar-based barbecue sauce or even white barbecue sauce in north Alabama; yellow mustard sauce in east Alabama; and thick, spicy red sauce everywhere in between.

History comes alive: From the Civil War to the civil rights movement, many chapters in history were written in Alabama. Battle sites throughout the state and the Edmund Pettus Bridge in Selma witnessed some of the nation's toughest struggles.

Golfer's paradise: Alabama has championship-caliber golf along the Robert Trent Jones Golf Trail. Better yet, the state-owned courses are much less expensive than comparable resort courses.

The U.S. Space and Rocket Center: Who knew rockets were made in Alabama? You can learn all about the U.S. space program, go on rides, and attend Space Camp at this museum in Huntsville.

Pristine beaches: Situated on the Gulf Coast, Alabama has white, sandy beaches in Dauphin Island, Gulf Shores, and Orange Beach to rival any in Florida but with fewer crowds.

Mobile and the Gulf Coast. Many people don't realize that Alabama has miles of white sandy beaches. Beach-goers can choose between the high-traffic areas of Gulf Shores and Orange Beach and the sparsely populated Dauphin Island. Mobile, which recently celebrated its tricentennial, is Alabama's port city.

PLANNING

WHEN TO GO

Although the state is a year-round haven, be advised that the summer heat and humidity can be overpowering, especially for those not used to it. The summer is, however, prime time for going to the beach and deep-sea fishing. The offshore breezes along the Gulf Coast help keep you comfortable.

Spring, when the azaleas are in full bloom, is perhaps the most beautiful time of all, and late spring is perfect for the wildflowers of northern Alabama along the Tennessee River basin and atop Lookout Mountain near Mentone. Fall visitors will find almost summerlike conditions along the coast until November. It may be a little cool at night, but the warm sunny days are ideal for strolling along the sand dunes.

Winters, although not severe, get a touch cold at times. Golf is played year-round, but wintertime golfers and bird-watchers might need a sweater or jacket to ward off the chill.

GETTING HERE AND AROUND

AIR TRAVEL

Birmingham International Airport, Montgomery Regional Airport, Huntsville International Airport, and Mobile Regional Airport are the major airports. Many visitors to the Gulf Coast find it convenient to fly into Pensacola Regional Airport, an hour east in Florida, or Gulfport-Biloxi Regional Airport, an hour west in Mississippi.

Airport Contacts Birmingham International Airport (☎ *205/599–0500* ⊕ *www.bhamintlairport.com*). **Gulfport-Biloxi Regional Airport** (☎ *228/863–5953* ⊕ *www.flygpt.com*). **Huntsville International Airport** (☎ *256/772–9395* ⊕ *www.hsvairport.org*). **Mobile Regional Airport** (☎ *251/633–0313* ⊕ *www.mobairport.com*). **Montgomery Regional Airport** (☎ *334/281–5040* ⊕ *www.montgomeryairport.org*). **Pensacola Regional Airport** (☎ *850/436–5000* ⊕ *www.flypensacola.com*).

CAR TRAVEL

Surrounded by Mississippi, Georgia, Tennessee, Florida, and the Gulf of Mexico, Alabama is accessible by a number of interstates. I–10 cuts across the southern tip of the state, providing a direct route from Mississippi on the west and the Florida Panhandle on the east. From Atlanta, I–85 takes you to the central part of the state, while I–20 brings you to Birmingham and points in north Alabama. The main north–south routes are I–65 coming down from Nashville and I–59 from the Chattanooga area. U.S. 80 cuts east–west across the state, connecting Demopolis, Selma, Montgomery, and Tuskegee. U.S. 82 runs northwest to southeast from Tuscaloosa through Montgomery and Eufaula.

Some sample mileages are as follows: Birmingham to Huntsville, 95 mi; Birmingham to Mobile, 253 mi; Birmingham to Montgomery, 90 mi; Birmingham to Gulf Shores, 274 mi.

RESTAURANTS

From the fresh seafood served along the coast to the traditional Southern comfort food found inland to the upscale modern Southern cuisine that helps define the state's cosmopolitan cities, Alabama has something for every taste. An abundance of catfish farms throughout the state ensures an ample supply of fresh fried fish, usually served with a hearty helping of hush puppies (deep-fried cornmeal dumplings). All over the state, you'll find heated discussions regarding which are the best barbecue joints. And even in the fanciest restaurants, no meal is complete without the ubiquitous sweet tea.

HOTELS

Lodging around Alabama falls into several categories. Country inns and bed-and-breakfasts are increasingly popular in many of the rural northern counties, whereas the cities contain a pleasant blend of remodeled older hotels and modern business complexes. Check out the B&B brochure available from the Alabama Bureau of Tourism and Travel to help with reservations. Along the coast, full-service resorts with their own golf courses provide a relaxing stay with a spectacular view of the Gulf of Mexico.

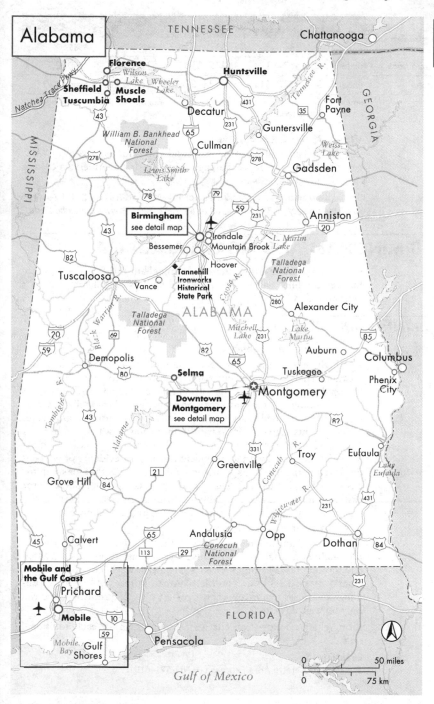

Alabama

TENNESSEE

Chattanooga

Natchez Trace Pkwy

Florence

Wilson Lake

Sheffield   Muscle   Wheeler Lake

Tuscumbia   Shoals

Huntsville

431

Fort Payne

35

43

Decatur

231

Guntersville

GEORGIA

MISSISSIPPI

William B. Bankhead National Forest

278

65

Cullman

278

Weiss Lake

Lewis Smith Lake

Gadsden

78

79

59

231

Anniston

Birmingham
see detail map

43

Irondale

20

Bessemer   Mountain Brook

L. Martin Lake

Vance

Hoover

Talladega National Forest

Tuscaloosa

♦ Tannehill Ironworks Historical State Park

82

ALABAMA

280

Alexander City

Talladega National Forest

Mitchell Lake

Lake Martin

85

20

69

82

201

Auburn

Columbus

59

Coosa R.

65

Demopolis

80

Tuskegee

Phenix City

43

Selma

✈ Montgomery

Downtown Montgomery
see detail map

82

21

331

Troy

Eufaula

Greenville

Conecuh R.

231

431

Lake Eufaula

Grove Hill

84

Black Warrior R.

Tombigbee R.

Alabama R.

Whitewater R.

45

Calvert

65

113

29

Andalusia

Conecuh National Forest

Opp

Dothan

84

231

Mobile and
the Gulf Coast

Prichard

✈

10

FLORIDA

Mobile

59

Mobile Bay

Gulf Shores

Pensacola

N

Gulf of Mexico

0 _____ 50 miles

0 _____ 75 km

WHAT IT COSTS				
	¢	$	$$	$$$	$$$$
Restaurant	under $7	$7–$11	$12–$16	$17–$22	over $22
Hotel	under $70	$70–$110	$111–$160	$161–$220	over $220

Restaurant prices are per person for a main course at dinner. Hotel prices are for a standard double room, excluding state and local taxes.

VISITOR INFORMATION

Call the Alabama Bureau of Tourism and Travel for a free copy of "Alabama's Black Heritage," a 56-page guide to African-American culture that includes hundreds of sites.

Visitor Information Alabama Bureau of Tourism and Travel (✉ *401 Adams Ave., Montgomery* ☎ *334/242–4169 or 800/252–2262* ⊕ *www.touralabama.org*).

BIRMINGHAM AND NORTH ALABAMA

From the Tennessee border south to Birmingham and Tuscaloosa, you'll find verdant hills, parks, natural beauty, and history all competing for your attention.

BIRMINGHAM

90 mi north of Montgomery.

Birmingham, set in a valley below the foothills of the Appalachians, blossomed due to the coal mines and the iron industry in the late 1800s. Its rapid growth earned it the nickname the "Magic City." Today its largest employer is the University of Alabama at Birmingham, which has a highly regarded medical center. In the 1960s, the city was a center for civil rights activity; Dr. Martin Luther King Jr. was jailed here for fighting racial inequality. By the 1990s, a diverse, progressive Birmingham had reconciled with its turbulent history, the evidence of which is displayed in the museums, churches, and landmarks that make up the city's Civil Rights District. Less densely populated than Atlanta to the east, Birmingham is a comfortably sprawling, easily navigable city with a growing reputation for sophisticated shopping and dining.

GETTING HERE AND AROUND

BUS TRAVEL   The Birmingham-Jefferson County Transit Authority (BJCTA) serves Birmingham. Bus fare is $1.25, plus 25¢ for transfers. Routes run Monday through Friday from 5 AM to 9 PM and on weekends and holidays from 5 AM to 12:30 PM. The Metro Area Express (MAX) serves Birmingham. Buses require exact change—$1 fare, 25¢ transfer—and run only on weekdays, 6–6.

TAXI TRAVEL   Birmingham's Yellow Cab charges $4.50 plus $2 for each additional mile.

ESSENTIALS

Bus Contacts Metro Area Express (☎ *205/521–0101*).

Alabama Facts

CLOSE UP

1

■ **State Name:** The Alabama, or Alibamu, were a Muskogean Indian tribe who lived in the center of what is now Alabama. The Alabama River was named after the tribe, and so too was the state.

■ **State Flower:** Camellia

■ **State Bird:** Yellowhammer

■ **State Nut:** Pecan

■ **State Horse:** Rocking Horse

■ **Highest point in Alabama:** Cheaha Mountain at 2,405 feet

■ **State Song:** Despite the tourism bureau's use of the slogan "Sweet Home Alabama," that hit by Lynyrd Skynyrd is not the state song. The official state song, "Alabama," was written by Edna Goeckel Gussen and Julia S. Tutwiler.

■ Known as Rocket City USA, Huntsville produced the rocket that first took humans to the moon. The U.S. Space and Rocket Center there is one of the world's largest space museums.

■ Montgomery was the first capital of the Confederate States of America. The capital was moved to Richmond, VA in May of 1861.

■ In 1836, Alabama became the first state to make Christmas an official holiday.

Taxi Contacts Yellow Cab (☎ *205/252–1131*).

Visitor Information Greater Birmingham Convention and Visitors Bureau (✉ *2200 9th Ave. N* ☎ *205/458–8000 or 800/458–8085* ⊕ *www.birmingha-mal.org*).

EXPLORING

❸ **16th Street Baptist Church.** On the morning of September 15, 1963, a bomb planted here by the Ku Klux Klan exploded, killing four young African American girls aged 11 to 14 who were attending Sunday school in the basement. In 1965, the FBI determined that four white men were responsible for bombing this black church that had been a hub for the civil rights movement. In 2000 and 2002 the last two men went to trial and were found guilty. A plaque erected in memory of the victims bears this legend: "MAY MEN LEARN TO REPLACE BITTERNESS AND VIOLENCE WITH LOVE AND UNDERSTANDING." ✉ *1530 Sixth Ave. N, Downtown* ☎ *205/251–9402* ✉ *Tour $5* ⊗ *Tues.–Fri. 10–4, Sat. by appointment.*

❶ ★ **Alabama Sports Hall of Fame.** Alabama has long been noted for its excellence in sports, and the Alabama Sports Hall of Fame, adjacent to the Convention Complex, displays memorabilia of such state heroes as coach Paul "Bear" Bryant, Jesse Owens, Willie Mays, Billy Williams, and Hank Aaron. ✉ *2150 Civic Center Blvd., Downtown* ☎ *205/323–6665* ✉ *$5* ⊗ *Mon.–Sat. 9–5.*

❽ **Birmingham Botanical Gardens.** Waterfalls cascade into pools with plants of every shade of green and flowers of every color imaginable under a great glass dome adjacent to the Birmingham Zoo. Outside, a quiet Japanese garden has small bridges over bubbling brooks and an authentic teahouse. Wear your best walking shoes: the gardens are

Birmingham

as extensive as they are beautiful. ✉*2612 Lane Park Rd., Mountain Brook* ☎*205/414–3900* ⊕*www.bbgardens.org* ✉*Free* ⊙*Daily sunrise–sunset.*

❹ **Birmingham Civil Rights Institute.** Tracing the roots of the civil rights move-
★ ment from the late 1800s through the troubled 1960s, when the city
was nicknamed "Bombingham," the institute shows its effect on the
present day via exhibits, multimedia presentations, music, and storytelling. Powerful exhibits include a replica of a Freedom Riders bus, an
integrated form of public transportation in which civil rights activists
crossed state lines to protest segregation; segregated water fountains;
and the door from the cell in which the Reverend Martin Luther King
Jr. wrote "Letter from Birmingham Jail." The institute has a research
gallery for public use and has conducted and preserved more than 400
interviews of movement leaders, participants, and historians as part of
its Oral History Project. ✉*520 16th St. N, Downtown* ☎*205/328–
9696* ⊕*www.bcri.org* ✉*$10* ⊙*Tues.–Sat. 10–5, Sun. 1–5.*

❷ **Birmingham Museum of Art.** The museum has one of the world's largest collections of Wedgwood, a comprehensive Asian art exhibit that
includes Vietnamese ceramics, a multilevel sculpture garden, and some
extraordinary examples of American art, plus Italian Renaissance and

pre-Columbian art. ✉*2000 8th Ave. N, Downtown* ☎*205/254–2565* ⊕*www.artsbma.org* ✉*Free* ⊗*Tues.–Sat. 10–5, Sun. noon–5.*

❼ Birmingham Zoo. The wooded zoo is home to some 800 exotic and endangered animals representing more than 200 species from around the world. Don't miss the black rhinoceroses, hippopotamuses, gorillas, giraffes, kangaroos, and llamas in outdoor exhibits; reptiles and tropical birds are indoors. Young visitors can also ride camels and play in the Foam Zone. ✉*2630 Cahaba Rd., Mountain Brook* ☎*205/879–0408* ⊕*www. birminghamzoo.com* ✉*$12* ⊗*Daily 9–5, with extended summer hrs.*

❻ Five Points South. This revitalized historic district just south of downtown has quaint shops and trendy restaurants. The neighborhood, named for the landmark circle where five streets converge, was one of Birmingham's first streetcar suburbs. Its various architectural styles include Spanish baroque, as seen in the **Highlands United Methodist Church** (✉*1045 20th St. S, Southside*), and art deco. ✉*Around 20th St., Magnolia Ave., and 11th Ave. S, Southside.*

❺ McWane Science Center. This four-story hands-on science learning center with an IMAX theater, a dinosaur exhibit, an aquarium, and science demonstrations is meant for kids, but adults will love it as well. The center also hosts traveling exhibits sure to pique the curiosity of young scientists. ✉*200 19th St. N, Downtown* ☎*205/714–8300 or 877/462–9263* ⊕*www.mcwane.org* ✉*Museum $11, IMAX $8.50, both $16, parking $5* ⊗*Sept.–May, weekdays 9–5, Sat. 10–6, Sun. noon–6; June–Aug., Mon.–Fri. 9–6, Sat. 10–6, Sun. noon–6.*

WHERE TO EAT

$$$–$$$$
MEDITERRANEAN

✗**Bottega.** Celebrated chef Frank Stitt's second restaurant is housed in an early-20th-century limestone building with high ceilings, warm walnut paneling, and a gleaming marble bar. A mezzanine overlooks the main dining room. The Italian-Mediterranean menu changes nightly to incorporate the freshest ingredients but could include lobster served with penne pasta and a saffron tomato sauce with garlic, chilies, and orange zest. Bottega's sister restaurant, Bottega Café, offers more casual dining, including gourmet pizza. ✉*2240 Highland Ave. S, Southside* ☎*205/939–1000* ⊕*www.bottegarestaurant.com* ☐*AE, MC, V* ⊗*Closed Sun. No lunch.*

$
SOUTHERN

✗**Dreamland Bar-B-Que.** This outpost of the original Dreamland in Tuscaloosa has a casual vibe and down home goodness like the original rib joint, but offers more choices on the menu. A long wooden bar, TVs tuned to sports, and license plates on the walls keep the focus on the main attraction here: pork ribs slathered in Dreamland's special sauce. The pulled pork sandwich and banana pudding are also stand outs. You can take home the sauce or have ribs shipped to you if you fall in love. ✉*1427 14th Ave. S, Downtown* ☎*205/933–2133* ⊕*www.dreamland-bbq.com* ⟋*Reservations not accepted* ☐*AE, D, MC, V.*

$$$–$$$$
SOUTHERN
Fodor'sChoice
★

✗**Highlands Bar & Grill.** Owner-chef Frank Stitt continues to achieve national acclaim with his innovative cooking that combines his love of "two Souths"—the rural southern fare of his childhood and the rustic cuisine of southern France. The dining room resembles a French bistro, with vintage posters and butter-yellow walls. The menu may include

How to Snack

Alabama, like everywhere in Dixie, is chock full of local delicacies to indulge in, so come hungry. One of the most iconic treats is a plate of fried green tomatoes at the **Irondale Café** in Irondale; the café was the inspiration for the Whistlestop Café in *Fried Green Tomatoes at the Whistlestop Café* by Fannie Flagg. For haute Southern cuisine in Birmingham, try Chef Frank Stitt's **Highlands Bar & Grill**, which was named the fifth best restaurant out of the top 50 in the U.S. by *Gourmet* magazine.

For fresh Gulf Coast seafood, including oysters on the half shell try **Wintzell's Oyster House** in Mobile. For barbecue, look for an iconic smoke stack and pigs decorating the counter, or head to one of **Dreamland Bar-B-Que's** locations throughout the state. The original, and some say the best, is located in Tuscaloosa.

pork rillettes with foie gras and spicy coleslaw; grilled grouper and Provençale pepper sauté with Niçoise olives; and roast Carolina quail and pork tenderloin with creamy grits, blackstrap molasses, and mustard greens. The crab cakes are a favorite of many customers. ✉*2011 11th Ave. S, Southside* ☎*205/939–1400* ⊕*www.highlandsbarandgrill.com* ⊟*AE, MC, V* ⊘*Closed Sun. and Mon. No lunch.*

$$$–$$$$ ✕**Hot and Hot Fish Club.** The unusual name of this upscale eatery can be
SOUTHERN traced to owner-chef Christopher Hastings's great-great-grandfather's gentlemen's club, the Hot and Hot. Hastings and his wife Idie, the co-owner, have decorated their West Coast–style restaurant with funky local artwork, including handmade bowls and plates. The menu changes nightly but may include shrimp and grits, seared tuna with Asian vegetable slaw, and pork and beans with collard greens and cracklin' corn bread. The cheese biscuits accent any meal, and the seasonal tomato salad is a big hit. End the evening with the chocolate soufflé with crème anglaise. ✉*2180 11th Court S, Southside* ☎*205/933–5474* ⊕*www. hotandhotfishclub.com* ⊟*AE, D, MC, V* ⊘*Closed Sun. and Mon. No lunch.*

¢–$ ✕**Irondale Café.** This homey little restaurant inspired the title establish-
SOUTHERN ment of Fannie Flagg's novel *Fried Green Tomatoes at the Whistlestop Café.* Of course, that dish is available, along with dozens of other fresh vegetables, several entrées, and a handful of desserts—all served cafeteria style. Unlike the tiny café in the book and movie, this now-sprawling restaurant has five dining rooms, the largest of which features photos and memorabilia of interest to fans of Flagg, whose great aunt ran the café from 1932 to 1972. ✉*1906 1st Ave. N (7 mi east of Birmingham), Irondale* ☎*205/956–5258* ⊕*www.irondalecafe.com* ⊟*MC, V* ⊘*No dinner weekends.*

WHERE TO STAY

$–$$ ⊡**Hotel Highland at Five Points South.** Formerly the Pickwick Hotel, this historic establishment was renovated and renamed in 2007. The eight-story hotel was built in the the Five Points South area in 1931 to hold offices; in the 1950s it held a fabulous nightclub that threw elaborate themed parties. Converted in 1986 to a hotel, it has Brazilian bed linens and furnishings and calls itself "uniquely hip." Don't miss the martini bar, which has signature cocktails and a vibrant ambience with brightly colored sofas and contemporary lighting. The guest rooms are calmer, with white comforters and gold accents. **Pros:** free Continental breakfast; unique decor; high-definition flatscreen TVs. **Cons:** no restaurant on-site but several within walking distance; $18 parking; minimum-stay requirements some weekends. ⊠ *1023 20th St. S, Southside* ☎*205/933–9555* ⊕*www.thehotelhighland.com* ⇥*35 rooms, 28 suites* ⋄*In-room: kitchen (some). In-hotel: parking (paid), no-smoking rooms* ⊟*AE, DC, MC, V* ⦿*CP.*

$$–$$$ 🏨 **The Tutwiler.** A National Historic Landmark, the Tutwiler was built
★ in 1913 as luxury apartments and converted into a hotel in 1986. A $9 million renovation in 2007 kept most of the charm, adding fireplaces and balconies to some of the rooms. Eclectic rooms have period reproduction furnishings, including armoires and high-back chairs, plus velour loveseats and crown molding. The elegant lobby has marble floors, chandeliers, brass banisters, antiques, and lots of flowers. The upper lobby level has black-and-white photographs detailing Birmingham's history through the civil rights movement. Visitors can listen to descriptions of the photographs with a headset available in the lobby. The hotel is considered a full-service Hampton Inn. **Pros:** historic charm; free, hot breakfast served on 8th floor with view of city; books and DVDs for checkout. **Cons:** hotel can book up fast; doors locked at night due to sketchy downtown neighborhood; $16 parking per day. ⊠*2021 Park Pl., Downtown* ☎*205/322–2100* ⊕*www.thetutwilerhotel.com* ⇥*149 rooms, 12 suites* ⋄*In-hotel: restaurant, room service, bar, gym, laundry service, Wi-Fi, parking (paid), no-smoking rooms* ⊟*AE, D, DC, MC, V* ⦿*BP.*

$$$–$$$$ 🏨 **Wynfrey Hotel.** The posh Wynfrey rises 15 stories above the sprawling
★ Riverchase Galleria mall. An Italian marble floor, Chippendale furniture, fresh flowers, and a brass escalator set a formal tone in the lobby. Spacious guest rooms have thick white comforters. Conference-goers have access to a 24-hour business center, while Spa Japonika and a rooftop swimming pool are perfect for those who prefer to unwind. For a hearty meal, try Shula's Steakhouse. **Pros:** long regarded as Birmingham's finest hotel; free airport shuttle by reservation. **Cons:** located at a busy mall; the staff could be friendlier. ⊠*U.S. 31, 1000 Riverchase Galleria, Hoover* ☎*205/987–1600 or 800/996–3739* ⊕*www.wynfrey. com* ⇥*290 rooms, 12 suites* ⋄*In-room: Internet. In-hotel: restaurant, room service, pool, gym, spa, laundry service, Wi-Fi, no-smoking rooms* ⊟*AE, D, DC, MC, V.*

NIGHTLIFE AND THE ARTS

For an up-to-date listing of happenings in the arts, get the current issue of *Birmingham* magazine on the newsstand.

Theatrical productions and music concerts are among the performances at the restored **Alabama Theatre for the Performing Arts** (⊠*1817 3rd Ave. N, Downtown* ☎*205/252–2262* ⊕*www.alabamatheatre.com*), built in 1927, where the summer film series brings classics back to the big screen. The **Birmingham-Jefferson Convention Complex** (⊠*2100*

Richard Arrington Jr. Blvd. N, Downtown ☎*205/458–8400* ⊕*www.
bjcc.org*)—a seven-block complex with an exhibition hall, a theater,
a concert hall, a conference center, a hotel, and an arena—presents
touring Broadway shows, major rock concerts, and exhibitions. The
covered amphitheater at **Sloss Furnaces** (✉*1st Ave. N and 32nd St.,
Downtown* ☎*205/324–1911*) hosts music concerts and seasonal civic festivals. National acts perform under the stars at **Verizon Wireless
Music Center** (✉*1000 Amphitheater Rd., U.S. 119 off I–65, Pelham*
☎*205/985–4900*).

FESTIVALS   In June the city hosts a music festival, **City Stages** (☎*205/251–1272*
⊕*www.citystages.org*), where concerts are held on nine stages and performance areas in and around downtown's Linn Park.

NIGHTLIFE   **The Comedy Club Stardome** (✉*1818 Data Dr., Hoover* ☎*205/444–0008*)
showcases nationally known and up-and-coming comedians nightly
except Monday.

SPORTS AND THE OUTDOORS

FISHING   There is excellent largemouth and spotted bass fishing 30 mi east of
Birmingham, on the Coosa River, at **Logan Martin Lake** (✉*I–20 east,
near Pell City*). There's fine fishing for crappie or bass at the lakes in
Oak Mountain State Park (✉*I–65 south, Exit 247 onto Cahaba Valley
Pkwy., Pelham* ☎*205/620–2520*).

GOLF   The 18-hole, par-72 course in **Oak Mountain State Park** (✉*I–65 south,
Exit 247 onto Cahaba Valley Pkwy., Pelham* ☎*205/620–2522*), just
south of Birmingham, is both scenic and challenging.

In the Birmingham area, the Robert Trent Jones Golf Trail continues
with the 18-hole, par-72 **Oxmoor Valley** (✉*100 Sunbelt Pkwy., Home-
wood* ☎*205/949–4444*).

HIKING AND   Joggers favor the quiet streets in and around the city's **Five Points South**
JOGGING   (✉*Around 20th St., Magnolia Ave., and 11th Ave. S, Southside*).

Oak Mountain State Park (✉*I–65 south, Exit 247 onto Cahaba Valley Pkwy., Pelham* ☎*205/620–2522*) is laced with trails for hiking or
jogging.

HUNTSVILLE

90 mi north of Birmingham via I–65.

The largest town in north Alabama, Huntsville is best known for the
center that helped produce a rocket that took astronauts to the moon,
but the Rocket City has a clutch of other attractions, including golf
courses, historic homes, and museums.

ESSENTIALS

Visitor Information Huntsville Convention and Visitors Bureau (✉*500
Church St.* ☎ *256/551–2230* ⊕ *www.huntsville.org*).

EXPLORING

☾ **U.S. Space and Rocket Center.** At this NASA research facility, you can learn
★ the fascinating story of space exploration and experience some of the
training that real astronauts undergo. The center offers a bus tour of
the NASA labs and shuttle test sites; hands-on exhibits in the museum;

space-travel simulators; the IMAX Spacedome Theater, with large-format films photographed in space as well as on earth; and an outdoor park filled with spacecraft, including a full-size model of a space shuttle. ⊠*1 Tranquility Base, West Huntsville* ☎*256/837–3400 or 800/637–7223* ⊕*www.space-camp.com/museum* ⊡*Museum $20, museum and IMAX $24.95* ⊙*Daily 9–5.*

☉ **EarlyWorks Museum Complex.** This hands-on history center is made up of three properties. The first, **Alabama Constitution Village**, is the site of Alabama's 1819 Constitutional Convention. Craftspeople in period dress demonstrate skills such as woodworking, printing, cooking, and weaving. In November and December, Santa Claus takes over the whole village with children's

WORD OF MOUTH

"You might try Huntsville. Stop off at either the Botanical Garden (located off I-565) where there is a fabulous children's garden that your children will enjoy. Or you could even just stay at Bridge Street at the Westin and let them enjoy the Carousel and the outdoor mall there. There are usually street performer–style entertainers out in the evenings as well, and they also have pedal boat rides. If you come all the way into Huntsville you could stay downtown at the Embassy Suites and go to EarlyWorks which is a hands-on museum geared to children, and they have two great spaces just for the younger set." —sanibella

activities. At the **EarlyWorks Children's Museum** you can hear stories from a talking tree, build a house at the Kidstruction Zone, play a tune on the giant instruments at the Alabama Bandstand, and examine a 46-foot keelboat. A few blocks from the village, **Huntsville's Historic Depot**, built in 1860, offers a glimpse of railroad life in the mid-19th century. Free guided walking tours of Huntsville's Twickenham Historic District, with its many antebellum homes, start here every Saturday at 10 AM. ⊠*404 Madison St., Downtown* ☎*800/678–1819 or 256/564–8100* ⊕*www.earlyworks.com* ⊡*One museum $10, all three museums $20* ⊙*Constitution Village and Historic Huntsville Depot, Tues.–Sat. 10–4; Children's Museum, Mon.–Sat. 9–4.*

WHERE TO EAT AND STAY

¢–$ ╳**Greenbrier Restaurant.** This rustic eatery in Madison was built by hand
SOUTHERN in 1952 by its founder, Jack Webb. The current owner, Jerry Evans,
★ who has been at the restaurant for more than 20 years, has kept the same dishes—catfish, ribs, and chicken served in generous portions—that made it a local favorite. The chicken is served with a special white barbecue sauce. Add tasty coleslaw and hot hush puppies, and you'll know why people drive long distances to eat here. ⊠*27028 Old Hwy. 20 (8 mi west of Huntsville, 2 mi off I-565), Madison* ☎*256/351–1800* ⊕*www.oldgreenbrier.com* ⊟*AE, D, MC, V.*

$$–$$$ ▦**Embassy Suites Huntsville Hotel and Spa.** Claiming a prize location downtown, this all-suites hotel opened in 2006 and is connected to the Von Braun Center and the Big Spring International Park via walkways. The spacious rooms, decorated in reds, oranges, golds and a hint of lime green, are warm and welcoming, and the hotel staff is gracious and waits to pamper you. The hotel has a Ruth's Chris steakhouse for

fine dining and offers a nightly manager's reception with free drinks. Pros: free cooked-to-order breakfast; free van service to area attractions; underground, secure parking garage; on-site spa. Cons: plan to dine early for best seating and shorter wait; limited restaurants and shopping nearby. ⊠ *800 Monroe St.* ☎*256/539–7373 or 800/362–2779* ⊕*www.embassysuites1.hilton.com* ⤳*295 suites* ♿*In-room: Internet. In-hotel: 2 restaurants, room service, pool, gym, laundry service, no-smoking rooms* ⊟*AE, D, DC, MC, V* ��*BP.*

SPORTS AND THE OUTDOORS

GOLF The three golf courses at **Hampton Cove** (⊠*450 Old Hwy. 431S, Owens Cross Rd.* ☎*256/551–1818*), 12 mi from Huntsville, are part of the Robert Trent Jones Golf Trail. All have 18 holes; two are par 72, and the third is par 54.

SHOPPING

Bridge Street Town Centre (⊠*6782 Old Madison Pike, Research Park* ☎*256/428–2022* ⊕*www.bridgestreethuntsville.com*) is a new outdoor shopping village with upscale shops and restaurants as well as a carousel, a gondola, and pedal boat rides. Monaco Pictures, an upscale movie theater, has 14 movie screens with leather seats, VIP balconies, an appetizer and dinner menu, and a full-service bar.

THE SHOALS

70 mi west of Huntsville.

The adjoining quad cities of Tuscumbia, Florence, Sheffield, and Muscle Shoals are known throughout Alabama simply as The Shoals. Spreading out on both sides of the Tennessee River basin, The Shoals is an attractive area rich in culture and history. Nearby Wilson Dam, on which construction was begun in 1918 to supply power to munitions plants in World War I, later became the cornerstone of the Tennessee Valley Authority (TVA). The dams and rivers built by this government agency, created in 1933, have greatly affected the economics of the area, providing both business and recreational opportunities.

EXPLORING

★ **Ivy Green.** This is the childhood home of Helen Keller, born in Tuscumbia in 1880. At the carriage house, behind the simple white-frame main house, Annie Sullivan taught young Helen the meaning of language. The annual **Helen Keller Festival** (☎*256/383–0783 or 800/344–0783* ⊕*www. helenkellerfestival.com*), held the third weekend in June, celebrates her life with arts and crafts, concerts, and performances of the play that tells her inspirational story, *The Miracle Worker,* which is staged on the grounds Friday and Saturday nights at 8 during June and July; on performance nights, the grounds open at 6:45 so that ticket holders can tour the house (no extra charge). ⊠*300 W. North Commons, Tuscumbia* ☎*256/383–4066* ⊕*www.helenkellerbirthplace.org* ☑*$6; The Miracle Worker $8–$10* ☉*Mon.–Sat. 8:30–4, Sun. 1–4.*

★ **Alabama Music Hall of Fame and Museum.** Here, you can wander through the history of Alabama's musical heritage and see the original contracts of Elvis Presley's deal with Sun Records, the actual touring bus of the

CLOSE UP

Robert Trent Jones Golf Trail

1

Alabama doesn't have much in the way of golf history, unlike Georgia, its neighbor to the east, which spawned golfing great Bobby Jones. But another Jones, the legendary and prolific golf architect Robert Trent Jones Sr., a namesake of but no relation to Bobby Jones, placed Alabama golf on the map with a series of scenic, challenging public golf courses spanning the state.

The **Robert Trent Jones Golf Trail** comprises 11 locations. Unlike most resort courses, where you are routed through a developer's maze of condos and town houses, only indigenous pines, oaks, rivers, streams, and lakes surround the Golf Trail courses. Wherever you are in Alabama, chances are you're not too far from one of the trail's stops.

Courses on the trail are often described as challenging—a euphemism for just plain hard. It's recommended that you move up one set of tees from your normal location, particularly for shorter hitters. Golf carts on the trail have global positioning systems (GPS), providing yardage measurements. Purchasing a yardage book with suggestions on how to play each hole is a good idea. Tee shots that don't find the fairway are often severely punished by a forest, a splash in a lake or creek, or a difficult hillside lie.

The three south-central Alabama locations make an excellent and convenient trip. **Capitol Hill** in Prattville, northwest of Montgomery, is the grandest course with the most layouts: three championship, 18-hole courses starting out from a fantastic clubhouse with a view of downtown Montgomery. **Cambrian Ridge** in

Greenville, about an hour south of Montgomery, also should not be missed. Three challenging 9-hole courses wind around the clubhouse, situated on the highest point in Butler County. Cambrian Ridge's Sherling Nine is stunningly serene and beautiful, particularly holes 3 through 7, which border placid, tree-lined Lake Sherling. Its Canyon Nine runs through an old deer-hunting site, starting off dramatically, with a 501-yard par 4 that plays 200 feet straight downhill. The parallel finishing holes for both the Sherling and Canyon Nines play uphill past weathered brown boulders in a gully separating the two fairways. **Grand National** in Opelika, near Auburn University, has two excellent championship courses that play along the banks of Lake Saughahatchee. The Lakes Course there has hosted the NCAA Golf Championships and is a regular stop on the professional Buy. com Tour Championship.

These state-owned golf courses are much more economical than comparable lush resort courses of the Southeast, with green fees ranging from $54 to a peak rate of $64 in springtime at the busier tracks. The courses also are well managed, and the pace of play is steady, even in peak times in April. The only way you can go wrong here is to hit poor shots.

Contacts Cambrian Ridge (✉ *101 Sunbelt Pkwy., Greenville* ☎ *334/382–9787*). **Capitol Hill** (✉ *2600 Constitution Ave., Prattville* ☎ *334/285–1114*). **Grand National** (✉ *3000 Robert Trent Jones Trail, Opelika* ☎ *205/749–9042*). **Robert Trent Jones Golf Trail** (☎ *800/949–4444* ⊕ *www.rtjgolf. com*).

—Sam Starnes

country music band Alabama, and exhibits on the likes of Hank Williams Sr., Lionel Richie, and Nat "King" Cole. ✉ *617 U.S. 72W, Tuscumbia* 📞*256/381–4417 or 800/239–2643* ⊕*www.alamhof.org* 🖳*$8* 🕓*Mon.–Sat. 9–5, Sun. 1–5.*

W.C. Handy Birthplace, Museum and Library. W. C. Handy (1873–1958), a mainly self-taught songwriter and bandleader known as the Father of the Blues, was one of the first to write down this genre of music. The cabin is furnished with items typical of his early life. Much of his memorabilia has been preserved in the museum, where you'll see his piano and famous golden trumpet and testimonials to his genius by such contemporaries as George Gershwin and Louis Armstrong. The annual **W. C. Handy Music Festival** (📞*256/766–7642* ⊕ *www.wchandymusicfestival.org*), held during the last week in July, draws thousands. ✉*620 W. College St., Florence* 📞*256/760–6434* 🖳*$2* 🕓*Tues.–Sat. 10–4.*

WHERE TO EAT AND STAY

$$$–$$$$ ✕**Dale's Restaurant.** Dine in comfort as red-jacketed waiters serve flame-
AMERICAN   grilled steaks seasoned with Dale's famous marinade. Chicken and
★   seafood dishes round out the menu. ✉*1001 Mitchell Blvd., Florence* 📞*256/766–4961* ▤*AE, DC, MC, V* 🕓*Closed Sun. No lunch.*

$–$$ 🏨**Joe Wheeler State Park Lodge.** This three-story fieldstone-and-redwood lodge, at the center of a 3,400-acre state park, slopes down a hill, giving every room a view of Wheeler Lake. All rooms have balconies; some suites have living rooms and tiny kitchenettes. Boats are available for trips on the lake, countless hiking trails lead to secluded spots and picnic areas, and redwood walkways connect the guest rooms with the pool area. Nearby are small, rustic brick or wood cabins, which are no-frills but comfortable; campsites are also available. **Pros:** secluded; scenic; plenty of outdoor activities. **Cons:** spotty cell phone reception; no phones or TVs in some rooms. ✉*U.S. 72, near Rogersville (between Athens and Florence), 4401 McLean Dr., Rogersville* 📞*256/247–5461 or 800/544–5639* ⊕*www.alapark.com/joewheeler* ⤴*75 rooms, 9 suites, 30 cabins, 10 lakeside cottages, 116 campsites* ⚒*In-room: no phone (some), kitchen (some), refrigerator (some), no TV (some). In-hotel: restaurant, golf course, tennis courts, pool, Wi-Fi, no-smoking rooms* ▤*AE, MC, V.*

MONTGOMERY AND CENTRAL ALABAMA

The flatlands of Alabama's central section, called the Black Belt region for its rich, fertile soil, provide the stage for stories of 19th-century plantation life, the Civil War, and the civil rights movement. Montgomery serves as a good base for exploring this region's Old South plantations, historic sites, and big fishing lakes.

MONTGOMERY

From the Civil War to the civil rights movement, Montgomery has been in the forefront of southern life. As you stand on the spot where Jefferson Davis took the oath of office as president of the Confederacy, you can gaze upon the Dexter Avenue King Memorial Baptist Church where

Dr. Martin Luther King Jr. preached his message of freedom. A century apart in time and worlds apart in symbolism, the two landmarks are a mere block apart geographically. Today Montgomery is the epitome of a progressive southern business city. New hotels and restaurants spring up frequently, along with skyscraper office complexes. Still, many historic homes and buildings remain. Alabama's capital city has a rich past and ambitions for a rich future.

GETTING HERE AND AROUND

BUS TRAVEL Montgomery has Montgomery Area Transit System (MATS) buses that run from 5:30 AM to 7 PM on weekdays and from 7:30 AM to 5:30 PM on weekends. The fare is $1.

CAR TRAVEL To drive downtown from Montgomery Regional Airport, turn north onto I–65, follow signs to I–85, and take the first exit, Court Street. To drive to the airport from downtown, take Exit 167 off I–65 to U.S. 80W and go 3 mi to airport entrance.

TAXI TRAVEL Taxis in Montgomery charge $3 for the first ⅙ mi, $1.80 for each additional mile. Try Yellow Cab.

ESSENTIALS

Bus Contacts MATS (☎ 334/262–7356).

Taxi Contacts Yellow Cab (☎ 334/262–5225).

Visitor Information Montgomery Visitors Center (✉ 300 Water St., Downtown ☎ 334/262–0013 or 800/240–9452 ⊕ www.visitingmontgomery.com).

EXPLORING

❶ **Alabama State Capitol.** Built in 1851, the state capitol served as the first
★ capitol for the Confederate States of America for a few months in 1861. On the front portico, a bronze star marks the spot where Jefferson Davis stood to take the oath of office as president of the Confederacy. The stairway curling up the sides of the circular hallway is freestanding, without visible support, and colorful murals capture the state's rich history. In the large House chamber and smaller Senate chamber are fireplaces with black Egyptian marble mantel pieces. ✉ 600 Dexter Ave., at Bainbridge St., Downtown ☎ 334/242–3935 ⊕ www.preserveala. org ⬚ Free ☉ Weekdays 9–5, Sat. 9–4.

❹ **Civil Rights Memorial.** The memorial, on the grounds of the Southern
★ Poverty Law Center, features water flowing over a table that bears the names of 40 people who gave their lives for racial equality. On a wall behind it appears a biblical quote Dr. Martin Luther King Jr. used in a speech: UNTIL JUSTICE ROLLS DOWN LIKE WATERS AND RIGHTEOUSNESS LIKE A MIGHTY STREAM. The sculptor, Maya Lin, also created the Vietnam Veterans Memorial in Washington, D.C. Visit the adjacent **Civil Rights Memorial Center** (⊕ www.splcenter.org/crm/crmc.jsp ⬚ $2 ☉ Weekdays 9–4:30, Sat. 10–4) to learn more about those who lost their lives during the civil rights movement. ✉ 400 Washington Ave., Downtown ☎ 334/956–8200 ⬚ Free ☉ 24 hrs ⊕ www.splcenter.org.

❺ **Dexter Avenue King Memorial Baptist Church.** Dr. Martin Luther King Jr. began his career as a minister in 1955 at this church, from which he directed the Montgomery bus boycott after Rosa Parks was arrested

Downtown
Montgomery

for refusing to give up her seat to a white man. The church's sanctuary and the basement Sunday-school rooms are open to visitors. A mural covering one basement wall depicts people and events associated with Dr. King and the civil rights movement. ✉ *454 Dexter Ave., Downtown* ☎ *334/263–3970* ⊕ *www.dexterkingmemorial.org* ✉ *$5* ⊙ *Tours Tues.–Fri. at 10, 11, 1, 2, and 3; Sat. 10, 11, noon, and 1.*

② **First White House of the Confederacy.** Built in 1840, this building across the street from the state capitol was occupied by Jefferson Davis and his family while the government of the Confederacy was being organized. Today it contains many of their possessions, plus other artifacts of the Civil War period. ✉ *644 Washington Ave., Downtown* ☎ *334/242–1861* ✉ *Free* ⊙ *Tours weekdays 8–4:30. Closed weekends.*

③ **Montgomery Museum of Fine Arts.** Alabama's oldest fine arts museum is housed in an impressive facility in the Wynton M. Blount Cultural Park, near the Alabama Shakespeare Festival theater. Highlights include works by important American artists such as Winslow Homer and Southern and folk art; ARTWORKS, hands-on galleries for children and adults; a permanent gallery exhibiting the Blount Collection of American Paintings; and a gift shop, auditorium, and print gallery, as well as galleries for changing exhibitions. You can eat lunch in Café M. ✉ *1 Museum Dr., East Montgomery* ☎ *334/244–5700* ⊕ *www.*

mmfa.org ☞*Free* ☉*Tues., Wed., Fri., and Sat. 10–5, Thurs. 10–9, Sun. noon–5.*

7 **Old Alabama Town.** About six blocks northwest of the capitol, between Madison Avenue and Columbus Street, this historic area consists of more than 50 restored houses, barns, stores, and other structures built between 1818 and circa 1920. History comes alive as volunteers dress in period costume to give visitors a glimpse of both the elegant town house lifestyle and rural pioneer living. The **Loeb Reception Center** has a self-guided walking tour that covers the 10 house museums clustered in the Living Block. The Italianate **Ordeman Townhouse** (✉*230 N. Hull St., Downtown*) is open for guided tours as are its restored outbuildings and gardens. The Working Block, just off Columbus Street on the district's north side, includes a gristmill, blacksmith shop, the **Cotton Gin and Cotton Museum,** and the **Rose-Morris Craft Center.** ✉*Loeb Reception Center, 301 Columbus St., Downtown* ☎*334/240–4500 or 888/240–1850* ⊕*www.oldalabamatown.com* ☞*Self-guided tour $8* ☉*Mon.–Sat. 9–3.*

6 **Rosa Parks Library and Museum.** This museum was built on the site where Parks refused to give up her seat on a city bus, sparking the 381-day Montgomery bus boycott that resulted in the U.S. Supreme Court decision in 1956 to desegregate the nation's public transportation system. The museum holds artifacts—including a replica of the bus—and documents from the era. ✉*251 Montgomery St., Downtown* ☎*334/241–8661* ⊕*montgomery.troy.edu/rosaparks/museum/* ☞*$5.50* ☉*Weekdays 9–5, Sat. 9–3, closed Sun.*

WHERE TO EAT

¢ ✕**Chris' Hot Dogs.** A Montgomery tradition since opening as a hot dog
AMERICAN stand in 1917, this eatery has booths and an old-fashioned lunch coun-
★ ter with stools. The famous sauce combines chili peppers, onions, and herbs to give the hot dogs a one-of-a-kind flavor. Try the hot dog with "kitchen chili," a heavy, hot chili of beans and onions. ✉*138 Dexter Ave., Downtown* ☎*334/265–6850* ⊕*www.chrishotdogs.com* ⌖*Reservations not accepted* ⊟*D, MC, V* ☉*Closed Sun.*

$$–$$$ ✕**Jubilee Seafood Company.** In a very pleasant small café, Bud Skinner
SEAFOOD cooks some of the finest and freshest seafood dishes in town, such as snapper prepared in several different ways, crab claws, and other delicacies. For a real treat, try the barbecued shrimp, which are marinated in a secret barbecue sauce, wrapped in bacon, and charbroiled. Bud also has a tasty West Indies salad with marinated crab. ✉*1057 Woodley Rd., Cloverdale* ☎*334/262–6224* ⊕*www.jubileeseafoodrestaurant.*

com ⚕ *Reservations not accepted* ☱ *AE, MC, V* ⊘ *Closed Sun.–Mon.*
No lunch.

$ ✕**Martin's Restaurant.** Martin's—a Montgomery institution since the
SOUTHERN 1940s—is a plain but comfortable "meat and three." Friendly servers
dish out generous helpings of home-cooked fresh vegetables, southern-
fried chicken, and delicious pan-fried catfish fresh from Alabama ponds.
The corn bread muffins melt in your mouth. ✉ *1796 Carter Hill Rd.,*
Downtown ☎ *334/265–1767* ☱ *No credit cards* ⊘ *Closed Sat.*

$$–$$$ ✕**Vintage Year.** Chef Derrick Huitt's innovative menu makes this Clo-
ECLECTIC verdale restaurant one of Montgomery's best. Start with an appetizer of
★ soft-shell crab with Worcestershire butter sauce or an asparagus salad
with blue cheese. Then try the New York strip steak marinated in molasses and served with a twice-baked potato, a fillet with crusted *panko*
(breadcrumb) shrimp, or shrimp and scallop linguini. ✉ *405 Cloverdale*
Rd., Cloverdale ☎ *334/264–8463* ☱ *AE, D, MC, V* ⊘ *Closed Sun. and*
Mon. No lunch.

WHERE TO STAY

$$ ⊞**Embassy Suites Hotel.** This all-suites high-rise hotel between the con-
★ vention center and the old railroad station pampers travelers with
sprawling rooms that include TVs and phones in the bedrooms as well
as the den area, plus kitchenettes. A spectacular atrium lobby filled
with plants resembles a tropical rain forest. Glass elevators give you a
bird's-eye view. **Pros:** free hot breakfast buffet; free manager's reception
nightly; location good for business, sightseeing; free parking; airport
shuttle. **Cons:** hear train whistle at night; downtown area gets sketchy
at night. ✉ *300 Tallapoosa St., Downtown* ☎ *334/269–5055* ⊕ *www.*
embassysuitesmontgomery.com ⇆ *237 suites* ⚭ *In-room: refrigerator,*
Internet. In-hotel: restaurant, pool, gym, laundry service, parking (free),
no-smoking rooms ☱ *AE, D, DC, MC, V* ◉|*BP.*

$$ ⊞**Red Bluff Cottage.** This bright, cheerful home in the heart of downtown overlooks the Alabama River plain with a raised porch that lets
you survey the view and a gazebo on the grounds. Each of the four guest
rooms—all on the ground floor—is decorated with antique furniture
and wall hangings and has a private bath; one has an adjacent children's
room. Owner Bonnie Ponstein cooks a full breakfast that may start
with a fruit parfait or baked bananas and include a wild rice waffle.
Pros: library with common TV, 1,000 books, and board games; homey
atmosphere; 600-thread-count sheets; fresh, hot breakfast. **Cons:** with
limited rooms, books up quickly; no TVs in rooms; few restaurants
nearby. ✉ *551 Clay St., Box 1026, Downtown* ☎ *334/264–0056 or*
800/551–2529 ⊕ *www.redbluffcottage.com* ⇆ *4 rooms* ⚭ *In-room: no*
TV, Internet. In-hotel: no-smoking rooms ☱ *AE, D, MC, V* ◉|*BP.*

THE ARTS

FESTIVALS Shakespearean plays, modern drama, and musicals are performed on
two stages at the **Alabama Shakespeare Festival** (☎ *334/271–5353 or*
800/841–4273 ⊕ *www.asf.net*) in the **Carolyn Blount Theatre** (✉ *1 Fes-*
tival Dr., East Montgomery) in the Wynton Blount Cultural Park on the
east side of Montgomery. The festival's season runs year round; tickets
cost $30–$60. While you're there, take time to smell the roses . . . and
other flowers and herbs planted in the **Shakespeare Garden.**

FILM Foreign and independent film buffs will enjoy Cloverdale's nonprofit **Capri Theatre** (✉ *1045 E. Fairview Ave., Cloverdale* ☎ *334/262–4858* ⊕ *www.capritheatre.org*), the city's first neighborhood theater, built in 1941, and now its only independent cinema.

SPORTS AND THE OUTDOORS

GOLF Montgomery is home to **Lagoon Park** (✉ *2855 Lagoon Park Dr., East Montgomery* ☎ *334/271–7000*), a flat 18-hole, par-72 course with some water hazards and trees, consistently rated by *Golf Digest* as one of the top 100 public courses in the United States. **River Run** (✉ *1501 Dozier Rd., East Montgomery* ☎ *334/271–2811*) has two courses: the first with 36 holes, a pro shop, putting greens, and a driving range that is lit at night, and the second an 18-hole, par-72 course adjacent to the Tallapoosa River.

SHOPPING

ANTIQUES **Herron House Antiques** (✉ *422 Herron St., Downtown* ☎ *334/265–2063*), Montgomery's oldest antiques shop, specializes in garden statuary as well as 18th- and 19th-century European furniture and accessories.

SELMA

15 mi west of Montgomery via U.S. 80.

Selma has played major roles in both Civil War and civil rights history. With the Confederacy's second-largest arsenal and foundry, the town was a target of Union attack in 1865, Alabama's only major inland Civil War battle. Almost 100 years later Selma came again to the forefront on March 21, 1965, as the stage of "Bloody Sunday." Civil rights protesters seeking to draw attention to the suppression of voting rights set out on a 50-mi march to Montgomery, where they intended to present their plight to lawmakers. At Edmund Pettus Bridge, they were beaten by state troopers with billy clubs as photographers captured the atrocities. Three weeks later, joined by some 20,000 supporters and led by civil rights leader Dr. Martin Luther King Jr., they accomplished a carefully guarded march to Montgomery, which resulted in the passing of the National Voting Rights Act. The path of that walk is an All-American Road and an official National Trail, and the city honors the event the first weekend in March at the annual Bridge Crossing Jubilee festival.

Among the sites worth visiting are **Old Town,** the largest historic district in the state, with more than 1,200 buildings, and **Martin Luther King Jr. Street,** a historic walking tour.

ESSENTIALS

Visitor Information **Selma–Dallas County Tourism and Convention Bureau** (✉ *912 Selma Ave., Selma* ☎ *334/875–7241 or 800/457–3562* ⊕ *www.selmaalabama.com*).

EXPLORING

The **National Voting Rights Museum and Institute** (✉ *1012 Water Ave.* ☎ *334/418–0800*) presents documents, photographs, and other exhibits that offer evidence of the important role of voting rights in the civil rights movement.

HISTORY YOU CAN SEE

In 1996, Congress established the **Selma to Montgomery National Historic Trail** to commemorate the 1965 Voting Rights March. Although the original marchers walked the 54-mi route, most visitors today drive the scenic byway. You can begin a civil rights tour in Selma, visiting the sights along the Martin Luther King Jr. Street walking tour as well as the National Voting Rights Museum, and Old Depot Museum.

Along the Selma to Montgomery National Historic Trail, be sure to stop at the **Lowndes County Interpretive Center** (*7002 Hwy. 80 W ✛ off Hwy. 80 at Mile Marker 106 in White Hall, Hayneville* ☎ *334/877–1984* ⊕ *www.nps.gov/semo* ☾ *Daily 9–4:30*). Through photos and personal artifacts, the center tells the story of the Voting Rights March and the larger struggle for civil rights.

In Montgomery, continue your tour with a visit to the Rosa Parks Library and Museum, Dexter Avenue King Memorial Baptist Church, and Civil Rights Memorial.

Memorabilia at the **Old Depot Museum** (⊠ *4 Martin Luther King Jr. St.* ☎ *334/874–2197*) offers a glimpse of life in Selma from 1820 through the 21st century.

The **Vaughan-Smitherman Museum** (⊠ *109 Union St.* ☎ *334/874–2174*) is an antebellum structure that houses the Art Lewis Civil War Collection of Civil War memorabilia and antiques.

In late April, one of the largest biannual **Civil War reenactments** (☎ *800/457–3562* ⊕ *www.battleofselma.com*) in the nation draws thousands to the site of the Battle of Selma, on the Alabama River.

In mid-March the **Historic Selma Pilgrimage and Antique Show** (☎ *800/457–3562* ⊕ *pilgrimage.selmaalabama.com*) takes visitors through antebellum homes, museums, and churches.

MOBILE AND THE GULF COAST

Mobile is the state's oldest city and one of its most graceful. A springtime explosion of azaleas beneath Spanish moss–draped oak canopies gives Mobile the name Azalea City. Just a short drive west of Mobile, Bellingrath Gardens is a not-to-be-missed public garden that's especially sensational in the spring. Nearby are the small communities of Mobile Bay.

The area of the Gulf Coast around Gulf Shores, to the south of Mobile, encompasses about 50 mi of pure white-sand beach, including Pleasure Island, formerly a peninsula, and Dauphin Island to the west. Though hotels and condominiums take up a good deal of the beachfront, some of it remains public. Here you'll find small-town Southern beach life, with excellent deep-sea fishing as well as freshwater fishing in the bays and bayous, water sports of all types, and world-class golf.

MOBILE

170 mi southwest of Montgomery on I–65.

Originally named Fort Condé by the French in 1711, Mobile was the site of the first white settlement in what is now Alabama. For eight years it was the capital of French colonial Louisiana, and it remained under French control until 1763, long after the capital had moved to New Orleans.

GETTING HERE AND AROUND

Fort Condé houses the official welcome center for Mobile.

Gray Line Tours, in Mobile, has excellent 1- to 3½-hour trolley or motor-coach tours, departing from Fort Condé daily to Mobile's historic points of interest as well as to Bellingrath Gardens and the USS *Alabama.*

ESSENTIALS

Tour Contacts Gray Line Tours (☎ 251/432–2229 or 800/338–5597 ⊕ www.grayline.com).

Visitor Information Fort Condé (✉ 150 S. Royal St., Downtown ☎ 251/434–7304). **Mobile Convention & Bay Visitors Bureau** (☎ 251/208–2000 or 800/566–2453 ⊕ www.mobile.org).

EXPLORING

Mobile, a busy international port, is noted for its tree-lined boulevards fanning westward from the riverfront. In the heart of busy downtown is Bienville Square, a park with an ornate cast-iron fountain shaded by centuries-old live oaks. One of the city's main thoroughfares, Dauphin Street, has many thriving restaurants, bars, and shops.

Condé-Charlotte Museum House. Next to Fort Condé, the museum was built from 1822 to 1824 as Mobile's first official jail and contains rooms furnished in the style of different periods of the city's history. ✉ 104 Theatre St., Downtown ☎ 251/432–4722 ⊠ $5 ⊘ Tues.–Sat. 10–4.

OFF THE
BEATEN
PATH

☾ **Estuarium at the Dauphin Island Sea Lab.** This facility on Dauphin Island, a 17-mi-long barrier island about 40 mi south of Mobile, spotlights the ecosystems of the Mobile Bay estuary, including the Mobile–Tensaw River Delta, Mobile Bay, the barrier islands, and the Gulf of Mexico. Outside, the Living Marsh Boardwalk has signs explaining the natural history of the state's marshes. Indoors are displays, interactive exhibits, a 9,000-gallon aquarium simulating the underwater environment of Mobile Bay, and a 16,000-gallon tank with sea life from the Gulf of Mexico. ✉ 101 Bienville Blvd.; take I–10 to Exit 17A, then Rte. 193S to Dauphin Island; turn left at the water tower and proceed 2.2 mi, Dauphin Island ☎ 251/861–7500 ⊕ www.disl.org ⊠ $7 ⊘ Sept.–Feb., Mon.–Sat. 9–5, Sun. 1–5; Mar.–Aug., Mon.–Sat. 9–6, Sun. noon–6.

Fort Condé. This fort in the center of town survives as a reminder of the city's beginnings. It was reconstructed at one third the original size when its remains were discovered—150 years after the fort was destroyed—during the building of the I–10 interchange. A portion of the fort, built from 1724 to 1735, houses the **visitor center** for the city and a museum. Brochures at the center outline excellent walking tours of the

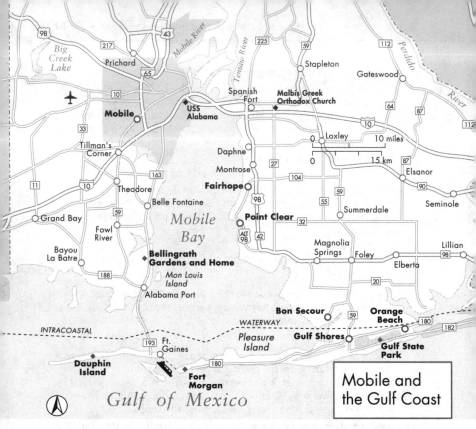

Mobile and
the Gulf Coast

city's historic districts, including De Tonti Square, Church Street East, and Dauphin Street. ⊠*150 S. Royal St., Downtown* ☎*251/434–7304* ◻*Free* ⊘*Daily 8–5.*

Gulf Coast Exploreum Science Center. Across from the Mobile Convention Center downtown is a science museum with a popular Hands On Hall, where kids of all ages can have fun while learning through interactive exhibits. Films in the state-of-the-art IMAX Dome Theater change every few months. Parking is at a premium in this area but is available in the lot across from Fort Condé off Royal Street. ⊠*65 Government St., Downtown* ☎*251/208–6873 or 877/625–4386* ⊕*www.exploreum. com* ◻*Exhibits $7–$8.75; IMAX theater $6–$7.75; both $10.75–$13* ⊘*Tues.–Fri. 9–5, Sat. 10–5, Sun. noon–5.*

Mobile Museum of Art. A $15 million expansion and renovation in 2002 tripled the Mobile Museum's former space. In addition to its impressive permanent collection of some 6,000 pieces of mostly American art, the museum hosts traveling exhibits. A branch gallery, **Mobile Museum of Art Downtown** (⊠*300 Dauphin St., Downtown* ☎*251/208–5200*), is near Cathedral Park. ⊠*Langan Park, 4850 Museum Dr., Spring Hill* ☎*251/208–5200* ⊕*www.mobilemuseumofart.com* ◻*$6* ⊘*Mon.–Sat. 10–5, Sun. 1–5.*

1

OFF THE BEATEN PATH

★**Bellingrath Gardens and Home** is famous for its magnificent azaleas, which are part of 65 acres of gardens in a 905-acre semitropical landscape. Showtime for the azaleas is late February through mid-March, when some 250,000 plantings of 200 different species are ablaze with color, but Bellingrath is a year-round wonder, with 2,500 rosebushes blooming in summer, 60,000 chrysanthemum

> **MOBILE'S MARDI GRAS**
>
> Mobilians boast that **Mardi Gras** (⊕ www.mobilemardigras.com) began here long before New Orleans ever celebrated Fat Tuesday, and the city still celebrates the pre-Lenten season, usually in February, with parades and merrymaking day and night.

plants cascading in the fall, and red fields of poinsettias brightening the winter. At the annual Magic Christmas in Lights event, holiday decorations in the gardens light up the night throughout December. Countless species and flowering plants spring up along Fowl River, and a free map lets you plan your own strolls along flagstone paths and across charming bridges. In April and October, large numbers of migratory birds drop by. One-hour **boat cruises** on Fowl River aboard the *Southern Belle* leave from the dock next to the Bellingrath Home at regular intervals. ✉*12401 Bellingrath Rd., Theodore* ☎*251/973–2217 or 800/247–8420* ⊕*www.bellingrath.org* ✍*Gardens $11; gardens and home $19; value pack (gardens, home, and cruise) $27* ⊙ *Gardens daily 8–sunset; home opens daily at 9 with closings varying by season.*

WHERE TO EAT

¢–$
AMERICAN
★

✕**Dew Drop Inn.** Mobile's oldest restaurant, the no-frills Dew Drop Inn is also one of the city's most popular places to meet and eat. The "world famous" Dew Drop Inn hot dog goes well with homemade onion rings or thick-cut steak fries. Daily specials include down-home favorites such as fried chicken or catfish, accompanied by perfectly seasoned vegetables. ✉*1808 Old Shell Rd., Midtown* ☎*251/473–7872* ⌦*Reservations not accepted* ▤*MC, V* ⊙*Closed Sun.*

$–$$
SEAFOOD

✕**Original Oyster House.** Destroyed during Hurricane Katrina, this Mobile Bay Causeway restaurant relocated a few months later about a mile from its original location, causing seafood lovers, who continue to pack the restaurant, to breathe a collective sigh of relief. Specialties include fried crab claws, Mike's grilled shrimp, shrimp and grits, and blackened mahimahi topped with fried crawfish tails and tasso ham cream sauce. ✉*3733 Battleship Pkwy., Spanish Fort* ☎*251/626–2188* ⊕*www.theoysterhouse.com* ▤*AE, D, MC, V* ⊙*Closed Mon.*

$$–$$$
AMERICAN

✕**The Pillars.** Chef Matt Shipp is a Mobile native who trained in kitchens from New York to New Orleans. Housed in a midtown mansion, the restaurant provides an intimate and elegant setting, excellent service, and the finest in steaks and seafood. The chef's Gulf Coast favorites such as turtle soup and shrimp and grits give a Southern twist to the menu. ✉*1757 Government St., The Loop* ☎*251/471–3411* ⊕*www.thepillars-mobile.com* ▤*AE, D, DC, MC, V* ⊙*No lunch on Sat.; Closed Sun.*

$$–$$$
SEAFOOD
★

✕ **Wintzell's Oyster House.** Fried, stewed, or nude—that's how this downtown Mobile landmark famously prepares its oysters. J. Oliver Wintzell opened the restaurant in 1938 as a six-stool oyster bar, and it now has several locations throughout the Mobile area, including Downtown, West Mobile, Saraland, Spanish Fort, and Fairhope. The walls are covered with Wintzell's nuggets of wisdom, including "Don't criticize your wife's judgment—look who she married" and "Generally, if you concentrate on rowing a boat, you won't have time to rock it." For lunch, try a bowl of gumbo or a shrimp or oyster po'boy. For dinner, the seafood platter or the catch of the day are good picks. ⊠ *605 Dauphin St., Downtown* ☎ *251/432–4605* ⊕ *wintzellsoysterhouse.com* ⊟ *AE, D, MC, V* ⊘ *Closed Mon.*

WHERE TO STAY

$$$–$$$$ ⊡ **The Battle House, a Renaissance Hotel.** The renovation of this 1852 hotel, once called the "living room of Mobile," returned a grand part of the city's history to use. The hotel, which was closed from the 1970s until 2007, retains some of its original charms, such as the Tiffany glass ceiling in the lobby of its restaurant, the Trellis Room ($$$$). Parting with tradition, the rooms have all the latest amenities, including flatscreen TVs, and Mobile's nicest spa is on-site. The lobby is classy and bright with hues of red, blue, yellow, and green. At the Whispering Arches on the second floor, you can send secret messages to someone across the way by whispering into the wall. **Pros:** nicest hotel in Mobile; all rooms have four-fixture bathrooms; beds have down comforters and plenty of pillows; you can pay $25 to enjoy "quiet rooms" with large Jacuzzis; on-site barber offers straight-razor shaves. **Cons:** hotel is separated into two towers, which are far away from each other; $16 valet parking only; $9.95 daily fee for Wi-Fi. ⊠ *26 N. Royal St., Downtown* ☎ *251/338–2000* ⊕ *www.rsabattlehouse.com* ⊃ *238 rooms, 31 suites* ⋔ *In-hotel: 3 restaurants, room service, bar, pool, gym, spa, no-smoking rooms* ⊟ *AE, D, MC, V.*

$–$$ ⊡ **Malaga Inn.** A delightful romantic getaway, the Malaga comprises
★   two town houses built by a wealthy landowner in 1862. The lobby opens onto a landscaped central courtyard with a fountain, and the rooms are large and airy. The Malaga, which is furnished with antiques, is on a quiet street downtown, within walking distance of the Museum of Mobile and the Gulf Coast Exploreum. **Pros:** historic charm; all rooms decorated differently; free continental breakfast. **Cons:** restaurant recently closed (no lunch/dinner); some rooms are more comfortable than others. ⊠ *359 Church St., Downtown* ☎ *251/438–4701 or 800/235–1586* ⊕ *www.malagainn.com* ⊃ *35 rooms, 3 suites* ⋔ *Inroom: Wi-Fi. In-hotel: pool, Wi-Fi, parking (free)* ⊟ *AE, D, MC, V* ⱺ *CP.*

NIGHTLIFE

Much of Mobile's nightlife centers around downtown's former commercial district, **Dauphin Street,** which has a number of restaurants and nightspots spread out over several blocks. Mobilians have taken to calling the area LoDa, short for "Lower Dauphin."

A quintessential neighborhood pub near downtown Mobile, **Callaghan's Irish Social Club** (⊠ *916 Charleston St., Oakleigh* ☎ *251/433–9374* ⊕ *www.callaghansirishsocialclub.com*) has live music and a friendly atmosphere. In midtown Mobile, the **Double Olive** (⊠ *2033 Airport*

Blvd., Midtown ☎*251/450–5001* ⊕*www.doubleolive.com*) is an artsy, urbane martini bar that draws hip crowds and has 26 signature martinis. **The Soul Kitchen** (⊠*219 Dauphin St., Downtown* ☎*334/433–5958* ⊕*www.soulkitchenmobile.com*) hosts local bands as well as a few national ones, drawing crowds of 20-somethings on Friday and Saturday nights.

SPORTS AND THE OUTDOORS

BOATING Named for the rivers that flow into Mobile Bay (Mobile, Spanish, Tensaw, Apalachee, and Blakeley), **5 Rivers** (⊠*30945 Five Rivers Blvd., Spanish Fort* ☎*251/625–0814* ⊕*www.outdooralabama.com*) offers visitors various ways to explore the delta. Daily boat rides may provide a glimpse of an alligator or a blue heron. You can rent a canoe or kayak or launch your own. The facility also has several nature paths and an exhibit hall.

GOLF The 18-hole, par-72 **Azalea City Golf Club** (⊠*1000 Gaillard Dr., Spring Hill* ☎*251/208–5150*) is operated by the city of Mobile. **Magnolia Grove** (⊠*7001 Lamplighter Dr., Northwest* ☎*251/645–0075 or 800/949–4444*), part of the Robert Trent Jones Golf Trail, has 54 holes of championship golf: two par-72 courses and an 18-hole, par-54 (each hole is par 3) course that is anything but easy. **Rock Creek** (⊠*140 Clubhouse Dr., Fairhope* ☎*251/928–4223*), in Fairhope, on the eastern shore of Mobile Bay, has 18 holes and is par 72. **TimberCreek** (⊠*9650 Timber-Creek Blvd., Daphne* ☎*251/621–9900*), in Daphne, has 27 holes and is par 72.

SHOPPING

Antiques buffs love Mobile because it offers more than 25 individual shops and malls that specialize in antiques. In the Loop area of midtown (where Government Street, Airport Boulevard, and Dauphin Island Parkway converge), several shops are within walking distance.

The seemingly endless **Antiques at the Loop** (⊠*2103 Airport Blvd., The Loop* ☎*251/476–0309*) has lamps, stained glass, furnishings, and garden accessories. The **Cotton City Antique Mall** (⊠*2012 Airport Blvd., The Loop* ☎*251/479–9747*) offers 12,000 square feet of antique furniture, vintage linens, clocks, and more. **Mary Parker Antiques** (⊠*418 Dauphin Island Pkwy., The Loop* ☎*251/473–9227*) has 8,000 square feet of antiques, from glassware and sewing machines to furniture. **Yellow House Antiques** (⊠*1902 Government St., The Loop* ☎*251/476–7382*) is an upscale shop with 18th- and 19th-century English, Continental, and American furniture and accessories.

FAIRHOPE AND POINT CLEAR

12 mi south of Malbis on U.S. 98A.

Clinging to the eastern shore of Mobile Bay, the quiet towns of Fairhope and Point Clear have restored clapboard houses with wide porches overlooking the bay and live oak trees cloaked with Spanish moss. Fairhope was settled around 1900 by a group of Midwesterners who established it as a utopian single-tax community (the system is still in use). Today Fairhope's streets are lined with seasonal flowers year-round—even the trash receptacles double as planters—and the downtown area has antiques shops, funky stores, art galleries, and B&Bs, making it a relaxing weekend escape. The Fairhope Municipal Pier, the centerpiece of town, offers fishing, boating, and marine services. Fairhope's Arts and Crafts Festival, held each March, is a large juried show that draws more than 200 exhibitors for a weekend.

Point Clear's incomparable Grand Hotel Marriott, operating since 1847, is a leading resort destination hidden away among million-dollar bayside estates. A stroll along the hotel's boardwalk provides a glimpse of the summer homes that line Mobile Bay.

> ### JUBILEE
>
> Sometime between June and September locals and visitors in Mobile Bay eagerly await the natural phenomenon known as a jubilee. During a jubilee the bay's inhabitants—fish, crabs, shrimp, and more—leave deeper water and scramble for shore usually in the middle of the night. Everyone grabs their nets to collect as many disoriented and oxygen-deprived fish as possible in the shallow water of the bay. Scientists aren't sure what makes the sea creatures leave their watery home, but it sure makes for good eats.

WHERE TO EAT AND STAY

$$$–$$$$
SOUTHERN

✕**The Fairhope Inn and Restaurant.** Owner-chef Tyler Kean's restaurant, inside a B&B, is fast becoming the place to dine in Fairhope. Elegant yet not stuffy, the small dining room extends onto an enclosed porch that overlooks a lush private courtyard. Kean's menu changes seasonally but may include pan-roasted grouper with asparagus and morel mushrooms in a red-wine sauce served over grits. Sunday brunch is quite popular. ✉ *63 S. Church St., Fairhope* ☎ *251/928–6226* ⊕ *www.thefairhopeinn. com* 🖃 *AE, D, DC, MC, V* ☉ *Closed Mon.*

$–$$
AMERICAN

✕**Manci's Antique Club, Inc.** The walls of this former produce warehouse turned gas station turned bar and grill are covered in antiques ranging from a large collection of Jim Beam decanters to farm implements; the parking area features hitching posts. The casual restaurant is known for its juicy Angus hamburgers, including the "Hurricane Burger," loaded with chili, cheese, bacon, onions, mushrooms, jalapeño peppers, and sour cream, and has oyster and shrimp po'boys and spider (soft-shell crab) sandwiches. For a laugh, ladies can go into the restroom and "lift the leaf," but be warned: the whole restaurant will know you peeked. ✉ *1715 Main St., Daphne* ☎ *251/626–9917* ⊕ *www.manci.net* 🖃 *AE, D, MC, V.*

$$–$$$

🛏**Bay Breeze Guest House.** A winding white-shell driveway leads through a camellia and azalea garden to this stucco-and-wood B&B owned by Bill and Becky Jones. The property, which was Becky's childhood home, fronts Mobile Bay not far from downtown Fairhope and has a 462-foot-long pier for fishing, crabbing, sunbathing, or just relaxing (on summer weekends breakfast is served at the end of the pier). Bedrooms in the main house have wood floors, brass queen-size beds, and antique furnishings. The cottage suites are light and spacious. **Pros:** private beach and pier; 3-acre garden for strolling. **Cons:** must call ahead to see if you can bring kids; no phones in rooms. ✉ *742 S. Mobile St., Box 526, Fairhope* ☎ *251/928–8976 or 866/928–8976* ⊕ *www.baybreeze.*

us ⌧*4 suites, 1 garden cottage room* &*In-room: no phone, kitchen (some), Wi-Fi. In-hotel: beachfront, bicycles, no-smoking rooms* ⊟*AE, D, MC, V* ⦿|*BP.*

$$$–$$$$ ⌧**Grand Hotel Marriott Resort, Golf Club & Spa.** Nestled amid 550 acres
★ of beautifully landscaped grounds on Mobile Bay, the Grand has been a cherished landmark since 1847 and is one of the South's premier resorts. The octagonal, two-story cypress-paneled and -beamed lobby serves as the hub for several wings. Its large three-sided fireplace, armchairs, and porcelain display evoke a casual elegance echoed in the half-moon dining room overlooking the bay. Renovations in 2002 and after Hurricane Katrina have expanded and improved the hotel, adding water fountains and a lagoon, a beach with a boat launch, a European spa, and contemporary suites. The resort's Lakewood Golf Club is the southernmost link in the Robert Trent Jones Golf Trail. **Pros:** peaceful location; kid-friendly activities; nice Sunday brunch; spa on-site. **Cons:** the beaches front a brackish bay, not ocean; limited parking (shuttle to remote lot). ⌧*1 Grand Blvd., just off Scenic 98, or 98A, Point Clear* ☎*251/928–9201 or 800/544–9933* ⦿*www.marriottgrand.com* ⌧*405 rooms, 30 suites* &*In-room: refrigerator (some), Wi-Fi. In-hotel: 5 restaurants, room service, bar, golf courses, tennis courts, pools, spa, beachfront, bicycles, children's programs (5–12), laundry service, parking (paid), no-smoking rooms* ⊟*AE, D, DC, MC, V.*

THE GULF COAST

50 mi south of Mobile via U.S. 90E and AL 59.

With sugary white sand and gentle, warm water, the Gulf Coast is by far one of the state's greatest attractions. The cooling offshore breezes provide a nice respite from the hot, humid summer temperatures. Although the Gulf Shores beach area has plenty of concessions and is usually crowded, those seeking isolated beach walks need only venture a couple of miles west. To the east is Orange Beach, a heavily developed coastal strip between the Gulf of Mexico and Perdido Bay.

ESSENTIALS

Visitor Information Alabama Gulf Coast Convention & Visitors Bureau
(⌧*23658 Perdido Beach Blvd., Orange Beach* ☎*251/968–7511 or 800/745–7263* ⦿*www.gulfshores.com).*

Bon Secour National Wildlife Refuge. Eight miles west of Gulf Shores, the 6,200 acres of this refuge are home to native and migratory birds and a number of endangered species, including the loggerhead sea turtle. You can hike or swim at some of the five units of the refuge. ⌧*12295 AL 180W, Bon Secour* ☎*251/540–7720* ⦿*www.fws.gov/bonsecour/.*

★ **Gulf State Park.** Along with 2½ mi of pure white beaches and glimmering dunes, the park has two freshwater lakes with fishing, plus biking, hiking, and jogging trails through pine forests; a gulf-front resort lodge and convention center; 496 full-hook-up campsites; 21 cottages; and a golf course. The park was undergoing renovations in 2009. ⌧*20115 AL 135, Gulf Shores* ☎*251/948–7275, 800/544–4853, or 800/252–7275* ⦿*www.alapark.com/GulfState/.*

☺ **Waterville USA.** Set on 17 acres, Waterville has a wave pool with 3-foot waves, 10 exciting waterslides, and a lazy river ride around the park. For younger children there are gentler rides in a supervised play area. The adjacent amusement park has a 36-hole miniature golf course, a video-game arcade, and an amusement park with roller coaster, NASCAR go-karts, kiddie area, "House of Bounce," trampoline, and flow rider—all priced per ride or game. ⊠*906 Gulf Shores Pkwy. (AL 59), Gulf Shores* ☎*251/948–2106* ⊕*www.watervilleusa.com* ☎*$30 (water park)* ☉ *Water park, Memorial Day–Labor Day, daily 10–6; amusement park, Mar.–Sept., daily 10–varies.*

> **WORD OF MOUTH**
>
> "The best time [to visit Gulf Shores] when it's not crowded and the weather is still nice would likely be shoulder seasons such as May (except for Memorial Day weekend) and September (after Labor Day weekend)."   —corli33

WHERE TO EAT

$$$–$$$$ ✕**Bayside Grill.** For fine dining overlooking the back bays that channel to
SEAFOOD the Gulf, you can't beat this choice. Caribbean cuisine is the chef's specialty, including fresh-caught seafood every night and a boiled seafood platter, but Bayside Grill also serves pasta, steak, salads, and chicken in large portions and a spectacular Sunday brunch. ⊠*27842 Canal Rd., Orange Beach* ☎*251/981–4899* ⊟*AE, D, MC, V.*

$$ ✕**Lulu's Homeport Marina.** With a famous brother lending celebrity status,
SEAFOOD and an enviable location on the Intracoastal Waterway, Lucy Buffett—Jimmy's sister—couldn't miss with her laid-back restaurant. Fortunately, the food is as good as the atmosphere. Start with the black-eyed-pea dip on crackers, known as "L.A. (Lower Alabama) caviar," and don't miss the blackened grouper po'boy topped with fried green tomato slices. Of course, there is a "Cheeseburger in Paradise" for Jimmy Buffet fans. There is also live music and other events on the weekends. ⊠*200 E. 25th Ave., Gulf Shores* ☎*251/967–5858* ⊕ *www.lulusathomeport. com* ⌂*Reservations not accepted* ⊟*AE, D, MC, V*

$$$$ ✕**Voyagers.** Roses and art deco touches set the tone for this airy, elegant
CONTINENTAL dining room. Two-level seating allows beach or poolside views from
★ every table. Chef James Freeman creates dishes such as trout with roasted pecans in Creole *meunière* sauce (dredged in flour with brown butter) and a rack of lamb seasoned with Dijon mustard and a Bordelaise sauce (red wine, marrow, shallots, and demi-glace). Finish up with a bread pudding soufflé with bourbon and vanilla whiskey sauce. Service is deft, and the wine selection is extensive. ⊠*Perdido Beach Resort, 27200 Perdido Beach Blvd., Orange Beach* ☎*251/981–9811 Ext. 112* ⊕*www.perdidobeachresort.com* ⊟*AE, D, DC, MC, V* ☉*Closed Mon. and Tues. Oct.–Mar. No lunch.*

WHERE TO STAY

$$$–$$$$ 🏨 **Gulf Shores Plantation.** This 320-acre family resort, 12 mi west of Gulf
★ Shores, faces the Gulf and has several condominium complexes as well as two-story duplex cottages that can accommodate up to 33 people each. Located next door, Kiva Dunes Golf Course is consistently ranked among the state's best by magazines such as *Golf Digest* and *Golf*. **Pros:**

family resort with lots of on-site activities; secluded; free Wi-Fi. **Cons:** not much within walking distance; parts of facility 25-plus years old. ⌧*805 Plantation Rd., Gulf Shores* ☎*251/540–5000 or 800/554–0344* ⊕*www.gulfshoresplantation.com* ⟳*524 units* ⌂*In-room: kitchen (some), refrigerator (some), Wi-Fi. In-hotel: tennis courts, pools, gym, beachfront, laundry facilities, no-smoking rooms* ▭*AE, D, MC, V.*

$$$–$$$$ 🏨**Original Romar House Bed and Breakfast Inn.** This unassuming beach cottage is filled with surprises—from the Caribbean-style upstairs sitting area to the Purple Parrot Bar to the art-deco-style guest rooms, each with a private bath. Built in 1924, the inn was closed and renovated after Hurricane Ivan in 2004, reopening in 2008. **Pros:** wine and cheese reception Monday through Saturday evenings; make-your-own-drinks honor bar; free Wi-Fi, even poolside. **Cons:** no TV in most rooms; no children under 16. ⌧*23500 Perdido Beach Blvd., Orange Beach* ☎*251/974–1625 or 800/487–6627* ⊕*www.bbonline.com/al/ romarhouse* ⟳*7 rooms* ⌂*In-room: no TV (some), Wi-Fi. In-hotel: bar, pool, beachfront, bicycles, no kids under 16, no-smoking rooms* ▭*AE, MC, V* ⎹◎⎹*BP.*

$$$–$$$$ 🏨**Perdido Beach Resort.** The eight- and nine-story towers of this resort
★ are faced with Mediterranean stucco and red tile, while the lobby is tiled in terra-cotta and decorated with a brass sculpture of gulls in flight and mosaics by Venetian artists. Rooms are furnished in coastal style, and all have a beach view and balcony. **Pros:** poolside bar; free parking; one of few hotels in area with conference facilities; delicious breakfast buffet at Café Palm Breeze. **Cons:** limited parking, so may have to park across street; no pay-per-view movies; closes for two weeks every year for renovations. ⌧*27200 Perdido Beach Blvd., Box 400, Orange Beach* ☎*251/981–9811 or 800/634–7263* ⊕*www.perdido-beachresort.com* ⟳*333 rooms, 12 suites* ⌂*In-hotel: 3 restaurants, bar, tennis courts, pool, gym, beachfront, laundry service, parking (free), no-smoking rooms* ▭*AE, D, MC, V.*

NIGHTLIFE AND THE ARTS

On the Alabama–Florida line is the sprawling **Flora-Bama Lounge** (⌧*17401 Perdido Key Dr., Pensacola, FL* ☎*251/980–5118 or 251/980–5119* ⊕*www.florabama.com*), home of the annual Interstate Mullet Toss, a fish-throwing competition. It's open 11 AM–2:30 AM, with live bands nightly and outdoor seating in summer.

SPORTS AND THE OUTDOORS

Gulf State Park (⌧*20115 AL 135, Gulf Shores* ☎*251/948–7275* ⊕*www. alapark.com*) has biking trails through pine forests and fishing spots.

FISHING   Deep-sea fishing from charter boats is popular, but take precautions
OUTFITTERS against sea sickness. Catches from deep-sea expeditions include king mackerel, amberjack, tuna, white marlin, blue marlin, grouper, bonito, sailfish, and red snapper.

Sand Roc Cay Marina (☎*800/806–7889* ⊕*www.sanroccay.com*) has fishing trips from $100 per person with specials in the off-season.

The complex at **Zeke's Landing** (☎*800/793–4044* ⊕*www.zekeslanding. com*) has a marina, restaurants, shops, and a fleet of charter boats for fishing trips.

GOLF Coastal Alabama has developed into one of the nicest golfing destinations in the Southeast. Prices for these courses range from about $35 to $70 for green fees and a cart.

The spectacular 18-hole, par-72 course adjacent to Gulf Shores Plantation Resort, **Kiva Dunes** (✉ *12 mi west of Gulf Shores on AL 180, Gulf Shores* ☎ *251/540–7000* ⊕ *www.kivadunes.com*), designed by Jerry Pate, combines oceanfront dunes golf with Scottish-style links golf. The complex **Craft Farms** (✉ *3840 Cotton Creek Cir., off AL 59 just north of Gulf Shores, Gulf Shores* ☎ *251/968–7500 or 800/327–2657* ⊕ *www.craftfarms.com*) has two 18-hole, par-72 courses designed by Arnold Palmer: Cotton Creek and Cypress Bend. About 12 mi north of Gulf Shores in Foley, the **Glenlakes Golf Club** (✉ *9530 Clubhouse Dr., Foley* ☎ *251/955–1220* ⊕ *www.glenlakesgolf.com*), a course designed by Bruce Devlin, has 18 challenging holes that play par 72 over 7,000 yards and another 9 holes that play par 35 stretching 3,100 yards. The 18-hole, par-72 course at **Gulf State Park** (✉ *20115 AL 135, Gulf Shores* ☎ *251/948–7275* ⊕ *www.alapark.com*), in Gulf Shores, is one of the area's oldest but most scenic and best-maintained courses along the coast.

SAILING AND WATER SPORTS Dolphin and nature cruises are available at **Cetacean Cruises** (☎ *251/550–8000* ⊕ *www.cetaceancruises.com*) in Orange Beach. Reservations are required to ride the glass-bottom boats. For a wild adventure, try parasailing above the Gulf of Mexico through **Chute 'Em Up Parasail** (☎ *251/981–7673*) in Orange Beach.

Scuba divers can catch a glimpse of the world-famous USS *Orinskany* aircraft carrier, which serves as an artificial reef, or more than 50 other wrecks and reefs in the Alabama–Florida waterways through **Down Under Dive Shop** (☎ *251/968–3483* ⊕ *www.downunderdiveshop.com*) in Gulf Shores. **Gary's Gulf Divers** (☎ *251/968–4279* ⊕ *www.gulfdiver.net*) is a full-service dive shop in Orange Beach.

SHOPPING

You can do everything from shop to catch a live concert at the Alabama Gulf Coast's newest shopping center, **The Wharf** in Orange Beach. The Wharf has 16 eateries, 40 shops, a nightclub, indoor miniature golf, a Ferris wheel, a 15-screen movie theater, and a 10,000-seat amphitheater. ✉ *23101 Canal Rd., Orange Beach* ☎ *251/980–4444* ⊕ *www. thewharfal.com*.

Florida

THE PANHANDLE AND SPACE COAST

WORD OF MOUTH

"The South Walton beaches along 30A are cooler than farther south that time of the year. Beautiful white sand, wonderful restaurants . . . a lot of things to do for all ages."

—Dana_M

"Any of the Florida state parks on the waterfront are worth seeing and spending time in and they all offer different amenities and levels of nature."

—newsbear

Updated By
Gary McKech-
nie and Kerry
Speckman

Florida's thin, green northwest corner snuggles up between the Gulf of Mexico and the Alabama and Georgia state lines. The Panhandle is sometimes called "the other Florida," since in addition to palm trees, what thrive here are the magnolias, live oaks, and loblolly pines common in the rest of the Deep South.

Until World War II, when activity at the Panhandle air bases took off, this section of the state was little known and seldom visited. But by the mid-1950s, the 100-mi stretch along the coast between Pensacola and Panama City was dubbed the Miracle Strip because of a dramatic property value rise. In the 1940s this beachfront land sold for less than $100 an acre; today that same acre can fetch hundreds of thousands of dollars. To convey the richness of the region, with its white sands and sparkling green waters, swamps, bayous, and flora, public-relations pros ditched the Redneck Riviera moniker that locals had created and coined the phrase Emerald Coast.

East of the Panhandle, northeastern Florida's primary draw is its beaches. Hugging the coast are long, slender barrier islands whose entire eastern sides make up a broad band of spectacular sand. The highlights of this area are Daytona Beach, the Spring Break Capital of the U.S., and the Kennedy Space Center.

ORIENTATION AND PLANNING

GETTING ORIENTED

The Panhandle is a large area, and the lack of sufficient air service can make it tough to access. However, from Pensacola, U.S. 98 generally skirts along the Gulf of Mexico through seaside towns and communities like Fort Walton Beach, Destin, Panama City Beach, Seaside, and Apalachicola.

About two hours south of Jacksonville on Interstate 95, Titusville, the entry point for the Kennedy Space Center, marks the northern perimeter of the Space Coast. If you take U.S. 1, it lengthens the trip, but the scenery makes up for the inconvenience. Route A1A (mostly called Atlantic Avenue south of St. Augustine) is the main road on all the barrier islands, and it's here that you find the best beaches.

The Emerald Coast. The Florida Panhandle beaches from roughly Pensacola Beach east to Apalachicola have been dubbed the Emerald Coast. Fort Walton Beach and Destin are two top vacation spots, while Grayton Beach is a good bet for a quieter destination. Farther east even the urban areas like Panama City Beach and Apalachicola have beaches that are well-preserved and inviting.

2

TOP REASONS TO GO

Snowy white beaches: Most of the Panhandle's Gulf Coast shoreline is relatively unobstructed by high-rise condos and hotels, and the white-powder sand is alluring.

A need for speed: Few things will get racing fans as revved up as the Daytona 500 Experience, the official attraction of NASCAR, and tours of Daytona International Speedway, home of the Daytona 500 and Coke Zero 400.

We have a liftoff: The John F. Kennedy Space Center and the United

States Astronaut Hall of Fame are must-see attractions for budding Buzz Aldrins or anyone who remembers the Apollo 11 moon landing.

Northeast Florid-aaah: Oceanfront destination spas like the Shores Resort & Spa in Daytona Beach are amusement parks of a different kind.

Good natured: A wealth of state and national parks means canoeing, fishing, sunbathing, hiking, bird-watching, and camping opportunities are just a stone's throw away.

Tallahassee. As the state capital (chosen because it was midway between the two earlier Spanish headquarters of St. Augustine and Pensacola), Tallahassee is worth visiting for its history, universities, and quite country charm.

Daytona Beach and the Space Coast. The Daytona 500, Bike Week, and spring break put it on the map, but Daytona Beach has become a popular family vacation destination. The Space Coast includes the Canaveral National Seashore, home to the John F. Kennedy Space Center and Cocoa Beach, the ultimate boogie-board beach town.

PLANNING

WHEN TO GO

Peak season is Memorial Day to Labor Day, with another spike during spring break. There's a "secret season" that falls around October and November. Things quiet down as students go back to school, but restaurants and attractions keep normal hours and the weather is moderate.

GETTING HERE AND AROUND

AIR TRAVEL

None of Florida's major airports are in the Panhandle, but Panama City, Pensacola, and Tallahassee make do with their smaller facilities. On the Northeast, Jacksonville International Airport (JAX) is the main hub with service to and from all major cities by the major carriers. Daytona Beach International (DAB) is a smaller operation with fewer flights. Although Orlando isn't part of the area, visitors to northeastern Florida often choose to arrive at Orlando International Airport (MCO) since cheaper flights are often available; however, the headache isn't always worth the savings.

Air Contacts Daytona Beach International Airport (DAB) (☎ 386/248–8069 ⊕ www.volusia.org/airport). **Jacksonville International Airport (JAX)** (☎ 904/741–4902 ⊕ www.jaa.aero). **Orlando International (MCO)**

(☎ 407/825-2001 ⊕ www.orlandoairports.net). **Panama City Bay County Airport** (☎ 850/763-6751 ⊕ www.pcairport.com). **Pensacola Gulf Coast Regional Airport** (☎ 850/436-5005 ⊕ www.flypensacola.com). **Tallahassee Regional Airport** (☎ 850/891-7800 ⊕ www.talgov.com/airport).

CAR TRAVEL

The main east–west arteries across the top of the state are Interstate 10 and U.S. 90. I–10 can be monotonous, but U.S. 90 piques your interest by routing you along the main streets of several county seats. U.S. 98 snakes eastward along the coast, splitting into 98 and 98A at Inlet Beach before rejoining at Panama City and continuing on to Port St. Joe and Apalachicola. The view of the gulf from U.S. 98 can be breathtaking, especially at sunset, but ongoing construction make it slow going most of the time. If you need to get from one end of the Panhandle to the other in a timely manner, drive inland to I–10, where the speed limit runs as high as 70 mph in places.

Along the east coast, if you want to drive as close to the Atlantic as possible and are not in a hurry, stick with Route A1A. It runs along the barrier islands, changing its name several times along the way.

RESTAURANTS

An abundance of seafood is served at coastal restaurants: oysters, crab, shrimp, scallops, and a variety of fish. Of course, that's not all there is on the menu. This part of Florida still impresses diners with old-fashioned comfort foods such as meat loaf, fried chicken, beans and cornbread, okra, and fried-green tomatoes. You'll also find small-town seafood shacks where you can dine "Florida Cracker"–style on deep-fried mullet, cheese grits, coleslaw, and hush puppies.

HOTELS

Many of the lodging selections here revolve around extended-stay options: resorts, condos, and time shares that allow for a week or more in simple efficiencies, as well as fully furnished homes. There are also cabins, such as the ones that rest between the dunes at Grayton Beach. During the summer and over holiday weekends, always reserve ahead for top properties.

WHAT IT COSTS				
	¢	$	$$	$$$	$$$$
Restaurant	under $10	$10–$14	$15–$19	$20–$30	over $30
Hotel	under $80	$80–$100	$101–$140	$141–$220	over $220

Restaurant prices are per person for a main course at dinner. Hotel prices are for a standard double room, excluding state and local taxes.

VISITOR INFORMATION

Contacts Visit Florida (✉ 2540 W. Executive Center Circle, Ste. 200, Tallahassee ☎ 850/488-5607 ⊕ www.visitflorida.com).

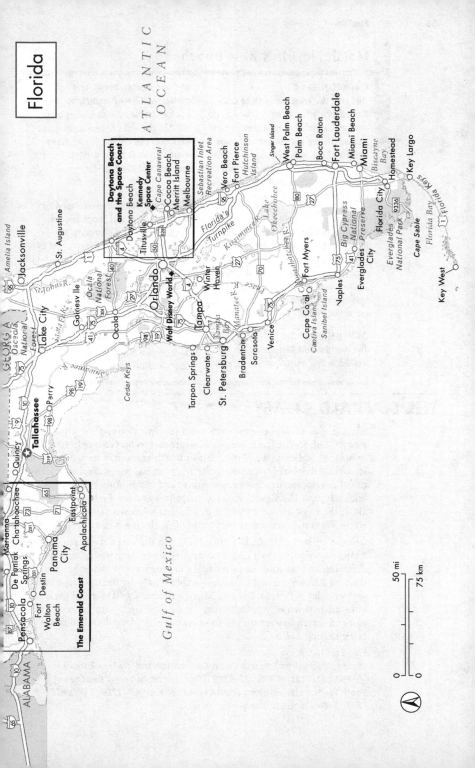

Florida

North Florida's Best Beaches

GRAYTON BEACH

This area will take you back to Old Florida where there are no condos, no strip malls, and no beach concessions. Instead, there's a state park that has preserved the area, big dunes, ample bird-watching and wildlife viewing, and on-the-water activities like canoeing, fishing, sailing, and swimming.

PANAMA CITY BEACH

If your visit to the Panhandle is based purely on beach access and activities, then this is where you want to be. A popular family retreat most times, families tend to steer clear during spring break, when it gets a bit crazy, but arrive in droves in the summer.

DAYTONA BEACH

The World's Most Famous Beach is fronted with a mixture of tall condos and apartments, hotels, low-rise motels, and flashy nightclubs. Traffic can get backed up, as driving on the sand is allowed (be careful, because cars can, and do, get stuck); areas marked no-car zones are less frenetic and more family-friendly.

COCOA BEACH

As home to Ron Jon Surf Shop (the world's largest surf shop) and the Cocoa Beach Surf Company (the world's largest surf complex), and the birthplace of eight-time world surfing champion Kelly Slater, it's only fitting that Cocoa Beach be dubbed "Surfing Capital of the East Coast." Stretching far over the Atlantic, the Cocoa Beach Pier (which extends 800 feet into the Atlantic) is an everyday gathering spot as well as a beachside grandstand for space-shuttle launches.

THE EMERALD COAST

On U.S. 98, several towns, each with its own personality, are strung along the shoreline from Pensacola southeast to St. George Island. The twin cities of Destin and Fort Walton Beach seemingly merge into one sprawling destination and continue to spread as more condominiums, resort developments, shopping centers, and restaurants crowd the skyline each year. The view changes drastically—and for the better—farther along the coast as you enter the quiet stretch known as the Beaches of South Walton, scattered along Route 30A, the main coastal road.

Continuing southeast on U.S. 98, you'll find Panama City Beach, whose "Miracle Strip" has just about completed a building frenzy with a new shopping and entertainment complex and new condos that have given the area a much-needed face-lift. Farther east, past the up-and-coming sleeper cities of Port St. Joe and Mexico Beach, you'll come to the quiet blue-collar town of Apalachicola, Florida's main oyster fishery. Here, you can watch oystermen ply their trade, using long-handled tongs to bring in their catch.

ESSENTIALS

Visitor Information Emerald Coast Convention and Visitors Bureau (☎ *850/651–7131 or 800/322–3319* ⊕ *www.destin-fwb.com*). **Beaches of South Walton Visitor Information Center** (☎ *850/267–1216 or 800/822–6877* ⊕ *www.beachesofsouthwalton.com*).

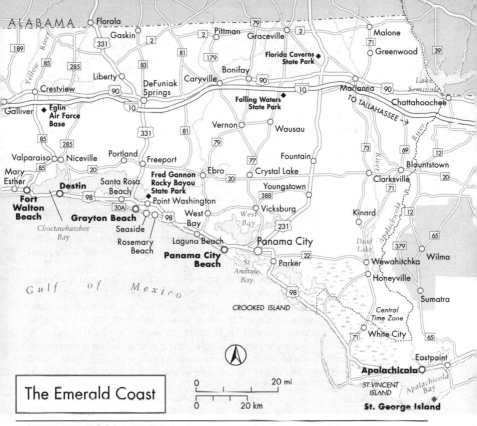

FORT WALTON BEACH

46 mi east of Pensacola via U.S. 98.

This coastal town dates from the Civil War but had to wait more than 75 years to come into its own. Patriots loyal to the Confederate cause organized Walton's Guard (named in honor of Colonel George Walton, onetime acting territorial governor of West Florida) and camped at a site on Santa Rosa Sound, later known as Camp Walton. In 1940 fewer than 90 people lived in Fort Walton Beach, but within a decade the city became a boomtown, thanks to New Deal money for roads and bridges and the development of Eglin Field during World War II. The military is now Fort Walton Beach's main source of income, but tourism runs a close second. Despite the inland sprawl of the town, independent merchants have created a cute little shopping district along U.S. 98.

EXPLORING

★ **Air Force Armament Museum.** The collection at this museum just outside the Eglin Air Force Base's main gate contains more than 5,000 armaments (a.k.a. missiles, bombs, and aircraft) from World Wars I and II and the Korean and Vietnam wars. Included are uniforms, engines, weapons, aircraft, and flight simulators. You can't miss the museum—there's a squadron of aircraft including a B-17 Flying Fortress, an SR-71

Blackbird, a B-52, a B-25, and helicopters parked on the grounds in front. A continuously playing 32-minute movie, *Arming the Future*, features current weapons and Eglin's history and its role in their development. ⌧*Rte. 85, Eglin Air Force Base* ☎*850/882–4062* ⊕*www. afarmamentmuseum.com* 🎫*Free* ⊙*Mon.–Sat. 9:30–4:30.*

WHERE TO EAT AND STAY

$$ ✕**Angler's.** Unless you sit in the water, you can't dine any closer to the
AMERICAN   gulf than at this casual beachside bar and grill next to the Gulfarium. Located at the entrance to Okaloosa Island Pier (and within a complex of other nightclubs and restaurants), Angler's houses the requisite sports bar with a million or more televisions (in the elevators and bathrooms even) broadcasting an equal number of sports events. Outside, a volleyball net tempts diners onto the sands. Snack on nachos and quesadillas or sample the fresh-catch dishes such as king crab and prawns, or "Anglers Elizabeth"—a fish fillet with shrimp, crabmeat, and hollandaise sauce. ⌧*1030 Miracle Strip Pkwy. SE* ☎*850/796–0260* ⊕*www. anglersbeachsidegrill.net* ⊟*AE, D, MC, V.*

$$$ ✕**Pandora's Steakhouse and Lounge.** On the Emerald Coast the name
STEAK   Pandora's is synonymous with prime rib. Steaks are cooked over a
★   wood-burning grill, and you can order your prime rib regular or extra-cut; fish aficionados should try the char-grilled yellowfin tuna or one of the daily specials. Cozy up in an alcove to enjoy your meal in peace or head to the lounge, where the mood turns a bit more gregarious with live entertainment Wednesday through Saturday. ⌧*1226 Santa Rosa Blvd.* ☎*850/244–8669* ⊕*www.pandorassteakhouse.com* ⊟*AE, D, DC, MC, V* ⊙*Closed Mon.*

$$$ ✕**Staff's.** Since 1913 folks have been coming to this garage-turned-
AMERICAN   eatery for steaks and seafood dishes like Florida lobster and char-grilled amberjack. Also on the chock-full menu are items including seafood gumbo with okra, grouper, soft-shell crabs, scallops, and oysters. The grand finale is a trip to the delectable dessert bar; try a generous wedge of cherry cheesecake. Sip a Tropical Depression or a rum-laced Squall Line while you peruse a menu tucked into the centerfold of a tabloid-size newspaper filled with snippets of local history and family memorabilia, including cute bathing beauty pix of the family's 1920 all-girl swim team. An even grander finale may be stopping in the quite authentic "Margaritaville-style" neighborhood lounge that features a pool table and a true Old Florida vibe. ⌧*24 Miracle Strip Pkwy. SE* ☎*850/243–3482* ⊕*www.staffrestaurant.com* ⊟*AE, D, MC, V.*

$$ 🛏**Aunt Martha's Bed and Breakfast.** While it is a new creation, Aunt Martha's can transport you back half a century, when Florida was still a sleepy little state. Placed smack dab on the banks of Santa Rosa Sound, its location is private and its atmosphere it neat as a pin. Five rooms feature floor to ceiling windows, a baby grand piano is poised to be played, and a library is stocked for guests. In the morning, the pampering continues with an old-fashioned southern breakfast. **Pros:** quiet sanctuary on the waterfront but with access to dining, shopping, and sites. **Cons:** not suited for kids and families; primarily for romance and privacy. ⌧*315 Shell Ave. SE* ☎*850/243–6702* ⊕*www.auntmarthasbedandbreakfast.com* ♿*In-hotel: laundry service* ⊟*AE, D, MC, V.*

2

$$–$$$ **Ramada Plaza Beach Resort.** If your family loves the water, splash down at this beachside extravaganza. Activity here revolves around a 194,000-gallon pool (allegedly the area's largest) with a separate grotto pool and bar and spectacular swim-through waterfall that tumbles down from an island oasis; there's also a separate kiddie pool, a beachwear and beach-toy shop, as well as an 800-foot private beach. It's a popular spot for conventions, spring break, and families on a budget: there's no charge for additional guests under 18, and roll-away beds are only an extra $10 per night. For an extra-special evening, book an odd-numbered room between 1133 and 1143—the back door of each opens right into the pool. **Pros:** extravagant offerings for a family-friendly vacation—the pool may please the kids more than the gulf. **Cons:** may be too busy for romance travelers or seniors seeking peace and quiet. ✉*1500 Miracle Strip Pkwy. SE* ☎*850/243–9161 or 800/874–8962* 🌐*www.ramadafwb.com* *309 rooms, 26 suites* *In-room: refrigerator. In-hotel: restaurant, bars, pools, gym, beachfront* *AE, D, DC, MC, V.*

NIGHTLIFE

The Boardwalk (✉*1450 Miracle Strip Pkwy.*) is a massive dining and entertainment complex at the entrance to the Okaloosa Island Pier and includes several restaurants (Crab Trap Seafood and Oyster House, Floyd's Shrimp House, and Angler's) as well as an assortment of nightclubs.

SPORTS AND THE OUTDOORS

Eglin Air Force Base Reservation. The size of Rhode Island—1,045 square mi, 463,448 acres—this base has 810 mi of creeks and plenty of challenging, twisting wooded trails. Outdoor enthusiasts hunt, fish, canoe, and swim here, and for $10 you can buy a day pass to camp or hike or mountain bike on the Timberlake Trail, which is open from 7 AM to 4:30 PM, Monday through Saturday. Permits can be obtained from the **Jackson Guard** (✉*107 Rte. 85 N, Niceville* 🌐*www.eglin.af.mil* ☎*850/882–4164*).

FISHING Don't miss a chance to go out to the end of the ¼-mi-long **Okaloosa Island Pier** (☎*850/244–1023* 🌐*www.okaloosaislandpier.com*). It costs only a buck to walk the plank, $7 if you'd like to fish (they sell bait, tackle, and rent poles).

GOLF The **Fort Walton Beach Golf Club** (✉*Rte. 189* ☎*850/833–9528*) is a 36-hole municipal course whose links (Oaks and Pines) lie about 400 yards from each other. The two courses are considered by many to be among Florida's best public layouts; green fee $32/$43 (with a shared cart). **Shalimar Pointe Country Club** (✉*302 Country Club Dr., Shalimar* ☎*850/651–1416* 🌐*www.shalimarpointe.com*) has 18 holes with a pleasing mix of water and bunkers; green fee $45/$59 (with cart).

DESTIN

8 mi east of Fort Walton Beach via U.S. 98.

Fort Walton Beach's neighbor lies on the other side of the strait that connects Choctawhatchee Bay with the Gulf of Mexico. Destin takes its name from its founder, Leonard A. Destin, a Connecticut sea captain who settled his family here sometime in the 1830s. For the next 100 years Destin remained a sleepy little fishing village until the strait, or East Pass, was bridged in 1935. Then recreational anglers discovered its white sands, blue-green waters, and abundance of some of the most sought-after sport fish in the world. More billfish are hauled in around Destin each year than from all other gulf-fishing ports combined, giving credence to its nickname, the World's Luckiest Fishing Village.

ESSENTIALS

Visitor Information Destin Chamber of Commerce (☎ *850/837–6241* ⊕ *www.destinchamber.com*).

EXPLORING

☺ **Big Kahuna's Lost Paradise.** The seasonal water park is the big draw here, with the Honolulu Half-pipe (a perpetual surfing wave), flume rides, steep and slippery slides, and assorted other methods of expending hydro-energy appealing to travelers who prefer freshwater thrills over the gulf (which is just across the street). This complex also has year-round family-friendly attractions: 54-hole miniature golf course, two go-kart tracks, an arcade, thrill rides for kids of all ages, and an amphitheater. ⊠ *U.S. 98 E* ☎ *850/837–4061* ⊕ *www.bigkahunas.com* ☞ *Grounds free, water park $37, miniature golf $5, go-karts $5.50, combination ticket (water park, golf, and two go-kart tickets) $55* ☉ *Water park: early May–Memorial Day, weekends 10–5; Memorial Day–mid-Sept., daily 10–10.*

WHERE TO EAT AND STAY

¢   ✕ **Broken Egg Café.** Follow the line and you'll find a local favorite break-
SEAFOOD   fast and lunch retreat. This is the kind of restaurant you crave when you're on the road, where they start each morning with platters of pancakes, waffles, and French toast and add special twists like blackberry grits and more than a dozen styles of omelettes including the "Hey Ricky," a Spanish omelette with avocado slices, green chiles, and onions. Crowded—and for a reason. ⊠ *104 Harbor Blvd. (U.S. 98)* ☎ *850/650–0499* ☰ *AE, D, MC, V* ☉ *No dinner. Closed Mon.*

$$$ ✕ **Marina Café.** A harbor view, impeccable service, and sophisticated
SEAFOOD   fare create one of the finest dining experiences on the Emerald Coast.
★   The ocean motif is expressed in shades of aqua, green, and sand accented with marine tapestries and sea sculptures. The chef calls his creations contemporary continental, offering diners a choice of thick USDA steaks, classic creole, Mediterranean, or Pacific Rim dishes. One regional specialty is the popular pan-seared yellow-edge grouper with a blue-crab-meat crust. A special sushi menu is available, the wine list is extensive, and happy hour runs from 5 to 7. ⊠ *404 U.S. 98 E* ☎ *850/837–7960* ☰ *AE, D, DC, MC, V* ☉ *No lunch.*

$$$$ ⊞ **Sandestin Golf and Beach Resort.** It's almost a city in itself and certainly
Fodor'sChoice   its own little world with shopping, charter fishing, spas, salons, tennis,
★   water sports, golf, and special events. Newlyweds, conventioneers, and families all find their fit in this 2,400-acre resort with accommodations spread across five areas: beachfront, beachside, village, bayside, and dockside. Each of the five neighborhood clusters offers a unique locale

2

with villas, cottages, condominiums, boat slips, and an inn. All rooms have a view, either of the gulf, Choctawhatchee Bay, a golf course, a lagoon, or a natural wildlife preserve. This resort accommodates an assortment of tastes, from the simple to the extravagant (the dial-up to the Wi-Fi), but the gigantic suites at the Westwinds are a cut above the rest. Baytowne Wharf is the "downtown" of the complex and has art galleries, wine stores, and a "festival marketplace" of shops and restaurants, so once you get here, you won't need—or want—to leave. **Pros:** has everything you'd ever need in a resort—and more. **Cons:** lacks the personal touches of a modest retreat. ⊠ *9300 Emerald Coast Pkwy. W* ☎ *850/267–8000 or 800/277–0800* ⊕ *www.sandestin.com* ⬤ *175 rooms, 250 condos, 275 villas* ⟐ *In-room: kitchen (some), refrigerator (some), Wi-Fi. In-hotel: 10 restaurants, bars, golf courses, tennis courts, pools, gym, beachfront, Internet terminal* ⊟ *AE, D, DC, MC, V.*

NIGHTLIFE

Folks come by boat and car to **AJ's Club Bimini** (⊠ *116 U.S. 98 E* ☎ *850/837–1913* ⊕ *www.ajs-destin.com*), a supercasual bar and restaurant overlooking the marina. Nightly live music means young, lively crowds pack the dance floor. **Harbor Docks** (⊠ *538 U.S. 98 E* ☎ *850/837–2506* ⊕ *www.harbordocks.com*) is another favorite with the local seafaring set. Here since 1979, the incredibly casual feel is marked by picnic tables and Hibachi grills, Destin's first sushi bar, and live music Thursday through Saturday. The **Hog's Breath Saloon** (⊠ *541 U.S. 98 E* ☎ *850/837–5991*), a chain hot spot with other locations in Key West and Destin, presents good live music Wednesday through Sunday. The food—steaks, burgers, salads—isn't bad, either.

SPORTS AND THE OUTDOORS

FISHING Destin has the largest charter-boat fishing fleet in the state. You can also pier-fish from the 3,000-foot-long Destin Catwalk and along the East Pass Bridge. **Adventure Charters** (⊠ *East Pass Marina, 288 U.S. 98 E* ☎ *850/654–4070* ⊕ *www.destinfishingservice.com*) represents more than 90 charter services that offer deep-sea, bay-bottom, and light-tackle fishing excursions. **Destin Dockside** (⊠ *East Pass Marina, 288 U.S. 98 E* ☎ *850/837–2622*) sells bait, tackle, and most anything else you'd need for a day of fishing. **Harbor Walk Marina** (⊠ *66 Harbor Blvd. U.S. 98 E* ☎ *850/337–8250* ⊕ *www.harborwalk-destin.com*) is a rustic-looking waterfront complex where you can get bait, gas, tackle, food, and anything else you might need for a day of fishing. Party-fishing-boat excursions cost as little as $65, a cheaper alternative to chartering or renting your own boat.

GOLF The **Indian Bayou Golf Club** (⊠ *1 Country Club Dr. E, off Airport Rd., off U.S. 98* ☎ *850/837–6191* ⊕ *www.indianbayougolf.com*) has a 27-hole course; green fee $55/$75 (with cart). The 18-hole **Kelly Plantation Golf Club** (⊠ *307 Kelly Plantation Dr.* ☎ *850/650–7600* ⊕ *www.kellyplantationgolf.com*), designed by Fred Couples and Gene Bates, is a semiprivate course that runs along Choctawhatchee Bay; green fee $142 (with cart). There's an 18-hole, semiprivate course at **Regatta Bay Golf and Country Club** (⊠ *465 Regatta Bay Blvd.* ☎ *850/337–8080* ⊕ *www. regattabay.com*); green fee $59/$129. For sheer number of holes, the

Sandestin Golf and Beach Resort (⊠*9300 U.S. 98 W* ☎*850/267–8211* ⊕*www.sandestin.com*) tops the list, with 72. There are four courses: **Baytowne Golf Club at Sandestin**, green fee: $105/$125; **Burnt Pines Course**, green fee: $109/$155; **Links Course**, green fee: $65/$115; and the **Raven Golf Club**, green fee: $75/$135.

SCUBA DIVING Scuba-diving and snorkeling instruction and outings are available through **Emerald Coast Scuba** (⊠*110 Melvin St.* ☎*850/837–0955 or 800/222–0955* ⊕*www.divedestin.com*). **The Scuba Shop** (⊠*348 S.W. Miracle Strip Pkwy. #19* ☎*850/243–1600* ⊕*www.thescubashopfwb. com*) offers dives and lessons.

SHOPPING

Don't call it a mall. **Destin Commons** (⊠*Mid-Bay Bridge and U.S. 98, Destin* ☎*850/337–8700* ⊕*www.destincommons.com*) is an "open-air lifestyle center." More than 70 high-end specialty shops are here, as well as a 14-screen theater, Hard Rock Cafe, a miniature train, and a nautical theme park for kids. The **Market at Sandestin** (⊠*9300 Emerald Coast Pkwy. W, Sandestin* ☎*850/267–8092*) has about two-dozen upscale shops that peddle such goods as expensive chocolates and designer clothes in an elegant minimall in a courtyard setting. **Silver Sands Factory Stores** (⊠*10562 Emerald Coast Pkwy. W* ☎*850/654–9771* ⊕*www. silversandsoutlet.com*) is one of the Southeast's largest retail designer outlets. More than 100 shops sell top-name merchandise.

GRAYTON BEACH

18 mi east of Destin via U.S. 98 on Route 30A.

The 26-mi stretch of coastline between Destin and Panama City Beach is referred to as the Beaches of South Walton.

EXPLORING

BEACH **Grayton Beach State Park.** One of the most scenic spots along the Gulf
Fodor'sChoice Coast, this 2,220-acre park is composed primarily of untouched Florida
★ woodlands within the Coastal Lowlands region. It also has salt marshes, rolling dunes covered with sea oats, crystal-white sand, and contrasting blue-green waters. The park has facilities for swimming, fishing, snorkeling, and camping, and there's an elevated boardwalk that winds over the dunes to the beach, as well as walking trails around the marsh and into the piney woods. An interesting sight is noticing that since the dunes shift frequently, the bushes you see are actually just the tops of full-sized slash pines and Southern magnolias. Even if you are just passing by, the beach here is worth the stop. Thirty fully equipped cabins are available for rent. ⊠*357 Main Park Rd., off Rte. 30A* ☎*850/231–4210* ⊚*$4 per vehicle, up to 8 people* ☉*Daily 8–sunset.*

WHERE TO EAT AND STAY

$$$$ ✕**Fish Out of Water.** Time your appetite to arrive at sunset and you'll wit-
AMERICAN ness the best of both worlds: sea oats lumbering on gold-dusted dunes
Fodor'sChoice outside and a stylish interior that sets new standards of sophistication
★ for the entire Panhandle. Colorful, handblown glass accent lighting that "grows" out of the hardwood floors, plush taupe banquettes, oversize handmade lamp shades, and a sleek bar area that screams New York

(complete with a cloud-white curtain-wall) create an atmosphere worthy of the inventive cuisine. Influences range from Asian (Thai-style grouper with lobster-coconut broth) to Southern (Low Country shrimp and scallops with creamy grits) to classic Continental (porcini-crusted osso buco), but all are convincingly wrought and carefully presented. Also look into the Berkshire pork chops, tuna saltimbocca, and black grouper. The extensive wine list keeps pace with the menu offerings. ⊠*34 Goldenrod Circle, 2nd fl. of WaterColor Inn* ☎*850/534–5008* ⊕*www.watercolorinn.com* ⊟*AE, D, DC, MC, V* ⊘*No lunch.*

$$ **✕Picolo Restaurant and Red Bar.** You could spend weeks here just taking
SEAFOOD in all the funky-junky, eclectic toy-chest memorabilia—from Marilyn Monroe posters to flags to dolls—dangling from the ceiling and tacked to every available square inch of wall. The contemporary menu is small, although it includes what you'd expect to find in the Panhandle: crab cakes, shrimp, crawfish, etc. They also serve breakfast. In season, they can seat a thousand people a day, so expect a wait. Blues and jazz musicians play nightly in the Red Bar. You can't make up a place like this. ⊠*70 Hotz Ave.* ☎*850/231–1008* ⊟*No credit cards.*

$$ 🏠**Cabins at Grayton Beach State Park.** Back-to-nature enthusiasts and
★ families love to retreat to stylish accommodations set among the sand pines and scrub oaks of this pristine state park. The two-bedroom duplexes (each named after a different species of tree found in the park) sleep up to six and have tin roofs, white trim, and tropical wooden-window louvers, and the beach is a leisurely five-minute walk away via a private boardwalk. Modern conveniences include central heat and air-conditioning and full-size kitchens complete with pots and pans. Gas fireplaces, barbecue grills, and screen porches add a homey touch. How homey? There is no daily maid service, you'll need to bring your own sheets and towels, and there are no room phones or televisions. Regardless, they're often booked solid as much as 11 months in advance, so call to check for cancellations. **Pros:** rare and welcome preservation of Old Florida; pure peace and quiet; what a gulf vacation is meant to be. **Cons:** if you're accustomed to abundant amenities, you won't find them here. ⊠*357 Main Park Rd.* ☎*800/326–3521 for reservations* ⊕*www. reserveamerica.com* ⤶*30 cabins* ♿*In-room: no phone, kitchen, no TV* ⊟*AE, MC, V.*

NIGHTLIFE

The **Red Bar** (⊠*70 Hotz Ave.* ☎*850/231–1008*), the local watering hole, presents red-hot blues or jazz acts every night. On Friday and Saturday nights it's elbow-to-elbow at the bar.

SHOPPING

Grayton Beach House of Art (⊠*26 Logan La.* ☎*850/231–9997* ⊕*www. house-of-art.com*) specializes in the works of Gordie Hinds, who gave up charter fishing and picked up a paintbrush in 2003. He paints what he knows best: fishing, seashores, piers, and marshes. The **Shops of Grayton** (⊠*Rte. 283 [Grayton Rd.], 2 mi south of U.S. 98* ☎*No phone*) is a colorful complex of eight Cracker-style cottages selling gifts, artwork, and antiques. At **Woodie Long Folk Art Gallery** (⊠*1066 B. N. Bay Dr. [Rte. 283], Santa Rosa Beach* ☎*850/231–9961*), in the living room of the artist's residence, you'll find a few of the 10,000 artworks the quirky local claims to have painted (a feature in *Smithsonian* magazine put Woodie on the art-world map). His folk paintings can be seen at the Cooperstown Museum, the Philadelphia Museum of Art, and on CD jackets and book covers.

PANAMA CITY BEACH

24 mi southeast of Grayton Beach via U.S. 98.

The dizzying number of high-rises built along the Miracle Strip—about two dozen in total—has led to the formation of a new moniker for this stretch of the Panhandle: the "Construction Coast." Invasive growth has turned the main thoroughfare, Front Beach Road, into a dense mass of traffic that peaks in spring and between June and August when college students descend en masse from neighboring states. The shoreline in town is 17 mi long, so even when a mile is packed with partying students, there are 16 more where you can toss a beach blanket. What's more, the beaches along the Miracle Strip, with their powder-soft sand and translucent emerald waters, are some of the finest in the state; in one sense, anyway, it's easy to understand why so many condos are being built here.

GETTING HERE AND AROUND

■ TIP➜When coming here, be sure to set your sights for Panama City Beach. Panama City is its beachless inland cousin. When navigating Panama City Beach by car, don't limit yourself to Front Beach Road—the stop-and-go traffic will drive you nuts. You can avoid the congestion by following parallel roads like Back Beach Road and U.S. 98. Also, anywhere along this long stretch of beachfront, look for "sunrise" signs that indicate an access point to the beach—they're a treasure to find, especially when you happen across one in the midst of a quiet residential neighborhood and know that a private and quiet beach experience is just a few feet away. The **Baytown Trolley** (☎850/769–0557) serves Bay County, including downtown Panama City and the beaches ($1.25).

ESSENTIALS

Visitor Information Panama City Beach Convention and Visitors Bureau (☎850/233–5070 or 800/722–3224 ⊕ www.thebeachloversbeach.com).

EXPLORING

♺ **Gulf World Marine Park.** It's certainly no SeaWorld, but with a tropical garden, tropical-bird theater, and alligator and otter exhibits, the park is still a winner with the kids. The stingray petting pool and the shark-feeding and scuba demonstrations are big crowd pleasers, and the old favorites—performing sea lions, otters, and bottle-nosed dolphins—still hold their own. If you're really nautically minded, consider the Trainer for a Day program, which allows you to go behind the scenes to assist in food preparation and training sessions and make an on-stage appearance in the Dolphin Show. ⊠15412 Front Beach Rd. ☎850/234–5271 ⊕www.gulfworldmarinepark.com ☙$24 ☉Late May–early Sept., daily 9 AM–7:30 PM; call for hrs at other times of year.

♺ **St. Andrews State Park.** At the eastern tip of Panama City Beach, the Fodor'sChoice 1,260-acre park includes beaches, pinewoods, and marshes. Complete ★ camping facilities are here and a snack bar, too, as well as places to

2

swim, pier-fish, and hike on clearly marked nature trails. Board a ferry to **Shell Island**—a 700-acre barrier island in the Gulf of Mexico with some of the best shelling north of Sanibel Island. A rock jetty creates a calm, shallow play area that is perfect for young children. Come to this spectacular park for a peek at what the entire beach area looked like before developers sank their claws into it. ✉ *4607 State Park La.* ☎ *850/233–5140* ⊕ *www.floridastateparks.org* 💲 *$5 per vehicle, up to 8 people* ⊘ *Daily 8–5.*

WHERE TO EAT AND STAY

$$
SEAFOOD
✕ **Billy's Steamed Seafood Restaurant, Oyster Bar, and Crab House.** Join the throng of locals who really know their seafood, then roll up your sleeves and dig into some of the gulf's finest blue crabs and shrimp seasoned to perfection with Billy's special recipe. Homemade gumbo, crawfish, shrimp, crab claws, fish tacos, whole lobsters, and the day's catch as well as sandwiches and burgers round out the menu. It's no-frills dining with no-frills decor, but you may get a kick out of hanging out with some real Florida folks who consider table manners optional. ✉ *3000 Thomas Dr.* ☎ *850/235–2349* ▤ *AE, D, MC, V.*

$$
SEAFOOD
✕ **Schooners.** Thanks to a clientele that's 90% local, this beachfront spot—which is really tucked away down a small avenue—bills itself as the "last local beach club," and more boldly, "the best place on Earth." It's actually a perfect place for a casual family lunch or early dinner: kids can have burgers and play on the beach while Mom and Dad enjoy grown-up drinks and more substantial fare such as homemade gumbo, steak, or simply prepared seafood like crab-stuffed shrimp, gulf-fresh grouper, and grilled tuna steaks. One sign of Schooner's casual atmosphere is the ceremonial firing of the cannon when the sun disappears into the gulf, a crowd favorite that fires up an all-around good vibe. Late-night folks pile in for live music and dancing. ✉ *5121 Gulf Dr.* ☎ *850/235–3555* ⊕ *www.schooners.com* ▤ *AE, D, MC, V.*

$$$–$$$$
Fodor's Choice
★
🏨 **Bay Point Golf Resort & Spa.** Across the Grand Lagoon from St. Andrews State Park, this expansive property exudes sheer elegance. The tropical-chic feel starts in the light-filled lobby, with its polished marble floors, glowing chandeliers, potted palms, and colorful floral paintings. Quiet guest rooms continue the theme with light-wood furnishings and armoires, floral-print fabrics, and private balconies or patios overlooking the lush grounds and peaceful bay. Rooms on the upper floors of the main building have expansive views of the bay and the gulf beyond, and villas are a mere tee-shot away from the hotel. A meandering boardwalk (which doubles as a jogging trail) leads to a private beach with an

---

HOW TO SNACK

Florida "Cracker" food is based on rudimentary ingredients that the pioneers ate, and that includes delicacies like swamp cabbage and possum. Thankfully, those don't appear on many menus, but a few of the holdouts—gator tail and frogs' legs—do.

Gator tail—usually breaded and deep-fried—tastes like chicken. On the other hand, frogs' legs taste like . . . chicken. The hardest part about eating frogs' legs is that they look precisely like frogs' legs, so if you can convince yourself that you're not eating an amphibian, you'll be better off.

open-air bar and water sports. The 12,000-square-foot spa offers massages, facials, manicures, pedicures, and waxing. **Pros:** quiet and away from the madness of Panama City Beach; complete range of services and activities. **Cons:** may be too expansive and generic for those seeking a small, intimate resort. ⊠*4200 Marriott Dr.* ☎850/236–6000 *or* 800/874–7105 ⊕*www.marriottbaypoint.com* ➷*316 rooms, 78 suites* ⚫*In-room: refrigerator (some), Wi-Fi. In-hotel: 5 restaurants, bars, golf courses, pools, gym* ⊟*AE, D, DC, MC, V.*

$$$–$$$$ ⊡**Legacy by the Sea.** Nearly every room at this 14-story, pastel-peach hotel has a private balcony with commanding gulf views. Rooms are designed with families in mind, from the fully equipped kitchens to the two televisions and waterproof sofa cushions, to the door that conveniently separates the bedroom area from the rest of the unit. There's a gulf-front pool and hot-tub area (with a kiddie pool), and freebies include Continental breakfast, daily newspaper, local calls, and an airport shuttle. A variety of water-sport options, including parasailing and jet-skiing, is offered by on-site concessionaires. The hotel's closed-circuit cable channel, airing nothing but live security-camera feeds (inside the elevator, around the pool, in the common areas), makes keeping an eye on the kids a breeze—and keeping an eye on unsuspecting adults a hoot. **Pros:** shopping, dining, and attractions are within walking distance; all the amenities a family (or college kids) need. **Cons:** in the heart of a crowded and congested district; can be difficult to access in peak seasons. ⊠*15325 Front Beach Rd.* ☎850/249–8601 *or* 888/886–8917 ⊕*www.legacybythesea.com* ➷*278 rooms, 78 suites* ⚫*In-room: kitchen, Wi-Fi. In-hotel: pool* ⊟*AE, D, DC, MC, V.* Ⓞ*CP.*

NIGHTLIFE

Boatyard (⊠*5325 North Lagoon Dr.* ☎850/249–9273 ⊕*www.boatyardclub.com*) is a multilevel, indoor-outdoor waterfront nightclub and restaurant that presents a regular lineup of bands, ranging from blues to steel drums to classic rock and beyond (DJs round out the entertainment roster). Courtesy of spring break, Panama City Beach features one of the nation's most famous clubs: **Club La Vela** (⊠*8813 Thomas Dr.* ☎850/234–4866 ⊕*www.clublavela.com*). While springtime finds it transformed into a hotbed of hedonism, a full slate of concerts, international DJs, 48 bar stations, swimming pools, and a tropical waterfall guarantees a full-tilt party in the Panhandle. **Pineapple Willy's** (⊠*9875 S. Thomas Dr.* ☎850/235–0928) is an eatery and bar geared to families and tourists—as well as sports fans.

SPORTS AND THE OUTDOORS

CANOEING Rentals for a trip down Econofina Creek, known as Florida's most beautiful canoe trail, are supplied by **Econofina Creek Canoe Livery** (⊠*Strickland Rd., north of Rte. 20, Youngstown* ☎850/722–9032). Kayaks can be rented for $25, canoes for $35.

DIVING Snorkeling and scuba diving are extremely popular in the clear waters here. If you have the proper certification, you can dive among dozens of ships sunk by the city to create artificial reefs. The **Panama City Dive Center** (⊠*4823 Thomas Dr., Panama City Beach* ☎850/235–3390 ⊕*www.pcdivecenter.com*) offers instruction, rentals, and charters.

SHOPPING

Occupying a huge swath of land that had once been an amusement park is **Pier Park** (✉*16230 Front Beach Rd.* ☎*850/236–9974* ⊕*www.simon.com*), an active and diverse 900,000-square-foot entertainment/shopping/dining complex that creates the downtown that Panama City Beach lacked.

TIME ZONE

If you are heading east to Apalachicola from the western Panhandle, remember to set your watch forward one hour. Apalachicola is in the Eastern Time Zone, whereas the west coast is in the Central Time Zone.

APALACHICOLA

65 mi southeast of Panama City Beach off U.S. 98.

It feels like a long haul between Panama City Beach and here. Add an odd name and a town's below-the-radar reputation to that long drive and you may be tempted to skip Apalachicola. But you shouldn't. It's a weirdly fascinating town that, for some reason, has a growing cosmopolitan veneer. And that makes it worth a visit.

Meaning "land of the friendly people" in the language of its original American Indian inhabitants, Apalachicola—known in these parts as simply Apalach—lies on the Panhandle's southernmost bulge. European settlers began arriving in 1821, and by 1847 the southern terminus of the Apalachicola River steamboat route was a bustling port town. Although the town is now known as the Oyster Capital of the World, oystering became king only after the local cotton industry flagged—the city's extra-wide streets, built to accommodate bales of cotton awaiting transport, are a remnant of that trade—and the sponge industry moved down the coast after depleting local sponge colonies. But the newest industry here is tourism, and visitors have begun discovering the Forgotten Coast, as the area is known, flocking to its intimate hotels and B&Bs, dining at excellent restaurants, and browsing in unique shops selling everything from handmade furniture to brass fixtures recovered from nearby shipwrecks. If you like oysters or want to go back in time to the Old South of Gothic churches and spooky graveyards, Apalachicola is a good place to start.

ESSENTIALS

Visitor Information Apalachicola Bay Chamber of Commerce (☎*850/653–9419* ⊕*www.apalachicolabay.org*).

EXPLORING

Drive by the **Raney House,** circa 1850, and **Trinity Episcopal Church,** built from prefabricated parts in 1838. The town is at a developmental turning point, pulled in one direction by well-intentioned locals who want to preserve Apalachicola's port-town roots and in the other by long-time business owners who fear preservation will inhibit commercial growth. For now, however, the city exudes a refreshing authenticity—think Key West in the early 1960s—that many others in the Sunshine State lost long ago, one that might be lost to Panama City Beach–style overdevelopment unless local government institutes an official historic-preservation committee.

WHERE TO EAT AND STAY

$$
SEAFOOD

✕**Boss Oyster.** "Shut up and shuck." That's the advice from this rustic Old Florida restaurant—and they should know. This is the top oyster restaurant in Florida's oyster capital. Located at the Apalachicola River Inn, this is where you can eat your oysters fried, Rockefeller-style, on the half-shell, or Greek, Mexican, English, with garlic, with shrimp, with crab, with hot peppers, with . . . oh, just eat 'em with gusto at this laid-back eatery overlooking the Apalachicola River. In addition to oysters, they lay down jumbo gulf shrimp, blue crabs, bay scallops, and fresh gulf grouper. Eat alfresco at picnic tables or inside in the busy, rustic dining room, but don't let the modest surroundings fool you—oysters aren't cheap here or anywhere in Apalach. The menu also includes such staples as steak and pizza. ✉*125 Water St.* ☎*850/653–9364* ▭*AE, D, DC, MC, V.*

$$$
LATIN AMERICAN
★

✕**Tamara's Cafe Floridita.** Mixing Florida flavors with South American flair, Tamara, a native Venezuelan, opened this colorful bistro more than a decade ago. Now owned by her daughter and son-in-law, the restaurant has new digs in a 1920s-era building, complete with stamped tin ceiling and original brick walls. For starters, try the creamy black-bean soup or the pleasantly spicy oyster stew; for dinner choose from seafood paella, prosciutto-wrapped salmon with mango-cilantro sauce, or margarita chicken and scallops with a tequila-lime glaze. All entrées come with black beans and rice, fresh vegetables, and focaccia bread, but if you still have room for dessert, try the fried-banana split or the *tres leches* (cake soaked in three types of milk), a South American favorite. The chef, who keeps watch over the dining room from an open kitchen, is happy to accommodate most any whim. ✉*71 Market St.* ☎*850/653–4111* ⊕*www.tamarascafe.com* ▭*AE, D, MC, V.*

$$–$$$

▦**Coombs Inn.** A combination of neighboring homes and a carriage house, this is an entire complex created with a Victorian flair. Seventeen fireplaces and an ornate oak staircase with lead-glass windows on the landing lend authenticity to this restored 1905 mansion. Of the 23 rooms in the collection, no two guest rooms are alike, but all are appointed with Victorian-era settees, four-poster or sleigh king beds, English chintz curtains, and Oriental rugs on polished hardwood floors. A full breakfast is served in the dining room, and an afternoon social includes tea and cookies. You can stay in the villa and beyond that a renovated carriage house. Popular for weddings and receptions, these may be the most elegant homes in Apalachicola. Free tours are offered in the afternoon if the accommodations are not in use. **Pros:** clean and comfortable; on-site, friendly owner who's happy to assist with travel tips and suggestions. **Cons:** be prepared to meet and greet other guests at the inn; if you favor complete privacy, a hotel may suit you better. ✉*80 6th St.* ☎*850/653–9199* ⊕*www.coombshouseinn.com* ⇆*23 rooms* ⚙*In-room: Wi-Fi. In-hotel: bicycles, no elevator, public Wi-Fi, no-smoking rooms* ▭*D, MC, V* ⦿*CP.*

SHOPPING

The **Tin Shed** (⊠*170 Water St.* ☎*850/653–3635*) has an impressive collection of antiques and knick-knacks, from brass luggage tags to 1940s nautical charts to sponge-diver wet suits to hand-glazed tiles and architectural elements salvaged from demolished buildings. Closed Sunday. The **Grady Market** (⊠*76 Water St.* ☎*850/653–4099*), on the first floor of the Consulate Inn, is a collection of more than a dozen boutiques, including several antiques dealers and the gallery of Richard Bickel, known for his stunning black-and-white photographs of local residents. **Avenue E** (⊠*15 Ave. E* ☎*850/653–1411*) is a stylish store specializing in reasonably priced antique and reproduction pieces, including furniture, lamps, artwork, and interior accessories.

FLORIDA FACTS

- **Nickname:** Sunshine state
- **State Capital:** Tallahassee
- **State Shell:** Horse conch
- **State Tree:** Sabal palm
- **State Flower:** Orange blossom
- **State Beverage:** Orange juice
- **State Rock:** Moon rock
- **State Freshwater Mammal:** Manatee
- **State Saltwater Mammal:** Dolphin
- **State Cat:** Florida panther

OFF THE BEATEN PATH

Pristine St. George Island sits 5 mi out into the Gulf of Mexico 8 mi south of Apalachicola via the Bryant Patton Bridge. The island is bordered by both Apalachicola Bay and the gulf, offering vacationers the best of both. The rich bay is an angler's dream, whereas the snowy-white beaches and clear gulf waters satisfy even the most finicky beachgoer.

On the east end of the island are 9 mi of undeveloped beaches and dunes on **St. George Island State Park** (*1900 E. Gulf Beach Dr.* ☎*850/927–2111* ⊕*www.floridastateparks.org/stgeorgeisland* ⊠*$4 per vehicle, up to 8 people* ☉*Daily 8–sunset*). Sandy coves, salt marshes, oak forests, and pines provide shelter for many birds, including bald eagles and ospreys. Spotless restrooms and plentiful parking make a day at this park a joy.

TALLAHASSEE

76 mi northeast of Apalachicola on U.S. 319.

Tallahassee maintains a tranquility quite different from the sun-and-surf coastal towns. Tallahassee is Florida with a Southern accent. The only Southern capital spared in the Civil War, Tallahassee has preserved its past. So along with Florida State University, the perennial Seminoles football champions, and FAMU's fabled "Marching 100" band, the city has more than a touch of the Old South.

GETTING HERE AND AROUND

Just 14 mi south of the Georgia border, Tallahassee is midway between Jacksonville and Pensacola and is nearer to Atlanta than Miami.

ESSENTIALS

Visitor Information Tallahassee Area Convention and Visitors Bureau
(☎ *850/413-9200 or 800/628-2866* ⊕ *www.visittallahassee.com*).

EXPLORING

Downtown Tallahassee Historic Trail. A route originally mapped and documented by an eager Eagle Scout as part of a merit-badge project, this trail has become a Tallahassee sightseeing staple. The starting point is the New Capitol, where you can pick up maps and descriptive brochures at the visitor center. You'll walk through the **Park Avenue and Calhoun Street historic districts,** which will take you back to territorial days and the era of postwar reconstruction. The trail is dotted with landmark churches and cemeteries, along with outstanding examples of Greek revival, Italianate, and prairie-style architecture. Some houses are open to the public.

Museum of Florida History. If you thought Florida was founded by Walt Disney, stop here. The displays explain Florida's past by highlighting the unique geological and historical events that have shaped the state. Exhibits include a mammoth armadillo grazing in a savanna, the remains of a giant mastodon found in nearby Wakulla Springs, and a dugout canoe that once carried American Indians into Florida's backwaters. Florida's history also includes settlements by the Spanish, British, French, and Confederates who fought for possession of the state. Gold bars, weapons, flags, maps, furniture, steamboats, and other artifacts underscore the fact that although most Americans date the nation to 1776, Florida's residents had been building settlements hundreds of years earlier. If this intrigues you, one floor up is the **Florida State Archives and Library,** where there's a treasure trove of government records, manuscripts, photographs, genealogical records, and other materials. ⊠ *500 S. Bronough St.* ☎ *850/245-6400, 850/245-6600 (library), and 850/245-6700 (archives)* ⊕ *www.flheritage.com* ✉ *Free* ⊙ *Weekdays 9-4:30, Sat. 10-4:30, Sun. noon-4:30.*

★ **New Capitol.** In the 1960s, when there was talk of relocating the capital to a more central location like Orlando, Panhandle legislators got to work and approved the construction of a 22-story modern skyscraper that would anchor the capital right where it was. It's perfectly placed at the crest of a hill, sitting prominently behind the low-rise Old Capitol. The governor's office is on the first floor, and House and Senate chambers on the fifth floor provide viewer galleries for when the legislative sessions take place (March to May). Catch a panoramic view of Tallahassee and the surrounding countryside all the way into Georgia from the fabulous 22nd-floor observation deck. Also on this floor is the Florida Artists Hall of Fame, a tribute to Floridians such as Ray Charles, Burt Reynolds, Tennessee Williams, Ernest Hemingway, and Marjorie Kinnan Rawlings. To pick up information about the area, stop at the Florida Visitors Center on the plaza level. There are guided tours from 9 to 3 on the hour (except at noon), on weekdays. ⊠ *400 S. Monroe St.* ☎ *850/488-6167* ✉ *Free* ⊙ *Visitor center weekdays 8-5.*

★ **Old Capitol.** The centerpiece of the capitol complex, this 1842 structure has been added to and subtracted from several times. Having been restored, the jaunty red-and-white-striped awnings and combination gas-electric lights make it look much as it did in 1902. Inside, it houses a must-see museum of Florida's political history as well as the old Supreme Court chambers and Senate Gallery—a very interesting peek into the past. ⊠ *S. Monroe St. at Apalachee Pkwy.* ☎ *850/487–1902* ⬛ *Free* ⊙ *Self-guided or guided tours weekdays 9–4:30, Sat. 10–4:30, Sun. noon–4:30.*

San Luis Archaeological and Historic Site. Long before New England's residents began gaining a foothold in America, the native Apalachee Indians as well as Spanish missionaries were settled down here. On the site of a 17th-century Spanish mission and Apalachee Indian town sites, this museum focuses on the archaeology of the late 1600s, when the Apalachee village here had a population of at least 1,400. By 1704, however, threatened by Creek Indians and British forces, the locals burned the village and fled. Although you can take self-guided tours and watch scientists conducting digs daily, it's more fun to hook up with one of the dozen or so living-history guides who will offer tours if you call in advance. ⊠ *2020 W. Mission Rd.* ☎ *850/487–3711* ⬛ *www. missionsanluis.org* ⬛ *Free* ⊙ *Tues.–Sun. 10–4.*

OFF THE BEATEN PATH

Fodor'sChoice ★ Edward Ball Wakulla Springs State Park. Fifteen miles south of Tallahassee on Route 61, this park is known for having one of the deepest springs in the world. This very picturesque and highly recommended park remains relatively untouched, retaining the wild and exotic look it had in the 1930s, when the films *Tarzan* and *Creature from the Black Lagoon* were shot here. Take a glass-bottom boat deep into the lush, jungle-lined waterways to catch glimpses of alligators, snakes, nesting limpkins, and other waterfowl. It costs $50 to rent a pontoon boat and go it alone—it may be worth it since an underground river flows into a pool so clear you can see the bottom more than 100 feet below. If you can't pull yourself away from this idyllic spot, spend the night in the 1930s Spanish-Mediterranean lodge. ⊠ *550 Wakulla Park Dr., Wakulla Springs* ☎ *850/926–0700* ⬛ *www.floridastateparks. org/wakullasprings* ⬛ *$4 per vehicle, up to 8 people; boat tour $6* ⊙ *Daily 8–sunset, boat tours hrly 9:30–4:30.*

DAYTONA BEACH AND THE SPACE COAST

Known as the spring-break and auto-racing capital of the U.S., Daytona is also a family-friendly destination. Travel just 75 mi to the south and you've got speeding rockets instead of speeding cars at the John F. Kennedy space Center. For beachlovers, this area is also home to the laid-back town of Cocoa Beach, which attracts visitors on weekends year-round since it's the closest beach to Orlando, 50 mi to the east.

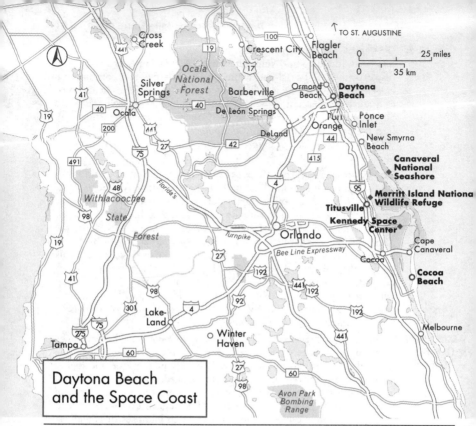

Daytona Beach
and the Space Coast

DAYTONA BEACH

65 mi south of St. Augustine.

Best known for the Daytona 500, Daytona has been the center of automobile racing since cars were first raced along the beach here in 1902. February is the biggest month for race enthusiasts, and there are weekly events at the International Speedway. During race weeks, bike weeks, spring-break periods, and summer holidays, expect extremely heavy traffic. On the mainland, near the inland waterway, several blocks of Beach Street have been "street-scaped," and shops and restaurants open onto an inviting, broad brick sidewalk.

GETTING HERE AND AROUND

DOTS Transit Service (☎*386/257–5411 or 800/231–1965*) has scheduled service connecting the Daytona Beach and Orlando International airports; fares are $35 one-way and $65 round-trip.

Daytona Beach has an excellent bus network, **Votran** (☎*386/756–7496* ⊕*www.votran.com*), which serves the beach area, airport, shopping malls including the Express Link to Orlando. Exact fare is required for Votran ($1–$2) and JTA ($1–$1.50).

ESSENTIALS

Visitor Information Daytona Beach Area Convention and Visitors Bureau (✉ *126 E. Orange Ave., Daytona Beach* ☎ *800/854–1234* ⊕ *www.daytona-beach.com*).

EXPLORING

Daytona Lagoon. Parents looking for a non-sandy way to occupy the kids for a few hours or a whole day may find their salvation at this colorful complex that features go-karts, miniature golf, laser-tag games, a video arcade with 100+ games, a water park with 10 different slides, and a 500,000-gallon tidal-wave pool. More adult entertainment—in the form of pool tables, dartboards, and plasma TVs—can be found in Gilligan's Sports Bar and Grill. ✉ *601 Earl St.* ☎ *386/254–5020* ⊕ *www. daytonalagoon.com* ✑ *Entertainment Center: free (fees for rides and games); Water Park: $27.99* ⊘ *Family Entertainment Center: Sun.– Thurs. 10–10, Fri. and Sat. 10–midnight; Water Park: call for hrs; Water Park closed early Oct.–late Mar.*

Daytona 500 Experience (formerly Daytona USA). The "official attraction of NASCAR" lets you experience the thrill of a race from the driver's seat with motion simulators like Daytona Dream Laps and Accelerator Alley, a highly realistic head-to-head racing experience in an 80%-scale stock car at speeds reaching 200 MPH. Participate in a pit stop on a NASCAR Winston Cup stock car or computer-design your own race car. There's also an exhibit of the history of auto racing with a rotating display of cars, an IMAX theater featuring "NASCAR 3D," and track tours. Daytona USA is also home to the **Richard Petty Driving Experience** (☎ *800/237–3889*), where you can ride shotgun in or drive a stock car at Daytona International Speedway (call for prices). ✉ *1801 W. International Speedway Blvd.* ☎ *386/681–6800* ⊕ *www.daytonausa.com* ✑ *$24* ⊘ *May–Sept., daily 9–7; Oct.–Apr., daily 9–5.*

WHERE TO EAT AND STAY

$$–$$$
SEAFOOD
✕ **Aunt Catfish's on the River.** Don't be surprised if your server introduces herself as your cousin, though you've never seen her before in your life. You see, everybody's "cousin" at Aunt Catfish's (as in, "Can I get you another mason jar of sweet tea, Cousin?"). The silly Southern hospitality is only one of the draws at this wildly popular seafood restaurant. The main lure, of course, is the food: fried chicken, fried shrimp, fried catfish, and crab cakes. Hot cinnamon rolls and hush puppies come with every entrée and can be a meal in themselves. Bring your appetite and your patience—a wait is practically guaranteed. Sunday brunch lures empty stomachs with made-to-order eggs and French toast, and a chocolate fountain. Aunt Catfish's is on the west bank of the Intracoastal Waterway (off U.S. 1, before crossing the Port Orange Causeway), just south of Daytona. ✉ *4009 Halifax Dr., Port Orange* ☎ *386/767–4768* ✑ *Reservations not accepted* ▭ *AE, MC, V.*

$–$$
AMERICAN
✕ **Daytona Brickyard.** It's not just the locals who swear that the Brickyard's charbroiled sirloin burgers are the best they've ever tasted—devotees have been known to drive from Georgia just for lunch. Given its name and location in the heart of NASCAR country, the popular bar and grill is covered in racing memorabilia. Dang, even the floor and the

Side Trip to St. Augustine

About an hour north from Daytona Beach off I–95, you'll find historic **St. Augustine.** Founded in 1565 by Spanish explorers, St. Augustine is the nation's oldest city; the historic district alone has more than 60 historic sites and attractions, plus 144 blocks of houses listed on the National Register of Historic Places.

If you're a history buff, a detour to St. Augustine is well worth your time. Pick up a map at the **St. Johns County Visitor Information Center** on San Marco Avenue between Castillo Drive and Orange Street, put on your walking shoes, and hit the sights along this walking tour.

From the visitor center, cross Orange Street to reach the **City Gate,** the entrance to the city's restored area. Walk south on St. George Street to the **Oldest Wooden Schoolhouse** (⊠ *14 St. George St.*), one of the nation's oldest schools. Directly across from it is the **Colonial Spanish Quarter Museum** (⊠ *29 St. George St.*), a living-history museum depicting the lives of Spanish soldiers and their families in the 1740s. Go out Fort Alley and cross San Marco Avenue to the impressive **Castillo de San Marcos National Monument** (⊠ *1 S. Castillo Dr.*). The fort was constructed of coquina, a soft limestone made of broken shells and coral and was built by the Spanish

to protect St. Augustine from British raids. Next, head west on Cuna Street and turn left on Cordova Street. Walk south three blocks to Valencia Street and turn right. At the end of the block is the splendid **Flagler Memorial Presbyterian Church** (⊠ *32 Sevilla St.*). Head one block south on Sevilla Street and turn left on King Street to find the **Government House Museum** (⊠ *48 King St.*), which houses a collection of more than 300 artifacts from archaeological digs and Spanish shipwrecks off the Florida coast. Henry Flagler built the **Lightner Museum** (⊠ *75 King St.*) and **Flagler College** (⊠ *74 King St.*) as luxury hotels in 1888. Don't miss the ornate antique music boxes at the Lightner. Continue two blocks east on King Street and turn right onto St. George Street to reach the **Ximenez-Fatio House Museum** (⊠ *20 Aviles St.*). Afterward, head a few blocks south down Aviles Street to St. Francis Street for a look at a microcosm of the city's history, the **Oldest House** (⊠ *14 St. Francis St.*). Head back north to the Bridge of Lions, the **Plaza de la Constitución** (⊠ *St. George St. and Cathedral Pl.*), and the **Cathedral Basilica of St. Augustine** (⊠ *40 Cathedral Pl.*). You have to cross the Bridge of Lions to get to Anastasia Island and the historic **St. Augustine Lighthouse & Museum** (⊠ *81 Lighthouse Ave.*), but it's worth the effort.

---

tablecloths are black-and-white checkered. But don't mistake the racing theme to mean the place merely serves greasy bar food to Joe Sixpacks. They're also known for feeding T-bone and NY strip steaks to doctors. ⊠ *747 International Speedway Blvd.* ☎ *386/253–2270* ♒ *Reservations not accepted* ⊟ *AE, MC, V.*

$$$–$$$$
Fodor'sChoice
★

🖼 **The Shores Resort & Spa.** Rustic furniture and beds swathed in mosquito netting lend themselves to the Old Florida decor at this 11-story beachfront resort, but there's nothing primitive about the hotel's amenities, including a luxury four-poster bed and a 42-inch plasma TV in every room, the Indonesian-inspired spa Indulge, and Azure restaurant and bar overlooking the ocean. Rooms are spacious and have views of either the ocean or the Intracoastal Waterway. **Pros:** beachfront; spa; friendly staff. **Cons:** expensive restaurant; crowded pool; not all rooms have balconies. ✉2637 S. Atlantic Ave., Daytona Beach Shores ☎386/767-7350 or 866/934-7467 ⊕www.shoresresort.com ➯212 rooms, 1 suite ♨In-room: safe, refrigerator (some), DVD, Wi-Fi. In-hotel: restaurant, room service, bars, pool, gym, spa, beachfront, laundry service, Wi-Fi, parking (free), some pets allowed, no-smoking rooms ☰AE, D, DC, MC, V.

$$$–$$$$ 🏨**Wyndham Ocean Walk Resort.** Kids definitely won't be bored at this high-rise beachfront resort that boasts four swimming pools, a waterslide, lazy river, game room, indoor miniature golf course, activities center, and the only traffic-free beach in Daytona Beach. Guests also appreciate the 1-, 2-, and 3-bedroom condominium-style units equipped with kitchens (dishware and utensils included), washers, and dryers, as well as the proximity to the shops and restaurants of Ocean Walk Village. Because the property doubles as a hotel and time-share resort, certain amenities such as room service and valet parking aren't offered. **Pros:** family-friendly; beachfront; spacious accommodations. **Cons:** no room service; very slow elevators. ✉300 N. Atlantic Ave. ☎386/323-4800 or 800/347-9851 ⊕www.oceanwalk.com ➯200 1-, 2-, and 3-bedroom suites ♨In-room: safe, kitchen, refrigerator, DVD (some), VCR. In-hotel: 2 restaurants, bars, golf course, pools, gym, spa, beachfront, water sports, children's programs age 5 and up, laundry facilities, Wi-Fi ☰AE, D, DC, MC, V.

NIGHTLIFE AND THE ARTS

THE ARTS Jazz, big band, blues, and folk acts perform at the outdoor, oceanfront **Daytona Beach Bandshell** (✉250 N. Atlantic Ave. ☎386/671-8250). Internationally acclaimed orchestras and soloists appear as part of the **Daytona Beach Symphony Society** (✉140 S. Beach St., Ste. 107 ☎386/253-2901). The **Ocean Center at Ocean Walk Village** (✉101 N. Atlantic Ave. ☎386/254-4500 or 800/858-6444) hosts concerts, conventions, boat shows, and rodeos, and is home to the Daytona ThunderBirds indoor football team. **Peabody Auditorium** (✉600 Auditorium Blvd. ☎386/671-3460) is used for concerts and programs year-round.

NIGHTLIFE **Ocean Walk** (✉250 N. Atlantic Ave. ☎386/258-9544) is a lively, always-hopping cluster of shops, restaurants, and bars right on the ocean, including **Adobe Gila's Margarita Fajita Cantina** (☎386/481-1000) and the **Mai Tai Bar** (☎386/947-2493). Spring breakers congregate by the thousands at **The Oyster Pub** (✉555 Seabreeze Blvd. ☎386/255-6348). At **Razzle's Nightclub** (✉611 Seabreeze Blvd. ☎386/257-6236), DJs play high-energy dance music from 8 PM to 3 AM.

SPORTS AND THE OUTDOORS

BEACH Billing itself as the World's Most Famous Beach, **Daytona Beach** permits you to drive your car right up to your beach site (from one hour after sunrise to one hour before sunset), spread out a blanket, and have all your belongings at hand (with the exception of alcohol which is prohibited); this is especially convenient for beachgoers who are elderly or have disabilities. However, heavy traffic during summer and holidays makes it dangerous for children, and families should be extra careful or stay in the designated car-free zones. The speed limit is 10 mph. ✛ *To get your car on the beach, look for signs on Route A1A indicating beach access via beach ramps. Sand traps are not limited to the golf course, though—cars can get stuck.*

AUTO RACING The massive **Daytona International Speedway** (✉*1801 W. International Speedway Blvd.* ☎*800/748–7467*), on Daytona's major east–west artery, has year-round auto and motorcycle racing, including the Daytona 500 in February and the Coke Zero 400 in July.

FISHING **Finest Kind II Sport Fishing Charters** (✉Inlet Harbor Marina, *133 Inlet Harbor Rd., Ponce Inlet* ☎*386/527–0732*) offers half-day, full-day, and night fishing excursions. **Sea Spirit Fishing** (✉Inlet Harbor Marina, *133 Inlet Harbor Rd., Ponce Inlet* ☎*386/763–4388*) has 4- to 10-hour private and group charters.

GOLF **Indigo Lakes Golf Club** (✉*312 Indigo Dr.* ☎*386/254–3607*) has 18 holes of golf; green fee $40/$65. The public courses at **LPGA International Legends Course** (✉*1000 Champions Dr., Daytona Beach* ☎*386/523–2001*) have 36 holes; green fee $120/$130. **Pelican Bay South Country Club** (✉*350 Pelican Bay Dr.* ☎*386/788–6496*) rents clubs and has a pro shop and a restaurant, in addition to 18 holes; green fee $35/$45. There's an 18-hole course at **Spruce Creek Golf & Country Club** (✉*1900 Country Club Dr., Port Orange* ☎*386/756–6114*), along with practice and driving ranges, rental clubs, a pro shop, and a restaurant; green fee $39/$49.

WATER SPORTS Catch air at **Daytona Beach Parasail** (✉*Silver Beach Ramp, Silver Beach Ave. and Rte. A1A* ☎*386/547–6067*). Rent surfboards or boogie boards at **Salty Dog Surf Shop** (✉*700 E. International Speedway Blvd.* ☎*386/258–0457)* or **Maui Nix** (✉*635 N. Atlantic Ave.,* ☎*386/253–1234*).

SHOPPING

Daytona Flea and Farmers Market (✉*2987 Bellevue Ave.* ☎*386/253–3330*) is one of the largest in the South.

CANAVERAL NATIONAL SEASHORE

★ Miles of grassy, windswept dunes and a virtually empty beach await you at this remarkable 57,000-acre park on a barrier island with 24 mi of undeveloped coastline spanning from New Smyrna to Titusville. The unspoiled area of hilly sand dunes, grassy marshes, and seashell-sprinkled beaches is a large part of NASA's buffer zone and is home to more than 1,000 species of plants and 300 species of birds and other animals. Surf and lagoon fishing are available, and a hiking trail leads to the top of an American Indian shell midden at Turtle Mound. For an additional charge, visitors can take a pontoon-boat tour ($20) or participate in the turtle-watch interpretive program ($14). Reservations required. A visitor center is on Route A1A at Apollo Beach. Weekends are busy, and parts of the park are closed before, during, and after launches, so call ahead.

ESSENTIALS

Visitor Information Canaveral National Seashore Visitor Center (✉ *7611 S. Atlantic Ave., Titusville* ☎ *386/428–3384* ⊕ *www.nps.gov/cana* ✉ *$3 per person* ⊙ *Nov.–Mar., daily 6–6; Apr.–Oct., daily 6 AM–8 PM*).

EXPLORING

Apollo Beach. In addition to typical beach activities (lifeguards are on duty May 30 to September 1), visitors to this beach on the northern end of Canaveral National Seashore can also ride horses here (with a permit), hike self-guided trails, and tour the historic Eldora Statehouse (currently closed for renovations). (✉ *Rte. A1A to the southern end of New Smyrna Beach* ☎ *386/428–3384* ✉ *$3 per person [admission to the National Seashore]* ⊙ *Nov.–Mar., daily 6–6; Apr.–Oct., daily 6 AM–8 PM.*

TITUSVILLE

67 mi east of Orlando, off I–95.

It's unusual that such a small, easily overlooked community of Titusville could accommodate what it does, namely the magnificent Merritt Island National Wildlife Refuge and the entrance to the Kennedy Space Center, the nerve center of the U.S. space program.

EXPLORING

ⓒ **Kennedy Space Center Visitor Complex.** This must-see attraction, just

Fodor'sChoice southeast of Titusville, is one of Central Florida's most popular sights.

★ Located on a 140,000-acre island 45 minutes outside Orlando, Kennedy Space Center is NASA's launch headquarters, where the space shuttle is prepared for flight, launched into space, and returns after its mission. The Visitor Complex gives guests a unique opportunity to learn about—and experience—the past, present, and future of America's space program.

Interactive programs make for the best experiences here, but if you want a low-key overview of the facility (and if the weather is foul) take the bus tour, included with admission. Buses depart every 15 minutes, and you can get on and off any bus whenever you like. Stops include the **Launch Complex 39 Observation Gantry,** which has an unparalleled view of the twin space-shuttle launchpads; the **Apollo/Saturn V Center,** with a don't-miss presentation at the Firing Room Theatre, where the launch of America's first lunar mission, 1968's *Apollo VIII,* is re-created with a ground-shaking, window-rattling liftoff; and the **International Space Station Center,** where NASA is building pieces of the space station; a mock-up of a "Habitation Module" is worth seeing.

Exhibits near the center's entrance include the **Early Space Exploration** display, which highlights the rudimentary yet influential *Mercury* and *Gemini* space programs; **Robot Scouts,** a walk-through exhibit of unmanned planetary probes; and the **Exploration in the New Millennium** display, which offers you the opportunity to touch a piece of Mars (it fell to the Earth in the form of meteorite). Don't miss the outdoor **Rocket Garden,** with walkways winding beside spare rockets, from early Atlas spacecraft to a *Saturn IB.* The redeveloped Children's Playdome enables kids to play among the next generation of spacecraft, climb a moon-rock wall, and crawl through rocket tunnels. Astronaut Encounter Theater has two daily programs where NASA astronaut corps share their adventures in space travel and show a short film. The most moving exhibit is the **Astronaut Memorial**. The 70,400-pound black-granite tribute to astronauts who lost their lives in the name of space exploration stands 42½ feet high by 50 feet wide.

More befitting Walt Disney World or Universal Studios (complete with the health warnings), the **Shuttle Launch Experience** is the center's newest and most spectacular attraction. Designed by a team of astronauts, NASA experts, and renowned attraction engineers, the 44,000-square-foot structure uses a sophisticated motion-based platform, special-effects seats, and high-fidelity visual and audio components to simulate the sensations experienced in an actual space-shuttle launch, including MaxQ, Solid Rocker Booster separation, main engine cutoff, and External Tank separation. The journey culminates with a breathtaking view of Earth from space.

The only back-to-back twin **IMAX theater** in the world is in the complex, too. The dream of space flight comes to life on a movie screen five stories tall with dramatic footage shot by NASA astronauts during missions. Realistic 3-D special effects will make you feel like you're in space with them. Films alternate throughout the year. Call for specific shows and times.

Add-on activities include **Lunch with an Astronaut** ($60.99, includes general admission), where astronauts talk about their experiences and engage in a good-natured Q&A; the typical line of questioning from kids—"How do you eat/sleep/relieve yourself in space?" **NASA Up Close** tour ($59, general admission included) brings visitors to sites seldom accessible to the public, such as the Vehicle Assembly Building, the shuttle landing strip, and the 6-million-pound crawler that transports the shuttle to its launchpad. Or see how far the space program has come with the **Cape Canaveral: Then and Now** tour ($59, includes general admission), which visits America's first launch sites from the 1960s and the 21st century's active unmanned-rocket program. ⊠*Rte. 405, Kennedy Space Center* ☎*321/449–4444* ⊕*www.kennedyspacecenter. com* ✉*General admission includes bus tour, IMAX movies, Visitor Complex shows and exhibits, and the Astronaut Hall of Fame, $38* ☉*Space Center opens daily at 9, closing times vary according to season (call for details), last regular tour 3 hrs before closing; closed certain launch dates.*

United States Astronaut Hall of Fame. The original *Mercury 7* team and the later *Gemini, Apollo, Skylab,* and shuttle astronauts contributed to make the United States Astronaut Hall of Fame the world's premium archive of astronauts' personal stories. Authentic memorabilia and equipment from their collections tell the story of human space exploration. You'll watch videotapes of historic moments in the space program and see one-of-a-kind items like Wally Schirra's relatively archaic *Sigma 7* Mercury space capsule, Gus Grissom's spacesuit (colored silver only because NASA thought silver looked more "spacey"), and a flag that made it to the moon. The exhibit **First on the Moon** focuses on crew selection for *Apollo 11* and the Soviet Union's role in the space race. Definitely don't miss the **Astronaut Adventure**, a hands-on

> ## SPACE INVADERS
>
> As fascinating as the exhibits and tours of Kennedy Space Center are, there's nothing like seeing a launch in person. Kennedy Space Center offers visitors two launch-viewing options for witnessing blast-off, one from the Visitor Complex ($28–$38), and another from a restricted-viewing site on NASA Causeway ($48–$58), the closest public viewing site to the launchpad. Ticket prices also include admission to the Visitor Complex. Check out ⊕ *www.kennedyspacecenter.com for launch schedules.*

discovery center with interactive exhibits that help you learn about space travel. One of the more challenging activities is a space-shuttle simulator that lets you try your hand at landing the craft—and afterward replays a side view of your rolling and pitching descent. If that gets your motor going, consider enrolling in **ATX (Astronaut Training Experience)**. Held at the Hall of Fame, this is an intense full-day experience where you can dangle from a springy harness for a simulated moonwalk, spin in ways you never thought possible in a multi-axis trainer, and either work Mission Control or helm a space shuttle (in a full-scale mock-up) during a simulated landing. Veteran astronauts helped design the program, and you'll hear first-hand from them as you progress through your training. Space is limited (no pun intended), so call well in advance. Included in the $250 program is your astronaut gear, lunch, and a VIP tour of the Kennedy Space Center. ⊠ *Rte. 405, Kennedy Space Center* ☎ *321/449–4444, 321/449–4400 ATX* ⊕ *www. kennedyspacecenter.com* 🖃 *$17* ☉ *Hall of Fame opens daily at 9, closing times vary according to season (call for details).*

WHERE TO EAT

$$$ ✕**Dixie Crossroads.** This sprawling restaurant is always crowded and
SEAFOOD   festive, but it's not just the rustic setting that draws the throngs—it's
★   the seafood. The specialty is the difficult-to-cook rock shrimp, which is served fried, broiled, or steamed. Diners with a hearty appetite can opt for the all-you-can-eat rock shrimp, small shrimp, tilapia, or catfish. Often the wait for a table can last 90 minutes, but if you don't have time to wait, you can order takeout or eat in the bar area. And a word to the wise: as tempting as those corn fritters dusted with powdered sugar are, don't fill up on them. ⊠ *1475 Garden St., 2 mi east of I–95 Exit 220* ☎ *321/268–5000* ⚘ *Reservations not accepted* 🖃 *AE, D, DC, MC, V.*

SPORTS AND THE OUTDOORS

Fodor's Choice   **Merritt Island National Wildlife Refuge.** Owned by the Florida Fish and
★   Wildlife Service as well as National Aeronautics and Space Administration (NASA), this 140,000-acre refuge, which adjoins the Canaveral
National Seashore, acts as a buffer around Kennedy Space Center while
protecting 1,000 species of plants and 500 species of wildlife, including
15 considered federally threatened or endangered. It's an immense area
dotted by brackish estuaries and marshes and patches of land consisting of coastal dunes, scrub oaks, pine forests and flatwoods, and palm
and oak hammocks. You can borrow field guides and binoculars at the
visitor center (4 mi east of Titusville) to track down falcons, ospreys,
eagles, turkeys, doves, cuckoos, owls, and woodpeckers, as well as loggerhead turtles, alligators, and otters. A 20-minute video about refuge
wildlife and accessibility—only 10,000 acres are developed—can help
orient you. You might take a self-guided tour along the 7-mi **Black
Point Wildlife Drive.** The dirt road takes you back in time, where there
are no traces of encroaching malls or mankind and it's easy to visualize the tribes who made this their home 7,000 years ago. On the **Oak
Hammock Foot Trail** you can see wintering migratory waterfowl and
learn about the plants of a hammock community. If you exit the north
end of the refuge, look for the **Manatee Observation Area** just north of
the Haulover Canal (maps are at the visitor center). They usually show
up in spring and fall. There are also fishing camps scattered throughout the area. Most of the refuge is closed 24 hours prior to a shuttle
launch. ⊠*Rte. 402, across Titusville Causeway* ☎*321/861–0667,
visitor center 321/861–0668* ⊕*www.fws.gov/merrittisland* ✉*Free
⊙Daily sunrise–sundown; visitor center weekdays 8–4:30, weekends
9–5 (Nov.–Mar.).*

COCOA BEACH

5 mi south of Cape Canaveral.

After crossing a long and high bridge just east of Cocoa Village, you'll
drop down upon a barrier island. A few miles farther and you'll reach
the Atlantic Ocean and picture-perfect **Cocoa Beach** at Route A1A. This
is one of the Space Coast's nicest beaches, with many wide stretches that
are excellent for biking, jogging, power walking, or strolling. In some
places there are dressing rooms, showers, playgrounds, picnic areas
with grills, snack shops, and surf-side parking lots. Beach vendors offer
necessities, and guards are on duty in summer. As the closest beach to
Orlando, Cocoa Beach is popular with Central Floridians looking for
a quick getaway or vacationers looking to extend their stay. The city is
also considered the capital of Florida's surfing community.

ESSENTIALS

Visitor Information Cocoa Beach Convention and Visitors Bureau (⊠*8501
Astronaut Blvd., Ste. 4, Cape Canaveral* ☎*321/454–2022 or 877/321–8474*
⊕*www.visitcocoabeach.com*).

WHERE TO EAT AND STAY

$-$$

SEAFOOD

✗**Oh Shucks Seafood Bar.** At the only open-air seafood bar on the beach, at the entrance of the Cocoa Beach Pier, the main item is oysters, served on the half shell. You can also grab a burger here, crab legs by the pound, or Oh Shucks' most popular item, coconut beer shrimp. Some diners complain that the prices don't jibe with the ultracasual atmosphere (e.g., plastic chairs), but they're also paying for the "ex-Pier-ience." There's live entertainment on Friday and Saturday. ⊠*401 Meade Ave., Cocoa Beach Pier* ☎*321/783–7549* ☐*AE, D, V.*

$$$

🏨**Hilton Cocoa Beach Oceanfront.** You can't get any closer to the beach than this seven-story oceanfront hotel. Most rooms have ocean views, but for true drama get a room on the east end, facing the water. If sand isn't your thing, enjoy the ocean breeze and live music on the 10,000-square-foot deck surrounding "the largest pool on the Space Coast." The property also offers a variety of water-sport rentals and surf lessons. With purple, gold, and green soft goods, room decor is more Mardi Gras than beach resort. Rooms also feature Hilton Serenity Beds. **Pros:** beachfront; friendly staff; clean. **Cons:** small bathrooms; no balconies; room windows don't open. ⊠*1550 N. Atlantic Ave.* ☎*321/799–0003* ⊕*www.hiltoncocoabeach.com* ⬳*285 rooms, 11 suites* ⌔*In-room: refrigerator, Wi-Fi. In-hotel: 3 restaurants, room service, bar, 2 pools, gym, beachfront, laundry facilities, laundry service, parking (free), no-smoking rooms* ☐*AE, D, DC, MC, V.*

$$$

★

🏨**Inn at Cocoa Beach.** One of the area's best, this charming oceanfront inn has spacious, individually decorated rooms with four-poster beds, upholstered chairs, and balconies or patios; most have ocean views. Deluxe rooms are much larger, with a king-size bed, sofa, and sitting area; most also have a dining table. Jacuzzi rooms are different sizes. Included in the rate are afternoon socials in the breezeway, evening wine and cheese, and a continental breakfast. **Pros:** quiet; romantic; honor bar. **Cons:** no on-site restaurant; "forced" socializing. ⊠*4300 Ocean Beach Blvd.* ☎*321/799–3460, 800/343–5307 outside Florida* ⊕*www. theinnatcocoabeach.com* ⬳*50 rooms* ⌔*In-room: safe, DVD (some), Wi-Fi. In-hotel: pool, beachfront, Wi-Fi, parking (free), no-smoking rooms* ☐*AE, D, MC, V* ⦿*CP.*

NIGHTLIFE

The **Cocoa Beach Pier** (⊠*401 Meade Ave.* ☎*321/783–7549)* is for locals, beach bums, surfers, and people who don't mind the weather-worn wood and sandy, watery paths. At the Mai Tiki Bar they claim that "No Bar Goes This Far," which is true, considering it's at the end of the 800-foot pier. Come to The Boardwalk Friday night for the Boardwalk Bash, with live acoustic and rock-and-roll music, drop in Saturday for more live music, and come back Wednesday evening to catch the reggae band. For great live jazz Tuesday through Sunday, head to **Heidi's Jazz Club** (⊠*7 Orlando Ave. N* ☎*321/783–4559).*

SPORTS AND THE OUTDOORS

BEACHES

Alan Shepard Park. Named for the former astronaut, this 5-acre oceanfront park, aptly enough, provides excellent views of shuttle launches. Facilities include 10 picnic pavilions, shower and restroom facilities, and more than 300 parking spaces (parking is $7 per day, $10 per day on weekends and holidays from early March through Labor Day). Shops and restaurants are within walking distance. ✉ *East end of Rte. 250* ☎ *321/868–3274.*

Sidney Fischer Park. The 10-acre oceanfront has showers, playgrounds, changing areas, picnic areas with grills, snack shops, and plenty of well-maintained, inexpensive surf-side parking lots. Beach vendors carry necessities for sunning and swimming. The parking fee is $5 for cars and RVs. ✉ *2100 block of Rte. A1A* ☎ *321/868–3252.*

FISHING The **Cocoa Beach Pier** (✉ *401 Meade Ave.* ⊕ *www.cocoabeachpier.com* ☎ *321/783–7549*) has a bait-and-tackle shop and a fishing area. There's a $1 charge to enter the fishing area at the end of the 800-foot-long boardwalk, and a $3.50 fishing fee. You can rent rods and reels here. ■ **TIP→ The pier is a great place to watch space-shuttle launches.**

KAYAKING Specializing in manatee encounters, **Adventure Kayak of Cocoa Beach** (☎ *321/480–8632*) takes guests on one- and two-person kayak tours of mangroves, channels, and islands.

SURFING If you can't tell a tri-skeg stick from a hodaddy shredding the lip on a gnarly tube, then you may want to avail yourself of the **Ron Jon Surf School** (✉ *150 E. Columbia La.* ☎ *321/868–1980*) or the **Cocoa Beach Surf Company** (✉ *4001 N. Atlantic Ave.* ☎ *321/799–9930*). They teach grommets (dudes) and gidgets (chicks) from kids to seniors in groups and one on one. **Ron Jon Watersports** (✉ *4275 N. Atlantic Ave.* ☎ *321/799–8888*) and the **Cocoa Beach Surf Company** (✉ *4001 N. Atlantic Ave.* ☎ *321/799–9930*) rent surfboards, body boards, and wet suits, as well as umbrellas, chairs, and bikes.

SHOPPING

Cocoa Beach Surf Company (✉ *4001 N. Atlantic Ave.* ☎ *321/799–9930*) is the world's largest surf complex with three floors of boards, apparel, sunglasses, and anything else a surfer or wannabe could need. Also on-site are a 5,600-gallon fish and shark tank, the Shark Pit Bar & Grill, and the **East Coast Surfing Hall of Fame and Museum.**

Fodor'sChoice It's impossible to miss the **Ron Jon Surf Shop** (✉ *4151 N. Atlantic Ave.,*
★ *Rte. A1A* ☎ *321/799–8888*). With a giant surfboard and an aqua, teal, and pink Art Deco facade, Ron Jon takes up nearly two blocks along Route A1A. What started in 1963 as a small T-shirt and bathing suit shop has evolved into a 52,000-square-foot superstore that's open every day 'round the clock. The shop has water-sports gear as well as chairs and umbrellas for rent and sells every kind of beachwear, surf wax, plus the requisite T-shirts and flip-flops. ■ **TIP→ For up-to-the-minute surfing conditions, call the store and press 3 and then 7 for the Ron Jon Surf and Weather Report.**

Georgia

ATLANTA, SAVANNAH, AND THE COAST

"The [Atlanta] CityPass allowed us to bypass the ticket line [at the Georgia Aquarium] which saved us standing in the Georgia heat. One tip: If there is not an event go up to the ballroom above the food court. It is not part of the traffic flow (and indeed signs say 'no live exhibits,' but the ballroom has a huge window to the beluga whale tank."

— palmettoprincess

"Well, my favorite is Jekyll Island, but it is decidedly NOT upscale. St. Simons is more so. Cumberland is deserted sans some campers and the Greyfield Inn. It's wonderful because it IS so deserted."

— starrs

www.fodors.com/community

Updated by
Eileen Robin-
son Smith and
Christine Van
Dusen

Geographically speaking, Georgia is the largest state east of the Mississippi River. Its varied terrain ranges from the foothills of the Appalachian Mountains, in the north, to the great coastal plain that stretches from the state's center toward the shore to the beaches of the Golden Isles and the Okefenokee National Wildlife Refuge, in the southeast.

Georgia's cities and towns define that famous Southern charm of fable in unique ways. Sprawling Atlanta, the state capital since the Civil War ended in 1865 is also the capitol of the New South, with the third largest concentration of Fortune 500 companies in the country. Colonial Savannah, with the nation's largest historic district, lures visitors with its cobblestone squares, parterre gardens, and historic homes. Georgia's 100-mi coast runs from the mouth of the Savannah River south to the mouth of the St. Marys River. The seaside resort communities blend Southern elegance with a casual sensibility. St. Simons Island, about 70 mi south of Savannah, attracts a laid-back crowd of anglers, beachgoers, golfers, and tennis players. On nearby Jekyll Island, the lavish lifestyle of America's early 19th-century rich and famous is still evident in their stately Victorian "cottages." Cumberland Island's protected forests and miles of sandy coastline and the dark waters of the Okefenokee are favorite haunts of nature lovers.

ORIENTATION AND PLANNING

GETTING ORIENTED

Atlanta lies just northwest of the center of the state and is easily accessible from most points via major interstates. Savannah is near the east coast, closest to the South Carolina border. The Golden Isles make up the stretch of Georgia sand between South Carolina and Florida, and the Okefenokee National Wildlife Refuge is at the south end of the state on the border with Florida.

Atlanta. Atlanta, the state's capital and seat of Fulton County, was founded in 1837 and sits on the Piedmont Plateau in northern Georgia. Though the metro area spans 8,000 square mi, don't let the sprawling size—or all the transplanted "Yankees"—fool you into thinking Southern hospitality is dead. It's alive and well in Atlanta's pith-helmeted downtown ambassadors, drawling coffee mug-fillers, waving neighbors, and good ol' boy politicians.

Savannah. Savannah's historic streets and link to the past is the main draw for travelers. The 2½-square-mi Landmark Historic District is the nation's largest. It is where the city's 22 squares and most of its accommodations, restaurants, and shops are located.

TOP REASONS TO GO

The Georgia Aquarium: Wildly successful after its opening in late 2005 in Atlanta, the world's largest aquarium draws visitors from all over the globe.

Following in King's footsteps: Home of Martin Luther King Jr., Atlanta was a hub of the civil rights movement. Not to be missed is a visit to the King Center and a tour through his childhood home on Auburn Avenue.

Intriguing architecture: Close to half of the 2,500 buildings in Savannah have architectural or historic significance. The many building styles—Georgian, Gothic Revival, Victorian, Italianate, Federal, and Romanesque—make strolling the tree-lined neighborhoods a delight. The 19th-century Telfairs's Owens-

Thomas house is a particular highlight.

Sapelo Island: When land was set aside as an independent state of freed slaves, it became known as Georgia's Black Republic. Vestiges of that community remain at Sapelo, and have made it an island of contrasts—rich in history and ecowilderness, and home to Hog Hammock, a one-of-a-kind community that echoes the culture and practices of its African slave heritage.

Horses of Cumberland: Cumberland Island is about as far removed from civilization as you can get, and seeing the majesty of these horses running wild across the shore is worth every effort of planning ahead. There are some 200 feral horses, descendants of those that were abandoned by the Spanish in the 1500s.

Coastal Isles and the Okefenokee. Coastal Georgia is a complex jigsaw wending its way from the ocean and tidal marshes inland along the intricate network of rivers. To truly appreciate the mystique of Georgia's coastal salt marshes and islands, make the 40-minute ferry crossing from Meridian to Sapelo Island.

PLANNING

WHEN TO GO

Atlanta isn't called "Hotlanta" for nothing—in the late spring and summer months the mosquitoes feast and the temperatures can reach a sticky and humid 99°F (thankfully, almost every place in the city is air-conditioned). The best time to visit is in the fall and early winter, when many other cities are beginning to get cold and gray but Atlanta typically maintains a steady level of sunshine and cool breezes.

There really is no bad time to visit Savannah. Spring and fall offer the best temperatures and most of the city's major arts festivals happen in September or October.

Early spring and late fall are ideal for visiting the coastal isles and the Okefenokee. By February, temperatures often reach into the 70s, while nights remain cool and even chilly, which keeps the bugs at bay. Because of the high demand to visit these areas before the bugs arrive and after they depart, you should book ferry reservations to Sapelo

Island and Cumberland Island National Seashore months in advance in spring and fall: without a reservation, you risk having to wait days for a cancellation.

GETTING HERE AND AROUND

AIR TRAVEL

Hartsfield-Jackson Atlanta International (ATL), the busiest passenger airport in the world, has reasonable airfares at most times of the year, given that the city is a transportation hub and most Atlanta attractions aren't seasonal. Savannah/Hilton Head International Airport is 18 mi west of downtown Savannah. The coastal isles are served by the Brunswick Golden Isles Airport. The closest major airports are in Savannah and Jacksonville, FL.

Airport Contacts **The Brunswick Golden Isles Airport** (⊠ *500 Connole St.* ☎ *912/265–2070* ⊕ *www.glynncountyairports.com*). **Hartsfield-Jackson Atlanta International Airport** (*ATL* ⊠ *6000 N. Terminal Pkwy., Atlanta* ☎ *404/530–7300* ⊕ *www.atlanta-airport.com*). **Savannah/Hilton Head International Airport** (⊠ *400 Airways Ave., West Chatham* ☎ *912/964–0514* ⊕ *www.savannahairport.com*).

RESTAURANTS

Atlanta is a city known for its food. Traditional Southern fare thrives, as do Asian fusion, Peruvian tapas, creative vegan, and mouth-scorching Indian food. Catch the flavor of the South at breakfast and lunch in modest establishments that serve only these meals. Reserve evenings for culinary exploration, including some of the new restaurants that present traditional ingredients and dishes in fresh ways. Waits at some hot dining locales can exceed an hour, especially if you arrive after 7 PM.

Savannah has excellent seafood restaurants, though locals also have a passion for spicy barbecued meats. Most of the River Street restaurants are high-volume and touristy. The Historic District yields a culinary cache. Sunday brunch is a beloved institution, but many restaurants close on Sunday night.

Restaurants in the coastal isles range from fish camps—normally rustic dockside affairs—to the more upscale eateries that tend to spawn around the larger towns.

HOTELS

One of America's most popular convention destinations, Atlanta offers plenty of variety in terms of lodgings. There are more than 76,000 rooms in metro Atlanta. Although Savannah has its share of chain hotels and motels, the city's most distinctive lodgings are in more than two dozen historic inns, guesthouses, and B&Bs gracing the Historic District. A Continental or full Southern breakfast is often included in the rate, as are afternoon refreshments (usually wine and cheese, sometimes elaborate hors d'oeuvres); these extras definitely help to justify some of the escalated prices. Hotels in the coastal isles run the gamut from Victorian mansions to Spanish-style bed-and-breakfasts to some of the most luxurious hotel–spa accommodations found anywhere. Since options are somewhat limited, make your reservations as far in advance as possible.

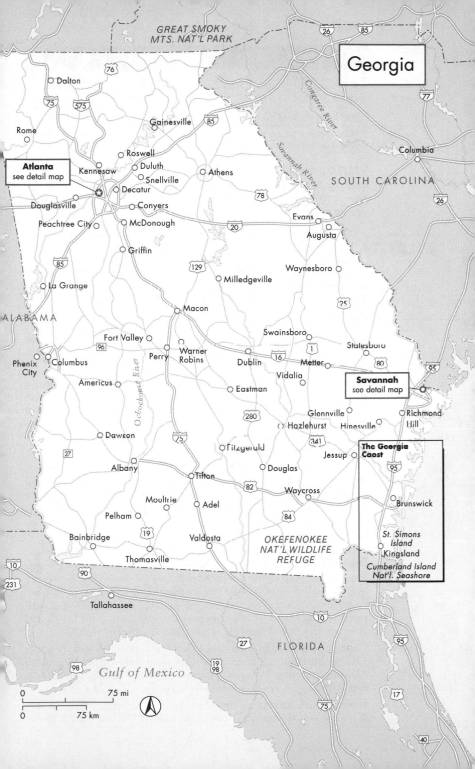

WHAT IT COSTS					
	¢	$	$$	$$$	$$$$
Restaurant	under $10	$10–$14	$15–$19	$20–$24	over $24
Hotel	under $100	$100–$150	$151–$200	$101–$250	over $250

Restaurant prices are per person for a main course at dinner. Hotel prices are for a standard double room, excluding state and local taxes.

VISITOR INFORMATION

Contacts Georgia Department of Economic Development (⊠ *75 5th St., Technology Square, Suite 1200, Atlanta, GA* ☎ *404/962–4000 or 800/847–4842* ⊕ *www.exploregeorgia.org*).

ATLANTA

A warm embrace greets visitors to Atlanta. Top-notch shopping, world-class dining, and major attractions are among the greatest rewards these days. The Georgia Aquarium, the largest in the world, draws visitors who want to get up close and personal with whale sharks. The Woodruff Arts Center is a cultural hub where you can catch a performance by the Atlanta Symphony Orchestra or gaze on treasures from the Louvre on loan at the High Museum of Art. And the fizzy World of Coke is dedicated to the hometown beverage.

Atlanta continues to experience explosive growth. The latest estimates place the city's population at 486,411. But the 20-county Atlanta Metropolitan Statistical Area counts more than 5 million residents. A good measure of the city's expansion is the ever-changing skyline; condominium developments appear to spring up overnight, while rundown properties seem to disappear in a flash.

Originally built as the terminus of the Western & Atlantic Railroad, Atlanta is still a transportation hub. The city now serves the world through Hartsfield-Jackson Atlanta International Airport—now ranked as the busiest in the world. It serves nearly 89 million passengers annually.

GETTING HERE AND AROUND

AIR TRAVEL Hartsfield-Jackson Atlanta International (ATL), the busiest passenger airport in the world, is 13 mi south of Downtown. Although an underground train and moving walkways help you reach your gate more quickly, budget extra time for negotiating the massive facility. Because of the airport's size, security lines can be long, especially during peak travel periods. MARTA, the regional subway system, is the fastest and cheapest way to and from the airport, but taxis are available.

CAR TRAVEL The city is encircled by Interstate 285. Three interstates also crisscross Atlanta: Interstate 85, running northeast–southwest from Virginia to Alabama; Interstate 75, running north–south from Michigan to Florida; and Interstate 20, running east–west from South Carolina to Texas.

Some refer to Atlanta as the "Los Angeles of the South," because driving is virtually the only way to get around. Atlantans have grown accustomed to frequent delays at rush hour—the morning and late-afternoon commuting periods seem to get longer every year.

Atlanta's lack of a grid system confuses many drivers, even locals. Some streets change their names along the same stretch of road, including the city's most famous thoroughfare, Peachtree Street, which follows a mountain ridge from downtown to suburban Norcross, outside Interstate 285: it becomes Peachtree Road after crossing Interstate 85 and then splits into Peachtree Industrial Boulevard beyond the Buckhead neighborhood and the original Peachtree Road, which heads into Chamblee. Adding to the confusion, dozens of other streets in the metropolitan area use "Peachtree" in their names.

SUBWAY TRAVEL MARTA has clean and safe subway trains with somewhat limited routes that link downtown with many major landmarks, like the CNN Center and the Martin Luther King Jr. Memorial. The system's two main lines cross at the Five Points station. MARTA uses a smart-card fare system called Breeze. The cards are available at RideStores and from vending machines at each station. The one-way fare is $1.75, but the cards offer several options, including weekend, weekly, and monthly passes.

Trains generally run weekdays 5 AM to 1 AM and weekends and holidays 6 AM to 12:30 AM. Most trains operate every 15 to 20 minutes; during weekday rush hours, trains run every 10 minutes.

■ TIP➔ Locals take MARTA to and from Hartsfield-Jackson International Airport, which has the traffic snarls common with larger airports. The $1.75 fare (plus a $0.50 charge for a Breeze Ticket or $5 for a reloadable Breeze Card) is a fraction of the amount charged by shuttles or taxis. Airport travelers should be careful about catching the right train. One line ends up at North Springs station to the north. The other at Doraville station, to the northeast. Daily parking is free at MARTA parking facilities. Long-term parking rates range from $4 to $7 daily. All stations do not have lots, however.

ESSENTIALS
Subway Contacts MARTA (☎ 404/848–5000 ⊕ www.itsmarta.com).

Visitor Information Atlanta Convention & Visitors Bureau (✉ 233 Peachtree St., Suite 100, Downtown ☎ 404/521–6600 ⊕ www.atlanta.net).

PLANNING YOUR TIME
Because it would take too long to explore the city end-to-end in one fell swoop, consider discovering Atlanta one pocket at a time. In Downtown you can stroll through the Georgia Aquarium, tour the CNN Center and meander through the World of Coca-Cola. Another good pocket includes three very walkable neighborhoods, all known for their canopies of trees, cute shops, and fun bistros: Virginia-Highland, Little Five Points, and Inman Park. Your third pocket should be Buckhead, and depending on when you go you will either see a neighborhood in metamorphosis or, if all goes according to plan, a shopper's mecca. Two constants there are Lenox Mall and Phipps Plaza, great shopping spots in their own right.

DISCOUNTS AND DEALS

Visitors can take advantage of the deal offered with **Atlanta CityPass**, "the ticket to a New and Old South vacation." As of this writing, an adult pass—which is valid for a nine-day period—cost $69 and provided access to six attractions: Georgia Aquarium, World of Coca-Cola, Zoo Atlanta, and a choice between Inside CNN Atlanta Studio Tour or Atlanta Botanical Garden, and a choice of either High Museum of Art or Atlanta History Center. Visit ⊕*www.citypass.com/city/atlanta.html* or call ☎*888/330–5008* for details.

EXPLORING

Atlanta proper has three major areas—Downtown, Midtown, and Buckhead—as well as many smaller commercial districts and intown neighborhoods. Atlanta's Downtown is filled with government staffers and office workers by day, but at night the visiting conventioneers—and, as city improvements take hold, residents—come out to play. Midtown, Virginia-Highland, Buckhead, and Little Five Points are the best places to go for dinner, nightclubs, and shows.

DOWNTOWN ATLANTA

❼ **Atlanta Cyclorama & Civil War Museum.** A building in Grant Park (named
★ for a New England–born Confederate colonel, not the U.S. president) houses a huge circular painting depicting the 1864 Battle of Atlanta, during which 90% of the city was destroyed. A team of expert European panorama artists completed the painting in Milwaukee, Wisconsin, in 1887; it was donated to the city of Atlanta in 1897. On the second level, a display called "Life in Camp" displays rifles, uniforms, and games soldiers played to pass the time. An outstanding bookstore has dozens of volumes about the Civil War. Guided tours are available every hour on the half hour. To get here by car, take Interstate 20 east to Exit 59A, turn right onto Boulevard, and then follow signs to the Cyclorama. The museum shares a parking lot and entrance walkway with Zoo Atlanta. ⊠*800C Cherokee Ave., Grant Park* ☎*404/658–7625* ⊕*www.atlantacyclorama.org* ⊠*$8* ⊗*Tues.–Sun. 9:30–4:30.*

❶ **Centennial Olympic Park.** This 21-acre swath of green was the central
⟳ venue for the 1996 Summer Olympics. The benches at the Fountain of
Fodor'sChoice Rings allow you to enjoy the water and music spectacle—eight tunes
★ are timed to coincide with water displays that shoot sprays 15 feet to 30 feet high. The All Children's Playground is designed to be accessible to kids with disabilities. Nearby is the world's largest aquarium and Imagine It! Children's Museum. The park also has a café, restrooms, and a playground, and typically offers ice-skating in winter. ■**TIP→ Don't miss seeing Centennial Olympic Park at night, when eight 65-foot-tall lighting towers set off the beauty of the park. These stylized reproductions represent the kind of markers that led ancient Greeks to significant public events.** ⊠*Marietta St. and Centennial Olympic Park Dr., Downtown* ☎*404/223–4412* ⊕*www.centennialpark.com* ⊗*Daily 7 AM–11 PM.*

❸ **CNN Center.** The home of Cable News Network occupies all 14 floors
★ of this dramatic structure on the edge of Downtown. The 55-minute CNN studio tour—difficult for some people because it descends eight

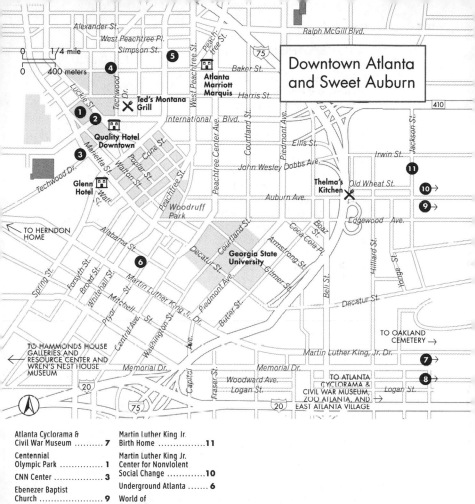

Downtown Atlanta
and Sweet Auburn

flights of stairs—is a behind-the-scenes glimpse of the control room, news rooms, and broadcast studios. Tours depart approximately every 10 minutes. You can make reservations by telephone or online. ✉*1 CNN Center, Downtown* ☎*404/827–2300* ⊕*www.cnn.com/studiotour* ✉*Tour $12* ⊘*Daily 9–5.*

② **Georgia Aquarium.** With 8 million gallons of water, this wildly popular attraction is the world's largest aquarium. The 550,000-square-foot building, an architectural marvel resembling the bow of a ship, has tanks of various sizes filled with more than 80,000 animals, representing 500 species. The aquarium's 6.3-million-gallon Ocean Voyager Gallery is the world's largest indoor marine exhibit, with 4,574 square feet

Fodor's Choice
★

of viewing windows. In the gigantic tanks you'll see dramatic white beluga whales, a favorite with many visitors, and massive whale sharks. Not everything has gills, however: there are also penguins, sea lions, sea otters, river otters, sea turtles, and giant octopi. As of this writing, the aquarium had announced plans to add a $110 million dolphin exhibit by 2010. Hordes of kids—and many adults—can always be found around the touch tanks. A cartoon show featuring Deepo, the aquarium mascot, is an extra $5.50 for adults and $4 for children. One-hour behind-the-scenes tours

WORD OF MOUTH

"Just returned from visiting our three-year-old grandson in Atlanta. The Children's Museum (Imagine It!) is wonderful. It is basically a very large room with different play areas (including one for babies and young toddlers). Lots of interactive play, plus places to sit and read. There is limited food available inside. Parking in one of the garages nearby ($12). It was a great way to spend a rainy day."   —TrvlMaven

are $50. Cafe Aquaria serves sandwiches, salads, and other light fare. There are often huge crowds, so arrive early or late for the best chance of getting a close-up view of the exhibits. ■TIP➜ **Purchase tickets at least a week ahead. Online ticketing is best, as you are e-mailed tickets you can print out at home.** ✉225 Baker St., Downtown ☎404/581–4000 or 877/434–7442 ⊕www.georgiaaquarium.org 🎟$23 ⊗Sun. to Fri. 10–5, Sat. 9–6.

❺ Imagine It! The Children's Museum of Atlanta. In this colorful and joyfully
ℭ noisy museum geared to children ages eight and younger, kids can build
★ sand castles, watch themselves perform on closed-circuit TV, operate a giant ball-moving machine, and get inside an imaginary waterfall (after donning raincoats, of course). Other exhibits rotate every few months. ✉275 Centennial Olympic Park Dr. NW, Downtown ☎404/659–5437 ⊕www.imagineit-cma.org 🎟$11 for ages 2 and above ⊗Weekdays 10–4, weekends 10–5.

❻ Underground Atlanta. Underground has seen more than its share of ups and downs. It was created from the web of subterranean brick streets, ornamental facades, and tunnels that fell into disuse in 1929, when the city built viaducts over the train tracks. The six-block district opened in 1969 as a retail and entertainment center and remained fairly popular until it was closed in 1980 for the MARTA train project. After a $142 million renovation, it reopened with eateries, retail, and specialty shops. In the following years, the spot's popularity waned. In 2005 the developers tried to revive interest in the district as a nighttime hot spot, opening six nightclubs on New Year's Eve, and saw mixed success. These days Underground remains relatively quiet during the daytime but hops at night for a largely African-American clientele, drawn to clubs like Sugar Hill and The House. As of this writing, the property was looking to charge $2 for entry to the district as a whole. ■TIP➜ **AtlanTIX, a half-price ticket outlet theater and cultural attractions, is in Underground Atlanta. It's open 11 to 6 Tuesday to Saturday, noon to 4 Sunday.** ✉50 Upper Alabama St., Downtown ☎404/523–2311 ⊕www.underground-atlanta.com.

④ World of Coca-Cola. Read all about it:
☾ New Coke replaces original Coke!
No, no—we're not referring to the
1980s marketing flop. The Atlanta-based beverage company closed
down its original museum and in
May 2007 emerged anew near the
Georgia Aquarium. This World of
Coca-Cola—a shrine to the brown
soda's image, products, and marketing—is, at 62,000 square feet, twice
the size of the previous building and
features more than 1,200 artifacts never before displayed to the public.
You can sip samples of Coca-Cola Company products from around the
world and peruse more than a century's worth of memorabilia from
the corporate archives. The gift shop sells everything from refrigerator magnets to evening bags. ■**TIP➔Visits begin with the screening of
a promotional movie. Some visitors love it; others see it as an annoyingly
long commercial.** ✉*121 Baker St. NW, Downtown* ☎*404/676–5151*
⊕*www.woccatlanta.com* ✂*$9* ☾*June–Aug., Mon.–Sat. 9–6, Sun.
11–5; Sept.–May, Mon.–Sat. 9–5, Sun. 11–5.*

> **HELP AT HAND**
>
> Need a helping hand—or simply
> directions—while exploring Downtown? Watch for a member of
> the **Atlanta Ambassador Force**
> (⊕ *www.atlantadowntown.com/
> ambassador.asp*). The members,
> easily recognized by their pith helmets, are a traveler's best friend.

③
3

⑧ Zoo Atlanta. This zoo has nearly 1,000 animals and 250 species living
☾ in naturalistic habitats. The gorillas and tigers are always a hit, as are
two giant pandas named Yang Yang and Lun Lun. Children can ride
the Nabisco Endangered Species Carousel and meet new friends at the
petting zoo; the whole family can take a ride on the Norfolk Southern
Zoo Express Train. To reach the zoo by car, take Interstate 20 east to
Exit 59A and turn right on Boulevard. Follow the signs to the zoo,
which is right near the Atlanta Cyclorama & Civil War Museum. ✉*800
Cherokee Ave. SE, Grant Park* ☎*404/624–5600* ⊕*www.zooatlanta.
org* ✂ *$17.99* ☾*Daily 9:30–5:30.*

SWEET AUBURN

⑨ **Ebenezer Baptist Church.** A Gothic Revival–style building completed in
Fodor'sChoice 1922, the church came to be known as the spiritual center of the civil
★ rights movement. Members of the King family, including the slain civil
rights leader, preached at the church for three generations. The congregation itself now occupies the building across the street. ■**TIP➔ A
federally funded restoration project is underway at the original church. Call
before visiting.** ✉*407 Auburn Ave. NE, Sweet Auburn* ☎*404/688–
7300* ✂*Free* ⊕*www.historicebenezer.org.*

⑪ **Martin Luther King Jr. National Historic Site and Birth Home.** The modest
Fodor'sChoice Queen Anne–style residence is where Martin Luther King Jr. was born
★ and raised. Besides items that belonged to the family, the house contains
an outstanding multimedia exhibit focused on the civil rights movement. To sign up for guided tours, go to the **National Park Service Visitor
Center** (✉*450 Auburn Ave., Sweet Auburn*), across the street from the
Martin Luther King Jr. Center for Nonviolent Social Change. Parking
is on the corner of John Wesley Dobbs Street and Boulevard, behind the
visitor center. ■**TIP➔ A limited number of visitors are allowed to tour the
house each day. Advance reservations are not possible, so sign up early in**

the day. ⊠*501 Auburn Ave., Sweet Auburn* ☎*404/331–6922* ⊕*www. nps.gov/malu* ⊠*Free* ☉*Tours: daily 10–5.*

⑩ **Martin Luther King Jr. Center for Nonviolent Social Change.** The Martin Luther King Jr. National Historic District occupies several blocks on Auburn Avenue, a few blocks east of Peachtree Street in the black business and residential community of Sweet Auburn. Martin Luther King Jr. was born here in 1929; after his assassination in 1968, his widow, Coretta Scott King, established this center, which exhibits such personal items as King's Nobel Peace Prize, bible, and tape recorder, along with memorabilia and photos chronicling the civil rights movement. In the courtyard in front of Freedom Hall, on a circular brick pad in the middle of the rectangular Meditation Pool, is Dr. King's white-marble tomb; the inscription reads; FREE AT LAST, FREE AT LAST, THANK GOD ALMIGHTY I'M FREE AT LAST. Nearby, an eternal flame burns. A chapel of all faiths sits at one end of the reflecting pool. Mrs. King, who passed away in 2006, is also entombed at the center. ⊠*449 Auburn Ave., Sweet Auburn* ☎*404/526–8900* ⊕*www.thekingcenter.org* ⊠*Free* ☉*Daily 9–5.*

MIDTOWN

⑮ **Atlanta Botanical Garden.** Occupying 30 acres inside Piedmont Park, the
Ⓒ grounds contain acres of display gardens, including a 2-acre interactive
Fodor'sChoice children's garden; a hardwood forest with walking trails; the Fuqua
★ Conservatory, which has unusual flora from tropical and desert climates; and the award-winning Fuqua Orchid Center, with a spectacular collection of tropical and high-elevation orchids. A variety of special exhibits take place throughout the year. ⊠*1345 Piedmont Ave., Midtown* ☎*404/876–5859* ⊕*www.atlantabotanicalgarden.org* ⊠*$12* ☉*Apr.– Oct., Tues.–Sun. 9–7, Thurs. 9–10; Nov.–Mar., Tues.–Sun. 9–5.*

⑬ **High Museum of Art.** This museum's permanent collection includes 19th-
★ and 20-century American works, including many by African-American artists. It also displays contemporary art. The building itself is a work of art; the American Institute of Architects listed the sleek structure, designed by Richard Meier, among the 10 best works of American architecture of the 1980s. An expansion designed by Renzo Piano, which opened in 2005, doubled the museum's size to 312,000 square feet with three new aluminum-paneled buildings. The roof features a system of 1,000 "light scoops" that filter light into the skyway galleries. A recent partnership with the Louvre Museum in Paris has brought hundreds of works from the Parisian museum's collection. ∎**TIP➔On the third Friday of every month, the museum is open for Friday Jazz until 10** PM. ⊠*Woodruff Arts Center, 1280 Peachtree St., Midtown* ☎*404/733– 4400, 404/733–4444 recorded information* ⊕*www.high.org* ⊠*$15* ☉*Tues., Wed., Fri., and Sat. 10–5, Thurs. 10–8, Sun. noon–5.*

⑫ **Margaret Mitchell House & Museum.** While she wrote her masterpiece, the author of *Gone With the Wind* lived in a turn-of-the-20th-century apartment house she called "the Dump." Volunteers gathered the funds necessary to restore the building in the early 1990s. To many Atlantans, the Margaret Mitchell House symbolizes the conflict between promoting the city's heritage and respecting its roots. The house has been struck by fire twice, in 1994 and 1996. Arson was strongly suspected but no

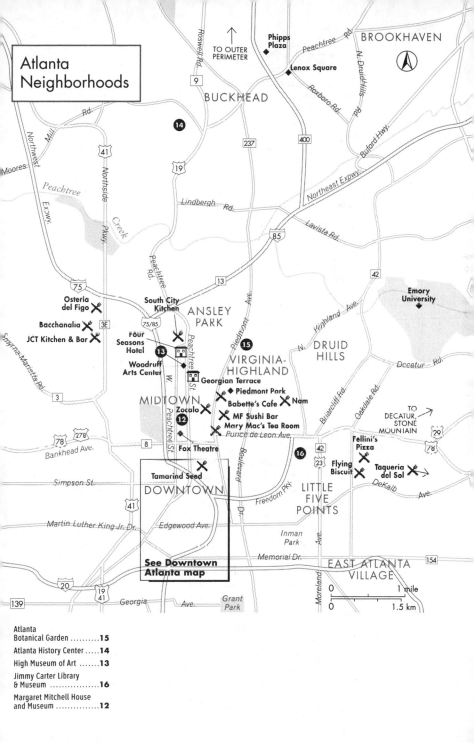

Atlanta Neighborhoods

TO OUTER PERIMETER

Phipps Plaza

Lenox Square

BROOKHAVEN

Roswell Rd.

Peachtree Rd.

N. Druid Hills Rd.

BUCKHEAD

Roxboro Rd.

9

237

400

Buford Hwy.

14

41

Northside Pkwy.

Northwest Mill Rd.

Moores

Peachtree Expwy.

Creek

Lindbergh Rd.

Northeast Expwy.

Lavista Rd.

19

85

42

Emory University

75

Osteria del Figo

South City Kitchen

Peachtree Rd.

13

ANSLEY PARK

Piedmont Ave.

Druid Rd.

Bacchanalia

3E

JCT Kitchen & Bar

75/85

Four Seasons Hotel

13

Peachtree St.

15

Decatur Rd.

Smyrna-Marietta Rd.

Woodruff Arts Center

Georgian Terrace

VIRGINIA-HIGHLAND

N. Highland Ave.

DRUID HILLS

3

MIDTOWN

Zocalo

12

Piedmont Park

Babette's Cafe

Nam

MF Sushi Bar

Mary Mac's Tea Room

Briarcliff Rd.

Oakdale Rd.

TO DECATUR, STONE MOUNTAIN

29

78

278

Peachtree St. W.

Ponce de Leon Ave.

Fellini's Pizza

78

8

Fox Theatre

16

42

23

Flying Biscuit

Taqueria del Sol

Bankhead Ave.

Tamarind Seed

Boulevard Dr.

DeKalb Ave.

Simpson St.

DOWNTOWN

LITTLE FIVE POINTS

41

Freedom Pkwy.

Martin Luther King Jr. Dr.

Edgewood Ave.

Inman Park

See Downtown Atlanta map

Memorial Dr.

EAST ATLANTA VILLAGE

154

20

0   1 mile

139

19 41

Georgia   Ave.

Grant Park

0   1.5 km

Moreland Ave.

HISTORY YOU CAN SEE

Gone With the Wind enthusiasts coming to Atlanta for the first time are often disappointed to discover that Scarlett O'Hara's beloved plantation, Tara, was no more real than Scarlett herself. But history buffs can find antebellum treasures in towns like Marietta and Kennesaw (about 20 mi northwest of Atlanta) and Roswell (about 23 mi north of Atlanta).

The **Marietta Gone With the Wind Museum** (⊠ *18 Whitlock Ave.* ☎ *770/794–5576* ⊕ *www.mariettaga.gov/gwtw/default.aspx*) pays homage to the movie with props and costumes.

The 2,884-acre **Kennesaw Mountain National Battlefield** (⊠ *Old U.S. 41 and Stilesboro Rd., Kennesaw* ☎ *770/427–4686* ⊕ *www.nps.gov/kemo*) was the site for crucial battles in 1864. The National Park Service maintains 16 mi of well-used hiking trails. A small museum has uniforms, weapons, and other items from the era.

The original furniture of the Archibald Smith family fills **Smith Plantation** (⊠ *935 Alpharetta St., Roswell* ☎ *770/640–3253* ⊕ *www.cvb. roswell.ga.us/smith-plantation-home. html*).

one was ever caught. Some say the city's most famous writer should not be lauded, as her book includes stereotypes of African-Americans during the Civil War. However, her fans point out that she helped to fund medical-school scholarships to Morehouse College for scores of African-American students. The visitor center exhibits photographs, archival material, and personal possessions. ⊠ *990 Peachtree St., at Peachtree Pl., Midtown* ☎ *404/249–7015* ⊕ *www.gwtw.org* ⊠ *$12* ☉ *Mon.–Sat. 9:30–5, Sun. 12–5.*

BUCKHEAD

⑭ **Fodor's Choice** ★ **Atlanta History Center.** Life in Atlanta, the South, and the Civil War are the focus of this fascinating museum. Displays are provocative, juxtaposing *Gone With the Wind* romanticism with the grim reality of Ku Klux Klan racism. Located on 33 acres in the heart of Buckhead, this is one of the Southeast's largest history museums with a research library and archives that annually serve more than 10,000 patrons. Visit the elegant 1928 **Swan House** mansion and the plantation house that is part of **Tullie Smith Farm.** The Kenan Research Center houses traveling exhibitions and an extensive archival collection. Lunch is served at the Swan Coach House, which also has a gallery and a gift shop. ⊠ *130 W. Paces Ferry Rd. NW, Buckhead* ☎ *404/814–4000* ⊕ *www.atlantahistorycenter.com* ⊠ *$15* ☉ *Mon.–Sat. 10–5:30, Sun. noon–5:30.*

VIRGINIA-HIGHLAND

⑯ ★ **Jimmy Carter Presidential Library & Museum.** This complex occupies the site where Union General William T. Sherman orchestrated the Battle of Atlanta (1864). The museum and archives detail the political career of former president Jimmy Carter. The adjacent Carter Center, which is not open to the public, focuses on conflict resolution and human rights issues. Outside, the Japanese-style garden is a serene spot to unwind. Both Carter and former First Lady Rosalynn Carter maintain offices here. ✉*441 Freedom Pkwy., Virginia-Highland* ☎*404/865–7100* ⊕*www.jimmycarterlibrary.org* 🎟*$8* ⊙*Mon.–Sat. 9–4:45, Sun. noon–4:45.*

OFF THE BEATEN PATH

Inman Park and Little Five Points. Since this neighborhood about 4 mi east of downtown was laid out by famous developer Joel Hurt in 1889, the area has faded and flourished a number of times, which explains the vast gaps in opulence evident in much of the architecture here. Huge, ornate Victorian mansions sit next to humble bungalows.

But no matter the exact address or style of home—be it modest or massive—Inman Park now commands considerable cachet among all types, from young families to empty-nesters to gays and lesbians. Here you'll also find the delightfully countercultural Little Five Points section, with funky boutiques, neighborhood bars, and gritty music venues that draw urban hipsters and suburban gawkers alike. Check out the kooky wigs, rubber corsets, and water pipes at **Junkman's Daughter** (✉*464 Moreland Ave. NE, Little Five Points* ☎*404/577–3188*), a funky-junky department store. The **Clothing Warehouse** (✉*420 Moreland Ave., Little Five Points* ☎*404/524–5070*) is one of the many colorful vintage-clothing stores here. Hot fashion can be found at **Cherry Bomb** (✉*1129 Euclid Ave., Little Five Points* ☎*404/522–2662*). If all that shopping makes you hungry, grab a bite—try the salt and vinegar popcorn or the hush puppies with smoked bacon and applesauce—at **The Porter Beer Bar** (✉*1156 Euclid Ave., Little Five Points* ☎*404/223–0393*). **A Cappella Books** (✉*484 Moreland Ave., Inman Park* ☎*404/681–5128*) stocks new and out-of-print titles. And don't miss **Charis Books** (✉*1189 Euclid Ave., Little Five Points* ☎*404/524-0304*), the South's oldest and largest feminist bookstore.

OTHER AREA ATTRACTIONS

It's essential to drive to these venues, so plan your visits with Atlanta's notorious rush hours in mind.

🌀 **Six Flags Over Georgia.** Georgia's major theme park, with heart-stopping roller coasters, family rides, and water attractions (best saved for last so you won't be damp all day), is a child's ideal playground. The new Goliath is a giant among roller coasters—at 200 feet, it's the largest in the Southeast. The heart-clenching ride hits speeds of 70 MPH. The park also has well-staged musical revues, concerts by top-name artists, and costumed characters such as the Justice League. ■**TIP➜ To get here, take MARTA's west line to the Hamilton Homes station and then hop aboard the Six Flags bus.** ✉*I–20W at 275 Riverside Pkwy., Austell* ☎*770/948–9290* ⊕*www.sixflags.com* 🎟*$29.99* ⊙*June–mid-Aug., open daily; mid-Aug.–Oct. and Mar.–May, open weekends; hrs vary.*

3

☼ **Stone Mountain Park.** At this 3,200-
★ acre state park you'll find the largest exposed granite outcropping on
earth. The Confederate Memorial
on the north face of the 825-foot-
high mountain is the world's largest sculpture, measuring 90 feet by
190 feet. There are several ways to
see the sculpture, including a cable
car that lifts you to the mountaintop and a steam locomotive that
chugs around the mountain's base.
Summer nights are capped with the

Lasershow Spectacular, an outdoor light display set to music and pro-
jected onto the side of Stone Mountain—attendance is a rite of passage
for new Atlantans. There are also a wildlife preserve, an antebellum
plantation, a swimming beach, two golf courses, a campground, a
hotel, a resort, several restaurants, and two Civil War museums. Crossroads, an entertainment complex with an 1870s-Southern-town theme,
offers costumed interpreters and a movie theater. The newest addition
is Sky Hike, a family-friendly ropes course at 12 feet, 24 feet, or 40
feet high. ⊠ *U.S. 78E, Stone Mountain Pkwy., exit 8, Stone Mountain*
☎ *770/498–5600* ⊕ *www.stonemountainpark.com* ⊠ *$8 per car, $25
per adult for an Adventure Pass* ⊙ *Daily 6 AM–midnight.*

WHERE TO EAT

DOWNTOWN

$–$$ ✕ **Ted's Montana Grill.** The Ted in question is CNN founder Ted Turner,
AMERICAN who has left a significant mark on this city. That's why Atlantans feel a
★ sense of ownership for this chain specializing in bison meat. Chicken,
beef, and salmon also play a role on the menu. Tin ceilings, a cheerful waitstaff, and mahogany paneling add to the comfortable feel. Ted
himself is known to stop by this location a lot; he lives in the building's
penthouse. ⊠ *133 Luckie St., Downtown* ☎ *404/521-9796* ⚐ *Reservations not accepted* ⊟ *AE, D, DC, MC, V.*

¢ ✕ **Thelma's Kitchen.** After losing her original location to make way for
SOUTHERN Centennial Olympic Park, Thelma Grundy moved her operation to
Auburn Avenue. The new location—more cheerful than the earlier
spot—serves favorites like okra pancakes, fried catfish, slaw, and macaroni and cheese, all of which are among the best in town. Thelma's
desserts, including lemon cheese pound cake, sweet-potato pie, red velvet cake, and pecan pie, are worth the trip. ⊠ *302 Auburn Ave., Sweet
Auburn* ☎ *404/688–5855* ⚐ *Reservations not accepted* ⊟ *No credit
cards* ⊙ *Closed Sun. No dinner.*

MIDTOWN

$$$$ ✕ **Bacchanalia.** Often called the city's best restaurant, Bacchanalia has
AMERICAN been a special-occasion destination since it opened in Buckhead in 1993.
Fodor'sChoice Chef-owners Anne Quatrano and Clifford Harrison helped transform
★ an industrial zone west of Midtown when they moved to their current

location in 2000. The renovated warehouse, known for its 20-foot ceilings, is decorated in deep, inviting tones. The kitchen focuses on locally grown organic produce and seasonal ingredients. Items on the prix-fixe menu change frequently, but could include crab fritters, wood-grilled beef tenderloin, and warm chocolate cake. ✉ *1198 Howell Mill Rd., West Midtown* ☎ *404/365–0410* ⟁ *Reservations essential* ▭ *AE, DC, MC, V* ✺ *Closed Sun.*

$$–$$$ ✕ **JCT Kitchen & Bar.** This comfortable, airy restaurant—with pale wood,
SOUTHERN white, and silver accents—is a welcome addition to the now-bustling
★ Westside Urban Market, home to the city's famed Bacchanalia restaurant and counter-service favorites Tacqueria del Sol and Figo. JCT, a "farmstead bistro" with Southern flair, is a great place for a business-casual lunch or a dinner date. The deviled eggs are to die for, as are the perfectly crisp truffle-Parmesan fries. Service is hit or miss. ✉ *1198 Howell Mill Rd., Suite 18, West Midtown* ☎ *404/355–2252* ⟁ *Reservations essential* ▭ *AE, DC, MC, V* ✺ *No lunch Sun.*

$ ✕ **Mary Mac's Tea Room.** Local celebrities and ordinary folks line up for
SOUTHERN the country-fried steak, fried chicken, and fresh vegetables. Here, in the Southern tradition, waitresses will call you "honey" and pat your arm to assure you that everything's all right. It's a great way to experience Southern food and hospitality all at once. ✉ *224 Ponce de Leon Ave., Midtown* ☎ *404/876–1800* ▭ *AE, MC, V.*

$$–$$$ ✕ **MF Sushibar.** The "MF" stands for Magic Fingers, and once you try
JAPANESE the spicy tuna tartar or the top-notch sushi rolls, you'll understand
Fodor's Choice why. Whether you take a seat at the bar or at one of the tables, you're
★ going to enjoy some of the best fish in town. Particularly popular is the Godzilla roll—shrimp tempura topped with smoked salmon, eel, and avocado. The ginger salad is a refreshing treat. ✉ *265 Ponce de Leon Ave., Midtown* ☎ *404/815–8844* ▭ *AE, D, DC, MC, V.*

$–$$ ✕ **Nam.** Brothers Alex and Chris Kinjo paid tribute to their mother's
VIETNAMESE homeland with this stylish eatery. Gauzy curtains separate the tables,
★ and sleek servers whisk by dressed in black and red. The crab-and-asparagus soup is packed with plenty of meat. Rich caramelized onions add mouthwatering depth to spicy clay-pot catfish. And the lemongrass tofu is just the right mix of crispy, spicy, and soft. ✉ *931 Monroe Dr., Suite A-101, Midtown* ☎ *404/541–9997* ▭ *AE, D, MC, V* ✺ *No lunch Mon. or weekends.*

¢–$ ✕ **Osteria del Figo.** High-quality counter-service restaurants like this one
ITALIAN have changed the face of Atlanta dining. In exchange for standing in a short line and paying up front, you get excellent food at a reasonable price. That's the concept behind this Italian eatery, which keeps it simple with pasta dishes, salads, and a few desserts. Try the bruschetta, which has a generous amount of fresh, juicy tomato chunks. Be sure to bring an appetite, as the portions are hefty. ✉ *1210 Howell Mill Rd., West Midtown* ☎ *404/351–3700* ⟁ *Reservations not accepted* ▭ *MC, V.*

$$–$$$ ✕ **South City Kitchen.** The culinary traditions of South Carolina inspire
SOUTHERN the dishes served at this cheerful restaurant. This is the place to get
★ fried green tomatoes with goat cheese, she-crab soup, or buttermilk fried chicken. The chef prepares catfish in many intriguing ways. Crab hash, served with poached eggs and chive hollandaise, is a classic.

Don't miss the chocolate pecan tart. Within walking distance of the Woodruff Arts Center, the spare, art-filled restaurant attracts a hip crowd. ⊠*1144 Crescent Ave., Midtown* ☎*404/873–7358* ⊟*AE, DC, MC, V.*

$$ ✗**Tamarind Seed.** All that is good
THAI about Thai flavors—refreshing lime, spicy basil, hot peppers, cooling coconut, and smoky fish sauces—is even better at this standout known for excellent service. Favorite dishes include chicken with green curry and sea bass with three-flavor sauce. Meals are served in a simple, subdued, but elegant setting. ⊠*1197 Peachtree St., Midtown* ☎*404/873–4888* ⊟*AE, MC, V* ⊗*No lunch Fri. and Sat.*

¢–$ ✗**Taqueria del Sol.** Don't let the long lines outside at this counter-service
MEXICAN eatery discourage you. They move quickly, and you'll soon be rewarded
★ with a full bar, a wide selection of tacos and enchiladas, unusual sides like spicy collard greens and jalapeño coleslaw, and a fabulous trio of salsas. Don't pass up the chunky guacamole. ⊠*1200-B Howell Mill Rd., West Midtown* ☎*404/352–5811* ⌧*Reservations not accepted* ⊟*AE, MC, V* ⊗*Closed Sun. No dinner Mon.*

$ ✗**Zocalo.** People come to this restaurant's inviting open-air patio—
MEXICAN warmed in the winter by giant heaters—for the city's best Mexican food. Order the guacamole, prepared tableside, as a starter before moving on to dishes like chicken breast simmered in a thick mole sauce or shrimp sautéed in chipotle salsa. The bar has an excellent selection of top-shelf tequilas. ■**TIP**➔ **There is also a location near the Decatur Courthouse on the square, and a new location will be opening near Grant Park.** ⊠*187 10th St., Midtown* ☎*404/249–7576* ⌧*Reservations not accepted* ⊟*AE, D, DC, MC, V* ⌧*123 East Court Sq., Decatur* ☎*404/270–9450* ⌧*Reservations not accepted* ⊟*AE, D, MC, V* ⊗*No lunch Sun.*

INMAN PARK AND CANDLER PARK

$$–$$$ ✗**Babette's Cafe.** Sunny yellow walls and back-porch seating add to
CONTINENTAL the homey charm of this renovated bungalow. The restaurant, which describes its cuisine as European country, offers such seasonal dishes as halibut with potato-leek gratin and beef tenderloin with Gorgonzola sauce. Loyal locals love the Sunday brunch. ⊠*573 N. Highland Ave., Inman Park* ☎*404/523–9121* ⊟*AE, D, DC, MC, V* ⊗*Closed Mon.*

¢ ✗**Fellini's Pizza.** This local chain, with seven parlors in the Atlanta area,
PIZZA puts together a mean 'za with a no-frills, order-at-the-counter approach. This particular location features a wide-open patio that looks out on the small and quirky commercial district in Candler Park. The slices are big and fresh. Some detractors say the stuff lacks flavor, but locals love the garlicky-good white pizza and the ham and pineapple combo.

✉*1634 McLendon Ave., Candler Park* ☎*404/687–9190* ▤*AE, D, DC, MC, V.*

¢–$ ✗**Flying Biscuit.** There's a long wait
SOUTHERN on weekends at this spot famous
★ for its biscuits served with cranberry-apple butter. Other huge hits include sausage made with free-range chicken and sage, and bean cakes with tomatillo salsa. Fancier dinners include roasted chicken and turkey meat loaf with pudge (mashed potatoes). There are also

WORD OF MOUTH

"Keep this in mind about staying at the Marriott Marquis downtown. You will not have to go outside your hotel to hop on the metro because it is connected to Peachtree Plaza. It is a big deal because July in Atlanta is hot and you can stay in the AC."

—GoTravel

3

plenty of vegetarian options. Next door is a bakery serving biscuits to go, as well as freshly baked muffins and cookies. Though this restaurant and its sister location in Midtown were purchased by a local chain, the service and food haven't suffered. ✉*1655 McLendon Ave., Candler Park* ☎*404/687–8888* ⌦*Reservations not accepted* ▤*AE, MC, DC, V.*

BUCKHEAD

¢¢¢¢ ✗**The Dining Room.** Chef Arnaud Berthelier's prix-fixe menu includes
CONTINENTAL dishes such as Four Story Hill Farm lamb, fried spinach and ricotta
Fodor's Choice raviolis with apricot chutney, and crispy Wild John Dory "pavé," morel
★ duxelle, wild asparagus, and chanterelle jus. The menu is served in an elegant dining room within the Ritz-Carlton featuring apple-green silk walls and floral upholstery with a slight Asian influence. The bronze sculpture that dominates the center of the room is a work by 18th-century French sculptor Paul Comolera, who helped create the Arc de Triomphe in Paris. ✉*Ritz-Carlton, Buckhead, 3434 Peachtree Rd. NE, Buckhead* ☎*404/237–2700* ⌦*Reservations essential. Jacket required* ▤*AE, D, DC, MC, V* ☯*Closed Sun. and Mon. No lunch.*

$$$$ ✗**Joël.** When founder and James Beard Award–winning chef Joël
FRENCH Antunes decided to leave this elegant brasserie to work at New York
Fodor's Choice City's Plaza Hotel, many a foodie worried that the French-inflected
★ menu would go downhill. But non. Antunes remains a partner in the Atlanta enterprise, and chef Cyrille Holota now occupies the famed dream kitchen, an immaculate and roomy 5,000-square-foot space so vast its creation almost halved the restaurant's seating capacity. Holata does Joël proud. The tomato tart is the perfect mix of fresh vegetables and basil on a crispy cracker, and the truffle grits are so creamy they feel like custard. The atmosphere is romantic, making a visit feel even more special. ✉*3290 Northside Pkwy, Buckhead* ☎*404/233–3500* ⌦*Reservations essential* ▤*AE, D, DC, MC, V* ☯*No lunch Sat. Closed Sun.*

WHERE TO STAY

DOWNTOWN

$$–$$$ 🏨**Atlanta Marriott Marquis.** Immense and coolly contemporary, the building seems to go up forever as you stand under the lobby's huge fabric sculpture that hangs from the skylighted roof 47 stories above. Guest

rooms, which open onto this atrium, are decorated in dark greens and tans. Fresh flowers fill the major suites, two of which have grand pianos and ornamental fireplaces. You don't even have to walk outside to reach the Peachtree Center MARTA station; it's connected via an indoor walkway. **Pros:** great views; convenient access to MARTA. **Cons:** lobby noise can carry to the lower floors. ⊠*265 Peachtree Center Ave., Downtown* ☎*404/521–0000 or 888/855–5701* ⊕*www.marriott.com* ↘*1,569 rooms, 94 suites* ⬩*In-room: Internet, Wi-Fi. In-hotel: 4 restaurants, bars, pool, gym, Internet terminal, parking (paid), no-smoking rooms* ⊟*AE, D, DC, MC, V.*

\$\$–\$\$\$ 🔤**Glenn Hotel.** This boutique hotel is a mix of New York sophistication and Miami sex appeal. The rooms are small, but a thoughtful renovation makes the best of the space. Glass walls between the oversize showers and the sleeping areas mean you won't miss a minute of the program on your plasma TV. The contemporary decor is sleek and sophisticated. **Pros:** new business center; complimentary Wi-Fi. **Cons:** dim lighting might be a bit dark for some guests. ⊠*110 Marietta St. NW, Downtown* ☎*404/521–2250 or 866/404–5366* ⊕*www.glennhotel.com* ↘*93 rooms, 16 suites* ⬩*In-room: Internet, Wi-Fi. In-hotel: restaurant, bar, gym, parking (paid)* ⊟*AE, D, DC, MC, V.*

¢–\$ 🔤**Quality Hotel Downtown.** This quiet, older downtown hotel two blocks off Peachtree Street is priced reasonably for its location; this, along with the hotel's proximity to the Georgia World Congress Center and the AmericasMart complex, makes the hotel popular during conventions. Note that prices go up when conventions are in town. Sofas and a grand piano fill the marble lobby. **Pros:** good breakfast; convenient to downtown attractions; check-in starts at 10 AM. **Cons:** one elevator, so it can take a while to get to your floor; little in the way of amenities. ⊠*89 Luckie St., Downtown* ☎*404/524–7991 or 888/729–7705* ⊕*www.qualityinn.com* ↘*75 rooms* ⬩*In-room: Internet, Wi-Fi. In-hotel: Internet terminal, parking (paid), no-smoking rooms* ⊟*AE, D, DC, MC, V* ⦾*BP.*

MIDTOWN

\$\$\$\$ 🔤**Four Seasons Hotel.** From the lobby a sweeping staircase leads up to
★ Park 75, the hotel's chic dining establishment. Rose-hue marble creates a warm feeling in the public spaces and lounges. Amenities abound throughout: marble bathrooms with extra-large soaking tubs, lemon or celadon color schemes, comfy mattresses, and brass chandeliers. The hotel prides itself on its immensely courteous staff—it's considered scandalous if a call to reception rings more than twice before it's answered. Stewards and other staff members are on hand the moment you need their help. **Pros:** staff is professional; dining options inside the hotel are quite good. **Cons:** fairly close to the action in Midtown, but you'll probably need to drive or take a cab to get to most of the bars, restaurants and clubs. ⊠*75 14th St., Midtown* ☎*404/881–9898* ⊕*www.fourseasons.com* ↘*226 rooms, 18 suites* ⬩*In-room: DVD, Internet, Wi-Fi. In-hotel: restaurant, bar, pool, gym, spa, Internet terminal, parking (paid), some pets allowed, no-smoking rooms* ⊟*AE, D, DC, MC, V.*

$$–$$$ 🏨**Georgian Terrace.** Enrico Caruso and other stars of the Metropolitan Opera once lodged in this 1911 hotel across the street from the Fox Theatre. The fine hotel, which has always housed the rich and famous, is now on the National Register of Historic Places. The columned lobby is striking, and breathtaking terraces traverse the exterior, making it a popular venue for wedding receptions. All the suites are pastel and plush, providing adequate if not luxurious comfort. **Pros:** the front terrace is a great place for people-watching, and having a glass of wine before a show at the Fox. **Cons:** some rooms are a little bit old-fashioned and cramped. ✉ *659 Peachtree St., Midtown* ☎ *404/897–1991* ⊕ *www.thegeorgianterrace.com* ↪ *308 rooms* ⎙ *In-room: kitchen (some), Internet, Wi-Fi. In-hotel: restaurant, pool, gym, Internet terminal, parking (paid)* ⊟ *AE, D, MC, V.*

BUCKHEAD

$–$$ 🏨**Doubletree Hotel Atlanta/Buckhead.** If the complimentary fresh-baked chocolate-chip cookies that welcome you don't convince you to stay here, maybe the excellent location, spacious rooms, and reasonable rates will. The hotel, which offers complimentary transportation within 3 mi, is adjacent to the Buckhead MARTA station. **Pros:** a warm welcome; comfortable beds. **Cons:** small bar; pay to park. ✉ *3342 Peachtree Rd., Buckhead* ☎ *404/231–1234 or 800/222–8733* ⊕ *www.doubletree.com* ↪ *230 rooms* ⎙ *In-room: Internet, Wi-Fi. In-hotel: restaurant, Internet terminal, parking (paid), no-smoking rooms* ⊟ *AE, D, DC, MC, V.*

$–$$ 🏨**Embassy Suites Hotel.** Just blocks from the shopping meccas of Lenox Square and Phipps Plaza is this modern high-rise. There are several different kinds of suites—from deluxe units with amenities like wet bars to more basic sleeping-and-sitting-room combinations. All of the rooms open onto a sunny atrium that towers 16 stories above the lobby. Rates include afternoon cocktails. **Pros:** location convenient to major shopping destinations. **Cons:** no flat-screen television, and Internet is not free. ✉ *3285 Peachtree Rd., Buckhead* ☎ *404/261–7733* ⊕ *www. embassysuites.com* ↪ *316 suites* ⎙ *In-room: Internet, Wi-Fi. In-hotel: restaurant, pool, gym, parking (paid), no-smoking rooms* ⊟ *AE, D, DC, MC, V* ⧌ *BP.*

$$$$ 🏨**The Mansion on Peachtree.** It's almost possible to forget you're in the
Fodor's Choice middle of bustling Buckhead when you sit down with a book or a cock-
★ tail in the English garden at this new hotel and residences. The floral oasis, with benches and a shallow reflecting pool, is just one of the many luxuries available here. Set back from the busy street, the 42-story tower features a sophisticated spa, a full-size fitness center and cozy seating areas decked out in soothing cream and brown tones. The expansive rooms feature several flat-screen televisions (including one that hides behind a painting, and another in the bathroom), a large soaking tub, and personal butler service. In-house eatery NEO is quiet and boasts impeccable service, but foodies are more excited about the soon-to-open Craft Atlanta, the latest venture from *Top Chef* judge and famed restaurateur Tom Colicchio. **Pros:** apartment-style living; delicious, fresh juices for breakfast at NEO; personalized service; relaxing spa. **Cons:** as of this writing, the indoor pool was not yet complete. ✉ *3376 Peachtree Rd., Buckhead* ☎ *404/995–7500* ⊕ *www.rwmansiononpeachtree.com*

⌐96 rooms, 31 suites, 45 residences ⟨In-room: Internet, Wi-Fi. In-hotel: restaurant, bar, gym, parking (fee) ⊟AE, D, DC, MC, V.

$$$$ ⊞**Ritz-Carlton, Buckhead.** Decorated with 18th- and 19th-century
Fodor'sChoice antiques, this elegant hotel is a regular stopover for visiting celebri-
★ ties. The richly paneled Lobby Lounge is a respite for shoppers from nearby Lenox Square and Phipps Plaza; afternoon tea and cocktails are popular. The Dining Room is one of the city's finest restaurants, and many of the area's top chefs have passed through its kitchen doors. The spacious guest rooms are furnished with traditional reproductions. The Club Level, with a separate lounge and concierge, showers you with everything from a bountiful continental breakfast in the morning to chocolates and cordials at night. The large gift shop, called the Boutique, sells everything from linens to luggage. As of this writing, a renovation was wrapping up, adding numerous guest rooms and six luxury suites. **Pros:** elegant; convenient to shopping; occasional celeb sightings. **Cons:** drab exterior doesn't seem very ritzy. ⊠ *3434 Peachtree Rd. NE, Buckhead* ☎*404/237–2700* ⊕*www.ritzcarlton.com* ⌐*453 rooms, incl. 58 suites, 6 luxury suites* ⟨*In-room: Internet, Wi-Fi. In-hotel: 3 restaurants, bar, pool, gym, spa, Internet terminal, parking (paid), no-smoking rooms* ⊟*AE, D, DC, MC, V.*

NIGHTLIFE AND THE ARTS

THE ARTS

For the most complete schedule of cultural events, check the weekly "Access Atlanta" section of the *Atlanta Journal-Constitution or the* city's lively and free alternative weekly, *Creative Loafing.* The *Atlanta Daily World,* serving the African-American community, is also published weekly.

AtlanTIX Ticket Services (☎*404/588–9890* ⊕*www.atlantaperforms.com/ discount-tickets/atlantix-half-price.html*), at Underground Atlanta and Lenox Square, sells half-price same-day tickets for performances as well as half-price same-day and next-day tickets for cultural events. Tickets are available Monday to Saturday 11 to 6, Sunday noon to 4.

DANCE The **Atlanta Ballet** (⊠*1400 W. Peachtree St., Midtown* ☎*404/892–3303* or *404/873–5811* ⊕*www.atlantaballet.com*), founded in 1929, is the country's oldest continuously operating ballet company. It has been internationally recognized for its productions of classical and contemporary works. Artistic director John McFall has choreographed such dance greats as Mikhail Baryshnikov and Cynthia Gregory; only the third director in the company's history, McFall brings a constant stream of innovative ideas and vision to the group. Most performances, except for the annual *Nutcracker,* are held at the Cobb Energy Performing Arts Centre.

PERFORMANCE **Chastain Park Amphitheatre** (⊠*4469 Stella Dr. NW, Buckhead* ☎*404/233–*
VENUES *2227* or *404/733–5000* ⊕*www.classicchastain.com*), home to Atlanta Symphony Orchestra's summer series and other pop concerts, feels more like an outdoor nightclub than a typical performance venue. Pack a picnic, bring a blanket if you've snagged some seats on the lawn, and prepare to listen to your favorite performers over the clink of dishes and

the chatter of dinner conversation. **Fox Theatre** (✉ *660 Peachtree St., Midtown* ☎ *404/881–2100* ⊕ *www.foxtheatre.org*), a dramatic faux-Moorish theater, is the principal venue for touring Broadway shows and national productions, as well as the home of the Atlanta Ballet. With a seating capacity of 21,000, **Philips Arena** (✉ *1 Philips Dr., Downtown* ☎ *404/878–3000* ⊕ *www.philipsarena.com*) is the major venue downtown. In addition to hosting the biggest musical acts, it's also the home of the Atlanta Hawks and the Atlanta Thrashers. The Philips Arena MARTA station makes getting here a snap. **Woodruff Arts Center** (✉ *1280 Peachtree St. NE, Midtown* ☎ *404/733–4200* ⊕ *www.woodruffcenter. org*) houses the Alliance Theatre and the Atlanta Symphony Orchestra.

THEATER **Actor's Express** (✉ *887 W. Marietta St. NW, Downtown* ☎ *404/607–7469*
★ ⊕ *www.actors-express.com*), an acclaimed theater group, presents an eclectic selection of classic and cutting-edge productions in the 150-seat theater of the King Plow Arts Center, a stylish artists' complex hailed by local critics as a showplace of industrial chic. **Alliance Theatre** (✉ *1280 Peachtree St. NE, Midtown* ☎ *404/733–5000* ⊕ *www.alliancetheatre. org*), Atlanta's premier professional theater, presents everything from Shakespeare to the latest Broadway and off-Broadway hits. It's in the Woodruff Arts Center. **Georgia Shakespeare** (✉ *4484 Peachtree Rd. NE, Buckhead* ☎ *404/264–0020* ⊕ *www.gashakespeare.org*), a tradition since 1986, brings plays by the Bard and other enduring authors to the 509-seat Conant Performing Arts Center, on the campus of Oglethorpe University, from June to November.

NIGHTLIFE

Atlanta has long been known for having more bars than churches, and in the South that's an oddity. The pursuit of entertainment—from Midtown to Buckhead—is known as the "Peachtree shuffle." Atlanta's vibrant nightlife includes everything from coffeehouses to sports bars, from country line dancing to high-energy dance clubs.

BARS You can't get a Budweiser or Coors at the **Brick Store Pub** (✉ *125 E. Court Sq., Decatur* ☎ *404/687–0990*), but you can choose from hundreds of other bottled and draft brews—including high-altitude beers—along with some very good burgers, salads, and sandwiches. The interior, particularly upstairs, is cavelike but comfortable. **East Andrews Cafe** (✉ *56 E. Andrews Dr., Suite 10, Buckhead* ☎ *404/869–1090*) offers upscale food, signature martinis and live indie, '80s, and party music at the bar and at the upstairs music venue. **Righteous Room** (✉ *1051 Ponce De Leon Ave., Virginia-Highland* ☎ *404/874–0939*) is tiny and nestled in between a movie theater and an Urban Outfitters store, but good things come in small packages: good grub (try the fried onion straws) and a jukebox with a moody playlist await. **TAP** (✉ *1180 Peachtree St., Midtown* ☎ *404/347–2221*) is one of Atlanta's few great gastropubs, serving upscale food like their mahimahi sandwich and watercress and cornichon salad alongside a variety of specialty brews and wine. One of the best features here is the patio—typically populated with after-work execs and trendy Midtowners—which sits out on busy Peachtree Street and provides ample opportunity for people-watching. **Vortex** (✉ *438 Moreland Ave., Little Five Points* ☎ *404/688–1828*) prides itself on being impolite—a look at the "rules" will show you they take no guff—but really it's a friendly bar with great burgers and fried zucchini. Just look for the huge skull, a landmark of Little Five Points, and you've found the front door.

COUNTRY   The 44,000-square-foot **Cowboys Concert Hall** (✉*1750 N. Roberts Rd., Kennesaw* ☎*770/426–5006*) attracts national talent twice a month. On Thursday to Sunday, line-dancing and couple-dancing lessons bring out the crowds. The cover is $7—more if an unusually high-profile act is slated. Billing itself as the nation's largest country-music dance club and concert hall, **Wild Bill's** (✉*2075 Market St., Duluth* ☎*678/473–1000*) has room for 5,000 dancin', drinkin', partyin' cowpokes. The cover is $8 to $10 most nights.

GAY AND   For up-to-the-minute information on the gay scene, pick up a free copy
LESBIAN   of *Southern Voice* (⊕*www.sovo.com*) throughout the city.

Blake's on the Park (✉*227 10th St., Midtown* ☎*404/892–5786*) is a favorite spot with weekly drag shows, a diverse crowd, and plenty of people-watching. **Burkhart's** (✉*1492 Piedmont Rd., Suite F, Ansley Square Shopping Center, Midtown* ☎*404/872–4403*) caters to a mostly male clientele with pool, karaoke, and drag shows. It's more of a neighborhood hangout than a dance club. **LeBuzz** (✉*585 Franklin Rd., Marietta* ☎*770/424–1337*) got new owners this year, and they're reinvigorating the place with contests and events like "Drag Idol" and
★   the "Men of Playgirl" revue from Las Vegas. Cover charges vary. **My Sister's Room** (✉*1271 Glenwood Ave., East Atlanta* ☎*770/424–1337*), a lesbian club formerly located in Decatur, is now located in East Atlanta and bills itself as the city's "most diverse ladies' bar," with hip-hop
★   music, DJs and karaoke. **Mary's** (✉*1287 Glenwood Ave., East Atlanta* ☎*404/624–4411*) is often mentioned as one of the best gay bars in Atlanta, known for hosting "Project Runway" viewing parties and a karaoke night they call "Mary-oke." **Woofs** (✉*2425 Piedmont Rd., Midtown* ☎*404/869–0112*) is Atlanta's first and only gay sports bar, with sports on 25 televisions, pool, darts, and Internet access.

JAZZ AND   **Blind Willie's** (✉*828 N. Highland Ave., Virginia-Highland* ☎*404/873–*
BLUES   *2583*) showcases New Orleans and Chicago blues groups. Cajun and zydeco are also on the agenda from time to time. The name honors Blind Willie McTell, a native of Thomson, Georgia; his original compositions include "Statesboro Blues," made popular by the Georgia-based Allman Brothers. Cover charges run $3 to $10. **Churchill Grounds** (✉*660 Peachtree St., Midtown* ☎*404/876–3030*) celebrates jazz with weekly jam sessions and great local and national acts. Cover charges typically range from $5 to $15. Resembling a ship, **Dante's Down the Hatch** (✉*3380 Peachtree Rd., Buckhead* ☎*404/266–1600*) is as popular for its music as it is for its sultry sensibility. Most nights music is provided by a jazz trio, which conjures silky-smooth tunes. **Sambuca** (✉*3102 Piedmont Rd., Buckhead* ☎*404/237–5299*), a lively bar with good blues and jazz music, attracts a young crowd.

ROCK   **10 High Club** (✉*816 N. Highland Ave., Virginia-Highland* ☎*404/873–3607*), a brick-walled space in the basement of the Dark Horse Tavern, hosts local and regional bands that are guaranteed to be loud. ■ **TIP→You can rock out to heavy-metal karaoke with the live band Metalsome backing you**

up a few nights a week. Covers rarely exceed $10. **Eddie's Attic** (✉ *515B N. McDonough St., Decatur* ☎ *404/377–4976*) is a good spot for catching local and some national rock, folk, and country-music acts. It has a full bar and restaurant and is near the Decatur MARTA station. Cover charges range from $5 to $20. **Smith's Olde Bar** (✉ *1578 Piedmont Ave., Midtown* ☎ *404/875–1522*) schedules different kinds of talent, both local and regional, in its acoustically fine performance space. Food is available in the downstairs restaurant. Covers vary depending on the

★ act, but are usually $5 to $15. **Star Community Bar** (✉ *437 Moreland Ave., Little Five Points* ☎ *404/681–9018*) is highly recommended for those who enjoy grunge and rockabilly. Bands play almost nightly, with covers of $5 to $8, depending on the act. The bar used to be a bank—the Elvis shrine in the vault must be seen to be believed.

SPORTS AND THE OUTDOORS

At almost any time of the year, in parks, private clubs, and neighborhoods throughout the city, you'll find Atlantans pursuing everything from tennis to soccer to rollerblading. The magazine *Atlanta Sports & Fitness* (☎ *404/843–2257* ⊕ *www.atlantasportsmag.com*), available free at many health clubs and sports and outdoors stores, is a good link to Atlanta's athletic community.

BASEBALL

Atlanta's most beloved team, Major League Baseball's **Atlanta Braves** (✉ *755 Hank Aaron Dr., Downtown* ☎ *404/522–7630* ⊕ *braves.mlb. com*), play in Turner Field, formerly the Olympic Stadium.

BIKING

Closed to traffic, **Piedmont Park** (✉ *Piedmont Ave. between 10th St. and Monroe Ave., Midtown* ⊕ *www.piedmontpark.org*) is popular for biking, running, dog-walking, and other recreational activities.

Connecting Atlanta with the Alabama state line, the **Silver Comet Trail** (☎ *404/875–7284* ⊕ *www.pathfoundation.org*) is very popular with bikers. The trail is asphalt and concrete.

Skate Escape (✉ *1086 Piedmont Ave., across from Piedmont Park, Midtown* ☎ *404/892–1292*) rents and sells bikes and in-line skates.

Part of the Atlanta–DeKalb trail system, the **Stone Mountain/Atlanta Greenway Trail** (☎ *404/875–7284* ⊕ *www.pathfoundation.org*) is a mostly off-road paved path that follows Ponce de Leon Avenue east of the city into Stone Mountain Park. The best place to start the 17-mi trek is the Jimmy Carter Presidential Library & Museum.

FOOTBALL

The **Atlanta Falcons** (✉ *1 Georgia Dome Dr., Downtown* ☎ *404/223–8000* ⊕ *www.atlantafalcons.com*) play at the Georgia Dome. In July and August, training camp is held in Flowery Branch, about 40 mi north of Atlanta. There's no charge to watch a practice session.

GOLF

Bobby Jones Golf Course. Named after the famed golfer and Atlanta native and occupying a portion of the site of the Civil War's Battle of Peachtree Creek, this is the only public course within sight of downtown

Atlanta. Despite having some of the city's worst fairways and greens, the immensely popular course is always crowded. ✉*384 Woodward Way, Buckhead* ☎*404/355–1009* ⚑*18 holes. 6455 yds. Par 71. Green Fee: $36/$39* ☞*Facilities: Driving range, putting green, pitching area, golf carts, pull carts, rental clubs, pro-shop, golf academy/lessons, restaurant, bar.*

North Fulton Golf Course. This course has one of the best layouts in the area. It's at Chastain Park, within the Interstate 285 perimeter. ✉*216 W. Wieuca Rd., Buckhead* ☎*404/255–0723* ⚑*18 holes. 6570 yds. Par 71. Green Fee: $36/$40* ☞*Facilities: golf carts, rental clubs, golf academy/lessons.*

Stone Mountain Golf Club. Stone Mountian has two courses: Stonemont and Lakemont. Stonemont, with several challenging and scenic holes, is the better of the two. ✉*1145 Stonewall Jackson Dr., Stone Mountain* ☎*770/465–3272* ⊕*www.stonemountaingolf.com* ⚑*18 holes. 6837 yds. Par 70. Green Fee: $49/$64* ☞*Facilities: Driving range, putting green, golf carts, pull carts, rental clubs, pro-shop, golf academy/lessons, restaurant, bar.*

RUNNING

Check the **Atlanta Track Club's** Web site (⊕*www.atlantatrackclub*.org) for weekly Atlanta area group runs.

The longest running path in **Piedmont Park** (✉*Piedmont Ave. between 10th St. and Monroe Ave., Midtown* ⊕*www.piedmontpark*.org) is the Park Loop, which circles the park in 1.68 mi.

SHOPPING

Atlanta's department stores, specialty shops, indoor malls, and antiques markets draw shoppers from across the Southeast. Most stores are open Monday through Saturday 10 to 9, Sunday noon to 6. The sales tax is 7% in the city of Atlanta and Fulton County and 6%–7% in the suburbs.

SHOPPING NEIGHBORHOODS

Nostalgic and cutting-edge at the same time, **Atlantic Station** was built to look like it's been around for a while. Actually, this combo of living, working, and recreational spaces opened in 2005. It covers about 10 square blocks, clustered around a green space known as Central Park. Retailers range from IKEA and Dillard's to Banana Republic and Z Gallerie. It's easy to reach by car, but is also accessible by free shuttle buses from the Arts Center MARTA station. An on-site concierge is happy to help you find your way around or make dinner reservations at the more than a dozen restaurants. ✉*1380 Atlantic Dr.* ☎*404/685–1841* ⊕*www.atlanticstation.com.*

Buckhead, a commercial district with many specialty shops and strip malls, is no minor shopping destination. Boutiques, gift shops, and some fine restaurants line East and West Paces Ferry roads, Pharr Road, East Shadowlawn Avenue, and East Andrews Drive. Cates Center has similar stores. Others are on Irby Avenue and Paces Ferry Place. And soon what once was the thriving entertainment district will become, according to its developers, the "Rodeo Drive of the South."

Decatur Square, a quaint town quad with a sophisticated, artistic vibe, is teeming with interesting specialty shops and delectable coffeehouses and cafés. Lively downtown Decatur, 8 mi east of Midtown Atlanta, is one of the metro area's favorite spots for sidewalk strolling and window-shopping.

Little Five Points attracts "junking" addicts who find happiness in Atlanta's version of Greenwich Village. There are vintage-clothing emporiums, used record and bookshops, and some stores that defy description.

Virginia-Highland is a wonderful urban neighborhood for window-shopping, thanks to its boutiques, antiques shops, and art galleries. Parking can be tricky in the evening, so be prepared to park down a side street and walk a few blocks.

MALLS

Lenox Square (✉ *3393 Peachtree Rd., Buckhead* ☎ *404/233–6767*), one of Atlanta's oldest and most popular shopping centers, has branches of Neiman Marcus, Bloomingdale's, and Macy's looming next to specialty shops such as Cartier and Mori. Valet parking is available at the front of the mall, but free parking is nearby. You'll do better at one of the several good restaurants in the mall—even for a quick meal—than at the food court. **The Mall at Peachtree Center** (✉ *231 Peachtree St., Downtown* ☎ *404/654–1296*) has specialty shops, such as International Records, Touch of Georgia, and the Atlanta International Museum gift shop. **Perimeter Mall** (✉ *4400 Ashford-Dunwoody Rd., Dunwoody* ☎ *770/394–4270*), known for upscale family shopping, has Nordstrom, Macy's, Dillard's, and Bloomingdale's and a plentiful food court. Its restaurants include the Cheesecake Factory, Goldfish, and Maggiano's Little Italy. **Phipps Plaza** (✉ *3500 Peachtree Rd., Buckhead* ☎ *404/262–0992*) has branches of Tiffany & Co., Saks Fifth Avenue, and Gucci, as well as such shops as Niketown and Teavana.

SPECIALTY SHOPS

ANTIQUES **Bennett Street** in Buckhead has antiques shops, home-decor stores such as John Overton Oriental Rugs-Antiques, and art galleries, including the Bennett Street Gallery. The Stalls on Bennett Street is a good antiques market. **Chamblee Antique Row** (☎ *404/606–3367* ⊕ *www.antiquerow. com*) is a browser's delight. At Peachtree Industrial Boulevard and Broad Street in the suburban town of Chamblee, it's just north of Buckhead and about 10 mi north of downtown. Buckhead's **Miami Circle,** is an upscale enclave with shops for antiques and decorative-arts lovers.

FOOD **Your DeKalb Farmers Market** (✉ *3000 E. Ponce de Leon Ave., Decatur* ☎ *404/377–6400*) has 175,000 square feet of exotic fruits, cheeses, seafood, sausages, breads, and delicacies from around the world. The cafeteria-style buffet, with a selection of earthy and delicious hot foods and salads, is alone worth the trip.

SAVANNAH

General James Oglethorpe, Savannah's founder, set sail for England in 1743, never to return. His last instructions, it's said, were, "Don't change a thing until I get back." That local joke holds more than a bit of truth. Savannah's elegant mansions, dripping Spanish moss, and sticky summer heat can make the city seem sleepy and stubbornly resistant to change. Which is exactly why many folks like the place.

Savannah, Georgia's oldest city, began its modern history on February 12, 1733, when Oglethorpe and 120 colonists arrived at Yamacraw Bluff on the Savannah River to found the 13th and last of the British colonies. As the port city grew, more settlers from England and Ireland arrived, joined by Scottish Highlanders, French Huguenots, Germans, Austrian Salzburgers, Sephardic and Ashkenazic Jews, Moravians, Italians, Swiss, Welsh, and Greeks.

GEORGIA FACTS
■ **State Capital:** Atlanta
■ **State Nickname:** Peach state
■ **State Insect:** Honey bee
■ **Highest Point:** Brasstown Bald, 4,784 feet above sea level
■ Georgia was named in honor of King George II of England.
■ Georgia joined the Confederacy on January 19, 1861.
■ "Georgia on My Mind" is the state song. It was performed on March 7, 1979 before the State Legislature by Georgia native, Ray Charles.

In 1793 Eli Whitney of Connecticut, who was tutoring on a plantation near Savannah, invented a mechanized means of "ginning" seeds from cotton bolls. Cotton soon became king, and Savannah, already a busy seaport, flourished under its reign. Waterfront warehouses were filled with "white gold," and brokers trading in the Savannah Cotton Exchange set world prices. The white gold brought in hard currency; the city prospered.

General William Tecumseh Sherman's army rampaged across Georgia in 1864, setting fire to railroads, munitions factories, bridges, and just about anything else between them and the sea. Rather than see the city torched, Savannahians surrendered to the approaching Yankees.

As the cotton market declined in the early 20th century, the city's economy collapsed. For decades Savannah's historic buildings languished; many were razed or allowed to decay. Cobwebs replaced cotton in the dilapidated riverfront warehouses. The tide turned in the 1950s, when residents began a concerted effort—which continues to this day—to restore and preserve the city's architectural heritage.

GETTING HERE AND AROUND

BUS TRAVEL The free CAT (Chatham Area Transit) Shuttle operates throughout the Historic District, running on a north–south route once an hour. For other Savannah buses, the fare is $1. The Dot is Savannah's other free downtown transportation system. In addition to the Savannah Belles Ferry, the Dot operates an Express Shuttle around downtown and historic 1930s River Street Streetcars, which began service in late 2008.

TAXI TRAVEL AAA Adam Cab Co., MC Transportation, and Yellow Cab Company are the three major taxi companies in Savannah; all can be hailed on the street or called, and all operate 24 hours a day. The standard taxi fare is $1.82 or $1.92 per mile; some companies offer flat rates to and from the airport and Tybee Island.

Savannah Pedicab is a bicycle rickshaw that costs $45 per hour or $25 per half-hour (you can also rent a pedicab for the day for $150). They operate from 11 AM to midnight (2 AM on weekends). They also rent cruiser-style bikes for $20 per day, and will deliver to your inn.

ESSENTIALS

Taxi Contacts AAA Adam Cab Incorporated (☎ 912/927–7466). **MC Transportation** ☎ 912/786–9191). **Savannah Pedicab** (☎ 912/232–7900 ⊕ www.savannahpedicab.com). **Yellow Cab** (☎ 912/236–1133).

Visitor Information Savannah Area Convention & Visitors Bureau (✉ 101 E. Bay St., Historic District ☎ 912/644–6401 or 877/728–2662 ⊕ www.savannahvisit.com). **Savannah Area Welcome Center** (✉ 301 Martin Luther King Jr. Blvd. ☎ 912/944–0455 ⊕ www.savannahvisit.com).

EXPLORING

THE HISTORIC DISTRICT

Georgia's sage founder, General James Oglethorpe, laid out the city on a perfect grid. It is as logical as a geometry solution. The Historic District is neatly hemmed in by the Savannah River, Gaston Street, East Street, and Martin Luther King Jr. Boulevard. Streets are arrow-straight, public squares of varying sizes are tucked into the grid at precise intervals, and each block is sliced in half by narrow, sometimes unpaved streets. Bull Street, anchored on the north by City Hall and the south by Forsyth Park, charges down the center of the grid and maneuvers around the five public squares that stand in its way. All the squares have some historical significance; many have elaborate fountains, monuments to heroes, and shady resting areas with park benches; all are bordered by beautiful homes and mansions that lovingly evoke another era.

❾ Andrew Low House. This residence was built in 1848 for Andrew Low, a native of Scotland and one of Savannah's merchant princes. The home later belonged to his son William, who inherited his wealth and married his longtime sweetheart Juliette Gordon. They lived in a baronial estate in the U.K. for decades before divorcing. It was after her former husband's death, that Juliette Gorden Low returned to this house and founded the Girl Scouts here on March 12, 1912. The house has 19th-century antiques, stunning silver, and some of the finest ornamental ironwork in Savannah. But it is the story and history of the family— even a bedroom named after the family friend and visitor General Robert E. Lee—that is fascinating and well-told by the tour guides. ✉ 329 Abercorn St., Historic District ☎ 912/233–6854 ✑ $8 ⊗ Mon.–Wed., Fri., and Sat. 10–4:30, Sun. noon–4.

❶ City Market. Although the 1870s City Market was razed years ago, city fathers are enacting a three-year plan to capture the authentic atmosphere and character of its bustling origins. Already a lively destination for art studios, open-air cafés, theme shops, and jazz clubs, this popular pedestrian-only area will become the ever more vibrant, youthful heart of Savannah's Historic District. You can rent a bike here or take a ride in a horse-drawn carriage. ✉ Between Franklin Sq. and Johnson

Savannah Historic District

Savannah River

Riverfront Plaza

River St.

Factors Walk

River St.

Factors Walk

✗ Vic's on the River

W. Bay St.

E. Bay St.

East Bay Inn

W. Bryan St.

E. Bryan St.

Ellis Sq.

W. Julian

Johnson Sq.

E. Julian

Reynolds Sq.

Warren Sq.

W. Congress St.

E. Congress St.

✗ Garibaldi

W. Broughton St.

E. Broughton St.

Cha Bella ✗

The Lady & Sons

Bistro Savannah

W. State St.

E. State St.

Telfair Sq.

W. President

Wright Sq.

E. President

Oglethorpe Sq.

Columbia Sq.

W. York St.

E. York St.

B. Matthews Eatery ✗

W. Oglethorpe Ave.

E. Oglethorpe St.

Ballastone Inn

Colonial Park Cemetery

Orleans Sq.

W. Hull

Chippewa Sq.

E. Hull

W. Perry

E. Perry

The Stephen Williams House

Harris Baking Company ✗

W. Liberty St.

E. Liberty St.

Noble Fare ✗

W. Harris St.

E. Harris St.

Pulaski Sq.

Madison Sq.

Lafayette Sq.

E. Macon St.

Troup Sq.

W. Charlton

St. John's Episcopal Church

E. Charlton

W. Jones St.

E. Jones St.

The Ziegler House Inn

Eliza Thompson House

W. Taylor St.

E. Taylor St.

Chatham Sq.

W. Wayne St.

Monterey Sq.

Calhoun Sq.

E. Wayne St.

Whitefield Sq.

W. Gordon St.

E. Gordon St.

Gastonian

W. Gaston St.

E. Gaston St.

✗ Blowin' Smoke BBQ

W. Huntingdon St.

Forsyth Park

E. Huntingdon St.

King-Tisdell Cottage

W. Hall St.

E. Hall St.

700 Drayton ✗

W. Gwinett St.

E. Gwinett St.

Mansion on Forsyth Park

0 ——— 1/4 mile

W. Park Ave.

E. Park Ave.

0 ——— 400 meters

W. Park Avenue Ln.

E. Park Avenue Ln.

✗ Locall 11ten

Montgomery St. · Jefferson St. · Barnard St. · Whitaker St. · Bull St. · Drayton St. · Abercorn St. · Lincoln St. · Habersham St. · Jefferson St. · Tattnall St.

Sq. on W. St. Julian St., Historic District ☎912/525–2489 *for current events.*

② **Factors Walk.** A network of iron crosswalks connects Bay Street with the multistory buildings that rise up from the river level, and iron stairways descend from Bay Street to Factors Walk. The area was originally the center of commerce for cotton brokers, who walked between and above the lower cotton warehouses. Cobblestone ramps lead pedestrians down to River Street. ■TIP→ These are serious cobblestones, so wear comfortable shoes. Also be aware that pedicabs cannot ride over these cobblestones. ⊠*Bay St. to Factors Walk, Historic District.*

DID YOU KNOW?

In Savannah many of the houses are named, but sometimes the name is the person who built the property rather than the person for whom it was built. For example, the Stephen Williams House, now restored as an elegant B&B, was named for its builder, Stephen Williams, rather than the owner, William Thorn Williams, six-time mayor of Savannah.

NEED A BREAK? The best place for an ice-cream soda is Leopold's (⊠ 212 E. Broughton St., Historic District ☎912/234–4442), a Savannah institution since 1919. It's currently owned by Stratton Leopold, grandson of the original owner and a Hollywood producer. Famed lyricist Johnny Mercer grew up a block away from Leopold's and was a faithful customer.

⑪ **Forsyth Park.** The park forms the southern border of Bull Street. On its 30 acres are a glorious white fountain dating to 1858, Confederate and Spanish-American War memorials, and the Fragrant Garden for the Blind, a project of Savannah garden clubs. There are tennis courts and a tree-shaded jogging path. Outdoor plays and concerts often take place here. At the northwest corner of the park, in **Hodgson Hall**, a 19th-century Italianate Greek Revival building, you can find the **Georgia Historical Society**, which shows selections from its collection of artifacts and manuscripts. ⊠*501 Whitaker St., Historic District* ☎912/651–2128 ⊕*www.georgiahistory.com* ⊗*Tues.–Sat. 10–5.*

⑩ **Green-Meldrim House.** Designed by New York architect John Norris and ★ built in 1850 for cotton merchant Charles Green, this Gothic Revival mansion cost $93,000 to build—a princely sum back then. The house was bought in 1892 by Judge Peter Meldrim, whose heirs sold it to St. John's Episcopal Church in the 1940s to use as a parish house. General Sherman lived here after taking the city in 1864. Sitting on Madison Square, the house has Gothic features such as a crenellated roof, oriels, and an external gallery with filigree ironwork. Inside are mantels of Carrara marble, carved black-walnut woodwork, and doorknobs and hinges of either silver plate or porcelain. ■TIP→ On Sunday admission is free after the 10:30 church service at St. John's and includes complimentary refreshments. ⊠*1 W. Macon St., Historic District* ☎912/233–3845 ⊠*$8* ⊗*Tues., Thurs., and Fri. 10–4, Sat. 10–1. Closed last 2 wks of Jan. and 2 wks before Easter.*

⑧ Isaiah Davenport House. The proposed demolition of this historic Savannah structure galvanized the city's residents into action to save their treasured buildings. By 1955 this home had a history of dilapidation that had lingered since the 1920s, when it had been divided into tenements. Semicircular stairs with some wrought iron lead to the recessed doorway of the redbrick Federal home that master builder Isaiah Davenport built for his family between 1815 and 1820. Three

> **PARK AND SAVE**
>
> Drivers be warned: Savannah patrollers are quick to dole out parking tickets. Visitors may purchase two-day parking passes ($8) at the Savannah Visitors Center and at some hotels and inns. Passes are valid in metered spots as well as in the city's lots and garages; they allow parkers to exceed the time in time-limit zones.

dormered windows poke through the sloping roof of the stately house, and the interior has polished hardwood floors and fine woodwork and plasterwork. Alas, neither the Davenports' furniture nor the pieces brought in to replicate theirs bespeak wealth. ⊠*324 E. State St., at Columbia Sq., Historic District* ☎*912/236–8097* ⊕*www.davenporthousemuseum.org* ⊠*$8* ⊙*Mon.–Sat. 10–4, Sun. 1–4.*

⑤ Jepson Center for the Arts. On Telfair Square is the Telfair Museum's
Fodor's Choice newest gallery (2006), an unexpectedly contemporary building amid
★ so many 18th- and 19th-century structures that are the city's hallmark. Within the steel-and-glass edifice you can find permanent hangings of Southern art, African-American art, and photography. There's a sculpture gallery and an outdoor sculpture terrace in addition to interactive, kid-friendly exhibits. ⊠*207 W. York St., Historic District* ☎*912/232–1177 or 912/790–8800* ⊕*www.telfair.org* ⊠*$10* ⊙*Mon. noon–5, Tues.–Sat. 10–5, Sun. 1–5.*

⑥ Juliette Gordon Low Birthplace/Girl Scout National Center. This majestic Regency town house, attributed to William Jay (built 1818–21), was designated in 1965 as Savannah's first National Historic Landmark. "Daisy" Low, founder of the Girl Scouts, was born here in 1860, and the house is now owned and operated by the Girl Scouts of America. Mrs. Low's paintings and other artwork are on display in the house, restored to the style of 1886, the year of Mrs. Low's marriage. ⊠*142 Bull St., Historic District* ☎*912/233–4501* ⊕*www.girlscouts.org/ birthplace* ⊠*$8* ⊙*Mon.–Sat. 10–4, Sun. 11–4.*

⑦ Owens-Thomas House & Museum. English architect William Jay's first
Fodor's Choice Regency mansion in Savannah is widely considered the country's finest
★ example of that architectural style. Built in 1816–19, the English house was constructed mostly with local materials. Of particular note are the curving walls of the house, Greek-inspired ornamental molding, half-moon arches, stained-glass panels, and Duncan Phyfe furniture and the hardwood "bridge" on the second floor. The carriage house includes a gift shop and rare urban slave quarters, which have retained the original furnishings and "haint-blue" paint made by the slave occupants. This house had indoor toilets before the White House and the Palace of Versailles. If you have to choose just one or two house-museums, let this be one. The house is owned by the Telfair Museum of Art. ⊠*124*

Abercorn St., Historic District ☎*912/233–9743* ⊕*www.telfair.org* 🎟*$10* ☉*Mon. noon–5, Tues.–Sat. 10–5, Sun. 1–5; last tour at 4:30.*

❸ **Riverfront Plaza.** Amid this nine-block brick concourse, you can watch a parade of freighters and pug-nosed tugs. Youngsters can play in the tugboat-shaped sandboxes. There is a steady stream of outlets for shopping and eating along the Savannah River. Savannah's Riverwalk is being extended 2,000 feet eastward from the Marriott hotel, with construction slated for completion in 2009. ✉*River St., between Abercorn and Barnard Sts., Historic District.*

❹ **Telfair Museum of Art.** The oldest public art museum in the Southeast was
★ designed by William Jay in 1819 for Alexander Telfair and sits across the street from Telfair Square. Within its marble rooms are American, French, and Dutch impressionist paintings; German tonalist paintings; a large collection of works by Kahlil Gibran; plaster casts of the Elgin Marbles, the Venus de Milo, and the Laocoön, among other classical sculptures; and some of the Telfair family furnishings, including a Duncan Phyfe sideboard and Savannah-made silver. During the Savannah Music Festival there are intimate, classical music performances here that are memorable. ✉*121 Barnard St., Historic District* ☎*912/232–1177* ⊕*www.telfair.org* 🎟*$10* ☉*Mon., Wed., Fri., and Sat. 10–5; Thurs. 10–8; Sun. 12–5.*

TYBEE ISLAND

Tybee Island is 18 mi east of Savannah and about 5 mi long and 2 mi wide, with seafood restaurants, chain motels, condos, and shops—most of which sprang up during the 1950s and haven't changed much since. *Tybee* is an Indian word meaning "salt." The Yamacraw Indians came to this island in the Atlantic Ocean to hunt and fish, and legend has it that pirates buried their treasure here. Tybee Island's entire expanse of taupe sand is divided into a number of public beaches, where you go shelling and crabbing, charter fishing boats, parasail, bike, jet ski, kayak, and swim. Nearby, the misnamed Little Tybee Island, actually larger than Tybee Island, is entirely undeveloped. **Tybee Island Lighthouse & Museum** (✉*30 Meddin Dr.* ☎*912/786–5801* ⊕*www.tybeelighthouse. org*) has been well restored; the Head Keeper's Cottage is the oldest building on the island, and should be on your list of must-sees on the island. The lighthouse opens daily at 9 AM, with the last tour at 4:30 PM; admission is $6. Kids will enjoy the **Marine Science Center** (✉*1510 Strand Ave.* ☎*912/786–5917* ⊕*www.tybeemsc.org*), which houses local marine life such as the Ogeechee corn snake, turtles, and the American alligator. It is open daily from 9 to 5 during the summer, from 10 to 5 otherwise; admission is $4. ✛*Tybee Island is 18 mi east of Savannah; take Victory Drive (U.S. 80)* ☎*800/868–2322 for Tybee Island Convention & Visitors Bureau* ⊕*www.tybeevisit.com.*

WHERE TO EAT

HISTORIC DISTRICT

$$$–$$$$
AMERICAN
★
✕**700 Drayton Restaurant.** This is a one-of-a-kind Savannah experience that begins as you walk up the stairs of the former Keyton Mansion into a lounge that dazzles with eclectic furnishings like a Versace leopard-

skin print chair, a suitable spot for a long power lunch or a romantic dinner. You will have a delectable meal made from regionally inspired cuisine utilizing fresh local produce. As an appetizer, the scallops with asparagus and mushrooms with a vanilla sauce are sublime. The Moroccan-spiced rack of lamb is one of the best entrées, but the lime-and-whiskey-marinated snapper, pan-seared with herb grits and tomatillo/lime sauce, is also divine. Leopold's has made the restaurant its own luscious ice cream flavor, "Old Savannah." Breakfast is also served daily, and the Sunday brunch is a local favorite for special occasions. ⊠*700 Drayton St., Historic District* ☎*912/721–5002 or 912/238–5158* ⌂*Reservations essential* ▭*AE, D, DC, MC, V.*

$$
SOUTHERN
Fodor's Choice
★

✕**B. Matthews Eatery.** A change of ownership has not changed the homey, neighborhood feel of this unpretentious restaurant, which continues to be an *in* spot for locals. Three meals a day are served, with Sunday brunch (reservations essential) and its bottomless mimosas renowned all over Savannah. Lunch (until 3) and dinner share the same menu, which is still star-worthy. Certain faves like the black-eyed-pea cake with Cajun remoulade and fried green tomato sandwiches (with oregano aioli) have been retained. Dinner entrées are an excellent value, and the lamb shanks with white-truffle risotto may make you moan. A good way to begin is with an exemplary wild-mushroom strudel. On Tuesdays there are half-price bottles of select wines; the wines by the glass are exceptional every day. Smoking is allowed after 10 PM and anytime at the patio tables. ⊠*325 E. Bay St., Historic District* ☎*912/233–1319* ▭*AE, D, MC, V.*

$$$
ECLECTIC
★

✕**Bistro Savannah.** High ceilings, burnished heart-pine floors, and gray-brick walls lined with local art—even undressed mannequins—contribute to the bistro qualities of this spot by City Market. The menu has specialties such as roasted Vidalia onion soup, which has a natural sweetness and is finished with cream and served with an herbed Parmesan crisp. Going international, Thai-spiced mussels with lemongrass, coconut, and red curry will heat you up after a nocturnal pedicab ride. The hanger steak is lean and flavorful, and the seared jumbo scallops are served over fresh crab succotash. The chef tries to use mostly local, organic veggies, chemical-free meats, and fresh, certified wild shrimp. Like most everything, ice creams, sorbets, and other desserts are made from scratch. Try Chef Scott Ostrander's twist on strawberry shortcake. ⊠*309 W. Congress St., Historic District* ☎*912/233–6266* ▭*AE, MC, V* ☽*No lunch.*

$
SOUTHERN
☽

✕**Blowin' Smoke BBQ.** The restaurant's name refers to the serious smoking of the meats and chicken over Georgia pecan wood, before the housemade barbecue sauce is slathered on. This is a hip, contemporary barbecue shop but based on the same Southern premise as the down-home barbecue joints that are candidly shown in the artsy black-and-white photos hung on the deep-purple and yellow walls. Fellow diners are usually 70% locals, students, and families with kids. The specialties here are pork ribs and hand-pulled pork. Of the fried appetizers, the mushrooms with smoky ranch dressing are the ticket. A must is one of the local craft beers. ⊠*514 Martin Luther King Jr. Blvd., Historic District* ☎*912/231–2385* ▭*AE, D, MC, V.*

$$$–$$$$
AMERICAN
Fodor's Choice
★ ✕ **Cha Bella.** "Organic is the only way," say chef/owner Matthew Roher and his partner Steve Howard, who do everything possible to conform their restaurant to this maxim as staunch supporters of the new Market at Trustee Gardens at The Morris Center. Surrounding the outdoor seating, sheltered by a tin roof, you'll find an aromatic herb garden; the restaurant also has two plots of land nearby where they grow much of their produce. The menu includes some excellent, unusual salads including grilled eggplant with warm plum tomatoes flavored with sweet basil and topped with a goat cheese cake. Among the pastas, the wild porcini pappardelle has a distinctive flavor and mix of textures. A local, all-star black grouper takes center stage, seared, over fresh succotash with lump crab meat. ✉ *10 E. Broad St., Historic District* ☎ *912/790–7888* ▤ *AE, D, MC, V* ⊘ *Closed Mon. No lunch.*

$$$–$$$$
ECLECTIC
Fodor's Choice
★ ✕ **Garibaldi.** This is a restaurant revered by the city's titans and Savannah's crème de le crème. There are such unforgettable appetizers as lamb ribs, slow-cooked with a sweet ginger sauce and a fuchsia pear-cabbage relish, and a salad with a poached pear, arugula, walnuts, and goat cheese fritters with a port-wine vinaigrette. Plump soft-shell crabs come with surprising glazes, and grouper and snapper with original treatments may be paired with house-made chutney and crab risotto. Have your knowledgeable and professional server suggest wine pairings. ✉ *315 W. Congress, Historic District* ☎ *912/232–7118* ⊜ *Reservations essential* ▤ *AE, D, MC, V* ⊘ *No lunch.*

¢
CAFÉ ✕ **Harris Baking Company.** Owner Sam Harris is the chief baker, and his raspberry-custard tarts and perfect éclairs will make your eyes roll back. Facing Drayton, look for the outdoor market umbrellas and tables; inside, the café is a minimalist study in gray, taupe, and chrome, with symbolic stalks of wheat in bud vases. All the baked goods are incredible, including the croissants and Euro-style artesian breads. But Sam also makes uncompromisingly good sandwiches, including a golden cibatta panini with roast beef, aioli, sautéed onions, mushrooms, and with provolone cheese. The lobster crab bisque, with homemade croutons, is particularly flavorful. And imagine banana bread pudding made with cinnamon buns and caramel sauce. ✉ *102 E. Liberty St., Historic District* ☎ *912/233–6400* ▤ *AE, D, MC, V* ⊘ *No dinner.*

$$$
SOUTHERN
Fodor's Choice
★ ✕ **The Lady & Sons.** Waiting in the long line at Food Network star Paula Deen's restaurant at 9:30 AM—simply to make a reservation for lunch or dinner—may set off your tourist-trap alarm. But have no fear, this place delivers. The outstanding buffet, stocked for both lunch and dinner, is the perfect primer to Southern soul food. Most people go back for seconds (or thirds—it's OK, Paula doesn't judge) of favorites like heavenly fried chicken, collard greens, ribs, mac-and-cheese, black-eyed peas, and creamed potatoes. The buffet also includes a dessert, though it's difficult to choose between classics like peach cobbler and banana pudding (our advice: get one of each and share). It's a relative bargain ($14 at lunch; $18 at dinner), but you can also order off the à la carte menu, which includes entrees like crab cake burgers at lunch and chicken potpie or barbecue grouper at dinner. ■TIP➔ **If you're in the large crowd waiting to be seated in the first lunch and dinner groups (11 AM and 5 PM), you may be treated to a visit from one of Paula's sons—or even the**

Lady herself! ✉*102 W. Congress St., Historic District* ☎*912/233–2600* ▭*AE, D, MC, V* ⏲*No dinner Sun.*

$$$$ AMERICAN ★ ✕**Local 11ten.** New Wave, American cuisine is served in what looks like an extension of the white-brick, American Legion post next door. A peek inside shows that it is light years away. Upbeat and contemporary, this is where several of the top young chefs in Savannah come on their nights off. The menu is seasonally driven and is continually changing depending on the availability of produce and the new chef's vision on any given day. Chef Bradley Daniels came here from the prestigious Blackberry Farm in Tennessee, and his cuisine is as Southern as the area's local favorites, including plump, soft-shell crabs, but his menu also has definite Italian and French influences. At this writing, a new rooftop bar is in the works that should be open by spring 2009. ✉*1110 Bull Street, Historic District* ☎*912/790–9000* ✍*Reservations essential* ▭*AE, D, MC, V* ⏲*Closed Sun., Mon. No lunch.*

$$$–$$$$ ECLECTIC Fodor's Choice ★ ✕**Noble Fare.** This is one superior fine-dining experience, all the way from the amuse-bouche to dessert. Most of the clientele are well-heeled, older residents out for a special occasion. The bread service includes honey butter, pistachio pesto, olive oil, and balsamic vinegar for your biscuits, flat breads, rolls, and foccacia, all of which are artistically presented on contemporary white dishes. A choice appetizer is tuna tartare with avocado, American caviar, and mango, drizzled with curry oil. The scallops are laudable, and fish is so fresh it practically moves on your plate, but if you are a venison lover go for the tenderloin with carrot puree, potatoes, greens, and Pinotage syrup. The molten love cake with raspberry sauce and custard ice cream is almost a requirement for dessert. The owners are Chef Patrick McNamara and his lovely bride Jenny, who runs the front of the house. A prix-fixe tasting menu is available. ✉*321 Jefferson St., Historic District* ☎*912/443–3210* ✍*Reservations essential* ▭*AE, D, MC, V* ⏲*No Lunch. Closed Sun. and Mon.*

$$$–$$$$ SOUTHERN ★ ✕**Vic's on The River.** This upscale Southern charmer is one of the hippest fine-dining rooms in town, where local residents congregate and tourists join in conversation at the bar as they listen to the talented pianists. Reserve a window table for the best views of the Savannah River. The young chef, Jay Cantrell, is becoming a local celebrity and is among those aggressively changing the dining scene for the better. Much of the menu is given over to classics like steaks and oysters Rockefeller. Pan-seared scallops are freshened up with crab and Andouille sausage risotto, wilted arugula, and lemon herb truffle butter. Lunch is popular with local business people and upscale tourists, and seafood po'boys and Angus burgers are sought after, as are the daily hot specials. Praline cheesecake is still very much in demand. ✉*16 E. River St., Historic District* ☎*912/721–1000* ✍*Reservations essential* ▭*AE, D, MC, V.*

TYBEE ISLAND

$$$ SOUTHERN ✕**Hunter House.** Built in 1910 as a family beach house, this renovated brick home with its wraparound veranda offers an intimate dining experience with a dose of Victorian ambience. Owner John Hunter operates one of the island's most consistently good restaurants, and that consistency has continued since the 1980s. Seafood dominates the menu and includes deliciously creative dishes such as a cognac-laced

seafood bisque and ahi tuna with a bourbon soy glaze, nori, and a wasabi drizzle. Meat eaters need not despair: chicken and steak options are available, and the restaurant offers a delicious pot roast as the perennial house special, served with mashed potatoes and gravy, red cabbage, carrots, and green beans, which remains the cheapest main course. The key lime tart is the perfect finish. ⊠ *1701 Butler Ave., Tybee Island* ☎ *912/786–7515* ▤ *AE, D, MC, V* ☉ *Closed mid-Dec.–mid-Jan. Closed Sun. Labor Day–mid-Dec. and mid-Jan.–Memorial Day.*

WHERE TO STAY

HISTORIC DISTRICT

$$$–$$$$
★
▦ **Ballastone Inn.** On the National Register of Historic Places, this sumptuous inn occupies an 1838 mansion that once served as a bordello. Rooms are handsomely furnished with antiques and fine reproductions; luxurious, scented linens and French down blankets on canopied beds; and a collection of original framed prints from *Harper's* scattered throughout. Garden (ground-floor) rooms are smaller but cozy, with exposed brick walls, beamed ceilings, and, in some cases, windows at eye level with the lush courtyard. Most rooms have working gas fireplaces, and three have whirlpool tubs. The aroma of fresh flowers permeates the air. Afternoon tea is served from a silver set and on fine china; the evening social hour features hors d'oeuvres; and a full bar stocks boutique wines. **Pros:** excellent location; romantic atmosphere; free passes to a downtown health club are included. **Cons:** limited off-street parking; this busy downtown area can be noisy. ⊠ *14 E. Oglethorpe Ave., Historic District* ☎ *912/236–1484 or 800/822–4553* ⊕ *www.ballastone.com* ⇗ *16 rooms, 3 suites* ⏦ *In-room: Wi-Fi (some). In-hotel: bar, parking (free), no kids under 16, no-smoking rooms* ▤ *AE, MC, V* ❑ *BP.*

$$
Fodor's Choice
★
▦ **East Bay Inn.** The charm of this tall, redbrick building with its hunter green shutters and awnings, its first-floor facade fashioned from cast iron, and the half-dozen American flags, is not lost on passersby. Built in 1852, this inn was once a series of early cotton warehouses and factory offices. The cast-iron, interior pillars were left and the brick walls exposed; the effect is handsome. The interior design is tasteful and professionally done with details that put it a step above what you will see in other similarly priced properties. Although the furnishings are reproductions, comfort has been emphasized, and all guest rooms look great. Each has one or two queen beds, a couch, and two comfy chairs, not to mention 18-foot ceilings. Breakfast is a good offering of cereals, meats, scrambled eggs, fresh fruit, and Danish. **Pros:** hospitality and service get very high marks; the evening reception goes farther than the requisite wine and cheese; great restaurant. **Cons:** not enough parking spaces (15) for the number of rooms; hallways, some art, and bathrooms are not as wonderful as the rooms; staff and clientele not as sophisticated as in more pricey inns. ⊠ *225 E. Bay St., Historic District* ☎ *912/238–1225 or 800/500–1225* ⊕ *www.eastbayinn.com* ⇗ *28 rooms* ⏦ *In-room: safe, Internet (some), Wi-Fi. In-hotel: restaurant, laundry service, Internet terminal, Wi-Fi, parking (free), some pets allowed, no-smoking rooms* ▤ *AE, D, MC, V* ❑ *BP.*

$$$–$$$$ ⊞ **Eliza Thompson House.** Eliza Thompson's loving husband Joseph built
★ this fine town house for her and their seven children in 1847, only
to leave her a widow, albeit a socially prominent one. This gracious
Victorian is one of the oldest B&Bs in Savannah, first transformed by
the first "new" owners in 1995, with furnishings and portraits in gold
leaf frames brought over from England. The rooms are handsomely
appointed, some with antiques and vintage beds, fine linens, and other
designer accents. The J. Stephen's Room with its aubergine walls, plaid
chairs, and Victorian couch look out to the mossy branches of a live
oak. Some of the back rooms are small. A full breakfast is taken in the
tranquil brick courtyard with its soothing fountains. Adjacent is the
New Orleans–esque carriage house, built in the 1980s; its 13 moder-
ately priced rooms have just been completely upgraded, furnishings
and all. Afternoon wine, cheese, and appetizers and, later, luscious
evening desserts and sherry are served in the atmospheric main parlor.
Pros: on one of Savannah's most beautiful brick-lined streets in a lively,
picturesque residential neighborhood; free parking passes are issued for
street parking; flat-screen TV with cable in every room. **Cons:** no private
parking lot; breakfast can be hit or miss; unattractive carpet in halls of
main house. ⊠ *5 W. Jones St., Historic District* ☎ *912/236–3620 or
800/348–9378* ⊕ *www.elizathompsonhouse.com* ⊲ *25 rooms* ♿ *In-
room: DVD, Wi-Fi. In-hotel: Internet terminal, parking (free), no kids
under 12, no-smoking rooms* ⊟ *AE, D, MC, V* ⊺⊙⊺ *BP.*

$$$–$$$$ ⊞ **Gastonian.** Many of the rooms in this atmospheric inn, built in 1868,
★ underwent an extensive remodeling in 2008. Fresh flowers throughout
and the outdoor covered arbor are unexpected pleasures. Guest rooms
are decorated with a mix of funky finds and antiques from the Georgian
and Regency periods; all have fireplaces, and most have whirlpool tubs.
In a second building, identical to the main house, where the dining and
socializing take place, the Lafayette Room has the most noteworthy
fireplace; the Caracalla Suite is named for the oversize whirlpool tub
built in front of its fireplace; the Low Room has a private wrought-iron
balcony looking out on the treetops. At breakfast you can have such hot
entrées as omelets with creamed spinach and goat cheese. Afternoon
tea, complimentary wine with cheese and hors d'oeuvres, and evening
cordials are among the treats. **Pros:** many rooms and suites are excep-
tionally spacious; the handsome and quiet Eli Whitney Room is one of
the least expensive; cordial and caring staff. **Cons:** accommodations on
the third floor are a hike; some of the furnishings are less than regal.
⊠ *220 E. Gaston St., Historic District* ☎ *912/232–2869 or 800/322–
6603* ⊕ *www.gastonian.com* ⊲ *14 rooms, 3 suites* ♿ *In-room: DVD,
Wi-Fi. In-hotel: Wi-Fi, parking (free), no kids under 12, no-smoking
rooms* ⊟ *AE, D, MC, V* ⊺⊙⊺ *BP.*

$$$$ ⊞ **Mansion on Forsyth Park.** Sophisticated, chic, and artsy only begin to
Fodor's Choice describe this Kessler property. The newer wings blend perfectly with its
★ historic surroundings and the original, 18,000-square-foot Victorian-
Romanesque, redbrick and terra-cotta mansion. Sitting on the edge of
Forsyth Park, its dramatic design, opulent interiors with a contempo-
rary edge, and magnificently diverse collection of some 400 pieces of
American and European art create a one-of-a-kind experience. Every

turn delivers something unexpected—the antique hat collection; the pool with its creative water wall, and a canopied patio that looks like it's out of the *Arabian Nights*; a Nordic-looking full-service spa; back-lighted onyx panels and 100-year-old Italian Corona–marble pillars. The 700 Drayton Restaurant offers contemporary fine dining and professional, attentive service. Upstairs, Casimir's Lounge, with live piano and jazz, is one of the city's hot spots. **Pros:** no real breakfast, but Starbuck's coffee, pastries, and bagels are gratis in the Bösendorfer Lounge every morning; an exciting, stimulating environment that transports you from the workaday world; complimentary Lincoln Town Car and driver (limited). **Cons:** very pricey, particularly for room service and phone calls; some of the art from the early 1970s is not appealing. ⊠ *700 Drayton St., Historic District* ☎ *912/238–5158 or 888/711–5114* ⊕ *www.mansiononforsythpark.com* ⇨ *126 rooms* ⚏ *In-room: safe, Internet, Wi-Fi. In-hotel: restaurant, room service, bars, spa, Internet terminal, Wi-Fi, parking (paid), no-smoking rooms* ☰ *AE, D, DC, MC, V* ⍓*EP.*

$$
FodorśChoice
★

⚏ **The Stephen Williams House.** Although named for its builder, this house was constructed for the honorable Mayor (six terms) William Thorn Williams in 1834. This wonderful Federal-style mansion is now owned by an equally exceptional retired physician, Dr. Albert Wall. Savannah-born, an inveterate storyteller, lover of history, antique collector, and survivor of seven historic preservation projects, he was determined to save this house, which had become one sad derelict. The sumptuous suite has an entirely separate parlor and a draped bed. The less expensive garden rooms, which share a bath, are characterized by beamed ceilings and exposed brick walls, and open out to the restored garden and walled courtyard with its lion's head fountain. Dr. Wall has a deep affection for his city, and as he pours morning coffee for his guests, he suggests his favorite things in Savannah for them to do and can arrange for bicycles to be delivered. The hotel is a superb wedding venue. **Pros:** elegant furnishings (a 45-year collection of period antiques, some museum-quality, some for sale); full Southern breakfast made from old Savannah recipes; beds triple-sheeted with Frette linens and choice of down pillows. **Cons:** occasional plumbing problems as befits an aged manse; no wine and hors d'oeuvres reception in the evening; rooms facing Liberty Street catch the bus and traffic noise. ⊠ *4 Barnard St., Historic District* ☎ *912/495–0032* ⊕ *www.thestephenwilliamshouse.com* ⇨ *4 rooms, 1 suite* ⚏ *In-room: Wi-Fi. In-hotel:, laundry service, Wi-Fi, parking (free), no kids under 12, no-smoking rooms* ☰ *AE, D, MC, V* ⍓*BP.*

$$$–$$$$
★

⚏ **The Zeigler House Inn.** This urban mansion on one of the city's most desirable brick-paved streets will have you fantasizing about living in such a place, just like the city's upper crust. Owner Jackie Heinz came from Atlanta for a weekend and put in an offer to buy the house before she left. It is her home now, and her taste is admirable, from the hanging baskets of rare flowers to the chocolate-brown ceilings in the main parlors that make the white ceiling medallions look like art. You can tap into Savannah's good life and have a romantic stay in a beautifully appointed room or, better yet, a suite with contemporary style juxtaposed with antiques, a custom-made king bed, and fine bedding. Jackie has a unique way of handling breakfast. Each room has a kitchenette or full kitchen with a coffeemaker; she stocks the fridge with juice and milk and bakes delectable pastries daily that she leaves for breakfast. A professional chef, she can prepare a gourmet, multicourse dinner for guests upon request. **Pros:** the privilege of being in such a lovable home; a stocked kitchen makes you feel like you really live here; lovely slate fireplaces and heart-pine floors and staircase. **Cons:** garden-level rooms have a subterranean feel; not a full-service hotel; no full, hot breakfast. ⊠*121 W. Jones St., Historic District* ☎*912/233–5307 or 866/233–5307* ⊕*www.zieglerhouseinn.com* ➟*4 rooms, 2 suites* ⑁*In-room: kitchen (some), refrigerator, DVD, Wi-Fi. In-hotel: Wi-Fi, parking (free), no kids under 12, no-smoking rooms* ▭*AE, MC, V* ⧉*CP.*

TYBEE ISLAND

If renting a 5-star beach house, a pastel island cottage, or a waterfront condo in a complex with a pool and tennis courts is more your Tybee dream, check out **Tybee Vacation Rentals** (⊠*1010 Hwy. 80E, Tybee Island* ☎*912/786–5853 or 866/359–0297* ⊕*www.tybeevacationrentals.com*).

NIGHTLIFE

Savannah's nightlife reflects the city's laid-back personality. Some clubs have live reggae, hard rock, and other contemporary music, but most stick to traditional blues, jazz, and piano-bar vocalists. After-dark merrymakers usually head for watering holes on Riverfront Plaza or the Southside.

BARS AND NIGHTCLUBS

A relatively new and certainly stellar nightspot, **Casimir Lounge** (⊠*700 Drayton St., Historic District* ☎*912/721–5061 or 912/238–5158*) is not as formal as the downstairs lounge at 700 Drayton, but its decor is gorgeous, too. The real draw is the live music that plays on Friday and Saturday nights (and sometimes Thursday or Sunday), beginning about 8:30. Jazz and blues are the norm. A gay bar, **Club One Jefferson** (⊠*1 Jefferson St., Historic District* ☎*912/232–0200* ⊕*www.clubone-online. com*) has been dubbed one of the city's best dance clubs by the locals, and the notorious Lady Chablis still does cameo appearances here. Drag shows are a feature, but mostly it's a DJ keeping the dancers in motion.

Fodor'sChoice There's no cover. **Planters Tavern** (⊠*23 Abercorn St., Historic District*
★   ☎*912/232–4286*), in the basement of the Olde Pink House, is one of Savannah's most romantic late-night spots for a nightcap. There's some kind of live entertainment every night. The decor never changes, and that is part of what makes the scene, especially the stone fireplace and the fox-hunt memorabilia.

LIVE MUSIC CLUBS

Jazz'd Tapas Bar (⊠*52 Barnard St., Historic District* ☎*912/236–7777*) is a chic, basement venue featuring a range of local artists are featured from Tuesday through Saturday. The tapas menu has healthy, contemporary small plates, and is one of the city's best values; the place usually opens at 4. No one under 21 can enter once the kitchen closes (10 PM weekdays, midnight on weekends); there's never a cover. **Vic's On the River** (⊠*26 E. Bay St. and 15 E. Bay St., Historic District* ☎*912/721–*

1000) is one of Savannah's best restaurants, which also happens to have an excellent bar. The piano is manned every night.

SPORTS AND THE OUTDOORS

BIKING

Island Bike (✉*14 W. State St., Historic District* ✉*205 Johnny Mercer Blvd., Wilmington Island* ☎*912/236–8808 or 912/897–7474*) rents single-speed adult bikes for $20 per day, kid's bikes for $15 per day, and multi-speed bikes for $25 per day at both locations. Helmets and locks are available only at the downtown location (for an extra charge). On Tybee Island you can enjoy a bike-friendly environment with ocean-view trails, at half the cost of biking downtown. **Tim's Beach Gear** (✉*Tybee Island* ☎*912/786–8467* ⊕*www.timsbeachgear.com*) rents bikes for adults and kids as well as in-tow carriers. This is strictly a drop-off service, offering free delivery and pickup on Tybee Island—for just $10 a day ($8 per day for multiday rentals), and that includes helmets.

BOATING AND FISHING

Explore the natural beauty and wildlife on a narrated boat tour with **Dolphin Magic Tours** (✉*101 River St., Historic District* ☎*800/721–1240* ⊕*www.dolphin-magic.com*). From River Street you go out to the marshlands and tidal creeks near Tybee Island. The search for dolphin encounters lasts two hours and sightings are guaranteed. Departure times vary according to the tides and the weather; the cruise costs $30. Bring sunscreen and beverages. **Lowcountry River Excursions** (✉*Bull River Marina, 8005 Old Tybee Rd. [Hwy. 80 E], Tybee Island* ☎*912/898–9222*), which operates out of Bull River Marina, allows you to experience an encounter with friendly bottlenose dolphins and enjoy the scenery and wildlife during a 90-minute cruise down the Bull River aboard a 40-foot pontoon boat. Restrooms are on board, and beverages, too. Call to confirm times and seasonal hours. Reservations are strongly advised. Capt. Judy Helmley, a long-time and legendary guide of the region, heads up **Miss Judy Charters** (✉*124 Palmetto Dr., Wilmington Island* ☎*912/897–4921 or 912/897–2478* ⊕*www.missjudycharters.com*) and provides packages ranging from two-hour sightseeing tours to 16-hour deep-sea fishing expeditions. Rates run about $500 for four hours and (up to) six people, and $650 for eight hours, and a 16-hour adventure will cost you $1,800. Most major credit cards accepted. Please don't forget to tip the mate 15% to 20%. **North Island Surf & Kayak** (✉*1C Old Tybee Rd., Tybee Island* ☎*912/786–4000* ⊕*www.northisland-kayak.com*) is a young and versatile operation, but they will open up a whole new world of kayaking with their sit-on-top kayaks that are virtually unsinkable. You can put in at the company's floating dock, or launch wherever you want. All rentals include paddles, life jackets, and seat backs. Prices are $40 per day for a single, $55 for a double; there are no hourly rentals. The company also offers ecotours; although these tours require a minimum of six adults ($50), you can often join a scheduled group if you are a couple or a single. You can also rent paddleboards here for $50 a day, or a surfboard for $30. Lessons are an extra $10 an hour.

SPAS

Magnolia Spa (⊠*Marriott Savannah Riverfront, 100 Gen. McIntosh Blvd., Historic District* ☎912/373–2039 ⊕*www.marriott.com*) is a secret mother lode of pampering services that the occasional visitor may not stumble upon in their wanderings since it is at the far end of the River Walk and within the Marriott and has not been open long. The very chic **Poseidon Spa** (□*The Mansion on Forsyth Park, 700 Drayton St., Historic District* ☎912/721–5004 ⊕*www.mansiononforsythpark. com*) is a first-class European-style spa, with a number of rejuvenating treatments and refinement services. It offers manicures, pedicures, skin and body treatments, massages, and access to a 24-hour fitness center. This truly is the town's glamour spa, though in truth prices run just a little more than the rest.

SHOPPING

Find your own Lowcountry treasures among a bevy of handcrafted wares—handmade quilts and baskets; wreaths made from Chinese tallow trees and Spanish moss; preserves, jams, and jellies. The favorite Savannah snack, and a popular gift item, is the benne wafer (from the African word for sesame seeds). These thin cookies are about the size of a quarter and come in different flavors.

SHOPPING DISTRICTS

For generations, **Broughton Street** (⊠*Between Congress and State Sts., Historic District*) was the main shopping street of the city. After a decades-long downturn, the area is thriving once again, not only with shops but with restaurants and coffeehouses, too. West of Bull Street are more shops; East of Bull, there are fewer stores, but you'll still find some high-end boutiques on both ends, as well as chain stores. **City Market** (⊠*W. St. Julian St. between Ellis and Franklin Sqs., Historic District*) takes its origins from a farmers' market back in 1755. Today it's a four-block emporium that has been involved in a renaissance program, and constitutes an eclectic mix of artists' studios, sidewalk cafés, jazz haunts, shops, and art galleries. **Riverfront Plaza/River Street** (⊠*Historic District*) is nine blocks of renovated waterfront warehouses (once the city's cotton exchange) containing more than 75 boutiques, galleries, restaurants, and pubs; you can find everything from popcorn to pottery here, and even voodoo spells! Leave your stilettos at home, or you'll find the street's cobblestones hard and dangerous work.

SPECIALTY SHOPS

ANTIQUES
Fodor's Choice
★
37th @ Abercorn Antique & Design (⊠*37th St., at Abercorn St., Historic District* ☎912/233–0064) is a one-stop shop that encompasses a city block of antiques and collectibles spanning 200 years. Stroll with a cup of java from the property's European café, and peruse through the area's largest collection of quilts, antique clocks, vintage costume jewelry, and museum-quality vintage children's clothes. Visit a primitive country kitchen displaying gadgets, enamelware, and 1950s-era linens. Original Persian rugs and antique sterling silver jewelry are among other unique items available.

BOOKS "The Book" Gift Shop and Midnight Museum (⊠*127 E. Gordon St., Historic District* ☎*912/233–3867*) sells all things related to *Midnight in the Garden of Good and Evil,* including souvenirs and author-autographed copies. It may not have a long life, in that the keen interest in the subject is on the wane. In the meantime, if you have never read this Savannah classic, you can pick it up here. Seeing the decline, the shop is now wisely capitalizing on the various ghost tours and has a lot of haunt-y items. **E. Shaver Booksellers** (⊠*326 Bull St., Historic District* ☎*912/234–7257*) is the source for 17th- and 18th-century maps and new books on regional subjects. It carries travel guides for Savannah and books on just about whatever you would want to know about the city, from its colonial beginnings to what there is for children to do. This shop occupies 12 rooms of an historic building, and it alone is something to see. The booksellers are knowledgeable about their wares.

**CLOTHING
FOR WOMEN
Fodor's**Choice
★ **Copper Penny** (⊠*22 W. Broughton St., Historic District* ☎*912/629–6800*) was conceptualized by owner Penny Vaigneur in Charleston (there's a store there and in Myrtle Beach). Carrying Trina Turk, Nanette Lapore, and Hudson Jeans, to name a few of the designers popular with young fashionistas, the more mature shopper comes to get some edgy pieces to contemporize her wardrobe. "Attached" is Copper Penny Shooz, where you'll find shoe fashion statements by BCB Girls, Kate Spade, Michael Kors, and the like. Great-looking purses complement the shoes; you'll find names like Francesco Biasia, Hype Handbags, and Tano. Love those Lucchese boots.

FOOD The Lady and her sons have another hit to their credit. They have transformed what was the grungiest of bars into the fabulous **Paula Deen Store** (⊠*108 W. Congress St., Historic District* ☎*912/232–1607*), which is filled with cookbooks by the Southern Queen of the Food Network. Two full floors of cooking goodies and gadgets are cleverly displayed against a backdrop of brick walls. The shop is adjacent to Deen's famous Southern-style restaurant, so you may get lucky, for her **Fodor's**Choice son Jamie may be signing cookbooks on your day. **River Street Sweets**
★ (⊠*13 E. River St., Historic District* ☎*912/233–6220*) opened in 1973, and it is Savannah's self-described "oldest and original" candy store. The aroma of creamy homemade fudge will draw you in, along with hot and fresh pralines, which are made all day long. The store is also known for milk-chocolate bear claws. It's a great place to find a unique, edible gift. You'll always receive excellent customer service here.

**HOME DECOR
Fodor's**Choice
★ **The Paris Market & Brocante** (⊠*36 W. Broughton St., Historic District* ☎*912/232–1500*) is a Francophile's dream, from the time you open the antique front door and take in the intoxicating aroma of lavender. This two-story emporium with chandeliers and other lighting fixtures is a classy version of the Paris flea market, selling furniture, vintage art, garden planters and accessories, and Euro-home fashions like boudoir accessories and bedding. And although the store will ship, there are numerous treasures that can be easily carried away, like the soaps, candles, vintage jewelry, kitchen and barware, and dried lavender.

THE COASTAL ISLES AND THE OKEFENOKEE

Georgia's coastal isles are a string of lush barrier islands meandering down the Atlantic coast from Savannah to the Florida border. Notable for their subtropical beauty and abundant wildlife, the isles also strike a unique balance between some of the wealthiest communities in the country and some of the most jealously protected preserves found anywhere. Until recently large segments of the coast were in private hands, and as a result much of the region remains as it was when the first Europeans set eyes on it 450 years ago. The marshes, wetlands, and waterways teem with birds and other wildlife, and they're ideal for exploring by kayak or canoe. Though the islands have long been a favorite getaway of the rich and famous, they no longer cater only to the well-heeled. There's mounting pressure to develop these wilderness shores and make them even more accessible.

GETTING HERE AND AROUND

Visiting the region is easiest by car, particularly Sapelo Island, because many of the outer reaches of Georgia are remote places with little in the way of transportation options. Touring by bicycle is an option for most of the region, but note that the ferries at Sapelo and Cumberland do not allow bicycles on board. Except for Little St. Simons, the Golden Isles are connected to the mainland by bridges around Brunswick and are the only coastal isles accessible by car. Sapelo Island and the Cumberland Island National Seashore can only be reached by ferry from Meridian and St. Marys, respectively.

BOAT AND FERRY TRAVEL   Cumberland Island and Sapelo Island are accessible only by ferry or private launch. The *Cumberland Queen* serves Cumberland Island and the *Anne Marie* serves Sapelo Island.

CAR TRAVEL   From Brunswick take the Jekyll Island Causeway ($3 per car) to Jekyll Island and the Torras Causeway to St. Simons. You can get by without a car on Jekyll Island, but you'll need one on St. Simons. You cannot bring a car to Cumberland Island or Sapelo.

TAXI TRAVEL   Courtesy Cab provides taxi service from Brunswick to and from the islands for a set rate that ranges from $15 to $25 to St. Simons and from $25 to Jekyll Island with a $2 per person surcharge to a maximum of seven persons. Island Cab Service can shuttle you around St. Simons for fares that range between $7 and $15 depending on your destination.

ESSENTIALS

Boat and Ferry Contacts Anne Marie (⊠ *Sapelo Island Visitors Center, Rte. 1, Box 1500, Darien* ☎ *912/437–3224* ⊕ *www.sapelonerr.org*). **Cumberland Queen** (⊠ *Cumberland Island National Seashore* ☐ *Box 806, 101 Wheeler St., St. Marys 31558* ☎ *912/882–4336 or 877/860–6787* ⊕ *www.nps.gov/cuis*).

Taxi Contacts Courtesy Cab (⊠ *4262B Norwich Exit, Brunswick* ☎ *912/264–3760*). **Island Cab Service** (⊠ *708 E. Island Square Dr., St. Simons* ☎ *912/634–0113*).

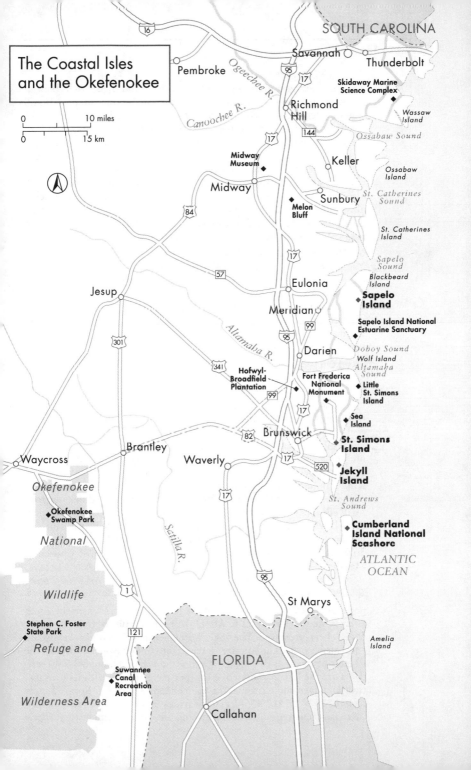

SAPELO ISLAND

68 mi south of Savannah via I-95.

The fourth-largest of Georgia's coastal isles—and bigger than Bermuda—Sapelo Island is a unique community in North America. It still bears evidence of the early-Paleo-Indians who lived here some 4,500 years ago, and is home to the Geechee, direct descendants of African slaves who speak a creole of English and various African languages. This rapidly dwindling community maintains many traditional African practices, including the making of sweetgrass baskets and the use of herbal medicines made from recipes passed down for generations. It's also a nearly pristine barrier island with miles of undeveloped beaches and abundant wildlife. To take the 40-minute ferry ride from Meridian on the mainland through the expanse of salt marshes to Sapelo Island is to enter a world seemingly forgotten by time.

GETTING HERE AND AROUND

You can explore many historical periods and natural environments here, but facilities on the island are limited. Note that you can't simply walk up to the dock and catch the ferry—you need to have a reservation for a tour, a campsite, or one of the island's lodgings (or have prearranged plans to stay with island residents). Bring insect repellent, especially in summer, and leave your pets at home. You can rent a bicycle on the island, but you cannot bring a bicycle on the ferry.

EXPLORING

Start your visit at the **Sapelo Island Visitor Center** in Meridian on the mainland near the Sapelo Island ferry docks. Here you can see exhibits on the island's history, culture, and ecology, and you can purchase tickets for a round-trip ferry ride and bus tour of the island. The sights that make up the bus tour vary depending on the day of the week, but always included are the marsh, the sand-dune ecosystem, and the wildlife management area. On Friday and Saturday the tour includes the 80-foot **Sapelo Lighthouse,** built in 1820, a symbol of the cotton and lumber industry once based out of Darien, a prominent shipping center of the time. To see the island's **Reynolds Mansion,** schedule your tour for Wednesday or Saturday. To get to the visitor center and Meridian Ferry Dock from downtown Darien, go north on Route 99 for 8 mi, following signs for the Sapelo Island National Estuarine Research Reserve. Turn right onto Landing Road at the Elm Grove Baptist Church in Meridian. The visitor center is about ½ mi down the road. ⊠ *Rte. 1, Box 1500, Darien* ☎ *912/437–3224, 912/485–2300 for group tours* ⊕ *www.sapelonerr.org.*

Hog Hammock Community is one of the few remaining sites on the south Atlantic coast where ethnic African-American culture from the slave era has been preserved. The "Salt Water Geechee," Georgia's sea-island equivalent to the Gullah, are descendants of slaves who worked the island's plantations during the 19th century. Hog Hammock's 40 residents are the last members of a disappearing culture with its own distinct language and customs. **The Spirit of Sapelo Tours** (⌂ *Box 7, Sapelo Island 31327* ☎ *912/485–2170*) provides private guided bus tours led by an island native who discusses island life, culture, and history. **Sapelo**

Culture Day (☎912/485–2197 ⊕*www.sapeloislandgeorgia.org*), a celebration of Geechee folklore, music, food, handcrafts, and art, takes place in Hog Hammock every year on the third weekend in October. Reservations are required.

WHERE TO EAT AND STAY

$$ ✕**Mudcat Charlie's.** This tabby-and-wood restaurant on the Altamaha
SEAFOOD River sits right in the middle of the Two Way Fish Camp and is a favor-
★ ite haunt of locals from nearby Darien. The restaurant overlooks the
boats moored in the marina, and the seafood is local. Crab stew, fried
oysters, and shrimp are the specialties, and the peach and apple pies
are made in-house. It's 1 mi south of Darien on U.S. 17, just after the
third bridge. Look for the Two Way Fish Camp sign. ✉*250 Ricefield
Way* ☎912/261–0055 ⊟*AE, D, MC, V.*

$$ ✕**Skipper's Fish Camp.** You can find this upscale take on the fish camp
SEAFOOD theme at the foot of Skipper's dock on the Darien River, where the
working shrimp boats moor. It has a beautiful courtyard pond that uses
water from the river and an open-air oyster bar. Popular menu items
include Georgia white shrimp, ribs, and fried flounder. There's usually
a wait on weekends, so get there early. At the southern end of Darien,
turn right at Broad just before the river bridge, then take the first left
down to the docks. ✉*85 Scriven St.* ☎912/437–3474 ⚄*Reservations
not accepted* ⊟*AE, D, MC, V.*

$–$$ 🖭**The Blue Heron Inn.** Bill and Jane Chamberlain's airy, Spanish-style
home sits on the edge of the marsh and is only minutes from the ferry
at the Sapelo Island Visitors Center. The downstairs dining and living
areas have an open, Mediterranean feel, with a large, rustic fireplace
and a sweeping view of the marsh. Guest rooms are simply decorated
with colorful quilts; most have four-poster beds, and all have a view of
the marsh. The proprietor, an Athens native, provides drinks and hors
d'oeuvres on the third-floor terrace overlooking the Doboy Sound every
evening, and his breakfast specialties include lime French toast and
sweet Georgia shrimp omelets. **Pros:** deliciously inventive breakfasts;
decks provide great views. **Cons:** the small number of rooms means the
place can book up fast. ✉*1 Blue Heron La., Meridian* ☎🖷912/437–
4304 ⊕*www.blueheroninngacoast.com* ⇄*4 rooms* ⚄*In-room: no
phone, no TV. In-hotel: Wi-Fi* ⊟*MC, V* 🍴❘*BP.*

¢ 🖭**The Wallow Lodge.** Cornelia Walker Bailey's memoir of life growing up
Geechee on Sapelo, *God, Dr. Buzzard, and the Bolito Man,* has made
her a folk hero and focused awareness on the disappearing communities
of descendants of African slaves. A stay at Bailey's Wallow Lodge offers
a chance to experience the island's distinct culture. Cotton chenille,
a tradition on Sapelo, and quilted spreads cover the beds. **Pros:** each
room is decorated with furniture and memorabilia from residents of the
island. **Cons:** the lodge has a communal kitchen, so unless you make
prior arrangements for meals, you must bring your own supplies from
the mainland. ✉*1 Main Rd., Box 34, Sapelo Island* ☎912/485–2206
🖷912/485–2174 ⊕*www.gacoast.com/geecheetours* ⇄*6 rooms, 5
with bath* ⚄*In-room: no phone, no TV* ⊟*No credit cards.*

NIGHTLIFE

It seems appropriate that the only watering hole in Hog Hammock is named the **Trough** (✉ *1 Main Rd.* ☎ *912/485–2206*). It's a small, bare-bones, belly-up-to-the-bar establishment, but owner Julius Bailey serves his beer ice-cold, and there's usually a good conversation going on. It's next to the Wallow Lodge (operated by Julius's wife, Cornelia), right "downtown."

ST. SIMONS ISLAND

40 mi south of Sapelo Island via U.S. 17.

St. Simons may be the Golden Isles' most developed vacation destination: here you can swim and sun, golf, hike, fish, ride horseback, tour historic sites, and feast on local seafood at more than 50 restaurants. (It's also a great place to bike and jog, particularly on the southern end, where there's an extensive network of trails.) Despite the development, the island has managed to maintain some of the slow-paced Southern atmosphere that made it such a draw in the first place. Upscale resorts and restaurants are here for the asking, but this island the size of Manhattan has only 20,000 year-round residents, so you can still get away from it all without a struggle. Even down in the village, the center of much of St. Simons's activity, there are unpaved roads and quiet back alleys of chalky white sand that seem like something out of the past.

GETTING HERE AND AROUND

Reach the island by car via the causeway from Brunswick. In the village area, at the more developed south end of the island, you can find shops, several restaurants, pubs, and a popular public pier. For $20 a quaint **"trolley"** (☎ *912/638–8954*) takes you on a 1½-hour guided tour of the island, leaving from near the pier at 11 AM and 1 PM in high season and at 11 AM in winter.

ESSENTIALS

Visitor Information Brunswick and the Golden Isles Visitors Center (✉ *4 Glynn Ave., Brunswick* ☎ *912/265–0620* ✉ *530 Beachview Dr., St. Simons* ☎ *912/638–9014* ☎ *800/809–1790* ⊕ *www.bgicvb.com*). **St. Simons Visitors Center** (✉ *St. Simons, F.J. Torras, Causeway at U.S. 17, St. Simons Island* ☎ *912/265–6620* ⊕ *www.bgicvb.com*).

EXPLORING

★ **St. Simons Lighthouse,** one of only five surviving lighthouses in Georgia, has become a symbol of the island. It's been in use since 1872; a predecessor was blown up to prevent its capture by Union troops in the Civil War. The **Museum of Coastal History,** occupying two stories of the lightkeeper's cottage, has period furniture and a gallery with photo displays illustrating the significance of shipbuilding on St. Simons, the history of the lighthouse, and the life of James Gould, the first lighthouse keeper. The keeper's second-floor quarters contain a parlor, kitchen, and two bedrooms furnished with period pieces, including beds with rope mattress suspension. ✉ *101 12th St.* ☎ *912/638–4666* ⊕ *www. saintsimonslighthouse.org* 🎫 *$5* ⊗ *Mon.–Sat. 10–5, Sun. 1:30–5.*

🕙 **Maritime History Museum.** At the restored 1936 Historic Coast Guard Station, this new center is geared as much to kids as adults. It features the life of a "Coastie" in the early 1940s through personal accounts of the military history of St. Simons Island and has illustrative displays on the ecology of the islands off the coast of Georgia. ✉*East Beach Causeway* ☎*912/638–4666* 🖼*$6* 🕙*Mon.–Sat. 10–5, Sun. 1:30–5.*

WHERE TO EAT

$ ✕**The Beachcomber BBQ and Grill.** No shoes, no shirt, no problem in this
BARBECUE small, rustic eatery where the walls are covered with reed mats and the barbecue smokes away on a cooker right beside the front door. Despite the name, it doesn't boast a beachfront location. However, it's one of the best barbecue joints on the island, offering everything from sandwiches to pulled pork, ribs, and brisket by the pound. ■**TIP→ The freshly squeezed lemonade is to die for.** ✉*319 Arnold Rd.* ☎*912/634–5699* ⊕*beachcomberbbq.com* ▭*AE, MC, V.*

$$ ✕**Bennie's Red Barn.** The steaks are cut fresh daily and cooked over an
AMERICAN oak fire in this barn of a restaurant that has been serving St. Simons for 50 years. Though there's room for 200 people, it feels just like family with the checkered tablecloths and the big open fireplace. There's also fresh local seafood. The pies are homemade. And there's music next door at Ziggy's on weekends. ✉*5514 Frederica Rd.* ☎*912/638–2844* ⊕*benniesredbarn.com* ▭*AE, D, MC, V* 🕙*No lunch.*

$$$ ✕**CARGO Portside Grill.** This superb bistro beside the port in Brunswick
SOUTHERN has a menu that reads like a foodie's wish list, with succulent coastal
★ fare from many ports. Chef Kate Buchanan puts a creative spin on Southern fare, whether it's sesame catfish, or pasta with grilled chicken in a chipotle cream sauce, or pork chops in a sauce flavored with Jack Daniels. Save room for the Georgia peach pound cake. ✉*1423 Newcastle St., Brunswick* ☎*912/267 7330* ⊕*cargoportsidegrill.com* ▭*AE, MC, V* 🕙*Closed Sun. and Mon. No lunch.*

$ ✕**Gnat's Landing.** There's more than a little bit of Margaritaville in this
AMERICAN Key West–style bungalow catering to the flip-flop crowd. Seafood is their specialty, with a gumbo that's outta sight. Besides being the strangest item on the menu, the fried dill pickle is also the most popular. Sandwiches and salads are also offered. And, of course, there's the "$8,000 margarita," which is about how much owner Robert Bostock spent in travel and ingredients coming up with the recipe. There's live music most Sunday nights, and once a year there's "Gnatfest," a party blowout with live bands for all those pesky regulars. ✉*310 Redfern Village* ☎*912/638–7378* ⊕*gnatslanding.com* ▭*AE, D, MC, V.*

$$$$ ✕**Halyards.** This elegant restaurant with a laid-back attitude makes
AMERICAN everything except the ketchup right on the premises. Chef-owner Dave
★ Snyder's devotion to quality has earned a faithful following of discerning locals. Slide into a cozy, tufted booth or sit at the sophisticated bar lined with photos of yachts. Headliners include the seared, sushi-grade tuna with a plum wine reduction and the Asian-style diver scallops. A tasting menu with five courses is paired with wines selected from the restaurant's impressive cellar. The signature coffee hits the mark with the coconut/lime panna cotta with a dark rum gelée layer. ✉*55 Cin-*

ema La. ☎912/638–9100 ⊕*halyardsrestaurant.com* ⚖*Reservations essential* ▤*AE, D, MC, V* ⊘*Closed Sun. No lunch.*

$$ ✕**Mullet Bay.** After 9 PM the older beach-bar crowd has this place hop-
AMERICAN ping, and on weekends the bar and wraparound porches can be stand-
ing-room only until the wee hours. By day, however, this spacious and
casual restaurant is great for families, serving a good selection of burg-
ers, pastas, and salads. The kids' menu starts at $1.95. ■**TIP**→**The plat-
ters of fried popcorn shrimp are delicious and perfect for sharing.** ⊠*512
Ocean Blvd.* ☎912/634–9977 ⊕*mulletbayrestaurant.com* ▤*AE, D,
MC, V.*

¢ ✕**Rafters.** If you're looking for cheap, delicious food and a raucous good
SEAFOOD time, this is the place. Revelers sit together at long tables and partake of
★ the offerings from the prodigious bar and the equally generous kitchen.
The restaurant serves ocean fare such as "u-shuck-'em" oysters, baked
mussels, and a shrimp quesadilla with caramelized papaya, lime, and
molasses. Rafters is open late and presents live entertainment Wednes-
day through Saturday. ⊠*315½ Mallery St.* ☎912/634–9755 ▤*AE,
D, MC, V* ⊘*Closed Sun.*

WHERE TO STAY

$ ▦**Holiday Inn Express.** With brightly decorated rooms at great prices,
this no-smoking facility is an attractive option in this price category. The
executive rooms have sofas and desks. **Pros:** good value. **Cons:** some
guests complain that the walls are too thin. ⊠*Plantation Village, 299
Main St.* ☎912/634–2175 or 888/465–4329 ⊕*www.hiexpress.com/
stsimonsga* ⇲*60 rooms* ♿*In-hotel: pool, bicycles, laundry service,
Wi-Fi, no-smoking rooms* ▤*AE, D, MC, V* ⫶⃝*BP.*

$$–$$$ ▦**King and Prince Beach & Golf Resort.** This resort is a cushy retreat with
spacious guest rooms and luxurious two- and three-bedroom villas.
Guests get golf privileges at the Hampton Club at the Hampton Plan-
tation on St. Simons, as well as access to many outdoor activities such
as sailing and tennis. The villas are all privately owned, so the total
number available for rent varies from time to time. **Pros:** sprawling
suites; access to Hampton Club; speedy room service. **Cons:** amenities
here are fairly basic. ■**TIP**→**The historic main building has been refur-
bished to include a Starbucks.** ⊠*201 Arnold Rd.* ☎912/638–3631 or
800/342–0212 ⊟912/634–1720 ⊕*www.kingandprince.com* ⇲*145
rooms, 2 suites, 41 villas* ♿*In-hotel: restaurants, room service, bar,
tennis courts, pools, bicycles, Wi-Fi* ▤*AE, D, MC, V* ⫶⃝*EP.*

$$$$ ▦**The Lodge at Sea Island Golf Club.** Simply put, this small resort over-
Fodor'sChoice looking the sea is one of the top golf and spa destinations in the country.
★ It has the feel of an English-country manor, with exposed ceiling beams,
walls covered with tapestries, hardwood floors softened by oriental
rugs, and your own private butler, on call 24 hours a day. Dashingly
decorated rooms and suites have water or golf-course views. The lodge
serves as the clubhouse for the Sea Island Golf Club (though the name
is misleading—all of the facilities are on St. Simons Island). Seaside, the
first of three courses built here, was inspired by St. Andrews in Scotland
and has breathtaking panoramas of coastal Georgia. **Pros:** fantastic
golfing; elegant interiors. **Cons:** only guests can visit the restaurants
or bars. ⊠*St. Simons Island* ☎888/732–4752 ⊕*www.seaisland.com*

➳*40 rooms, 2 suites* ☾*In-room: refrigerator, DVD, Internet. In-hotel: restaurant, bar, golf courses, tennis court, pool, spa, children's programs (ages 3–19)* ▤*AE, D, DC, MC, V.*

$–$$ ▦ **Sea Palms Golf and Tennis Resort.** If you're looking for an active getaway, this contemporary complex could be the place for you—it has golf, tennis, a fitness center loaded with state-of-the-art equipment, a beach club, sand-pit volleyball, horseshoes, and bicycling. The guest rooms, touted to be the largest standard rooms in the Golden Isles, have balconies with views of the Marshes of Glynn and the golf course. **Pros:** guests have beach club privileges. **Cons:** the furnishings are somewhat unimaginative. ⊠*5445 Frederica Rd.* ☎*912/638–3351 or 800/841–6268* ⊕*www.seapalms.com* ➳*112 rooms, 23 suites, 11 villas* ☾*In-hotel: 2 restaurants, golf course, tennis courts, pools, gym, bicycles* ▤*AE, DC, MC, V.*

SPORTS AND THE OUTDOORS

BIKING   St. Simons has an extensive network of bicycle trails, and you can ride on the beach as well. **Ocean Motion** (⊠*1300 Ocean Blvd.* ☎*912/638–5225 or 800/669–5215*) rents bikes for the entire family, from trail bikes to beach bikes to seats for infants. At **Wheel Fun** (⊠*532 Ocean Blvd., just off intersection with Mallory St.* ☎*912/634–0606*) you can rent anything from multispeed bikes to double surreys with bimini tops that look like antique cars and carry four people.

GOLF   The top-flight golf facilities at the Lodge at Sea Island are available only to members and guests, but St. Simons has two other high-quality courses open to the general public. **The Hampton Club** (⊠*100 Tabbystone St.* ☎*912/634–0255* ⊕*www.hamptonclub.com*), at the north end of St. Simons on the site of an 18th-century cotton, rice, and indigo plantation, is a *Golf Digest* "Places to Play" 4-star winner. The par-72 course designed by Joe Lee lies amid towering oaks, salt marshes, and lagoons. **Sea Palms Golf and Tennis Resort** (⊠*5445 Frederica Rd.* ☎*912/638–3351 or 800/841–6268* ⊕*www.seapalms.com*), on a former cotton plantation, offers 27 holes of golf and a driving range.

KAYAKING AND SAILING   After an instructional clinic, head off to explore the marsh creeks, coastal waters, and beaches with **Ocean Motion** (⊠*1300 Ocean Blvd.* ☎*912/638–5225 or 800/669–5215*), which has been giving kayaking tours of St. Simons for more than 20 years. If sailing is your thing, try **Barry's Beach Service** (⊠*On the beach, near the Beach Club North Breaker Condominiums* ☎*912/638–8053 or 800/669–5215*) for Hobie Cat rentals and lessons in front of the King and Prince Beach and Golf Resort on Arnold Road. Barry's also rents kayaks, boogie boards, and beach funcycles (low, reclining bikes), and conducts guided ecotours.

JEKYLL ISLAND

18 mi south of St. Simons Island, 90 mi south of Savannah.

For 56 winters, between 1886 and 1942, America's rich and famous faithfully came south to Jekyll Island. Through the Gilded Age, World War I, the Roaring '20s, and the Great Depression, Vanderbilts and Rockefellers, Morgans and Astors, Macys, Pulitzers, and Goodyears shuttered their 5th Avenue castles and retreated to elegant "cottages" on their wild coastal island. It's been said that when the island's distinguished winter residents were all "in," a sixth of the world's wealth was represented. Early in World War II the millionaires departed for the last time. In 1947 the state of Georgia purchased the entire island for the bargain price of $675,000.

Jekyll Island is still a 7½-mi playground, but it's no longer restricted to the rich and famous. A water park, picnic grounds, and facilities for golf, tennis, fishing, biking, and jogging are all open to the public. One side of the island is lined by nearly 10 mi of hard-packed Atlantic beaches; the other by the Intracoastal Waterway and picturesque salt marshes. Deer and wild turkeys inhabit interior forests of pine, magnolia, and moss-veiled live oaks. Egrets, pelicans, herons, and sandpipers skim the gentle surf. Jekyll Island's clean, mostly uncommercialized public beaches are free and open year-round. Bathhouses with restrooms, changing areas, and showers are open at regular intervals along the beach. Beachwear, suntan lotion, rafts, snacks, and drinks are available at the Jekyll Shopping Center, facing the beach at Beachview Drive. Visitors must pay a fee of $3, which is used to support conservation of the island's natural and cultural resources.

GETTING HERE AND AROUND
Jekyll Island is connected to the mainland by the Sidney Lanier Bridge. Once on the island, you'll need a car or a bicycle to get around.

ESSENTIALS
Visitor Information Jekyll Island Welcome Center (⊠ *1 Downing Musgrove Causeway, Jekyll Island* ☎ *912/635–3636* ⊕ *www.jekyllisland.com*).

EXPLORING
The **Georgia Sea Turtle Center,** a new must-see on Jekyll Island, aims to increase awareness of habitat and wildlife conservation challenges for the endangered loggerhead turtles through turtle rehabilitation, research, and education programs. The center includes educational exhibits and a "hospital," where visitors can view rescued turtles, which lay their eggs along Jekyll Island beaches from May through August, and read their stories. ⊠ *214 Stable Rd.* ☎ *912/635–4444* ⊕ *www. georgiaseaturtlecenter.org* ⊠ *$6* ☉ *Daily 10–6.*

The **Jekyll Island History Center** gives tram tours of the Jekyll Island National Historic Landmark District. Tours originate at the museum's visitor center on Stable Road four times a day. Tours at 11 and 2 include two millionaires' residences in the 240-acre historic district. Faith Chapel, illuminated by stained-glass windows, including one Tiffany original, is open daily 2–4. ⊠ *100 Stable Rd., I–95, Exit 29* ☎ *912/635–4036* 🖶 *912/635–4004* ⊕ *www.jekyllisland.com* ⊠ *$10–$17.50* ☉ *Daily 9–5; tours daily, 10, 11, 2, and 4.*

☾ **Summer Waves** is an 11-acre park using more than a million gallons of water in its 18,000-square-foot wave pool, water slides, children's activity pool with two slides, and circular river for tubing and rafting. Inner tubes and life vests are provided at no extra charge. ⊠ *210 S. Riverview Dr.* ☎ *912/635–2074* ⊕ *www.summerwaves.com* ⊠ *$19.95* ☉ *Late May–early Sept., Sun.–Thurs. 10–6, Sat. 10–8; hrs vary at beginning and end of season.*

**OFF THE
BEATEN
PATH**

Driftwood Beach. If you've ever wondered about the effects of erosion on barrier islands, head at low tide to this oceanfront boneyard on North Beach, where live oaks and pines are being consumed by the sea at an alarming rate. The snarl of trunks and limbs and the dramatic, massive root systems of upturned trees are an eerie and intriguing tableau of nature's slow and steady power. It's been estimated that nearly 1,000 feet of Jekyll's beach have been lost since the early 1900s. ■TIP→**Bring your camera; the photo opportunities are terrific and this is the best place to shoot St. Simons Lighthouse.** ⊹ *Head to far north of Jekyll on Beach-view Dr. to large curve where road turns inland. When ocean is visible through forest to your right, pull over and take one of the many trails through trees to beach.*

WHERE TO EAT

$$$$
SOUTHERN
★

✕**Grand Dining Room.** The colonnaded Grand Dining Room of the Jekyll Island Club maintains a tradition of fine dining first established in the 19th century. The huge fireplace, views of the pool, and sparkling silver and crystal all contribute to the sense of old-style elegance. Signature dishes are the pistachio-crusted rack of lamb, grouper flamed with hazelnut liqueur, and the filet mignon. The menu also includes local seafood and regional dishes such as Southern fried quail salad. The wine cellar has its own label cabernet, merlot, white zinfandel, and chardonnay, made by Round Hill Vineyards. ⊠*Jekyll Island Club, 371 Riverview Dr.* ☎*912/635–2400* ⌖*Reservations essential* ☞*Jacket required* ☐*AE, D, DC, MC, V.*

$$$
SEAFOOD

✕**Latitude 31.** Right on the Jekyll Island Club Wharf, in the middle of the historic district, Latitude 31 wins the prize for best location. The menu has everything from oysters Rockefeller to seafood crepes to bourbon peach- and pecan-glazed pork tenderloin. There's also a kids' menu. ⊠*Jekyll Island Club Wharf* ☎*912/635–3800* ☐*D, MC, V* ⊗*Closed Mon.*

$$
SEAFOOD
★

✕**The Rah Bar.** A tiny swamp shack right on the end of the Jekyll Island Club Wharf (connected to Latitude 31), the Rah Bar is the place for a hands-on experience. It's elbow-to-elbow dining (unless you eat at the tables outside on the wharf) with "rah" oysters, "crawdaddies," and "u peel 'em" shrimp. As you eat, you look out on the shrimp boats and the beautiful salt-marsh sunsets. ⊠*Jekyll Island Club Wharf* ☎*912/635–3800* ☐*D, MC, V* ⊗*Closed Mon.*

$$
SEAFOOD
♺

✕**SeaJay's Waterfront Café & Pub.** A casual tavern overlooking the Jekyll Harbor Marina, SeaJay's serves delicious, inexpensive seafood, including a crab chowder that locals love. This is also the home of the wildly popular Lowcountry boil buffet: an all-you-can-eat feast of local shrimp, corn on the cob, smoked sausage, and new potatoes. There's live music Thursday through Saturday night. ■TIP→**Bring the kids, their special menus run from $3.95.** ⊠*1 Harbor Point Rd., Jekyll Harbor Marina* ☎*912/635–3200* ☐*AE, D, MC, V.*

WHERE TO STAY

$$–$$$

▦**Beachview Club.** Grand old oak trees shade the grounds of this luxury, all-suites lodging. Rooms are either on the oceanfront or have a partial ocean view; some rooms are equipped with hot tubs and gas fireplaces. Efficiencies have one king-size or two double beds, a desk, and a kitchenette. The interior design reflects an understated island theme, and the unique meeting room in the Bell Tower accommodates up to 35 people for business events. Higher-end suites have full kitchens. **Pros:** friendly and eager staff; property near the beach. **Cons:** room decor is somewhat out of date; not much for kids to do here. ⊠*721 N. Beachview Dr.* ☎*912/635–2256 or 800/299–2228* 🖷*912/635–3770* ⊕*www.beachviewclub.com* ⇒*38 rooms, 6 suites* ☐*In-room: kitchen (some). In-hotel: bar, pool, bicycles, Wi-Fi, parking (free)* ▤*AE, D, DC, MC, V.*

$$$–$$$$ 🖾 **Jekyll Island Club Hotel.** This sprawling 1886 resort was once described
★ as "the richest, the most exclusive, the most inaccessible club in the world." Not so today. The comfortable resort's focal point is a four-story clubhouse, with its wraparound verandas and Queen Anne–style towers and turrets. Rooms, suites, apartments, and cottages are decorated with mahogany beds, armoires, and plush sofas and chairs. Two beautifully restored former "millionaires' cottages"—the Crane and the Cherokee— add 23 elegant guest rooms to this gracefully groomed compound. The B&B packages are a great deal. **Pros:** on the water; old-world charm, with traditional room keys; close proximity to restaurants, shopping, and sea-turtle center. **Cons:** room decor and some appliances could use an update. ⊠*371 Riverview Dr.* ☎*912/635–2600 or 800/535–9547* 🖷*912/635–2818* ⊕*www.jekyllclub.com* ⇒*138 rooms, 19 suites* ☐*In-room: Internet, Wi-Fi. In-hotel: restaurant, bar, pool, beachfront, bicycles, Wi-Fi, parking (free)* ▤*AE, D, DC, MC, V.*

SPORTS AND THE OUTDOORS

BIKING The best way to see Jekyll is by bicycle: a long, paved trail runs right along the beach, and there's an extensive network of paths throughout the island. **Jekyll Island Mini Golf and Bike Rentals** (⊠*N. Beachview Dr. at Shell Rd.* ☎*912/635–2648*) has a wide selection, from the surrey pedal cars, which can hold four people, to lay-down cycles, to the more traditional bikes. **Wheel Fun** (⊠*60 S. Oceanview Dr.* ☎*912/635–9801*) sits right in front of the Days Inn and is easy to get to Jekyll's southern beachfront.

FISHING With 40 years of experience in local waters, Captain Vernon Reynolds of **Coastal Expeditions** (⊠*Jekyll Harbor Marina* ☎*912/265–0392* ⊕*www.coastalcharterfishing.com*) provides half-day and full-day trips in-shore and offshore for fishing, dolphin-watching, and sightseeing. Aside from his ample angling skills, Larry Crews of **Offshore Charters** (⊠*Jekyll Harbor Marina* ☎ *912/265–7529* ⊕*www.offshore-charters. com*) also offers his services as captain to tie the knot for anyone who's already landed the big one.

GOLF The **Jekyll Island Golf Club** (⊠*322 Capt. Wylly Rd.* ☎*912/635–2368*) has 63 holes, including three 18-hole, par-72 courses, and a clubhouse. Green fees are $40, good all day, and carts are $17 per person per course. The 9-hole, par-36 **Oceanside Nine** (⊠*N. Beachview Dr.* ☎*912/635–2170*) is where Jekyll Island millionaires used to play. Green fee is $22, and carts are $7.25 for every nine holes.

TENNIS The **Jekyll Island Tennis Center** (⊠*400 Capt. Wylly Rd.* ☎*912/635–3154* ⊕*www.gate.net/~jitc*) has 13 clay courts, with seven lighted for nighttime play. The facility hosts six USTA-sanctioned tournaments throughout the year and provides lessons and summer camps for juniors. Courts cost $18 per hour daily 9 AM to 10 PM. Reservations for lighted courts are required and must be made prior to 6 PM the day of play.

CUMBERLAND ISLAND NATIONAL SEASHORE

Fodor's Choice *47 mi south of Jekyll Island; 115 mi south of Savannah to St. Marys*
★ *via I–95; 45 min by ferry from St. Marys.*

Cumberland, the largest of Georgia's coastal isles, is a national treasure. The 18-mi spit of land off the coast of St. Marys is a nearly unspoiled sanctuary of marshes, dunes, beaches, forests, lakes, and ponds. And although it has a long history of human habitation, it remains much as nature created it: a dense, lacework canopy of live oak shades sand roads and foot trails through thick undergrowths of palmetto. Wild horses roam freely on pristine beaches. Waterways are homes for gators, sea turtles, otters, snowy egrets, great blue herons, ibises, wood storks, and more than 300 other species of birds. In the forests are armadillos, wild horses, deer, raccoons, and an assortment of reptiles.

In the 16th century the Spanish established a mission and a garrison, San Pedro de Mocama, on the southern end of the island. But development didn't begin in earnest until the wake of the American Revolution, with timbering operations for shipbuilding, particularly construction of warships for the early U.S. naval fleet. Cotton, rice, and indigo plantations were also established. In 1818 Revolutionary War hero Gen. "Lighthorse" Harry Lee, father of Robert E. Lee, died and was buried near the Dungeness estate of General Nathaniel Greene. Though his body was later moved to Virginia to be interred beside his son, the gravestone remains. During the 1880s the family of Thomas Carnegie (brother of industrialist Andrew) built several lavish homes here. In the 1950s the National Park Service named Cumberland Island and Cape Cod as the most significant natural areas on the Atlantic and Gulf coasts. And in 1972, in response to attempts to develop the island by Hilton Head–developer Charles Fraser, Congress passed a bill establishing the island as a national seashore. Today most of the island is part of the national park system.

GETTING HERE AND AROUND

The only access to the island is on a National Park Service ferry, the *Cumberland Queen.* Ferry bookings are heavy in summer. Cancellations and no-shows often make last-minute space available, but don't rely on it. You can make reservations up to six months in advance. ■ TIP➔ **Note that the ferry does not transport pets, bicycles, kayaks, or cars.**

EXPLORING

Though the **Cumberland Island National Seashore** is open to the public, the only public access to the island is via the *Cumberland Queen,* a reservations-only, 146-passenger ferry based near the National Park Service Information Center at St. Marys. From the Park Service docks at the island's south end, you can follow wooded nature trails, swim and sun on 18 mi of undeveloped beaches, go fishing and bird-watching, and view the ruins of Thomas Carnegie's great estate, **Dungeness.** You can also join history and nature walks led by Park Service rangers.

Bear in mind that summers are hot and humid and that you must bring everything you need, including your own food, soft drinks, sunscreen, and insect repellent. There's no public transportation on the island. ⑦ *Cumberland Island National Seashore, Box 806, St. Marys 31558* 🕾 *912/882–4335 Ext. 254* ⊕ *www.nps.gov/cuis* 🖃 *Round-trip ferry $17, day pass $4* ⊘ *Mar.–Sept., ferry departure from St. Marys daily 9* AM *and 11:45* AM; *from Cumberland, Sun.–Tues. 10:15* AM *and 4:45* PM, *Wed.–Sat. 10:15* AM, *2:45* PM, *4:45* PM. *Oct. and Nov., ferry departure from St. Marys daily 9* AM *and 11:45* AM; *from Cumberland 10:15* AM *and 4:45* PM. *Dec.–Feb., Thurs.–Sun., ferry departure from St. Marys 9* AM *and 11:45* AM, *from Cumberland 10:15* AM *and 4:45* PM.

OFF THE BEATEN PATH

The First African Baptist Church. This small, one-room church on the north end of Cumberland Island is where John F. Kennedy Jr. and Carolyn Bessette were married on September 21, 1996. Constructed of white-washed logs, it's simply adorned with a cross made of sticks tied together with string and 11 handmade pews seating 40 people. It was built in 1937 to replace a cruder 1893 structure used by former slaves from the High Point–Half Moon Bluff community. The Kennedy–Bessette wedding party stayed at the Greyfield Inn, built on the south end of the island in 1900 by the Carnegie family. ✉ *North end of Cumberland near Half Moon Bluff.*

WHERE TO EAT AND STAY

$$
SEAFOOD

✕ **Lang's Marina Restaurant.** Everything's made from scratch at this popular waterside restaurant, including the desserts. And the seafood comes fresh from the owner's boats. You can order shrimp, scallops, and oysters, or opt for the Captain's Platter and get some of everything. Fish is available fried, grilled, or blackened. ✉ *307 W. St. Marys St., near waterfront park, St. Marys* 🕾 *912/882–4432* ⊟ *MC, V* ⊘ *Closed Sun. and Mon. No dinner Tues. No lunch Sat.*

$
SEAFOOD

✕ **The Williams' Saint Marys Seafood and Steak House.** Don't let the tabby-and-porthole decor fool you. In a region rife with seafood restaurants, this one's full of locals for a reason. The food is fresh, well prepared, and plentiful, and the price rarely gets so right. The menu includes frogs' legs and alligator tail for more adventurous eaters. ✉ *1837 Osborne Rd., St. Marys* 🕾 *912/882–6875* ⊟ *MC, V.*

$$$$
★

🏠 **Greyfield Inn.** Once described as a "Tara by the sea," this turn-of-the-last-century Carnegie family home is Cumberland Island's only accommodation. Built in 1900 for Lucy Ricketson, Thomas and Lucy Carnegie's daughter, the inn is filled with period antiques, family portraits, and original furniture that evoke the country elegance of a bygone era. And with a 1,000-acre private compound, it offers a solitude that also seems a thing of the past. Prices include all meals, transportation, tours led by a naturalist, and bikes. Nonguests can dine at the restaurant ($$$$) on delicious dishes that change daily. **Pros:** air-conditioned during summer; lack of telephone service means complete solitude. **Cons:** no stores on Cumberland; communications to the mainland are limited. ✉ *Cumberland Island* 🕾 *904/261–6408 or 866/401–8581* ⊕ *www. greyfieldinn.com* ⌁ *16 rooms, 4 suites* ⌂ *In-room: no phone, no TV. In-hotel: restaurant, bar, bicycles* ⊟ *D, MC, V* ⍓ *FAP.*

SPORTS AND THE OUTDOORS

KAYAKING Whether you're a novice or skilled paddler, **Up The Creek Xpeditions** (⊠*111 Osborne St., St. Marys* ☎*912/882–0911*) can guide you on kayak tours through some of Georgia and Florida's most scenic waters. Classes include navigation, tides and currents, and kayak surfing and racing. Trips include Yulee, the St. Marys River, and the Cumberland Sound. The sunset dinner paddle includes a meal at Borrell Creek Restaurant overlooking the marsh.

OKEFENOKEE NATIONAL WILDLIFE REFUGE

Larger than all of Georgia's barrier islands combined, the Okefenokee National Wildlife Refuge covers 730 square mi of southeastern Georgia and spills over into northeastern Florida. From the air, all roads and almost all traces of human development seem to disappear into this vast, seemingly impenetrable landscape, the largest intact freshwater wetlands in the contiguous United States. The rivers, lakes, forests, prairies, and swamps all teem with seen and unseen life: alligators, otters, bobcats, raccoons, opossums, white-tailed deer, turtles, bald eagles, red tailed hawks, egrets, muskrats, herons, cranes, red-cockaded woodpeckers, and black bears all make their home here. The term *swamp* hardly does the Okefenokee justice. It's the largest peat-producing bog in the United States, with numerous and varied landscapes, including aquatic prairies, towering virgin cypress, sandy pine islands, and lush subtropical hammocks.

During the last Ice Age, 10,000 years ago, this area was part of the ocean flow. As the ocean receded, a dune line formed, which acted as a dam, forming today's refuge. The Seminole Indians named the area "Land of the Quivering Earth." And if you have the good fortune to walk one of the many bogs, you can find the earth does indeed quiver like Jell-O in a bowl.

GETTING HERE AND AROUND

There are three gateways to the refuge: an eastern entrance at the U.S. Fish and Wildlife Service headquarters in the Suwannee Canal Recreation Area, near Folkston; a northern entrance at the Okefenokee Swamp Park near Waycross; and a western entrance at Stephen C. Foster State Park, outside the town of Fargo. Visiting here can feel frustrating, because none of the parks encompass everything the refuge has to offer; you need to determine what your highest priorities are and pick your gateway on that basis. The best way to see the Okefenokee up close is to take a day trip from whichever gateway you choose. You can take an overnight canoeing-camping trip into the interior, but be aware that access is restricted by permit. Plan your visit between September and April to avoid the biting insects that emerge in May, especially in the dense interior.

SUWANNEE CANAL RECREATION AREA

8 mi southwest of Folkston via Rte. 121.

The east entrance of the Okefenokee near Folkston offers access into the core of the refuge by way of the man-made Suwannee Canal. The most extensive open areas in the park—Chesser, Grand, and Mizell

Prairies—branch off the canal and contain small natural lakes and gator holes. The prairies are excellent spots for sport fishing and birding, and it's possible to take one- and two-hour guided boat tours of the area leaving from the Okefenokee Adventures concession, near the visitor center. The concession also has equipment rentals and food at the Camp Cornelia Cafe. The visitor center has a film, exhibits, and a mechanized mannequin that tells stories about life in the Okefenokee (it sounds hokey but it's surprisingly informative). A boardwalk takes you over the water to a 50-foot observation tower. Hikers, bicyclists, and private motor vehicles are welcome on the Swamp Island Drive; several interpretive walking trails may be taken along the way. Picnicking is permitted. ⊠*Rte. 2, Box 3330, Folkston* ☎*912/496–7836* ⊕*www.fws. gov/okefenokee* ⊡*$5 per car* ⊙*Refuge: Mar.–Oct., daily ½ hr before sunrise–7:30* PM; *Nov.–Feb., daily ½ hr before sunrise–5:30* PM.

OKEFENOKEE SWAMP PARK

ℭ *8 mi south of Waycross via U.S. 1.*

This park serves as the northern entrance to the Okefenokee National Wildlife Refuge, offering easy access as well as exhibits and orientation programs good for the entire family. The park has a 1-mi nature trail, observation areas, wilderness walkways, an outdoor museum of pioneer life, and boat tours into the swamp that reveal its unique ecology. A boardwalk and 90-foot tower are excellent places to glimpse cruising gators and birds. A 1½-mi train tour (included in the admission price) passes by a Seminole village and stops at Pioneer Island, a re-created pioneer homestead, for a 30-minute walking tour. ⊠*5700 Okefenokee Swamp Park Rd., Waycross* ☎*912/283–0583* ⊟*912/283–0023* ⊕*www.okeswamp.com* ⊡*$12, plus $4–$16 for boat tours* ⊙*Daily 9–5:30.*

STEPHEN C. FOSTER STATE PARK

18 mi northeast of Fargo via Rte. 177.

Named for the songwriter who penned "Swanee River," this 80-acre island park is the southwestern entrance to the Okefenokee National Wildlife Refuge and offers trips to the headwaters of the Suwannee River, Billy's Island—site of an ancient Indian village—and a turn-of-the-20th-century town built to support logging efforts in the swamp. The park is home to hundreds of species of birds and a large cypress-and-black-gum forest, a majestic backdrop for one of the thickest growths of vegetation in the southeastern United States. Park naturalists lead boat tours and recount a wealth of Okefenokee lore while you observe alligators, birds, and native trees and plants. You may also take a self-guided excursion in a rental canoe or a motorized flat-bottom boat. Campsites and cabins are available. ⊠*Rte. 1, Box 131, Fargo* ☎*912/637–5274* ⊕*gastateparks.org/info/scfoster* ⊡*$5 per vehicle for National Wildlife Refuge* ⊙*Mar.–mid-Sept., daily 6:30* AM*–8:30* PM; *mid-Sept.–Feb., daily 7* AM*–7* PM.

Kentucky

LOUISVILLE TO LEXINGTON

WORD OF MOUTH

"In spite of being a KY native, I've only done the Derby once, five years ago. The one thing we had not known ahead of time—and it could have cost us—is that you need to show proof of your SS# in order to collect. As much as I enjoyed the races—all the color, sounds, hats both elegant and crazy—the highlight for me was seeing Walter Cronkite and his wife passing 2 feet in front of me in a golf cart! At the track, I highly recommend two things (both alcohol-related, as it turns out): a Bloody Mary at the Finlandia booth, and a mint julep, preferably from the vendor roving in the stands. On a hot day in May, there's nothing better."

—lifes2short

Updated by
Susan Reigler

Postcard views along U.S. superhighways are rare, but that's exactly what travelers zipping along Interstate Highways 64 and 75 in central Kentucky see. For many miles, the routes are bounded by rolling, fenced pastures of emerald green bluegrass where Kentucky's famous Thoroughbred racehorses graze.

Homesteading farmers brought the seeds for bluegrass, *Poa pratensis,* with them to Kentucky, where it thrived in the calcium-rich limestone soil. In the distance you can see the graceful outlines of horse owners' mansions and the equally expensive equine residences (most barns in horse country are climate-controlled).

This picturesque landscape is so famous that it's hard to imagine it as a product of agriculture, not nature. When Daniel Boone and other settlers came to the area in the 18th century, herds of bison roamed where horses now graze, and tall native cane covered fields that are now pastureland. When cities and plantations replaced stockades and log cabins, the frontier tradition of sheltering travelers evolved into the Southern hospitality still characteristic of Kentucky.

ORIENTATION AND PLANNING

GETTING ORIENTED

Visitors to Kentucky will find ample opportunities to interact with horses. You can attend horse races in Lexington or Louisville, visit museums dedicated to horses, or just enjoy the horse-rich scenery while driving along quieter roads, including Old Frankfort Pike, which meanders between farmsteads.

Louisville. Kentucky's largest city and the nation's northernmost Southern city, Louisville is best known for the Kentucky Derby, which takes place the first Saturday in May. Its handsome homes and tree-lined streets are especially beautiful in the spring.

Midway and Versailles. These two charming small towns have main streets lined with shops and restaurants and make fine stops when traveling between Louisville and Lexington.

Lexington. The state's second largest city lies in the heart of the Bluegrass region and is the center of Thoroughbred horse racing in the United States. Lexington contains several charming, historic neighborhoods; offers a variety of good restaurants; and reaps the intellectual and cultural benefit of the state's largest university.

TOP REASONS TO GO

Horse farm scenery: Tree-shaded lanes wind though some of the world's most beautiful landscape, home to the elegant Thoroughbreds that graze on the state's famous bluegrass.

Kentucky Derby Festival: Two weeks of nonstop partying lead up to the first Saturday in May and the "Most Exciting Two Minutes in Sports."

One-of-a-kind museums: You can find the world's largest baseball bat at the Louisville Slugger Museum and tiny, priceless bibelots at the Headley-Whitney Museum.

Kentucky haute cuisine: The region's chefs use locally produced ingredients in tried-and-true dishes and contemporary creations often laced with the state beverage, bourbon.

Relaxing getaways: Pamper yourself with a stay in one of Kentucky's historic bed-and-breakfasts or hotels.

4

PLANNING

WHEN TO GO

Springtime in the Kentucky Bluegrass is stunning. The pastures are deep green, bordered by blooming dogwoods and redbuds in all their white and pink glory, and foals born the previous winter frolic near their mothers in the pastures. Fall is also a fine season, and you'll be rewarded with colorful foliage along the country lanes. Summer, especially July, August, and most of September, can be hot and humid. The **Kentucky Derby Festival** takes place in the two weeks prior to **Derby Day** (the first Saturday in May) at Churchill Downs in Louisville. The annual international cross-country and steeplechase **Rolex Three-Day Event** is held during the later part of April at the Kentucky Horse Park outside Lexington.

GETTING HERE AND AROUND

AIR TRAVEL

Two airports—and virtually every American airline—serve central Kentucky. Louisville International Airport is just south of the city's downtown. Blue Grass Airport, with considerably fewer flights than Louisville, serves Lexington. The two cities are an hour apart by car.

Airport Contacts Blue Grass Airport (⊕ *www.bluegrassairport.com*). **Louisville International Airport** (⊕ *www.louintlairport.com*).

BICYCLE TRAVEL

If you ride, bring your bike to the Bluegrass. Many of the rolling, two-lane roads that run along the horse farm boundaries are favorite routes for cyclists.

CAR TRAVEL

Several interstate highways converge in Kentucky, and automobile access to the central portion of the state is excellent. I–64 passes straight through the center of Bluegrass Country, running east–west. Access from the north or the south is along I–75, which intersects with I–64 at Lexington. Take I–64 exit 58 or exit 65 for access to horse country drives. Exits 113 and 115 on the merged I–64/75 will take you into downtown Lexington. I–64 passes through downtown Louisville; the 3rd Street exit (5C) gives the best access to downtown attractions.

RESTAURANTS

There's much, much more to Kentucky cuisine than fried chicken, though the true, panfried version is one of America's great dishes. Sample traditional favorites such as salty, smoke-cured country ham, flavorfully sweet Bibb lettuce, cheddar grits, panfried quail, and, in season, venison. The must-have dessert is bread pudding with bourbon sauce. Treat yourself to a snifter of really fine bourbon as an after-dinner drink. In general, bourbons are characterized by vanilla and caramel notes and can range from fruity to spicy.

HOTELS

There are dozens of small inns and B&Bs in Kentucky, the majority of which are located in historic properties ranging from 18th-century stone houses and log cabins to ornate Victorian mansions. Just a century ago, Kentucky was dotted with 18th- and 19th-century coaching inns and the 20th-century equivalent, the cozy neocolonial motor lodge. While some of these remain, lodging options today are dominated by chains, ranging from high-end to budget.

WHAT IT COSTS				
¢	$	$$	$$$	$$$$
Restaurant	under $7	$7–$11	$12–$16	$17–$22	over $22
Hotel	under $70	$70–$110	$111–$160	$161–$220	over $220

Restaurant prices are per person for a main course at dinner. Hotel prices are for a standard double room, excluding state and local taxes.

VISITOR INFORMATION

Contacts Kentucky Department of Tourism (☎ *800/225-8747* ⊕ *www.kentuckytourism.com*).

LOUISVILLE

176 mi north of Nashville on I–65; 421 mi north of Atlanta via I–75; 560 mi west of Richmond via I–64.

Kentucky's largest city is famous for Churchill Downs racetrack and the Kentucky Derby. It's also the hometown of boxing legend Muhammad Ali. Louisville was founded in 1778 when George Rogers Clark, leading a group of settlers and soldiers, decided to stop at the Falls of the Ohio, a rock outcropping into a river containing the world's largest exposed Devonian fossil bed. Louisville is often considered the "Gateway to the South" as a Midwestern sensibility pervades this most northern of southern cities.

Natives can't seem to agree on how to pronounce its name: "*Loo*-uh-vuhl" is common, as is "*Lull*-vuhl." Don't get caught pronouncing it "*Lew*-is-ville," which is all wrong, considering the city was named after

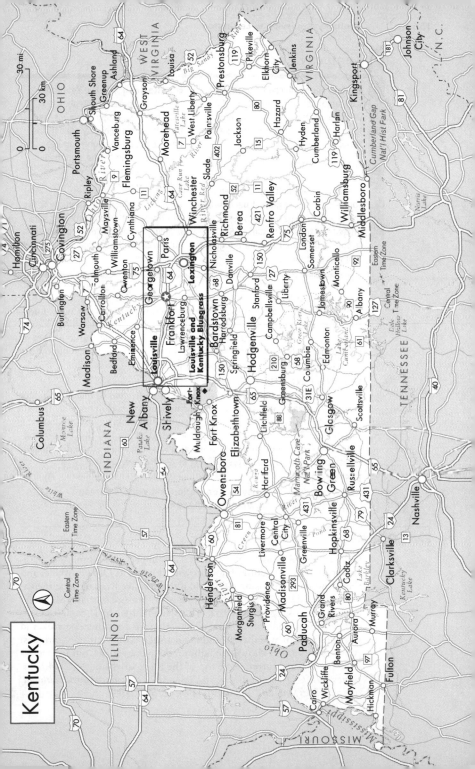

Kentucky

CLOSE UP

Kentucky Facts

■ **State Name:** Accounts of the origin vary, but most agree that Kentucky is an Indian name—possibly Wyandot for "Land of Tomorrow" or Iroquois for "Land of Meadows."

■ **State Capital:** Frankfort. This small city of 27,000 on the Kentucky River is approximately halfway between Louisville and Lexington. It became the capital in 1792 when its residents offered the then-hefty sum of $3,000 to state legislators to locate the government seat there.

■ **State Song:** "My Old Kentucky Home," composed by Stephen Collins Foster, was supposedly inspired by visits to his Kentucky cousins in Bardstown. It's the song you hear sung every year by the sentimental, bourbon-dampened crowd at the Kentucky Derby.

■ **Greatest Paradox:** Kentucky is the world's largest producer of bourbon, distilling about 95% of all produced, but almost half the state's 120 counties are dry.

King Louis XVI by veterans of the American Revolutionary War in gratitude for the help France gave the colonies. That's the same Louis who was married to Marie Antoinette and who lost his head in his own country's revolution. There's a larger-than-life marble statue of him at the corner of 6th and Jefferson Streets in downtown Louisville on the grounds of City Hall, head firmly in place.

GETTING HERE AND AROUND
You'll need a car to get around in Louisville. All areas of the city connect via expressways and parkways leading out from downtown. Transit Authority of River City (TARC) provides bus service throughout the city but is only convenient along a handful of routes. Beware of Spaghetti Junction, the tangle of ramps and looping lanes at the downtown riverfront where Interstates 65, 71, and 64 converge.

ESSENTIALS
Visitor Information Louisville Convention and Visitors Bureau (☎ *800/626–5646* ⊕ *www.gotolouisville.com*).

EXPLORING

Conrad–Caldwell House. The residential neighborhood of imposing Victorian mansions just south of downtown is known as Old Louisville, and there's no more imposing edifice than the massive Romanesque revival Conrad–Caldwell House, at the corner of St. James Court and Magnolia Street, overlooking Central Park. The opulent home of Theophilus Conrad, who made millions in timber, has elaborate exterior stonework and intricate interior woodwork and is furnished with Victorian antiques. Alas, visitors aren't allowed to light up their stogies on Conrad's smoking balcony, on a turret at the top of the three-story house. ✉ *1402 St. James Ct., Old Louisville* ☎ *502/636–5023* ⊕ *www.conradcaldwell. org* ✉*$5* ☾*Sun. and Wed.–Fri. noon–4, Sat. 10–4.*

★ **Falls of the Ohio Fossil Beds.** Cross the Second Street Bridge to Clarksville, Indiana, to visit the Falls of the Ohio State Park, site of the world's largest exposed Devonian fossil bed. Four hundred million years ago this was an inland sea full of flora and fauna; today this layer of limestone contains the fossil record of 600 plant and animal species, such as corals and armored fishes. It is best to visit in late summer, when the water level is low. There is an admission fee to the Interpretive Center, but no charge to walk about the park. ⊠ *201 Riverside Dr., Clarksville, IN* ☎ *812/280–9970* ⊕ *www.fallsoftheohio.org* ⛳ *$5* ☯ *Mon.–Sat. 9–5, Sun. 1–5.*

> ### HISTORY YOU CAN SEE
>
> Kentucky was the 15th state and the first west of the Appalachian Mountains. General George Rogers Clark, who founded Louisville, captured the Northwest Territory from the British during the Revolutionary War. Frontiersman Daniel Boone traversed the state, and many historic markers in Kentucky document his activities. The countryside still contains many 18th- and 19th-century stone or brick buildings and even a few log cabins. Most of the historic home museums in the region are linked to important Civil War–era figures, such as Abraham Lincoln and members of the Clay family.

Fodor's Choice **Kentucky Derby Museum.** The horse
★ race itself lasts only two minutes, but the exhibits at the Derby Museum will keep you enthralled for hours. The Greatest Race—a heart-pounding movie shown on a 360-degree screen—depicts the drama and traditions of training a Thoroughbred to race in the Derby. Interactive exhibits encourage you to place a bet, shoe a horse, and even mount a scale-model racehorse with a "jockeycam" to show you a rider's perspective. ⊠ *704 Central Ave., South Louisville* ☎ *502/637–1111* ⊕ *www.derbymuseum.org* ⛳ *$10* ☯ *Mar. 15–Nov. 30, Mon.–Sat. 8–5, Sun. 11–5; Dec. 1–Mar. 14, Mon.–Sat. 9–5, Sun. 11–5.*

★ **Locust Grove.** About 15 minutes east of downtown on River Road (a Kentucky Scenic Byway) is a stoplight at Blankenbaker Lane with signs pointing to Locust Grove. The Georgian mansion, one of the area's earliest residences, was built in 1790 by William Croghan, who was married to Louisville founder George Rogers Clark's sister Lucy. Situated on 55 rolling acres, the plantation includes a formal garden and several outbuildings. The house is furnished with period antiques and contains an impressive ballroom, a marvelously elegant space in this very civilized frontier house. ⊠ *561 Blankenbaker La., St. Matthews* ☎ *502/897–9845* ⊕ *www.locustgrove.org* ⛳ *$8* ☯ *Mon.–Sat. 10–4:30, Sun. 1–4:30.*

☯ **Louisville Science Center.** This refurbished dry goods warehouse, sporting a brightly painted cast-iron facade, contains hands-on natural history and technology exhibits. Highlights include a space gallery with a replica of an Apollo capsule and an exhibit on human anatomy and physiology. The four-story IMAX theater, which shows a changing selection of nature-based films, has separate admission. ⊠ *727 W. Main St., Downtown* ☎ *502/561–6100* ⊕ *www.louisvillescience.org* ⛳ *$12* ☯ *Mon.–Thurs. 9:30–5, Fri. and Sat. 9:30–9, Sun. noon–6.*

Louisville Slugger Museum & Factory. You can't miss this place—a seven-story baseball bat leans against the building housing the museum and bat factory. (An appropriately sized baseball is embedded in one window of the plate-glass factory next door, too.) Step up to the plate at the scary virtual pitching diamond, and see autographed bats of virtually every baseball great. The last tour begins one hour before close. ☒*800 W. Main St., Downtown* ☎*502/588–7228* ⊕*www.sluggermuseum.org* ⛫*$10* ⊙*Mid-Aug.–June 30, Mon.–Sat. 9–5, Sun. noon–5; July 1–mid-Aug., Mon.–Sat. 9–6, Sun. noon–6.*

Louisville Zoo. More than 1,300 animals from around the world live in these landscaped settings, including the Gorilla Forestand Lorikeet Landing, where birds will perch on your shoulder. Other zoo residents include polar bears, lions, tigers, penguins, timber wolves, and Komodo dragons. ☒*1100 Trevilian Way, Highlands* ☎*502/459–2181* ⊕*www.louisvillezoo.org* ⛫*$12* ⊙*Mar.–June, daily 10–5; July and Aug., Sun.–Wed. 10–5, Thurs.–Sat. 10–8; Sept.–Feb., daily 10–4.*

Speed Art Museum. More than 6,000 years of art history are represented in this extremely accessible museum located at the edge of the University of Louisville's campus. Notable installations include the Satterwhite Gallery of Renaissance and baroque tapestries and textiles, European and American paintings, a modern sculpture court, and an interactive gallery for children called Art Sparks. The museum regularly hosts traveling exhibits of national and international significance. ☒*2035 S. 3rd St., Old Louisville* ☎*502/634–2700* ⊕*www.speedmuseum.org* ⛫*Free; fee for special exhibits* ⊙*Tues., Wed., and Fri. 10:30–4, Thurs. 10:30–8, Sat. 10:30–5, Sun. noon–5.*

OFF THE BEATEN PATH

Abraham Lincoln Birthplace National Historic Site. The 16th president was born in a one-room log cabin on his parents' Kentucky farm on February 12, 1809. A replica log cabin inside a stone memorial is reached by climbing 56 steps, one for each year of Lincoln's life. The visitor center has a series of exhibits, including a short film about the Great Emancipator. ☒*2995 Lincoln Farm Rd. (U.S. 31E), Hodgenville* ☎*270/358–3137* ⊕*www.nps.gov/abli* ⛫*Free* ⊙*Daily Labor Day–Memorial Day, 8–4:45; Memorial Day–Labor Day, 8–6:45.*

Fodor's Choice ★

Mammoth Cave National Park. This cave system, which began forming 350 million years ago when what is now the southeastern United States was located 10 degrees south of the equator and was covered by a shallow tropical ocean, is the longest in the world. More than 365 mi of passageways have been explored, and the deepest level is 379 feet below the surface. A variety of guided tours at different levels, from an easy 1¼-hour tour to a strenuous six-hour tour, are offered, emphasizing geology, history, or animal life. ☒*1 Mammoth Cave Pkwy.* ⊹*take the Park City exit off I-65 and follow the signs to the park* ☎*270/758–2180* ⊕*www.nps.gov/maca/index.htm* ⛫*Cave tours $5–$48* ⊙*Daily 8–6:15.*

WHERE TO EAT

$$$$
AMERICAN
Fodor's Choice
★

✕ 211 Clover Lane Restaurant. The light, airy interior and pebble-covered patios of this restaurant evoke the South of France, and its menu takes advantage of the traditions of the American South with a suitably Continental accent. Chicken fricassee is laced with garlic, and trout meunière (dredged in flour, fried, and served with a brown butter sauce) is made with local fish. The wine list has been carefully selected to complement the cuisine. ⊠*211 Clover La., St. Matthews* ☎*502/896–9570* ⊟*AE, MC, V* ⊕*www.211cloverlane.com* ⊘*Closed Mon. No dinner Sun.*

$$$$
SOUTHERN
★

✕ Bourbon's Bistro. If you want to learn more about Kentucky's amber elixir, this is the place to come—it has virtually every bourbon currently in production (more than 130 of them) and offers tasting flights of different styles. The menu, which ranges from a stacked burger to lobster cakes, includes southern favorites like pan-seared pork chop and bacon-wrapped scallops. Naturally, bourbon is an ingredient in many dishes. ⊠*2255 Frankfort Ave., Crescent Hill* ☎*502/894–8838* ⊕*www.bourbonsbistro.com* ⊟*AE, MC, V.*

$$$–$$$$
FRENCH
Fodor's Choice
★

✕ Lilly's. Chef–proprietor Kathy Cary is Kentucky's most honored chef. She emphasizes local ingredients in dishes with Southern and Continental influences, reflecting her twin loves of Europe and her native Kentucky. Cary's creations range from Kentucky tapas to a nightly version of veal scallopine (sauces and sides change). Lovers of lamb will always be happy with that dish's preparation here. Menus change with the seasons to take advantage of local produce. The intimate, contemporary purple and deep green dining rooms will make you feel like you're dining in an elegant private home. ⊠*1147 Bardstown Rd., Highlands* ☎*502/451–0447* ⊕*www.lillyslapeche.com* ⊟*AE, MC, V* ⊘*Closed Sun. and Mon.*

$$$$
AMERICAN
Fodor's Choice
★

✕ Limestone. This restaurant serves up high-end comfort food, including a flatiron steak and grilled chicken with white beans and country ham. Grilled chops or fish come with sides such as crawfish corn pudding or the "grits du jour." Traditional à la carte Southern sides include fried green tomatoes and buttermilk mashed potatoes. Both the wine and bourbon lists are excellent. ⊠*10001 Forest Green Blvd., Lyndon* ☎*502/426–7477* ⊕*www.limestonerestaurant.com* ⊟*AE, D, MC, V* ⊘*No dinner Sun.*

$–$$
SOUTHERN

✕ Lynn's Paradise Cafe. Formica and Bakelite are the decorator materials, not to mention the toys and mismatched salt and pepper shakers on the tables. You'll know you've arrived at the right place when you see the concrete animals in the parking lot. Big portions at breakfast, lunch, and dinner are a hallmark. Southern specialties in the morning include biscuits and gravy and pancakes made with grits. Comfort food at lunch and dinner ranges from meatloaf to roast turkey in the evening. ⊠*984 Barret Ave., Highlands* ☎*502/583–3447* ⊕*www.lynnsparadisecafe.com* ⊟*AE, MC, V*

$$$$
AMERICAN

✕ The Oakroom. The beautiful, oak-lined, formal dining room of the Seelbach Hotel was originally the luxury hostelry's billiards room. The private nook off of the main room housed card games, including those played by visitor Al Capone. Dishes are in a haute Kentucky style: spoonfish caviar, bourbon mash bread, farm-raised buffalo, Kentucky lamb, and Appalachian-foraged ginger. The most extensive wine cellar in the state has some 1,400 bottles. Sunday brunch is as elegant as the dinners. ✉ *500 S. 4th St., Downtown* ☎ *502/585–3200* ⊕ *www.seelbachhilton.com* ⚑ *Reservations essential* ☰ *AE, D, MC, V.* ⊙ *Closed Sun. No lunch Mon.*

$$$$ ✕ **Pat's Steak House.** Tender, bacon-wrapped fillets come with traditional
STEAK sides such as baked potatoes and lima beans. If you're not in a red meat
★ mood, both the fried chicken and rich fried chicken livers are first-rate, too. The former coach stop housed in a two-story brick structure near downtown has many cozy dining rooms. Bourbon Manhattans are excellent and generously portioned. ✉ *2437 Brownsboro Rd., Clifton* ☎ *502/893–2062* ⊕ *www.patssteakhouselouisville.com* ☰ *No credit cards* ⊙ *Closed Sun.*

$$–$$$ ✕ **Science Hill Inn.** Country ham, panfried chicken, and grits soufflé
SOUTHERN dominate the traditional menu at Science Hill Inn, where the Georgian dining room was once part of an exclusive girls' college preparatory school. Be sure to try the splendid hot water corn bread—crunchy on the outside and tender within. Naturally you should end your meal with the bread pudding with bourbon sauce. ✉ *525 Washington St., Shelbyville* ☎ *502/633–2825* ⚑ *Reservations essential* ☰ *AE, MC, V* ⊙ *Closed Mon.*

$$ ✕ **Uptown Cafe.** Pasta dishes, including the signature duck ravioli, come
AMERICAN in whole or half portions. This stylish café serves up many hot sandwiches as well as grilled entrées, excellent dinner salads and veal, seafood, beef, and vegetarian dishes. Most of the very reasonably priced wines are available by the glass. ✉ *1624 Bardstown Rd., Highlands* ☎ *502/458–4212* ⊕ *www.uptownlouisville.com* ☰ *AE, D, MC, V* ⊙ *Closed Sun.*

WHERE TO STAY

$$$$ 🏨 **Brown Hotel.** Opened in 1923, this grand-but-intimate hotel has a
Fodor'sChoice gilded second-floor lobby that gleams with marble and polished wood.
★ Rooms are furnished with fine reproductions and luxurious bedding. A special Louisville dish, the Hot Brown, was invented here—you can order the turkey, bacon, and cheese sandwich–casserole hybrid from room service. **Pros:** great bar in lobby with lots of comfortable seating; outstanding concierge service; airport shuttle. **Cons:** hotel restaurant, English Grill, closed on Sunday and Monday. ✉ *335 W. Broadway, Downtown* ☎ *502/583–1234* ⊕ *www.brownhotel.com* ⇒ *293 rooms* ⚑ *In-room: refrigerator (some), DVD (some), Internet. In-hotel: 3 restaurants, room service, 2 bars, gym, laundry service, Wi-Fi, parking (paid), some pets allowed, no-smoking rooms* ☰ *AE, D, DC, MC, V.*

$$ 🏨 **Central Park Bed & Breakfast.** This welcoming limestone Italianate house built in 1884 overlooks Louisville's Central Park. Period details include ornate plaster and woodwork throughout. The eight spacious guest rooms (some are suites) are furnished with antiques, and all have private baths and working fireplaces. Full breakfast is one of many creature comforts. **Pros:** overlooks Olmsted-designed park with walking/jogging paths and tennis courts; close to downtown; quiet. **Cons:** no elevator; on-street parking. ✉ *1353 S. 4th St., Old Louisville*

☎502/638–1505 🌐*www.centralparkbandb.com* 8 *rooms* *In-room: DVD, Internet* *AE, D, MC, V* *BP.*

$$–$$$ **The Galt House.** The 25-story Galt House is the only hotel on Louisville's riverfront and has all kinds of welcoming public areas, including a top-floor restaurant, a bourbon bar, and a lounge inspired by London's Crystal Palace. **Pros:** river view; 24-hour deli; spacious rooms; airport shuttle. **Cons:** slow elevators, especially when a convention is in residence. ✉*140 N. 4th St.* ☎*502/589–5201* 🌐*www.galthouse.com* *1,290 rooms* *In-room: refrigerator (some), DVD (some), Internet. In-hotel: 3 restaurants, room service, 3 bars, gym, laundry service, Wi-Fi, parking (paid), no-smoking rooms* *AE, D, DC, MC, V.*

LOUISVILLE'S RIVER WALK

To explore Louisville's river heritage, set aside some time to walk the 6.9-mi **River Walk,** which stretches west from Waterfront Park to Chickasaw Park. In some spots the paved pathway is right down by the water, and in others it winds through bosky parkland; you'll forget you're so close to a city. Best of all is the overlook near 26th Street of the McAlpine Lock & Dam, where coal barges and passenger boats are eased around the Falls of the Ohio.

$$–$$$ ★ **Inn at the Park.** This impressive, red stone, Richardson Romanesque mansion next to Central Park has five rooms and two suites, all with private baths, and is decorated throughout with period antiques, reproductions, and fine art. A full breakfast is served and may be requested for early morning. **Pros:** one-touch working fireplaces in some rooms; exceptionally large rooms; private garden. **Cons:** on-street parking. ✉*1332 S. 4th St., Old Louisville* ☎*502/637–6930* 🌐*www.innatpark.com* *8 rooms* *In-room: DVD, Internet* *AE, D, MC, V* *BP.*

$$$ FodorsChoice ★ **Seelbach Hilton Hotel.** Seven U.S. presidents and such notables as gangster Al Capone and author F. Scott Fitzgerald (who set a scene of his novel *The Great Gatsby* here) have stayed at this historic hotel, which celebrated its 100th anniversary in 2005. Check out the live jazz in the bar off the lobby before retiring to your four-poster for the night. **Pros:** central location; great bourbon list in bar. **Cons:** next door to entertainment district full of chain restaurants and noisy crowds on weekends. ✉*500 S. 4th St.* ☎*502/585–3200* 🌐*www.seelbachhilton.com* *321 rooms* *In-room: refrigerator (some), Internet. In-hotel: 3 restaurants, room service, 2 bars, gym, spa, laundry service, parking (paid), some pets allowed, no-smoking rooms* *AE, D, DC, MC, V.*

$–$$ ★ **Tucker House Bed & Breakfast.** This 1840s farmhouse is on five wooded acres about 20 minutes from downtown Louisville and an hour from horse country. The owners, who serve multicourse gourmet breakfasts (you won't be hungry again until dinnertime), have handsomely furnished the house with period antiques. ■ **TIP→Weekday rates are lower than weekend stays.** **Pros:** beautifully restored house; quiet at night. **Cons:** nearby industrial park is expanding and encroaching on the view. ✉*2406 Tucker Station Rd., Jeffersontown* ☎*502/297–8007* 🌐*www.tuckerhouse1840.com* *4 rooms* *In-hotel: pool* *AE, MC, V* *BP.*

4

NIGHTLIFE AND THE ARTS

Louisville's two entertainment centers are Downtown (with the main performing arts center, restaurants, hotels, and Louisville Slugger Field) and along the Bardstown Road corridor just east of Downtown (with restaurants, a street scene, and boutique shops). Fourth Street Live, two blocks bounded by Jefferson Street and Muhammad Ali Boulevard., contains many restaurants, clubs, and bars.

Kentucky Center (⊠ *5 Riverfront Plaza at Main St., Downtown* ☎ *502/584–7777* ⊕ *www.kentuckycenter.org*) is home to the Louisville Orchestra, Kentucky Opera, Louisville Ballet, and the traveling Broadway Series.

More than 200 plays have had their premiers at **Actors Theatre** (⊠ *316 W. Main St., Downtown* ☎ *502/584–1205* ⊕ *www.actorstheatre.org*) during the annual Humana Festival of New American Plays (March). The Tony Award–winning regional company stages a variety of plays throughout the year.

SPORTS AND THE OUTDOORS

The family-friendly **Louisville Slugger Field** (⊠ *401 E. Main St., Downtown* ☎ *502/212–2287* ⊕ *www.batsbaseball.com*) is the home of the AAA-International League Louisville Bats, the main feeder team to the major League Cincinnati Reds.

Churchill Downs (⊠ *700 Central Ave., South Louisville* ☎ *502/636–4400* ⊕ *www.churchilldowns.com*), the historic race track with trademark Twin Spires, is the home of the Kentucky Derby. Racing is held for several weeks each spring and fall.

SHOPPING

In many ways, Louisville's true "downtown" is **Bardstown Road** (⊠ *At the east terminus of Broadway and going east to Taylorsville Rd., Highlands*) with its variety of locally owned eateries, coffee houses, shops, and a colorful street scene.

MIDWAY AND VERSAILLES

60 mi east of Louisville on I–64.

Set among the picturesque horse farms of the Inner Bluegrass, the historic towns of Midway and Versailles each have Main Streets lined with antiques shops and eclectic eateries that are lovely places to stop for lunch and a little shopping while sightseeing in horse country.

Equus Run Vineyards. Thirty-five rolling acres are planted with several kinds of grapes, but you won't mistake this for Napa Valley. As the name suggests, horses are grazing in the bluegrass pasture just over the fence. A tasting room and gift shop offer the estate-made wines, and in summer you can enjoy the gardens and evening concerts in the amphitheater. ⊠ *1220 Moore's Mill Rd., Midway* ☎ *859/846–9463*

CLOSE UP

Kentucky Bourbon

An important component of dining and entertaining in Kentucky is the "sippage." Given the ready supply of corn for fermenting and white oak for making barrels, Kentucky became an important whiskey-making center early in its history. By law bourbon is distilled from fermented grain that must be at least 51% corn. Other grains in the formula (the "mash bill") are barley and rye or wheat; wheated bourbons tend to be fruitier, while those containing rye are spicier. After fermentation, the whiskey must be aged in charred, never-before-used white oak barrels for at least two years. Most are aged for five to seven years.

Bourbon is definitely the state beverage. Locals drink it before dinner with a splash of water ("bourbon and branch") or in cocktails such as the old-fashioned (invented in Louisville in the 19th century) or the Manhattan. Favorite brands are Woodford Reserve, Maker's Mark, and Buffalo Trace. After dinner, high-proof bourbons with multiple layers of flavors are savored in snifters. Pappy Van Winkle, Wild Turkey Russell's Reserve, and Booker's are among the best; a drop or two of water releases their complex bouquets.

To get a taste of it all, you can tour eight distilleries—Buffalo Trace, Four Roses, Heaven Hill, Jim Beam, Maker's Mark, Tom Moore, Wild Turkey, and Woodford Reserve—along the **Kentucky Bourbon Trail** (⊕ *www.kybourbontrail.com*).

4

⊕ *www.equusrunvineyards.com* ✉ *Free; additional charge for concerts* ☉ *Nov.–Mar., Tues.–Sat. 11–5; Apr.–Oct., Tues.–Sat. 11–7.*

Fodor's Choice **Woodford Reserve Distillery.** Limestone buildings dating from the early
★ 19th century have been restored to operation for distilling, aging, and bottling Woodford Reserve bourbon. At the end of the distillery tour, guests 21 and over can sample the whiskey—the only Kentucky bourbon made in copper stills like those used to produce scotch. This distillery is one of eight along the Kentucky Bourbon Trail. ✉ *7855 McCracken Pike, Versailles* ☎ *859/879–1812* ⊕ *www.woodfordreserve.com* ✉ *$5* ☉ *Apr.–Oct., Tues.–Sat. 9–5, Sun. 12:30–4:30.*

WHERE TO EAT AND STAY

$$$–$$$$ ✕**Bistro La Belle.** The decor here is half horse country, half Left Bank, and
SOUTHERN completely welcoming. There's a very good wine list to pair with entrées that include lamb, duck, quail, trout, and pike. Cornmeal-crusted oysters are a recommended starter, and many of the desserts are laced with bourbon. ✉ *121 E. Main St., Midway* ☎ *859/846–4233* ⊕ *bistrolabelle.googlepages.com* ▤ *D, MC, V* ☉ *Closed Sun.–Tues.*

$$$$ ✕**Holly Hill Inn.** Chef-owner Ouita Michel uses locally grown meats and
ECLECTIC produce to create her five-course prix-fixe menus, which change every
Fodor's Choice two weeks and may be southern, French, Southwestern, or any cuisine
★ that strikes her fancy. The restaurant has multiple dining rooms in an old southern mansion with a wraparound porch, where alfresco dining is offered in summer. Wine pairings are available for an additional

charge. ⊠*426 N. Winter St., Midway* ☎*859/846–4732* ⊕*www.hollyhillinn.com* ✍ *Reservations essential* ☰*AE, MC, V* ⊗*Closed Mon. and Tues.*

¢ ✕**Wallace Station.** This popular breakfast and lunch spot in a former
AMERICAN train depot serves homemade soups and gourmet sandwiches, with offerings that will appeal to both vegetarians and meat-eaters. You can often see exercise riders from nearby horse farms eating here in coveralls graced with farm logos. ⊠*3854 Old Frankfort Pike, Versailles* ☎*859/846–5161* ⊕*www.wallacestation.com* ☰ *AE, MC, V.*

$$$–$$$$ ▦**A Storybook Inn.** This house in downtown Versailles built in 1843 has a spacious garden accented with stone fences and a well-stocked library that add to the relaxing atmosphere. Some of the luxuriously appointed bedroom suites furnished with antiques also have working fireplaces. **Pros:** quiet; private. **Cons:** car needed to visit any Bluegrass region attractions; restaurant only serves breakfast. ⊠*227 Rose Hill Ave., Versailles* ☎*877/270–2563* ⊕*www.storybook-inn.com* ⌑*5 rooms* ⌕*In-room: no phone, refrigerator, DVD. In-hotel: restaurant, bar, Internet terminal, parking (free), no-smoking rooms* ☰*AE, D, MC, V* ⊗*Closed Christmas Eve to Valentine's Day.*

LEXINGTON

Known as the "Horse Capital of the World," the countryside surrounding Lexington is home to nearly 500 farms breeding Thoroughbred and standardbred horses. If you want to devote your trip to touring equine-related attractions, this is the place to start. The images most outsiders conjure when they think of Kentucky—rolling green countryside dotted with manicured horse farms and antebellum mansions—can be found here in abundance. About half of the state's renowned bourbon distilleries are in this area, too.

Arts and education thrive in this modern city, home to many historic sites, museums, a resident symphony orchestra, art galleries, and the University of Kentucky. Victorian Square, a complex of restored red-brick 19th-century warehouses, contains retail stores and restaurants. A good way to get a feel for Lexington is to tour some of its many historic houses.

GETTING HERE AND AROUND

Public transportation is limited, so a car is essential for getting around the city and nearby attractions. The tree-lined, two-lane roads—notably Paris Pike and Old Frankfort Pike—that wind through horse farm country are very popular with bicyclists, too.

Downtown streets are mostly one-way. Don't make the mistake of getting on New Circle Road thinking you'll skirt around the city center. It's a strip-mall-lined nightmare with closely spaced stoplights.

ESSENTIALS

Visitor Information Lexington Convention and Visitors Bureau
(☎*800/845–3959* ⊕ *www.visitlex.com*).

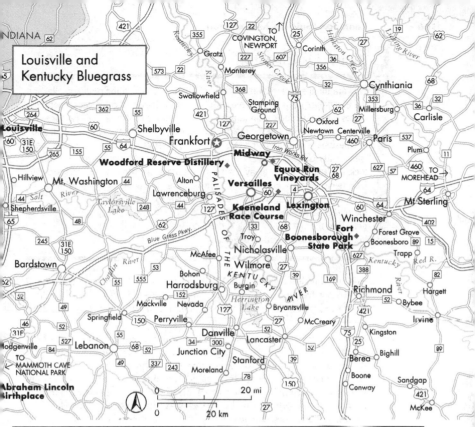

EXPLORING

Ashland. This 18-room brick mansion was the country home of Senator Henry Clay and his family for more than four decades. The tour highlights antebellum Kentucky plantation life and the political achievements of Clay, who served in both the U.S. House of Representatives as Speaker and the U.S. Senate. The current site is about 20 acres (at one point the estate covered more than 600 acres) and includes gardens, a gift shop, and a café. The last tour begins at 4. ✉ 120 Sycamore Rd., Chevy Chase 🕿 859/266–8581 ⊕ www.henryclay.org 🎫 $7 ⊙ Feb., weekends by appointment; Mar., Nov., and Dec., Tues.–Sat., 10–4, Sun. 1–4; Apr.–Oct., Mon.–Sat. 10–4, Sun. 1–4.

Bluegrass Tours. Lexington's oldest tour company takes visitors to horse farms, Keeneland racetrack, and historic venues. It's an excellent introduction to the area, especially if you only have a day or two in the region. ✉ 817 Enterprise Dr., Downtown 🕿 800/755–6956 ⊕ www.bluegrasstours.com 🎫 $30 ⊙ Daily tours at 9:30 and 1:30 must be booked at least 3 days in advance.

★ **Headley-Whitney Museum.** George W. Headley was a prominent designer of jewelry and small objects of decorative art known as bibelots. Dozens of his pieces are on display here in this museum on his former estate. Extraordinarily detailed dollhouses commissioned by Headley's sister-

Kentucky Limestone

Why are there so many horse farms in the Bluegrass? It's the soil. Limestone makes up the geological underpinning of central Kentucky. The mineral found in limestone is calcium carbonate, and when water comes in contact with the rock, it gradually wears away the surface, releasing calcium into the topsoil and the stream water, which means the bluegrass on which the horses graze and the water they drink is rich in the mineral they need to develop strong bones in their long, fragile racing legs. This chemical property of limestone is also responsible for Kentucky's famed cave region, about 100 mi west of the Bluegrass, where the limestone was worn away beneath surface sandstone to create Mammoth Cave—the world's longest at more than 365 mapped mi.

in-law Marylou Vanderbilt Whitney, the artist's library, and a shell grotto are well worth a couple of hours. ⊠ *4435 Old Frankfort Pike, East Lexington* ☎ *859/255–6653* ⊕ *www.headley-whitney.org* ⊠ *$7* ⊙ *Tues.–Fri. 10–5, weekends noon–5.*

Hunt-Morgan House. John Wesley Hunt, the first millionaire west of the Appalachians, built this Federal-style house in Lexington's Gratz Park district in the early 1800s. His grandson, John Hunt Morgan, served as an officer in the Confederate cavalry, and the house also has a small Civil War museum. A portrait of another family member, Thomas Hunt Morgan, who won the Nobel Prize in Physiology or Medicine for his genetics discoveries, hangs in one room. The last tour of the house departs one hour before closing. ⊠ *201 N. Mill St., Gratz Park* ☎ *859/233–3290* ⊕ *www.bluegrasstrust.org/hunt-morgan.html* ⊠ *$7* ⊙ *Mar.–Nov., Wed.–Fri. 1–5, Sat. 10–4, Sun. 1–4.*

Ⓒ **Kentucky Horse Park.** Tour the **International Museum of the Horse**, run
Fodor'sChoice in cooperation with the Smithsonian Institution. In addition to view-
★ ing the many exhibits on the ancient relationship between people and horses, you'll also be able to get close to real horses. There's a Parade of Breeds, horse-drawn carriage rides, and a 45-minute trail ride around the park suitable even for those who've never ridden before. The park also houses the **American Saddlebred Museum** (that's the breed used for dressage). Tours of nearby horse farms are available for an extra fee. ⊠ *4089 Iron Works Pike, North Lexington* ☎ *859/233–4303* ⊕ *www. kyhorsepark.com* ⊠ *$15* ⊙ *Mar. 15–Oct. 31, daily 9–5; Nov. 1–Mar. 14, Wed.–Sun. 9–5.*

Mary Todd Lincoln House. This two-story Georgian house, built from 1803 to 1806, was originally an inn. Abraham Lincoln courted Mary Todd, who lived here with her parents, when he came to visit Kentucky friends. This house was the first historic site to be restored in honor of a first lady. The last tour is offered at 3. ⊠ *578 W. Main St., Downtown* ☎ *859/233–9999* ⊕ *www.mtlhouse.org* ⊠ *$7* ⊙ *Mar. 15–Nov. 30, Mon.–Sat. 10–4.*

Fort Boonesborough State Park. The stockade built on the banks of the Kentucky River by Daniel Boone and his followers was the second permanent settlement in Kentucky. This replica of the original fort has and tours that include costumed reenactors. ✉ *4375 Boonesborough Rd., Richmond* ☎ *859/527–3131* 💲 *$6* 🕐 *Apr. 1–Oct. 31, daily 9–5:30.*

WHERE TO EAT

$–$$

VEGETARIAN

✗ **Alfalfa.** The original location of this organic café with many vegetarian offerings was across from the main entrance to the University of Kentucky campus. Now downtown, the restaurant still serves favorites such as red beans and rice and the avocado grill, a grilled sandwich with avocado and cheese. Live, mostly folk, music adds to the ambience. ✉ *141 E. Main St., Downtown* ☎ *859/253–0014* 🌐 *www.alfalfarestaurant.com* 🚫 *AE, MC, V* 🕐 *No dinner Sun.–Tues.*

$$$$

AMERICAN

✗ **Dudley's.** The historic Dudley School building on the edge of downtown houses shops and this handsome restaurant with wood-paneled dining rooms and a working fireplace. The brick-walled patio is a favorite local outdoor dining venue. The varied menu features pasta dishes, chops, steaks, and sautéed and grilled seafood, while appetizers and salads are perfect light choices for warm weather. The Kentucky lamb burger is a satisfying cool-weather choice. ✉ *380 S. Mill St., Downtown* ☎ *859/252–1010* 🌐 *www.dudleysrestaurant.com* 🚫 *AE, MC, V.*

$$$–$$$$

SOUTHERN

✗ **Merrick Inn.** Housed in an antebellum farmhouse that was the center of a horse farm, the Merrick Inn's dining rooms are filled with antiques. Traditional Kentucky ingredients, including Bibb lettuce and bourbon, are much in evidence. Southern-fried chicken, pork tenderloin, and rainbow trout are traditional favorites, but you can also get steak or lobster tail. The old-fashioned desserts include peach Melba and bread pudding. ✉ *3380 Tates Creek Rd., Tates Creek* ☎ *859/269–5417* 🌐 *www.murrays-merrick.com* 🚫 *AE, MC, V* 🕐 *Closed Sun.*

$$$$

ITALIAN

★

✗ **Portofino's.** Elegant pasta dishes, including gnocchi, form the centerpiece of the menu. Non-pasta entrées include duck, seafood, and veal dishes. The upscale casual restaurant is located in a handsomely renovated 19th-century building. The award-winning wine list includes many half bottles. ✉ *249 E. Main St., Downtown* ☎ *859/253–9300* 🌐 *www.portofinolexington.com* 🚫 *AE, MC, V* 🕐 *Closed Sun.*

WHERE TO STAY

$$$–$$$$

🏨 **George Clark House.** High Victorian opulence is the rule at this B&B near the University of Kentucky campus. Built in 1890 as a private home, the turreted mansion is furnished with period antiques, and rooms are equipped with gas fireplaces. Four resident cats preside over the house. **Pros:** gourmet breakfast; attentive service; friendly resident cats. **Cons:** cancellation window expands from seven to 45 days during Keeneland racing dates. ✉ *131 Woodland Ave., University* ☎ *859/254–2500* 🌐 *www.innsnorthamerica.com/ky/GeorgeClarkHouse.htm* 🛏 *4 rooms* 🔧 *In-room: Internet. In-hotel: no-smoking rooms* 🚫 *AE, MC, V* 🍽 *BP.*

$$$-$$$$ **Gratz Park Inn.** This small, European-style hotel is on the edge of
Fodor's Choice historic Gratz Park. The Federalist–Georgian architecture and decor
★ are inviting, and the house reportedly is home to a friendly ghost. **Pros:**
excellent restaurant; first-rate service; central location. **Cons:** smaller
rooms can feel overcrowded with furniture. ⊠ *120 W. 2nd St., Gratz
Park* ☎ *800/752–4166* ⊕ *www.gratzparkinn.com* ⇆ *44 rooms* ⓑ *In-
room; refrigerator (some), Internet. In-hotel: restaurant, room service,
bar, laundry service, parking (free), no-smoking rooms* ⊟ *AE, D, DC,
MC, V.*

$$$ **Lexington Downtown Hotel.** Located in the center of downtown, this
modern 22-story hotel dominates the skyline and is connected by sky-
walks to major convention halls and the sports arena. **Pros:** location;
stop for Bluegrass Tours. **Cons:** city's biggest convention hotel; generic
atmosphere. ⊠ *369 W. Vine St., Downtown* ☎ *859/231–9000* ⊕ *www.
lexingtondowntownhotel.com* ⇆ *367 rooms* ⓑ *In-room: refrigerator
(some), Wi-Fi. In-hotel: 2 restaurants, room service, bar, pool, gym, spa,
laundry service, parking (paid), no-smoking rooms* ⊟ *AE, D, MC, V.*

NIGHTLIFE AND THE ARTS

The arts of nightlife of Lexington center, not unnaturally, around the
University of Kentucky campus where there are lots of student and
faculty hangouts. Downtown restaurant and nightlife have picked up
in recent years, but is still rather sedate.

Concert and recital halls and an art gallery provide rotating series
of performances and exhibits, both professional and student at the
Singletary Center for the Arts (⊠ *Rose St. and Euclid Ave., University*
☎ *859/257–4929*).

SPORTS AND THE OUTDOORS

The **Keeneland Race Course** (⊠ *4201 Versailles Rd., Keeneland* ☎ *859/
254–3412* ⊕ *www.keeneland.com*) was used in location filming for
Seabiscuit. In addition to spring and fall racing dates, annual sales of
Thoroughbreds take place on the grounds.

SHOPPING

Victorian Square (⊠ *401 W. Main St., Downtown* ☎ *859/252–7575*
⊕ *www.victoriansquareshoppes.com*), a city block of handsome 19th-
century redbrick buildings, has been refurbished and contains galleries,
clothing stores, restaurants, and specialty shops.

Louisiana

NEW ORLEANS TO CAJUN COUNTRY ·

WORD OF MOUTH

"NOIA is different things for different people, which is what made it so great. You can party, learn history, walk around and look at gorgeous buildings, see cemeteries and enjoy weather that is typically better than much of the country."

—cancankant

"In general, NO is one of the rare cities where locals and tourists eat well at the same places. The Central Grocery and Acme and Galatoire's are all full of locals and tourists, and for good reason."

—Ackislander

Updated
by Michelle
Delio, Paul A.
Greenberg,
Molly Jahncke,
David Parker
Jr., Kandace
Power Graves,
and Sue
Strachan

Louisiana is a state divided, both physically and philosophically. North Louisiana, with its rolling hills and piney woods, is strongly Southern in flavor. The flatter, marshy land in South Louisiana is Cajun Country, with sharp differences in food, music, and even language. Riverboats ply the mighty Mississippi, and antebellum homes line the wayside in both regions, but it's New Orleans, home of the famous Mardi Gras festivities, that garners the lion's share of attention, drawing most visitors to South Louisiana.

New Orleans and its environs were settled by the French in the early 18th century, and 22 parishes of South Louisiana were settled soon after by Cajuns. Cajuns are descendants of the French who colonized Acadia—present day Nova Scotia and New Brunswick, Canada. In the mid-1700s the British expelled the Acadians, who resettled in the Louisiana Territory and became known as Cajuns. In 1803 President Thomas Jefferson purchased not just New Orleans, but the entire Louisiana Territory, from Napoléon Bonaparte.

New Orleans's many charms—Mardi Gras, fine dining, gracious living, and exciting nightlife to name a few—are well known. Outside New Orleans, in Cajun Country, you can ride a *pirogue* (a small, flat-bottom boat) poled through a bayou, kick your heels to fiddles, and eat at tables laden with crawfish, jambalaya, and gumbo.

ORIENTATION AND PLANNING

GETTING ORIENTED

South Louisiana encompasses all of the region south of Alexandria and extending east to the "instep" of this boot-shaped state. Almost all of South Louisiana is considered Cajun Country, or French Louisiana, except for the region north of Baton Rouge.

New Orleans. A city of neighborhoods, the French Quarter has been the geographic and cultural heart of New Orleans since the early 1700s. The Quarter is a vibrant commercial and residential hodgepodge of wrought-iron balconies, beckoning courtyards, antiques shops—and, of course, tawdry Bourbon Street. Faubourg Marigny, New Orleans's first suburb, has nightclubs, cafés, and some lovingly restored Creole cottages; grittier Bywater, despite gentrification, retains its working-class credentials while accommodating a burgeoning arts scene. Most of the city's newer hotels are clustered in Central Business District (CBD) and the Warehouse District, near Canal Street or the sprawling Morial Convention Center. There also are classy museums, fine restaurants, a

TOP REASONS TO GO

Mardi Gras: The quintessential party in America's party town.

French Quarter strolls: Walking amid New Orleans's historic buildings, you'll meet buskers and drunks, artists and ghosts. It's one of the most intriguing neighborhoods in the country.

All that jazz: Entire chapters of America's musical history were written here—and you can still see some of the country's best artists perform here in incredibly intimate settings.

Soul food: Eating in New Orleans is like going on a taste safari. There's Creole, Cajun, and southern comfort food, as well as ethnic eats and countless fusion cuisines.

Cajun culture: It's alive and well in South Louisiana's smaller burgs, where locals celebrate their heritage in food and song. Saturday morning and afternoon are devoted to Cajun music and Zydeco rocks back-road barns and country clubs on Friday and Saturday nights.

bustling casino, and the city's most adventurous art galleries. Stunning early-19th-century mansions make the Garden District a great neighborhood for walking, followed by an afternoon browsing the shops and cafés along bustling Magazine Street.

Plantation Country. Hit the tour-bus trail up the Mississippi to see how Louisiana's wealthy planters once lived.

Cajun Country. Awesome food, rockin' dance halls, more festivals than you can shake a crawfish net at—and in Lafayette, a surprisingly sophisticated cultural scene—await.

PLANNING

WHEN TO GO

Perhaps the best time to visit the area is early spring. Days are pleasant, except for seasonal cloudbursts, and nights are cool. May through September is hot and humid—double 100 days (100F and nearly 100% humidity) aren't uncommon. If you're looking for a deal and can take the heat, hotel prices are lower during sticky July and August. June through November there are heavy rains and occasional hurricanes. Although winters are mild compared with those in northern climes, the high humidity can put a chill in the air December through February.

GETTING HERE AND AROUND

AIR TRAVEL

Most major and a few regional airlines serve Louis Armstrong International Airport in Kenner, 15 mi east of downtown New Orleans.

Airport Information Louis Armstrong New Orleans International Airport (⊠ *900 Airline Dr., Kenner* ☎ *504/464–0831* ⊕ *www.flymsy.com*).

CAR TRAVEL

If you don't plan to drive outside New Orleans's city limits, you probably won't need a car—you'll save money traveling by streetcar, cab, and on foot. If you do decide to drive in New Orleans, keep in mind that some streets are in ragged condition, traffic lights routinely malfunction, and parking in the Quarter is tight (and parking regulations vigorously enforced). You'll need a car to venture outside the city to see the plantations and Cajun Country.

RESTAURANTS

New Orleans is known as much for its sensory expression as it is for its *joie de vivre*, and nowhere is this more evident than in the stellar cuisine offered at local restaurants. Traditional Louisiana dishes, such as jambalaya, red beans and rice, gumbo, and étouffée are readily available, but the delectable surprise of dining in New Orleans is the diversity of dishes and cuisines that are available, not to mention the culinary ingenuity on display.

HOTELS

Accommodations in Louisiana run from homey bed-and-breakfasts to chain motels, from luxury hotels to elegant antebellum mansions. Louisiana has well over 100 B&Bs; Cajun Country is loaded with charming ones. In New Orleans, the French Quarter has a plethora of guest houses that emphasize old-world ambience in 19th-century town houses and carriage houses. As one of the nation's favorite convention cities, New Orleans also has a plethora of high-rise convention hotels and luxury chain hotels.

WHAT IT COSTS				
	¢	$	$$	$$$	$$$$
Restaurant	under $9	$9–$16	$17–$25	$26–$35	over $35
Hotel	under $100	$100–$149	$150–$199	$200–$275	over $275

Restaurant prices are per person for a main course at dinner. Hotel prices are for a standard double room, excluding state and local taxes.

NEW ORLEANS

Mark Twain called New Orleans one of four unique American cities, a distinction that the Crescent City still deserves today. This is a vibrant, colorful, over-the-top place, a city of excess filled with music, food, drink, and fun. The calendar is packed with festivals celebrating everything from jazz to gumbo to Tennessee Williams, but spontaneous parties can pop up at any time, for *any* reason—people even dance in the street after funerals here.

And while this party atmosphere was once the dominant image associated with the city, today Hurricane Katrina is the first thing that comes to mind when people think of New Orleans. The city was crippled by the storm, and though it's still not back to 100%—whole neighborhoods are gone, and the residents who remain are fighting hard to rebuild their homes—the heart of New Orleans remains. It beats a little stronger each month. Today there are more restaurants in the city than before Katrina, and almost as many hotel rooms. The most popular parts of the city—the French Quarter and the Garden District—are

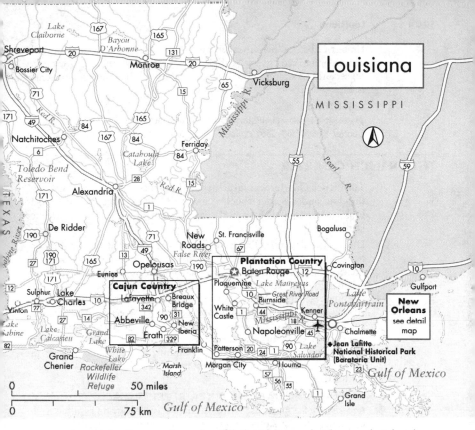

completely up and running, filled with unusual sights, opulent hotels, delicious food, and soul-stirring music. So come on down for a visit. You'll help this historic city get back on its feet and, more importantly, you'll find out what Mark Twain was talking about.

GETTING HERE AND AROUND

STREETCAR TRAVEL Streetcars are a great way to see the city. The St. Charles line runs from Canal Street to the intersection of Claiborne and Carrollton avenues; along the way it passes the Garden District, Audubon Park, and Tulane and Loyola universities. The Riverfront line skirts the French Quarter along the Mississippi, from Esplanade Avenue to the Ernest N. Morial Convention Center. Some Canal line streetcars make a straight shot from the Quarter to the cemeteries at City Park Avenue; others take a spur at Carrollton Avenue that goes to City Park and the New Orleans Museum of Art.

Fares for streetcars are $1.25 ($1.50 for express lines); VisiTour visitors' passes have one-day unlimited rides for $5 and a three-day unlimited pass for $12. For route maps, timetables, and more information, visit ⊕*www.norta.com.*

TAXI TRAVEL Taxis are often the most convenient way to move around, and drivers are used to short trips, so don't hesitate to grab a cab if you're leery about walking back to your hotel at night. Most locals will recommend

United Cabs, Yellow Checker, and Veterans. Don't get into an unlicensed/unmarked "gypsy" cab. Rates are $1.60 per mi or 20¢ for every 40 seconds of waiting, plus a base of $2.50; each additional passenger is $1.

ESSENTIALS

Visitor Information Louisiana Office of Tourism (⊠ 529 St. Ann St., French Quarter ☎ 504/568–5661 ☉ Tues. Sat. 9 5).

THE FRENCH QUARTER

The French Quarter was largely spared Katrina's destruction. Although flooding and disorder touched its Canal Street edge, you'll have to look closely to find signs of damage elsewhere within its well-defined borders.

During the day, the Quarter offers several different faces to its visitors. Decatur Street is a strip of tourist shops and hotels uptown from Jackson Square; downtown from the square, it becomes an alternative hangout for leather-clad regulars drawn to shadowy bars, vintage clothing resellers, and novelty shops. Chartres Street is a relatively calm stretch of inviting shops and eateries. Royal Street is the address of sophisticated antiques shops and many of the Quarter's finest homes. Bourbon Street claims the sex shops, extravagant cocktails, and music clubs filmmakers love to feature. Dauphine and Burgundy streets are more residential, with just a few restaurants and bars serving as retreats for locals.

JACKSON SQUARE AND THE RIVERFRONT

7 **Aquarium of the Americas.** Power failures during Katrina resulted in the major loss of the Aquarium's collection of more than 7,000 aquatic creatures. In a dramatic gesture of solidarity, aquariums around the country joined together with the Aquarium of the Americas in an effort to repopulate its stock. The museum, now fully reopened, has four major exhibit areas—the Amazon Rain Forest, the Caribbean Reef, the Mississippi River, and the Gulf Coast—all of which have fish and animals native to that environment. A special treat is the Seahorse Gallery, which showcases seemingly endless varieties of these beautiful creatures. The aquarium's spectacular design allows you to feel part of the watery worlds by providing close-up encounters with the inhabitants. A gift shop and café are on the premises. ⊠ 1 Canal St., French Quarter ☎ 504/581–4629 or 800/774–7394 ⊕ www.auduboninstitute. org ☜ Aquarium $18; combination ticket with IMAX $23.50; combination ticket for aquarium, zoo, and round-trip cruise $41 ☉ Aquarium Tues.–Sun. 10–5.

6 **Canal Street.** Canal Street, 170 feet wide, is the widest main street in the United States and one of the liveliest—particularly during Carnival parades. It was once scheduled to be made into a canal linking the Mississippi River to Lake Pontchartrain; plans changed, but the name remains. In the early 1800s, after the Louisiana Purchase, the French Creoles residing in the French Quarter were segregated from the Americans who settled upriver from Canal Street. The communities had

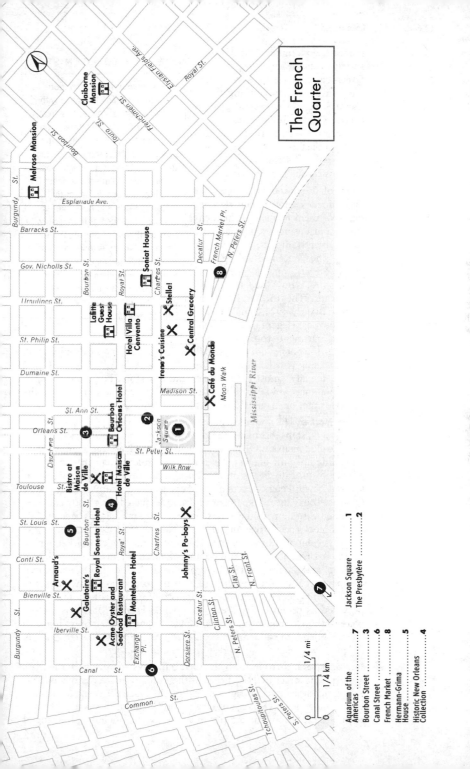

The French Quarter

Claiborne Mansion

Melrose Mansion

Bourgundy St.

Esplanade Ave.

Barracks St.

Gov. Nicholls St.

Bourbon St.

Ursulines St.

Soniat House

St. Philip St.

Lafitte Guest House

Hotel Villa Convento

Dumaine St.

Irene's Cuisine ✕

Stella! ✕

✕ Central Grocery

Elysian Fields Ave.

Royal St.

Toulo St.

Frenchmen St.

Royal St.

Chartres St.

Decatur St.

French Market Pl.

N. Peters St.

⑧

✕ Café du Monde

Moon Walk

Madison St.

Bourbon Orleans Hotel

②

St. Ann St.

Orleans St.

③

Dauphine St.

Jackson Square ①

St. Peter St.

Wilk Row

Bistro at Maison de Ville ✕

Hotel Maison de Ville

④

Toulouse

Bourbon St.

Royal St.

Chartres St.

Mississippi River

St. Louis St.

Royal Sonesta Hotel

⑤

Johnny's Po-boys ✕

Clay St.

N. Front St.

Conti St.

Arnaud's ✕

Galatoire's ✕

Monteleone Hotel

Decatur St.

Bienville St.

Acme Oyster and Seafood Restaurant ✕

Clinton St.

N. Peters St.

Burgundy St.

Iberville St.

Exchange Pl.

Dorsiere St.

⑦

↙

Canal St.

⑥

Common St.

Tchoupitoulas St.

St. Peters St.

0 — 1/4 mi
0 — 1/4 km

separate governments and police systems, and what is now Canal Street—and, most specifically, the central median running down Canal Street—was neutral ground between them. Today, animosities between these two groups are history, but the term "neutral ground" has survived as the name for all medians throughout the city.

Some of the grand buildings that once lined Canal Street remain, many of them former department stores and businesses now serving as hotels, restaurants, or souvenir shops. The Werlein Building (605 Canal Street), once a multilevel music store, is now the Palace Café restaurant. The former home of Maison Blanche (921 Canal Street), once the most elegant of the downtown department stores, is now a Ritz-Carlton hotel, with a ground floor devoted to an upscale mini-mall. One building still serving its original purpose is Adler's (722 Canal Street), the city's most elite jewelry and gift store. For the most part, these buildings are faithfully restored, so you can still appreciate the grandeur that once reigned on this fabled strip.

> **HISTORY YOU CAN SEE**
>
> When Thomas Jefferson negotiated the Louisiana Purchase with Napoleon Bonaparte, he was really after New Orleans, a strategic post near the mouth of the Mississippi River. Throughout the 19th century, the port city blossomed into one of the nation's largest and most significant, a beneficiary of the cotton industry and brisk international trade (much of it, tragically, built on the backs of slaves). New Orleans's heyday is long past, but many visible remnants of its Colonial and Antebellum past remain, from the French Quarter to the elegant plantation homes dotting the Mississippi.

8 French Market. The sounds, colors, and smells here are alluring: street performers, ships' horns on the river, pralines, muffulettas, sugarcane, and Creole tomatoes. Originally a Native American trading post, later a bustling open-air market under the French and Spanish, the French Market historically began at Café du Monde and stretched along Decatur and North Peters streets all the way to the downtown edge of the Quarter. Today the market's graceful arcades have been mostly enclosed and filled with shops and eateries, and the fresh market has been pushed several blocks downriver, under sheds built in 1936 as part of a Works Progress Administration project. This area of the French Market, which begins at Ursulines Street and contains a large **flea market** as well as a farmers' market area and its own praline and food stands, was slated for major renovation even before Katrina tore away its awnings and the 2005 hurricane season devastated the farming communities that provided its produce. The newly renovated French Market is a great place to shop for cheap souvenirs, sunglasses, or beads; it's also home to an expanded farmers' market. ⊠ *Decatur St., French Quarter* ☉ *Daily 6–6; hrs may vary depending on season and weather.*

1 Jackson Square. Surrounded by historic buildings and plenty of the city's atmospheric street life, the heart of the French Quarter is this beautifully landscaped park. Originally called the Place d'Armes, the square was founded in 1718 as a military parade ground. It was also the site of public executions carried out in various styles, including burning at the stake, beheading, breaking on the wheel, and hanging. A **statue of Andrew Jackson,** victorious leader of the Battle of New Orleans in the War of 1812, commands the center of the square; the park was renamed for him in the 1850s. The words carved in the base on the cathedral side of the statue—THE UNION MUST AND SHALL BE PRESERVED—are a lasting reminder of the federal troops who occupied New Orleans during the Civil War and who inscribed them. ⊠ *French Quarter* ⊙ *Park daily 8 AM–dusk; flagstone paths on park's periphery open 24 hrs.*

② **The Presbytère.** One of twin Spanish colonial–style buildings flanking **Fodor's Choice** St. Louis Cathedral, this one, on the right, was designed to house the ★ priests of the cathedral; instead, it served as a courthouse under the Spanish and later under the Americans. It is now a museum showcasing a spectacular collection of Mardi Gras memorabilia, and displays highlight both the little-known and popular traditions associated with New Orleans's most famous festival. The building's cupola, destroyed by a hurricane in 1915, was restored in 2005 to match the one atop its twin, the Cabildo. ⊠ *Jackson Sq., French Quarter* ☎ *504/568–6968* ⊕ *lsm.crt.state.la.us* ⊡ *$5* ⊙ *Tues.–Sun. 9–5.*

INSIDE THE VIEUX CARRÉ

③ **Bourbon Street.** Ignore your better judgment and take a stroll down Bourbon Street, past the bars, restaurants, music clubs, and novelty shops that have given this strip its reputation as the playground of the South. The bars of Bourbon Street were among the first businesses of the city to reopen after the storm; catering to the off-duty relief workers, they provided a different form of relief. On most nights, the crowds remain lighter here than in recent years, but the spirit of unbridled revelry is back in full swing. The noise, raucous crowds, and bawdy sights are not family fare; if you go with children, do so before sundown. Although the street is usually well patrolled, it is wise to stay alert to your surroundings. The street is blocked to make a pedestrian mall at night; often the area is shoulder to shoulder, especially during major sports events and Mardi Gras.

⑤ **Hermann-Grima House.** One of the largest and best-preserved examples of ☾ American architecture in the Quarter, this Georgian-style house has the **Fodor's Choice** only restored private stable and the only working 1830s Creole kitch-★ en in the Quarter. American architect William Brand built the house in 1831. The house fortunately sustained only minor damage during Katrina and is open for visits and tours. Cooking demonstrations on the open hearth are held here all day Thursday from October through May. You'll want to check the gift shop, which has many local crafts and books. ⊠ *820 St. Louis St., French Quarter* ☎ *504/525–5661* ⊡ *$10, combination ticket with the Gallier House $18* ⊙ *Tours Thurs.–Tues. 10, 11, noon, 2, 3.*

④ **Historic New Orleans Collection.** This private archive and exhibit complex, ★ with thousands of historic photos, documents, and books, is one of the finest research centers in the South. It occupies the 19th-century town house of General Kemper Williams and the 1792 Merrieult House. Changing exhibits focus on aspects of local history. History tours and home tours of the houses, grounds, and archives are offered several times daily. A museum shop sells books, prints, and gifts. Children under 12 are not admitted. ✉ *533 Royal St., French Quarter* ☎ *504/523–4662* ⊕ *www.hnoc.org* ✑ *Exhibit and research library (410 Chartres St.) free, tour of houses or archive galleries $5* ⊙ *Tues.–Sat. 9:30–3.*

WAREHOUSE DISTRICT

Bordered by the river, St. Charles Avenue, Poydras Street, and the Interstate 10 expressway and filled with former factories and cotton warehouses, the Warehouse District began its renaissance when the city hosted the World's Fair here in 1984. Old abandoned buildings were renovated to host the fair and its events, setting the scene for future development. Structures that housed the international pavilions during the fair now make up the New Orleans Morial Convention Center and a number of hotels, restaurants, bars, and music clubs. Today, the Warehouse District remains one of the hottest residential and arts-and-nightlife areas of the city, dotted with modern renovations of historic buildings, upscale loft residences, excellent eateries, and a number of bars and music clubs.

EXPLORING

Fodor's Choice ★ **Blaine Kern's Mardi Gras World at Kern Studios.** Mardi Gras World's entertainment complex moved from Algiers Point to join Blaine Kern Studios and new private-event venues on the east bank of New Orleans in early 2009. Located just upriver of the New Orleans Convention Center, the massive 400,000-square-foot complex occupies the former Delta Queen Steamboat terminal and River City Casino sites right along the Mississippi River. The new Mardi Gras World brings the fun of its west bank predecessor closer to the city center with an enhanced guided tour through a maze of video presentations, decorative sculptures, and favorite megafloats from Mardi Gras parades such as Bacchus, Rex, and Endymion. Visitors enter through a plantation alley that is part Cajun swamp-shack village, part antebellum Disneyworld (Kern was a friend of, and inspired by, Walt Disney). If you're not here for the real thing, Mardi Gras World is a fun (and family friendly) backstage look at the history and artistry of Carnival. Admission includes cake and coffee. ✉ *1380 Port of New Orleans Pl., Warehouse District* ☎ *504/361–7821 or 800/362–8213* ⊕ *www.mardigrasworld.com* ✑ *$18* ⊙ *Daily 9:30–5.*

Fodor's Choice ★ **National World War II Museum.** Exhibits take visitors from the Normandy invasion to the sands of Pacific Islands and the Home Front. The brainchild of historian and writer Dr. Stephen Ambrose, who taught for many years at the University of New Orleans until his death in 2002, this moving, well-executed examination of World War II covers far more ground than simply D-Day. The seminal moments are re-created through propaganda posters and radio clips from the period; biographical sketches of the military personnel involved; a number of short documentary films (including one bitterly sad film on the Holocaust, featuring interviews with survivors); and collections of weapons, personal items, and other artifacts from the war. The exhibits occupy a series of galleries spread through the interior of a huge warehouse space. One spotlighted exhibit, in a large, open portion of the warehouse near the entrance, is a replica of the Higgins boat troop landing craft, which were manufactured in New Orleans. In 2005 the museum announced a $300 million expansion plan to quadruple the size of the facility in several phases. Across the street from the current facility, a 4-D theater experience produced by Tom Hanks and a canteen featuring live period entertainment are set to open in November. This is the first of six new pavilions proposed for the expanded campus, due to be completed in 2015. Check the Web site for updates on the expansion and a list of current movies, lectures, events, and programs. ⊠*925 Magazine St. (main entrance on Andrew Higgins Dr.), Warehouse District* ☎*504/527–6012* ⊕*www.nationalww2museum.org* ⊡*$14* ⊗*Oct.–June, daily 9–5; July–Sept., Tues.–Sun. 9–5.*

GARDEN DISTRICT

With its beautifully landscaped gardens surrounding elegant antebellum homes, the Garden District lives up to its name. Although its homes aren't open to the public, outside of occasional special-event tours, enjoying the sights from outside the cast-iron fences is well worth the visit.

The Garden District is divided into two sections by Jackson Avenue. Upriver from Jackson is the wealthy **Upper Garden District,** where the homes are meticulously kept. Below Jackson, the **Lower Garden District** is rougher in areas, though the homes here are often structurally just as beautiful and are increasingly being restored. Still, the streets are less well patrolled and best toured during the day. **Magazine Street,** lined with antiques shops, boutiques, restaurants, and cafés, serves as a southern border to the Garden District. St. Charles Avenue forms the northern border. Take the historic streetcar here—it's a fun and leisurely way to see the sights along the avenue. A number of companies also offer walking tours.

EXPLORING

Brevard House. Though Anne Rice moved out of the elegant Garden District home in 2004, the famous novelist's fans still flock to see the house that inspired the Mayfair Manor in her series *Lives of the Mayfair Witches.* The house is a three-bay Greek Revival, extended over a luxurious side yard and surrounded by a fence of cast-iron rosettes that earned the estate's historical name, Rosegate. ⊠*1239 1st St., Garden District.*

Colonel Short's Villa. Occupied for a brief time by the Union governor of post–Civil War Louisiana, the house was stylistically influential in the district because the two-story galleries of its dining room wing had railings made of cast iron rather than wood. The fence, with a pattern of morning glories intertwining with cornstalks, is the most famous example of cast iron in the Garden District. Legend has it that Colonel Short purchased the fence for his wife, who was homesick for Kentucky. A similar cornstalk fence appears in the French Quarter at 915 Royal Street. ⊠*1448 4th St., Garden District.*

Robinson House. Styled after an Italian villa, this home built in the late 1850s is one of the largest in the district. Doric and Corinthian columns support the rounded galleries. It is believed to be the first house in New Orleans with "waterworks," as indoor plumbing was called then. Years

New Orleans Cemeteries

New Orleans's "cities of the dead," with rows of crypts like little houses and streets organized with signs, are some of the city's most enduring images. Of the metropolitan area's 42 cemeteries, 15 are examples of the aboveground burial practices of the French and Spanish. The two which are safest to tour on your own are listed below. For organized cemetery tours that are detailed and accurate, try nonprofit group **Save Our Cemeteries** (☎504/525–3377 ⊕www. saveourcemeteries.org).

Lafayette Cemetery No. 1. Begun around 1833, this was the first planned cemetery in the city, with symmetrical rows, roadways for funeral vehicles, and lavish aboveground vaults and tombs for the wealthy families who built the surrounding mansions. In 1852, 2,000 yellow-fever victims were buried here. Movies such as *Interview with the Vampire* and *Easy Rider* have used this walled cemetery for its

eerie beauty. The cemetery is open to the public, and you can wander the grounds on your own or take an organized tour. ⊠*1400 block of Washington Ave., Garden District* ⊠*Cemetery free, tour $6* ⊙*Weekdays 7–2:30, Sat. 7–noon; Save Our Cemeteries tours Mon., Wed., Fri., and Sat. at 10:30.*

Lake Lawn Metairie Cemetery. The largest cemetery in the metropolitan area, known to locals simply as Metairie Cemetery, is the final resting place of nine Louisiana governors, seven New Orleans mayors, three Confederate generals, and musician Louis Prima. Many of New Orleans's noted families are also interred here in elaborate monuments ranging from Gothic crypts to Romanesque mausoleums to Egyptian pyramids. Walk the grounds or drive along named streets to see them. In the mid-1800s, this was the site of the Metairie Racetrack and Jockey Club. ⊠*5100 Pontchartain Blvd., Metairie* ⊙*Daily 8–5.*

of extensive renovation based on the original plans culminated with a re-landscaping in 2005. ⊠*1415 3rd St., Garden District.*

UPTOWN

Lying west of the Garden District, Uptown is the residential area on both sides of St. Charles Avenue along the streetcar route, upriver from Louisiana Avenue. It includes many mansions as sumptuous as those in the Garden District, as well as Loyola and Tulane universities and a large urban park named for John James Audubon. Traveling along the avenue from downtown to uptown provides something of a historical narrative: the city's development unfolded upriver, and the houses grow more modern the farther uptown you go.

EXPLORING

☺ **Audubon Park.** Formerly the plantation of Etienne de Boré, the father of ★ the granulated sugar industry in Louisiana, **Audubon Park** is a large, lush stretch of green between St. Charles Avenue and Magazine Street, continuing across Magazine Street to the river. Designed by John Charles Olmsted, nephew of Frederick Law Olmsted (who laid out New York

City's Central Park), it contains the world-class **Audubon Zoo**; a 1.7-mi track for running, walking, or biking; picnic and play areas; Audubon Park Golf Course; a tennis court; horse stables; and a river view. Calm lagoons wind through the park, harboring egrets, catfish, and other indigenous species. The park and zoo were named for the famous ornithologist and painter John James Audubon, who spent many years working in and around New Orleans. None of the original buildings from its former plantation days remain; in fact, none of the buildings that housed the 1884–85 World's Industrial and Cotton Centennial Exposition have survived. The only reminder of the city's first World's Fair is Exposition Boulevard, the street address assigned to houses that front the park along the downtown side. ⊠*Riverview Dr., off of Magazine St., Uptown* ☎*504/861–3527* ⊕*www.auduboninstitute.org* ✉*Free.*

BAYOU ST. JOHN AND MID-CITY

Above the French Quarter and below the lakefront, neither Uptown nor quite downtown, Mid-City is an amorphous yet proud territory embracing everything from the massive, lush City Park to gritty storefronts along Carrollton Avenue. It is a neighborhood of tremendous ethnic and economic diversity. Here you'll find great restaurants, cultural landmarks such as Rock and Bowl, restored former plantation homes, and crumbling inner city neighborhoods. Actual sights are few and far between in Mid-City, and the neighborhood suffered heavily from flooding during Hurricane Katrina, but the area is recovering. The neighborhood around Bayou St. John near City Park is still one of the more picturesque in town and is fruitful for walks.

EXPLORING

City Park. City Park, a 150-year-old, 1,500-acre expanse of moss-draped oaks and gentle lagoons 2 mi from the French Quarter, suffered mightily in Hurricane Katrina's winds and flooding. The storm felled or damaged more than 1,000 trees, destroyed an 18-hole golf course, ravaged vegetation, and forced the park to lay off 90% of its staff. Nevertheless, the park has been rebuilt with the help of hundreds of local and visiting volunteers and is again a great place to walk or jog, play tennis, feed the ducks, visit one of its attractions, or simply relax. Just beyond the main entrance at the end of Esplanade Avenue stands the **New Orleans Museum of Art** and an adjacent sculpture garden; tucked elsewhere in the sprawling park are tennis courts, a sports stadium and running track, baseball diamonds and playgrounds, equestrian stable and golf course, along with miles of meandering walking paths and gentle lagoons rife with waterfowl. The park's art-deco benches, fountains, bridges, and ironwork are remnants of a 1930s Works Progress Administration refurbishment, and whimsical sculptures by renowned New Orleans artist Enrique Alferez dot the **New Orleans Botanical Garden.** The train garden here, operating on weekends only, is still a fun stop for the kids. Other children's favorites, Storyland and Carousel Gardens, are also open seasonally on weekends. Most attractions are clustered near the museum, but a stroll or picnic anywhere in the park is a wonderful way to relax. A popular drive-through Christmas holiday

Fodor's Choice
★

light display had to be scaled down after Katrina, but a walking tour and activities beginning annually after Thanksgiving pack in holiday revelers. Call ahead or check the park's Web site for revised hours and available activities. ⊠ *Bordered by City Park Ave., Robert E. Lee Blvd., Marconi Dr., and Bayou St. John Mid-City* ☎ *504/482–4888* ⊕ *www. neworleanscitypark.com.*

Fodor'sChoice **Pitot House.** One of the few surviving houses that lined the bayou in the
★ late 1700s, and the only Creole-colonial style house in the city open to the public, Pitot House is named for James Pitot, who bought the property in 1810 as a country home for his family. Pitot built one of the first cotton presses in New Orleans and served as the city's mayor from 1804 to 1805 and later as parish court judge. The Pitot House was restored and moved a block to its current location in the 1960s to make way for the expansion of Cabrini High School. It is noteworthy for its stucco-covered brick-between-post construction, an example of which is exposed on the second floor. The house is typical of the West Indies style brought to Louisiana by early planters, with galleries around the house that protect the interior from both rain and sunshine. There aren't any interior halls to stifle ventilation, and opposing doors encourage a cross breeze. The house is furnished with period antiques from the United States, and particularly Louisiana. ⊠ *1440 Moss St., Bayou St. John* ☎ *504/482–0312* ⊕ *www.louisianalandmarks.org* ⊠ *$7* ⊙ *Wed.– Sat. 10–3 or by appointment.*

WHERE TO EAT

FRENCH QUARTER

$ ✕ **Acme Oyster and Seafood Restaurant.** A rough-edge classic in every way,
SEAFOOD   this no-nonsense eatery at the entrance to the French Quarter is a prime
ⓒ   source for cool and salty raw oysters on the half shell; shrimp, oyster, and roast-beef po'boys; and tender, expertly seasoned red beans and rice. Table service, once confined to the main dining room out front, is now provided in the rear room as well. Expect lengthy lines outside, often a half-block long (trust us though, it's worth it). Crowds lighten in the late afternoon. ⊠ *724 Iberville St., French Quarter* ☎ *504/525– 1160* ⊕ *www.acmeoyster.com* ⟜ *Reservations not accepted* ⊟ *AE, D, DC, MC, V.*

$$$ ✕ **Arnaud's.** This grande dame of classic Creole restaurants still sparkles.
CREOLE   In the main dining room, ornate etched glass reflects light from charm-
Fodor'sChoice   ing old chandeliers while the late founder, Arnaud Cazenave, gazes from
★   an oil portrait. The adjoining jazz bistro offers the same food but is a more casual and music-filled dining experience. The ambitious menu includes classic dishes as well as more contemporary ones. Always reliable are Shrimp Arnaud—cold shrimp in a superb rémoulade—and Oysters Bienville, Petit Filet Lafitte, and praline crepes. Jackets are requested in the main dining room. Be sure to visit the Mardi Gras museum upstairs. ⊠ *813 Bienville St., French Quarter* ☎ *504/523–5433* ⊕ *www.arnauds.com* ⟜ *Reservations essential* ⊟ *AE, D, DC, MC, V* ⊙ *No lunch Sat.*

$$$ ✕**Bistro at Maison de Ville.** Forget
CREOLE everything you thought you knew
★ about hotel restaurants. "The Bis-
tro," as locals refer to it, defies
convention with its charming, Euro-
pean-inspired decor, intimate dining
room that seats 44, and a kitchen so
tiny it would fit in the average util-
ity closet. Still, chef Greg Picolo's
dishes, like fine sautéed Louisiana
gulf fish, osso buco, bouillabaisse,
and bacon-wrapped filet mignon,
are so well conceived that one might
picture an operation much larger
and more sophisticated. The wine
list is legendary in these parts, and
the ambience is as well suited to a

marriage proposal as it is to a power lunch. The Bistro may just be the
best-kept secret in the French Quarter. ✉*727 Toulouse St, French Quar-
ter* ☎*504/528–9206* ⊕*www.hotelmaisondeville.com/dining* ▭*AE, D,
DC, MC, V.*

¢ ✕**Café du Monde.** No trip to New Orleans is complete without a cup of
CAFÉ chicory-laced café au lait and addictive sugar-dusted beignets in this ven-
erable Creole institution. The tables under the green-and-white-striped
awning are jammed at every hour with locals and tourists feasting on
powdery doughnuts and views of Jackson Square. ■TIP→**If there's a line
for table service, head around back to the takeout window and get your cof-
fee and beignets to go. Enjoy them overlooking the river right next door, or
in Jackson Square.** The magical time to go is just before dawn, when the
bustle subsides and you can hear the birds in the crepe myrtles across
the way. Five satellite locations (Riverwalk Marketplace in the CBD,
Lakeside Shopping Center in Metairie, Esplanade Mall in Kenner, Oak-
wood Mall in Gretna, and Veterans Blvd. in Metairie) are convenient but
lack the character of the original. ✉*800 Decatur St., French Quarter*
☎*504/525–4544* ⊕*www.cafedumonde.com* ▭*No credit cards.*

$ ✕**Central Grocery.** This old-fashioned Italian grocery store produces
CAFÉ authentic muffulettas, one of the gastronomic gifts of the city's Italian
immigrants. Good enough to challenge the po'boy as the local sandwich
champ, it's made by filling round loaves of seeded bread with ham,
salami, mozzarella, and a salad of marinated green olives. Sandwiches,
about 10 inches in diameter, are sold in wholes and halves. ■TIP→**The
muffulettas are huge! Unless you're starving, you'll do fine with a half.** You
can eat your muffuletta at a counter, or get it to go and dine on a bench
on Jackson Square or the Moon Walk along the Mississippi riverfront.
The Grocery closes at 5:30 PM. ✉*923 Decatur St., French Quarter*
☎*504/523–1620* ▭*D, MC, V* ☻*No dinner.*

$$$ ✕**Galatoire's.** Galatoire's has always epitomized the old-style French-
CREOLE Creole bistro. Many of the recipes date to 1905. Fried oysters and bacon
Fodor'sChoice en brochette are worth every calorie, and the brick-red rémoulade sauce
★ sets a high standard. Other winners include veal chops in béarnaise

5

sauce, and seafood-stuffed eggplant. The setting downstairs is a single, narrow dining room lighted with glistening brass chandeliers; bentwood chairs and white tablecloths add to its timelessness. You may reserve a table in the renovated upstairs rooms, though the action is on the first floor, where partying regulars inhibit conversation but add good people-watching entertainment value. Friday lunch starts early and continues well into early evening. A jacket is required. ⊠*209 Bourbon St., French Quarter* ☎*504/525–2021* ⊕*www.galatoires.com* ⊟*AE, D, DC, MC, V* ⊙*Closed Mon.*

$$
ITALIAN
★
✕**Irene's Cuisine.** Its walls are festooned with enough snapshots, garlic braids, and crockery for at least two more restaurants, but it all just adds to the charm of this cozy Italian-Creole eatery. From Irene DiPietro's kitchen come succulent roasted chicken brushed with olive oil, rosemary, and garlic; original, velvety soups; and fresh shrimp, aggressively seasoned and grilled before joining linguine glistening with herbed olive oil. Waits here can stretch to the 60-minute mark during peak dinner hours, which is just enough time for a bottle of wine in the convivial little piano bar. It easily has the friendliest service personnel in the French Quarter. ⊠*539 St. Philip St., French Quarter* ☎*504/529–8811* ⊗*Reservations not accepted* ⊟*AE, MC, V* ⊙*No lunch.*

$
CAFÉ
☼
✕**Johnny's Po-boys.** Strangely enough, good po'boys are hard to find in the French Quarter. Johnny's compensates for the scarcity with a cornucopia of them, even though the quality is anything but consistent, and the prices are somewhat inflated for the tourist trade. Inside the soft-crust French bread come the classic fillings, including lean boiled ham, well-done roast beef in garlicky gravy, and crisply fried oysters or shrimp. The chili may not cut it in San Antonio, but the red beans and rice are the real deal. The surroundings are rudimentary. ⊠*511 St. Louis St., French Quarter* ☎*504/524–8129* ⊕*www.johnnyspoboy. com* ⊟*No credit cards* ⊙*No dinner.*

$$$
ECLECTIC
Fodor's Choice
★
✕**Stella!** Chef Scott Boswell has evolved into one of the city's most innovative and daring culinarians. Try Louisiana gulf shrimp and chanterelle and lobster mushroom risotto. The porcini-crusted rack of Australian lamb and lamb rib eye is strictly upscale comfort food, the perfect prelude to chocolate cake with hot buttered pink lemonade. Stella! now sits comfortably among New Orleans's best fine-dining restaurants. ⊠*1032 Chartres St., French Quarter* ☎*504/587–0091* ⊕*www.restaurantstella. com* ⊟*AE, D, DC, MC, V* ⊙*No lunch.*

CBD AND WAREHOUSE DISTRICT

$$$
SOUTHERN
★
✕**August.** If the Gilded Age is long gone, someone forgot to tell the folks at August, whose main dining room shimmers with masses of chandelier prisms, thick brocade fabrics, and glossy woods. Service is anything but stuffy, however, and chef John Besh's modern technique

HOW TO SNACK

New Orleans boasts some superb fine dining establishments—including a few that have been around for more than a century—but people here are just as proud of the simple fare that has fueled the working classes for generations. You can get a plate of red beans and rice most any day, but it's traditionally served on Monday (and still shows up as the Monday special on many café menus). Legend has it that Monday was set aside for laundry, so home cooks needed something they could throw in a pot and forget about while they went about the laborious task of washing.

While the origins of the *muffuletta* sandwich are debatable, there's no doubt about the durability of this gut-busting sandwich. Locals and visitors alike queue up at **Central Grocery** for whole- or half-muffulet-tas, Italian bread loaves stuffed with ham, salami, provolone, and a layer of olive salad.

The po'boy—sliced meat, fried seafood, or even fried potatoes crammed into a loaf of French bread and slathered in mayonnaise or gravy—is another must-try for visitors, who throng **Mother's** and **Johnny's Po-boys** at lunchtime.

For sweets, it's hard to beat the beignets at **Café du Monde,** where the fried French-style "doughnuts" come dusted in powdered sugar and accompanied by chicory-laced café au lait. And then there's the praline, traditionally a wafer of sugar, butter, cream, and pecans, now available in nontraditional flavors such as chocolate, coconut, peanut butter, and rum. They're available in shops all over the French Quarter, some of which offer a view of the candy chef in action.

adorns every plate. Nothing is mundane here: handmade gnocchi with blue crab and winter truffle shares menu space with slow-cooked pork belly and butter-poached main lobster with black truffles. Expect the unexpected—like slow-roasted Kobe beef short ribs with Jerusalem arti-chokes. The sommelier is happy to confer with you on the surprisingly affordable wine list. ✉*301 Tchoupitoulas St., CBD* ☎*504/299–9777* ⊕*www.restaurantaugust.com* ⌂*Reservations essential* ▭*AE, MC, V* ☽*No lunch Sat.–Thurs.*

$$$ ✗**Cuvée.** With a name that refers to a blend of wines, this restaurant
SOUTHERN   divides its inspirations between France's Champagne region and south
Fodor's Choice   Louisiana. The menu rests on a firm French foundation, but the flavors
★   are often distinctively New Orleans. Talented chef Robert Iacovone sometimes seems unstoppable, like when he fashions the city's most elegant cane syrup and smoked duck breast paired with walnut and blue cheese risotto, or when he presents his pork tenderloin with juni-per and Gruyère apple strudel. Main courses are gutsy and inspired, as is the wine list. The space is defined by exposed brick and gilt-framed paintings. ✉*322 Magazine St., CBD* ☎*504/587–9001* ⊕*www.restau-rantcuvee.com* ⌂*Reservations essential* ▭*AE, DC, MC, V* ☽*Closed Sun. No lunch Mon., Tues., and Fri.*

$$$ ✗**Emeril's.** Celebrity-chef Emeril Lagasse's urban-chic flagship restaurant
AMERICAN   is always jammed. A wood ceiling in a basket-weave pattern muffles

Food Glossary

Andouille (pronounced ahn-*dooey*). A mildly spiced Acadian smoked sausage of lean pork, it often flavors gumbos, red beans and rice, and jambalayas.

Beignet (pronounced ben-*yay*). Although a beignet was originally a rectangular puff of fried dough sprinkled with powdered sugar, the term can also refer to fritters or crullers containing fish or seafood.

Boulette (pronounced *boo*-let). This is minced, chopped, or pureed meat or fish shaped into balls and fried.

Café brûlot (pronounced broo-*loh*). Cinnamon, lemon, clove, orange, and sugar are steeped with strong coffee, then flambéed with brandy and served in special pedestaled cups.

Chicory coffee. The ground and roasted root of a European variety of chicory is added to ground coffee in varying proportions. Originally used for reasons of economy, coffee with chicory is now favored by many New Orleanians. It lends an added bitterness to the taste.

Dirty rice. In this cousin of jambalaya, bits of meat, such as giblets or sausage, and seasonings are added to white rice before cooking.

Dressed. A po'boy "dressed" contains lettuce, tomato, pickles, and mayonnaise or mustard.

Étouffée (pronounced ay-too-*fay*). Literally "smothered," the term is used most often for a thick stew of crawfish tails cooked in a roux-based liquid with crawfish, fat, garlic, and green seasonings.

Gumbo. From an African word for okra, it can refer to any number of stewlike soups made with seafood or meat and flavored with okra or ground sassafras and myriad other seasonings. Frequent main ingredients are combinations of shrimp, oysters, crab, chicken, andouille, duck, and turkey. A definitive gumbo is served over white rice.

Jambalaya (pronounced jam-buh-*lie*-uh). Rice is the indispensable ingredient in this relative of Spain's paella. The rice is cooked with a mix of diced meat and seafood in tomato and other seasonings. Shrimp and ham make frequent appearances, as do sausage, green pepper, and celery.

Meunière (pronounced muhn-*yehr*). This method of preparing fish or soft-shell crab entails dusting it with seasoned flour, sautéing it in brown butter, and using the butter with lemon juice as a sauce. Some restaurants add a dash of Worcestershire sauce.

Muffuletta. The city's southern Italian grocers created this round-loaf sandwich traditionally filled with ham, salami, mozzarella, and a layer of chopped, marinated green olives. Muffulettas are sold whole and in halves or quarters.

Po'boy. A hefty sandwich, the po'boy is made with the local French bread and any number of fillings: roast beef, fried shrimp, oysters, ham, meatballs in tomato sauce, and cheese are common. A po'boy "dressed" contains lettuce, tomato, pickles, and mayonnaise or mustard.

Tasso (pronounced *tah*-so). Acadian cooks developed this lean, intensely seasoned ham. It's used sparingly to flavor sauces and gumbos.

much of the clatter and chatter. The ambitious menu gives equal emphasis to Creole and modern American cooking—try the barbecue shrimp here for one of the darkest, richest versions of the local specialty. Desserts, such as the renowned banana cream pie, verge on the gargantuan. Service is meticulous, and the wine list's depth and range should soothe even the most persnickety imbiber. ⊠ *800 Tchoupitoulas St., Warehouse District* ☎ *504/528–9393* ⊕ *www.emerils.com* ⌖ *Reservations essential* ☰ *AE, D, DC, MC, V* ⊘ *No lunch weekends.*

$ ✕**Mother's.** Tourists line up for down-home eats at this island of blue-
CAFÉ collar sincerity amid downtown's glittery hotels. Mother's dispenses delicious baked ham and roast beef po'boys (ask for "debris" on the beef sandwich and the bread will be slathered with meat juices and shreds of meat), home-style biscuits and jambalaya, and a very good chicken gumbo in a couple of bare-bones—yet charming—dining rooms. Breakfast service is a bit slow, but that doesn't seem to repel the hordes fighting for seats at peak mealtimes. Service is cafeteria style, with a counter or two augmenting the tables. ⊠ *401 Poydras St., CBD* ☎ *504/523–9656* ⊕ *www.mothersrestaurant.net* ⌖ *Reservations not accepted* ☰ *AE, MC, V.*

GARDEN DISTRICT/UPTOWN

$$$ ✕**Brigtsen's.** Chef Frank Brigtsen's fusion of Creole refinement and Aca-
CREOLE dian earthiness reflects his years as a Paul Prudhomme protégé. His
Fodor's Choice dishes represent some of the best south Louisiana cooking you'll find
★ anywhere. Everything is fresh and filled with deep, complex tastes. The butternut shrimp bisque defines comfort food. Rabbit and chicken dishes, usually presented in rich sauces and gravies, are full of robust flavor. The roux-based gumbos are thick and intense, and the warm bread pudding is worth every calorie. Trompe l'oeil murals add whimsy to the intimate spaces of this turn-of-the-20th-century frame cottage. Ask for a table on the enclosed front sun porch. ⊠ *723 Dante St., Uptown* ☎ *504/861–7610* ⊕ *www.brigtsens.com* ⌖ *Reservations essential* ☰ *AE, DC, MC, V* ⊘ *Closed Sun. and Mon. No lunch.*

$ ✕**Casamento's.** Tiled in gleaming white and cream-color ceramic, Casa-
SEAFOOD mento's has been a haven for Uptown seafood lovers since 1919. Family members still wait tables and staff the immaculate kitchen out back, while a reliable handful of oyster shuckers ensure that plenty of cold ones are available for the standing-room-only oyster bar. Specialties from the diminutive menu include oysters lightly poached in seasoned milk; fried shrimp, trout, and soft-shell-crab platters; and fried oysters, impeccably fresh and greaseless, served between thick slices of white toast. Everything is clean, and nothing is superfluous. Even the houseplants have a just-polished look. ⊠ *4330 Magazine St., Uptown* ☎ *504/895–9761* ⊕ *www.casamentosrestaurant.com Reservations not accepted* ☰ *No credit cards* ⊘ *Closed Sun., Mon., and early June–late Aug.*

$$$ ✕**Commander's Palace.** No restaurant captures New Orleans's gastro-
CREOLE nomic heritage and celebratory spirit as well as this one, long considered
Fodor's Choice the grande dame of New Orleans's fine dining. The recent renovation
★ has added new life, especially upstairs, where the Garden Room's glass walls have marvelous views of the giant oak trees on the patio below; other rooms promote conviviality with their bright pastels. The menu's

5

classics include sugarcane-grilled pork chops; a spicy and meaty turtle soup; terrific bourbon-lacquered Mississippi quail; and a wonderful griddle-seared gulf fish. Among the addictive desserts is the bread-pudding soufflé. Weekend brunches are a New Orleans tradition. Jackets are preferred at dinner. ⊠*1403 Washington Ave., Garden District* ☎*504/899–8221* ⊕*www.commanderspalace.com* ⚑*Reservations essential* ▤*AE, D, DC, MC, V.*

WHERE TO STAY

FRENCH QUARTER/FAUBOURG MARIGNY

$$$ **Bourbon Orleans Hotel.** Located in the absolute center of the French Quarter, this property has been exquisitely renovated. The lobby level exudes turn-of-the-20th-century New Orleans glamour, and includes the consistently outstanding Paillard's Restaurant. Guest rooms are spacious and well-appointed, but those that face the street are a bit hard on the ears, due to the nightly activity on Bourbon Street. Business travelers will appreciate ergonomic office chairs and in-room Wi-Fi. The lobby-level Bourbon Oh! bar is a quiet place to have cocktails and people-watch through wall-to-wall windows, and Napoleon's Itch bar is great for late-night Bourbon Street fun. **Pros:** recent meticulous renovation; outstanding restaurant. **Cons:** lobby level is often crowded and noisy with curious passersby; hotel is steps from loud, 24-hour Bourbon Street bars. ⊠*717 Orleans Ave., French Quarter* ☎*504/523–2222* ⊕*www. bourbonorleans.com* ⟿*346 rooms, 16 suites* ⚐*In-room: Wi-Fi. In-hotel: restaurant, bars, gym, parking (paid)* ▤*AE, D, DC, MC.*

$$ **Claiborne Mansion.** Enormous rooms with high ceilings, canopy or four-poster beds, polished hardwood floors, and rich fabrics embellish this handsome 1859 mansion in the Faubourg Marigny, on the fringe of the French Quarter. The house overlooks Washington Square Park and has a lush, dramatically lighted rear courtyard and pool. Although it's spacious and elegant, the charming house still feels intimate. Celebrities regularly book it for the privacy, but families appreciate its suites with separate bedrooms. Think of the mansion as an authentic mid-19th-century home—with cable and air-conditioning. **Pros:** elegant alternative to hotels and B&Bs; within walking distance of several great restaurants and jazz clubs. **Cons:** street parking only. ⊠*2111 Dauphine St., Faubourg Marigny* ☎*504/949–7327* ⊕*www.claibornemansion.com* ⟿*2 rooms, 5 suites* ⚐*In-hotel: pool* ▤*AE, MC, V* ⍧*BP.*

$$ **Hotel Maison de Ville.** Delightfully secluded amid the hustle and bustle
Fodor's Choice   of the French Quarter, this property oozes refined elegance and romance.
★   Tapestry-covered chairs, a gas fire burning in the sitting room, and antiques-furnished rooms all contribute to a 19th-century atmosphere. Some rooms are in former slave quarters in the courtyard; others are on the upper floors of the main house. Breakfast is served on a silver tray, and port and sherry are available in the afternoon. For a special hideaway, book one of the hotel's Audubon Cottages. The Bistro at Maison de Ville is one of the best-kept culinary secrets in the French Quarter. **Pros:** unique rooms; personal and consistently above-average service. **Cons:** tough to get a reservation. ⊠*727 Toulouse St., French Quarter* ☎*504/561–5858 or 800/634–1600* ⊕*www.maisondeville.com* ⟿*14*

CLOSE UP

Louisiana Facts

■ As of late 2007, the population of New Orleans was hovering at about 300,000—roughly two-thirds what it was before Hurricane Katrina.

■ At 450 feet, Louisiana's State Capitol building in Baton Rouge, the brainchild of Gov. Huey P. Long, is the tallest in the U.S.

■ The St. Charles Avenue streetcar has been running in one form or another—from locomotives to mule-drawn cars to the electric-powered cars used today—since 1835, making it the oldest continually used transit line in the country.

■ Unlike the other 49 states, Louisiana is divided into parishes, not counties.

■ The official colors of Mardi Gras—purple, green, and gold—represent justice, faith, and power, respectively, and were introduced by the Krewe of Rex in 1892 (appropriately, their theme that year was "Symbolism of Colors").

rooms, 2 suites, 7 cottages ⌂In-room: Wi-Fi. In-hotel: pool, parking (paid), no kids under 12 ☰AE, D, DC, MC, V ⎸⎹CP.

$ 🏨**Hotel Villa Convento.** The Campo family provides around-the-clock service in this four-story 1848 Creole town house. Although it's just blocks from the Quarter's tourist attractions, shopping, and great restaurants, this guesthouse is on a surprisingly quaint, quiet street, close to the Old Ursuline Convent. Each morning you can have croissants and fresh-brewed coffee on the lush patio, or just step across the street to the charming Croissant d'Or. Rooms, which are furnished with reproductions of antiques, vary in price; some have balconies, chandeliers, or ceiling fans. **Pros:** located in the quieter residential section of the French Quarter; local legend says the hotel was once a high-traffic bordello. **Cons:** room decor and linens need updating. ✉616 Ursulines St., French Quarter ☎504/522–1793 ⊕www.villaconvento.com ⟐25 rooms ⌂In-room: Wi-Fi ☰AE, D, DC, MC, V ⎸⎹CP.

$$ 🏨**Lafitte Guest House.** A four-story 1849 French-style manor house, the Lafitte is meticulously restored, with rooms decorated with period furnishings. Room 40 takes up the entire fourth floor and overlooks French Quarter rooftops. Room 5, the loft apartment, overlooks the beautiful courtyard. Breakfast can be brought to your room, served in the Victorian parlor, or enjoyed in the courtyard; wine and hors d'oeuvres are served each evening. **Pros:** feels like a historic mansion; "Mansion rooms" with balcony are spectacular; new furnishings. **Cons:** located on a high-traffic corner of Bourbon Street. ✉1003 Bourbon St., French Quarter ☎504/581–2678 or 800/331–7971 ⊕www.lafitteguesthouse. com ⟐14 rooms, 2 suites ⌂In-room: Wi-Fi. In-hotel: no-smoking rooms ☰AE, D, DC, MC, V ⎸⎹CP.

$ 🏨**Melrose Mansion.** Down pillows and fine-milled soaps; a full breakfast served poolside, in a formal dining room, or in your room; and rooms filled with 19th-century Louisiana antiques are among the attractions of this handsome 1884 Victorian mansion. Rooms and suites are spacious,

Fodor'sChoice

★

with high ceilings and polished hardwood floors. Cocktails are served each evening in the formal drawing room. Baths are sumptuous affairs; those in suites have hot tubs. All but one of the rooms have a wet bar, and one has a private patio. **Pros:** pure luxury; very private; lots of pampering. **Cons:** unreasonable refund policy on reservations—and full room charges must be paid in advance. ⊠ *937 Esplanade Ave., French Quarter* ☎ *504/944–2255* ⊕ *www.melrosegroup.com* ⇤ *8 rooms, 4 suites* ⅄ *In-room: Wi-Fi. In-hotel: bar, pool* ☐ *AE, D, MC, V* ⦿ *BP.*

$$$$ ⚏ **Monteleone Hotel.** The grande dame of French Quarter hotels—with
Fodor'sChoice its ornate baroque facade, liveried doormen, and shimmering lobby
★ chandeliers—was built in 1886 and renovated in 2004. A stellar addition is the full-service Spa Aria. Rooms are extra large and luxurious, with rich fabrics and a mix of four-poster beds, brass beds, and beds with traditional headboards. Junior suites are spacious; sumptuous VIP suites come with extra pampering. The slowly revolving Carousel piano bar in the lobby is a local landmark, and the first-rate dinner in the hotel's Hunt Room Grill is one of the city's best-kept secrets. There's live jazz every night in the lounge. **Pros:** ideal central location offering access to French Quarter and downtown locations; civilized, old New Orleans feel; recently renovated. **Cons:** while the Hunt Room Grill is nice, the hotel's more casual restaurant offers mediocre food and poor service. ⊠ *214 Royal St., French Quarter* ☎ *504/523–3341 or 800/535–9595* ⊕ *www.hotelmonteleone.com* ⇤ *600 rooms, 55 suites* ⅄ *In-room: Wi-Fi. In-hotel: 2 restaurants, bar, pool, gym, spa, Wi-Fi* ☐ *AE, D, DC, MC, V.*

$$$$ ⚏ **Royal Sonesta Hotel.** Step from the revelry of Bourbon Street into
Fodor'sChoice the marble elegance of this renowned hotel's lobby, where lush plants
★ enhance a cool, serene atmosphere. Most guest rooms are of average size, furnished with light-color reproduction antiques: many have French doors that open onto balconies or patios. Rooms facing Bourbon Street are noisy, but most are sufficiently soundproof. Begue's Restaurant is locally beloved and presents one of the city's best Sunday buffet brunches; the charming Desire Oyster Bar, on the lobby level, faces Bourbon Street and serves local seafood delicacies. **Pros:** outstanding service; bustling, cavernous lobby; great balcony views of the Quarter. **Cons:** consistent high occupancy can lead to slow elevator service; rooms facing Bourbon street are noisy. ⊠ *300 Bourbon St., French Quarter* ☎ *504/586–0300 or 800/766–3782* ⊕ *www.royalsonestano. com* ⇤ *500 rooms, 32 suites* ⅄ *In-room: Wi-Fi. In-hotel: 2 restaurants, bar, pool, gym, parking (paid)* ☐ *AE, D, DC, MC, V.*

$$$$ ⚏ **Soniat House.** This singularly handsome property comprises three
Fodor'sChoice meticulously restored town houses built in the 1830s. Polished hard-
★ wood floors, Oriental rugs, and American and European antiques are complemented by contemporary artwork. Amenities include Annick Goutal toiletries, goose-down pillows, and Egyptian cotton sheets. Some rooms and suites have hot tubs. Exotic plants fill two secluded courtyards, where afternoon cocktails and an unforgettable breakfast ($12.50 extra) of homemade biscuits and strawberry jam, fresh-squeezed orange juice, and café au lait can be enjoyed, weather permitting. An on-site antiques shop carries exquisite European furnishings. Many

regular New Orleans visitors consider this the city's finest hotel. **Pros:** sheer refined elegance; incomparable privacy; expert service; afternoon wine service that is as civilized as it gets. **Cons:** while the breakfast is delicious, portions and menu options are limited. ✉*1133 Chartres St., French Quarter* ☎*504/522–0570 or 800/544–8808* ⊕*www.soniathouse.com* ↪*20 rooms, 13 suites* ⌂*In-room: Wi-Fi. In-hotel: parking (paid)* ▭*AE, MC, V.*

CBD

$

Fodor'sChoice

★

🖵**Harrah's New Orleans Hotel.** Located directly across the street from Harrah's New Orleans Casino, this 26-story hotel is richly appointed with marble floors, exquisite chandeliers, plush furnishings, and artwork selected and installed by local gallery owner Arthur Roger. The lobby-level restaurant, Ruth's Chris Steak House, is considered by locals to be among the best steak restaurants in the city. Guest rooms are larger than the local norm and have extras like refrigerators, high-definition televisions, cordless phones, and Wi-Fi. The Fulton Street Corridor, a four-block promenade featuring shops, private party spaces, and live entertainment areas, is connected to the hotel. **Pros:** well-trained staff provides above-average service; guests without cars can easily walk to Riverfront, CBD, and French Quarter attractions. **Cons:** the hustle and bustle of this part of town might not suit travelers seeking peace and quiet. ✉*Poydras St. at Fulton St., CBD* ☎*504/533–6000 or 800/847–5299* ⊕*www.harrahs.com* ↪*450 rooms, 81 suites* ⌂*In-room: refrigerator, Wi-Fi. In-hotel: restaurant, bar, pool, gym, spa, laundry service* ▭*AE, D, DC, MC, V.*

$$$

Fodor'sChoice

★

🖵**Loews New Orleans Hotel.** A refashioned bank building in the heart of downtown is home to this plush 21st-century hotel. The West Indies–style lobby provides a welcoming atmosphere, and bright, oversized rooms are enriched with local artwork and soothing colors. The guest rooms are among the largest and most well appointed in the city. Café Adelaide and the Swizzlestick Bar, both on the lobby level, are operated by the same family that owns the legendary Commander's Palace Restaurant. This may look like a typical chain hotel on the outside—but inside it's singular in its quality and consistency. **Pros:** well managed; accessible to everything that counts downtown; reliable service and product. **Cons:** located in one of the most high-traffic downtown areas. ✉*300 Poydras St., CBD* ☎*504/595–5310 or 800/235–6397* ⊕*www.loewshotels.com* ↪*273 rooms, 12 suites* ⌂*In-room: Wi-Fi. In-hotel: restaurant, bar, pool, gym, spa, laundry service* ▭*AE, D, DC, MC, V.*

$$$

Fodor'sChoice

★

🖵**Windsor Court Hotel.** Exquisite, gracious, elegant, eminently civilized—these words are frequently used to describe Windsor Court, but all fail to capture the wonderful essence of this hotel. From Le Salon's delightful afternoon tea—the city's only authentic European presentation, served daily in the lobby—to the unbelievably large rooms, this is one of *the* places to stay in New Orleans. Plush carpeting, canopy and four-poster beds, fully stocked wet bars, marble vanities, and mirrored dressing areas are just a few of the many amenities. The Grill Room is considered the premiere fine-dining room in the city, and the Polo Lounge has one of the best martini presentations to be found

5

anywhere, as well as a highly imaginative appetizer menu. The hotel is four blocks from the French Quarter and easy walking distance to the Riverfront and fabulous shopping options. **Pros:** old-world elegance; superior service. **Cons:** lobby is on the 11th floor; only two elevators from ground level to lobby. ⊠*300 Gravier St., CBD* ☎*504/523–6000 or 800/262–2662* ⊕*www.windsorcourthotel.com* ⌖*58 rooms, 266 suites, 1 penthouse* ♿*In-room: Wi-Fi. In-hotel: 2 restaurants, bar, pool, gym, laundry service, parking (paid)* ⊟*AE, D, DC, MC, V.*

GARDEN DISTRICT/UPTOWN

$

Fodor'sChoice

★

Chimes Bed and Breakfast. Jill and Charles Abbyad's charming Uptown residence has rooms in the main house and a converted carriage house, with hardwood or slate floors. The Abbyads maintain a homey environment with all the conveniences of a large hotel: hair dryers, irons, stereos, coffeemakers, and private entrances. A Continental breakfast is served in the airy dining room; afterward, you can relax in the butterfly garden in the courtyard. English, French, Arabic, and Spanish are spoken in the house, and children are welcome. All rooms have private entrances onto the courtyard. **Pros:** premises and guest rooms are extremely well kept and clean. **Cons:** noise carries easily from room to room. ⊠*1146 Constantinople St., Uptown* ☎*504/899–2621* ⊕*www. chimesneworleans.com* ⌖*5 rooms* ♿*In-room: Internet, Wi-Fi. In-hotel: some pets allowed, no-smoking rooms* ⊟*AE, MC, V* ⎟⊙⎟*CP.*

¢

1896 O'Malley House. This house is sheer elegance. Rooms are furnished with beautiful antiques, with heavy cypress doors, hardwood floors, granite bathroom counters, and oversize windows with plush draperies. The owners have paid attention to every detail, down to the chocolates delivered with the evening turndown service—on a silver tray. Step outside and board the Canal Street streetcar for a quick ride downtown. This place is a true find. **Pros:** surprisingly low rates; steps away from the Canal Street streetcar line. **Cons:** some distance from downtown and French Quarter attractions. ⊠*120 S. Pierce St., Uptown* ☎*504/488–5896 or 866/226–1896* ⊕*www.1896omalleyhouse.com* ⌖*8 rooms* ♿*In-room: Wi-Fi* ⊟*AE, MC, V* ⎟⊙⎟*CP.*

$$

Fodor'sChoice

★

Grand Victorian Bed & Breakfast. Just a block and a half from Commander's Palace Restaurant, the Grand Victorian more than lives up to its lofty name. Each lavishly appointed room evokes old Louisiana with period pieces and distinctive private baths. The Greenwood Suite includes a hot tub, stained-glass windows, and a private balcony that extends across the front of the house and overlooks historic St. Charles Avenue. An oak-shaded common balcony on the second floor stands atop a traditional New Orleans garden. A Continental breakfast is served in either the dining room or on the balcony. **Pros:** true elegance; rooms are exquisitely appointed; possibly the best B&B value in the area. **Cons:** located on a high-traffic street. ⊠*2727 St. Charles Ave., Garden District* ☎*504/895–1104 or 800/977–0008* ⊕*www.gvbb.com* ⌖*8 rooms* ♿*In-room: Wi-Fi. In-hotel: restaurant* ⊟*AE, D, MC, V.*

$

Maison Perrier Bed & Breakfast. This 1890s Victorian mansion reportedly housed a gentlemen's club, and rooms have been named after the ladies of the evening who entertained here. Comfortable, spacious rooms have high ceilings and exceptionally large, well-appointed private baths;

some have private balconies and sitting rooms. The daily homemade breakfast may include waffles and praline French toast. Fresh-baked brownies and tea are served in late afternoon; complimentary wine, beer, and cheese are served in the charming front parlor on Friday and Saturday evening. **Pros:** recent redecorating has truly brought the place up a notch; the lavender "Dolly's Room" is one of the most beautiful rooms in town; fantastic balconies for Mardi Gras parade watching. **Cons:** rooms that face St. Charles Avenue can be noisy. ⊠*4117 Perrier St., Uptown* ☎*504/897–1807 or 888/610–1807* ⊕*www.maisonperrier. com* ➡*9 rooms* ♿*In-room: Wi-Fi* ⊟*AE, D, MC, V.*

NIGHTLIFE

People come here to eat, listen to live music, and party; and the city still delivers on all three counts. No American town places such a premium on pleasure as New Orleans. From swank hotel lounges to sweaty dance clubs, refined jazz clubs, and raucous Bourbon Street bars, this city is serious about frivolity—and famous for it. Partying is more than an occasional indulgence in this city—it's a lifestyle.

BARS AND LOUNGES

Fodor'sChoice
★ **Columns Hotel.** An evening cocktail on the expansive front porch of the Columns, shaded by centuries-old oak trees and overlooking the St. Charles Avenue streetcar route, is one of the more romantic New Orleans experiences. The Victorian Lounge, with period decor and a fireplace, and plenty of decaying elegance, draws a white-collar crowd of all ages. Live jazz combos play Monday through Wednesday evenings. ⊠*3811 St. Charles Ave., Uptown* ☎*504/899–9308.*

Crescent City Brewhouse. This convivial brewpub makes five specialty brews on the premises and one seasonal selection. The suds pair well with oysters on the half shell and other pub grub. Jazz combos set up near the entrance most afternoons, and seating on a second-floor balcony affords a nice view of the Mississippi River and busy Decatur Street. ⊠*527 Decatur St., French Quarter* ☎*504/522–0571.*

French 75. Sophistication awaits in the form of rich cigars and fine liquor served up in cozy French-style surroundings. The specialty here is the French 75, made with brandy and premium champagne. After a round or two, venture upstairs to the Germaine Wells Mardi Gras Museum, showcase for many ball gowns worn by the original owner's daughter. ⊠*813 Bienville St., French Quarter* ☎*504/523–5433.*

★ **Lafitte's Blacksmith Shop.** Probably the most photographed building in the Quarter after St. Louis Cathedral, this 18th-century cottage was, according to legend, once a blacksmith shop that served as a front for the eponymous pirate's less legitimate business ventures. Today, it's a popular and atmospheric piano bar with a rustic, candlelit interior and a small outdoor patio that has banana trees and a sculpture by the late Enrique Alferez (whose work also decorates City Park). ⊠*941 Bourbon St., French Quarter* ☎*504/522–9397.*

Napoleon House Bar and Cafe. This vintage watering hole has long been popular with writers, artists, and various other free spirits; even locals who don't venture often into the French Quarter will make it a special destination. It's a living shrine to the New Orleans school of decor: faded grandeur. Chipped wall paint, diffused light, and a tiny courtyard with a trickling fountain and lush banana trees create a timeless escapist mood. The house specialty is a Pimm's Cup (Pimm's No. 1, juice, and club soda—a sort of fizzy, spiked lemonade); a menu including sandwiches, soups, salads, and cheese boards is also available. This is the perfect place for late-afternoon people-watching. ⊠ *500 Chartres St., French Quarter* ☎ *504/524–9752.*

> ## GET A "GO CUP"
>
> If you're on foot, you can get your beverage to go from any bar in the city. Open containers of alcohol are allowed on the streets, as long as they're not in glass containers. So when you're ready to leave, ask your bartender for a "go cup," pour your drink into the plastic cup, and head out the door to the next venue, drink in hand.

Pat O'Brien's. Sure, it's touristy, but there are reasons Pat O's has been a must-stop on the New Orleans cocktail trail for so long. For one thing, there's plenty of room to spread out, from the elegant side bar and piano bar that flank the carriageway entrance to the lush (and in winter, heated) patio. Friendly staff, an easy camaraderie among patrons, and a signature drink—the pink, cloying, and extremely potent Hurricane, which comes with a souvenir glass—make this French Quarter stalwart a pleasant afternoon diversion. ⊠ *718 St. Peter St., French Quarter* ☎ *504/525–4823.*

The Sazerac Bar. Located in the historic and newly renovated Roosevelt Hotel, this is one of the most famous bars in Louisiana, providing libations and inspiration since 1893. Drawn to the signature Sazerac cocktails and ramos gin fizzes, a famous and intriguing clientele has graced the bar over the years, including Governor Huey P. Long, who in the 1930s built a 90-mi highway between New Orleans and the state capital, so, many believe, he could get directly to the hotel lounge for his signature drink. ⊠ *123 Baronne St., CBD* ☎ *504/648–1200.*

FESTIVALS

Fodor's Choice ★ **Mardi Gras.** There's simply nothing quite like Mardi Gras, which takes place in February or March. The biggest event in the city's busy festival calendar has been around for well over a century, and for a celebration of frivolity, people here take Carnival very seriously. There are almost daily parades—even one for dogs, the Krewe of Barkus—in the two weeks leading up to Fat Tuesday, when pretty much the entire city takes the day off, gets in costume, and hits the streets. ⊕ *www.mardigrasneworleans.com.*

New Orleans Jazz & Heritage Festival. Top-notch local and international talent take to several stages the last weekend of April and first weekend of May. The repertoire covers much more than jazz, with big-name pop stars in the mix, and there are dozens of lectures, quality arts and crafts, and awesome food to boot. Next to Mardi Gras, Jazz Fest is the city's biggest draw; book your hotel as far in advance as possible. ☎ *504/410–4100* ⊕ *www.nojazzfest.com.*

MUSIC VENUES

First-time visitors to New Orleans are often bowled over by the amount of both musical talent the city contains and the opportunities to witness it live—in clubs, coffee shops, at festivals, even on the street. Use the following list as a starting point: the venues selected here host good bands on a regular basis, but represent just a fraction of the opportunities you'll have to hear live music.

WORD OF MOUTH

"I walked past the French Quarter through part of Marigny the residential area and Frenchmen's Reef, a street of jazz bars which my bartender last night told me to explore—much nicer than Bourbon Street."   —NeoPatrick

★ **Donna's Bar & Grill.** Donna's is a great place to hear traditional jazz, R&B, and the city's young brass bands in an informal neighborhood setting. On Monday night many of the city's top musicians stop by after their regular gigs to sit in for the diverse sets of drummer Bob French; free red beans and rice are served. ⊠ *800 N. Rampart St., French Quarter* ☎ *504/596–6914.*

House of Blues. Despite its name, blues is a relatively small component in the booking policy, which also embraces rock, jazz, country, soul, funk, world music, and more, performed by everyone from local artists to international touring acts. The adjoining restaurant has an eclectic menu, with classic Southern cuisine, served in ample portions at reasonable prices. The **Parish,** a smaller, more intimate offshoot upstairs from the main house, hosts local and touring groups. ⊠ *225 Decatur St., French Quarter* ☎ *504/529–2583 concert line.*

Fodor'sChoice ★ **Maple Leaf.** The phrase "New Orleans institution" gets thrown around a lot, but this place deserves the title. It's wonderfully atmospheric, with pressed-tin walls and a lush tropical patio, and one of the city's best venues for blues, New Orleans–style R&B, funk, zydeco, and jazz. On Sunday, the bar hosts the South's longest-running poetry reading. It's a long haul from the French Quarter, but worth the trip, especially if combined with a visit to one of the restaurants clustered near this commercial stretch of Oak Street. ⊠ *8316 Oak St., Uptown* ☎ *504/866–9359.*

Preservation Hall. The jazz tradition that flowered in the 1920s is enshrined in this cultural landmark by a cadre of distinguished New Orleans musicians, most of whom were schooled by an ever-dwindling group of elder statesmen. There is limited seating on benches—many patrons end up squatting on the floor or standing in back—and no beverages are served or allowed. Nonetheless, the legions of satisfied customers regard an evening here as an essential New Orleans experience. Cover charge is $10, but can run a bit higher for special appearances. Call ahead for performance times; sometimes the show ends before you even begin pre-partying. ⊠ *726 St. Peter St., French Quarter* ☎ *504/522–2841 or 504/523–8939.*

★ **Snug Harbor.** This intimate club is one of the city's best rooms for soaking up modern jazz, blues, and R&B. It is the home base of such esteemed talent as vocalist Charmaine Neville and pianist-patriarch Ellis Marsalis (father of Wynton and Branford). The dining room serves good

5

local food but is best known for its burgers. Budget-conscious types can listen to the band through speakers in the bar without paying the rather high cover charge. ⊠ *626 Frenchmen St., Faubourg Marigny* ☎ *504/949–0696.*

Fodor's Choice
★ **Spotted Cat.** Jazz, funk, and blues bands perform nearly every night, with early-afternoon sets weekends, at this rustic club right in the thick of the Frenchmen Street action. A rattan seat near the front window makes for good people-watching. ⊠ *623 Frenchmen St., Faubourg Marigny* ☎ *504/943–3887.*

Tipitina's. A bust of legendary New Orleans pianist Professor Longhair, or "Fess," greets visitors at the door of this Uptown landmark, which takes its name from one of his most popular songs. As the concert posters pinned to the walls attest, Tip's hosts a wide variety of touring bands and local acts. The long-running Sunday-afternoon Cajun dance still packs the floor. The Tipitina's Foundation has an office and workshop upstairs, where local musicians affected by Hurricane Katrina can network, gain access to resources, and search for gigs. ⊠ *501 Napoleon Ave., Uptown* ☎ *504/895–8477.*

SHOPPING

The main shopping areas in the city are the **French Quarter,** with narrow, picturesque streets lined with specialty, gift, fashion, and antiques shops and art galleries; the **Central Business District** (CBD), populated mostly with specialty and department stores; the **Warehouse District,** best known for contemporary-arts galleries and cultural museums; **Magazine Street,** home to antiques shops, art galleries, home-furnishings stores, dining venues, fashion boutiques, and specialty shops; and the **Riverbend/Maple Street** area, which offers clothing, jewelry, and bookstores, as well as some specialty shops.

ANTIQUES

Bush Antiques. Antique beds are the specialty, but you'll also find religious artifacts, Continental furniture, architectural elements, ironwork, and lighting. The shop displays its beds, furniture, and accessories in vignettes in 12 rooms on two floors. A courtyard in the back holds a bounty of antique garden accoutrements. ⊠ *2109 Magazine St., Uptown* ☎ *504/581–3518* ⊕ *www.bushantiques.com.*

★ **Lucullus.** The entire store is focused on the art of food—preparing it, serving it, and eating it—and is filled with French tables, English china, cooking and serving utensils, linens, lighting, food-related art, snuff boxes and more, including oddities like Lady Sarah Churchill's picnic set. Items are mainly from the 18th and 19th centuries. The shop is owned by Patrick Dunne, author of *Epicurean Collector.* ⊠ *610 Chartres St., French Quarter* ☎ *504/528–9620* ⊕ *www.lucullusantiques.com.*

Fodor's Choice
★ **M.S. Rau.** Historically significant items, such as furniture and other pieces from royal families, are spotlighted among 18th- and 19th-century French, American, and English furniture, sterling silver, cut glass, statuary, and jewelry in this 30,000-square-foot store, which opened in 1912. ⊠ *630 Royal St., French Quarter* ☎ *504/523–5660 or 800/544–9440* ⊕ *www.rauantiques.com.*

ART AND CRAFTS GALLERIES

Fodor's Choice ★ **Arthur Roger Gallery.** One of the most respected names among art aficionados, Arthur Roger has compiled a must-see collection of local contemporary artworks by Lin Emery, Jacqueline Bishop, and Willie Birch, as well as such national names as glass artist Dale Chihuly and filmmaker-photographer John Waters. ✉*432 Julia St., Warehouse District* ☎*504/522–1999* ✉*730 Tchoupitoulas St., Warehouse District* ☎*504/524–9393* ⊕*www.arthurrogergallery.com.*

LeMieux Gallery. Gulf Coast artists from Louisiana to Florida display art and crafts here alongside work by the late New Orleans abstract artist Paul Ninas. ✉*332 Julia St., Warehouse District* ☎*504/522–5988* ⊕*www.lemieuxgalleries.com.*

★ **RHINO Contemporary Crafts.** The name stands for Right Here In New Orleans, which is where most of the artists whose arts and crafts are displayed in this co-op live and work. You'll find original paintings in varying styles, metalwork, sculpture, ceramics, glass, functional art, jewelry, fashion accessories, and artwork made from found objects. The gallery also holds art classes for children. ✉*333 Canal St., Shops at Canal Place, CBD* ☎*504/523–7945* ⊕*www.rhinocrafts.com.*

BOOKS

Librairie Book Shop. Set up like a library with well-stocked shelves of old, new, and hard-to-find volumes, this spot carries the Quarter's largest selection of books, posters, and postcards of local lore. ✉*823 Chartres St., French Quarter* ☎*504/525–4837.*

CLOTHING

★ **Trashy Diva Boutique.** Boutique owner/designer Candice Gwinn puts a retro-romantic spin inspired by the 1920s to 1950s on the women's fashions she creates. You'll find dresses, blouses, skirts, coats, jewelry, upscale shoes, and hats. The Trashy Diva Lingerie Boutique next door (831 Chartres St.) features corsets and romantic evening wear. ✉*829 Chartres St., French Quarter* ☎*504/581–4555* ✉*2048 Magazine St., Uptown* ☎*504/299–8777* ⊕*www.trashydiva.com.*

JEWELRY

Fodor's Choice ★ **Katy Beh Contemporary Jewelry.** The owner's penchant for unusual, finely crafted contemporary jewelry is evident in the display cases that hold national and emerging artists' delicate and sometimes bold pins, bracelets, earrings, rings, and pendants. ✉*3708 Magazine St., Uptown* ☎*504/896–9600 or 877/528–9234* ⊕*www.katybeh.com.*

MUSIC

★ **Louisiana Music Factory.** A favorite haunt for locals looking for New Orleans's and regional music—new and old—this retail store has records, tapes, CDs, DVDs, sheet music, and books as well as listening stations, music-oriented T-shirts, original art of musicians, and a stage for live concerts. ✉*210 Decatur St., French Quarter* ☎*504/586–1094* ⊕*www.louisianamusicfactory.com.*

PLANTATION COUNTRY

The area designated Plantation Country envelops a cascade of plantations along the Great River Road leading west from New Orleans. Louisiana plantations range from the grandiose Nottoway on River Road to the humbler owner-occupied homes.

The River Road plantations are closely tied to New Orleans's culture and society: it was here that many of the city's most prominent families made their fortunes generations ago, and the language and tastes here are historically French. Baton Rouge, the state capital, has some interesting sights of its own.

GETTING HERE AND AROUND

From New Orleans, the fastest route to the River Road plantations is Interstate 10 west to Interstate 310 to Exit 6, River Road. Alternatives to the Great River Road are to continue on either Interstate 10 or U.S. 61 west; both have signs marking exits for various plantations. Route 18 runs along the west bank of the river, Route 44 on the east.

THE GREAT RIVER ROAD

The Old South is suspended in an uneasy state of grace along the Great River Road, where the culture that thrived here during the 18th and 19th centuries, both elegant and disturbing, meets the blunt ugliness of the industrial age. Between New Orleans and Baton Rouge, beautifully restored antebellum plantations along the Mississippi are filled with period antiques, ghosts of former residents, and tales of Yankee gunboats. Yet industrial plants mar the scenery, and the man-made levee, constructed in the early 20th century in a desperate ploy to keep the mighty Mississippi on a set course, obstructs the river views that plantation residents once enjoyed. Still, you can always park your car and climb up on the levee for a look at Ol' Man River.

The Great River Road is also called, variously, Route or LA 44 and 75 on the east bank of the river and Route or LA 18 on the west bank. "LA" and "Route" are interchangeable; we use Route throughout this chapter. Alternatives to the Great River Road are Interstate 10 and U.S. 61; both have signs marking exits for various plantations. All the plantations described are listed on the National Register of Historic Places, and some of them are B&Bs. Plantation touring can take anywhere from an hour to two days, depending upon how many houses you want to see.

DESTREHAN PLANTATION

23 mi west (upriver) of New Orleans.

The oldest plantation left intact in the lower Mississippi Valley, this simple West Indies–style house, built in 1787 by a free man of color, is typical of the homes built by the earliest planters in the region. The plantation is notable for the hand-hewn cypress timbers that were used in its construction and for the insulation in its walls, made of *bousillage,* a mixture of horsehair, Spanish moss, and mud. Some days bring period demonstrations of indigo dying, candle making, or open-

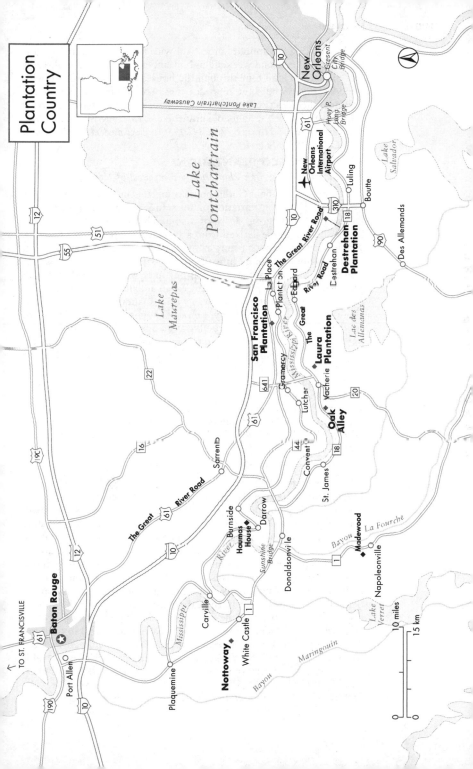

Plantation Country

TO ST. FRANCISVILLE

Baton Rouge

Port Allen

Plaquemine

Carville

White Castle

Nottoway ◆

Bayou Maringouin

Mississippi River

Sunshine Bridge

Donaldsonville

Napoleonville

Lake Verret

Bayou La Fourche

Madewood ◆

Houmas House ◆

Burnside

Darrow

St. James

Convent

Oak Alley ◆

Vacherie

The Laura Plantation ◆

Lutcher

Gramercy

San Francisco Plantation

The Great River Road

Mississippi River

The Great River Road

Planter on Great River Road

La Place

Edgard

Castrehan

Destrehan Plantation

River Road

Boutte

Luling

New Orleans International Airport

Lake Maurepas

Lake Pontchartrain

Lake Pontchartrain Causeway

New Orleans

Crescent City Bridge

Huey P. Long Bridge

Lake Salvador

Lac des Allemands

Des Allemands

Sorrento

Lake Pontchartrain

10 miles

15 km

hearth cooking; an annual fall festival with music, crafts, and food is held during the second weekend in November. A costumed guide leads you on a 45-minute tour through the house, which is furnished with period antiques and some reproductions. You are free to explore the grounds, including several smaller structures and massive oak trees borne down by their weighty old branches. ✉ *13034 River Rd., Destrehan* ☎ *985/764–9315 or 877/453–2095* ⊕ *www.destrehanplantation. org* 🎫 *$10* 🕐 *Daily 9–4.*

SAN FRANCISCO PLANTATION

18 mi west of Destrehan Plantation, 35 mi west of New Orleans.

An elaborate Steamboat Gothic house completed in 1856, San Francisco presents an intriguing variation on the standard plantation styles, with galleries resembling the decks of a ship. The house was once called St. Frusquin, a name derived from a French slang term, *sans fruscins,* which means "without a penny in my pocket"—the condition its owner, Valsin Marmillion, found himself in after paying exorbitant construction costs. Valsin's father, Edmond Bozonier Marmillion, had begun the project. Upon his father's death, Valsin and his German bride, Louise von Seybold, found themselves with a plantation on their hands. Unable to return to Germany, Louise brought German influence to south Louisiana instead. The result was an opulence rarely encountered in these parts: ceilings painted in trompe l'oeil, hand-painted "toilets" with primitive flushing systems, and cypress painstakingly rendered as marble. Tour guides impart the full fascinating story on the 45-minute tour through the main house. An authentic one-room schoolhouse and a slave cabin have been installed on the grounds, which you can tour at your leisure. Louisiana novelist Frances Parkinson Keyes used the site as the model for her book *Steamboat Gothic.* ✉ *2646 River Rd., Garyville* ☎ *985/535–2341 or 888/322–1756* ⊕ *www.sanfranciscoplantation.org* 🎫 *$15* 🕐 *Nov.–Mar., daily 9–4; Apr.–Oct., daily 9:30–4:30.*

LAURA PLANTATION

10 mi west of San Francisco Plantation, 57 mi west of New Orleans.

Laura Plantation provides a more intimate, well-documented presentation of Creole plantation life than any other property on River Road. The narrative of the guides is built on first-person accounts, estate records, and original artifacts from the Locoul family, who built the simple, Creole-style house in 1805. Laura Locoul, whose grandmother founded the estate, kept a detailed diary of plantation life, family fights, and the management of slaves. The information from Laura's diary and the original slave cabins and other outbuildings (workers on the plantation grounds lived in the cabins into the 1980s) provide rare insights into slavery under the French. The plantation gift shop stocks a large selection of literature by and about slaves and slavery in southern Louisiana and the United States. Senegalese slaves at Laura are believed to have first told folklorist Alcee Fortier the tales of Br'er Rabbit; his friend Joel Chandler Harris used the stories in his Uncle Remus tales. ✉ *2247 River Rd. (Rte. 18), Vacherie* ☎ *225/265–7690 or 888/799–7690* ⊕ *www.lauraplantation.com* 🎫 *$15* 🕐 *Daily 10–4.*

OAK ALLEY

3 mi west of Laura Plantation, 60 mi west of New Orleans.

Built between 1837 and 1839 by Jacques T. Roman, a French-Creole sugar planter from New Orleans, Oak Alley is the most famous of all the antebellum homes in Louisiana and an outstanding example of Greek Revival architecture. The 28 gnarled oak trees that line the drive and give the columned plantation its name were planted in the early 1700s by an earlier settler, and the oaks proved more resilient than the dwelling he must have built here. A guided tour introduces you to the grand interior of the manor, furnished with period antiques. Be sure to take in the view from the upper gallery of the house and to spend time exploring the expansive grounds. A number of late-19th-century cottages behind the main house provide simple overnight accommodations and a restaurant is open daily for breakfast (8:30–10:30) and lunch (11–3). ⊠ *3645 River Rd. (Rte. 18), Vacherie* ☎ *225/265–2151 or 888/279–9802* ⊕ *www.oakalleyplantation.com* 🗏 *$15* ⊗ *Weekdays 10–4, weekends 10–5.*

NOTTOWAY

Fodor's Choice
★ *33 mi northwest of Madewood, 70 mi west of New Orleans.*

The South's largest plantation house, Nottoway, should not be missed. Built in 1857, the mansion is a gem of Italianate style. With 64 rooms, 22 columns, and 200 windows, this white castle (the town of White Castle was named for it) was the crowning achievement of architect Henry Howard. It was saved from destruction during the Civil War by a Northern officer (a former guest of the owners, Mr. and Mrs. John Randolph). An idiosyncratic layout reflects the individual tastes of the original owners and includes a grand ballroom, famed in these parts for its crystal chandeliers and hand-carved columns. You can stay here overnight, and a formal restaurant serves lunch and dinner daily. ⊠ *31025 Hwy. 1, 2 mi north of White Castle* ☎ *225/545–8632 or 866/527–6884* ⊕ *www.nottoway.com* 🗏 *$15* ⊗ *Daily 9–5.*

BATON ROUGE

80 mi northwest of New Orleans via I-10.

Hemmed in as it is by endless industrial plants, Baton Rouge does not look like much from the road. However, Baton Rouge, the state capital, has several interesting and readily accessible sights, including the attractive capitol grounds and an educational planetarium. This is the city from which colorful, cunning Huey P. Long ruled the state; it is also the site of his assassination. Even today, more than half a century after Long's death, legends about the controversial governor and U.S. senator abound.

ESSENTIALS

Visitor Information Baton Rouge Visitors & Conventions Bureau ⊠ *730 North Blvd., Baton Rouge* ☎ *225/383–1825 or 800/527–6843* ⊕ *www.visitbatonrouge.com.* **Louisiana Visitor Information Center** ⊠ *900 N. 3rd St., Baton Rouge* ☎ *225/342–7317* ⊕ *www.louisianatravel.com.*

EXPLORING

♻ **Louisiana Arts & Science Museum and Irene W. Pennington Planetarium.**
Housed in a 1925 Illinois Central railroad station near the Old State
Capitol, this idiosyncratic but high-quality museum brings together a
contemporary art gallery, an Egyptian tomb exhibit, a children's museum and discovery zone, and a state-of-the-art planetarium, which is
also kid-friendly. The planetarium presents regular shows, as does the
ExxonMobil Space Theater. The museum also hosts traveling exhibits, and houses the nation's second-largest collection of sculptures by
20th-century Croatian artist Ivan Mestrovic, many of which adorn the
entrance hall. ⊠ *100 S. River Rd.* ☎ *225/344–5272* ⊕ *www.lasm.org*
▭ *$6, $8 including planetarium show* ⊗ *Tues.–Fri. 10–4, Sat. 10–5
(planetarium 10–8), Sun. 1–5.*

Louisiana State Museum—Baton Rouge. This museum showcases the history
of Louisiana through two exhibits: "Grounds for Greatness: Louisiana
and the Nation," which relates Louisiana history to the nation and the
world, from the Louisiana Purchase to World War II; and the "Louisiana Experience: Discovering the Soul of America," a road-trip-like
exhibit that courses through the different regions of the state. There is
also a gallery for changing exhibits. ⊠ *660 N. 4th St.* ☎ *800/568–6968*
▭ *$6* ⊗ *Tues.–Sat. 9–5, Sun. noon–5.*

Old Governor's Mansion. This Georgian-style home was constructed for
Governor Huey P. Long in 1939, and nine governors have since lived
there. The story goes that Long instructed the architect to design it to
resemble the White House, representing Long's unrealized ambition to
live in the real one. Notable features on the guided tour include Long's
bedroom and a secret staircase. ⊠ *502 North Blvd.* ☎ *225/387–2464*
⊕ *www.oldgovernorsmansion.org* ▭ *$6* ⊗ *Tues.–Fri. 10–3, or by
appointment.*

Old State Capitol. When this Gothic Victorian fantasia was completed
in 1850, it was declared by some to be a masterpiece, by others a
monstrosity. No one can deny that the restored building is colorful
and dramatic. In the entrance hall a stunning purple, gold, and green
spiral staircase winds toward a stained-glass atrium. The building now
holds the **Louisiana Center for Political and Governmental History,** an
education and research facility with audiovisual exhibits. The "assassination room," an exhibit covering Huey Long's final moments, is a
major draw. ⊠ *100 North Blvd., at River Rd.* ⊕ *www.sec.state.la.us/
osc* ▭ *$4* ⊗ *Tues.–Sat. 10–4, Sun. noon–4.*

State Capitol Building. Still called the "New State Capitol," this building has housed the offices of the governor and Congress since 1932. It
is a testament to the personal influence of legendary Governor Huey
Long that the funding for this massive building was approved during
the Great Depression, and that the building itself was completed in a
mere 14 months. You can tour the first floor, richly decked with murals
and mosaics, and peer into the halls of the Louisiana legislature. Huey
Long's colorful personality eventually caught up with him: he was assassinated in 1935, and the spot where he was shot (near the rear elevators)
is marked with a plaque. At 34 stories, this is America's tallest state

capitol; an observation deck on the 27th floor affords an expansive view of the Mississippi River, the city, and the industrial outskirts. ✉ *900 N. 3rd St.* ☎ *225/342–7317* ✉ *Free* ☉ *Daily 8–4:30 (tower until 4).*

WHERE TO EAT

$$$
SOUTHERN
★

✗ **Juban's.** An upscale bistro with a lush courtyard and walls adorned with art, Juban's is a family-owned and -operated restaurant not far from the LSU campus. Tempting main courses of seafood, beef, and veal dishes, as well as roasted duck, rabbit, and quail, highlight the sophisticated menu. The Hallelujah Crab (soft-shell stuffed with seafood and topped with "creolaise" sauce) is a specialty, and Juban's own mango tea is delicious. The warm bread pudding is something to write home about. ✉ *3739 Perkins Rd. (Acadiana Shopping Center)* ☎ *225/346–8422* ⊕ *www.jubans.com* ▭ *AE, D, DC, MC, V* ☉ *Closed Sun. No lunch Mon. and Sat.*

$$
SOUTHERN

✗ **Mike Anderson's.** This lively seafood spot manages to be a lot of things to a lot of people: first-daters, families, groups of friends, and solo diners all find a warm welcome here. Locals of every stripe praise the seafood, and it is true that the food is good, fresh, served in large portions, and consistent. The South Louisiana Combo—fried shrimp, oysters, crawfish tails, catfish, and stuffed crab served with french fries, hush puppies, and a choice of salad or coleslaw (pick the coleslaw!)—is a best bet. ✉ *1031 W. Lee Dr.* ☎ *225/766–7823* ⊕ *www.mikeandersonsbr. com* ▭ *AE, D, MC, V.*

CAJUN COUNTRY

French Louisiana, lying amid the bayous, rice paddies, and canebrakes to the west of New Orleans, has become famous in the rest of the country for its food (jambalaya and blackened fish) and music (both Cajun and zydeco). Cajun culture is decidedly rural, rooted in a smattering of tiny towns and in the swamps and bayous that wind among them. Driving from one village to the next, antiques shoppers and nature lovers alike will find bliss. Live oaks with ragged gray buntings of Spanish moss form canopies over the bottle-green bayous. Country roads follow the contortions of the Teche (pronounced *tesh*), the state's longest bayou, and meander through villages where cypress cabins rise up out of the water on stilts and moored fishing boats and pirogues scarcely bob on the sluggish waters. At the centers of these same villages are wonderful bakeries, historic churches, fresh oyster bars, and regional antiques for sale in small, weathered shops.

Many visitors to this region are surprised to hear the dialect for the first time. Cajun French is an oral tradition in which French vocabulary and approximate grammar encounter the American accent, and it differs significantly from what is spoken in France. English is also spoken throughout Cajun Country, but you will hear Gallic accents and see many signs that read ICI ON PARLE FRANÇAIS (French spoken here).

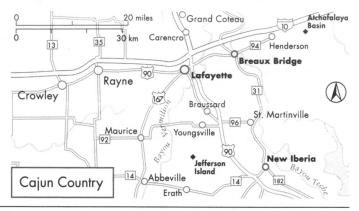

Cajun Country

LAFAYETTE

137 mi northwest of New Orleans via I–10, 60 mi west of Baton Rouge via I–10.

Lafayette (pronounced lah-fay-*ette*), 136 mi west of New Orleans and the largest city in Cajun Country, is a major center of Cajun life and lore, the "big city" in the middle of the countryside. It's an interesting and enjoyable town, with some worthwhile historical and artistic sights. The simulated Cajun villages at **Vermilionville** and **Acadian Village** provide evocative introductions to the traditional Cajun way of life. Excellent restaurants and B&Bs make Lafayette a good jumping-off point for exploring the region. The city has also had an infusion of new restaurants and nightclubs—particularly downtown, which is lively even on weekend nights.

ESSENTIALS

Visitor Information Lafayette Convention and Visitors Commission (⊠ *1400 N.W. Evangeline Thruway [Box 52066], Lafayette* ☎ *337/232–3737 or 800/346–1958* ⊕ *www.lafayettetravel.com*).

EXPLORING

Alexander Mouton House and Lafayette Museum. Built in 1800 as the *maison dimanche,* or "Sunday house," of town founder Jean Mouton, this galleried town house with a mid-19th-century addition now preserves local history. The older section is an excellent example of early Acadian architecture and contains artifacts used by settlers. The main museum contains Civil War–era furnishings and memorabilia and a Mardi Gras exhibit. ⊠ *1122 Lafayette St.* ☎ *337/234–2208* 🎟 *$3* ⊗ *Tues.–Sat. 9–4:30, Sun. 1–4.*

Children's Museum of Acadiana. Good on a rainy day or to soak up extra energy in the kids, this museum is basically a large indoor playground, with educational games and interactive exhibits such as a grocery store, a kid's-size TV news studio, a bubble exhibit, and more. ⊠ *201 E. Congress St.* ☎ *337/232–8500* 🎟 *$5* ⊗ *Tues.–Sat. 10–5.*

Jefferson Street Market. A collective of artists, artisans, and dealers fills the deep hall of this market. Antiques and mod kitsch, refined gifts and quirky artwork—this market has it all. Changing contemporary art exhibits claim the central gallery space. ⊠*538 Jefferson St.* ☎*337/233–2589* ⊘*Mon.–Sat. 10–5.*

Lafayette Courthouse. The courthouse contains an impressive collection of more than 2,000 historical photographs of life in the Lafayette area. There are images of famous politicians such as Dudley LeBlanc and Huey Long working the stump and scenes from the great flood of 1927. Many of the pictures are displayed on the second floor. ⊠*800 Buchanan St.* ☎*337/233–0150* ⊘*Weekdays 8:30–4:30.*

☾ **Lafayette Natural History Museum and Planetarium.** Opened in 2003, this sparkling natural-history museum includes changing exhibitions and lots of fun hands-on science for

CREOLE VS. CAJUN

Cajun cuisine relies on locally available ingredients, such as rabbit, mirliton, and rice. Most dishes have the "holy trinity" of celery, bell pepper, and garlic as a base; traditional examples include boudin and maque choux (a corn stew, usually served with crawfish tails). Creole cuisine is more cosmopolitan, incorporating French, Spanish, Italian, African, and French Caribbean influences. While many dishes use the same holy trinity, Creole dishes, like their French counterparts, are defined by their sauces. Examples include shrimp Creole, crawfish bisque, and oysters Rockefeller.

kids. ⊠*433 Jefferson St.* ☎*337/291–5544* ⊕*www.lnhmpmuseum.org* ⊠*$5* ⊘*Tues.–Fri. 9–5, Sat. 10–6, Sun. 1–6.*

Murals. There are several outdoor murals by Robert Dafford in the center of Lafayette. A Louisiana swamp scene is across from **Dwyer's Café** (⊠*323 Jefferson St.*), and splashy cars and TVs with vignettes of Cajun life are on the **Jefferson Tower Building** (⊠*556 Jefferson St.*). The microcosm of Lafayette inside the garage at **Parc Auto du Centre Ville,** at the corner of Polk and Vermilion streets, is the work of local artist Tanya Falgout.

WHERE TO EAT

$$$
CAJUN

✕**Café Vermilionville.** This 19th-century inn with crisp white napery and old-brick fireplaces serves French and Cajun fare to a well-dressed crowd. Among the specialties are Gulf fish Acadien and grilled duck breast. This is a favorite spot for special occasions among Lafayette residents. ⊠*1304 W. Pinhook Rd.* ☎*337/237–0100* ⊕*www.cafev.com* ⊟*AE, D, DC, MC, V* ⊘*Closed Sun. No lunch Sat.*

$$
CAJUN
★

✕**Prejean's.** Oyster shuckers work in a cozy bar at this local favorite along Interstate 49, north of central Lafayette. Three meals are served in this cypress house with a wide front porch. People gather at tables with red-and-white-check cloths to partake of Prejean's seafood platter (gumbo, fried shrimp, oysters, catfish, crab cakes, and maque choux) and some of its legendary gumbo (you can pick from four varieties). There's a Black Angus steak for meat lovers, too. There's live Cajun music, and usually dancing, nightly. ⊠*3480 U.S. I–49 N* ☎*337/896–3247* ⊕*www.prejeans.com* ⊟*AE, D, DC, MC, V.*

WHERE TO STAY

$$–$$$ ⊞**Bois des Chênes Inn.** This B&B is housed in the 19th-century Mouton
★ Plantation, in a quiet residential area of Lafayette. An upstairs suite
can accommodate five, and has early Acadian antiques; downstairs, the
Louisiana Empire Suite has a queen-size bed, and the Victorian Suite a
double bed. Breakfast is prepared by owner Marjorie Voorhies, and her
husband, Coerte Voorhies, conducts unusually informative boat tours
through the surrounding swamps. A complimentary glass of wine and a
tour through the home is included in the room rate. **Pros:** nice owners;
pretty grounds. **Cons:** rooms feel like they could benefit from a good air-
ing out. ⊠ *338 N. Sterling St.* ☎*337/233–7816* ⊃*5 rooms* ☆*In-hotel:
some pets allowed, no-smoking rooms* ⊟*AE, MC, V* ⦿*BP.*

$$ ⊞**T'Frere's House.** Built in 1880 of native cypress and handmade bricks,
"little brother's house" has been a B&B since 1985. About 2 mi south of
the Oil Center, the Acadian-style house with Victorian trim is furnished
with French and Louisiana antiques. Additional accommodations are
in an Acadian-style cottage behind the main house. You are greeted
with a complimentary "T'julep" and "Cajun canapés," hors d'oeuvres
made with boudin. The Cajun breakfast combines regional ingredients
with traditional Southern cuisine. **Pros:** charming decor; owners like
to feed their guests well; great if you are looking to get away from it
all but still want to be near 21st-century amenities. **Cons:** it feels a bit
far from everything; not a good option if you're on a diet. ⊠ *1905
Verot School Rd.* ☎*337/984–9347 or 800/984–9347* ⦿*www.tfreres.
com* ⊃*9 rooms* ⊟*AE, D, MC, V* ⦿*BP.*

BREAUX BRIDGE

★ *10 mi northeast of Lafayette.*

A dyed-in-the-wool Cajun town, Breaux Bridge is known as the Craw-
fish Capital of the World. During the first full weekend in May, the
Crawfish Festival draws more than 100,000 visitors to this little village
on Bayou Teche. Once a wild place, old Breaux Bridge has attracted a
small arts community that includes renowned Louisiana photographer
Debbie Fleming Caffery and has traded its honky tonks for B&Bs,
antiques shops, and restaurants.

ESSENTIALS

Visitor Information Chamber of Commerce (⊠ *314 E. Bridge St. 70517*
☎ *337/332–5406* ⦿ *www.breauxbridgelive.com*).

WHERE TO EAT AND STAY

$$ ✗**Café des Amis.** The culinary heart and soul of downtown Breaux
CAJUN Bridge rests in this large, renovated storefront just a block from Bayou
★ Teche where locals and visitors gather to enjoy hospitality that is second
only to the food. Sample the ambience over cocktails or coffee at the
bar, or take a table and try the extraordinary turtle soup or the crawfish
corn bread. Breakfast here should be savored, from the fresh-squeezed
orange juice to the *oreille de cochon* (pastry-wrapped boudin), *couche-
couche* (corn-bread-based cereal), and black java. Saturday mornings
bring the popular Zydeco Breakfast, featuring a band and dancing.

✉*140 E. Bridge St.* ☎*337/332–5273* ⊕*www.cafedesamis.com* ▤*AE, D, MC, V* ✪*Closed Mon. and Tues. No dinner Sun.*

¢ ✗**Poche's.** At this no-frills operation, order your authentic Cajun cook-
CAJUN ing at the counter, then eat in or take away. Daily specials are stick-to-
your ribs Cajun food. Boudin, sausage, cracklings, and stuffed chicken
are just a few of the items to take out. ✉*33015-A Main Hwy., 2 mi
from center of Breaux Bridge* ☎*337/332–2108* ▤*MC, V.*

$$$ 🛏**Maison des Amis.** The owners of Café des Amis renovated this 19th-
Fodor'sChoice century house on the bank of Bayou Teche with comfort and relaxation
★ in mind. Each room has a private entrance and a queen-size bed cov-
ered with luxurious linens and pillows. A pier and gazebo are perfect
for watching moonlight over the bayou. The complimentary Cajun
breakfast at Café des Amis is not to be missed. **Pros:** just steps from
Cafe des Amis and its famous brunch; located in downtown Breaux
Bridge. **Cons:** not all rooms have private bathrooms. ✉*111 Washington
St.* ☎*337/507–3399* ⊕*www.maisondesamis.com* ⇆*3 rooms, 1 suite*
▤*AE, D, MC, V* ⭗*BP.*

NIGHTLIFE
La Poussière (✉*1215 Grand Point Rd.* ☎*337/332–1721*) is an ancient
Cajun honky tonk with live music on Saturday and Sunday.

NEW IBERIA

★ *14 mi south of St. Martinville.*

The town of New Iberia is the hub of lower Cajun Country, second
only to Lafayette as an arts-and-culture draw. The grand homes of
sugarcane planters dominate the residential section of Main Street, just
off Bayou Teche, pointing to a glorious past at the center of a booming
sugar industry and anchoring the current cultural revival taking place
here. Park downtown or stay in one of the numerous B&Bs here and
you can easily walk to the bayou, restaurants, art galleries, and shops
in the historic business district. Downtown stretches eight blocks east
and west on Main Street (Route 182) from the intersection of Center
Street (Route 14). The Shadows-on-the-Teche plantation home is at this
intersection and is a good place to park.

Check with the **Acadiana Arts Council** (☎*337/233–7060* ⊕*www.
artscouncil.org*) for the latest information on performances at the inti-
mate **Sliman Theater for the Performing Arts** (☎*337/369–2337*), on
Main Street. It is the site for the "Louisiana Crossroads" concert series,
which features mainly Louisiana musicians, but also showcases musi-
cians from out of state who are influenced by the region.

The **Conrad Rice Mill** is the country's oldest rice mill still in operation,
dating from 1912, and it produces a distinctive wild pecan rice. Tours
are conducted on the hour between 10 AM and 3 PM. The adjacent
Konriko Company Store sells Cajun crafts and foods. ✉*307–309 Ann
St.* ☎*337/367–6163 or 800/551–3245* ⊕*www.conradricemill.com*
⭕*Mill $4* ✪*Mon.–Sat. 9–5.*

★ **Shadows-on-the-Teche,** one of the South's best-known plantation homes,
was built on the bank of the bayou for wealthy sugar planter David

Weeks in 1834. In 1917 his descendant William Weeks Hall conducted one of the first history-conscious restorations of a plantation home. Truckloads of original documents were deliberately preserved. The result is one of the most fascinating tours in Louisiana. Weeks Hall willed the property to the National Trust for Historic Preservation in 1958, and each year the trust selects a different historical topic to emphasize. Surrounded by 2 acres of lush gardens and moss-draped oaks, the two-story rose-hue house has white columns, exterior staircases sheltered in cabinet-like enclosures, and a pitched roof pierced by dormer windows. The furnishings are 85% original to the house. ⊠*317 E. Main St.* ☎*337/369–6446* ⊕*www.shadowsontheteche.org* ⊠*$7* ☉*Mon.–Sat. 9–4:30, Sun. noon–4:30.*

WHERE TO EAT AND STAY

$$
CAJUN

✕**Clementine.** Named for folk artist Clementine Hunter, with an insignia based on her signature, Clementine favors cuisine that might be called nouveau-Cajun: inspired by local ingredients and traditions, but subtly seasoned and artfully presented. Changing art exhibits by locals are introduced at bimonthly openings featuring wine and hors d'oeuvres. Clementine hosts live music on Friday and Saturday nights. ⊠*113 E. Main St.* ☎*337/560–1007* ⊕*www.clementinedowntown.com* ⊟*AE, D, MC, V* ☉*Closed Sun. No lunch Sat. No dinner Mon.*

$

⌂**Bayou Teche Guest Cottage.** There could scarcely be a better way to appreciate the Queen City of the Teche than to spend a night in this simple, two-room, 18th-century cottage on the bank of the bayou, down the road from downtown attractions. Guests are left on their own, with self-service breakfast items provided in the refrigerator. You can explore the 3 acres of quiet grounds or sit in the front-porch rocking chairs and watch towboats ply the waters. The house canoe is also at your disposal. **Pros:** pretty views; good location to explore New Iberia; if you want to be alone, this is the place. **Cons:** depending on what you expect from a B&B, you'll either find it charming—or a bit worn around the edges. ⊠*100 Teche St.* ☎*337/364–1933* ⤢*1 cottage* �*In-room: refrigerator* ⊟*No credit cards.*

Mississippi

THE GULF COAST, NATCHEZ TRACE, AND THE MISSISSIPPI DELTA

WORD OF MOUTH

"We flew into Nashville and rented a car, headed to New Orleans via the Natchez Trace Parkway. If you're driving the Trace (or exploring anywhere in Mississippi River country), buy and read Mark Twain's *Life on the Mississippi* before you go. Visited Elvis's house and watched all of the other tourists. Next day we took our time along the trail to Jackson before cutting south to New Orleans for a business conference. Fantastic BLT (with homemade garlic-Tabasco mayo) at French Camp. We give French Camp an unequivocal 'Eat lunch here if you drive this road.' We can't say enough how much we enjoyed this drive."

—PhotoDad

Updated by
Michael Ream

Mississippi is deep in the heart of Dixie. As you enter the lush Magnolia State, listen for the gentle drawl of an authentic Southern welcome. Stop in small towns, rich with historic houses and museums. Mississippians honor tradition, which manifests itself in everything from the meticulous upkeep of stately old homes—which you can tour—to the preservation of front-porch stories passed down from generation to generation.

Mississippi is a gold mine for history buffs, with numerous Civil War sites and some of the best-preserved examples of antebellum architecture in the South. The Natchez Trace Parkway, strung with magnolia trees and hilltop vistas, cuts across the state, passing through Tupelo, Jackson, and Natchez, where echoes of the great wealth of the antebellum era can be seen in the numerous grand mansions. The mighty Mississippi forms the western border of the state, winding slowly through the Delta, where it has defined river towns like Vicksburg. Along the Gulf Coast, the "Playground of the South" beckons with casinos, boating, and historical sites, including Beauvoir, home of Jefferson Davis and one of the best places in the country to get a sense of the history of the Confederacy. The area was battered by Hurricane Katrina in 2005 and is slowly recovering. While the casinos have reopened, many sights are still struggling to rebuild, and some, especially beachside restaurants that were completely destroyed, are gone forever.

ORIENTATION AND PLANNING

GETTING ORIENTED

The Gulf Coast, where the good times roll day and night, has a somewhat New Orleans flavor, whereas the Delta—the rich area of farmland periodically delivered by Mississippi River floods—is more like Memphis: genteel and polite, with a small-town, conservative manner. A trip along the Natchez Trace, which stretches from Natchez northeast through Jackson, the state capital, and Tupelo, then on to Nashville, will carry you back to a time of settlers, outlaws, traveling preachers, and post riders. Oxford is a cosmopolitan little town in northern Mississippi with a strong literary tradition. Jackson, the state capital, maintains the heart of a small Southern town even as it grows into a sprawling city.

The Gulf Coast. The coast is coming back from damage wrought by Hurricane Katrina, with visitors flocking to casinos stacked along the beach in Biloxi and pleasure boats plying Mississippi Sound. Nearby Ocean Springs offers a slower pace, with the feel of an artists' colony.

TOP REASONS TO GO

History you can see: Mississippi has several Civil War sites, including the massive battle of Vicksburg and the longtime home of Jefferson Davis in Beauvoir. Natchez offers an up-close look at antebellum life, with guides in historic costume at numerous columned mansions.

Find a groove: The spawning ground for both the blues and rock 'n' roll, Mississippi counts music icons B. B. King and Elvis Presley as native sons. Elvis's boyhood home is preserved in Tupelo, and the sounds of the blues still spill out of the doors of a few clubs in the Delta.

Look for lady luck: Casinos have taken over the Gulf Coast and the Delta, making Mississippi a challenger to Las Vegas. Table games and slots are within arm's reach in Biloxi, Vicksburg, and Tunica, as are Vegas-style entertainment and golf.

Take it easy: The Gulf Coast is built for relaxation. Kick back and watch the shrimp boats, head out onto the water on one of the local cruisers, or go for a swim on Ship Island.

Indulge Southern style: You don't have to look far to find delicious barbecue, fried catfish, and rich desserts. Along the Gulf Coast, fresh seafood is the norm, with numerous restaurants serving the catch of the day.

The Natchez Trace. An old trail for Mississippi Native Americans and river traders, the trace passes through wild emerald forests and the occasional city, including Tupelo, which gave the world Elvis.

Holly Springs and Oxford. The Old South lives on in the stately old homes of Holly Springs, while another slice of Southern heritage is seen in Rowan Oak, the Oxford home of William Faulkner. Oxford also offers college town charm centered on its famous square.

Mississippi Delta. The birthplace of the blues has old country roads winding through landscapes that look the same as when cotton was king in Mississippi. Today, the focus is gambling, with Tunica's majestic casinos rising into the sky like a Vegas of the cotton fields.

PLANNING

WHEN TO GO

The Gulf Coast's casinos keep the action rolling year-round, but other coastal attractions, such as boat trips on Mississippi Sound, are best from late spring to early fall. Natchez's pilgrimage of historic homes typically runs from early March to mid-April and late September to mid-October. Prepare for the weather—Mississippi's fairly fickle. Spring and fall can be glorious, while summer days can be murderously hot and sweaty, calling for cool drinks on a shady veranda. Now and then, a winter cold snap sends porch sitters scurrying inside.

GETTING HERE AND AROUND

AIR TRAVEL

Gulfport-Biloxi Regional Airport; Golden Triangle Regional Airport, between Columbus and Starkville near the north end of the Natchez Trace; Jackson-Evers International Airport; and Tupelo Regional Airport serve the state. If you're heading for the casinos on the Gulf Coast, it's easiest to fly into Gulfport-Biloxi. Another possibility is to fly into Jackson, at the intersection of two major interstate highways and, thus, a good base for exploring different regions of the state. Still another option if you want to check out the Delta, Tupelo, Oxford, or Tunica is to fly into Memphis, which is just a couple hours' drive from all four places.

Airport Information Golden Triangle Regional Airport (⊠ *U.S. 82, 10 mi west of Columbus, Columbus* ☏ *601/327–4422*). **Gulfport-Biloxi Regional Airport** (⊠ *Airport Rd. off U.S. 49, Gulfport* ☏ *228/863–5951*). **Jackson-Evers International Airport** (⊠ *100 International Dr., Jackson* ☏ *601/939–5631*). **Memphis International Airport** (⊠ *2491 Winchester Rd., Whitehaven* ☏ *901/922–8000* ⊕ *www.mscaa.com*). **Tupelo Regional Airport** (⊠ *2704 West Jackson St., Tupelo* ☏ *662/841–6571*).

BUS TRAVEL

Coast Transit Authority provides local service throughout the Gulf Coast area.

Bus Information Coast Transit Authority (⊠ *333 DeBuys Rd., Gulfport* ☏ *228/896–8080* ⊕ *www.coasttransit.com*).

CAR TRAVEL

You can drive across the Gulf Coast in roughly 1½ hours via I–10. It takes a little longer on U.S. 90. From Gulfport, it takes just over an hour to reach New Orleans and about three hours to get to Jackson via U.S. 49.

A car is the only way to tour the Natchez Trace properly, though you can reach major cities by plane and by bus. Corinth is at the intersection of U.S. 72 and U.S. 45, and Tupelo is 5 mi south of the Natchez Trace Parkway at the intersection of U.S. 45 and U.S. 78.

Jackson is accessed by I–55, I–20, and U.S. 49. Natchez, at the beginning of the Natchez Trace Parkway, is served by U.S. 61.

RESTAURANTS

Fresh Gulf seafood, particularly redfish, flounder, and speckled trout, stars in coast restaurants. Soft-shell crab is a coast specialty, and crab claws are a traditional appetizer. Locals are fond of quaffing Biloxi-born Barq's root beer with their seafood. In Tupelo, Jackson, and Natchez you can find everything from caviar to chitlins. Jackson has several elegant restaurants. Southern breakfasts, featuring biscuits and gravy, and served in antebellum opulence, are a Natchez trademark. All in all, good food and drink are required in Mississippi; fancy surroundings aren't. Dress is casual unless otherwise noted.

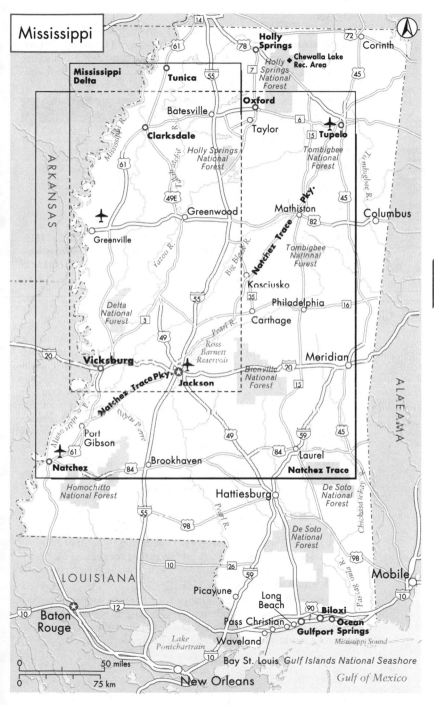

HOTELS

Business at casino hotels on the Gulf Coast is booming even as the area still struggles to recover from the damage of Hurricane Katrina, so reservations are a good idea. National hotel and motel chains are found throughout the state. Historic mansions converted to bed-and-breakfasts add variety in Jackson, Natchez, and Vicksburg.

WHAT IT COSTS					
	¢	$	$$	$$$	$$$$
Restaurant	under $7	$7–11	$12–$16	$17–$22	over $22
Hotel	under $70	$70–$110	$111–$160	$161–$220	over $220

Restaurant prices are for a main course at dinner. Hotel prices are for a standard double room, excluding state and local taxes.

VISITOR INFORMATION

Contacts Mississippi Gulf Coast Convention and Visitors Bureau (✉ *11975 Seaway Rd., Gulfport* ☎ *228/896–6699 or 888/467–4853* ⊕ *www.gulfcoast. org*). **Mississippi Welcome Center** (✉ *U.S. 82 at Reed Rd., Box 6022, Greenville* ☎ *662/332–2378* ⊕ *www.visitmississippi.org*).

THE GULF COAST

Until Hurricane Katrina, the Mississippi Gulf Coast was a honky-tonk paradise, bedecked with gleaming casino boats and full of cruising fun seekers soaking up the sun and running pleasure craft on Mississippi Sound. When Katrina stormed ashore at the end of August 2005, casinos, hotels, restaurants, and other tourist spots were wiped out—as were the homes of tens of thousands of people who helped run these mainstays of the tourism economy that made the coast hum. Empty foundations still stand as a haunting reminder of Katrina's wrath, even as the area has slowly begun to recover.

The coast extends for about 75 mi along the Gulf of Mexico from Alabama to Louisiana. Although I–10 runs the length of the area, it's better to drive U.S. 90 (Beach Boulevard) to experience the coast. The crush of casinos and condos occasionally breaks to give a view of lazy, drooping oaks and the still waters of the Mississippi Sound. On a clear day, if you have good eyesight or a good imagination, you can see some of the barrier islands that separate the sound from the Gulf of Mexico. Their names (from east to west) are Petit Bois (anglicized as "Petty Boy"), Horn, East and West Ship, and Cat. Two others, Round and Deer, lie within the sound.

Enjoy wondrous walks along the beachfront, but take your cue from the locals and ignore any urge to swim. The Mississippi Sound is murky at best, and the stagnant Gulf Waters can be unpleasantly hot. For swimming, take a ride out to Ship Island and its wonderful beach.

OCEAN SPRINGS

60 mi west of Mobile, 90 mi east of New Orleans.

Ocean Springs offers an antidote to the sensory overload found along Casino Row in nearby Biloxi. Just east of the Biloxi Bay Bridge (completely rebuilt after it was destroyed by Hurricane Katrina and popular for strolls and jogs), Ocean Springs is one of the oldest towns in America—it was founded in 1699 as Fort Maurepas, France's first permanent outpost in Louisiana. Known as an artists' colony, the town offers visitors a quaint and quiet old downtown, with streets shaded by live oaks perfect for strolling and shopping.

GETTING HERE AND AROUND

Ocean Springs's Visitor Center is just off the corner of U.S. 90 and Washington, and is in the town's historic L & N (Louisville & Nashville) train station.

ESSENTIALS

Visitor Info Ocean Springs Chamber of Commerce and Visitor Center (✉ *1000 Washington Ave.* ☎ *228/875–4424* ⊕ *www.oceanspringschamber.com*).

EXPLORING

★ **Gulf Islands National Seashore** (✉ *3500 Park Rd.* ☎ *228/875–0074* ⊕ *www.nps.gov/guis*), which includes Horn, Petit Bois, and Ship Islands, each about 10 mi off the coast, has a visitor center on Ocean Springs's Davis Bayou. The area includes nature trails, a 51-site campground with electric and water hookups, and a sewage dump station. Primitive camping is available on East Ship, Horn, and Petit Bois, which can be reached by private or charter boat—check with the visitor center for a list of boat operators. These islands are designated wilderness areas, with limited or nonexistent water, communications, or shelter facilities available. West Ship Island, reached via regularly scheduled excursion boats from Gulfport, has water and limited food service, as well as guided tours of Fort Massachusetts in summer. A swimming beach is on the south side of West Ship Island, which can be reached via boardwalk and has full facilities for visitors. The sun's rays on the islands can get very intense—bring sunscreen, a hat, and lightweight, loose-fitting protective clothing.

Walter Anderson (1903–65), an artist of genius and grand eccentricity, made his home in Ocean Springs, as did his two brothers, also artists. Drawings and watercolors, some not discovered until after his death, are on display at the **Walter Anderson Museum of Art.** Down a narrow gravel road, within a forest near the waterfront, stands **Shearwater Pottery and Showroom** (✉ *102 Shearwater Dr.* ☎ *228/875–7320* 🖃 *Free* ☉ *Mon.–Sat. 9–5:30, Sun. 1–5:30.*), which has long served as the Anderson family's workshop and has several rooms of pottery for sale. ✉ *510 Washington Ave.* ☎ *228/872–3164* ⊕ *www.walterandersonmuseum.org* 🖃 *$7* ☉ *Mon.–Sat. 9:30–4:30, Sun. 12:30–4:30.*

WHERE TO EAT

$–$$

SEAFOOD

✕ **Aunt Jenny's Catfish Restaurant.** This down-home, family-style place is in a house built in 1852 by Old Fort Bayou north of downtown. The simple menu features fried or broiled catfish, of course, as well as gulf

6

Mississippi Facts

- **Population:** Mississippi had an estimated population of nearly 3 million in 2008. The state has the largest proportion of African-Americans of any state, nearly 40% of the population.

- **State Symbols:** Mississippi's state tree and flower is the beautiful magnolia—the spreading leaves and white flowers of these massive trees are ubiquitous. The teddy bear also has a history in Mississippi—Teddy Roosevelt refused to shoot a captured bear on a hunting trip here, leading toymakers to create stuffed bears with his name.

- **Highest Point:** Woodall Mountain, in the northeast corner of the state, at 806 feet.

- **Lowest Point:** Sea level at the Gulf of Mexico.

- **Greatest Paradox:** The Mississippi Delta has some of the richest farmland in the world as well as some of the worst poverty—as recently as 1990, Tunica County had more than 50% of its population living below the poverty line, the largest percentage in the United States, and one in four families did not have indoor plumbing.

---

shrimp, fried chicken, and plenty of Southern side dishes piled high. Several menu choices are all-you-can-eat. There's also a cocktail lounge in the basement. ⊠*1217 Washington Ave.* ☎*228/875–9201* ⊕*www.coastseafood.com* ☐*D, MC, V* ⊗*No lunch Mon.*

$$–$$$
SEAFOOD
★
✕**Jocelyn's Restaurant.** The restaurant has limited hours—it's open for dinner only from Thursday through Saturday—but the food is worth it: this is as good as coast seafood gets. Fresh crabmeat fixed three or four ways, trout, flounder, and, when available, snapper are subtly seasoned and served with garnishes as bright and original as modern art. Stuffed eggplant is another favorite. ⊠*1608 Bienville Blvd. (U.S. 90)* ☎*228/875–1925* ⌂*Reservations not accepted* ☐*No credit cards* ⊗*No lunch. Closed Sun.–Wed.*

SHOPPING

Hillyer House (⊠*920 Washington Ave.* ☎*228/875–8065* ⊗*Mon.–Sat. 10–5*) which relocated to Ocean Springs after its store in Pass Christian was destroyed by Katrina, sells handmade jewelry, pottery, glass, and brass made by local and regional artists.

At **Realizations** (⊠*1000 Washington Ave., in the old Train Depot* ☎*228/875–0503*) you can buy Walter Anderson prints and clothing printed with his unique designs.

BILOXI

2 mi west of Ocean Springs.

Sitting on a peninsula bracketed by Mississippi Sound and an inlet known as the Back Bay, Biloxi (pronounced bi-*lux*-i) is perhaps the most vibrant, ethnically diverse city on the Mississippi coast.

The city served as the capital of the Louisiana Territory from 1720 until 1723, when it was changed to New Orleans. By the 1890s, Biloxi was a center of the seafood industry, drawing immigrants from as far as Croatia, Slovenia, and Czechoslova- kia and as near as Louisiana to fish and process the Gulf of Mexico's huge stores of shrimp and oysters. Numerous canneries and seafood factories sprouted in the Back Bay area north of the beachfront, and roads and railroads ran paral- lel to the water. Keesler Air Force Base opened in 1941 and is one of numerous military facilities on the coast. More immigrants arrived in the 1970s, as Vietnamese came to work as shrimp fishermen and stayed to form a significant community.

KATRINA MEMORIAL

Biloxi's Katrina Memorial is close to the beach on the Biloxi Town Green, which fronts on the Mis- sissippi Sound opposite the Hard Rock Casino (look for the giant guitar). The simple black granite wall stands 12 feet high, the maximum height of Katrina's tidal surge in Biloxi. A memorial erected after Hurricane Camille in 1969 is several blocks away.

Casinos, which arrived in 1992, transformed what had been a low-key vacation area into a noisy high rise gambling mecca: the majority of the coast's casinos are in Biloxi, including several major players in gam- bling. After Hurricane Katrina demolished the floating casino boats, their operators simply moved ashore, throwing up high-rise towers just steps from the beach.

Away from the freewheeling atmosphere inside the casinos, Biloxi's his- toric downtown offers a slower pace. The centerpiece of downtown is the Vieux Marche (Old Market), which extends for roughly four blocks along Howard Avenue. History buffs will find a fascinating piece of American history on the coast road west of Biloxi at Beauvoir, Jefferson Davis's home after the Civil War.

GETTING HERE AND AROUND

It's tough avoiding traffic tie ups on Beach Boulevard, which is the only major street serving all the casinos. One possibility is to park in the old downtown area and walk from casino to casino along the beachfront, which has several pleasant strolling areas.

The Biloxi Visitor Center, which like the rest of the city was hit hard by Hurricane Katrina, is temporarily housed just west of the Vieux Marche in the Bond-Grant House.

ESSENTIALS

Biloxi Visitors Center (✉ *932 Howard Ave.* ☎ *228/374–3105* ⊕ *www.biloxi. ms.us*).

EXPLORING

Erected in 1848, the 48-foot-tall **Biloxi Lighthouse** is a local landmark. During the Civil War, Union forces, operating from Ship Island, block- aded the Mississippi Sound and cut Biloxi off from much-needed sup- plies. When the Yankees demanded that Biloxi submit or starve, they were told that the Union would have to "blockade the mullet" first. Ever since, smoked mullet fish with syrup has been known as "Biloxi bacon." The city defended itself with what appeared to be a formidable cannon array near the lighthouse but was actually only two cannons and many logs painted black. Today, the lighthouse stands alone in the middle of U.S. 90 at Porter Avenue, just west of the Beau Rivage Casino. ✉ *U.S. 90 at Porter Ave., Casino Row* ⊗ *Closed.*

The **Biloxi Schooners**, two replica 19th-century oyster schooners, cruise the waters of Mississippi Sound for 2½ hours, typically twice a day, at 2 and sunset. The schooners sail from the Schooner Pier Complex, 1 mi east of the Beau

Rivage casino and just west of the Grand Casino. ✉ *Schooner Pier Complex, 367 Beach Blvd., Casino Row* ☎ *228/435–6320* ⊕ *www. maritimemuseum.org/schooners/schooners.php* ☑ *$25* ⊗ *Sails at 2 and 5 or 6.*

For a taste of the shrimping life, the **Biloxi Shrimping Trip** gives visitors 70 minutes as a shrimper pulling nets through the Gulf waters. Trips aboard the tour boat *Sailfish* depart from Biloxi's small craft harbor, in the shadow of the Hard Rock Casino. The boat typically goes out on three trips a day, at 10, noon, and 2. ✉ *Hwy. 90 and Main St., Biloxi Small Craft Harbor* ☎ *228/385–1182 or 800/289–7908* ⊕ *www.gcww. com/sailfish* ☑ *$15* ⊗ *Daily trips at 10, noon, and 2.*

★ **The Ohr–O'Keefe Museum of Art** commemorates both Georgia O'Keefe and George Ohr, the flamboyant, eccentric, and prolific "mad potter" of Biloxi. Since it was destroyed in Hurricane Katrina, the museum, now housed temporarily in Biloxi's Glenn L. Sweatman House, displays only a small collection of Ohr's pottery. The remainder of the collection is in storage awaiting completion of the museum's new campus designed by architect Frank Gehry, scheduled to be completed in 2011. ✉ *1596 Glenn L. Sweetman Dr., near Casino Row* ☎ *228/374–5547* ⊕ *www. georgeohr.org* ☑ *Free* ⊗ *Mon.–Sat. 9–4:30.*

WHERE TO EAT AND STAY

Many casinos have several restaurants on-site, and you can still find no-frills seafood shacks away from the beach.

$$$$
CAJUN
★
✕ **Mary Mahoney's Old French House Restaurant.** Locals swear by it, not only for the history behind the place (the New Orleans–style restaurant opened in 1964), but also for the food. Start off with a bowl of rich, dark gumbo and move on to the stuffed flounder or one of the steak selections. The bread pudding drenched in rum sauce is unforgettable. ✉ *110 Rue Magnolia (700 block of Beach Blvd., 2 blocks east of I–110), Casino Row* ☎ *228/374–0163* ⊕ *www.marymahoneys.com* ▤ *AE, D, DC, MC, V* ⊗ *Closed Sun.*

$$$
SEAFOOD
✕ **Ole Biloxi Schooner.** Up and running at a new location post-Katrina, this popular seafood joint is back to serving up platters of fried shrimp and oysters and stuffed crab. Wash it all down with a Barq's root beer. The Schooner is open for breakfast, lunch, and dinner. ✉ *871 Howard Ave., Vieux Marche* ☎ *228/435–8071* ⊕ *schooner.biloxi.tk* ▤ *No credit cards* ⊗ *Closed Sun.*

$$$–$$$$ ⊞**Beau Rivage.** MGM Mirage pulled out all the stops when it built this
★ impressive, multiple amenity facility, the grandest Las Vegas–style hotel
casino on the Gulf Coast. In the lobby, majestic magnolia trees line the
inside walkway that leads from the entrance to the casino. The mag-
nolia theme continues to the spacious modern rooms with Italian mar-
ble floors. With 12 restaurants on the property and a tropical-themed
pool with Roman decor, this hotel is the antithesis of understated. For
entertainment, there's the 24-hour casino with table games and slot
machines, a 1,500-seat theater that draws top entertainers, and a chic
nightclub. **Pros:** a huge slate of entertainment and activities to choose
from; concierge. **Cons:** a little overwhelming in its assault on the senses;
no airport shuttle. ⊠*875 Beach Blvd., Casino Row* ☎*228/386–7111
or 888/567–6667* ⊕*www.beaurivage.com* ⟳*1,645 rooms, 95 suites*
⏁*In-room: DVD (some), Internet. In-hotel: 12 restaurants, room ser-
vice, bars, golf course, pool, gym, spa, laundry service, Wi-Fi, parking
(free), no-smoking rooms* ▭*AE, D, MC, V.*

$$–$$$ ⊞**Grand Biloxi.** At this low-key casino hotel, some rooms have views
of the Biloxi Bay Bridge, and you can catch a gorgeous sunset over
the Mississippi Sound from the outdoor pool (though not for long—a
new casino is going up on the beach). The hotel's nearby Grand Bear
golf course is an 18-hole championship course designed by Jack Nick-
laus. **Pros:** great views; a good value for a casino hotel. **Cons:** rooms a
little on the small side; no airport shuttle. ⊠*280 Beach Blvd., Casino
Row* ☎*228/436–2946 or 800/946–2946* ⊕*www.grandcasinobiloxi.
com* ⟳*454 rooms, 40 suites* ⏁*In-room: kitchen (some), refrigerator
(some), Wi-Fi. In-hotel: 3 restaurants, room service, bar, pool, spa, laun-
dry service, Wi-Fi, parking (free and paid), no-smoking rooms* ▭*AE,
D, MC, V.*

6

GULFPORT

13 mi west of Biloxi.

Gulfport is a bit gritty compared to Biloxi's glittering casino strip, but it
offers a water park, children's museum, and access to one of the Gulf's
most historic islands, making it a nice stop for families.

EXPLORING

☉ **Gulf Islands Waterpark** offers a variety of waterslides for children of all
ages, as well as a wave pool and a lazy river that flows throughout the
park. Several concession stands are on-site. ⊠*17200 16th St.* ⊹*Exit
I–10 at Hwy. 49 N to Landon Rd. W* ☎*228/328–1266 or 866/485–
3386* ⊕*www.gulfislandswaterpark.com* ▨*$2–$28* ☉*Daily mid-May–
mid-Aug.; weekends only late Apr.–mid-May and late Aug.–mid-Sept.*

☉ The **Lynn Meadows Discovery Center** offers more than 15,000 square feet
of hands-on learning activities, including science experiments and a
port, train station, and tree house. ⊠*246 Dolan Ave. (off U.S. 90/Beach
Blvd.)* ☎*228/897–6039* ⊕*www.lmdc.org* ▨*$7* ☉*Tues.–Sat. 10–5.*

★ If you have time for only one activity on this part of the coast, make
it a getaway to **Ship Island** on the passenger ferry from the **Gulfport
Yacht Harbor.** Founded in the 1920s by a Croatian immigrant to the

HISTORY YOU CAN SEE

Fodor's Choice ★ On U.S. 90, about 6 mi west of downtown Biloxi and 7 mi east of downtown Gulfport is **Beauvoir**, the antebellum beach-front home where Jefferson Davis spent the last 12 years of his life. It was here that the president of the Confederacy wrote his memoirs *The Rise and Fall of the Confederate Government* and *A Short History of the Confederate States of America*. The serene, raised-cottage-style house, which later served as a home for elderly Confederate veterans, is set on a broad lawn facing the Mississippi Sound. A Confederate cemetery on the grounds includes the **Tomb of the Unknown Soldier of the Confederacy**. The house and grounds have been largely restored since being seriously damaged in Hurricane Katrina. ✉ *2244 Beach Blvd.* ☎ *228/388–4400* ⊕ *www.beauvoir.org* *$9* ⊙ *Daily 9–5.*

Gulf Coast, the ferry runs once or twice a day from March through October, and the trip takes about an hour. Watch for dolphins during the 11-mi crossing, and don't forget sunscreen and protective clothing. At Ship Island, a part of Gulf Islands National Seashore, a U.S. park ranger will guide you through **Ft. Massachusetts**, built in 1859 and used by Union troops to blockade the Mississippi Sound during the Civil War. The rangers will treat you to tales of the island's colorful past, including the story of the *filles aux casquettes*—young women sent by the French government as brides for the lonely early colonists. Each girl (*fille*) carried a small hope chest (*casquette*) with her. Spend the day sunning, swimming in the dazzlingly clear waters, and combing the beaches for treasures washed up by the surf. Beach chair and umbrella rentals are available on the island as well as refreshment stands. ✉ *Ticket office at Gulfport Yacht Harbor at intersection of Hwy. 49 and U.S. 90* ☎ *228/864–1014 or 866/466–7386* *www.msshipisland.com* ⛴ *Ferry $22 round-trip* ⊙ *Mar.–Oct.*

WHERE TO EAT

$$–$$$ ✕ **The Dock.** This super-casual open-air seafood joint overlooks Gulfport
SEAFOOD Lake, an extension of the Back Bay of Biloxi. Try the fried speckled trout, panfried lump crab cake, or wasabi-seared tuna with seaweed salad. Po'boys and selections from the oyster bar are also good choices. It can get a little noisy around the bar and during live music shows. ✉ *13247 Seaway Rd.* ☎ *228/276–1500* ⊕ *www.thedockgulfport.com* ▭ *AE, D, MC, V* ⊙ *Closed Mon. and Tues.*

¢–$ ✕ **Lil Ray's.** Relocated from Waveland after Katrina, this old favorite
SEAFOOD is back dishing up its signature lunchtime specials like po'boys, fried oysters, and shrimp along with lighter fare like grilled mahimahi and chicken. ✉ *500-A Courthouse Rd.* ☎ *228/896–9601* ⊕ *www.lilrays-restaurant.com* ⌖ *Reservations not accepted* ▭ *MC, V* ⊙ *Closed Sun. No dinner Mon.–Thurs.*

$$$–$$$$ ✕ **Vrazel's.** The interior of this charming brick building has a sooth-
SEAFOOD ing intimacy about it, with soft lighting and dining nooks with large windows facing the beach or overlooking exquisite gardens. Choose from a substantial list of coastal water fare: red snapper, Gulf trout,

Mississippi's Golf Coast

A year-round mild climate allows for excellent opportunities to hit the links on the "golf coast" and golf packages are offered by many coast hotels and motels.

The **Bridges Golf Resort** (⊠ *The Bridges at Hollywood Casino Bay St. Louis, 711 Hollywood Blvd., Bay St. Louis* ☎ *866/758-2591* ⊕ *www.hollywoodcasinobsl.com*) has an 18-hole course (par 72) designed by Arnold Palmer. The course encompasses more than 17 lakes and 14 acres of wetlands. Golf carts come equipped with computers that give pro tips on how to play each hole. The resort is also the site of the **Arnold Palmer Golf Academy. Diamondhead's Pine and Cardinal** courses (⊠ *7600 Golf Club Circle, Diamondhead* ☎ *800/346-8741* ⊕ *www.diamondheadms.org*) are two 18-hole courses (both par 72) that challenge even the pros. Wooded, gently rolling, and well kept, they are ringed by the large, elegant houses and condominiums of the Diamondhead resort community.

Grand Casino's lavish **Grand Bear** (⊠ *1240 Grand Way Blvd., Saucier* ☎ *228/539-7806* ⊕ *www.harrahsgolf.com*) is a Jack Nicklaus–designed beauty that caters to resort guests only. The course (par 72) is on 650 acres that include natural wetland terrain, two rivers, and a man-made lake. Beautifully landscaped **Mississippi National Golf Club** (⊠ *900 Hickory Hill Dr., Gautier* ☎ *228/497-2372* ⊕ *www.mississippinational.com*) has fairways lined with whispering pines, tall oaks, magnolias, and dogwoods on an 18-hole course (par 72). The **Oaks Gulf Club** (⊠ *24384 Club House Dr., off Menge Ave., Pass Christian* ☎ *228/452-0909* ⊕ *www.theoaksgolfclub.com*), an 18-hole, par-72 championship course, has been praised by *Golf Digest*. **Windance Country Club** (⊠ *19385 Champion Cir., Gulfport* ☎ *228/832-4871 Ext. 26* ⊕ *www.windancecc.com*), owned by Island View Casino, has an 18-hole, par-72 course that has hosted the Ben Hogan and Nike tours.

6

flounder, and shrimp prepared every which way. A full slate of steaks is on the menu as well. End your meal with one of Vrazel's famous flaming deserts. ⊠ *3206 W. Beach Blvd. (U.S. 90)* ☎ *228/863-2229* ⊕ *www.vrazels.com* ⊟ *AE, D, DC, MC, V* ☉ *Closed Sun. No lunch Sat.*

SHOPPING

Prime Outlets of Gulfport (⊠ *Exit 34A off I-10, 1000 Factory Shops Blvd.* ☎ *228/867-6100*) has more than 80 famous shops offering factory-outlet prices and connected by a covered walkway. A food court, tourist information booth, and playground are also on the premises.

EN ROUTE The landscape grows increasingly uncluttered, wild, and lovely west of Gulfport. From Long Beach through to Pass Christian, U.S. 90 bisects stretches of stately homes to the north and shimmering water to the south.

THE NATCHEZ TRACE

The flower-sprigged and forested Natchez Trace Parkway is a vast and verdant living history lesson. This enchanted path between Nashville and Natchez is said to be about 8,000 years old. It follows the early trails worn by Natchez, Choctaw, and Chickasaw Native Americans, itinerant preachers, post riders, soldiers, and settlers. Landscaped by the National Park Service, the trace winds through straight pines, haunting cypresses, peaceful vistas of reeds, and still waters with dense woodlands.

The trace is almost 450 mi long, with 313 mi in Mississippi. The Mississippi segment begins in the state's northeast corner, between Iuka and Belmont. Mile markers are posted along the way to help drivers navigate. There are no billboards on the trace, and commercial vehicles are forbidden to use it. Motels can be found in the many towns that lie near its route. Park rangers are serious about the posted speed limits; you'll probably get acquainted with one if you drive any faster.

> ## WORD OF MOUTH
>
> "Shhhhh! Don't tell anyone else about this wonderful, quiet road. We enjoyed driving [the Natchez Trace Parkway] from Nashville, TN, south to Natchez, MS, last November in our motor home—taking our time and do very few miles each day. We are on the road most of the year and we can tell you that it's one of our favorite trips. We were disappointed to miss lunch at French Camp (we were there too early in the day), but we enjoyed walking the grounds. The quiet, the serenity, the road itself were a gift."
> —EastEileen

ESSENTIALS

The Natchez Trace Parkway Visitor Center, 6 mi north of Tupelo on the trace, distributes a four-foot-long *Official Map and Guide,* which has mile-by-mile information from Nashville to Natchez. The center has exhibits, some of which are geared toward kids, and shows a 12-minute film relating to the Parkway.

Visitor Information Natchez Trace Parkway Visitor Center (⊠ *2680 Natchez Trace Pkwy., Tupelo* ☎ *800/305–7417* ⊕ *www.nps.gov/natr*).

TUPELO

90 mi southeast of Memphis, 70 mi east of Oxford.

The largest city in north Mississippi, Tupelo (named after the tupelo gum tree), was founded in 1859 and is a city of accomplishment—it was the first city to provide its residents power through the Tennessee Valley Authority, in 1934. Tupelo is even better known as the birthplace of Elvis Presley, born in his family's tiny shotgun shack in 1935.

Today, Tupelo has a population of about 36,000, with the surrounding area at nearly 135,000. A thriving downtown centers on a copper-domed courthouse. Work is underway outside of the city on a Toyota assembly plant, to open in 2010 or 2011, and an interstate highway to link Tupelo with Memphis and Birmingham is planned. The city is also a center of the furniture industry.

GETTING HERE AND AROUND

The Natchez Trace runs along the northwest and west sides of Tupelo. U.S. Highways 45 and 78 intersect north of downtown, and U.S. 78 runs to Memphis, about a two-hour drive. U.S. 278 (Main Street) runs west to Oxford, about a one-hour drive. The Elvis Presley Birthplace is east of downtown on U.S. 278, off Veterans Boulevard.

ESSENTIALS

Visitor Information Tupelo Convention and Visitors Bureau (✉ *399 E. Main St., Box 47, Tupelo* ☎ *601/841–6521 or 800/533–0611* ⊕ *www.tupelo.net* ⊙ *Mon.–Fri. 8–5).*

EXPLORING

★ The **Elvis Presley Birthplace** is anchored by the tiny, two-room shotgun-style house built by Presley's father, Vernon, for just $180. Elvis Aaron Presley was born here on January 8, 1935. The home has been restored and furnished much as it was when the Presleys lived in it but is now surrounded by Elvis Presley Park, land purchased with proceeds from Elvis's 1956 concert at the Mississippi–Alabama Fair. The park includes granite markers that commemorate significant events in Elvis's life and a memorial fountain. Also on-site are a gift shop (stocked with Elvis souvenirs) and the Elvis Presley Museum, which stores more than 3,000 pieces of Elvis memorabilia. The **Elvis Presley Memorial Chapel,** suggested by the singer in 1971 as a place for his fans to meditate, was dedicated in 1979, two years after Presley's death. ✉ *306 Elvis Presley Dr., off E. Main St.* ☎ *662/841–1245* ⊕ *www.elvispresleybirthplace.com* ✉ *Birthplace $4, chapel $6, museum $8* ⊙ *May–Sept., Mon.–Sat. 9–5:30, Sun. 1–5; Oct.–Apr., Mon.–Sat. 9–5, Sun. 1–5.*

The **Oren Dunn City Museum** displays local history memorabilia, including an 1870s dogtrot cabin, church, and school; two Tupelo fire trucks; a 1948 Lee County bookmobile; Dudie's Diner, a Memphis trolley car turned local eatery; and a Frisco caboose. ✉ *689 Rutherford Rd. 38803* ☎ *662/841–6438* ⊕ *www.orendunnmuseum.org* ✉ *$3* ⊙ *Closed Sun. and Mon.*

Tupelo National Battlefield, on Main Street west of downtown, commemorates the Civil War's Battle of Tupelo with monuments and displays. In 1864 Union general A. J. Smith marched 14,000 troops against Nathan Bedford Forrest's forces near Tupelo. Smith's goal was to end the constant Confederate harassment of supply lines to Sherman's army and thereby secure the Union invasion of Atlanta. The battle, on July 14, 1864, was the last major one in Mississippi and one of the bloodiest. ✉ *W. Main St. (MS 6)* ☎ *662/680–4025 or 800/305–7417* ⊕ *www.nps. gov/tupe* ⊙ *Daily sunrise–sunset.*

WHERE TO EAT AND STAY

Virtually all motels in Tupelo, including several national chains, are clustered around the intersection of Gloster Drive (MS 145) and U.S. 78.

$–$$ ✕ **Grill at Fairpark.** Fish is the best option at this restaurant with black-
AMERICAN lacquered booths, designer light fixtures, and a lively bar. Lobster

Natchez Trace Parkway

The Natchez Trace winds past forests and fields for more than 300 mi through Mississippi, entering the state at Tishomingo State Park. The trip from Tupelo to Jackson, which has most of the interesting sights along the Parkway, takes three hours if you don't stop. It can easily take an entire day, however, if you pause to read the wooden markers, explore nature trails, and admire the neat fields, trees, and wildflower meadows. The parkway is incomplete from Mile Markers 101.5 to 87.0. Connecting routes are I–55, I–20, and I–220. To reach Jackson, follow I–55 south from the trace.

Bynum Mounds (Mile Marker 232.4) are ceremonial hills that were constructed between 100 BC and AD 200 by prehistoric people. Exhibits describe their daily existence.

At **French Camp** (Mile Marker 180.7), where Frenchman Louis LeFleur established a stand in 1812, you can watch sorghum molasses being made on Saturday in late September and October. Native American and French artifacts are housed inside the authentic dogtrot-style cabin.

Cypress Swamp (Mile Marker 122.0), a pleasure today, was a treacherous, mosquito-infested morass for early travelers. A 20-minute self-guided nature walk takes you through the tree-canopied tupelo/bald cypress swamp.

The **Mississippi Crafts Center at Ridgeland** (Mile Marker 102.4) displays and sells high-quality crafts in a dogtrot log cabin. Members of the Craftsmen's Guild of Mississippi have created pewter and silver jewelry, pottery, hand-woven and hand-screened clothing, whimsical wooden toys, highly prized Choctaw baskets, and

other interesting items. The center sponsors free demonstrations (usually on weekends) of basket weaving, wood carving, pottery, and quilting. There are restrooms and picnic tables on-site. ⊠ *950 Rice Rd., Natchez Trace at Ridgeland, Ridgeland* ☎ *662/856–7546* ⊕ *www.mscrafts.org* ☐ *Free* ⊙ *Daily 9–5.*

Post riders stopped during the early 1800s at the Natchez Trace's **Rocky Springs** (Mile Marker 54.8). General Grant's army camped here on its march to Jackson and Vicksburg during the Civil War. Trails meander through the woods and up a steep hill to a tiny old cemetery and **Rocky Springs Methodist Church** (1837), where services are still held on Sunday.

At Mile Marker 41.5 is a portion of **Sunken Trace,** a short section of the original Native American trace of loess soil (easily eroded and compacted earth). You can park and walk along it for a short way.

Emerald Mound (Mile Marker 10.3) is the second-largest Native American mound in the country, covering almost 8 acres. It was built around 1300 for religious ceremonies practiced by ancestors of the Natchez Native Americans.

As you near Natchez, the Natchez Trace Parkway abruptly ends, putting you on U.S. 61. You'll pass through the little town of Washington, capital of the Mississippi Territory from 1802 to 1817. In 1802 **Jefferson College** (☎ *601/442–2901*) was chartered as the territory's first educational institution; its historic buildings have been meticulously restored.

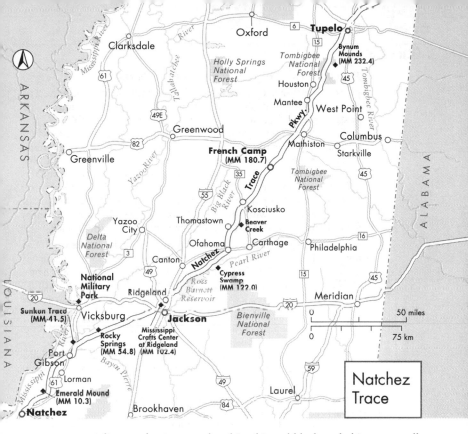

ravioli, macadamia-crusted mahimahi, and blackened ahi tuna are all standouts, as are the burgers. ✉ 343 E. Main St. ☎ 662/680–3201 ⊕ www.eatwithus.com ▭ AE, D, MC, V.

$$–$$$
AMERICAN

✕**Harvey's.** A unassuming white brick exterior hides a dimly lit, sophisticated dining room. The menu includes steaks, chops, and other all-American favorites. The house special is prime rib, and seafood selections include almond-crusted grouper and fresh fish of the day. Lots of plants and warm wood tones add to the appeal. ✉ 424 S. Gloster St. ☎ 662/842–6763 ⊕ www.eatwithus.com ▭ AE, D, MC, V ⊗ Closed Sun.

$$–$$$
MEDITERRANEAN

✕**Vanelli's.** A big, family-owned restaurant north of most of Tupelo's motels, Vanelli's serves Mediterranean specials like pasta, veal, eggplant Parmesan, and souvlaki, as well as pizzas. ✉ 1302 N. Gloster St. ☎ 662/844–4410 ⊕ www.vanellis.com ▭ AE, D, MC, V.

$

▦**Quality Inn.** This is the best choice among Tupelo's chain motels. It has large, spartan rooms and many free amenities. **Pros:** free Continental breakfast; free Wi-Fi; short drive to Elvis Presley Birthplace. **Cons:** no concierge; hotel is a little bland. ✉ 1011 N. Gloster St. ☎ 662/841–2222 ⊕ www.qualityinn.com ⇥ 111 rooms, 3 suites ⎙ In-room: refrigerator, Wi-Fi. In-hotel: pool, gym, laundry service, Wi-Fi, parking (free), no-smoking rooms ▭ AE, D, M, V ⊚|CP.

JACKSON

180 mi southwest of Tupelo, 45 mi east of Vicksburg.

Jackson is at heart a sleepy Southern city that is striding into the 21st century. The city is named for Andrew Jackson, who was popular with Mississippians long before he became president. As Major General Jackson, he helped negotiate the Treaty of Doak's Stand, according to which the Choctaw ceded large chunks of Mississippi to the United States on October 18, 1820. President Thomas Jefferson recommended that the town be laid out in a checkerboard pattern of alternating squares of buildings and parks. Peter A. Van Dorn proposed the city plan for Jackson and submitted a map for the new city in April 1822; today the Old Capitol, along with the Capitol Green on which it sits and nearby Smith Park, is one of the few remaining examples of the scheme.

A major transportation and manufacturing center during the Civil War, notably of tent fabric for Confederate troops, Jackson was completely destroyed in July 1863 following a punishing siege by the Union Army. Only a handful of buildings were left standing, including the governor's mansion, which served as General Sherman's headquarters during the Union occupation.

Jackson was home to civil rights activist Medgar Evers, a Mississippi native who worked to ensure voting rights and to desegregate the University of Mississippi. In June 1963, Evers was assassinated by a white supremacist. His home in Jackson has been preserved and offers exhibits about his life.

The city did not escape the wrath of Hurricane Katrina in 2005. The storm ripped the roof off the Old State Capitol and severely damaged the 19th-century Greek revival structure. The building reopened in 2009 and features several new exhibits related to Mississippi history.

GETTING HERE AND AROUND

At the intersection of I–55 and I–20, Jackson is about a 3-hour drive from New Orleans and a 3½-hour drive from Memphis. Jackson International Airport is just east of the city.

ESSENTIALS

Visitor Information Jackson Convention and Visitors Bureau (⊠ *111 East Capitol St., Suite 102* ☎ *601/960–1891 or 800/354–7695* ⊕ *www.visitjackson. com* ⊙ *Mon.–Fri. 8–5*).

EXPLORING

Jackson's neat, tree-shaded neighborhoods are excellent for walking, jogging, or Sunday driving, especially the **Belhaven area** bounded by Riverside Drive, I–55, Fortification Street, and North State Street. **Carlisle, Poplar, Peachtree,** and **Fairview streets** are distinguished by fine homes.

The **Eudora Welty House** was the home of Jackson's most famous writer for 76 years, from age 16 until her death in 2001. The handsome Tudor revival home overlooks the spreading oaks and white colonnaded buildings of Belhaven College across the street. Welty wrote in her bedroom on the second floor and entertained guests around the dining room table. The house features several pieces from her art collection. ⊠ *1119*

Pinehurst Pl., Belhaven ☎*601/353–7762* ⊕*www.mdah.state.ms.us/ welty* 🖅*$5* ⊙*Tours Wed.–Fri. at 9, 11, 1, and 3.*

The **Medgar Evers Home and Museum** sits on a quiet residential street in North Jackson, and has been restored to look largely as it did when the civil rights leader lived there with his wife and young children in the early 1960s. Inside are displays about Evers's remarkable life, ranging from his service in Europe in World War II, including the D-Day invasion, to his struggle to integrate the University of Mississippi. In June 1963, Evers was assassinated by a white supremacist as he stepped out of his car into the house's carport. The house is open by appointment only; contact the registrar at Tougaloo College (phone number below) to arrange a tour. A statue of Evers also stands outside the library named after him nearby at 4215 Medgar Evers Boulevard. ⊠*2332 Margaret Walker Alexander Dr., Downtown* ☎*601/977–7839 or 601/977–7700* 🖅*Free.*

The **Mississippi Governor's Mansion,** built in 1841, is a National Historic Landmark. Like the Old State Capitol down the street, it was built in the Greek revival style. The two floors include a state dining room and several parlors with cornice molding and Duncan Phyfe furniture. Tours are given Tuesday through Friday on the half hour from 9:30 to 11 AM. **Smith Park** (⊠*Bounded by Amite, West, Congress, and Yazoo Streets, Downtown*), behind the governor's mansion, is the only public square that remains from the original city plan for Jackson from 1822. The park was named after James Smith, a Scottish manufacturer, Confederate benefactor, and Jackson resident from 1834 to 1855. Eudora Welty used the park as the setting for her short story "The Winds." ⊠*300 E. Capitol St., Downtown* ☎*601/359–3175* 🖅*Free* ⊙*Tours Tues.–Fri. 9:30–11.*

The **Mississippi Museum of Art** moved into its new $14 million home in June 2007. The permanent collection features a wealth of works focused on Mississippi, while the museum also has works by Georgia O'Keeffe, Mary Cassatt, Andy Warhol, and other artists, as well as a collection of pre-Columbian ceramics. ⊠*380 S. Lamar St., Downtown* ☎*601/960–1515* ⊕*www.msmuseumart.org* 🖅*Free* ⊙*Tues.– Sat. 10–5, Sun. noon–5.*

The **Mississippi State Capitol** sits in Beaux-Arts splendor at the junction of Mississippi, High, President, and West streets, its dome surmounted by a gold-plated copper eagle with a 15-foot wingspan. Completed in 1903 at what was then the enormous cost of $1 million, the capitol underwent a $19 million renovation from 1979 to 1983. Built on the site of the old state penitentiary, it was designed by the architect Theodore C. Link, who was influenced by the design of the U.S. Capitol in Washington, D.C. The center dome rises 180 feet, and the building features pronounced cornices and enriched moldings, as well as a Roman portico with six Corinthian columns. ⊠*400 High St., Downtown* ☎*601/359–3114* 🖅*Free* ⊙*Weekdays 8–5.*

The **Old Capitol,** severely damaged by Hurricane Katrina, stands at the head of Capitol Street, where it is flanked by the **War Memorial Building** to the north and the **Mississippi Archives Building** to the south. Constructed in 1839 in the Greek revival style with simple columns and elegant proportions, it served as the state capitol from 1839 to 1903. The building has been renovated since Katrina and now contains a museum showcasing Mississippi's state government. ⊠*100 S. State St., Downtown* ☎*601/576–6920* ⊕*www.mdah.state.ms.us* ⊑*Free* ⊙*Tues.–Sat. 9–5, Sun. 1–5.*

The **Smith Robertson Museum and Cultural Center** on the edge of Farish Street, Jackson's original African-American business district, has artifacts and exhibits depicting the history of black life in Mississippi, including displays on the migration of blacks from the rural South to Northern cities in the 20th century. The building once housed the first public school for African-American children in Jackson. ⊠*528 Bloom St., Farish Street* ☎*601/960–1457* ⊑*$4.50* ⊙*Weekdays 9–5, Sat. 10–1, Sun. 2–5.*

> **HOW TO SNACK**
>
> It's never difficult to find a roadside stand serving up fried catfish or barbecue drenched in spicy sauce. Interestingly, tamales are a common foodstuff in Mississippi, and many towns have a stand or trailer purveying the cornmeal tubes filled with hot, seasoned ground beef. You may also stumble across pickles in Kool-Aid in Clarksdale or slugburgers—ground beef mixed with cornmeal then deep fried—in northeast Mississippi. The po'boy, made famous in New Orleans and a Gulf Coast staple, typically features fried shrimp and oysters with mayonnaise, lettuce, and tomato on crusty French bread.

WHERE TO EAT

$$–$$$
ITALIAN
✕**BRAVO!** This cheery, bustling restaurant is tucked inside an upscale shopping center just off the interstate. Traditional regional Italian cuisine—zesty pastas, wood-fired pizza, homemade breads, and antipasti—shares the menu with grilled meats topped with unique sauces, chutneys, and herb rubs. The menu changes frequently but is consistently good. ⊠*244 Highland Village, I–55 exit 100, North Jackson* ☎*601/982–8111* ⊕*www.bravobuzz.com* ⊟*AE, D, DC, MC, V* ⊙*Closed Mon.*

$–$$
CAFÉ
✕**Broad Street Baking Co. & Café.** You can enjoy breakfast, lunch, or dinner at this restaurant where some dozen different breads are baked fresh daily using European and old family recipes. The menu has a wide variety of sandwiches and salads. Changing daily specials include penne with blackened chicken or shrimp and asparagus, crawfish po'boys, and southwestern Cobb salad. ⊠*101 Banner Hall, 4465 I–55N, just south of Northside Dr., North Jackson* ☎*601/362–2900* ⊟*AE, D, MC, V* ⊙*No dinner Sun.*

$$
SOUTHERN
★
✕**Julep.** An eclectic, gourmet take on Southern cooking: crawfish egg rolls with black-eyed-pea salsa, blackened catfish tacos with caramelized onions and remoulade, and shrimp and grits with crème sauce are some of the offerings. Southern standbys like fried chicken and crawfish étouffée are here, too. A well-heeled crowd packs into one of Jackson's hippest bars, which offers numerous specialty drinks. The restaurant stays open late every night but Sunday. ⊠*4500 I–55 N, Suite 105, corner of I–55 and Northside Dr. in Highland Village, North Jackson* ☎*601/362–1411* ⊕*www.juleprestaurant.com* ⊟*AE, D, MC, V.*

$$$–$$$$ ✗**Nick's.** Locals pile into this popular, relaxed dining room hidden away
SEAFOOD   in an office building near the agriculture and sports museums. Innova-
tive seafood dishes include tilapia with pecan butter and roasted mahi-
mahi with a chipotle butter sauce. There's a large selection of steaks
and dinner salads, as well as the restaurant's famous seafood gumbo.
Desserts are wonderful, too, especially the white-chocolate mousse with
raspberry sauce. ✉*1501 Lakeland Dr., North Jackson* ☎*601/981–
8017* ⊕*www.nicksrestaurant.com* ⊟*AE, DC, MC, V* �⊘*Closed Sun.*

$$$–$$$$ ✗**Primos.** Family owned since 1929, this cozy and comfy eatery in Ridge-
AMERICAN   land, just outside of Jackson, serves up blue plate specials to hungry
diners. House specialties are fresh seafood and prime rib, sandwiches
include a catfish po'boy, and several seafood salads are available. The
in-house bake shop turns out pound cake, caramel brownies, and other
sweet treats. Breakfast is popular as well. ✉*515 Lake Harbour Dr.,
Ridgeland* ☎*601/898–3600* ⊕*www.primoscafe.com/primos_home.
html* ⊟*AE, DC, MC, V* ⊘*Closed Sun.*

$$$$ ✗**Schimmel's.** A Jackson institution popular with politicos and local
SEAFOOD   power brokers, Schimmel's specializes in prime meat and fresh Gulf sea-
food. Signature dishes include steaks, grilled lamb chops, Cajun shrimp
with pepper jack grits, and Parmesan-and-crab-crusted Gulf snapper.
The restaurant transforms into a blues club on Saturday nights. ✉*2615
N. State St., Fondren* ☎*601/981–7077* ⊕*www.schimmelsonline.com*
⊟*AE, D, MC, V* ⊘*Closed Sun. and Mon.*

WHERE TO STAY

$$–$$$ 🛏**Fairview Inn.** Listed on the National Register of Historic Places, this
stately colonial revival mansion is in Jackson's prestigious Belhaven
section, conveniently situated near many of the major attractions yet
secluded enough to suggest a country retreat, with sculpted hedges on
a rolling lawn. Tapestries and period antiques fill the public rooms,
and the guest rooms are decked out in chintz and Laura Ashley fab-
rics. Southern breakfast is included in the rate. **Pros:** concierge; some
rooms have sun porches. **Cons:** some rooms have no elevator access;
no airport shuttle. ✉*734 Fairview St., Belhaven* ☎*601/948–3429 or
888/948–1908* ⊕*www.fairviewinn.com* 📞*7 rooms, 10 suites* ⚲*In-
room: Wi-Fi. In-hotel: restaurant, room service, bar, gym, spa, Wi-Fi,
parking (free), no-smoking rooms* ⊟*AE, D, MC, V* ⦿*BP.*

$$–$$$ 🛏**Hilton Jackson.** Just off I–55N, on the border between Jackson and
rapidly developing Ridgeland and Madison, this sleek and contempo-
rary high-rise hotel underwent a $7 million renovation in 2008. Rooms
are comfortable and stylish, with mahogany furniture. **Pros:** excellent
restaurants; free airport shuttle. **Cons:** no concierge; nearly 10 mi
from downtown sights. ✉*1001 East County Line Rd., North Jackson*
☎*601/957–2800 or 888/263–0524* ⊕*www.hiltonjackson.com* 📞*265
rooms, 11 suites* ⚲*In-room: refrigerator (some), Wi-Fi. In-hotel: 2 res-
taurants, room service, bar, pool, gym, laundry service, Wi-Fi, parking
(free), no-smoking rooms* ⊟*AE, D, DC, MC, V.*

$$–$$$ 🛏**Jackson Marriott.** This standard chain business hotel has a convenient
downtown location. East-facing rooms have fabulous views of the state
capitol, and guests receive chocolates on their pillows. **Pros:** execu-
tive floors; lots of amenities. **Cons:** no airport shuttle; no concierge.

✉*201 E. Amite St., Downtown* ☎*601/969–5100* ⊕*www.marriott. com* ➥*300 rooms, 3 suites* ⅃*In-room: Wi-Fi. In-hotel: restaurant, room service, bar, pool, gym, laundry service, Wi-Fi, parking (paid), some pets allowed, no-smoking rooms* ⊟*AE, D, MC, V.*

$-$$ ▦**Old Capitol Inn.** Rooms are tastefully designed, with muted tones and
★ elegant accents at this charming boutique hotel. The redbrick building has decorative wrought-iron balconies, and all rooms have separate sitting areas. A marble fountain gurgles tranquilly in the lobby appointed with hip modern furniture. Breakfast is included. **Pros:** good location on the edge of downtown; complimentary happy hour; free Wi-Fi. **Cons:** no airport shuttle; no concierge. ✉*226 N. State St., Downtown* ☎*601/359–9000 or 888/359–9001* ⊕*www.oldcapitolinn.com* ➥*22 rooms, 2 suites* ⅃*In-room: refrigerator (some), Wi-Fi. In-hotel: restaurant, laundry service, Wi-Fi, parking (free), no-smoking rooms* ⊟*AE, MC, V.*

NIGHTLIFE AND THE ARTS

930 Blues Cafe (✉*930 N. Congress Street, Downtown* ☎*601/948–0888*) a great, down-home blues club in a converted house, draws all types to its weekend shows and Thursday night blues jam. **Hal and Mal's** (✉*200 S. Commerce St., Downtown* ☎*601/948–0888*) is a downtown brewpub that often has live music. **The Quarter** (✉*1855 Lakeland Dr., North Jackson*) is a dining and entertainment complex with several restaurants and bars.

SHOPPING

The **Fondren District,** where Old Canton Road forks off N. State Street in North Jackson, offers a full slate of shopping, with numerous small boutiques.

ANTIQUES For antiques, the **Antique Market** (✉*3009 N. State St., Fondren* ☎*601/982–5456*) features numerous shops. **Brent's Drugs** (✉*655 Duling Ave., Fondren* ☎*601/366–3427*) in business since 1946, has been converted to a gift shop but retains an old-fashioned soda fountain. **Fondren Beverage Emporium** (✉*3030 N. State St., Fondren* ☎*601/321–0806*) stocks an assortment of sodas, sweets, and snacks in an aqua and orange edifice that also has several other funky shops. **Highland Village** (✉*4500 I–55N, North Jackson* ☎*601/982–5861*), just east of the Northside Drive exit on I–55, offers numerous upscale merchants and several restaurants.

BOOKS Books by Mississippi authors and about Mississippi are available on the other side of the interstate from knowledgeable booksellers at **Lemuria** (✉*202 Banner Hall, 4465 I–55N, at Northside Dr., North Jackson* ☎*601/366–7619*).

NATCHEZ

★ *103 mi southwest of Jackson via the Natchez Trace Parkway.*

Natchez's quiet streets give little indication of the bustle and wealth that once surrounded one of the richest towns in America. In the years leading up to the Civil War, Natchez had more millionaires than New York, Boston, or Philadelphia. Strategically located on a bluff overlooking a broad and deep channel of the Mississippi, with relatively easy navigation to the Gulf of Mexico, Natchez grew increasingly prosperous following the introduction of steamboats on the Mississippi in the early 1800s. Cotton grown around Natchez steamed down the river to New Orleans and eventually to the textile mills of New England and the United Kingdom, and Natchez

> **WORD OF MOUTH**
>
> "Consider visiting Natchez during Spring Pilgrimage (www.natchez-pilgrimage.com/spring.htm). There are several antebellum homes open during that time and the azaleas should be in bloom."
> —notbob

became a capital of conspicuous consumption, as cotton barons constructed stunning mansions with impressive architecture stocked with the finest antiques. Meanwhile, river pilots, speculators, and rogues and ruffians of all stripes flocked to "Natchez-Under-the-Hill," a flat stretch of riverbank that offered every manner of vice to those looking to make their fortune on the river.

While Natchez was largely unscathed by the Civil War and saw commerce resume at the war's end, its fortunes declined as the century drew to a close and steamboats lost out to railroads. Today barges ply the river, but the only steamboat is the casino permanently anchored opposite Natchez-Under-the-Hill.

The **Natchez Pilgrimage,** begun in 1932 by the women of the city's garden club, gives visitors the opportunity to see the cotton planters' homes restored to their grandeur. Guides costumed in hoopskirts escort visitors through numerous houses around town. The pilgrimage is held twice a year, in spring and fall, and there is also a Christmas program. In addition, many houses are open for tours year-round and several have been converted to B&Bs.

GETTING HERE AND AROUND

Natchez is at the southern terminus of the Natchez Trace, about a 2½-hour drive from Jackson (it's actually closer to Baton Rouge, Louisiana), and lies along the "Great River Road," or U.S. 61, which heads north along the Mississippi to Vicksburg.

The old downtown is laid out in a tight grid on the riverbank, but most of the stately old homes are on the outskirts of downtown or even farther out. A car is essential. The visitor center is a short drive south of downtown, in the shadow of the Mississippi River Bridge.

ESSENTIALS

Visitor Information Natchez Visitor Center (✉ *640 S. Canal St., Natchez* ☎ *601/446-6345 or 800/647-6724* ⊕ *www.natchez.ms.us* ☺ *Mon.–Sat. 8:30–5, Sun. 9–4*).

EXPLORING

Forks of the Road was once a center of the slave trade in the United States. The second largest slave market in the South, it later became a refuge for slaves freed after Union troops occupied Natchez in July 1863. Located in an outlying commercial area, it has several displays on the history of the slave market and slavery in the area. ✉ *On Liberty Rd., between St. Catherine St. and D'evereaux Dr.* ▨ *Free.*

The **Grand Village of the Natchez Indians** archaeological park and museum depict the culture of the Natchez Native Americans, which reached its zenith in the 1500s. ✉ *400 Jefferson Davis Blvd.* ☎ *601/446–6502* ⊕ *mdah.state.ms.us/hprop/gvni.html* ✉ *Free* ⊘ *Mon.–Sat. 9–5, Sun. 1:30–5.*

Contact **Natchez Pilgrimage Tours** at the Natchez Visitor Center, next to the Mississippi River Bridge, for tickets and information on house tours. Hours vary for each house and begin on either the hour or half hour. House tours are $10 for one house or three for $24. **Auburn** (✉ *400 Duncan Ave.* ☎ *601/442–5981* ⊕ *www.auburnmuseum.org*) is a Greek revival mansion, with one of the most intriguing features of any house in Natchez or anywhere else: a spiral staircase that winds unsupported up to the second floor. The 12-room mansion, built in 1812, has Ionic columns and intricate moldings. **Magnolia Hall** (✉ *215 S. Pearl St.* ☎ *601/442–6672*) was shelled by the Union gunboat *Essex* during the Civil War. A shell reportedly exploded in a soup tureen, scalding several diners at the table. The Greek revival mansion has stucco walls and fluted columns topped with curving Ionic capitals. Note the plaster magnolia blossoms on the parlor ceiling. **Rosalie** (✉ *100 Orleans St.* ☎ *601/445–5676*), circa 1820, is the quintessential Southern plantation house, with its white columns, hipped roof, and red bricks. Restored by the Natchez Garden Club, the house serves as the state home of the Daughters of the American Revolution. Furnishings purchased for the house in 1858 include a famous Belter parlor set. **Stanton Hall** (✉ *401 High St.* ☎ *601/442–6282*) is one of the most palatial and most photographed houses in America. Built in 1857, its four giant fluted Corinthian columns support double porticoes enclosed by delicate, lacy wrought-iron railings. The five-story house features a nearly 17-foot-high main hallway. This magnificent preservation project of the Pilgrimage Garden Club is furnished with Natchez antiques. ✉ *640 S. Canal St.* ☎ *601/446–6631 or 800/647–6742* ⊕ *www.natchezpilgrimage.com* ⊘ *Daily 8:30–5* .

The **William Johnson House** tells a fascinating account from local history. Born a slave in 1809, Johnson was freed by his master at age 11 and went to work as a barber. With a sharp eye for business, he prospered, operating as a farmer and land speculator, and owning several slaves of his own. Throughout his adult life, Johnson kept diaries of his daily activities, leaving behind the most comprehensive account by a free black man before the Civil War. His recollections give a picture of life in Natchez down to the most telling details. ✉ *210 State St.* ☎ *601/445–5345* ⊕ *www.nps.gov/natc/* ✉ *Free* ⊘ *Daily 9–4:30.*

WHERE TO EAT
Several of Natchez's B&Bs have on-site restaurants; check with managers about hours and special events.

$$–$$$

SOUTHERN

✗**Biscuits & Blues.** This is a fun, boisterous place to chow down to the sounds of the blues and rock 'n' roll. One of two locations (the other one's in San Francisco), this dark-wood-and-brass-rail saloon-type eatery features barbecue and New Orleans–style seafood, with a wide selection of po'boys. Try the eggplant Orleans, a crisp eggplant on a bed of spicy tomato coulis topped with Gulf shrimp in a light garlic cream sauce and garnished with fried oysters. The incessant music makes for a noisy dining room, but that's why you came to a restaurant with "blues" in the name—right? ⊠ *315 Main St.* ☎*601/446–9922* ▤*AE, D, MC, V* ⊗*Closed Mon.*

$–$$ ✕**Carriage House Restaurant.** On the grounds of Stanton Hall, the Carriage
SOUTHERN House serves up fried chicken, baked ham, and its famous mouthwatering miniature biscuits. The restaurant has a delightful Victorian-parlor interior. ⊠ *401 High St.* ☎*601/445–5153* ⊕*www.stantonhall.com* ▤*AE, MC, V* ⊗*No dinner. Closed Tue. and Wed.*

$–$$ ✕**Cock of the Walk.** In a marvelous old train depot overlooking the Mis-
SOUTHERN sissippi River, this longtime dining spot specializes in fried catfish fillets, fried dill pickles, hush puppies, mustard greens, and coleslaw. Blackened or grilled catfish and chicken are also offered. ⊠ *200 N. Broadway, on bluff* ☎*601/446–8920* ⊕*www.cockofthewalk.biz* ▤*AE, D, MC, V* ⊗*Closed Sun. No lunch Sat.*

$$$–$$$$ ✕**Magnolia Grill.** Hidden in Natchez-Under-the-Hill, this spot is a favor-
SEAFOOD ite with locals, who come for the relaxed atmosphere and several varieties of seafood, including baked, fried, or grilled catfish or shrimp, as well as redfish topped with crawfish étouffée. Mouthwatering desserts may include cheesecake with fresh strawberries, blueberries, or peaches and bread pudding. An enclosed deck gives diners a view of the Mississippi lazily flowing by. ⊠ *49 Silver St.* ☎*601/446–7670* ⊕*www. magnoliagrill.com* ▤*AE, D, MC, V.*

6

WHERE TO STAY

$$–$$$ 🏨**The Briars Inn.** Once the home of Varina Howell, the wife of Jefferson Davis, this B&B sits on a promontory overlooking the Mississippi River. The 19 acres of landscaped grounds are a perfect place for peaceful strolling, and the inn's rooms are beautifully decorated with period furnishings imparting a gracious plantation feel. A Southern breakfast is served in the dining room. **Pros:** wonderfully landscaped grounds; great river views. **Cons:** not within walking distance of downtown; rooms may be a little worn around the edges. ⊠ *31 Irving La. (behind hotel)* ☎*601/446–9654 or 800/634–1818* ⊕*www.thebriarsinn.com* ⤴*14 rooms, 3 suites* ♿*In-room: refrigerator (some), kitchen (some), Wi-Fi. In-hotel: Wi-Fi, parking (free), no-smoking rooms* ▤*AE, D, MC, V* ♚ *BP.*

$$–$$$ 🏨**Dunleith.** Stately, colonnaded Dunleith is a popular Natchez B&B inn with elegant, plantation-style rooms furnished with four-poster beds and antiques. The breakfast room/restaurant is a former poultry house with old brick walls. Beautiful gardens enhance the grounds. A kitchenette is available in the estate's former dairy barn, and Dunleith also has rooms at Riverview Suites in downtown at 100 Main Street. **Pros:** comfortable beds; delicious breakfast. **Cons:** dairy barn rooms are a little noisy; bathrooms show some signs of age. ⊠ *84 Homochitto St.* ☎*601/446–8500 or 800/433–2445* ⊕*www.dunleith.com* ⤴*26 rooms, 1 suite* ♿*In-room: kitchen (some), refrigerator (some), Wi-Fi. In-hotel: restaurant, pool, parking (free), no kids under 14.* ▤*AE, D, MC, V* ♚ *BP.*

$–$$ 🏨**Eola Hotel.** Open since 1927, this six-story hotel sits quietly in downtown Natchez. The lobby is suitably grand, if a little faded, and some rooms have riverview balconies. **Pros:** great location for downtown strolls; helpful staff for sightseeing. **Cons:** a little noisy in some rooms; in general a little worn around the edges. ✉ *110 N. Pearl St.* ☎ *601/445–6000 or 866/445–3652* ⊕ *www.natchezeola.com* ⌖ *125 rooms, 6 suites* ⌂ *In-room: Wi-Fi. In-hotel: restaurant, room service, bar, gym, laundry service, Wi-Fi, parking (free), some pets allowed (paid)* ▤ *AE, D, MC, V.*

$$$–$$$$
Fodor's Choice
★
⊞ **Monmouth Plantation.** Travelers rave about this majestic Greek revival plantation house, built in 1818 and converted into a luxury B&B. A National Historic Landmark, you have a choice of rooms in the main house of the antebellum mansion or in outlying buildings on the 27 acres of beautifully landscaped grounds. You can almost hear the theme music from *Gone With the Wind* as you approach the main house, but don't get any ideas about turning the curtains into a ball gown. Some rooms are decorated with antiques from the original owners, the Quitman family, and some have working fireplaces and Jacuzzi tubs. The room rate includes a full Southern breakfast served in the dining room, hors d'oeuvres in the evening, and a tour of the mansion. **Pros:** very peaceful and relaxing; lots of history in this property; Wi-Fi; dinner available in the restaurant. **Cons:** some rooms a little worn around the edges; some rooms can be noisy. ✉ *36 Melrose Ave.* ☎ *601/442–5852 or 800/828–4531* ⊕ *www.monmouthplantation.com* ⌖ *15 rooms, 15 suites* ⌂ *In-room: Wi-Fi. In-hotel: restaurant, Wi-Fi; no kids under 14* ▤ *AE, D, MC, V* ⎇ *BP.*

NIGHTLIFE AND THE ARTS
King's Tavern (✉ *619 Jefferson St.* ☎ *601/446–8845*) is in the oldest house in the Natchez Territory (1789). The lounge is rustic and inviting, especially if you're an "Old Natchez" aficionado. The **Under-the-Hill Saloon** (✉ *25 Silver St.* ☎ *601/446–8023*) has live entertainment—from blues to folk—on weekends in one of the few original buildings left in Natchez-Under-the-Hill.

HOLLY SPRINGS AND OXFORD

Holly Springs and Oxford, just east of I–55 in northern Mississippi, are sophisticated versions of the Mississippi small town; both are courthouse towns incorporated in 1837. They have historic architecture, arts and crafts, literary associations, and the unhurried pleasures of Southern life that remain constant from generation to generation: entertaining conversation, good food, and nostalgic walks at twilight.

HOLLY SPRINGS

40 mi southeast of Memphis via I–55, 61 mi northwest of Tupelo via U.S. 78.

Holly Springs arose from a crossroads of old Native American trails originally called Spring Hollow. Chickasaw Indians and travelers stopped to rest here and bathe in medicinal spring waters sheltered by holly trees. Settlers came from the Carolinas, Virginia, and Georgia in the 1830s, and Holly Springs became an educational, business, and cultural center as the newly arrived planters began to rake in profits. Cotton barons built palatial mansions and handsome commercial buildings. Today Holly Springs has more than 200 structures (61 of which are antebellum homes) listed on the National Register of Historic Places.

At least 50 raids befell Holly Springs during the Civil War. The worst took place in December 1862, when the Confederate army, under General Earl Van Dorn, destroyed $1 million worth of Union supplies intended to aid General Ulysses S. Grant in his march against Vicksburg. Bent on reprisals against the city, Grant ordered General Benjamin Harrison Grierson to burn it to the ground. A clever Holly Springs matron, Maria Mason, invited General Grierson into her home to chat, and they discovered that they shared a love of music and had studied piano under the same teacher; so instead of destroying Holly Springs, Grierson enjoyed its hospitality at a series of afternoon gatherings and piano concerts.

Many of Holly Springs' historic homes are open only during **Spring Pilgrimage** (the third weekend in April), but their exteriors alone are quite spectacular. On Salem Avenue, you'll find Cedarhurst and Airliewood, brick houses constructed in the Gothic style popularized in the 1850s by Andrew Jackson Downing. General Grant used Airliewood as his headquarters during his occupation of Holly Springs.

GETTING HERE AND AROUND

A 30-minute drive from Memphis, Holly Springs is in north Mississippi near the Tennessee state line on U.S. 78 and MS 4, MS 7, and MS 311. Oxford is another half hour's drive south on MS 7.

ESSENTIALS

Visitor Information Holly Springs Tourism (⊠ *104 E. Gholson Ave.* ☎ *662/252–2515 or 888/687–4765*).

EXPLORING

Hill Crest Cemetery (⊠ *380 S. Maury St.38635*) contains the graves of 13 Confederate generals. Many of the iron fences surrounding the graves were made locally before the Civil War.

The **Kate Freeman Clark Art Gallery** is dedicated solely to the work of Holly Springs resident Kate Freeman Clark, who was trained as a painter in New York City during the 1890s. Clark completed more than 1,000 works, including landscapes and portraits. She returned to Holly Springs in the 1920s and never painted again. Many of her friends did not know of her talent until her paintings were discovered after her death. In her will she left funds to establish a museum. Call for information on hours and admission charges. ⊠*292 E. College Ave.* ☎*662/252–4211* ⊗*By appointment.*

Montrose (1858), which serves as headquarters for the Holly Springs Garden Club, has an elegant spiral staircase, elaborate cornices, and plaster ceiling medallions. The grounds have been designated a state arboretum. Tours are by appointment with the Holly Springs Chamber of Commerce or Tourism Office. ⊠*307 E. Salem Ave.* ☎*662/252 2943* ⊠*$10.*

Rust College (⊠*N. Memphis St.* ☎*662/252–4661*), founded in 1866, contains **Oak View** (circa 1860), one of the oldest buildings in the area. Metropolitan Opera star Leontyne Price, a native of Laurel, Mississippi, gave a brief concert in 1966 that raised money to build the library named for her. It houses the extensive memorabilia of civil rights leader Roy Wilkins.

The **Yellow Fever House** (⊠*104 E. Gholson Ave.*), built in 1836, was Holly Springs' first brick building. It was used as a hospital during the 1878 yellow fever epidemic.

WHERE TO EAT

¢ ×**Phillips Grocery.** The building housing Phillips Grocery was construct-
AMERICAN   ed in 1882 next to the railroad tracks as a saloon for railroad workers. Today the restaurant is decorated with antiques and crafts and serves big, old-fashioned hamburgers. ⊠*541A Van Dorn St., across from old depot* ☎*662/252–4671* ⚐*Reservations not accepted* ▤*No credit cards* ⊗*Closed Sun. No dinner.*

OXFORD

60 mi southeast of Memphis via I–55, 50 mi east of Tupelo via MS 6.

Oxford and Lafayette County were immortalized as the Jefferson and Yoknapatawpha County Oxford native William Faulkner's novels, but even if you're not a Faulkner fan, this is a great place to experience small-town living. You won't be bored: the characters who fascinated Faulkner still live here, and the University of Mississippi keeps things lively.

Faulkner received the 1949 Nobel Prize for Literature, and his readers will enjoy exploring the town that inspired *The Hamlet, The Town,* and *The Mansion.* "I discovered that my own little postage stamp of native soil was worth writing about, and that I would never live long enough to exhaust it," said Faulkner. "I created a cosmos of my own."

GETTING HERE AND AROUND

Traffic gets heavy around Courthouse Square throughout the day and into the evening, and good luck finding a parking place on the square, at least when the university is in session. Fortunately, many motels and restaurants are within walking distance.

ESSENTIALS

Visitor Information Oxford Convention and Visitors Bureau (✉ *102 Ed Perry Blvd.* ☎ *662/232–2367* ⊕ *www.oxfordcvb.com*). **Oxford Tourism Council** (✉ *107 Courthouse Square, inside City Hall* ☎ *662/232–2477* ⊕ *www.oxfordms. net/departments/otc.htm*).

EXPLORING

You can easily meet Faulkner in **Courthouse Square,** a National Historic Landmark in the center of town—albeit only a statue of him lounging, pipe in hand, on a bench in front of **City Hall,** on the northeast corner of the square, which also houses the local tourism office. At the center of the square is the white-sandstone **Lafayette** (pronounced luh-*fay*-it) **County Courthouse** named for the French Revolutionary hero the Marquis de Lafayette. The courthouse was rebuilt in 1873 after Union troops burned it down; on its south side is a monument to Confederate soldiers, donated by the Faulkner family. **Neilson's** (*119 Courthouse Sq.*) is the oldest continually operating department store in the South.

University Avenue, running west from South Lamar Boulevard just south of Courthouse Square to the University of Mississippi, is one of the state's most beautiful sights when the trees flame orange and gold in the fall or when the dogwoods bloom white and pink in the spring.

The **University Museums** display the brightly colored paintings of local artist Theora Hamblett. Hamblett gained international fame for her works depicting dreams and visions, Mississippi landscapes, and scenes from her childhood. The museum also has a collection of Greek and Roman antiquities and a quirky exhibit of 19th-century scientific exhibits, and its cultural center hosts regional and national art exhibits year-round. ✉ *University Ave. at 5th St.* ☎ *662/915–7073* 🎫 *Free* 🕐 *Tues.–Sat. 9:30–4:30, Sun. 1–4:30.*

"Ole Miss," or the **University of Mississippi,** opened in 1848 with 80 students. The **Grove,** the tree-shaded heart of the campus, is as important in Oxford as Courthouse Square—on football weekends, it fills up with tailgaters gearing up to cheer on the Rebels in nearby Vaught-Hemingway stadium. Contact the school's **public relations department** (☎ *662/915–7236*) for information about university's plays, lectures, sporting events, and special events.

The **Center for the Study of Southern Culture** (☎ *662/915–5993* ⊕ *www.olemiss.edu/depts/south/*), housed in antebellum Barnard Observatory, facing the Grove, is a groundbreaking institution dedicated to regional studies. Its conferences attract scholars from around the world, and it publishes the remarkable *Encyclopedia of Southern Culture,* as well as *Living Blues* magazine. The **J. D. Williams Library** (☎ *662/915–5858*) contains a permanent exhibit on Faulkner, including his Nobel Prize medal; first editions of books by other Mississippi authors, such as Eudora Welty, Richard Wright, and Barry Hannah; an extensive blues archive.

Fodor's Choice ★ **Rowan Oak** was William Faulkner's home from 1930 until his death in 1962. Although it's one of Mississippi's most famous attractions, there are no signs to direct you and only an unobtrusive historic marker at the site. The house and its surrounding 32 acres are as serene and private

William Faulkner

Nobel Prize–winning author William Faulkner lived in Oxford from age five until his death in 1962, and based much of his writing on observations of his hometown. Yoknapatawpha County, setting of many Faulkner novels and stories, is a thinly disguised version of Oxford's Lafayette County, and Faulkner's novels like *The Sound and the Fury* and *As I Lay Dying* deal with the social and racial tensions of Yoknapatawpha residents.

Though Faulkner is one of the greats of Southern literature, he had little financial success for much of his writing career. He supplemented his income with jobs in a power plant and as a postmaster at the University of Mississippi. He spent so much of his time in the post office writing, playing cards, and ignoring customers that he was eventually forced to resign. He said famously of this experience: "I reckon I'll be at the beck and call of folks with money all my life, but thank God I won't ever again have to be at the beck and call of every son of a bitch who's got two cents to buy a stamp."

as they were when Faulkner lived and wrote here. Built about 1848 by Colonel Robert Sheegog, the two-story, white-frame house with square columns represents the primitive Greek revival style of architecture common to many Mississippi antebellum homes. After the Civil War it fell into disrepair, but in 1930 it was purchased by Faulkner and his bride of one year, Estelle Oldham Franklin.

The house was both a sanctuary and a financial burden to the author, it is now a National Historic Landmark owned by the University of Mississippi. Faulkner wrote an outline for his novel *A Fable* on the walls of the study, which is reputed to be the most photographed room in the state. The days of the week are neatly printed over the head and length of the bed, and to the right of the door leading into the room is the notation TOMORROW. ⊠ *Old Taylor Rd.* ☎ *662/234–3284* ✉ *$5* ⊙ *Tues.–Sat. 10–4, Sun. noon–4.*

Faulkner's funeral was held at Rowan Oak, and he was buried in the family plot in **St. Peter's Cemetery,** at Jefferson and North 16th Streets, beside his relatives. Also buried here is Caroline Barr, "Mammy Callie," Faulkner's childhood nurse. The tomb of the author's brother, Dean Faulkner, who was killed in an airplane crash, bears the same epitaph as the one Faulkner gave to John Sartoris in the novel *Pylon.*

William Faulkner was married at **College Hill Presbyterian Church,** a little church 8 mi northwest of Oxford on College Hill Road, on June 20, 1929. The original pews are intact, and it's believed that Sherman stabled horses here during his occupation of College Hill in 1862. Behind the church is one of north Mississippi's oldest cemeteries. ⊠ *339 County Road 102* ☎ *662/234–5020.*

WHERE TO EAT

$–$$ ✗ **Ajax Diner.** This great Southern diner has funky touches, like folk art
SOUTHERN on the walls. The savory meatloaf is stuffed with garlic and pepper jack
cheese, mashed potatoes are creamy and flavorful, and the crust on the
jalapeño corn bread is just right. There's a rib eye, a buffalo porterhouse pork chop, and fried catfish (of course), as well as a variety of
vegetarian plates. ✉ *118 Courthouse Sq.* ☎ *662/232–8880* 🍽 *AE, D,
MC, V* ⊘ *Closed Sun.*

¢–$ ✗ **Bottletree Bakery.** This is the closest to crusty European-style bread that
CAFÉ you'll find in Mississippi. If that isn't reason enough to stop in, check
out the saucer-size cinnamon rolls. The bakery serves breakfast and
lunch as well as pastries and specialty coffees. ✉ *923 Van Buren Ave.*
☎ *662/236–5000* 🍽 *MC, V* ⊘ *Closed Mon. No dinner.*

$$$$ ✗ **City Grocery.** What was once a grocery store is now a trendy bis-
CAJUN tro on Oxford's historic Courthouse Square. Chef and New Orleans
★ native John Currence has been constantly innovating since 1992, and
the changing menu has seen peanut-crusted pork chop, grilled Gulf of
Mexico red snapper, and shrimp and grits. Bananas Foster is a wonderful dessert. ✉ *152 Courthouse Sq.* ☎ *662/232–8080* 🌐 *www.citygro-
ceryonline.com* 🍽 *AE, D, MC, V* ⊘ *Closed Sun.*

$$$–$$$$ ✗ **Downtown Grill.** With its comfortable plaid chairs and dark walls, the
SOUTHERN Grill's bar could be a club in Oxford, England, but then there's the light
and airy balcony overlooking the square—pure Oxford, Mississippi.
Specialties include catfish Lafitte (fried and topped with shrimp, juli-
enned ham, and a savory cream sauce), grilled mahimahi, filet mignon,
and rich desserts. ✉ *110 Courthouse Sq.* ☎ *662/234–2659* 🍽 *AE, D,
MC, V* ⊘ *Closed Sun.*

WHERE TO STAY

$$ 🏨 **Downtown Oxford Inn and Suites.** This standard motel just a few blocks
north of the square has a shaded outdoor terrace that overlooks the
courthouse. **Pros:** complimentary breakfast; good downtown location.
Cons: somewhat standard rooms; no concierge. ✉ *400 N. Lamar Blvd.*
☎ *662/234–3031* 🌐 *www.downtownoxfordinnandsuites.com* 🛏 *65
rooms, 35 suites* ♿ *In-room: refrigerator (some), Wi-Fi. In-hotel: restaurant, bar, pool, gym, laundry service, Wi-Fi, parking (free), no-smoking rooms* 🍽 *AE, D, MC, V* 🍴 *CP.*

$ 🏨 **Inn at Ole Miss.** The inn is slowly establishing itself following the con-
struction of a new, eight-story building overlooking The Grove on the
university campus. The building is a bit institutional, but the rooms are
quiet and comfortable. This is where Barack Obama and John McCain
both prepped for their 2008 debate at Ole Miss. **Pros:** evening shuttle
service to downtown; free Wi-Fi. **Cons:** not within walking distance
of Courthouse Square; no concierge; very limited breakfast. ✉ *Alumni Dr.* ☎ *662/234–2331* 🌐 *innatolemiss.com* 🛏 *93 rooms, 36 suites*
♿ *In-room: kitchen (some), refrigerator, DVD (some), Wi-Fi. In-hotel:
pool, laundry service, Wi-Fi, parking (free and paid), no-smoking rooms*
🍽 *AE, MC, V.*

$–$$ 🏨 **Puddin' Place.** This Victorian house has a wonderful back porch with
swings and rockers, as well as a backyard with hammocks and a tree
house. The two suites—each with sitting room, separate bedroom, and

private bath—are thoughtfully furnished with antiques. There's a one-room cottage out back popular with honeymooners that has breakfast delivered to the door. **Pros:** very cozy rooms; excellent Southern breakfast. **Cons:** rooms a little on the older side; no credit cards. ✉*1008 University Ave.* ☎*662/234–1250* ⬅*2 suites, 1 cottage* ⚐*In-room: refrigerator (some), DVD (some), Wi-Fi. In-hotel: Wi-Fi, parking (free), no smoking rooms* ▬*No credit cards* ⦿ *BP.*

NIGHTLIFE AND THE ARTS

The **Faulkner and Yoknapatawpha Conference,** held in July on the Ole Miss campus, includes lectures by Faulkner scholars and field trips to the sites of the fictional Yoknapatawpha County. The annual **Oxford Conference for the Book,** held in March, has an emphasis on Southern authors.

Proud Larry's (✉*211 S. Lamar Blvd.* ☎*662/236–0050* ⊕*www.proud-larrys.com*) regularly schedules regional bands playing blues, folk, funk, jazz, and rock.

MISSISSIPPI DELTA

"The Delta begins in the lobby of the Peabody Hotel in Memphis and ends on Catfish Row in Vicksburg," quipped Greenville journalist David Cohn. In between is a vast agricultural plain created by the Mississippi River, famous as the birthplace of the blues. U.S. 61, the Blues Highway, rambles through the cotton fields and hard-luck towns of the Delta, cruising past many sites of blues history. Some say the rural crossroads where bluesman Robert Johnson allegedly sold his soul to the devil in return for prowess at guitar is out there somewhere on the highway.

If you have only one day in the Delta, use it to cruise down U.S. 61 and the Great River Road (MS 1). Gamble your way through Tunica. Stop for lunch and a swing through the Delta Blues Museum in Clarksdale. If you can, stay for a show at the Ground Zero Blues Club. Then pick up the blues on the radio about the time you glimpse the first kudzu near Vicksburg.

TUNICA

30 mi south of Memphis via U.S. 61.

This region is a gambler's paradise. Huge casino hotels have sprung up along an otherwise empty and somewhat barren strip of Delta highway, barely a half hour's drive from downtown Memphis. The view of these entertainment and hotel complexes emerging from the cotton fields is surreal, but step inside and you'll think you're in Vegas or Atlantic City. If you're not interested in gambling, you can still take advantage of good entertainment at the casinos—everything from comedy acts to blues and country music.

GETTING HERE AND AROUND

U.S. 61 runs from Memphis through the Delta to Vicksburg and Natchez and to Baton Rouge, Louisiana. The Great River Road (MS 1) parallels U.S. 61 and the river through part of this route.

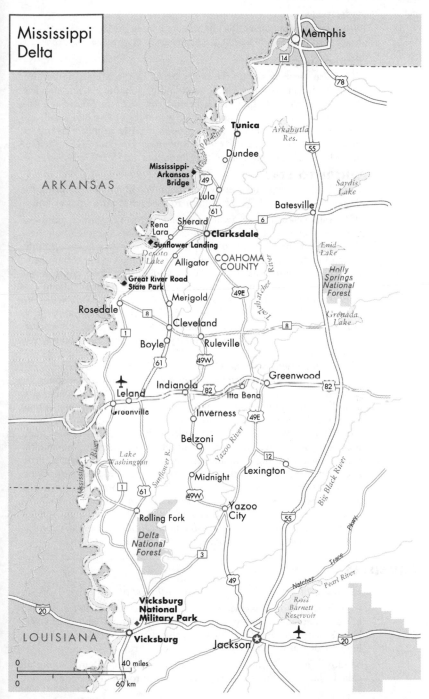

Mississippi
Delta

Memphis
14
78
ARKANSAS
Tunica
Arkabutla
Res.
55
Dundee
Mississippi-
Arkansas
Bridge
49
Lula
Sardis
Lake
61
Batesville
Sherard
6
Rena
Lara
Clarksdale
Sunflower Landing
Desoto
Lake
Alligator
COAHOMA
COUNTY
Enid
Lake
Great River Road
State Park
Merigold
49E
Holly
Springs
National
Forest
6
Rosedale
8
Cleveland
Grenada
Lake
8
Boyle
61
Ruleville
1
49W
Greenwood
Leland
Indianola
82
Itta Bena
82
Greenville
Inverness
49E
Belzoni
Yazoo River
Lake
Washington
Sunflower R.
12
Midnight
Lexington
49W
Yazoo
City
Big Black River
1
61
55
Rolling Fork
Delta
National
Forest
3
Mississippi River
49
Natchez
Pearl River
Vicksburg
National
Military Park
Ross
Barnett
Reservoir
Trace Pkwy.
20
LOUISIANA
Vicksburg
Jackson
20

0   40 miles
0   60 km

ESSENTIALS

Visitor Info Tunica Convention and Visitors Bureau (⊠ *13625 U.S. 61N, Tunica Resorts* ☎ *662/363–3800 or 888/488–6422* ⊕ *www.TunicaMiss.com).*

EXPLORING

The **Tunica RiverPark** sits on the sandy banks of the Mississippi, with a nature trail winding through the surrounding wetlands. A museum features a huge fish tank showcasing the aquaculture of the Mississippi River, displays on area history, and interactive exhibits like a diving bell and a river pilot simulator. The *Tunica Queen* departs from the river park for scenic river cruises. ⊠ *Box 99, 1 River Park Dr.* ☎ *662/357–0050 or 866/517–4837* ⊕ *www.TunicaRiverPark.com* ☜ *$5* ⊙ *Daily 9–5.*

WHERE TO STAY

Casino rates change frequently and are often much lower during the week—it's best to call (or go online) and see what rates are available.

$$$ 🏨 **Harrah's Tunica.** This sprawling complex features the largest gambling floor between Las Vegas and Atlantic City. Rooms are spread out over three separate buildings, two of which are a short drive away from the casino building. A 2,500-seat theater presents big-time entertainment. One of the restaurants is the Paula Deen Buffet. **Pros:** comfortable rooms; concierge. **Cons:** some rooms are nowhere near the casino; no airport shuttle. ⊠ *13615 Old U.S. 61, Tunica Resorts* ☎ *800/946–4946* ⊕ *www.harrahstunica.com* ☜ *998 rooms, 350 suites* ⊘ *In-room: refrigerator, Wi-Fi. In-hotel: 5 restaurants, room service, bars, golf course, tennis courts, pools, gym, spa, laundry service, Wi-Fi, parking (free), no-smoking rooms* ⊟ *AE, D, DC, MC, V.*

$$ 🏨 **Sam's Town Hotel & Casino – Tunica.** An Old West theme pervades this mammoth hotel-casino-entertainment complex. Rooms and suites are adjacent to the casino, which contains more than 1,500 slot machines as well as table games and live poker and keno. Past performers at the 1,600-seat River Palace Arena have included Bill Cosby, Wynonna Judd, and Wayne Newton. River Bend Links is the adjacent 18-hole championship golf course. The four restaurants at Sam's, including Smokey Joe's, serve everything from juicy Angus steaks to spicy barbecue. **Pros:** good restaurants and nightlife; near other casinos and river park. **Cons:** no airport shuttle; no concierge. ⊠ *1477 Casino Strip Resorts Blvd., Robinsonville* ☎ *800/456–0711* ⊕ *www.samstowntunica.com* ☜ *837 rooms, 32 suites* ⊘ *In-room: refrigerator (some), Wi-Fi. In-hotel: 4 restaurants, room service, bars, golf course, pool, gym, laundry service, Wi-Fi, parking (free), no-smoking rooms* ⊟ *AE, D, DC, MC, V.*

CLARKSDALE

60 mi southwest of Memphis, 30 mi southwest of Tunica via U.S. 61.

As a child, author Tennessee Williams spent time in Clarksdale visiting his grandfather, the rector of St. George's Episcopal Church. In Williams's play *Cat on a Hot Tin Roof,* the character Brick was running high hurdles at nearby Friars Point when he broke his leg.

Muddy Waters, John Lee Hooker, Ike Turner, and Sam Cooke all called Clarksdale home before heading north to Memphis and beyond in search of fame and fortune. The town still has the Riverside Hotel (*615 Sunflower Ave.*), where many blues musicians stayed when playing Clarksdale's impressive selection of juke joints, most of which have sadly since closed down.

ESSENTIALS

Visitor Info Coahoma County Tourism Commission (⌧ *1540 De Soto Ave., Box 160, Clarksdale* ☎ *662/627–7337* ⊕ *www.clarksdaletourism.com*).

EXPLORING

The **Delta Blues Museum** is a testament to the important role played by Clarksdale and Coahoma County in the history of the blues. Exhibits and programs trace the influence of the blues on rock, jazz, and pop music through videotapes, slides, records, and books. The museum is housed in the restored Illinois Central Freight Train Depot. ⌧ *1 Blues Alley* ☎ *662/627–6820* ⊕ *www.deltabluesmuseum.org* ⌧ *$7* ☉ *Mar.–Oct., Mon.–Sat. 9–5; Nov.–Feb., Mon.–Sat. 10–5.*

WORD OF MOUTH

"Are you by any chance a fan of the blues or of the other King, B. B.? If so, you could combine a visit to Memphis with a short drive down Hwy 61 to Clarksdale, visit the Delta Blues Museum and have some BBQ at Abe's. If you plan to sell your soul, this is the place. Next time (and there will be) we'll stay at the Shack Up Inn."

—Gardyloo

6

WHERE TO EAT AND STAY

$$$
BARBECUE

✕ **Abe's BBQ.** This no-frills barbecue shack sits in the shadow of the sign commemorating the "crossroads" where bluesman Robert Johnson allegedly sold his soul to the devil in return for fame and skill on the guitar. The menu is simple—pork and beef sandwiches, ribs, and Mississippi tamales. Usually a locals spot, it fills up with blues fans during Clarksdale's annual juke joint festival in April. ⌧ *616 State St. (U.S. 61) at DeSoto St. (U.S. 49)* ☎ *662/624–9947* ⊕ *www.abesbbq.com* ⌧ *Reservations not accepted* ☐ *AE, D, MC, V.*

$$$–$$$$
SOUTHERN

✕ **Madidi.** Morgan Freeman is a partner in this fine-dining restaurant, as well as in Clarksdale's Ground Zero Blues Club. The menu is inventive, with dishes like pan-seared sea bass and pecan-crusted Colorado lamb chops. ⌧ *164 Delta Ave.* ☎ *662/627–7770* ⊕ *www.madidires.com* ☐ *AE, D, MC, V* ☉ *No lunch. Closed Sun. and Mon.*

$–$$
MEDITERRANEAN

✕ **Rest Haven.** The Delta's large Lebanese community is reflected in the eclectic fare at this restaurant. Among the favorites are kibbe (seasoned lean ground lamb with cracked wheat), spinach and meat pies, and cabbage rolls. Daily plate-lunch specials include chicken and dumplings and red beans and sausage over rice. ⌧ *419 N. State St. (MS 161)* ☎ *662/624–8601* ⊕ *www.clarksdale.com/resthaven* ☐ *No credit cards* ☉ *Closed Sun.*

¢–$
★

▥ **Shack Up Inn.** This former cotton plantation transformed into a "bed-and-beer" is unlike any other lodging. Guests sleep in nine converted sharecroppers' shotgun shacks, complete with rusting tin roofs, ramshackle front porches, worn lawn chairs, and country kitsch furnishings. Although they've been equipped with electricity and plumbing, it's still a far cry from a luxury or even budget hotel. Their motto, after all, is the "the Ritz we ain't." More modern rooms are available in the Cotton

Gin Inn, as well as in a tractor shed converted into a three-bedroom, two-bathroom house. The converted cotton gin also features space for music performances. The shacks and rooms fill up fast—call well ahead. **Pros:** unique lodging; lots of outdoor space. **Cons:** certainly not for everyone; a bit of a drive from downtown; no phones in most rooms. ✉*Hopson-Pixley Rd., off U.S. 49S, about ½ mi south of the intersection with U.S. 61, Clarksdale* ☎*662/624–8329* ⊕*www.shackupinn. com* 🛏*20 rooms* ⚙*In-room: no phone, kitchen (some), refrigerator (some), no TV (some), Wi-Fi. In-hotel: laundry facilities, Wi-Fi, parking (free), some pets allowed* ⊟*AE, D, MC, V.*

NIGHTLIFE AND THE ARTS

★ The **Ground Zero Blues Club** (✉*0 Blues Alley [364 Delta Ave.]* ☎*662/621–9009* ⊕*www.groundzerobluesclub.com*), partly owned by Morgan Freeman, is just down the street from the Delta Blues Museum. Bands play Wednesday through Saturday nights, and the kitchen turns out no-frills Southern cooking like catfish and shrimp sandwiches as well as good burgers.

VICKSBURG

147 mi southwest of Clarksdale via U.S. 61, 35 mi west of Jackson via I–20.

Vicksburg began as a mission founded by the Reverend Newitt Vick in 1814. He chose a spot high on the bluffs above a bend in the Mississippi River, a location that would have important consequences for the young city during the Civil War.

In June 1862 the Union had control of the Mississippi River, with the exception of Vicksburg, which was in Confederate hands. Ulysses S. Grant's men doggedly slogged through canals and bayous in five futile attempts to capture the city, which was called the Gibraltar of the Confederacy because of its impregnable natural defenses. Then, in a series of raids and battles, Grant laid waste the area between Vicksburg and Jackson to the east and Port Gibson to the south before returning to Vicksburg. His attacks were repulsed once again; he then laid siege to the city for 47 days as its residents, hiding in caves, slowly starved. On July 4, 1863, the city surrendered: the Union had split the Confederacy, gaining control of the river, a key development in its eventual victory.

Today, Vicksburg National Military Park features a driving tour that passes key points in the siege as well as monuments to the military units from numerous states that fought for control of Vicksburg.

Downtown Vicksburg has made a comeback in recent years, with art galleries, shops, and a boutique hotel springing up on Washington Street and adjoining blocks. Several casinos stand along the riverbank, where you can see the Yazoo River flow into the Mississippi. A children's play area stands on the site of catfish row, once an important catfish market. Nearby are several murals depicting important historical events in Vicksburg. Many historic homes in town have been converted to inns and B&Bs.

ESSENTIALS

Visitor Info **Vicksburg Convention and Visitors Bureau** (✉ *3300 Clay St. [just west of I-20], Box 110, Vicksburg* ☎ *601/636-9421 or 800/221-3536* ⊕ *www.visitvicksburgcvb.com*).

EXPLORING

★ **Vicksburg National Military Park** nearly encircles Vicksburg, following the line of the Confederate fortifications. The park comprises 1,800 acres of fortifications and earthworks lined with monuments and markers tracing battle positions. A driving tour winds 16 mi through the park; one-hour audio tours are available for purchase at the visitor center, which also has exhibits and a film on the siege. About 7 mi into the park is the USS *Cairo*, a Union gunboat raised from the Yazoo River; restored. Civil War artifacts recovered from the *Cairo* are on display at the adjacent USS *Cairo* Museum. Vicksburg National Military Cemetery contains the graves of nearly 17,000 Union soldiers; Confederate dead from the siege were buried in the Vicksburg City Cemetery ✉ *3201 Clay St.* ☎ *601/636-0583 for main switchboard, 601/636-2199 for USS Cairo* ⊕ *www.nps.gov/vick* ✎ *$8 per car* ⊙ *Apr. 1–Oct. 1: tour road daily 7:30–7; visitor center daily 8–5; USS Cairo ship and museum daily 9:30–6. Oct. 1–Apr. 1: tour road, visitor center, and USS Cairo ship and museum daily 8–5.*

WHERE TO EAT AND STAY

$$$–$$$$ ✗ **Rusty's Riverfront Grill.** At this classic riverfront fish house frequented
SEAFOOD by locals, selections include stuffed flounder and grilled or blackened amberjack, as well as a house special of blackened redfish with crawfish cream sauce. The menu also has steaks and chicken. The small dining room fills up fast, especially on weekends, and the open kitchen and crowded tables can make for noisy dining. ✉ *901 Washington St.* ☎ *601/638-2030* ♨ *Reservations not accepted* ☰ *AE, D, MC, V.*

$$–$$$ ✗ **Walnut Hills Restaurant.** An example *par excellence* of a uniquely
SOUTHERN Southern place: the round-table restaurant. Take a seat with a group
★ of friendly fellow diners at one of the large round tables topped with a lazy Susan, upon which sits a platter of fried chicken or country-fried steak and heaping side dishes of Dixie favorites like mustard greens, okra, red beans and rice, and purple-hulled peas. Finish it off with a dish of divine chocolate or lemon pudding. Servers move briskly through the dining rooms in the rambling converted house, filling glasses with sweet tea. An à la carte menu has steaks, chops, seafood, gumbo, and po'boys. ✉ *1214 Adams St., at Clay St.* ☎ *601/638-4910* ⊕ *www.walnuthillsms.net* ♨ *Reservations not accepted* ☰ *AE, D, MC, V* ⊙ *Closed Sat. No dinner Sun.*

$$–$$$ ⊞ **Cedar Grove Mansion Inn.** An entire city block is consumed by this
★ 1840s mansion, outbuildings, and grounds reborn as a B&B. All rooms are furnished with period antiques and Civil War artifacts, the most impressive of which is the Union cannonball still lodged in the parlor wall. You can hear nearby river traffic at night from the otherwise quiet,

gaslit grounds and survey the watery scene during the day from the rooftop veranda. VCRs are available for rooms. **Pros:** lots of amenities; delicious Southern breakfast. **Cons:** some distance from downtown; outdoor pool is unheated. ⊠*2200 Oak St.* ☎*601/636–1000 or 800/862–1300* ⊕*www.cedargroveinn.com* ⌐*22 rooms, 11 suites* ⌂*In-room: kitchen (some), refrigerator (some). In-hotel: restaurant, room service, bar, tennis court, pool, laundry service, Wi-Fi, parking (free), some pets allowed, no-smoking rooms* ⊟*AE, D, DC, MC, V*◎⏢*BP.*

$$–$$$ ⊞**The Ware House.** This truly unique boutique hotel opened in 2008 in
★   the heart of downtown Vicksburg looks as though it was transplanted from a much more cosmopolitan locale. The sumptuous theme suites have oak or black granite countertops and track lighting; some have fireplaces, and others include touches like a bearskin rug or a baby grand piano. Curved leather sofas are typical. A sports bar and cocktail lounge are part of the two-story courtyard complex. **Pros:** great value for what's included; very convenient for strolling downtown and the riverfront. **Cons:** still establishing itself, with plans to add more amenities; front desk is off-duty after 5. ⊠*1412 Washington St.* ☎*601/634–1000* ⊕*www.thewarehouse.ms* ⌐*3 rooms, 10 suites* ⌂*In-room: kitchen (some), refrigerator, Wi-Fi. In-hotel: 2 bars, Wi-Fi, parking (free), some pets allowed (paid), no smoking rooms* ⊟*AE, D, MC, V.*

SHOPPING

H.C. Porter Gallery (⊠*1216 Washington St.* ☎*601/661–9444*) features the paintings, prints, and photography of acclaimed Mississippi artist H. C. Porter, much of whose work has focused on the landscapes of her home state.

North Carolina

THE COAST, THE TRIANGLE, AND ASHEVILLE

WORD OF MOUTH

"Weather in the OBX is great to the end of September, except for the occasional hurricane system. There is not a lot of nightlife in the OBX. But the beaches are nice and the water is warm."

—nohomers

"The Triangle area in general is great—three hours from mountains and 2½ from the beach . . . great food, travel, weather, art, sports (colleges are dominant), parks, university/college stuff (lectures, etc.), outdoor recreation. There is no shortage of stuff to do. Plus, you get that Southern hospitality. People are so friendly and helpful. You can't go wrong."

—jspence

Updated
by Liz Biro,
Amber
Nimocks, and
Lan Sluder

Unlike many other states, North Carolina does not have one city that stands head and shoulders above the rest, nor are the cities gritty, noisy, or oversize. Instead, the pace is a bit slower, manners still count, and canopies of hardwoods and pine trees characterize cities and countryside alike. Thanks to its temperate climate, world-class schools, and a dynamic economy, North Carolina is one of the top places to live in the U.S.

In 1524 the explorer Giovanni da Verazano landed on what is now North Carolina's shore and wrote in his log that it was "as pleasant and delectable [a land] to behold as is possible to imagine." Sixty years later the New World's first English-speaking settlers found their way to the state's eastern edge, which is bordered by 300 mi of beaches, islands, and inlets. Hernando de Soto searched for gold in the western part of the state, an area bounded by two ranges of the southern Appalachians, the Blue Ridge Mountains, and the Great Smoky Mountains. Several centuries later, in 1799 the first gold rush in the United States got its start in the Piedmont region when young Conrad Reed discovered a 17-pound nugget of gold. And although North Carolina was the last state to secede during the Civil War, the state provided more troops and supplies to the Confederacy than any other Southern state and suffered the most casualties. Thanks to efforts of the state and many determined citizens, this history and more has been carefully preserved.

ORIENTATION AND PLANNING

GETTING ORIENTED

Solitude in the form of miles of pristine shore, along with boating, scuba diving, and fishing are the main pastimes in the Outer Banks along the North Carolina coast. The Triangle (Raleigh, Durham, and Chapel Hill), in the central Piedmont, is the hub of higher education, scientific research, and state-sponsored cultural resources. Charlotte, the state's largest city, is known as a center of high finance in the South, and prides itself on its cosmopolitan flair. In the western mountains, anchored by Asheville, you'll find everything from hiking trails to the Biltmore Estate.

The North Carolina Coast. Long stretches of wild beach are intermingled with small towns on this ribbon of sand known as the Outer Banks. The north end is a tourist mecca of shops, resorts, restaurants, beach cottages, and historic sites. Quiet villages and open, undeveloped beach mark the south end where travelers often hear nothing but surf and shorebirds. On the Crystal Coast, history ranges from Colonial to Civil

TOP REASONS TO GO

Water, water everywhere: Surfers delight in Cape Hatteras's mighty waves. Kayakers and boaters prefer the Crystal Coast's sleepy estuaries and rippling inlets. Beach strollers love Ocracoke's remote, unspoiled shore. The landscape variety lets you choose your own adventure, whether it's boating, trekking, sunning, or simply observing.

Lighting the darkness: North Carolina's seven lighthouses have individual personalities, from the masculine elegance of Currituck's brick facade to the iconic spiral of Hatteras. You'll want to take time to see them all.

Raleigh museums: More than a dozen museums and historical sites—several within an easy walk of one another—cover every aspect of North Carolina life, from its prehistoric roots to its arts achievements and sports heroes.

Biltmore Estate: The 250-room Biltmore House, modeled after the great Renaissance châteaus of the Loire Valley in France, is the largest private home in America. The 8,000-acre estate, with extensive gardens, a deluxe hotel, and restaurants, is the most-visited attraction in North Carolina.

Blue Ridge Parkway: This winding two-lane road, which ends at the edge of the Great Smokies and shows off the highest mountains in eastern America, is the most scenic drive in the South.

7

War sites. Farther south, Wilmington is both cosmopolitan and historic, with a 200-block National Register historic district and a revitalized waterfront with shops, cafés, and nightlife.

The Triangle. Since the region is home to Duke University, North Carolina State University, and the University of North Carolina at Chapel Hill, life in the Triangle revolves around basketball and higher education. Leafy campuses offer architectural delights, and the surrounding communities reflect the universities' progressive spirits with a vibrant farm-to-table food scene and a passion for learning and the arts.

Charlotte. The Queen City's contemporary facade dazzles, and its skyline gleams with the most impressive modern architecture in the state. Alongside fans cheering the NFL's Carolina Panthers and hipsters hitting the city's sleek nightspots in this New South metropolis, you'll find traditional Southern hospitality.

Asheville. Set in a valley surrounded by the highest mountains in Eastern America, Asheville is a base for exploring the region, but it is also a destination unto itself. Here you can tour America's largest home and discover why Asheville has a national reputation for its arts, crafts, and music scenes.

PLANNING

WHEN TO GO

North Carolina's coast shines in spring (April and May) and fall (September and October), when the weather is most temperate and the water reasonably warm. Traveling during these times means you can avoid the long lines and higher prices associated with peak tourist season. The Piedmont and the mountains around Asheville are also beautiful in the spring, and leaf peepers crowd the mountain roads in the fall.

GETTING HERE AND AROUND

AIR TRAVEL

The closest large, commercial airports to the Outer Banks are Raleigh-Durham, a 5-hour drive, and Norfolk International in Virginia, a 1½-hour drive. Wilmington International Airport serves the Cape Fear Coast. To reach the Triangle, the Raleigh-Durham International Airport, off Interstate 40 between the two cities, is served by most major airlines. Charlotte-Douglas International Airport is west of Charlotte off Interstate 85. Asheville Regional Airport is one of the most pleasant and most modern airports in the South.

Airport Contacts Asheville Regional Airport (AVL ✉ 708 Airport Rd., Fletcher ☏ 828/684–2226 ⊕ www.flyavl.com). **Charlotte-Douglas International Airport** (CLT ✉ 5501 Josh Birmingham Pkwy., Airport/Coliseum, Charlotte ☏ 704/359–4013 ⊕ www.charlotteairport.com). **Norfolk International** (✉ 2200 Norview Ave. ☏ 757/857–3351 ⊕ www.norfolkairport.com). **Raleigh-Durham International Airport** (RDU ✉ 1600 Terminal Blvd., Morrisville ☏ 919/840–2123 ⊕ www.rdu.com). **Wilmington International Airport** (✉ 1740 Airport Blvd. ☏ 910/341–4125 ⊕ www.flyilm.com).

BOAT AND FERRY TRAVEL

From Ocracoke in the Outer Banks, car ferries take off to Hatteras Island, Cedar Island, and the mainland's Swan Quarter. You need to reserve some ferries by calling the NC Department of Transportation's ferry division.

Boat and Ferry Contacts North Carolina Department of Transportation Ferry Information (☏ 800/293–3779).

CAR TRAVEL

On the one hand, navigation in the Outer Banks is a snap because there's only one road—Route 12. On the other, traffic can make that single road two lanes of pure frustration on a rainy midsummer day when everyone is looking for something besides sunbathing. Low-lying areas of the highway are also prone to flooding.

Charlotte is a transportation hub; Interstate 77 comes in from Columbia, South Carolina, to the south, and then continues north to Virginia, intersecting Interstate 40 on the way. U.S. 1 runs north–south through the Triangle and links to Interstate 85 going northeast. U.S. 64, which makes an east–west traverse across the Triangle, continues eastward all the way to the Outer Banks.

Interstate 40 runs east–west through Asheville. Interstate 240 forms a perimeter around the city. The Blue Ridge Parkway runs northeast from

North Carolina

Downtown Asheville see detail map

The Triangle and Charlotte

The Crystal Coast and Wilmington

The Outer Banks

VIRGINIA

SOUTH CAROLINA

GEORGIA

ATLANTIC OCEAN

Cape Lookout Nat'l Seashore

Cape Hatteras Nat'l Seashore

GREAT SMOKY MTS. NAT'L PARK

Black River

0   75 mi
0   75 km

Elizabeth City · Southern Shores · Manteo · Kitty Hawk · Hertford · Edenton · Columbia · Belhaven · Swan Quarter · Engelhard · Beaufort

Windsor · Plymouth · Washington · Greenville · New Bern · Havelock · Swansboro

Roanoke Rapids · Rich Square · Rocky Mount · Goldsboro · Kinston · Jacksonville · Surf City

Henderson · Oxford · Durham · Raleigh · Garner · Smithfield · Warsaw · Elizabethtown · Wilmington · Carolina Beach · Kure Beach

Roxboro · Reidsville · Greensboro · Burlington · Chapel Hill · Dunn · Fayetteville · Rockingham · Lumberton · Bladenboro · Whiteville · South Port

Winston-Salem · High Point · Lexington · Albemarle · Pinehurst · Sanford · Wadesboro

Elkin · Statesville · Hickory · Gastonia · Concord · Charlotte · Mathews · Monroe · Rock Hill

Boone · Lenoir · Shelby · Chapin · Williston

Mars Hill · Black Mountain · Asheville · Greenville · Columbia · Evans

Knoxville

Florence · North Charleston · Charleston

Athens · Duluth · Atlanta · Conyers · McDonough

12 · 64 · 13 · 95 · 40 · 421 · 24 · 1 · 74 · 85 · 77 · 26

Great Smoky Mountains National Park to Shenandoah National Park in Virginia, passing Asheville.

RESTAURANTS

Along the coast, raw bars serve oysters and clams on the half shell; seafood houses sell each day's local catch, be it tuna, wahoo, mahi-mahi, mackerel, shrimp, or blue crabs. In the Piedmont area, where the Triangle and Charlotte are located, it's as easy to grab a bagel, empanada, or spanakopita as a biscuit. The region is still the home of barbecue: wood-fired, pit-cooked, chopped or sliced pork traditionally served with coleslaw and hush puppies. Asheville chefs, trained at leading culinary programs, are creating innovative dishes. At many places the emphasis is on "slow food"—made with locally grown, often organic, ingredients.

NORTH CAROLINA FACTS
■ **State Capital:** Raleigh
■ **State Motto:** Esse quam videri ("To be, rather than to seem")
■ **State Flower:** Dogwood
■ **State Shell:** Scotch bonnet
■ **State Reptile:** Eastern box turtle
■ **State Beverage:** Milk
■ **State Dog:** Plott hound
■ **State Vegetable:** Sweet potato
■ **State Fruit:** Scuppernong grape
■ **State Wildflower:** Carolina lily
■ **State Folk Dance:** Clogging

HOTELS

Hundreds of rental properties are available along the coast. Small beach cottages can be had, but increasingly, so-called "sand castles," large multistory homes, suit large groups. Motels and hotels clustered all along the Outer Banks are still the more affordable way to go. Accommodations in the Piedmont include everything from roadside motels to sprawling resorts to lovely bed-and-breakfasts. Bed-and-breakfasts bloom in the mountains like wildflowers; Asheville alone has more than three dozen. The mountains also have a few large resorts, of which the Grove Park Inn in Asheville is the prime example.

WHAT IT COSTS				
	¢	$	$$	$$$	$$$$
Restaurant	under $10	$10–$14	$15–$19	$20–$24	over $24
Hotel	under $100	$100–$150	$151–$200	$201–$250	over $250

Restaurant prices are for a main course at dinner. Hotel prices are for two people in a standard double room in high season excluding state and local taxes.

VISITOR INFORMATION

Contacts North Carolina Travel & Tourism Division (✉ *301 N. Wilmington St., Raleigh, NC* ☎ *919/715–5900 or 800/847–4862* ⊕ *www.visitnc.com*).

THE NORTH CAROLINA COAST

North Carolina's 300-plus mi of coastline are fronted by a continuous series of fragile barrier islands. Broad rivers lead inland from the sounds, along which port cities have grown. Lighthouses, dunes, and vacation homes (often built by out-of-staters) dot the water's edge. There are battle sites from the American Revolution and the Civil War, elegant golf links, and kitschy putt-putt courses. Aquariums, fishing charters, and museum outreach programs put you up close and personal with the seashore critters. North Carolina's small towns (mostly of 1,000 to 3,000 people) offer genuine warmth and hospitality.

The coast is generally divided into three broad sections that include islands, shoreline, and coastal plains: the Outer Banks (Corolla south through Ocracoke, including Roanoke Island), the Crystal Coast (Core and Bogue Banks, Beaufort, Morehead City, and the inland river city of New Bern), and the greater Cape Fear region (Wrightsville Beach through the Brunswick County islands, including Wilmington). The Outer Banks are visible from space: a thin, delicate tracing of white are the barrier islands, which form a buffer between the Atlantic Ocean and the mainland. Although other states' coasts have turned into wall-to-wall hotels and condominiums, much of North Carolina's coast belongs to the North Carolina Division of Parks and Recreation.

THE OUTER BANKS

North Carolina's Outer Banks stretch from the Virginia state line south to Cape Lookout. Think of the OBX (a shorthand used on popular bumper stickers) as a series of stepping stones in the Atlantic Ocean. Throughout history the treacherous waters surrounding these islands have been the nemesis of shipping, gaining them the nickname "Graveyard of the Atlantic." A network of lighthouses and lifesaving stations, which grew around the need to protect seagoing craft, attracts curious travelers, just as the many submerged wrecks attract scuba divers. The islands' coves and inlets, which sheltered pirates—the notorious Blackbeard lived and died here—now give refuge to anglers, bird-watchers, and sunbathers.

The region is divided into four coastal sections: the Northern Beaches, beginning with Corolla, followed by Roanoke Island, Hatteras Island, and then Ocracoke Island. For many years the Outer Banks remained isolated, with only a few hardy commercial fishing families. Today the islands are linked by bridges and ferries, and much of the area is included in the Cape Hatteras and Cape Lookout national seashores.

NORTHERN BEACHES
Corolla: 91 mi south of Norfolk, VA, via U.S. 17, U.S. 158, and Rte. 12; 230 mi east of Raleigh via U.S. 64, U.S. 17, and Rte. 12. Duck: 16 mi south of Corolla. Kitty Hawk: 19 mi south of Corolla, 7 mi south of Duck.

The small northern beach settlements of Corolla and Duck are largely seasonal, residential enclaves full of summer rental condominiums. Drive slowly in Corolla: here freely wandering wild horses always have

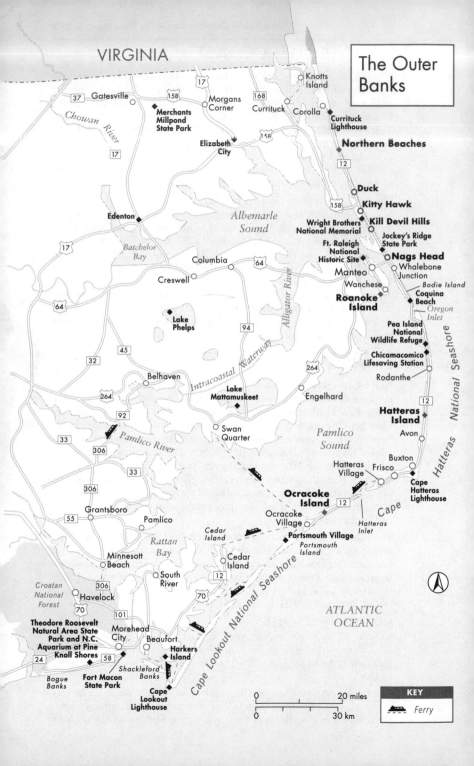

HOW TO SNACK

Although plenty of famous food items have originated in North Carolina—Krispy Kreme Doughnuts, Pepsi-Cola, Texas Pete hot sauce, and Cheerwine (a cherry-flavor soda) among them—the Outer Banks isn't the sight of any truly groundbreaking culinary creations. But walk down the street in any of its small towns on a humid summer night, and you can see one foodstuff over and over again: ice cream. Whether it's stuffed in cups, ladled into shakes, or balanced on cones, it's the dessert that people here like to end their days with.

There are also snacks from the sea (after all, this is the coast). Raw bars serve oysters and clams on the half shell; seafood houses sell fresh crabs (soft shells in the early summer season) and whatever local catch—tuna, wahoo, mahimahi, mackerel, shrimp—has been hauled in that day. Increasingly, highly trained chefs are settling in the region and diversifying menus. Fish dishes—broiled, fried, grilled, or steamed—are listed alongside entrées fusing Asian flavors and traditional Southern ingredients such as black-eyed peas.

the right of way. Upscale Duck has lots of restaurants and shops. Kitty Hawk, with a few thousand permanent residents, is among the quieter beach communities with fewer rental accommodations. Given these communities' contiguous nature and similar looks, the uninitiated may not realize when they've crossed from Kitty Hawk into Kill Devil Hills. The towns' respective roles in the drama of the first powered flight occasionally create some confusion as well. When arriving at the Outer Banks, the Wright brothers first stayed in the then-remote fishing village of Kitty Hawk, but their flight took place some 4 mi south on Kill Devil Hill, a gargantuan sand dune where today the Wright Brothers National Memorial stands.

GETTING HERE AND AROUND Most people drive to the northern beaches via U.S. 17, 64, and 264, which all link to the local U.S. 158 and Rte. 12. Some commercial and charter flights are available from nearby airports. Plan your time wisely, as heavy traffic can lead to long travel delays in summer. Marked paths and wide shoulders accommodate bikers and walkers. Guided tours are available, too. Still, a car is essential for getting around on your own time.

ESSENTIALS **Visitor Information Aycock Brown Welcome Center** (⊠ *5230 North Croatan Highway MM 1, Kitty Hawk* ☎ *877/629–4386*).

EXPLORING

The **Currituck Beach Lighthouse** is the northernmost lighthouse on the Outer Banks. Except in high winds or thunderstorms, you can climb 214 steps to the top. Completed in 1875 of around 1 million bricks, the lighthouse is unpainted. ⊠ *1101 Corolla Village Rd., Rte. 12, north of Whalehead club sign, Corolla* ☎ *252/453–8152* ⊕ *www.currituck-beachlight.com* ⊠ *$7* ☉ *Easter–Thanksgiving, daily 9–5.*

The **Wright Brothers National Memorial,** a 60-foot granite monument that resembles the tail of an airplane, stands as a tribute to Wilbur and

HISTORY YOU CAN SEE

Outer Banks residents take great pride in their "First in Flight" moniker, and they won't hesitate to threaten fisticuffs with folks from Ohio who claim the title. (The Wright Brothers lived in the Buckeye State and experimented and built their airplane in their Dayton bicycle shop, but it *flew* in North Carolina.)

The Wright Brothers National Memorial, in Kill Devil Hills, includes the 60-foot granite pylon that marks the spot where Orville and Wilbur

began experimenting with their glider; actual models of their 1902 glider and 1903 flying machine are on display. You can also build and fly your own paper airplane to see how aerodynamics work.

Outside, the steady winds that drew the brothers to North Carolina are still blowing strong.

Orville Wright. The two bicycle mechanics from Ohio took to the air here on December 17, 1903. You can see a replica of the *Flyer* and stand on the spot where it made four takeoffs and landings, the longest flight a distance of 852 feet. Exhibits and an informative talk by a National Park Service ranger bring the event to life. The Wrights had to bring in the unassembled airplane by boat, along with all their food and supplies for building a camp. They made four trips to the site beginning in 1900. The First Flight is commemorated annually. ⊠*1401 National Park Dr., off U.S. 158 between MM 7 and MM 8, 5 mi south of Kitty Hawk, Kill Devil Hills* ☎*252/441–7430* ⊕*www.nps.gov/wrbr* ☜*$4* ⊙*Sept.–May, daily 9–5; June–Aug., daily 9–6.*

WHERE TO EAT AND STAY

$$–$$$ ✕**Blue Point Bar & Grill.** This upscale spot with an enclosed porch over-
SEAFOOD looking Currituck Sound is as busy as a diner and as boldly colorful—
★ with a red, black, and chrome interior. The menu mixes Southern style
with local seafood, including the ever-popular she-crab soup, a thick
and rich concoction made with cream, sherry, herbs, Old Bay seasoning, and, of course, crab roe. Lunch is served Tuesday–Sunday. ⊠*1240
Duck Rd., Duck* ☎*252/261–8090* ⊕*www.thebluepoint.com* ▤*AE,
MC, V.*

$$$–$$$$ ✕**Nicoletta's Italian Café.** White linen tablecloths, flowers, and a view of
ITALIAN the Currituck Beach Lighthouse mean atmosphere with a capital A. For
more than a decade, Nicoletta's has been known for fresh seafood and
southern Italian pasta dishes, and owner Pasquale Anzalone carries on
the tradition. Off-season hours may vary. ⊠*106 Corolla Light Town
Center, Rte. 12, Corolla* ☎*252/453–4004* ▤*MC, V* ⊙*No lunch.*

$$$–$$$$ 🏨**Advice 5¢.** A roof with varied pitches and eaves tops this contempo-
★ rary steely blue-gray beach house with white trim and multipane win-
dows rising from the sandy dunes. Although the name is lighthearted,
Advice 5¢ is very serious about guest care. Beds in each room are dressed
with crisp, colorful linens. All rooms have private decks, ceiling fans, and
baths stocked with thick cotton towels. The suite has a whirlpool bath,

sitting area, and cable TV. You have use of the tennis courts, swimming pool, and the beach access at Sea Pines, a nearby resort. From the North Beach area you can easily walk to downtown shops and restaurants. **Pros:** on-site massage therapy; quiet and secluded but walking distance to commercial area. **Cons:** no ocean view. ⊠ *111 Scarborough La., Duck* ☎ *252/255–1050 or 800/238–4235* ⊕ *www.advice5.com* ⏎ *4 rooms, 1 suite* ⇘ *In-room: no phone. In-hotel: restaurant, no-smoking rooms* ⊟ *MC, V* ⊗ *Closed mid-Nov.–mid-Mar.* ❑ *BP.*

NAGS HEAD
9 mi south of Kitty Hawk.

It's widely accepted that Nags Head got its name because pirates would tie lanterns around the necks of their horses to lure merchant ships onto the shoals hoping to wreck them and profit from the cargo. Dubious citizenry aside, Nags Head was established in the 1830s as North Carolina's first tourist haven.

The town—one of the largest on the Outer Banks, yet still with a population of only about 3,000 people—lies between the Atlantic Ocean and Pamlico Sound, along and between U.S. 158 ("the bypass") and Route 12 ("the beach road" or Virginia Dare Trail). Both roads are congested in the high season, and the entire area is commercialized. Many lodgings, whether they're dated cottages, shingled older houses, or sprawling new homes with plenty of bells and whistles, are available through the area's plentiful vacation rentals. Numerous restaurants, motels, hotels, shops, and entertainment opportunities keep the town hopping day and night.

Nags Head has 11 mi of beach with 40 public access points from Route 12, some with paved parking and some with restrooms and showers. ■ TIP→ **It's easy to overlook the flagpoles stationed along many area beaches; but if there's a red flag flying from one of them, it means the water is too rough even for wading.** These are not a suggestion—ignoring them can mean hefty fines.

GETTING HERE AND AROUND From the east, arrive by car on U.S. 64/264 or from the north on U.S. 17 and U.S. 158. Although many people cycle and walk on designated paths, most exploring requires a car.

ESSENTIALS **Visitor Information Whalebone Welcome Center** (⊠ *2 N.C. 12 Highway MM 17, Nags Head* ☎ *877/441–6644*).

EXPLORING
The first North Carolina Historic Shipwreck Site, the 175-foot **USS Huron**, lies in 20 feet of water off the Nags Head Pier and is a favorite with scuba divers. The iron-hulled ship sank in a November storm in 1877, taking all but a handful of her 124-man crew with her. ⊠ *Offshore between MM 11 and MM 12.*

Jockey's Ridge State Park has 426 acres that encompass the tallest sand dune on the East Coast (about 80 to 100 feet). Walk along the 384-foot boardwalk from the visitor center to the edge of the dune. The climb to the top is a challenge; nevertheless, it's a popular spot for hang gliding, kite flying, and sand boarding. You can also explore an estuary, a museum, and several trails through the park. In summer, join the free Sunset on the Ridge program: watch the sun disappear while you sit on the dunes and learn about their local legends and history. Covered footwear is a wise choice here, as the loose sand gets quite hot in the summer months. ⊠ *U.S. 158, MM 12* ☏*252/441-7132* ⊕*www.jockeysridgestatepark.com* ☒*Free* ⊙*Daily 8–sunset.*

> ### SIFTING ECOLOGY
>
> The vegetation on the sand dunes is practically all that's keeping them from blowing away in the wind. Dune conservation is very serious for the survival of the beaches, and the vegetation also provides shelter to turtles, rabbits, snakes, and other wildlife. Please don't disturb it!

Coquina Beach, in the Cape Hatteras National Seashore, is considered by locals to be the loveliest beach in the Outer Banks. The wide-beam ribs of the shipwreck *Laura Barnes* rest in the dunes here. Driven onto the Outer Banks by a nor'easter in 1921, she ran aground north of this location; the entire crew survived. The wreck was moved to Coquina Beach in 1973 and displayed behind ropes, but subsequent hurricanes have scattered the remains and covered them with sand, making it difficult to discern. Free parking, public changing rooms, showers, and picnic shelters are available. ⊠ *Off Rte. 12, MM 26, 8 mi south of U.S. 158.*

WHERE TO EAT AND STAY

$$$–$$$$

SEAFOOD

★

✕**Basnight's Lone Cedar Café.** Hearts were broken when this 25-year-old restaurant, owned by powerful North Carolina Senator Marc Basnight and family, burned in 2007, but the new contemporary setting with simple pine tables and a huge glass-walled wine rack in the main dining room is sleeker and larger than the original. Big windows all around allow everyone a chance to see the osprey mother and chicks that nest on a waterfront piling outside. North Carolina produce and seafood are the stars here. Soft-shell crabs in season come from an on-site shedding facility, and a stunning, extensive herb garden provides fresh seasoning. Beef, chicken, pork, and pastas are also on the menu. ⊠ *Nags Head–Manteo Causeway, 7623 S. Virginia Dare Trail* ☏*252/441-5405* ⊕*www.lonecedarcafe.com* ⌲*Reservations not accepted* ▭*D, MC, V* ⊙*Closed Jan.*

$$$–$$$$

SEAFOOD

Fodor'sChoice

★

✕**Owens' Restaurant.** A classic clapboard cottage with pine paneling hosts this half-century-old restaurant that has been in the same family and location since 1946. Stick with the seafood or beef, at which the kitchen staff excels. Miss O's crab cakes are ever-popular, as is the filet mignon topped with lump crabmeat and asparagus with béarnaise sauce. Pecan-encrusted sea scallops are plump and tender. The 16-layer lemon and chocolate cakes are delicious. In summer arrive early and expect to wait. The brass-and-glass Station Keeper's Lounge has entertainment Thursday, Friday, and Saturday nights in summer. ⊠ *U.S. 158, MM 16.5, 7114 S. Virginia Dare Trail* ☏*252/441-7309* ⊕*www.owensrestaurant.com* ⌲*Reservations not accepted* ▭*AE, D, MC, V* ⊙*Closed Jan. and Feb. No lunch.*

¢–$

SEAFOOD

✕**Sam & Omie's.** This no-nonsense niche is named after two fishermen who were father and son. Opened in 1937, it's one of the oldest restaurants on the Outer Banks. Fishing illustrations hang on the walls, and country music plays in the background. It's open daily 7 to 10, serving every imaginable kind of seafood, and then some. Try the fine marinated tuna steak, Cajun tuna bites, or frothy crab-and-asparagus soup. You might catch owner Carol Sykes munching fresh peach cake with pecans if you call in July, and the chef has been using the same recipe for the she-crab soup for 22 years. Locals love breakfast here. ■ TIP➔ **Die-hard fans claim that Sam & Omie's serves the best oysters on the beach.** ⊠ *U.S. 158, MM 16.5, 7228 Virginia Dare Trail* ☎*252/441–7366* ⊕*www. samandomies.net* ⚖*Reservations not accepted* ⊟*D, MC, V* ⊗*Closed Dec.–Feb.*

$$–$$$
Fodor'sChoice
★

⊞ **First Colony Inn.** Stand on the verandas that encircle this old, three-story, cedar-shingle inn and admire the ocean views. Two rooms have wet bars and kitchenettes; others have four-poster or canopy beds, hand-crafted armoires, and English antiques. All rooms contain extras, such as heated towel bars. The story of this landmark's near demolition, its rescue, and the move to the present site is told in framed photographs, letters, and news accounts lining the sunny dining room. In fall and winter, Nature Conservancy birding weekends include excursions to the Pea Island Wildlife Refuge. **Pros:** homey accommodations feel like grandma's house; some in-room hot tubs. **Cons:** you'll have to cross a road to get to the beach; no elevator. ⊠ *U.S. 158 MM 16, 6720 S. Virginia Dare Trail* ☎*252/441–2343 or 800/368–9390* ⊕*www.firstcolonyinn. com* ⇌*26 rooms* ⚷*In-room: kitchen (some), refrigerator. In-hotel: restaurant, pool, no-smoking rooms* ⊟*AE, D, MC, V* ⦿*BP.*

ROANOKE ISLAND

10 mi southwest of Nags Head.

On a hot July day in 1587, 117 men, women, and children left their boat and set foot on Roanoke Island to form the first permanent English settlement in the New World. Three years later, when a fleet with supplies from England landed, the settlers had disappeared without a trace, leaving a mystery that continues to baffle historians. Much of the 12-mi-long island, which lies between the Outer Banks and the mainland, remains wild. Of the island's two towns, Wanchese is the fishing village, and Manteo is more tourist-oriented, with sights related to the island's history, as well as an aquarium.

GETTING HERE AND AROUND
From the east, drive to the island on U.S. 64/264; from the Outer Banks, follow U.S. 158 to U.S. 64/264. Although Manteo's main drag and downtown waterfront have sidewalks, a car is useful for visiting the town's various sites. Charter flights are available at Dare County Regional Airport.

ESSENTIALS
Visitor Information Outer Banks Welcome Center on Roanoke Island (⊠*1 Visitors Center Circle, Manteo* ☎*877/629–4386*).

EXPLORING

☾ A history, educational, and cultural-arts complex, **Roanoke Island Festival Park** sits on the waterfront in Manteo. Costumed interpreters conduct tours of the 69-foot ship, *Elizabeth II*, a representation of a 16th-century vessel. The complex also has an interactive museum and shop, a recreated 16th-century settlement site, a fossil pit, plays, concerts, arts-and-crafts exhibitions, and special programs. ⊠ *Waterfront,* *off Budleigh St., Manteo* ☎ *252/475–1500, 252/475–1506 for event hotline* ⊕ *www.roanokeisland.com* ✉ *$8* ☉ *Nov.–Dec. and Feb.–Mar., daily 9–5; Apr.–Oct., daily 9–6.*

★ **Fort Raleigh National Historic Site** is a restoration of the original 1585
☾ earthworks that mark the beginning of English-colonial history in America. ■ TIP➔ **Be sure to see the orientation film and then take a guided tour of the fort.** A nature trail through the 513-acre grounds leads to an outlook over Albemarle Sound. Native American and Civil War history is also preserved here. *The Lost Colony* (✉ *1409 U.S. 64/264, 27954* ☎ *252/473–3414 or 800/488–5012* ⊕ *www.thelostcolony.org* ✉ *$16*), Pulitzer Prize–winner Paul Green's drama, was written in 1937 to mark the 350th birthday of Virginia Dare. Except from 1942 to 1947, it has played every summer since in Fort Raleigh National Historic Site's Waterside Theatre. It reenacts the story of the first colonists, who settled here in 1587 and mysteriously vanished. Cast alumni include Andy Griffith and Lynn Redgrave. Reservations are essential. ✉ *1401 National Park Dr., off U.S. 64/264, 3 mi north of downtown Manteo* ☎ *252/473–5772* ⊕ *www.nps.gov/fora* ✉ *Free* ☉ *Sept.–May, daily 9–5; June–Aug., daily 9–6.*

☾ The **North Carolina Aquarium at Roanoke Island,** overlooking Croatan Sound, occupies 68,000 square feet of space. There are touch tanks, but *The Graveyard of the Atlantic* is the centerpiece exhibit. It's a 285,000-gallon ocean tank containing the re-created remains of the USS *Monitor*, sunk off Hatteras Island. The aquarium hosts a slew of activities and field trips, from feeding fish to learning about medicinal aquatic plants to kids' workshops. ✉ *374 Airport Rd., off U.S. 64, 3 mi northeast of Manteo* ☎ *252/473–3493, 866/332–3475 for aquarium, 252/473–3494 for educational programs* ⊕ *www.ncaquariums.com* ✉ *$8* ☉ *Daily 9–5.*

WHERE TO EAT AND STAY

$$–$$$ ✕ **Full Moon Café.** Colorful stained-glass panels hang in the large front
AMERICAN   windows of this wonderfully cheerful bistro renovated from a gas sta-
★   tion. The herbed hummus with roasted pita is fantastic, as are the fat crab cakes and baked crab-dip appetizer. The kitchen uses fresh local seafood and never deep fries the catch. Other choices include salads, veggie wraps, Cuban-style enchiladas, burgers of all kinds, Angus beef, and a dozen innovative and hearty sandwiches. Light eaters beware: even the Waldorf salad comes with a million pecans and apples; expect lots of cheese on any dish that includes it. ■ TIP➔ **The café also serves specialty cocktails and maintains a thoughtfully selected wine list.** ✉ *207 Queen Elizabeth Ave., Manteo* ☎ *252/473–6666* ⊕ *www.thefullmoon-cafe.com* ▭ *AE, D, MC, V.*

¢   ✕ **Magnolia Grille.** Freddy and Pam Ortega, cheerful New York trans-
AMERICAN   plants, run the immensely popular restaurant on Manteo's downtown waterfront. The place is hopping, even at breakfast; lunch gets the over-flow from nearby Festival Park. ■ TIP➔ **If it's too busy, get takeout and savor your sandwich by the waterfront.** You can choose from char-grilled chili cheeseburgers, quesadillas, salads, assorted sandwiches including a fried oyster sandwich, and hearty chicken dishes; some dishes are intended—and others can be modified—for vegetarians. ✉ *408 Queen*

Elizabeth Ave., Manteo ☎*252/475–9877* ▤*AE, D, MC, V* ☽*No dinner Sun. and Mon.*

¢–$ ⚏**Scarborough Inn.** Two stories of wraparound porches surround the Scarborough, which is modeled after a turn-of-the-20th-century inn. Outside each room are benches and rocking chairs; inside, each is decorated differently, with family heirlooms as well as modern conveniences, like coffeemakers. Room refrigerators come stocked with ready-made, packaged breakfast items. The property is within walking distance of popular shops and restaurants and about 5 mi from the beach. **Pros:** nicely groomed garden areas; B&B feel at a good price. **Cons:** located on a busy road; small lobby; innkeeper may step out and lock front office. ⊠*524 U.S. 64/264, Manteo* ☎*252/473–3979* ⊕*www.scarborough-inn.com* ⇆*14 rooms* ⚒*In-room: refrigerator. In-hotel: no-smoking rooms* ▤*AE, D, MC, V* ⦿*EP.*

$$$–$$$$ ⚏**Tranquil House Inn.** This charming 19th-century-style inn sits water-
⟳ front, a few steps from shops, restaurants, and the Roanoke Island Festi-
★ val Park. The individually decorated rooms have classic, clean lines and muted colors; some have comfy sitting areas. Complimentary wine and cheese are served in the evening. The popular restaurant, 1587 ($$$$), is known for its chop-house-style cuts and inventive entrées, such as pan-roasted, chipotle-spiced duck breast and grilled tuna over spicy Thai noodles. **Pros:** easy walking distance from shops and restaurants; complimentary evening wine reception; child-friendly. **Cons:** located on a busy commercial waterfront; small, cramped lobby; no elevator. ⊠*405 Queen Elizabeth Ave., Box 2045, Manteo* ☎*252/473–1404 or 800/458–7069* ⊕*www.1587.com* ⇆*25 rooms* ⚒*In-hotel: restaurant, bicycles no-smoking rooms* ▤*AE, D, MC, V* ⦿*BP.*

SPORTS AND THE OUTDOORS
Oregon Inlet Fishing Center (⊠*98 Rte. 12, north end of Oregon Inlet Bridge* ☎*252/441–6301 or 800/272–5199*) is a full-service marina that leads fishing excursions and has supplies such as bait, tackle, ice, and fuel for the fisherman. The National Park Service maintains an adjacent boat launch.

CAPE HATTERAS NATIONAL SEASHORE

Longtime visitors to the Outer Banks have seen how development changes these once unspoiled barrier islands, so it's nice to know that the 70-mi stretch of the Cape Hatteras National Seashore will remain protected. Its pristine beaches, set aside as the first national seashore in 1953, stretch from the southern outskirts of Nags Head to Ocracoke Inlet, encompassing three narrow islands: Bodie, Hatteras, and Ocracoke.

Some of the best fishing and surfing on the East Coast are in these waters, which also are ideal for other sports such as windsurfing, diving, and boating. Parking is allowed only in designated areas. Fishing piers are in Rodanthe, Avon, and Frisco.

With 300 mi of coastline, there are plenty of beaches that don't have lifeguards on duty. ▪**TIP→To identify beaches with trained staff, contact the Ocean Rescue in the town, or if you're in a National Park, the Park Service.**

HATTERAS ISLAND
15 mi south of Nags Head

The Herbert C. Bonner Bridge arches for 3 mi over Oregon Inlet and carries traffic to Hatteras Island, a 42-mi-long curved ribbon of sand jutting out into the Atlantic Ocean. At its most distant point (Cape Hatteras), Hatteras is 25 mi from the mainland. About 85% of the island belongs to Cape Hatteras National Seashore, and the remainder is privately owned in seven small, quaint villages strung along Route 12, the island's fragile lifeline to points north. Among its nicknames, Hatteras is known as the blue marlin (or billfish) capital of the world. The fishing's so great here because the Continental Shelf is 40 mi offshore, and its current, combined with the nearby Gulf Stream and Deep West Boundary Current, create an unparalleled fish habitat. The total population of the towns—Rodanthe, Waves, Salvo, Avon, Buxton, Frisco, and Hatteras Village—is around 4,000.

GETTING HERE AND AROUND From the north, reach Hatteras Island via U.S. 158. From the east, take U.S. 64/264 to U.S. 158. South of the Outer Banks, U.S. 70 leads to Rte. 12 and requires a couple of ferry rides. Some commercial and charter flights are available from nearby airports.

EXPLORING

Pea Island National Wildlife Refuge is made up of more than 5,800 acres of marsh on the Atlantic Flyway. To bird-watchers' delight more than 365 species have been sighted from its observation platforms and spotting scopes and by visitors who venture into the refuge. Pea Island is home to threatened peregrine falcons, piping plovers, and tundra swans, which winter here. A visitor center on Route 12 has an information display and maps of the two trails. ■ TIP→ Remember to douse yourself in bug spray, especially in spring. Guided canoe tours are available for a fee. ⊠ *Pea Island Refuge Headquarters, Rte. 12, 5 mi south of Oregon Inlet* ☎ *252/987–2394* ⊕ *www.fws.gov/peaisland* 🎟 *Free* ⊙ *June–Aug., daily 9–5; Mar.–May and Sept.–Nov., daily 9–4; Dec.– Feb., hrs vary, call ahead.*

ⓒ ★ **Cape Hatteras Lighthouse** was the first lighthouse built in the region, authorized by Congress in 1794 to help prevent shipwrecks. The original structure was lost to erosion and Civil War damage; this 1870 replacement is, at 208 feet, the tallest brick lighthouse in the world. Endangered by the sea, in 1999 the lighthouse was actually raised and rolled some 2,900 feet inland to its present location. A visitor center is located near the base of the lighthouse. In summer the principal keeper's quarters are open for viewing, and you can climb the lighthouse's 257 steps (12 stories) to the viewing balcony. ■ TIP→ Children under 42 inches in height aren't allowed in the lighthouse. Offshore lay the remains of the USS *Monitor*, a Confederate ironclad ship that sank in 1862. ⊠ *Off Rte. 12, 30 mi south of Rodanthe, Buxton* ☎ *252/995–4474* ⊕ *www. nps.gov/caha* 🎟 *Visitor center and keeper's quarters free, lighthouse tower $6* ⊙ *Visitor center and keeper's quarters: daily 9–5. Lighthouse tower: Apr.–mid-Oct., daily 10–5.*

WHERE TO EAT AND STAY

$$-$$$
SEAFOOD

✗**Breakwater.** Fat Daddy crab cakes, rolled in potato chips then fried and served with pineapple jalapeño salsa, is one of the more creative signature dishes. You also get more standard seafood options, such as shrimp fried or broiled with white wine and butter. The restaurant sits atop Oden's Dock. Given the casual nature of life here, Breakwater stands out with tables dressed in white linen. The dining room is a bit small, but waiting for a table in comfortable chairs on the deck overlooking Pamlico Sound is not a chore. ⊠ *Waterfront, Rte. 12, Hatteras Village* ☎*252/986-2733* ⊕*www.odensdock.com* ⊟*AE, D, MC, V* ⊘*Closed Sun.–Wed. Labor Day–Memorial Day. No lunch.*

$$-$$$
AMERICAN

✗**The Captain's Table.** South of the entrance for the Cape Hatteras Light-house, this place is popular for its well-prepared food and homey manner. In addition to offering the usual seafood, the menu has pork barbecue, chicken, and beef. It's also a popular breakfast spot. ⊠ *Rte. 12, Buxton* ☎*252/995-5988* ⊟*MC, V* ⊘*Closed Dec.–early Apr. No lunch.*

$-$$

☷**Sea Gull Motel.** The 1950s-era, family-operated Sea Gull was renovated in 2004 with comfort in mind. Adjacent cottage properties, each of which sleeps up to six, rent ($$$$) by the week during high season. The 15 rooms, about 50 yards from the beach, all have at least a mini-refrigerator and microwave; a two-bedroom suite with a full kitchen is also available. Ask about corner room No. 116 with ocean views on two sides. **Pros:** quiet setting; oceanfront pool; family-friendly. **Cons:** remote location; no breakfast; no Wi-Fi. ⊠*56883 N.C. Hwy 12, between MM 70 and 71, Hatteras Village* ☎*252/986-2550* ⊕*www.seagullhatteras.com* ⇨*15 rooms, 1 suite, 2 cottages* ⚒*In-room: kitchen (some), refrigerator, Internet. In-hotel: pool, beachfront, no-smoking rooms* ⊟*D, MC, V.*

OCRACOKE ISLAND

Ocracoke Village: 15 mi southwest of Hatteras Village.

Fewer than 1,000 people live on this, the last inhabited island in the Outer Banks, which can be reached only by water or air. The village itself is in the widest part of the island, around a harbor called Silver Lake. Man-dredged canals form the landscape of a smaller residential area called Oyster Creek.

Centuries ago, however, Ocracoke was the stomping ground of Edward Teach, the pirate known as Blackbeard. A major treasure cache from 1718 is still rumored to be hidden somewhere on the island.

GETTING HERE
AND AROUND

The only way to reach Ocracoke Island is by private boat or ferry. State car ferries land at either end of the island and depart as late as 10 PM to Cedar Island and midnight to Hatteras Island. Only one road, Rte.12, traverses the island. Quiet streets shoot off to the left and right at the south end. Lots of cyclists come to Ocracoke, and many inns have bikes guests may use, but be careful when biking Rte. 12 from one end of the island to the other in summer; traffic can be heavy, and there are no designated bike paths along the highway.

ESSENTIALS

Visitor Information National Park Service Visitor Center (⊠*Rte. 12, Ocracoke Island* ☎*252/928-4531).*

EXPLORING

Ocracoke Island **beaches** are among the least populated and most beautiful on the Cape Hatteras National Seashore. Four public access areas have parking as well as off-road vehicle access. ⊠ *Off Rte. 12.*

Look out from the **Ocracoke Pony Pen** observation platform at the descendants of the Banker Ponies that roamed wild before the island came under the jurisdiction of Cape Hatteras National Seashore. The Park Service took over management of the ponies in 1960 and has helped maintain the population of about 30 animals; the wild herd once numbered nearly 500. All the animals you see today were born in captivity and are fed and kept on a 180-acre range. Legends abound about the arrival of the island's Banker Ponies. Some believe they made their way to the island after the abandonment of Roanoke's Lost Colony. Others believe they were left by early Spanish explorers or swam to shore following the sinking of the *Black Squall,* a ship carrying circus performers. ⊠ *Rte. 12, 6 mi southwest of Hatteras-Ocracoke ferry landing.*

Built in 1823, **Ocracoke Lighthouse** is the second-oldest operating lighthouse in the U.S. (Sandy Hook, New Jersey, has the oldest.) It was first fueled by whale oil, then kerosene, and finally electricity. ■ **TIP→ The squat whitewashed structure, 77 feet, 5 inches tall, is unfortunately not open to the public for climbing, but the base is open between Memorial Day and Labor Day. The lighthouse is a photographer's dream.** ⊠ *Off Rte. 12, Live Oak Rd., Ocracoke Village* ⊕ *www.nps.gov/caha/ocracokelh.htm.*

WHERE TO EAT AND STAY

$$–$$$ ✕ **The Pelican Restaurant and Patio Bar.** This 19th-century harborfront
SEAFOOD home in a grove of twisted oak trees has a patio next to an outdoor bar: many people take a seat here and don't leave for a long while. Jumbo shrimp stuffed with cream cheese and jalapeño peppers and lump crab cakes are two of the most requested food items. "Shrimp Hour," which is really two hours every day (3 to 5), draws crowds because large steamed shrimp sell for 15¢ each. The Pelican also serves breakfast—cereal, egg dishes, biscuits with homemade jelly, and corned beef hash—until 11 AM. Acoustic music plays at times during the off-season but seven nights a week in summer. ⊠ *305 Irvin Garrish Hwy., Ocracoke* ☎ *252/928–7431* ⊟ *AE, D, MC, V.*

$$ ⊞ **Island Inn and Dining Room.** This white-clapboard inn on the National Register of Historic Places was built as a private lodge back in 1901. It's starting to show its age a bit, but is full of Outer Banks character. The rooms in the modern wing are good for families. The large rooms in the Crow's Nest, on the third floor, have cathedral ceilings and look out over the island. One- and two-bedroom villas ($$$$) with full kitchens, living rooms, and laundry facilities are also available. **Pros:** quiet taste of old Ocracoke; spectacular views from the Crow's Nest; walking distance to shops and restaurants; heated pool. **Cons:** starting to show its age; no-frills rooms and some with no television. ⊠ *Lighthouse Rd. and Rte. 12, Box 9* ☎ *252/928–4351, 877/456–3466* ⊕ *www.ocracokeislandinn.com* ⌨ *28 rooms, 4 villas* ♿ *In-room: no TV (some). In-hotel: pool, no-smoking rooms* ⊟ *AE, MC, V.*

SHOPPING

In 1920 Albert Styron set up **Styron's General Store** (✉ *Lighthouse Rd.* ☎ *252/928–2609*) in Ocracoke; three generations later, the store is a place to pick up not dry goods and fishing equipment but souvenirs and gifts. An old, red Coca-Cola cooler today holds big jars of nickel candy.

OFF THE
BEATEN
PATH

★ **Cape Lookout National Seashore.** Extending for 55 mi from Portsmouth Island to Shackleford Banks, Cape Lookout National Seashore includes 28,400 acres of uninhabited land and marsh. The remote, sandy islands are linked to the mainland by private ferries. Loggerhead sea turtles nest here. To the south, wild ponies roam Shackleford Banks and Cape Lookout Lighthouse continues to help sailors navigate the treacherous waters. There are primitive cabins (with and without electricity, no linens or utensils) with bunk beds and campgrounds. Ferry service is available from Harkers Island to the Cape Lookout Lighthouse area, from Davis to Shingle Point, from Atlantic to an area north of Drum Inlet, and from Ocracoke Village to Portsmouth Village. A list of authorized ferry services can be found at the park's Web site: ⊕ *www.nps.gov/calo/ planyourvisit/ferry.htm.*

THE CRYSTAL COAST

Carteret County, with nearly 80 mi of ocean coastline, is known as the Crystal Coast. It's composed of the south-facing beaches along the barrier island Bogue Banks (Atlantic Beach, Pine Knoll Shores, Indian Beach, Salter Path, and Emerald Isle), three major mainland townships (Morehead City, Beaufort, and Newport), and a series of small, unincorporated "down-east" communities traversed by a portion of U.S. 70, designated a Scenic Byway.

ESSENTIALS

Visitor Information Crystal Coast Visitor Center (✉ 3409 Arendell St., Morehead City ☎ 877/206–0929 ⊕ www.sunnync.com).

BEAUFORT

20 mi west of Harkers Island–Cape Lookout ferry; 150 mi southeast of Raleigh.

There's a feeling of having stepped back in time in the small seaport with a bustling boardwalk; residents take great pride in the city's restored public buildings and homes—and in their homes' histories, which sometimes include tales of sea captains and pirates. Established in 1713, the third-oldest town in North Carolina was named for Henry Somerset, duke of Beaufort, and it's hard to miss the English influence here. Streets, at least those in the historic district, are named after British royalty and colonial leaders.

GETTING HERE
AND AROUND

Beaufort is near the far eastern end of U.S. 70, which links to U.S. 17. The town has a small airstrip, but no commercial flights. For boaters, it's located along the Intracoastal Waterway, and downtown docks are available. The closest major airport is in New Bern. The town is a perfect park-and-stroll location, with historic sites, museums, and a retail center all within walking distance of each other.

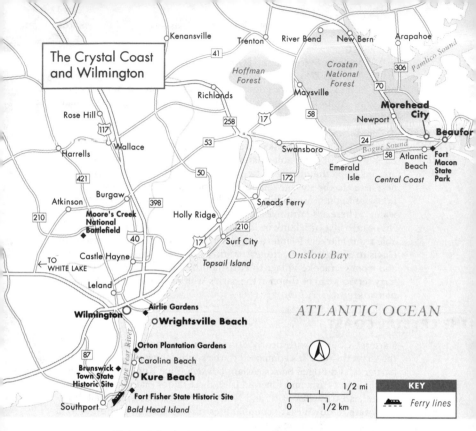

Visitor Information Beaufort Historic Site Visitor Center (✉ *130 Turner St.,
Beaufort* ☎ *252/728–5225*).

EXPLORING

The **Beaufort Historic Site,** in the center of town, consists of 10 buildings
dating from 1778 to 1859, eight of which have been restored, including the 1796 **Carteret County Courthouse** and the 1859 **Apothecary
Shop and Doctor's Office.** Don't miss the **Old Burying Grounds** (1709),
where Otway Burns, a privateer in the War of 1812, is buried under
his ship's cannon; a nine-year-old girl who died at sea is buried in a
rum keg; and an English soldier saluting the king is buried upright in
his grave. The required tours, either on an English-style double-decker
bus or by guided walk, depart from the visitor center. ✉ *130 Turner
St.* ☎ *252/728–5225 or 800/575–7483* ⊕ *www.beauforthistoricsite.
org* ✉ *$8 tour* ☉ *Mon.–Sat., walking tours at 10, 11:30, 1, and 3:30.
Bus tour: Apr.–Oct., Mon., Wed., Fri., and Sat. at 11 and 1:30. Burying
Ground tour: June–Sept., Tues.–Thurs. at 2:30.*

☾
★ **North Carolina Maritime Museum** documents the state's seafaring history. An exhibit about the infamous pirate Blackbeard includes artifacts
recovered from the discovery of his flagship, *Queen Anne's Revenge,*
near Beaufort Inlet. Other exhibits focus on local fossils and duck
decoys. The associated **Watercraft Center,** across the street, has lectures

on boat-building and stargazing, birding treks, and fossil hunting tours. ✉ *315 Front St.* ☎ *252/728-7317* ⊕ *www.ncmaritime.org* 🎫 *Free* ⊗ *Weekdays 9–5, Sat. 10–5, Sun. 1–5.*

WHERE TO EAT AND STAY

$$–$$$
SEAFOOD

✕ **The Net House.** Once upon a time, the Net House, a long, low-slung building with few windows, was just that—a place where fishing nets were made, repaired, and stored. Today people, not fishing gear, occupy every corner of the building, which is divided into dining rooms with walls of weathered pine. Hungry diners spill onto the sidewalk waiting to get into this family-owned restaurant to sample specialties such as steamed shellfish and broiled or lightly battered and fried oysters, shrimp, and other seafood. Locals tout the clam chowder, broiled grouper Dijon, and key lime pie for good reason. Call in the off-season to make sure it's open; hours vary. ✉ *133 Turner St.* ☎ *252/728–2002* 🍽 *Reservations not accepted* 🖃 *MC, V.*

$$–$$$
SEAFOOD

✕ **The Spouter Inn.** Dining at a shaded table on the Spouter's deck overlooking Beaufort Harbor and Taylor's Creek is one of life's treats. Boats glide by, you see a wild horse or two on Carrot Island just across the way, and a waiter appears with a cool drink and plate of shrimp caught that day. The prime rib and steak are popular alternatives to seafood. The attached bakery produces all kinds of cakes and pies: the banana-cream crepe may make you forget all other desserts for a while. Sunday brunch choices include quiche, omelets, and eggs Benedict with crab cakes. There's indoor seating as well. ✉ *218 Front St.* ☎ *252/728–5190* ⊕ *www.thespouterinn.com* 🖃 *AE, MC, V* ⊗ *Closed Mon. Labor Day–Memorial Day. Closed Jan.*

¢–$

🛏 **Captain's Quarters Bed & Biscuit.** Richard (Capt. Dick) and Ruby (Miss Ruby) Collins, and their daughter Polly, welcome guests with an enthusiasm that is as genuine as their passion for Beaufort and Carteret County, an area Dick first came to know during his years as a Navy pilot in World War II. Each morning, along with a weather report, the captain serves breakfast, which includes fresh biscuits his wife and daughter make from an old family recipe. Antiques, most of them family heirlooms, fill the 19th-century home that the family restored. Reading material and reading lights are just two of the thoughtful touches you'll find. **Pros:** quiet home; a large white wraparound porch with a sky-blue ceiling has cozy rockers; the innkeeper is a great source of sea stories; major historic sites across the street. **Cons:** located on a busy street; common rooms can be a little warm in summer. ✉ *315 Ann St.* ☎ *252/728–7711 or 800/659–7111* ⊕ *www.captainsquarters.us* 📻 *3 rooms* ⚓ *In-room: no phone, no TV. In-hotel: restaurant, no kids under 10, no-smoking rooms* 🖃 *MC, V* 🍴 *BP.*

MOREHEAD CITY
3 mi west of Beaufort via U.S. 70.

The quiet commercial waterfront at Morehead City is dotted with restaurants and shops that have put new life in its old buildings. The largest town on the Crystal Coast, it hosts a state port and charter fishing arena. It's also home to sizeable marine research facilities for the National Oceanic and Atmospheric Administration, the University of North Carolina at Chapel Hill, and North Carolina State University.

Outside the city, you can fish, swim, picnic, and hike at Fort Macon State Park. Route 58 passes through all the beach communities on Bogue Banks, a barrier island across Bogue Sound from Morehead City.

GETTING HERE AND AROUND

Morehead City is near the far east end of U.S. 70. Arendell Street (U.S. 70) is Morehead City's main drag. Running parallel to the waterfront, it and some side streets contain the Fish Walk, a series of colorful sculptures in clay relief depicting indigenous fish and other types of sea life as well as gift shops and restaurants.

EXPLORING

The centerpiece of **Fort Macon State Park** is the 1834 pentagonal fortress used first to protect the coast against foreign invaders and pirates, then against Yankees during the Civil War. You can explore on your own or take a guided tour. The 365-acre park set in a maritime forest also offers picnicking areas, hiking trails, a mile-long beachfront with a large bathhouse and refreshments, and summer concerts. Rangers offer a wide selection of nature talks and walks, including Civil War weapons demonstrations, bird or butterfly hikes, and beach explorations. Follow the boardwalk over the dunes to the beach, which, due to strong currents, has lifeguards on duty June through Labor Day from 10 to 5:45. A bathhouse locker costs $4. ⊠ *East end of Rte. 58, Bogue Banks, 3 mi south of Morehead City, 2300 E. Fort Macon Road, Atlantic Beach* ☎ *252/726–3775* ⊕ *www.ncparks.gov/visit/parks/foma/main.php* ⊠ *Free* ☉ *Fort: daily 9–5:30. Grounds: Mar.–May, Sept., and Oct., daily 8–7; June–Aug., daily 8–8.*

The **North Carolina Aquarium at Pine Knoll Shores.** A recent $25 million renovation tripled the facility's size. Exhibits include a touch pool with live horseshoe crabs; river otters; and a 306,000-gallon, 64-foot-long Living Shipwreck of a German submarine sunk off the North Carolina coast in 1942. There's a large selection of programs, walks, and excursions. You can take a nighttime stroll on the beach looking for loggerhead turtles or kayak the Theodore Roosevelt Natural Area. Kids will love seeing the aquarium menagerie getting fed or spending a night at a slumber party in front of the Living Shipwreck exhibit. ☎ *252/247–4003, 866/294–3477 for activities* ⊠ *U.S. 58, Atlantic Beach, 1 Roosevelt Blvd.* ⊕ *www.ncaquariums.com* ⊠ *$8* ☉ *Daily 9–5.*

Fodor's Choice
★

WHERE TO EAT AND STAY

$$–$$$
ECLECTIC
★

✕ **Bistro by the Sea.** An atrium in the bar is decorated as a grape arbor, which says a lot about the importance of wines to the dining experience here. The stonework and stucco exterior hint at the Mediterranean style within, but the cuisine defies any particular theme. Beef, chicken, and seafood all share space on the menu—but the flavor is as likely to be Asian as Italian. Don't miss the tuna sushi served the same day it is caught. There's a vodka and piano bar as well as a cigar patio. ⊠ *4031 Arendell St.* ☎ *252/247–2777* ⊕ *www.bistro-by-the-sea.com* ⊟ *AE, D, MC, V* ☉ *Closed Sun. and Mon. No lunch.*

$$–$$$
SEAFOOD

✕ **Sanitary Fish Market.** In 1938, when the Sanitary was founded, many fish houses were ill kept. The owners wanted to signal that theirs was different; clean, simple, and generous are still the bywords at this waterfront place where diners sit at long wooden tables. It can get busy (waits of an hour) and noisy (the restaurant seats 600), but people from around the world (their photos, many celebrities among them, line the walls) gush about the seafood and don't mind the fine-dining prices with the no-frills atmosphere. Have seafood prepared almost any way you want it—steamed, fried, grilled, or broiled. The two-course Deluxe Shore dinner has, among other things, shrimp, oysters, crabs, and fish. Hush puppies and coleslaw come with every meal. ⊠*501 Evans St.* ☎*252/247–3111* ⊕*www.sanitaryfishmarket.com* ▤*AE, D, MC, V* ⊘*Closed mid-Dec. and Jan.*

$$ ▦**Windjammer Inn.** What you get here is straightforward—a comfort-
🖐 able, large room with a private balcony, an ocean view, and easy access to the beach. The five-story glass elevator sets the inn apart from typical beach lodging. There's a two-night minimum stay on summer weekends; great off-season rates. **Pros:** outdoor Jacuzzi; all rooms are oceanfront; beach is right outside the door and feels private. **Cons:** small lobby; no breakfast. ⊠*103 Salter Path Rd., Atlantic Beach* ☎*252/247–7123 or 800/233–6466* ⊕*www.windjammerinn.com* ⇝*46 rooms* ⌂*In-room: refrigerator. In-hotel: pool, no-smoking rooms* ▤*AE, D, MC, V.*

SPORTS AND THE OUTDOORS

Two wreck sites popular for scuba diving are the former German gun-
ship *Schurz*, seized by the United States and sunk following a collision in 1918, and the *Papoose*, a 412-foot tanker sunk by a German torpedo in 1942, which is now inhabited by docile sand sharks. **Olympus Dive Center** (⊠*713 Shepard St.* ☎*252/726–9432* ⊕*www.olympusdiving.com*) has two dive boats and offers full- and half-day charters, special charters for divers seeking decompression certification, equipment rental, and lessons. ■**TIP→ In addition to wreck excursions, it sponsors photography dives, spearfishing charters, and shark expeditions.**

SHOPPING

The oldest continuously operating curb market in North Carolina, **Carteret County Curb Market** (⊠*13th and Evans Sts., Morehead City* ☎*252/222–6359*) is open each Saturday from May to Labor Day from 7:30 AM to 11:30 AM. It's the place to find everything from flowers to flounder, locally grown vegetables, fresh seafood, baked goods of all descriptions, and a variety of North Carolina crafts.

Dee Gee's Gifts & Books (⊠*508 Evans St., Morehead City* ☎*252/726–3314 or 800/333–4337*) offers a wide variety of books with regional interest and frequently holds book signings by local authors. This is also the place to look for North Carolina crafts, cards, gifts, candy, nautical charts, and art.

WILMINGTON

89 mi southwest of New Bern via U.S. 17 and 117; 130 mi south of Raleigh via I–40.

The city's long history, including its part in the American Revolution, is revealed in sights downtown and in the surrounding area. The Cotton Exchange and Water Street Market are old buildings now used as shopping and entertainment centers. *Henrietta II,* a paddle-wheeler similar to those that plied the waters of the Cape Fear River, has been put into service as a tourist vessel.

GETTING HERE AND AROUND
Wilmington is at the crossroads of U.S. 17 and the I–40 terminus. Commercial flights land at Wilmington International Airport. The downtown historic district along the riverfront is very walkable. As you move away from this immediate area, however, a car becomes necessary for visits to places such as the USS *North Carolina* Battleship Memorial. In summer the major thoroughfare can be fairly busy, so allow more time than the distance would indicate. Route 132, the main north–south road through town, continues south where I–40 leaves off. U.S. 76 runs from downtown east to Wrightsville Beach; U.S. 421 goes south to Carolina and Kure beaches.

EXPLORING

Burgwin-Wright Museum House. The house General Cornwallis used as his headquarters in April 1781 was built in 1770 on the foundations of a jail. After a fine, furnished restoration, this colonial gentleman's town house was turned into a museum that includes seven distinct period gardens. ⊠*224 Market St., Downtown* ☎*910/762–0570* ⊒*$10* ⊘*Tues.–Sat. 10–4.*

Cape Fear Museum of History and Science. Trace the natural, cultural, and social history of the lower Cape Fear region from its beginnings to the present. One exhibit follows the youth of one of Wilmington's most famous native sons, basketball superstar Michael Jordan. Another is about the fossilized skeleton of an ancient (1.5 million years old), giant (20 feet long, 6,000 pounds) sloth discovered in 1991 during the construction of a Wilmington retention pond. ⊠*814 Market St., Downtown* ☎*910/798–4350* ⊕*www.capefearmuseum.com* ⊒*$5* ⊘*Late May–early Sept., Mon.–Sat. 9–5, Sun. 1–5; mid-Sept.–mid-May, Tues.–Sat. 9–5, Sun. 1–5.*

Cotton Exchange. In an area along the Cape Fear River that has flourished as a trading center since pre–Civil War days stands a shopping mall in a rambling renovated warehouse, once headquarters of the largest cotton exporter in the world. There are also several restaurants on-site. ⊠*321 N. Front St., Downtown* ☎*910/343–9896* ⊕*www.shopcottonexchange.com* ⊘*Mon.–Sat. 10–5:30, Sun. 1–5.*

Louise Wells Cameron Art Museum. The museum, formerly known as the St. John's Museum of Art, is dedicated to the fine art and crafts of North Carolina from the 18th to the 20th centuries. Its permanent collection, contained in a sleek 40,000-square-foot facility, includes originals by Mary Cassatt, master potter Ben Owen, and folk artist Clyde Jones. On the 10-acre grounds are restored Confederate defense mounds built during a battle in the waning days of the Civil War. ⊠*3201 S. 17th St., 4 mi south of downtown, South Metro* ☎*910/395–5999* ⊕*www.cameronartmuseum.com* ⊒*$7* ⊘*Tues. and Fri.–Sun. 11–5, Thurs. 11–9.*

ↂ **USS *North Carolina* Battleship Memorial.** Take a self-guided tour of a ship that participated in every major naval offensive in the Pacific during World War II. Exploring the floating city, with living quarters, a post office, chapel, laundry, and even an ice-cream shop, takes about two hours. A 10-minute orientation film is shown throughout the day. ■ TIP➔ **A climb down into the ship's interior is not for the claustrophobic.** The ship can be reached by car or by taking the river taxi from Riverfront Park, Memorial Day through Labor Day, at a cost of $4 per person. ✉ *1 Battleship Rd., junction of U.S. 74/76 and U.S. 17 and 421, west bank of Cape Fear River, Downtown* ☎ *910/251–5797* ⊕ *www. battleshipnc.com* 🖅 *$12* ⊗ *Memorial Day–Labor Day, daily 8–8; early Sept.–late May, daily 8–5.*

WHERE TO EAT

$ | SEAFOOD | ✕ **Catch.** A Wilmington native, chef-owner Keith Rhodes knows where to find fresh, local seafood and how to cook it so that the flavor is not trumped by other ingredients. Asian and Southern influences dictate the menu at this tiny, casual lunchtime venue that is sometimes open for dinner. Curried almonds give crunch to hickory smoked shrimp salad, and blackened mahimahi is served with maple-cinnamon sweet potatoes. Locals love the fried seafood platters of shrimp, flounder, and oysters, or some combination of the three. Arrive early to grab a seat, as lots of downtown professionals lunch here. ✉ *215 Princess St.* ☎ *910/762–2841* 🥢 *Reservations not accepted* ▭ *MC, V* ⊗ *No dinner most nights.*

¢–$ | SOUTHWESTERN | ✕ **K38 Baja Grill.** Named for a popular surfers' point break in Baja, Mexico, where some friends once shared memorable roadside fish tacos, the K38 menu heavily references Baja culinary traditions. You won't find Americanized Mexican fare here. Standard Mexican dishes feature seafood, such as the tacos with crisp beer-battered fish. Chicken and beef are also available. The restaurant also has two nearby outposts—Tower 7 at Wrightsville Beach and K38 Baja Grill in north Wilmington. ✉ *5410 Oleander Dr., Midtown* ☎ *910/395–6040* ▭ *AE, D, MC, V* 🖅 *Porter's Neck Shopping Center, 8211 Market Street, North Wilmington* ☎ *910/686–8211* ▭ *AE, D, MC, V* ✉ *4 N. Lumina Ave., Wrightsville Beach* ☎ *910/256–8585* ▭ *AE, D, MC, V.*

$–$$ | AMERICAN | ✕ **Water Street Restaurant & Sidewalk Café.** A restored two-story brick waterfront warehouse dating from 1835 holds a contemporary restaurant and outdoor café with an impressive wine list of more than 50 labels. Incredibly tender grilled free-range chicken is topped with zesty gremolata. Housemade apple-sage sausage patties perch atop fluffy cheese grits with a Tabasco bite. Crisp shoestring fries are irresistible, and seafood chowder is made daily on the premises. Sidewalk and balcony diners are right on the waterfront, making sunset a nice time to linger over cheesy crab dip and a glass of wine. ■ TIP➔ **There's live music most nights, including a popular jazz Sunday brunch.** ✉ *5 Water St., Downtown* ☎ *910/343–0042* ⊕ *www.5southwaterstreet.com* ▭ *AE, MC, V.*

WHERE TO STAY

$$$–$$$$ | 🏨 **Graystone Inn.** Less B&B than elegant country manor, Graystone is downtown, but feels as quiet and remote as the countryside. The turn-of-the-20th-century home was built by the widow of a successful merchant, and she wasted no expense when it came to architectural detail—it's rich with ceiling coffers, columns, moldings, fireplaces, and other decorative touches. A covered veranda is inviting even if the

weather doesn't cooperate for a stroll through the gardens. Bedrooms are stately and comfortable without being overdone. Suite bathrooms are unusually modern and roomy. Continental breakfast items are available for those who can't make the 8:30 to 9 cooked meal. **Pros:** luxurious lobby; considerate touches like umbrellas at the door; spacious rooms. **Cons:** on a busy street; smoking is permitted on outdoor verandas; "proper attire" required in common areas that means clean shoes, neat shirts, and no swimsuits; no red wine allowed. ⊠ *100 S. 3rd St., Downtown* ☎ *910/763–2000 or 888/763–4773* ⊕ *www.graystoneinn. com* ↙ *6 rooms, 3 suites* ⚒ *In-room: Wi-Fi. In-hotel: restaurant, no kids under 12* ⊟ *AE, D, MC, V* ⊙ *BP.*

¢–$ ⊡ **Jameson Inn.** Midway between downtown Wilmington and Wrightsville Beach, this small hotel with large rooms offers all the comforts of home, including recliners in some rooms. Across the street from a Target-anchored shopping center, there are plenty of restaurant choices within walking distance. Jameson's deluxe Continental breakfast includes make-your-own Belgian waffles. **Pros:** pet-friendly, near two key thoroughfares, walking distance to shopping and chain restaurants. **Cons:** small bathrooms, far from the downtown historic district, surrounded by congested roads. ⊠ *5102 Dunlea Ct., Market* ☎ *910/452–5660 or 800/526–3766* ⊕ *www.jamesoninns.com* ↙ *67 rooms* ⚒ *In-room: refrigerator (some), Wi-Fi. In-hotel: pool, gym, some pets allowed, no-smoking rooms* ⊟ *AE, D, MC, V* ⊙ *BP.*

$$–$$$ ⊡ **The Wilmingtonian.** Members of the entertainment industry often
★   frequent the Wilmingtonian. Luxurious suites each have a different theme—classic movies, nautical heritage, country French, and so on. Rooms are spread throughout four buildings set in gardens, including a convent. ■ **TIP→ Request ground-floor accommodations if stairs are a problem; there are no elevators.** **Pros:** walking distance to downtown business district; private courtyard; celebrity spottings. **Cons:** no breakfast; near noisy downtown nightclubs. ⊠ *101 S. 2nd St., Downtown* ☎ *910/343–1800 or 800/525–0909* ⊕ *www.thewilmingtonian.com* ↙ *40 suites* ⚒ *In-room: kitchen (some), refrigerator, Wi-Fi. In-hotel: restaurant, laundry facilities, some pets allowed, no-smoking rooms* ⊟ *AE, D, MC, V.*

NIGHTLIFE AND THE ARTS

Level 5 at City Stage (⊠ *21 S. Front St., Downtown* ☎ *910/342–0272* ⊕ *www.citystageatlevel5.com*). Part bar, part theater, Level 5 is all entertainment. At the top of an old Masonic temple, the facility includes a 250-seat venue for offbeat productions and comedy troupes as well as a rooftop bar with live music. Campy, good fun is the order of the night at **Rum Runners: Dueling Piano Bar** (⊠ *21 N. Front St., Downtown* ☎ *910/815–3846* ⊕ *www.rumrunnersusa.com*), a 6,000-square-foot tiki bar where embarrassingly fruit-filled punches and margaritas are mandatory. When the dueling pianists take the stage and demand you sing along to hits from the past 40 years, you just have to go with the flow. **Thalian Hall Center for the Performing Arts** (⊠ *310 Chestnut St., Downtown* ☎ *910/343–3664 or 800/523–2820*), a restored opera house in continuous use since 1858, hosts dozens of theater, dance, stand-up comedy, cinema society, and musical performances each year.

SPORTS AND THE OUTDOORS

Wrecks such as the World War II oil tanker *John D. Gill,* sunk by ◡ mans in 1942 on her second-ever voyage, make for exciting scuba divinₑ off the Cape Fear Coast. **Aquatic Safaris** (⊠*6800-1A Wrightsville Ave., Wilmington* ☎*910/392–4386* ⊕*www.aquaticsafaris.com*) leads trips to see the wrecks and rents scuba equipment.

From April through December, **Cape Fear Riverboats, Inc.** (⊠*101 S. Water St., Downtown* ☎*910/343–1611 or 800/676–0162* ⊕*www. cfrboats.com*) runs several types of cruises aboard a three-deck, 156-foot riverboat, the *Henrietta III,* which departs from docks at Water and Dock streets.

OFF THE BEATEN PATH

The Cape Fear Coast. The greater Cape Fear region stretches from Topsail Island north of Wilmington south to Southport. The Cape Fear River Basin begins in the Piedmont region and meanders several hundred miles before spilling into the Atlantic Ocean about 30 mi south of downtown Wilmington. **Wrightsville Beach** and **Kure Beach** are good day trips from Wilmington, with miles of beaches for sunning, swimming, surfing, and surf fishing.

THE TRIANGLE

The cities of Raleigh, Durham, and Chapel Hill are known collectively as the Triangle, with Raleigh to the east, Durham to the north, Chapel Hill to the west, and, in the center, Research Triangle Park—a cluster of public and private research facilities set in 6,800 acres of lake-dotted pineland—attracts scientists, academics, and businesspeople from all over the world. Throughout the Triangle, an area that has been characterized as "trees, tees, and PhDs," politics and basketball are always hot topics. The NCAA basketball championship has traded hands among the area's three major universities.

7

RALEIGH

85 mi east of Greensboro; 143 mi northeast of Charlotte.

Raleigh is Old South and New South, down-home and upscale, all in one. Named for Sir Walter Raleigh, who established the first English colony on the coast in 1585, it's the state capital and one of the country's fastest growing cities. Many of the state's largest and best museums are here, as are North Carolina State University and six other universities and colleges.

GETTING HERE AND AROUND

Like Washington, D.C., Raleigh has a highway that loops around the city. The terms "Inner Beltline" and "Outer Beltline" refer to your direction: The Inner Beltline runs clockwise; the Outer Beltline runs counterclockwise. Don't confuse the Outer Beltline with the Outer Loop, which refers to Interstate 540.

You can board a trolley run by **Historic Raleigh Trolley Tours** (☎*919/857–4364*) for a narrated hour-long tour of historic Raleigh. Between March and December, the trolley runs Saturday at 10 and 11 AM and 12, 1:30,

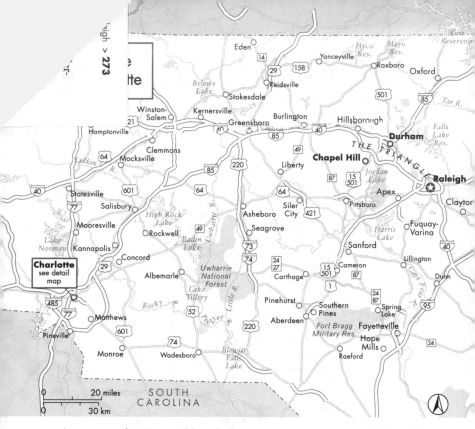

and 2:30 PM. Although the tour starts and ends at Mordecai Historic Park, you can hop aboard at any stop along the route, including the State Capital Bicentennial Plaza, the Joel Lane House, and City Market. The cost is $8 per person.

ESSENTIALS

Visitor Information **Greater Raleigh Convention and Visitors Bureau** (✉ *Bank of America Bldg., 421 Fayetteville St. Mall, Suite 1505* ☎ *919/834–5900* ⊕ *www.raleighcvb.org*). **Capital Area Visitor Services** (✉ *5 E. Edenton St., Raleigh* ☎ *919/807–7950* ⊕ *ncmuseumofhistory.org/vs/index.html*).

EXPLORING

Artspace. A nonprofit visual-arts center, Artspace offers open studios where the artists are happy to talk to you about their work. The gift shop showcases the work of the resident artists. ■ **TIP➔The place bustles with visitors during the monthly First Friday art walk, when galleries and museums throughout the city host public receptions to show off new work.** ✉ *201 E. Davie St., Downtown* ☎ *919/821–2787* ⊕ *www.artspacenc.org* ☞ *Free* ☾ *Tues.–Sat. 10–6.*

City Market. Specialty shops, art galleries, restaurants, and a small farmers' market are found in this cluster of cobblestone streets. A free trolley shuttles between City Market and other downtown restaurant and nightlife locations from 5:30 PM to 11:30 PM Thursday through

Saturday. ✉ *Martin and Blount Sts., Downtown* ☎ *919/821–1350* ⊙ *Most stores Mon.–Sat. 10–5:30; most restaurants Mon.–Sat. 7 AM–1 AM, Sun. 11:30–10.*

Ⓒ **Marbles Kids Museum.** Two museums merged to create this 84,000-square-foot cathedral of play and learning. Everything is hands-on, so your little one is free to fill a shopping cart in the marketplace, don a fireman's

HOOFING IT

It's easy to get around downtown Raleigh, as the streets are laid out in an orderly grid around the State Capitol. A good place for a stroll is the Oakwood Historic District, a 19th-century neighborhood with dozens of restored homes.

hat, clamber through the cab of a city bus, scale the crow's nest of a three-story pirate ship, or splash in numerous water stations. Older children can don costumes in a backstage dressing room and make a big entrance on a child-size stage, play chess with two-foot pawns, perform simple science experiments or create Web pages with their pictures on them. The wide-open design of the space and its architectural details, including a suspension bridge and a courtyard with a 6-foot marble fountain give adults something to look at as well. There's also an IMAX theater. ✉ *201 E. Hargett St., Downtown* ☎ *919/834–1040* ⊕ *www.marbleskidsmuseum.org* ✉ *Museum $5; museum and IMAX $9.50–$12.95* ⊙ *Tues.–Sat. 9–5, Sun. noon–5.*

North Carolina Museum of History. Founded in 1898, the museum is now in a state-of-the-art facility on Bicentennial Plaza. It houses the N.C. Sports Hall of Fame, which displays memorabilia from 260 inductees, from college heroes to pro superstars to Olympic contenders. You can see Richard Petty's race car, Arnold Palmer's Ryder cup golf bag, and Harlem Globetrotter Meadowlark Lemon's uniforms. ■TIP➔ **The Capital Area Visitor Services, in the museum's lobby, is a great place to plan your downtown itinerary, pick up brochures, or arrange area tours.** ✉ *5 E. Edenton St., Downtown* ☎ *919/807–7900* ⊕ *www.ncmuseumofhistory.org* ✉ *Free* ⊙ *Mon.–Sat. 9–5, Sun. noon–5.*

Ⓒ **North Carolina Museum of Natural Sciences.** At 200,000 square feet, this
★ museum is the largest of its kind in the Southeast. Exhibits and dioramas celebrate the incredible diversity of species in the state's various regions. There are enough live animals and insects—including butterflies, hummingbirds, snakes, and a two-toed sloth—to qualify as a small zoo. One display contains rare whale skeletons. The pièce de résistance, however, is the "Terror of the South" exhibit, featuring the dinosaur skeleton of "Acro," a giant carnivore that lived in the region 110 million years ago. ✉ *11 W. Jones St., Downtown* ☎ *919/733–7450 or 877/462–8724* ⊕ *www.naturalsciences.org* ✉ *Free* ⊙ *Mon.–Sat. 9–5, Sun. noon–5.*

Oakwood Historic District. Several architectural styles—though the Victorian structures are especially notable—can be found in this tree-shaded 19th-century neighborhood. Brochures for self-guided walking tours of the area, which encompasses 20 blocks bordered by Person, Edenton, Franklin, and Watauga–Linden streets, are available at the Capital Area Visitor Services on Edenton Street. Adjacent to historic Oakwood is **Oakwood Cemetery** (✉ *701 Oakwood Ave., Downtown*

☎919/832–6077). Established in 1869, it's the resting place of 2,800 Confederate soldiers, Civil War generals, governors, and numerous U.S. senators. The grounds are carefully cultivated and feature willows, towering oaks, and crepe myrtles. The House of Memory next to the Confederate burial ground recalls North Carolinians' involvement in the U.S. military.

WHERE TO EAT

¢ ✕**Big Ed's City Market Restaurant.** This place was founded by Big Ed Watkins, who claims some of the recipes were handed down from his great-grandfather, a Confederate mess sergeant. Southern cooking doesn't get much more traditional than this place; make sure you indulge in the biscuits. The restaurant is filled with antique farm implements and political memorabilia, including snapshots of presidential candidates who have stopped by. Every Saturday morning a Dixieland band plays. ⊠*220 Wolfe St., City Market, Downtown* ☎*919/836–9909* ⌒*Reservations not accepted* ⊟*AE, D, MC, V* ⊘*Closed Sun. No dinner.*

SOUTHERN

$$ ✕**Enoteca Vin.** As the French–Italian name indicates, wine takes center stage at this sophisticated but unpretentious restaurant. The sleek interior—part of the old Pine State Creamery—consists of warm maple, stainless steel, and exposed brick. The eclectic menu emphasizes organic ingredients that are local (flounder, goat cheese) and seasonal (okra, peaches), complemented by food-friendly wines from all over the world. The ever-changing Sunday brunch menu might include French toast with fresh strawberries or shrimp with goat cheese, papaya, avocado, and cherry tomatoes in a red-pepper vinaigrette. ⊠*410 Glenwood Ave., Suite 350, Downtown* ☎*919/834–3070* ⊕*www.enotecavin.com* ⊟*AE, MC, V* ⊘*Closed Mon. No lunch.*

ECLECTIC

$$–$$$ ✕**Irregardless Café.** This café's menu—a combination of dishes for meat eaters as well as vegetarians and vegans—changes daily. You might find chicken breast coated with crushed cashews and marinated in a lemon-tahini dressing, for example, or mushroom ravioli in a smoked tomato cream sauce. Salads are amply portioned, and the breads, soups, and yogurts are made on the premises. There's live music every night, and dancing on Saturday and brunch on Sunday spice things up. The blond wood, brightly hued contemporary art, sunny dining areas, and well-spaced tables all add to the relaxing vibe. The restaurant is midway between North Carolina State University and downtown. ⊠*901 W. Morgan St., University* ☎*919/833–8898* ⊕*www.irregardlesscafe.com* ⊟*AE, D, MC, V* ⊘*No lunch Sat. No dinner Sun. Closed Mon.*

AMERICAN

$$$ ✕**Margaux's.** Eclectic is the best way to describe the cuisine at this North Raleigh fixture. The menu changes daily and might include peppercorn-crusted beef fillet with crispy fried oysters or phyllo-wrapped salmon with Brie, cranberry jam, and asparagus. A stone fireplace warms the room in winter, and modern sculpture stands and hangs here, there, and everywhere. ⊠*Brennan Station Shopping Center, 8111 Creedmoor Rd., North Hills* ☎*919/846–9846* ⊕*www.margauxsrestaurant.com* ⊟*AE, D, MC, V.*

ECLECTIC
★

$$$$ ✕**Second Empire.** Wood paneling, muted lighting, and well-spaced tables make for a calming and elegant dining experience in this restored 1879 historic house. The menu, which changes seasonally, has a regional

AMERICAN
★

flavor; the food is intricately styled so that colors, textures, and tastes fuse. For an entrée you might order pan-roasted sea scallops served with grits and applewood-smoked bacon, or five-spiced duck confit with green lentils and orzo. A brick tavern on the lower level has a less expensive menu that includes braised lamb shank and grilled trout. ⊠ *330 Hillsborough St., Downtown* ☎ *919/829–3663* ⊕ *www.second-empire.com* ⊟ *AE, D, MC, V* ⊘ *Closed Sun. No lunch.*

WHERE TO STAY

$ ⊡ **North Raleigh Hilton.** This freshly renovated hotel is a favorite spot for corporate meetings. Large rooms invite you to kick back on the sofa for some TV or soak in the extra-deep tub, but if you need to work, the ergonomic desk chair is quite accommodating. Lofton's Cafe is open for breakfast, and the Skybox Grill & Bar has several dozen flat-screen televisions so fans won't miss a second of the action. The fitness center has exercise bikes, treadmills, and a whirlpool. **Pros:** newly redone rooms are comfortable, and the hotel is close to I–440; a free airport shuttle is available between 6 AM and 10 PM. **Cons:** busy location makes getting in and out of the hotel at rush-hour tough. ⊠ *3415 Wake Forest Rd., North Hills* ☎ *919/872–2323 or 800/445–8667* ⊕ *www.hilton.com* ◁ *338 rooms, 7 suites* ♿ *In-room: Internet, Wi-Fi. In-hotel: restaurant, room service, bars, pool, gym, laundry service* ⊟ *AE, D, MC, V.*

$$ ⊡ **Oakwood Inn.** This 1871 Victorian B&B, one of the first to be built in what is now the Oakwood Historic District, is listed on the National Register of Historic Places. Each of the individually decorated guest rooms has a working fireplace. Rosewood antiques fill one room; another has a queen-size sleigh bed as its centerpiece. Wine and sweets are always on hand, so guests can enjoy refreshments on the front porch overlooking a yard filled with irises and star magnolias. Walkers may find themselves drawn to the nearby Krispy Kreme; as the sweet scent of doughnuts cooking fills the morning air. **Pros:** fans of Victorian architecture can get their fill of sights on a morning walk through the neighborhood. **Cons:** Victorian decor dominates the interior, so this would be a poor fit for fans of sleek, modern surroundings. ⊠ *411 N. Bloodworth St., Downtown* ☎ *919/832–9712 or 800/267–9712* ⊕ *www.oakwood-innbb.com* ◁ *6 rooms* ♿ *In-room: Wi-Fi* ⊟ *AE, D, MC, V* ⊙ *BP.*

NIGHTLIFE

The **Berkeley Café** (⊠ *217 W. Martin St., Downtown* ☎ *919/821–0777*) hosts live music, including rock and roll, metal, and electronic. **Goodnight's Comedy Club** (⊠ *861 W. Morgan St., University* ☎ *919/828–5233*) combines dinner with a night of laughs. Past performers include Jerry Seinfeld, Chris Rock, and Ellen DeGeneres. Faces of early-20th-century newsboys stare out from a 20-foot photo mural covering one wall at **The Raleigh Times Bar** (⊠ *14 E. Hargett St., Downtown* ☎ *919/833–0999*), a 1906 newspaper office that's been artfully restored as a gastropub. The bar features a great selection of Belgian beers and thoughtful wine and cocktail lists.

7

SPORTS AND THE OUTDOORS

GOLF **Hedingham Golf Club.** Designed by architect David Postlethwait, this semiprivate course has water hazards on eight holes. Watch out for hole 9, where a large pond affects your play three times. ⊠ *4801 Harbour Towne Dr.* ☎ *919/250–3030* ⊕ *www.hedingham.org* ⚑ *18 holes. 6609 yds. Par 71. Green Fee: $20–$39* ⚲ *Facilities. Golf carts, golf academy/lessons.*

Lochmere Golf Club. Designed by Carolina PGA Hall of Famer Gary Hamm, this course meanders through the tree-lined links, challenging players with several different types of water hazards. A tiered green makes Hole 3 a difficult par 3. ⊠ *2511 Kildaire Farm Rd., Cary* ☎ *919/851–0611* ⊕ *www.lochmere.com* ⚑ *18 holes. 6136 yds. Par 71. Green Fee: $20–$49* ⚲ *Facilities: Driving range, putting green, golf carts, rental clubs, pro shop, golf academy/lessons, restaurant.*

Neuse Golf Club. About 20 minutes from downtown Raleigh, this semiprivate course feels far from the city's hustle and bustle. The 1993 John LaFoy–designed course follows the Neuse River and is characterized by rolling fairways and rock outcroppings. ⊠ *918 Birkdale Dr., Clayton* ☎ *919/550–0550* ⊕ *www.neusegolf.com* ⚑ *18 holes. 7010 yds. Par 72. Green Fee: $40–$60* ⚲ *Facilities: Driving range, putting green, rental clubs, pro shop, golf academy/lessons.*

SHOPPING

SHOPPING CENTERS Raleigh's first shopping center, **Cameron Village Shopping Center** (⊠ *1900 Cameron St., Cameron Village* ☎ *919/821–1350*) is an upscale assemblage of boutiques and restaurants. The **Triangle Town Center** (⊠ *5959 Triangle Town Blvd., North Raleigh* ☎ *919/792–2222*) contains some 165 stores, including Abercrombie & Fitch, Coldwater Creek, Lindt Chocolates, Saks Fifth Avenue, and Williams-Sonoma.

FOOD Open year-round, the 60-acre **State Farmers' Market** (⊠ *1201 Agriculture St., Southwest Metro* ☎ *919/733–7417*) is the place to go for locally grown fruits and vegetables, flowers and plants, and North Carolina crafts. The cavernous down-home restaurant is a great place to grab a bite.

DURHAM

23 mi northwest of Raleigh.

Although its image as a tobacco town lingers, Durham is now also known for the medical facilities and research centers associated with the city's prestigious Duke University. With more than 20,000 employees, Duke is the largest employer in this city of 188,000, and residents and visitors alike can take advantage of the lectures, art activities, and sports events associated with the university. Durham has more than a dozen historic sites, including several of North Carolina's 38 National Historic Landmarks.

GETTING HERE AND AROUND

Durham's city center has grown rather haphazardly around its universities and commercial districts in the past 100 years. One-way streets and roads that change names can make navigation tricky. Using Durham

Freeway, aka Highway 147 as a guide helps. This thoroughfare bisects the city diagonally, connecting Interstates 85 and 40, and most places of interest can be reached via its exits.

ESSENTIALS

Visitor Information Durham Convention and Visitors Bureau (☒ *101 E. Morgan St.* ☎ *919/687-0288 or 800/446-8604* ⊕ *www.durham-nc.com*).

EXPLORING

Bennett Place State Historic Site. In April 1865 Confederate General Joseph E. Johnston surrendered to U.S. General William T. Sherman in this house, 17 days after Lee's surrender to Grant at Appomattox. The two generals then set forth the terms for a "permanent peace" between the South and the North. Live historical events are held throughout the year, demonstrating how Civil War soldiers drilled, lived in camps, got their mail, and received medical care. ☒ *4409 Bennett Memorial Rd., Downtown* ☎ *919/383-4345* ⊕ *www.nchistoricsites. org/bennett/bennett.htm* ☒ *Free* ☉ *Tues.–Sat. 9–5.*

Brightleaf Square (☒ *Main and Gregson Sts., Duke University* ☎ *919/682–9229*), in the former Watts and Yuille warehouses, is named for the tobacco that once filled these buildings. The two long buildings—filled with stores like James Kennedy Antiques, Offbeat Music, Shiki Pottery, and Wentworth and Leggett Rare Books and Prints—sandwich an attractive brick courtyard.

★ **Duke Chapel.** A Gothic-style gem built in the early 1930s, this chapel is the centerpiece of Duke University. Modeled after England's Canterbury Cathedral, it has a 210-foot-tall bell tower. Weekly services are held here Sunday at 11 AM. ■ TIP➔The chapel is a popular wedding spot, so check the Web site for tour availability before going on Saturday. ☒ *Chapel Dr., West Campus, Duke University* ☎ *919/681-1704* ⊕ *www.chapel.duke. edu* ☉ *Sept.–May, daily 8 AM–10 PM; June–Aug., daily 8–8.*

Duke Homestead. Washington Duke, patriarch of the now famous Duke family, moved into this house in 1852. It wasn't until he heard how the Union soldiers were enjoying smoking his tobacco that he decided to market his "golden weed." Explore the family's humble beginnings at this State Historic Site, which includes the first ramshackle "factory" as well the world's largest spittoon collection. Guided tours demonstrate early manufacturing processes; the visitor center exhibits early tobacco advertising. ☒ *2828 Duke Homestead Rd., Downtown* ☎ *919/477-5498* ⊕ *www.ah.dcr.state.nc.us* ☒ *Free* ☉ *Tues.–Sat. 9–5.*

Duke University. A stroll along the tree-lined streets of this campus, founded in 1924, is a lovely way to spend a few hours. The university, known for its Georgian and Gothic Revival architecture, encompasses

---

WORD OF MOUTH

"There is a beautiful 'mall' area next to the Durham Bulls ballpark, where there is usually live music on Friday evenings from 6–8 PM. There is also often music at Brightleaf Square—where a number of restaurants have outdoor patios you can sit and eat and listen. Durham has the exquisite Duke Gardens adjoining the campus of Duke. One of our favorite historic sites is the Bennett Place Farm (where the biggest surrender in the Civil War occurred)."
—uhoh_busted

7

525 acres in the heart of Durham. A highlight of any visit is the **Nasher Museum of Art** (⊠ *2001 Campus Dr., Duke University* ☎ *919/684–5135* ⊕ *www.nasher.duke.edu*), which displays African, American, European, and Latin American artwork from various eras. The collection includes works by Rodin, Picasso, and Matisse. Tours of the campus, available during the academic year, can be arranged in advance. ⊠ *Office of Special Events, Smith Warehouse, 114 Buchannan Blvd.* ☎ *919/684–3710* ⊕ *www.duke.edu*.

☉ ★ **North Carolina Museum of Life and Science.** Here you can ride in a flying machine, sail a radio-controlled boat on an outdoor pond, view artifacts from space missions, and ride a train through a wildlife sanctuary. The nature center contains such animals as black bears, red wolves, and lemurs. The three-story Magic Wings Butterfly House lets you walk among tropical species in a rain-forest conservatory. In the Insectarium you can see and hear live insects under high magnification and amplification. ⊠ *433 Murray Ave., off I–85, Downtown* ☎ *919/220–5429* ⊕ *www.ncmls.org* 🎫 *Museum $10.85, train ride $2* ☉ *Mon.–Sat. 10–5, Sun. noon–5. Closed Mon. Sept.–Dec.*

★ **Sarah P. Duke Gardens.** A wisteria-draped gazebo and a Japanese garden with a lily pond teeming with fat goldfish are a few of the highlights of these 55 acres in Duke University's West Campus. More than 5 mi of pathways meander through formal plantings and woodlands. The Terrace Café serves lunch Monday through Friday and brunch Saturday and Sunday. ⊠ *426 Anderson St. at Campus Dr., West Campus, Duke University* ☎ *919/684–3698* ⊕ *www.hr.duke.edu/dukegardens* 🎫 *Free* ☉ *Daily 8–dusk.*

WHERE TO EAT

$$$
ECLECTIC

✕ **George's Garage.** This restaurant defies pigeonholing. It's part nouvelle restaurant, part prepared-food market, part bar, and part bakery—all in a cavernous, pumped-up room. Fresh fish and Mediterranean fare are specialties, but you can also dine on grilled chicken, pork, lamb, and beef. Live entertainment and dancing make this a popular after-hours hangout. Don't miss brunch every Sunday. ⊠ *737 9th St., Downtown* ☎ *919/286–1431* ▭ *AE, D, MC, V.*

$–$$
SEAFOOD

✕ **Kemp's Seafood House.** Everything about Kemp's is big, especially the platters of shrimp, stuffed crab, and flounder. This counter-service hot spot serves seafood cooked in a variety of ways, but the specialty of the house is calabash style, lightly battered and fried. Hush puppies and sweet tea round out the experience. ⊠ *115 Page Point Circle, Southeast Metro* ☎ *919/957–7155* ⊱ *Reservations not accepted* ▭ *AE, D, MC, V.*

$$$–$$$$
MODERN
SOUTHERN
Fodor'sChoice
★

✕ **Magnolia Grill.** This bistro is consistently one of the area's finest, most innovative places to dine. The food created by chef-owners Ben and Karen Barker is as eye-catching as the art on the walls. The daily menu, which maintains a Southern sensibility, may include spicy green-tomato soup with crab and country ham or striped bass with oyster stew. ⊠ *1002 9th St., Downtown* ☎ *919/286–3609* ▭ *AE, MC, V* ☉ *Closed Sun. and Mon. No lunch.*

$$
MODERN
SOUTHERN
★

✕**Watts Grocery.** When slow food enthusiasts say "eat local," this is what they mean. The menu of dressed-up Southern dishes at Watts Grocery, which reflects both the chef's Southern roots and her French training, relies on the freshest seasonal ingredients and locally raised meats. The smooth and savory meat terrines served with homemade pickles, and the grilled pork tenderloin over corn pudding are standouts on the summer menu. The decor is stylish but understated with comfortable banquettes and local artwork. Sunday brunch draws a crowd with dishes like andouille sausage and stewed chilies Benedict, and a toasted pimento cheese sandwich with local tomatoes and bacon. ✉*1116 Broad St., Trinity Park* ☎*919/416–5040* ⊟*AE, MC, V* ☾*Closed Mon.*

WHERE TO STAY

$$–$$$

🏨**Arrowhead Inn.** Brick chimneys and tall Doric columns distinguish this Federal Revival plantation situated on 6 acres dotted with 200-year-old magnolias. Antiques and working fireplaces in every room create a cozy environment, and the whirlpool tubs and steam showers in many rooms lend an air of luxury. **Pros:** comfortable inn offers suites and roomy cottages. **Cons:** it's a bit removed from the city center. ✉*106 Mason Rd., North Metro* ☎*919/477–8430 or 800/528–2207* ⊕*www. arrowheadinn.com* ➦*7 rooms, 1 cabin, 1 cottage* ♿*In-room: Wi-Fi* ⊟*AE, D, MC, V* ⦿*BP.*

$–$$

🏨**Blooming Garden Inn.** With its yellow exterior, this B&B is literally and figuratively a bright spot in the Holloway Historic District. Inside, the inn explodes with color and warmth, thanks to exuberant hosts Dolly and Frank Pokrass. Your gourmet breakfast might be walnut crepes with ricotta cheese and warm raspberry sauce. At the Holly House, a restored Victorian home across the street, the Pokrasses accommodate extended stays. **Pros:** great location near downtown; highly regarded service. **Cons:** quiet setting may be too sedate for those seeking nightlife action. ✉*513 Holloway St., Downtown* ☎*919/687–0801 or 888/687–0801* ⊕*www.bloominggardeninn.com* ➦*3 rooms, 2 suites* ♿*In-room: Internet, Wi-Fi* ⊟*AE, D, MC, V* ⦿*BP.*

$$$$
★

🏨**Washington Duke Inn & Golf Club.** On the campus of Duke University, this luxurious hotel evokes the feeling of an English country inn. Guest rooms with plaid bedspreads and creamy wall coverings overlook either a park or a Robert Trent Jones and Rees Jones–designed golf course. On display in the public rooms are memorabilia belonging to the Duke family, for whom the hotel and university are named. At the quietly sophisticated Fairview restaurant ($$$$) you can dine on poached tiger shrimp and mango cocktail sauce followed by prosciutto-wrapped monkfish with goat-cheese grits. **Pros:** well appointed and service-oriented; luxury travelers will feel right at home. **Cons:** the stately setting may make you feel like you need to mind your p's and q's. ✉*3001 Cameron Blvd., Duke University* ☎*919/490–0999 or 800/443–3853* ⊕*www. washingtondukeinn.com* ➦*271 rooms, 42 suites* ♿*In-room: Internet, Wi-Fi. In-hotel: restaurant, room service, bar, golf course, tennis courts, pool, gym, laundry service* ⊟*AE, D, MC, V.*

7

NIGHTLIFE AND THE ARTS

THE ARTS Performances that are part of the internationally known **American Dance Festival** (☎919/684–6402 ⊕ *www.americandancefestival.org*), held annually in June and July, take place at various locations around town.

The Beaux-Arts **Carolina Theatre** (⊠ *309 W. Morgan St., Downtown* ☎919/560–3030 ⊕ *www.carolinatheatre.org*), dating from 1926, hosts classical, jazz, and rock concerts, as well as April's Full Frame Film Festival and August's North Carolina Gay and Lesbian Film Festival. **ManBites Dog Theater** (⊠ *703 Foster St., Downtown* ☎919/682–3343 ⊕ *www. manbitesdogtheater.org*) performs edgy, socially conscious plays.

NIGHTLIFE **The American Tobacco Complex** (⊠ *318 Blackwell St., Downtown* ☎919/433–1566 ⊕ *www.americantobaccohistoricdistrict.com*), adjacent to the Durham Bulls Athletic Park, houses offices, bars and restaurants in a series of beautifully refurbished warehouses left over from the city's cigarette-rolling past. Free summer concerts are staged on a central lawn, in the shadow of a freshly painted Lucky Strike water tower. A new performing arts center hosting touring Broadway shows was on track to open in December 2008. With 19 beers on tap, the **James Joyce Irish Pub** (⊠ *912 W. Main St., Downtown* ☎919/683–3022) is a popular meeting place. Live musical acts perform at 10 PM on Friday and Saturday.

SPORTS AND THE OUTDOORS

BASKETBALL Durham's Atlantic Coast Conference team is Duke's **Blue Devils** (☎919/681–2583 ⊕ *www.goduke.com*), which plays its home games at the 8,800-seater Cameron Indoor Stadium.

GOLF **Duke University Golf Club.** Twice host of the NCAA men's championship, this course was designed in 1955 by the legendary Robert Trent Jones; his son, Rees Jones, completed a renovation of the links in 1994. The whopping 442-yard par 4 on Hole 18 separates serious players from duffers. ⊠ *3001 Cameron Blvd., at Science Dr.* ☎919/490–0999 or 800/443–3853 ⊕ *www.washingtondukeinn.com/golfclub.html* ⚑ *18 holes. 6868 yds. Par 72. Green Fee: $30–$100* ⚐ *Facilities: Driving range, golf carts, rental clubs, pro shop, golf academy/lessons, restaurant, bar.*

Hillandale Golf Course. The oldest course in the area, Hillandale was designed by the incomparable architect Donald Ross, but was redesigned by George Cobb following the course's move in 1960. The pro shop is consistently named one of the best in the country. The course, with a couple of doglegs and a slew of water hazards, gives even experienced golfers a strategic workout. ⊠ *1600 Hillandale Rd.* ☎919/286–4211 ⊕ *www.hillandalegolf.com* ⚑ *Reservations essential* ⚑ *18 holes. 6339 yds. Par 71. Green Fee: $20–$44* ⚐ *Facilities: Driving range, golf carts, rental clubs, pro shop, golf academy/lessons, restaurant, bar.*

SHOPPING

Durham's funky **9th Street** (⊠ *9th St. at Markham Ave., West Durham* ☎919/572–8808) is lined with shops and restaurants. The **Streets of Southpoint Mall** (⊠ *6910 Fayetteville Rd., off I–40, Southeast Metro* ☎919/572–8808) dominates Durham's shopping scene with its village look, restaurants, movie theaters, and upward of 150 stores, including Nordstrom and Restoration Hardware.

CRAFTS **One World Market** (⊠*811 9th St., Duke University* ☎*919/286–2457*) holds 2,000 square feet of unique, affordable arts and crafts collected from around the world, from home accessories to children's toys. As a nonprofit enterprise, the market sells crafts from fair trade vendors, which aim to provide artisans in developing countries a living wage.

FOOD **Parker and Otis** (⊠*112 S. Duke St., Downtown* ☎*919/683–3200*) stocks local produce and specialty foods as well as international spices, wines, chocolates, teas, coffees, and scads of candy. Gourmet breakfast and lunch dishes are served until 7 PM. Gift baskets can be shipped all over the country and internationally.

CHAPEL HILL

28 mi northwest of Raleigh; 12 mi southwest of Durham.

Chapel Hill may be the smallest city in the Triangle, but its reputation as a seat of learning looms large. This is the home of the nation's first state university, the University of North Carolina, which opened its doors in 1795. Despite the large number of students and retirees, Chapel Hill retains the feel of a quiet village. Franklin Street, with its interesting mix of trendy bars, tasty eateries, and oddball stores, has always been the heart of downtown Chapel Hill.

GETTING HERE AND AROUND

Chapel Hill is a wonderful place to walk around, and a terrible place to park a car. Find a parking space in one of the lots along Rosemary Street, one block off Franklin, and give yourself a chance to enjoy the Carolina blue skies. Start at the Old Well on Cameron Avenue and wander through campus, or eat, sip and shop your way down Franklin Street, beginning at the Old Post Office, heading west to Carrboro

ESSENTIALS

Visitor Information Chapel Hill/Orange County Visitors Bureau (⊠*501 W. Franklin St., Chapel Hill* ☎*919/968-2060* ⊕*www.visitchapelhill.org*).

EXPLORING

Franklin Street runs along the northern edge of the **University of North Carolina** campus, which is filled with oak-shaded courtyards and stately old buildings. The **Ackland Art Museum** (⊠*Columbia and Franklin Sts., University* ☎*919/966–5736* ⊕*www.ackland.org*) showcases one of the Southeast's strongest collections of Asian art, plus an outstanding selection of drawings, prints, and photographs as well as old-master paintings and sculptures. The **Louis Round Wilson Library** (⊠*Polk Pl., between E. Cameron Ave. and South Rd., University* ☎*919/962–0114* ⊕*www.lib.unc.edu/wilson*) houses the largest single collection of state literature in the nation.

Morehead Planetarium and Science Center where the original Apollo astronauts trained, is one of the largest in the country. You can see planetarium shows, science demonstrations, and exhibits for children and adults. ⊠*250 E. Franklin St., University* ☎*919/962–1236* ⊕*www.*

moreheadplanetarium.org 🖢*$6* ⊘ *Open daily; hrs vary by season. Call or check Web site before visiting.*

The **North Carolina Botanical Garden,** south of downtown, has the largest collection of native plants in the Southeast. Nature trails wind through a 300-acre Piedmont forest. The herb garden and carnivorous-plant collection are impressive. A new visitor education center is slated to open in summer 2009. ⊠ *Totten Center, Old Mason Farm Rd., South Metro* ☎*919/962–0522* ⊕*www.ncbg.unc.edu* 🖢*Free* ⊘ *Weekdays 8–5; Mar.–Oct., Sat. 9–6, Sun. 1–6; Nov.–Feb., Sat. 9–5, Sun. 1–5.*

WHERE TO EAT

$$–$$$ ╳**Crook's Corner.** In business since 1982, this small restaurant has been
SOUTHERN an exemplar of Southern chic. The menu, which changes nightly, high-
★ lights local produce and regional specialties such as green-pepper chick-
en with hoppin' john (black-eyed peas), crab gumbo, buttermilk pie, and honeysuckle sorbet. A wall of bamboo and a waterfall fountain make the patio a delightful alfresco experience (it's heated for winter-time dining). Look for the faded pink pig atop the building. ⊠*610 W. Franklin St., Downtown* ☎*919/929–7643* ⊟*AE, D, MC, V* ⊘*Closed Mon. No lunch.*

¢–$ ╳**Mama Dip's Country Kitchen.** In Chapel Hill, Mildred Edna Cotton
SOUTHERN Council—better known as Mama Dip—is just about as famous as
★ Michael Jordan. That's because she and her eponymous restaurant, which serves authentic home-style Southern meals in a roomy but sim-ple setting, have been on the scene since the early '60s. Everything from chicken and dumplings, ribs, and country ham to fish, beef, salads, a mess of fresh vegetables, and melt-in-your-mouth buttermilk biscuits appear on the lengthy menu. ■TIP→ **Mama Dip's two cookbooks explain her famed "dump cooking" method and offer up more than 450 recipes.** ⊠*408 W. Rosemary St., Downtown* ☎*919/942–5837* ⊟*MC, V.*

$$ ╳**Weathervane Café.** This 30-year-old eatery, tucked into an expansive
AMERICAN fine-foods shop, uses those top-notch ingredients for such dishes as mustard-glaze salmon and goat-cheese risotto. There's plenty of com-fortable seating around the open kitchen, but the spacious courtyard, filled with plants and fountains, is why people stand in line. The all-day Sunday brunch is a big draw; French toast stuffed with mascarpone and strawberries is popular, as are poached eggs and crabmeat on a but-termilk biscuit. ⊠*Eastgate Shopping Center, 201 S. Estes Dr., North Metro* ☎*919/929–9466* ⊟*AE, D, MC, V.*

WHERE TO STAY

$$$$ 🏨**Fearrington House Country Inn.** A member of the prestigious Relais
★ & Châteaux group, this inn sits on a 200-year-old farm that has been remade to resemble a country village. "Oreo" cows (Belted Galways that are black on the ends, white in the middle) roam the pasture near the entrance. Carefully chosen antiques, English-pine furnishings, and oversize tubs fill the inn's modern guest rooms, which overlook a courtyard and the gardens. Some suites have a whirlpool or fireplace. The prix-fixe restaurant ($$$$) serves contemporary cuisine, including seared scallops with parsnip puree, black trumpet mushrooms, salsify, and blood-orange butter. Guests can choose a full English breakfast

or homemade granola. The hotel is in Pittsboro, 8 mi south of Chapel Hill. **Pros:** feels like a country inn but with up-to-date luxuries. **Cons:** the setting, while pristine, can feel a bit contrived. ⊠ *2000 Fearrington Village Center, Pittsboro* ☎ *919/542–2121* ⊕ *www.fearringtonhouse. com* ⟿ *35 rooms, 8 suites* ⌂ *In-room: Wi-Fi. In-hotel: 2 restaurants, tennis courts, pool, laundry service* ⊟ *AE, MC, V* ⬥○|*BP.*

$$$–$$$$
Fodor's Choice
★

⊡ **The Franklin Hotel.** A boutique hotel minutes from UNC's campus, The Franklin has helped sustain a renaissance on Franklin Street's west end since it opened in 2007. Its posh amenities, including marble bathrooms, in-room spa services, iPod docks, a pillow menu, and on-site parking (truly a luxury in Chapel Hill), lend an air of sophistication, while the understated elegant design of the building blends with the neighborhood's village aesthetic. Guests can people-watch from room balconies or mingle with the after-work crowd at Roberts, the cushy ground floor bar and patio. Service is spot-on, from the friendly hosts behind the counter to the well-versed bartender. The setting and the luxury combine to make guests feel at once part of the college scene but also far-removed from their everyday lives. **Pros:** high-tech in-room facilities include iPod docks and flat-screen TVs. **Cons:** Franklin Street location can get noisy when the campus is buzzing with students. ⊠ *311 W. Franklin St., University* ☎ *919/442–9000* ⊕ *www.franklinhotelnc. com* ⟿ *67 rooms, 7 suites* ⌂ *In-room: Wi-Fi. In-hotel: restaurant, room service, bar, gym, spa* ⊟ *AE, D, MC, V.*

NIGHTLIFE

The Chapel Hill area is the place to hear live rock and alternative bands. The stalwart of the club scene is the dark and funky **Cat's Cradle** (⊠ *300 E. Main St., Carrboro* ☎ *919/967–9053*), which has nightly entertainment primarily from local and regional bands. The **West End Wine Bar** (⊠ *450 W. Franklin St., Downtown* ☎ *919/967–7599*) attracts a more affluent crowd with its comprehensive wine list (more than 100 by the glass), dinner menu, and rooftop patio. The downstairs speakeasy-style Cellar has three pool tables, eight draft beers, and a 1,200-song jukebox.

SPORTS AND THE OUTDOORS

GOLF **UNC Finley Golf Course.** This public golf course was designed by golf legend Tom Fazio, who gave the links wide fairways and fast greens. ⊠ *Finley Golf Course Rd.* ☎ *919/962–2349* ⊕ *www.uncfinley.com* ⚐ *18 holes. 6231 yds. Par 72. Green fee: $47–$80* ⚲ *Facilities: Driving range, putting green, golf carts, pro shop, golf academy/lessons, restaurant.*

SHOPPING

Minutes from downtown, the lively **Eastgate Shopping Center** (⊠ *E. Franklin St. at U.S. 15/501 bypass, North Metro*) sells everything from antiques to wine. **Fearrington Village** (⊠ *2000 Fearrington Village Center, Pittsboro* ☎ *919/542–4000*), 8 mi south of Chapel Hill on U.S. 15/501 in Pittsboro, has upscale shops selling art, garden items, handmade jewelry, and more.

BOOKS At the independent **McIntyre's Bookstore** (⊠ *Fearrington Village, 2000 Fearrington Village Center, Pittsboro* ☎ *919/542–3030*) you can read by the fire in one of the cozy rooms. McIntyre's has a big selection of mysteries, as well as gardening and cookbooks. The store also hosts some 125 readings throughout the year.

FOOD   **A Southern Season** (⊠*Eastgate Shopping Center, 201 S. Estes Dr., North Metro* ☎*919/929–7133 or 800/253–3663*) stocks a dazzling variety of items for the kitchen, from classic recipe books to the latest gadgets. Many of the foods, such as barbecue sauces, peanuts, and hams, are regional specialties. Custom gift baskets can be sent anywhere in the world.

CHARLOTTE

Although it dates from Revolutionary War times (it's named for King George III's wife), Charlotte is definitely part of the New South. Uptown Charlotte has broad streets and a skyline of gleaming skyscrapers. It also has some fashionable historic neighborhoods that are noted for their architecture and their winding, tree-shaded streets. Public art— such as the sculptures at the four corners of Trade and Tryon streets—is increasingly displayed in the city. Erected at Independence Square, the sculptures symbolize Charlotte's roots and aspirations: a gold miner (commerce), a mill worker (the city's textile heritage), a railroad builder (transportation), and a mother holding her baby aloft (the future).

Heavy development has created some typical urban problems. Outdated road systems in this metropolis make traffic a nightmare during rush hours, and virtually all the city's restaurants are packed on weekends. But the locals' Southern courtesy is contagious, and people still love the laid-back pleasures of jogging, picnicking, and sunning in Freedom Park.

GETTING HERE AND AROUND

Charlotte is a driver's town, but a new light rail system has made going sans car a much more palatable option for commuters and visitors. The LYNX blue line is clean and fast, and runs from Uptown Charlotte, through the convention center, to I–485. Check for routes and schedules at ⊕*www.charmeck.org/departments/cats/lynx*.

You'll be able to walk around Uptown and the historic Fourth Ward.

ESSENTIALS

Visitor Information Visit Charlotte/Main Street Charlotte (⊠ *330 S. Tryon St., Uptown* ☎ *704/331–2700* ⊕ *www.charlottesgotalot.com*).

EXPLORING

UPTOWN CHARLOTTE

Uptown Charlotte is ideal for walking. The city was laid out in four wards around Independence Square, at Trade and Tryon streets. The Square, as it is known, is the center of the Uptown area.

➏ **Afro-American Cultural Center.** In a 1911 house of worship, this is a showcase for art, music, drama, and dance. ■ **TIP➔ Come on Sunday, when admission is free.** ⊠*401 N. Myers St., Uptown* ☎*704/374–1565* ⊕*www.aacc-charlotte.org* ⊠*$5; free Sun.* ☉*Tues.–Sat. 10–5, Sun. 1–5.*

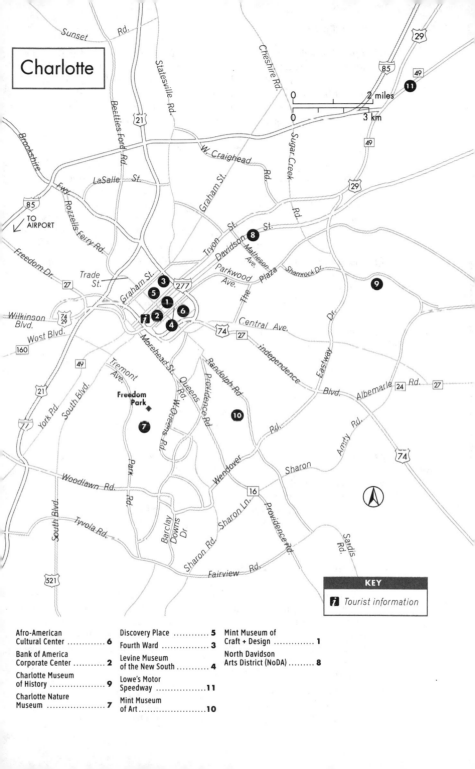

Charlotte

KEY

🛈 Tourist information

② Bank of America Corporate Center. Architecture fans should make time for a trip to see one of the city's most striking buildings. The Cesar Pelli–designed structure rises 60 stories to a crownlike top. The main attractions are three monumental lobby frescoes by world-renowned Ben Long, whose themes are making/building, chaos/creativity, and planning/knowledge. Also in the tower are the **North Carolina Blumenthal Performing Arts Center** and the restaurants, shops, and exhibition space of **Founders Hall.** ⊠ *100 N. Tryon St., Uptown.*

⑤ Discovery Place. Allow at least two hours for the **aquariums,** the three-story **rain forest,** and the **IMAX Dome Theater.** A ham-radio room, a puppet theater, and plenty of hands-on science experiments are other highlights. Check the schedule for special exhibits. ⊠ *301 N. Tryon St., Uptown* ☎ *704/372–6261 or 800/935–0553* ⊕ *www.discoveryplace. org* ⊠ *$10* ☉ *Labor Day–May, weekdays 9–5, Sat. 10–6, Sun. 12:30–6; June–Labor Day, Mon.–Sat. 10–6, Sun. 12:30–6.*

③ Fourth Ward. Charlotte's popular old neighborhood began as a political subsection created for electoral purposes in the mid-1800s. The architecture and sensibility of this quiet, homespun neighborhood provide a glimpse of life in a less hectic time. A brochure includes 18 places of historic interest.

④ Levine Museum of the New South. With its 8,000-square-foot centerpiece exhibit "Cotton Fields to Skyscrapers: Charlotte and the Carolina Piedmont in the New South" as a jumping-off point, this museum offers a comprehensive interpretation of post–Civil War Southern history. Interactive exhibits and different "environments"—a tenant farmer's house, an African-American hospital, a bustling street scene—bring to life the history of the region. ■ **TIP→ Admission is free on Sunday.** ⊠ *200 E. 7th St., Uptown* ☎ *704/333–1887* ⊕ *www.museumofthenewsouth. org* ⊠ *$6* ☉ *Mon.–Sat. 10–5, Sun. noon–5.*

① Mint Museum of Craft + Design. This museum is a showplace for contemporary crafts. In addition to the 16,000-square-foot gallery, with its spectacular 40-foot-tall glass wall, the permanent collections of ceramics, glass, fiber, metal, and wood make this one of the country's major crafts museums. ■ **TIP→ Use your ticket stub from the crafts museum for free same-day admission to the Mint Museum of Art.** ⊠ *220 N. Tryon St., Uptown* ☎ *704/337–2000* ⊕ *www.mintmuseum.org* ⊠ *$6* ☉ *Tues.–Sat. 10–5, Sun. noon–5.*

Fodor's Choice ★

GREATER CHARLOTTE

⑨ Charlotte Museum of History. Built in 1774, this stone building is the oldest dwelling in the county. Hezekiah Alexander and his wife Mary reared 10 children in this house and farmed the land. Seasonal events commemorate the early days. Permanent and rotating exhibits in the museum span 300 years of southern Piedmont history. ■ **TIP→ Admission is free on Sunday.** ⊠ *3500 Shamrock Dr., East Charlotte/Merchandise Mart* ☎ *704/568–1774* ⊕ *www.charlottemuseum.org* ⊠ *Tues.–Sat. $6; Sun. free* ☉ *Tues.–Sat. 10–5, Sun. 1–5.*

⑦ Charlotte Nature Museum. You'll find a butterfly pavilion, bugs galore, live animals, nature trails, a puppet theater, and hands-on exhibits just for children at this museum affiliated with Discovery Place. ⊠ *1658*

Sterling Ave., next to Freedom Park, Uptown ☎*704/372–0471* ⊕*www. discoveryplace.org* ✉*$4* ⊙*Weekdays 9–5, Sat. 10–5, Sun. 1–5.*

Fodor's Choice
★

⓫ **Lowe's Motor Speedway.** This state-of-the-art facility, holding 167,000 fans, is considered the heart of NASCAR. An estimated 90% of driving teams live within 50 mi. Hosting more than 350 events each

year, this is one of the busiest sports venues in the United States. Racing season runs April to November, and tours are offered on non-race days. The Speedway Club, an upscale restaurant, is on the premises. ■ TIP→ When there's a race, the population of Concord can jump from 60,000 to more than 250,000. Make sure you book your lodging well in advance. ✉*5555 Concord Pkwy. S, northeast of Charlotte, Concord* ☎*704/455–3200 or 800/455–3267* ⊕*www.lowesmotorspeedway.com.*

★ If you want to indulge the driver in you, you can take lessons through the **Richard Petty Driving Experience** (☎*704/455–9443* ⊕*www.1800bepetty. com*). You can drive a NASCAR-style stock car at speeds up to 155 mph around the Lowe's track. If you want the thrill of the ride without being in the driver's seat, you can ride with an instructor and go up to 165 mph. Classes are available throughout the year, though only when there's no event at Lowe's Motor Speedway. Prices vary, but start at $400 for eight laps around the track. ■ TIP→ You must have a valid driver's license and be able to drive a manual (stick shift) transmission car to drive, and you'll need to reserve ahead of time.

Slated to open in early 2010, the 50,000-square-foot **NASCAR Hall of Fame** will celebrate the only sport born in North Carolina. Visitors will be able to watch films on NASCAR history, see cars that ran the speedways, view changing exhibits, and experience simulations of what racing is like for NASCAR drivers and crews. It will also serve as the ceremony site for the legends inducted into the Hall. ✉*Martin Luther King Blvd. and Brevard St., Uptown* ⊕*www.nascarhall.com.*

⓾ **Mint Museum of Art.** Built in 1836 as the first U.S. Mint, this build-
★ ing has been a home for art since 1936. Among the holdings in its impressive permanent collections are American and European paintings, furniture, and decorative arts; African, pre-Columbian, and Spanish-colonial art; porcelain and pottery; and regional crafts and historic costumes. ■ TIP→ Your ticket stub gets you free admission to downtown's Mint Museum of Craft + Design. ✉*2730 Randolph Rd., East Charlotte/ Merchandise Mart* ☎*704/337–2000* ⊕*www.mintmuseum.org* ✉*$6* ⊙*Tues. 10–9, Wed.–Sat. 10–5, Sun. noon–5.*

⓼ **North Davidson Arts District.** Charlotte's answer to SoHo or TriBeCa is NoDa, a neighborhood as funky as Uptown is elegant. Creative energy flows through the reclaimed textile mill and mill houses, cottages, and commercial spaces of this north Charlotte neighborhood, where you'll find both the kooky and the conformist—artists, musicians, and dancers; street vendors; and restaurateurs—sharing space.

WHERE TO EAT

$–$$　✕**300 East.** The gentrified neighborhood in which this casual spot resides
ECLECTIC　doesn't lack for charming older houses. Even so, 300 East makes its
★　mark, and not just because of its brightly hued signage. The bold contemporary menu—pork tenderloin with banana-mango salsa and saffron rice, for instance, or penne with duck and lobster—attracts a hip
and eclectic bunch. Choose a table in one of the private dining nooks
and crannies, or outside on the open-air patio. Here people-watching is
as much fun as eating. ⊠*300 East Blvd., SouthPark* ☎*704/332–6507*
▤*AE, D, MC, V.*

$$$–$$$$　✕**Bentley's on 27.** Where to look? To one side is the city skyline, viewed
FRENCH　from the 27th floor. To the other is the impressive display at the *gueri-
don,* a French cooking cart. The food itself is elegant in its simplicity:
a salad of baby greens, shallots, pearl tomatoes, and a champagne vin-
aigrette dressing, for instance, or a filet mignon with roasted potatoes,
pearl onions, wild mushrooms, spinach leaf, and red wine reduction,
grilled asparagus, baby carrots, roasted pears, and blue-cheese risot-
to. You'd close your eyes to savor the taste, but then you'd miss the
view. ⊠*Charlotte Plaza, 201 S. College St., Uptown* ☎*704/343–9201*
▤*AE, MC, V.*

$$–$$$　✕**Latorre's.** The emphasis at this downtown eatery is on the heat, color,
LATIN AMERICAN　and flavor of Latin America. Art splashed with vibrant shades of mango,
lemon, and papaya complements exposed-brick walls and hardwood
floors. Live salsa and merengue is the perfect backdrop for the likes of
orange-and-cumin-encrusted salmon over black-bean rice cakes, and
tender grilled *chimichurri* (a piquant Argentinian herb sauce) flank steak
served with tortillas and three salsas. On weekends the place is open
for dancing until 2:30 AM. ⊠*118 W. 5th St., Uptown* ☎*704/377–4448*
▤*AE, MC, V* ✹*Closed Sun.*

¢　✕**Mert's Heart and Soul.** Talk about the New South. Business execu-
SOUTHERN　tives and arts patrons make their way to Mert's—named for Myrtle, a
Fodor'sChoice　favorite customer with a sunny disposition. Owners James and Renee
★　Bezzelle serve large portions of Low Country and Gullah staples, such
as fried chicken with greens, macaroni and cheese, and corn bread.
Lowcountry specialties include shrimp-and-salmon omelets and red
beans and rice. Buckwheat and sweet-potato pancakes draw a weekend
brunch crowd. ⊠*214 N. College St., Uptown* ☎*704/342–4222* ▤*AE,
MC, V* ✹*No dinner Mon. and Tues.*

¢　✕**Price's Chicken Coop.** If you want to know where the locals eat, just
SOUTHERN　follow the scent of oil to this storefront institution in the historic South
End neighborhood, just across I–277 from Uptown. The place isn't
much to look at, but that's OK because the food is to-go only. And
the chicken is the reason to go—and go again and again. A light crispy
coating cuddles succulent meat so juicy you'll begin to understand that
there is indeed an art to running a deep fryer. Take some back to your
hotel in Uptown and make everyone on the elevator jealous with the
scent of Southern-fried goodness. ⊠*1614 Camden Rd., South End*
☎*704/333–9866* ⬥*Reservations not accepted* ▤*No credit cards*
✹*Closed Sun. and Mon.*

WHERE TO STAY

$-$$ 🏨**Omni Charlotte Hotel.** This 16-story hotel is in the heart of downtown, within walking distance of the convention center as well as many arts and sports venues. An escalator whisks you to the OverStreet Mall, where you'll find shops, restaurants, and a lounge. Many guest rooms have glass walls overlooking the city skyline. Satin hangers and rainfall showers are among the ways a guest feels pampered. You can also request a "Get Fit" room with a portable treadmill. **Pros:** location and amenities are great for downtown. **Cons:** busy setting might be too much for some travelers. ✉*132 E. Trade St., Uptown* ☎*704/377–0400 or 800/843–6664* ⊕*www.omnicharlotte.com* 🛏*374 rooms, 33 suites* ⚏*In-room: Internet, Wi-Fi. In-hotel: restaurant, bar, pool, laundry service* ▭*AE, D, MC, V.*

$-$$ 🏨**Westin Charlotte.** The Westin Charlotte is a study in modern comfort. The vast medallion chandelier in the lobby is as striking as the hotel's gleaming green-glass facade. Rooms feature ultra-comfy beds and roomy showers in marble bathrooms as well as stunning views of the city. The concierges know the area well, from where the best touring Broadway shows are to where to find baby supplies in a pinch. A stop for the new LYNX light rail is just outside the hotel door. Both service and comfort are delivered at very high levels. **Pros:** helpful staff and beautiful surroundings; in-room spa services. **Cons:** parking in the on-site deck is not included in room rate. ✉*601 S. College St., Uptown* ☎*704/375–2600* ⊕*www.westin.com/charlotte* 🛏*700 rooms* ⚏*In-room: Internet. In-hotel: restaurant, room service, bar, gym, pool, laundry service, parking (paid)* ▭*AE, D, MC, V.*

BED-AND-BREAKFASTS

$$$-$$$$ 🏨**Duke Mansion.** Coming up the boxwood-lined drive of the Duke Mansion feels like going back in time. The well-preserved property was once home to Duke University benefactor James Buchanan Duke. The inn, which changed hands many times since Duke's death, is now run by a nonprofit organization. Some of the rooms have original fixtures, including bathtubs and vanities. Spacious sleeping-porch balconies overlook the well-maintained grounds. Modern amenities include flat-screen TVs, comfortable beds, and cozy robes. In the morning, a full breakfast is served in the dining room. Staying at the Duke Mansion seems more like borrowing a wealthy friend's estate than spending a night in a hotel. **Pros:** guests get a real sense of history and a neighborhood feel. **Cons:** older bathroom fixtures do not perform to modern standards. ✉*400 Hermitage Rd., Myers Park* ☎*704/714–4400* ⊕*www.dukemansion. com* 🛏*20 rooms* ⚏*In-room: Wi-Fi* ▭*MC, V.*

NIGHTLIFE AND THE ARTS

THE ARTS

With the 2,100-seat Belk Theatre, the **North Carolina Blumenthal Performing Arts Center** (✉*130 N. Tryon St., Uptown* ☎*704/372–1000* ⊕*www. performingartsctr.org*) houses several resident companies, such as the Charlotte Symphony Orchestra, North Carolina Dance Theatre, and Opera Carolina. At Paramount's Carowinds, the **Paladium Amphitheater**

(⊠*14523 Carowinds Blvd., South Charlotte/Pineville* ☎*704/588–2600 or 800/888–4386* ⊕*www.paramountparks.com*) presents family-friendly acts spring to fall. The **Verizon Wireless Amphitheater** (⊠*707 Pavilion Blvd., Speedway* ☎*704/549–5555* ⊕*www.verizonwirelessamphitheater.com*) spotlights big-name concerts—Norah Jones, Tim McGraw, Melissa Etheridge—spring through fall.

NIGHTLIFE

In business since 1973, the **Double Door Inn** (⊠*1218 Charlottetown Ave., Uptown* ☎*704/376–1446*) is a staple of the national blues circuit. Eric Clapton, Junior Walker, and Stevie Ray Vaughn are among the legends who've played at this laid-back venue. **Ri Ra** (⊠*208 N. Tryon St., Uptown* ☎*704/333–5554*), Gaelic for "uproar," serves up traditional food, ale, and, on Thursday to Sunday night, live music.

SPORTS AND THE OUTDOORS

AUTO RACING

NASCAR races, such as May's Coca-Cola 600, draw huge crowds at the **Lowe's Motor Speedway** (⊠*5555 Concord Pkwy. S, northeast of Charlotte, Concord* ☎*704/455–3200 or 800/455–3267* ⊕*www.lowesmotorspeedway.com*).

GOLF

Larkhaven Golf Club. The oldest public course in Charlotte, Larkhaven opened in 1958. Mature trees have narrowed the fairways, and there's a 60-foot elevation drop on Hole 9, a par 3. ⊠*4801 Camp Stewart Rd.* ☎*704/545–4653* ⊕*www.larkhavengolf.com* ⚑*18 holes. 6328 yds. Par 72. Green Fee: $32–$45* ⚲*Facilities: golf carts, pro shop.*

Paradise Valley Golf Center. This short course is perfect for players without much time, as a round usually takes just an hour. But don't let that fool you: this course can challenge the best of them. Unique elements include two island tees. There's also a miniature golf course called the Lost Duffer set in a 19th-century mining town. ⊠*110 Barton Creek Dr.* ☎*704/548–1808* ⊕*www.charlottepublicgolf.com/paradise-valley. php* ⚑*18 holes. 1264 yds. Par 54. Green Fee: $8–$17* ⚲*Facilities: golf carts.*

Woodbridge Golf Links. This semiprivate course is lovely to look at and challenging to play. You have to be careful with the water hazards; there are water features on 13 holes. ⊠*7107 Highland Creek Pkwy.* ☎*704/875–9000* ⊕*www.highlandcreekgolfclub.com* ⚑*18 holes. 6520 yds. Par 72. Green Fee: $49–$69* ⚲*Facilities: driving range, putting green, golf carts, pro shop, restaurant, bar.*

SHOPPING

Charlotte is the largest retail center in the Carolinas. Most stores are in suburban malls; villages and towns in outlying areas have shops selling regional specialties.

SHOPPING MALLS

Two-story **Carolina Place Mall** (⊠ *11025 Carolina Place Pkwy., off I–485, South Charlotte/Pineville* ☎ *704/543–9300*) is on the interstate. Destination shopping has been raised to an art form at **Concord Mills** (⊠ *8111 Concord Mills Blvd., off I–85, Concord* ☎ *704/979–5000*), which sells hundreds of brand names and discounted designer labels. Look for stores carrying Ralph Lauren, Louis Vitton, Burburry, and OshKosh B'Gosh. **SouthPark Mall** (⊠ *4400 Sharon Rd., SouthPark* ☎ *704/364–4411*) has such high-end stores as Tiffany & Co., Montblanc, Coach, and Hermes.

SPECIALTY STORES

ANTIQUES The nearby towns of Waxhaw, Pineville, and Matthews are the best places to find antiques. You can find a good selection of antiques and collectibles at the sprawling **Metrolina Expo** (⊠ *7100 N. Statesville Rd., off I–77, North Charlotte/Lake Norman* ☎ *704/596–4643*) on the first weekend of the month.

FOOD The **Charlotte Regional Farmers Market** (⊠ *1801 Yorkmount Rd., Airport/Coliseum* ☎ *704/357–1269*) sells produce, eggs, plants, and crafts.

ASHEVILLE

Asheville is the hippest city in the South. At least that's the claim of Asheville's fans, who are legion. Visitors flock to Asheville to experience the arts and culture scene, which rivals that of Santa Fe, and to experience the city's blossoming downtown, with its myriad restaurants, coffeehouses, museums, galleries, bookstores, antiques shops, and boutiques.

Named "the best place to live" by many books and magazines, Asheville is also the destination for retirees escaping the cold North, or of "half-backs," those who moved to Florida but who are now coming half the way back to the North. Old downtown buildings have been converted to upmarket condos for these affluent retirees, and, despite the housing slowdown, new residential developments are springing up south, east, and west of town. As a result of this influx, Asheville has a much more cosmopolitan population than most cities of its size (70,000 people in the city, about 400,000 in the metro area).

Asheville has a diversity you won't find in many cities in the South. There's a thriving gay community, many aging hippies, and young alternative-lifestyle seekers. People for the Ethical Treatment of Animals (PETA) has named Asheville the most vegetarian-friendly city in America.

The city really comes alive at night, with the restaurants, sidewalk cafés, and coffeehouses; so visit after dark to see the city at its best. Especially on warm summer weekends, Pack Square, Biltmore Avenue, Haywood Street, Wall Street, and Battery Park Avenue are busy until well after midnight.

GETTING HERE AND AROUND

From the east and west, the main route to Asheville is I–40. The most scenic route to Asheville is via the Blue Ridge Parkway, which meanders between Shenandoah National Park in Virginia and the Great Smoky Mountains National Park near Cherokee, NC. Interstate 240 forms a freeway perimeter around Asheville, and Pack Square is the center of the city.

While a car is virtually a necessity to explore Asheville thoroughly, the city does have a metropolitan bus system with 24 routes radiating from the Transit Center in downtown. Asheville also has a sightseeing trolley service; tickets are available at the Asheville Convention and Visitors Bureau. Asheville is highly walkable, and the best way to see downtown is on foot.

ESSENTIALS

Visitor Information **Asheville Convention and Visitors Bureau** (⊠ *36 Montford Ave., Box 1010* ☎ *828/258–6101 or 888/247–9811* ⊕ *www.exploreasheville.com).*

DOWNTOWN ASHEVILLE

A city of neighborhoods, Asheville rewards careful exploration, especially on foot. You can break up your sightseeing with stops at the more than 50 restaurants in downtown alone, and at any of hundreds of unique shops.

Downtown Asheville has the largest extant collection of art deco buildings in the Southeast outside of Miami Beach, most notably the S&W Cafeteria (1929), Asheville City Hall (1928), First Baptist Church (1927), and Asheville High School (1929). It's also known for its architecture in other styles: Battery Park Hotel (1924) is neo-Georgian; the Flatiron Building (1924) is neoclassical; the Basilica of St. Lawrence (1912) is Spanish baroque; and Pack Place, formerly known as Old Pack Library (1925), is in the Italian-Renaissance style.

❹ Basilica of St. Lawrence. A collaboration of Biltmore House–head architect Richard Sharp Smith and the Spanish engineer-architect Rafael Gustavin, this elaborate Catholic basilica was completed in 1908. It follows a Spanish-Renaissance design, rendered in brick and polychrome tile, and has a large, self-supporting dome with Catalan-style vaulting. ⊠ *97 Haywood St., Downtown* ☎ *828/252–6042* ⊡ *Free* ☉ *Weekdays 9–4.*

❷ Black Mountain College Museum + Arts Center. Famed Black Mountain College (1933–56), 16 mi east of Asheville, was important in the development of several groundbreaking 20th-century art, dance, and literary movements. Some of the maverick spirits it attracted in its short lifetime include artists Willem and Elaine de Kooning, Robert Rauschenberg, Josef and Anni Albers, Ben Shahn, M.C. Richards, and Franz Kline; dancer Merce Cunningham; musician John Cage; filmmaker Arthur Penn; and writers Kenneth Noland, Charles Olson, and Robert Creeley. A museum and gallery dedicated to the history of the radical college occupies a small space in downtown Asheville. It puts on occasional

Downtown
Asheville

exhibits and publishes material about the college. Call ahead to find out what's currently happening. ⌧*54 Broadway, Downtown* ☎*828/299–9306* ⊕*www.blackmountaincollege.org* ⌧*Varies, depending on the exhibit; usually $5–$10* ⊙*Wed.–Sat. noon–4.*

5 Grove Arcade Public Market. When it opened in 1929, the Grove Arcade was trumpeted as "the most elegant building in America" by its builder, W. E. Grove, the man also responsible for the Grove Park Inn. With the coming of the Great Depression and World War II, the Grove Arcade evolved into a dowdy government building. In late 2002 its polished limestone elegance was restored, and it reopened as a public market patterned in some ways after Pike Place Market in Seattle. The market covers a full city block and has about 50 locally owned stores and restaurants, along with apartments and office space. A new Arts & Heritage Gallery features interactive exhibits and regional crafts and music. The building is an architectural wonder, with gargoyles galore, and well worth a visit even if you don't shop or dine here. ⌧*1 Page Ave., Downtown* ☎*828/252–7799* ⊕*www.grovearcade.com* ⌧*Free* ⊙*Mon.–Sat. 10–6, Sun. noon–5; store hrs vary.*

1 Pack Place Education, Arts & Science Center. This 92,000-square-foot complex in downtown Asheville houses the **Asheville Art Museum, Colburn Earth Science Museum, Health Adventure,** and **Diana Wortham**

Theatre. The **YMI Cultural Center**, also maintained by Pack Place, and focusing on the history of African-Americans in western North Carolina, is across the street. The Health Adventure has 11 galleries with hands-on exhibits, all of interest to children. The Asheville Art Museum stages major exhibits several times a year, with some highlighting regional artists. The Colburn Earth Science Museum displays local gems and minerals. The intimate 500-seat Diana Wortham Theatre hosts musical concerts and dance and theater performances year-round. ⊠ *2 S. Pack Sq., Downtown* 🕾 *828/257–4500*

⊕ *www.packplace.org* ⊠ *Art museum $6, Health Adventure $8.50, earth science museum $4, YMI Cultural Center $5* ⊙ *Tues.–Sat. 10–5, Sun. 1–5 (art museum open until 8 Fri.).*

❸ **Thomas Wolfe Memorial.** Asheville's most famous son, novelist Thomas Wolfe (1900–38), grew up in a 29-room Queen Anne–style home that his mother ran as a boardinghouse. The house, a state historic site, was badly damaged in a 1998 fire (a still-unsolved case of arson); it reopened in mid-2004 following a painstaking $2.4 million renovation. Though about one-fourth of the furniture and artifacts were lost in the fire, the house—memorialized as "Dixieland" in Wolfe's novel *Look Homeward, Angel*—has been restored to its original 1916 condition, including a light canary yellow paint on the exterior. You'll find a visitor center and many displays, and there are guided tours of the house and heirloom gardens. The admission, at only a dollar, is one of the best bargains in town. ⊠ *52 Market St., Downtown* 🕾 *828/253–8304* ⊕ *www.wolfememorial.com* ⊠ *$1* ⊙ *Tues.–Sat. 9–5, Sun. 1–5.*

Fodor'sChoice ★

GREATER ASHEVILLE

North Asheville, the historic Montford section (home to more than a dozen B&Bs), and the Grove Park neighborhood all have fine Victorian-era homes, including many remarkable Queen Anne houses. Biltmore Village, across from the entrance to the Biltmore Estate, was constructed at the time that Biltmore House was being built, and is now predominantly an area of retail boutiques and galleries. The River District, along the French Broad River, is an up-and-coming arts area, with many studios and lofts. Across the river, West Asheville has suddenly become the hottest part of the city, with its main artery, Haywood Road, sporting new restaurants, edgy stores, and popular clubs, though much of West Asheville retains its low-key, slightly scruffy, 1950s ambience.

Fodor'sChoice ★ **Biltmore Estate.** Built in the 1890s as the private home of George Vanderbilt, the astonishing 250-room French-Renaissance château is America's largest private residence. (Some of Vanderbilt's descendants still live on the estate, but the bulk of the home and grounds are open to visitors.) Richard Morris Hunt designed it, and Frederick Law Olmsted landscaped the original 125,000-acre estate (now 8,000 acres), which faces Biltmore Village. It took 1,000 workers five years to complete the gargantuan project. On view are the priceless antiques and art collected by the Vanderbilts, including notable paintings by Renoir and John Singer Sargent, along with 75 acres of gardens and formally landscaped grounds. You can also see the state-of-the-art winery and an 1890s-era farm, River Bend. Candlelight tours of the house are offered at Christmastime. Also on the grounds are a deluxe hotel, five restaurants open to the public, and an equestrian center. Each year in August, Biltmore Estate hosts music concerts with nationally known entertainers such as B.B. King and REO Speedwagon. Biltmore House's fourth floor, whose rooms are now open to the public, includes an observatory with sweeping views of the surrounding landscape, an architectural model room housing Hunt's 1889 model of the house, and servants' bedrooms and meeting hall, so you can see how the staff lived. Most people tour the house on their own, but guided tours are available ($15 additional). Note that there are a lot of stairs to climb, but much of the house is accessible for guests in wheelchairs or with limited mobility. ■TIP→ **If possible, avoid visiting on weekends during fall color season and the weeks between Thanksgiving and Christmas, when crowds are at their largest. Save by booking online rather than buying at the gate.** Saturday admission prices are higher than weekday rates, but, if you come back, the second visit in two days is only $10. The best deal is the annual pass, allowing unlimited admission for a year and costing only about twice as much as a one-day admission. ⊠ *Exit 50 off I-40, South Metro* ☎ *828/255–1700 or 800/411–3812* ⊕ *www.biltmore.com* ☜ *$47, Sun.–Fri.; $51, Sat.; $59 flex ticket for any day of the year; $99 unlimited visit annual pass; $15 extra for guided group tours of the house; $150 extra for premium tour with personal guide and visits to areas not normally open to the public* ⊙ *Admission gate and reception and ticket center: Jan.–Mar., daily 9–4; Apr.–Oct., daily 8:30–5; Nov.–Dec., daily 8:30–8.*

Biltmore Village. Across from the Biltmore Estate, Biltmore Village is a highly walkable collection of restored English village–style houses, now mostly shops and galleries. Badly flooded in 2004, with many buildings damaged and shops closed, the Village has come back to life, with nearly all shops now reopened. Of particular note is **All Souls Cathedral,** one of the most beautiful churches in America. It was designed by Richard Morris Hunt following the traditional Norman cross plan and opened in 1896. ⊠ *3 Angle St., South Metro* ☎ *828/274–2681* ☜ *Free* ⊙ *Daily, hrs vary.*

Ⓒ **North Carolina Arboretum.** Part of the original Biltmore Estate, these 434
Fodor'sChoice acres completed Frederick Law Olmsted's dream of creating a world-
★ class arboretum in the western part of North Carolina. Highlights include southern Appalachian flora in stunning settings, such as the Blue Ridge Quilt Garden, with bedding plants arranged in patterns reminiscent of Appalachian quilts, and sculptures set among the gardens. An extensive network of trails is available for walking or mountain biking.

A bonsai exhibit features miniature versions of many native trees. The 16,000-square-foot Baker Exhibit Center, which opened in late 2007, hosts traveling exhibits on art, science, and history. ■TIP→ **For an unusual view of the arboretum, try the Segway tour, where you can glide through the forest for two hours on the gyroscopically controlled "Human Transporter" invented by Dean Kamen.** The cost ($45 weekdays, $55 Saturdays) includes training on the Segway. Riders must be at least 18 years old and weigh between 80 and 250 pounds. Tours are at 10 and 2 Monday–Saturday. ⊠*100 Frederick Law Olmsted Way, 10 mi southwest of downtown Asheville, at Blue Ridge Pkwy. (MM 393), near I–26 and I–40, South Metro* ☎*828/665–2492* ⊕*www.ncarboretum. org* ⊠*$6 per car parking fee; free Tues.* ☉ *Visitor education center: Mon.–Sat. 9–5, Sun. noon–5. Gardens and grounds: Apr.–Oct., daily 8 AM–9 PM; Nov.–Mar., daily 8 AM–7 PM.*

WNC Farmers Market. The highest-volume farmers' market in North Carolina is a great place to buy local jams, jellies, honey, stone-ground grits and cornmeal, and, in season, local fruits and vegetables. In spring look for ramps, a wild cousin of the onion with a very strong odor. A wholesale section below the main retail section (both are open to all) offers produce in bulk. ⊠*570 Brevard Rd., 5 mi southwest of downtown Asheville, off I–40, South Metro* ☎*828/253–1691* ⊠*Free* ☉*Apr.–Oct., daily 8–6; Nov.–Mar., daily 8–5.*

WHERE TO EAT

Because of the large number of visitors to Asheville and the many upscale retirees who've moved here, the city has a dining scene that's much more vibrant and varied than its size would suggest. You'll find everything from Greek to Vietnamese, Moroccan to Southern soul food, and barbecue to sushi. Asheville has more vegetarian restaurants per capita than any other city, and there are coffeehouses on many corners.

DOWNTOWN

$$$
SEAFOOD
✗**Bistro 1896.** Bistro 1896 (in a building on Pack Square dating from that year) focuses on seafood but also offers other dishes. Start with oysters on the half shell, so fresh you can smell the salt air, or fried calamari, then jump to seafood-stuffed salmon or sesame-encrusted tuna. The bistro look comes from the period photos on the walls and glass-top tables with fresh flowers. On Sunday there's a brunch with a build-it-yourself Bloody Mary bar. Sidewalk seating lets you take in the street performers on bustling Pack Square. ⊠*7 Pack Sq., Downtown* ☎*828/251–1300* ⊟*AE, MC, V.*

$
SOUTHERN
✗**Early Girl Eatery.** Named after an early-maturing tomato variety, Early Girl Eatery is casually Southern, with a cheerfully chic twist. A wall of south-facing windows provides wonderful light most of the day. No white tablecloths here: you eat on brown butcher paper. The dinner menu runs to items like seared duck breast with collard greens. At breakfast, choose huge stacks of buttermilk pancakes or Creole catfish and stone-ground grits. ⊠*8 Wall St., Downtown* ☎*828/259–9592* ⊟*MC, V.*

$
ECLECTIC
★
✕**Greenlife.** Asheville's wildly popular organic and natural foods grocery is *the* place to stock up on healthful, delicious picnic supplies. In addition to groceries, Greenlife has an extensive prepared food and takeout section, featuring a variety of soups of the day (including several vegan soups), hot lunch items, fresh sushi, and made-to-order sandwiches on organic breads. Greenlife also has the friendliest employees in town. ✉*70 Merrimon Ave., Downtown* ☎*828/254–5440* ⊟*MC, V.*

¢–$
VEGETARIAN
✕**Laughing Seed Café.** You'll get more than brown rice and beans at this vegetarian eatery, with a bold mural on one wall and a bar. The extensive menu ranges from fruit drinks to sandwiches and pizzas to dinner specialties influenced by the flavors of India, Thailand, Mexico, and Morocco. Fruits and vegetables come from local organic farms during the growing season. Breads are baked daily on premises. There's outdoor dining on charming Wall Street. ✉*40 Wall St., Downtown* ☎*828/252–3445* ⊟*AE, D, MC, V* ◔*Closed Tues.*

$$$$
MODERN
SOUTHERN
✕**The Market Place.** Clean lines, neutral colors, and brushed-steel mobiles create a sophisticated style at one of Asheville's longest-lived fine-dining establishments. (It opened in 1979.) The food offers refreshing twists on ingredients indigenous to the mountains, such as game and trout, and the South in general. Possible entrées are pan-seared red trout with corn fritters and squash slaw, and wood-grilled pork chop with sautéed greens, herbed quinoa, and strawberry-ginger compote. Iron gates open onto an exterior courtyard and dining patio. On the casual side of the restaurant, Bar 100 offers a bar menu of snacks and lighter dishes, all made with ingredients from within 100 mi of Asheville. ✉*20 Wall St., Downtown* ☎*828/252–4162* ⌕*Reservations essential* ⊟*AE, MC, V* ◔*Closed Sun. No lunch.*

$–$$
INDIAN
★
✕**Mela Indian Restaurant.** Mela opened in 2005 and quickly established itself as the best Indian restaurant in the city. Rather than specialize in one type of Indian cuisine, it offers dishes from across the country. The tandoori dishes (chicken, salmon, or lamb) are especially delicious. Entrées are served with basmati rice, lentil stew, and *papadum* (lentil wafers). Portions are large, making this one of the best values downtown. The space is unexpectedly modern, with rough tile walls and a high ceiling, though accented with woodwork, doors, and furnishings from India. ✉*70 N. Lexington, Downtown* ☎*828/225–8880* ⊟*AE, D, MC, V.*

¢
EASTERN
EUROPEAN
✕**Old Europe.** The Hungarian owners, Zoltan and Melinda Vetro, bring a European sensibility to this immensely popular pastry shop and coffeehouse. It's often jammed; the crowd spills over to the courtyard, slurping coffee—served with a piece of chocolate—and liqueurs and downing delicious tortes, cakes, and other European pastries. Although full meals are served, you're better off sticking to the desserts and coffees. There's live entertainment on weekends, in a nightclub upstairs. ✉*41 N. Lexington Ave., Downtown* ☎*828/252–0001* ⊟*MC, V.*

¢–$
LATIN AMERICAN
✕**Salsa's.** In an expanded space with a slightly retro-hippie look, you'll find spicy and highly creative Mexican and Caribbean fare in huge portions. Pan-fried fish tacos, roast pumpkin empanadas, and organic chicken enchiladas are among the recommended entrées. ✉*6 Patton Ave., Downtown* ☎*828/252–9805* ⊟*AE, D, MC, V* ◔*Closed Sun.*

7

$–$$ ✗ **Tupelo Honey Café.** Hello, darlin'! This is the place for down-home
SOUTHERN   Southern cooking with an uptown twist. Owner Sharon Schott delivers
ⓒ   a lot more than grits, with dishes like seared salmon with corn bread,
and hormone-free pork chop with mashed sweet potatoes. Breakfast
is served anytime, and there is a jar of tupelo honey available on every
table. The atmosphere is loud and a little funky, and there's often a
line. Kids are welcome; they can entertain themselves by drawing on
the paper tablecloths. ⊠ *12 College St., Downtown* ☎ *828/255–4863*
⌕ *Reservations not accepted* ☰ *AE, MC, V* ⊘ *Closed Mon. No lunch
Fri. and Sat.*

$$–$$$ ✗ **Zambras.** Sophisticated tapas selections, such as grilled scallops with
SPANISH   parsnip-potato gratin, prosciutto-wrapped medjool dates with goat
★   cheese, pan-seared local trout with hazelnuts and oranges, and steamed
mussels make this one of the most interesting restaurants in the mountains. There are also several varieties of paella and other dishes, many
influenced by the cuisine of Mediterranean Spain and North Africa,
and a wine list featuring unusual Spanish wines and sherries. Volup-
tuous Moorish colors and live gypsy music (and belly dancers on weekends) lend an exotic air. ⊠ *85 Walnut St., Downtown* ☎ *828/232–1060*
⌕ *Reservations essential* ☰ *AE, D, MC, V* ⊘ *No lunch.*

BILTMORE VILLAGE

$$$ ✗ **Rezaz.** With abstract art displayed on the cinnamon- and apricot-
MEDITERRANEAN   color walls and waiters dressed in black rushing around pouring wine,
★   you'd never know this sophisticated Mediterranean restaurant is in
the site of a former hardware store. Try the veal osso buco milanese or
the aborio-crusted sea scallops. There are daily specials, such as goat-
cheese ravioli on Monday and seared ahi tuna on Friday. You enter
the restaurant through Enoteca, Rezaz's wine bar, which serves panini
sandwiches, antipasti, and other less-expensive fare in a casual setting.
⊠ *28 Hendersonville Rd., Biltmore Village* ☎ *828/277–1510* ☰ *AE,
MC, V* ⊘ *Closed Sun.*

WHERE TO STAY

The Asheville area has a nice mix of B&Bs, motels, and small owner-
operated inns. There are more than three dozen B&Bs, one of the larg-
est concentrations in the South. Most are in the Montford area near
downtown and the Grove Park area north in the city. At least eight
B&Bs in the area promote themselves as gay-owned and actively seek
gay and lesbian guests, and an equal number advertise that they are
gay-friendly. More than 100 chain motel properties are dotted around
the metropolitan area, with large clusters on Tunnel Road near the
Asheville Mall, on U.S. Highway 25 and Biltmore Avenue near the Bilt-
more Estate, and southwest near Biltmore Square Mall. Also, you'll find
inns and boutique hotels, both downtown and around the city. In rural
areas around the city are a few lodges and cabin colonies.

DOWNTOWN

$$$–$$$$ 🏨**Haywood Park Hotel.** Location is the main draw of this downtown hotel, which was once a department store. Once ensconced in a suite here, you're within walking distance of many of Asheville's shops, restaurants, and galleries. The lobby has golden oak woodwork accented with gleaming brass. The suites are spacious, with baths done in Spanish marble. The long-popular Flying Frog Café, with an astonishingly eclectic menu—mixing French, Indian, and German cuisine—is in the hotel. There's a small shopping galleria in the atrium, and a very popular sidewalk café. **Pros:** great central downtown location; expansive suites. **Cons:** limited parking (valet); somewhat outdated decor in rooms and lobby; service sometimes spotty; no pool. ⊠*1 Battery Park Ave., Downtown* ☎*828/252–2522 or 800/228–2522* ⊕*www.haywoodpark. com* ⌂*33 suites* ⚭*In-room: safe (some), refrigerator, Wi-Fi. In-hotel: restaurant, room service, bar, gym, laundry service, no-smoking rooms* ▤*AE, D, DC, MC, V* ¶⊙|*BP.*

NORTH METRO

$$$–$$$$ 🏨**1900 Inn on Montford.** Guests are pampered at this Arts and Crafts–
Fodor's Choice style B&B, where most rooms have whirlpool baths, some have big-
★ screen plasma TVs, and all have fireplaces. There are lots of nooks and corners in the expansive public spaces for snuggling up with a book. The inn has a social hour every evening. Innkeepers Ron and Lynn Carlson say that the Cloisters—a 1,300-square-foot suite in their carriage house out back—is the largest suite in Asheville. Younger children are discouraged in the main house. **Pros:** well-run and deluxe B&B; antiques but also modern amenities. **Cons:** not for families with small children. ⊠*296 Montford Ave., North Metro* ☎*828/254–9569 or 800/254–9569* ⊕*www.innonmontford.com* ⌂*5 rooms, 3 suites* ⚭*In-room: refrigerator (some), DVD, Internet, Wi-Fi. In-hotel: Wi-Fi, no kids under 12, no-smoking rooms* ▤*AE, D, MC, V* ¶⊙|*BP.*

$$$–$$$$ 🏨**Albemarle Inn.** Famed Hungarian composer Béla Bartók lived here
★ in the early 1940s, creating his Third Piano Concerto, the "Asheville Concerto." You can stay in his room on the third floor, although Juliet's Chamber, with its private balcony overlooking lovely gardens, may appeal more to modern Romeos. Owners Cathy and Larry Sklar left their jobs as lawyers in Connecticut in order to turn this 1907 Greek Revival mansion in a quiet North Asheville residential area into one of the top B&Bs in the region. Some rooms have working fireplaces and canopied beds. Gourmet breakfasts are prepared by the inn's chef. **Pros:** delightfully upscale B&B; lovely residential neighborhood; excellent breakfasts. **Cons:** old-fashioned claw foot tubs in some rooms make showering difficult. ⊠*86 Edgemont Rd., 1 mi north of I–240, North Metro* ☎*828/255–0027 or 800/621–7435* ⊕*www.albemarleinn.com* ⌂*10 rooms, 1 suite* ⚭*In-room: Wi-Fi. In-hotel: no kids under 12, no-smoking rooms* ▤*D, MC, V* ¶⊙|*BP.*

$$$–$$$$ 🏨**Black Walnut Inn.** The Biltmore House supervising architect Richard Sharp Smith built this 1899 home in Asheville's Montford section. Today it's a B&B on the National Register of Historic Places. Most of the rooms—all redone in 2004 by owners Peter and Lori White—have working fireplaces. Parts of the 2000 movie *28 Days* were filmed here. (The star, Sandra Bullock, stayed in the Dogwood Room.) **Pros:** a gem of a B&B; charming antique-filled house; excellent breakfast and afternoon wine and appetizer hour included. **Cons:** grounds are not large, with only a small garden. ⊠ *288 Montford Ave., North Metro* ☎ *828/254–3878 or 800/381–3878* ⊕ *www.blackwalnut.com* ⤳ *6 rooms, 1 cottage* ⌂ *In-room: VCR. In-hotel: Wi-Fi, no-smoking rooms* ☰ *D, MC, V* ⍫ *BP.*

$$$$ 🏨 **Grove Park Inn Resort & Spa.** Asheville's premier large resort is an
★ imposing granite edifice that dates from 1913 and has panoramic views of the Blue Ridge Mountains. Henry Ford, F. Scott Fitzgerald (who stayed in room 441), and Michael Jordan, as well as eight U.S. presidents from Woodrow Wilson to George H. W. Bush, have stayed here. It's furnished with oak antiques in the Arts and Crafts style, and the lobby fireplaces are as big as cars. Four restaurants offer plenty of choices. The spa is one of the finest in the country. As the hotel's main focus is on group meetings, alas, sometimes individual guests get short shrift. Rooms in the original section are mostly smaller but have more character than those in the newer additions. **Pros:** imposing historic hotel; wonderful setting; magnificent mountain views; first-rate spa and golf course. **Cons:** individual guests sometimes play second fiddle to large group meetings. ⊠ *290 Macon Ave., North Metro* ☎ *828/252–2711 or 800/438–5800* ⊕ *www.groveparkinn.com* ⤳ *498 rooms, 12 suites* ⌂ *In-room: Internet, Wi-Fi. In-hotel: 4 restaurants, bars, golf course, tennis courts, pools, gym, spa, laundry service, Wi-Fi, no-smoking rooms* ☰ *AE, D, DC, MC, V.*

$$–$$$ 🏨 **The Lion and the Rose.** One of the characters in Thomas Wolfe's *Look Homeward, Angel* lived in this house, an 1898 Queen Anne–Georgian in the historic Montford Park area near downtown. It couldn't have looked any better then than it does now. A special detail is a 6-foot Palladian-style stained-glass window at the top of oak stairs. Innkeepers Jim and Linda Palmer keep the heirloom gardens and five guest rooms looking gorgeous. The landscaping around the house is striking. For snacks and wine, guests have 24-hour access to a a well-stocked pantry. For the most privacy, choose the Craig-Toms suite, which occupies the entire third floor. **Pros:** comfortable small B&B; impressively landscaped grounds; good value. **Cons:** as at all the B&Bs in Montford, it's a bit of a walk to downtown. ⊠ *276 Montford Ave., North Metro* ☎ *828/255–6546 or 800/546–6988* ⊕ *www.lion-rose.com* ⤳ *4 rooms, 1 suite* ⌂ *In-room: refrigerator (some), DVD, Wi-Fi. In-hotel: Wi-Fi, no kids under 12, no-smoking rooms* ☰ *D, MC, V* ⍫ *BP.*

SOUTH METRO

$$$–$$$$ 🏨 **Bohemian Hotel.** You can't stay any closer to the Biltmore Estate than at this hotel, unless you are on the Estate grounds. New in late 2008, the Bohemian is steps from the Estate's main gate, and close to all the shops and restaurants in Biltmore Village. The down side is that this is a congested area, with frequent delays due to a nearby train track crossing on Biltmore Avenue; you'll need the hotel's valet parking. The Tudor style of the hotel is designed to blend with the architecture of Biltmore Village, though some say it reminds them of Hogwarts school in the Harry Potter movies and novels. Spacious rooms have sumptuous velvet

fabrics, antique mirrors, and plasma TV. **Pros:** new upscale hotel; at Biltmore Estate gate, near Biltmore Village. **Cons:** located in a congested area with heavy traffic. ⊠*11 Boston Way, South Metro* ☎*828/505– 2949* ⊕*www.bohemianhotelasheville.com* ⤴*104 rooms* ⌂*In-room: refrigerator (some), Wi-Fi. In-hotel: restaurant, bar, gym, spa, Wi-Fi, no-smoking rooms* ⊟*AE, D, MC, V.*

$$$$
Fodor's Choice
★ ⊡**Inn on Biltmore Estate.** Many people who visit the Biltmore mansion long to stay overnight; if you're one of them, your wish is granted in the form of this posh hilltop property. The hotel mimics the look of Biltmore House with natural stone and copper. French manor houses inspired the interior. Nice touches include afternoon tea in the library. The dining room, reserved for hotel guests only, is bookended by large windows with mountain views and a massive fireplace. Menus deftly blend local and international ingredients. Available packages include admission to Biltmore Estate for the length of your stay and free shuttles to all parts of the estate. **Pros:** deluxe hotel on Biltmore Estate grounds; exclusive restaurant; top-notch service. **Cons:** very expensive; atmosphere can be a bit formal. ⊠*Biltmore Estate, Exit 50 off I–40, South Metro* ☎*800/922–0084* ⊕*www.biltmore.com/inn* ⤴*204 rooms, 9 suites* ⌂*In-room: refrigerator (some), Internet, Wi-Fi. In-hotel: restaurant, room service, bar, pool, spa, gym, bicycles, Wi-Fi, no-smoking rooms* ⊟*AE, D, DC, MC, V.*

$$$–$$$$
★ ⊡**The Residences at Biltmore.** Located not far from the gates of Biltmore Estate, these suites-style accommodations are some of the most luxe in Asheville. Studio and one-bedroom condo apartments (some two- and three-bedroom units are available), tastefully decorated with Arts and Crafts touches, have fully equipped kitchens with granite countertops and stainless-steel appliances, stacked stone gas fireplaces, hardwood floors, wall mounted flat screen TVs, and washers and dryers. Most units have whirlpool baths. **Pros:** luxury suites with fully equipped kitchens; convenient location near both Biltmore Estate and downtown Asheville; well-managed with helpful staff. **Cons:** on-site restaurant planned but not yet open; a bit of a hike to restaurants in Biltmore Village. ⊠*700 Biltmore Ave., South Metro* ☎*828/350–8000 or 866/433–5594* ⊕*www.residencesatbiltmore.com* ⤴*55 suites* ⌂*In-room: kitchen, DVD, Wi-Fi. In-hotel: pool, gym, Wi-Fi, no-smoking rooms* ⊟*AE, D, MC, V.*

NIGHTLIFE AND THE ARTS

For the latest information on nightlife, arts, and entertainment in the Asheville area, get a copy of *Take 5,* an entertainment tabloid in Friday's *Asheville Citizen-Times* or the weekly free newspaper, *Mountain Express.*

THE ARTS

The Asheville area has about 40 theaters and theater companies. Asheville also has a vibrant art and crafts gallery scene, with about two dozen galleries. Most of the galleries are within a block or two of Pack Square, while some, especially working studios, are in the River District. Biltmore Village also has several galleries.

One of the oldest community theater groups in the country, **Asheville Community Theatre** (⊠ *35 E. Walnut St., Downtown* ☎*828/254–1320*) stages professional plays year-round in its own theater building. The biggest art gallery in town, with 14,000 square feet of exhibit space, **Blue Spiral 1** (⊠*38 Biltmore Ave., Downtown* ☎*800/291–2513*) has about 30 exhibits of sculpture, paintings, and photographs each year.

In the Pack Place complex, the 500-seat **Diana Wortham Theatre** (⊠*2 S. Pack Sq., Downtown* ☎*828/257–4530*) is home to more than 100 musical and theatrical events each year. As the headquarters of the prestigious Southern Highland Craft Guild, the **Folk Art Center** (⊠*Blue Ridge Pkwy., MM 382* ☎*828/298–7298*), regularly puts on exceptional quilt, woodworking, pottery, and other crafts shows and demonstrations. This is a top spot to purchase very high quality (and expensive) traditional crafts, such as quilts, baskets, and pottery. In a 1928 landmark building decorated with polychrome terra-cotta tile, **Kress Emporium** (⊠*19 Patton Ave., Downtown* ☎*828/281–2252*) is a place for more than 75 craftspeople to show and sell their crafts. The space is not air-conditioned and can be hot in summer. Owned by arts entrepreneur John Cram, **New Morning Gallery** (⊠*7 Boston Way, Biltmore Village* ☎*828/274–2831 or 800/933–4438*) has 12,000 square feet of exhibit space, focusing on more popular ceramics, garden art, jewelry, furniture, and art glass. In a tiny, 99-seat theater, **North Carolina Stage Company** (⊠*33 Haywood St., Downtown* ☎*828/350–9090*) is a professional company that puts on edgy, contemporary plays. With professional summer theater that often celebrates mountain culture, **Southern Appalachian Repertory Theatre (SART)** (⊠*Owen Hall, Mars Hill College* ☎*828/689–1239*) produces plays such as William Gregg and Perry Deane Young's *Mountain of Hope,* about the 1835 controversy over whether or not Mt. Mitchell is the highest peak east of the Rockies. In a 1938 building that housed a five-and-dime, **Woolworth Walk** (⊠*25 Haywood St., Downtown* ☎*828/254–9234*) features the work of 150 crafts artists in 20,000 square feet of exhibit space on two levels, and there's even a soda fountain, built to resemble the original Woolworth luncheonette.

The 2,400-seat **Thomas Wolfe Auditorium** (⊠*87 Haywood St., Downtown* ☎*828/259–5736*), in the Asheville Civic Center, hosts larger events including traveling Broadway shows and performances of the Asheville Symphony. The Civic Center, which is showing its age, is looking at a $140 million expansion to include a new performing-arts theater.

NIGHTLIFE

More than a restaurant, more than a movie theater, **Asheville Pizza and Brewing Company** (⊠*675 Merrimon Ave.* ☎*828/254–1281*), also called Brew 'n' View, is a wildly popular place to catch a flick while lounging on a sofa, drinking a microbrew, and scarfing a veggie pizza. In a renovated downtown appliance store, the ever-popular **Barley's Taproom** (⊠*42 Biltmore Ave.* ☎*828/255–0504*) has live bluegrass and Americana music three or four nights a week. The bar downstairs has about two dozen microbrew beers on draft, and you can play pool and darts upstairs in the Billiard Room. The camp decor at **Club Hairspray** (⊠*38 N. French Broad Ave.* ☎*828/258–2027*) will make you feel like you're back in 1961, though the music is contemporary. The crowd is diverse but predominately gay. Billed as a "listening room," **Grey Eagle** (✉*185 Clingman Ave.* ☎*828/232–5800*), in the River Arts District area, features popular local and regional bands four or five nights a week, with contra dancing on some other nights. **The Orange Peel Social Aid and Pleasure Club** (✉*101 Biltmore Ave.* ☎*828/225–5851*) is far and away the number one nightspot in downtown Asheville. Bob Dylan, Hootie and the Blowfish, and Steve Winwood have played here in an intimate, smoke-free setting for audiences of up to 950. In 2008 *Rolling Stone* named it one of the top five rock clubs in the U.S. For smaller events, it also has a great dance floor, with springy wood slats.

Asheville's best-known gay and lesbian club, **Scandals** (✉*11 Grove St.* ☎*828/252–2838*), has a lively dance floor and drag shows on weekends. In a 1913 downtown building, the jazz and blues club **Tressa's** (✉*28 Broadway* ☎*828/254–7072*) is nominally private, but lets nonmembers in for a small cover charge. There's a quieter, no-smoking room upstairs. In happening West Asheville, the smoke-free **Westville Pub** (✉*777 Haywood Rd.* ☎*828/225–9782*) has about 50 different beers on the menu, and a different band plays nearly every night.

SPORTS AND THE OUTDOORS

GOLF

Asheville Municipal Golf Course (✉*226 Fairway Dr.* ☎*828/298 1867*) is a par-72, 18-hole public municipal course designed by Donald Ross. Affordable fees start at $30. **Broadmoor** (✉*101 French Broad La., Fletcher* ☎*828/687–1500*), 15 mi south of Asheville, is a public Scottish-style links course, playing to 7,111 yards, par 72. **Apple Valley at Colony Lake Lure Golf Resort** (✉*201 Blvd. of the Mountains, Lake Lure* ☎*828/625–2888 or 800/260–1040*), 25 mi from Asheville, has two 18-hole, par-72 courses known for their beauty.

Grove Park Inn Resort (✉*290 Macon Ave.* ☎*828/252–2711 Ext. 1012 or 800/438–5800*) has a par-70 course that's more than 100 years old. You can play the course ($85 if you start after 2 PM) even if you're not a guest at the hotel. **Southern Tee** (✉*111 Howard Gap Rd., Fletcher* ☎*828/687–7273*) is an 18-hole, par-3 course with attractive rates—$22 with cart even on weekends in peak season.

SHOPPING

Biltmore Village (✉*Hendersonville Rd.* ☎*828/274–5570*), across from the Biltmore Estate, is a cluster of specialty shops, restaurants, galleries, and hotels in an early-20th-century-English-hamlet style. You'll find everything from children's books to music, antiques, and wearable art. **New Morning Gallery,** a jewelry, crafts, and art gallery at 7 Boston Way attracts customers from all over the Southeast.

Shopping is excellent all over **Downtown Asheville,** with at least 200 stores, including about 30 art galleries and over a dozen antiques shops. Several streets, notably **Biltmore Avenue, Lexington Avenue,** and **Wall Street** are lined with small, independently owned stores.

The **Grove Arcade Public Market** (✉ *1 Page Ave., Downtown* ☎ *828/252–7799*), one of America's first indoor shopping centers, originally opened in 1929. The remarkable building, which covers an entire city block, was totally redone and reopened in 2002 as a collection of some 50 local specialty shops and restaurants.

Grovewood Gallery at the Homespun Shops (✉ *111 Grovewood Rd.* ☎ *828/253–7651*), adjacent to the Grove Park Inn and established by Mrs. George Vanderbilt, sells furniture and contemporary and traditionally crafted woven goods made on the premises.

Great Smoky Mountains National Park

WORD OF MOUTH

"There are so many hiking trails in the Smokies, including the Appalachian Trail. It's a great place . . . to enjoy nature. Numerous peaks over 6,000 ft in the park . . . pretty spectacular. Once you get to even the most basic trails in the park you'll find the crowds quickly evaporate."

—tmd63

"The Smokies are just an absolutely gorgeous place. There are more places to hike, picnic, and enjoy the mountains than you will have time for. Cade's Cove is gorgeous, you can also take horseback rides there, and we spent a lazy afternoon tubing in Townsend as well."

—Hellion

www.fodors.com/community

Updated by
Michael Ream
and Lan Sluder

Great Smoky Mountains National Park is one of the great wild areas of the eastern United States and the most-visited national park in the U.S. From a roadside lookout or from a clearing in a trail, in every visible direction you can see the mountains march toward a vast horizon of wilderness.

Some of the tallest mountains in the East are here, including 16 peaks over 6,000 feet. The highest in the park, Clingmans Dome, was reputedly the original inspiration for the folk song "On Top of Old Smoky." It rises 6,643 feet above sea level and 4,503 feet above the valley floor. These are also some of the oldest mountains in the world, far older than those in the Rockies, the Alps, or the Andes. Geologists say the building of what are now the Great Smokies began about a billion years ago.

Today, the park hosts over 9 million visitors each year, almost twice as many as the second-most-visited national park, the Grand Canyon. Even so, with more than 814 square mi of protected land, if you get out of your car you can soon be in a remote cove where your closest neighbors are deer, bobcats, and black bears.

ORIENTATION AND PLANNING

GETTING ORIENTED

The good news is that it's easy to get to the Great Smoky Mountains National Park. In some ways, that's also the bad news, as the Smokies are within a day's drive of some of America's largest cities, resulting in traffic during peak travel periods such as summer and fall weekends. The closest sizeable cities to the park are Asheville, NC, to the east and Knoxville, TN, to the west. The Smokies are split almost evenly between North Carolina and Tennessee, and the Appalachian Trail runs along most of the border between the two states. Depending on traffic, it can take an hour or more to get from one side of the park to the other, via the only route through the park, Newfound Gap Road.

North Carolina Side. The North Carolina side boasts the highest mountain in the park—Clingmans Dome—as well as the historic Cataloochee Valley, many scenic overlooks and great hiking opportunities. It also connects to the famed Blue Ridge Parkway near Cherokee, NC.

Tennessee Side. This side of the park is where the action is, and also the crowds. The top attraction is Cades Cove. Despite the traffic, Cades Cove is well worth the time; it's undoubtedly the most beautiful valley in the park, with wide, open fields and many preserved settlers' buildings.

What's Nearby in North Carolina. Sometimes called "the quiet side of the park," the North Carolina side of the Smokies is edged with a collection of small, low-key towns. The most appealing of these are Bryson City and Waynesville.

TOP REASONS TO GO

Witness the wilderness: Great Smoky Mountains National Park is one of the last remaining big chunks of wilderness in the East. Get away from civilization in more than 800 square mi of tranquility, with old-growth forests, clear streams, meandering trails, wildflowers, and panoramic vistas from mile-high mountains.

Get your endorphins going: Outdoor junkies can bike, boat, camp, fish, hike, ride horses, raft white water, watch birds and wildlife, and even ski cross-country.

Experience mountain culture: Visit restored mountain cabins and tour "ghost towns" in the park, with old frame and log buildings preserved much as they were 100 years ago.

Spot wildlife: You can see black bears, elk, white-tailed deer, wild turkeys, and other wildlife. Biologists estimate there are more than 1,500 bears, 6,000 deer, and nearly 100 elk now in the park, so your chances of seeing these beautiful wild creatures, while not guaranteed, is quite good.

Learn something new: Take advantage of the interpretive talks and walks and Junior Ranger programs for kids.

What's Nearby in Tennessee. Near the western edge of the park are the towns of Gatlinburg and Pigeon Forge, virtually synonymous with the tourist trade. Here you'll find souvenir shops, outlet malls, country music theaters, mini-golf courses, amusement parks like Dollywood, chain motels, and plenty of restaurants.

PLANNING

WHEN TO GO

There's not a bad time to visit the Smokies, though summer and the month of October are the busiest times. Weekends in October are especially crowded, and you should expect traffic delays on Newfound Gap Road (U.S. 441) and traffic jams in Cades Cove. Beat the crowds by coming on weekdays and also early in the day, before 10 AM. Late spring is a wonderful time to visit the park, as wildflowers are in bloom, and it's before the heat, humidity, and crowds of summer.

GETTING HERE AND AROUND
AIR TRAVEL

The closest airport with national air service is Asheville Regional Airport (AVL), about 60 mi east of the Cherokee entrance.

Airport Information Asheville Regional Airport (*AVL* ✉ *708 Airport Rd., Fletcher* ☎ *828/684–2226* ⊕ *www.flyavl.com*).

CAR TRAVEL

Coming either from the east or west, I–40 is the main access route to the Smokies; from the north and south, I–75, I–81, and I–26 are primary arteries.

A wonderfully pleasant route to the Smokies from North Carolina is the **Blue Ridge Parkway**, which has its southern terminus at Cherokee.

U.S. 441, also called Newfound Gap Road, is the main road through the park, and the only paved road that goes all the way through. It travels 31 mi between Cherokee and Gatlinburg, crossing Newfound Gap at nearly a mi high.

PARK ENTRANCES

Gatlinburg, TN: From I–40 take Exit 407 to TN 66 South. At the Sevierville intersection, continue straight onto U.S. 441 South and follow it into the park.

Townsend, TN: From I–40, take Exit 386B to U.S. 129 South to Alcoa/Maryville. At Maryville take U.S. 321 North/TN 73 East through Townsend; continue straight on TN 73 into the park.

Cherokee, NC: Follow U.S. 441/U.S. 23 North. At Dillsboro merge on U.S. 74 West/U.S. 441 North. At Exit 74 merge onto U.S. 441 into the park.

RESTAURANTS

The closest thing to fine dining you can find in the park is a hot dog at the snackbar in Cades Cove or a Coke from a vending machine at a visitor center. You'll have to make your own fine dining with an alfresco picnic at one of the park's attractive picnic areas or leave the park for a meal.

Outside the park you'll find many more dining options, from fast food to fine dining, the latter especially in Asheville.

HOTELS AND CAMPGROUNDS

The only accommodations actually in the park, besides camping, are at one remote, rustic, and remarkable mountain lodge on the Tennessee side, LeConte Lodge. Camping, however, is abundant and reasonably priced. The park has 947 tent and RV camping spaces at 10 developed campgrounds, in addition to more than 100 backcountry campsites and shelters. The cost ranges from free (backcountry sites and shelters) to $14–$23 per night for front-country sites. Developed campgrounds range from creekside sites in historic valleys to a campground among evergreens at over a mile high. All but one of the campgrounds accept RVs and trailers, though most have size limits. Immediately outside the park are many commercial campgrounds and RV parks.

Outside the park, you have a good selection of hotels of every ilk. In the larger cities, like Gatlinburg and Pigeon Forge, you'll find the usual chain motels and hotels. For more of a local flavor, look at the many mountain lodges and inns in small towns like Bryson City and Waynesville.

WHAT IT COSTS					
	¢	$	$$	$$$	$$$$
Restaurant	under $10	$10–$14	$15–$19	$20–$24	over $24
Hotel	under $100	$100–$150	$151–$200	$201–$250	over $250
Camping	under $10	$10–$14	$15–$19	$20–$24	over $24

Restaurant prices are per person for a main course at dinner. Hotel prices are for a standard double room, excluding state and local taxes. Camping prices are for campsites that usually include a tent pad or parking area for RVs/trailer, fire pit or grate and/or raised grill, bear-proof food-storage lockers at some campgrounds, and picnic table; potable water and restrooms with flush toilets and running water will be nearby.

PLANNING YOUR TIME

NORTH CAROLINA SIDE IN 1 DAY If you only have a day to visit the Smokies, start early, pack a picnic lunch, and drive to the **Oconaluftee Visitor Center,** to pick up orientation maps and brochures. While you're there, spend an hour or so exploring the **Mountain Farm Museum.** Then, drive the ½ mi to **Mingus Mill** and see corn being ground into meal in an authentic working gristmill. Head up **Newfound Gap Road** and, via Clingmans Dome Road, to **Clingmans Dome.** Stretch your legs and walk the ½-mi paved, but fairly steep, trail to the observation tower on Clingmans Dome, the highest point in the Smokies. If you've worked up an appetite, head back down the mountain and stop for a leisurely picnic at **Collins Creek Picnic Area** (MM 25.4).

TENNESSEE SIDE IN 1 DAY Start early, pack a picnic lunch, and drive to the **Sugarlands Visitor Center** to orient yourself to the park. Head to the **Cades Cove Loop Road** and drive the 11-mi loop, stopping to explore the preserved farmsteads and churches. Spend some time in the **Cable Mill** area, visiting the grist mill, **Gregg-Cable House,** and other outbuildings. Depending on your timing, you can picnic at one of the stops in Cades Cove or Metcalf Bottoms. Take **Newfound Gap Road** up to **Newfound Gap.** Technically, **Clingmans Dome Road** is just over the state line, but if you've come this far you'll want to drive up. Return down Clingmans Dome and Newfound Gap roads and walk the self-guided trail around the **Noah "Bud" Ogle** farm. Then, proceed on to **Roaring Fork Motor Nature Trail.** At Auto Tour site number 5, park in the parking lot at the Trillium Gap trailhead and—if you have the time and are up to a moderate 2.6-mi (round-trip) hike— walk to **Grotto Falls.**

VISITOR INFORMATION

Contacts Cades Cove Visitor Center (✉ *Cades Cove Loop Rd.* ☎ *865/436-1200* ⊘ *Dec. and Jan., daily 9–4:30; Feb. and Nov., daily 9–5; Mar., Sept., and Oct., daily 9–6; Apr.–Aug., daily 9–7*). **Oconaluftee Visitor Center** (✉ *U.S. 441, 1½ mi from Cherokee* ☎ *865/436–1200* ⊘ *Nov.–Apr., daily 8–4:30; May, daily 8:30–5:30; June–Aug., daily 8–6; Sept. and Oct., daily 8:30–6* ✑ *Free*). **Sug-arlands Visitor Center** (✉ *U.S. 441, 2 mi inside the park* ☎ *865/436–1200* ⊘ *Dec.–Feb., daily 8–4:30; Mar. and Nov., daily 8–5; Apr., May, Sept., and Oct., daily 8–6; June–Aug., daily 8–7*).

8

FLORA AND FAUNA

A profusion of vegetation defines the Great Smokies; it has one of the richest and most diverse collections of flora in the world. The park is about 95% forested, home to almost 6,000 known species of wildflowers, plants, and trees.

Many call the Smokies the "wildflower national park," as it has more flowering plants than any other U.S. national park. You can see wildflowers in bloom virtually year-round, from the ephemerals such as trillium and columbine in late winter and early spring, the bright red cardinal flowers, orange butterfly weed, and black-eyed Susans in summer, and Joe-pye weed, asters, and mountain gentian in the fall. However, the best time to see wildflowers in the park is the spring, especially April and early May. The second-best time to see the floral display is early summer. From early to mid-June to mid-July, the hillsides and heath balds blaze with the orange of flame azaleas, the white and pink of mountain laurel, and the purple and white of rhododendron. In the fall, typically in October, hundreds of thousands of visitors jam the roads of the park to view the autumn leaf color.

Living in Great Smoky Mountains National Park are some 66 species of mammals, over 200 varieties of birds, 50 native fish species, and more than 80 types of reptiles and amphibians.

The North American black bear is the symbol of the Smokies. Bear populations vary year to year, but biologists think that up to 1,600 bears are in the park, a density of about two per square mile. Many visitors to the park see bears, although sightings are never guaranteed.

The National Park Service has helped reintroduce elk, river otters, and peregrine falcons to the Smokies. Because of the high elevation of much of the park, you'll see birds here usually seen in more northern areas, including the common raven and the ruffed grouse.

For a few short weeks, usually from late May to mid-June, synchronous fireflies put on an amazing light show. In this illuminated mating dance, the male Photinus fireflies blink 4 to 8 times in the air, then wait about 6 seconds for the females on the ground to return a double-blink response. The Joyce Kilmer Memorial Forest just outside the park is a great place to see them.

NORTH CAROLINA SIDE

The North Carolina side of the park provides you with a great variety of sights and experiences, from high peaks to historical houses. Right at the Oconaluftee Visitor Center at the entrance to the park is the Mountain Farm Museum, one of the best-preserved collections of historic log buildings in the region. If you're interested in seeing wildlife, Cataloochee, like Cades Cove on the Tennessee side, is a beautiful valley where you can spot deer, wild turkeys, and even elk. Even if you never leave your car, Newfound Gap Road offers plenty of scenic views. If, however, you're ready to lace up your hiking boots, there are hundreds of miles of hiking trails to be explored, from the paved trail to the top of Clingmans Dome to the granddaddy of all trails, the

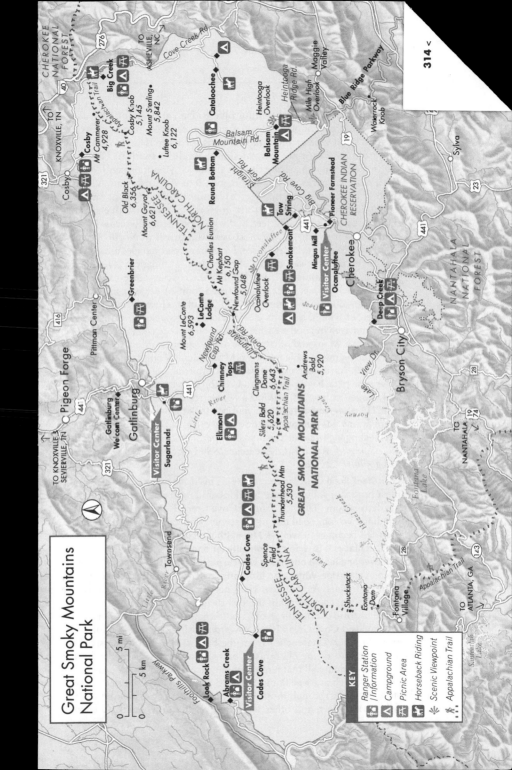

Great Smoky Mountains National Park

KEY
Ranger Station / Information
Campground
Picnic Area
Horseback Riding
Scenic Viewpoint
Appalachian Trail

Appalachian Trail, which skims 71 mi of the ridges along the North Carolina–Tennessee border.

SCENIC DRIVES

Fodor'sChoice
★ **Blue Ridge Parkway.** The beautiful Blue Ridge Parkway (or BRP as it's known on local bumper stickers) gently winds through mountains and meadows and crosses mountain streams for more than 469 mi on its way from the north near Waynesboro, Virginia, south to Cherokee, North Carolina, connecting the Great Smoky Mountains and Shenandoah national parks. Beginning at mile 0 at Rockfish Gap, Virginia, the BRP crosses the Virginia–North Carolina border at about mile 217. About 252 mi of the Parkway are in North Carolina. With elevations ranging from 649 to 6,047 feet, and with more than 250 scenic lookout points, it is truly one of the most beautiful drives in North America. Admission to the Parkway is free. No commercial vehicles are allowed, and the entire Parkway is free of billboards, although in a few places residential or commercial development encroaches close to the road. The BRP, which has a maximum speed limit of 45 MPH, is generally open year-round but sections of it, or all of it, close during inclement weather. In winter, sections can be closed for weeks at a time due to snow, and even in good weather fog and clouds occasionally make driving difficult. Maps and information are available at information centers along the highway. Mile markers (MMs) identify points of interest and indicate the distance from the Parkway's starting point in Virginia (MM 0). A new park headquarters and visitor center near Asheville at MM 384 opened in late 2007. It has a "green roof" with plants growing on it. ■TIP→Remember to fill up your gas tank before you get on the BRP. There are no gas stations on the scenic drive, but you'll find stations at intersecting highways near exits. ⊡*Superintendent, Blue Ridge Pkwy., 199 Hemphill Knob Rd., Asheville 28803* ☎*828/298–0398* ⊕*www.nps.gov/blri* ☒*Free.*

★ **Cove Creek Road** (*Old Highway 284*). This drive takes you to one of the most beautiful valleys in the Smokies, and to one of the most interesting destinations. The first 7 mi of Cove Creek Road is a mostly paved, winding two-lane road through a scenic rural valley. Entering the park, the road becomes gravel. ■TIP→Although in the park this is a two-way road, in places it is wide enough only for one vehicle, so you may have to pull over and let the oncoming vehicle pass. At points the curvy road hugs the mountainside, with steep drop-offs, making it unsuitable for large RVs or travel trailers. As you near the Cataloochee Valley, suddenly you're on a nice, paved road again. Follow the paved road, as it is a short cut to the historic old buildings of Cataloochee. (You can also continue on the unpaved Cove Creek Road toward Crosby, TN, and in about 5 mi you can enter Cataloochee from the back side.) Follow the signs for a driving tour of the old houses, barns, churches, a school, and other buildings that are all that remain of the once-thriving Cataloochee community, which at its peak in 1910 had about 1,200 residents. You can stop and walk through most of the buildings. Keep a lookout for elk, wild turkey, deer, and other wildlife here. If you haven't had enough driving for the day, from Cataloochee you can continue on the unpaved Cove Creek Road to Big Creek campground near the North Carolina–Tennessee line, where you can reconnect with I–40 at Exit 451 on the Tennessee side.

Newfound Gap Road (*U.S. 441*). Newfound Gap Road is the busiest road in the park by far, with more than a million vehicles making the 16-mi climb from 2,000-foot elevation near Cherokee to almost a mile high at Newfound Gap (and then down to Gatlinburg on the Tennessee side). It's the only road that goes all the way through the center of the park, and the only fully paved road. While it's not a route to escape from the crowds, the scenery is memorable. If you don't have time to explore the back roads or to go hiking, Newfound Gap Road will give you a flavor of the richness and variety of the Smokies. Unlike other roads in the park, Newfound Gap Road has mile markers; however, the markers run "backwards" (as far as North Carolinians are concerned), starting at 0 at the park boundary near Gatlinburg to 31.1 at the border of the park at the entrance to the Blue Ridge Parkway near Cherokee. Among the sites on the road are: Oconaluftee Visitor Center and Mountain Farm Museum (MM 30.3); Mingus Mill (MM 29.9); Smokemont Campground and Nature Trail (MM 27.2); Web Overlook (MM 17.7), from which there's a good view almost due west of Clingmans Dome; and Newfound Gap (MM 14.7), the start of the 7-mi road to Clingmans Dome.

WHAT TO SEE

HISTORIC SIGHTS

Fodor's Choice ★ **Cataloochee Valley.** This is one of the most memorable and eeriest sites in all of the Smokies. At one time Cataloochee was a community of more than 1,200 people, in some 200 buildings. After the land was taken over in 1934 for the national park, the community dispersed. Although many of the original buildings are now gone, more than a dozen houses, cabins, and barns, two churches, and other structures have been kept up. You can visit the Palmer Methodist Chapel, a one-room schoolhouse, Beach Grove School, and the Woody and Messer homesteads. It's much like Cades Cove on the Tennessee side, but much less visited. On a quiet day you can almost hear the ghosts of the former Cataloochee settlers. You will almost always spot a few elk here, especially in the evening and early morning. Cataloochee is one of the most remote parts of the Smokies reachable by car, via a narrow, winding, gravel road. ⊠ *Cataloochee Community, via U.S. 276 near Maggie Valley, off Exit 20 of I–40, to Cove Creek Rd.*

★ **Mountain Farm Museum.** This museum at the Oconaluftee Visitors Center is perhaps the best re-creation anywhere of a mountain farmstead. The nine farm buildings, all dating from around 1900, were moved here from locations within the park. Besides a furnished two-story log cabin, there is a barn, apple house, corn crib, smokehouse, chicken coop, and other outbuildings. In season, corn, tomatoes, pole beans, squash, and other mountain crops are grown in the garden, and park staff sometimes put on demonstrations of pioneer activities, such as

8

making apple butter and molasses. ✉ *U.S. 441 at Oconaluftee Visitors Center* ☎ *828/497–1904.*

Mingus Mill. In its time, the late 19th century, this was the state-of-the-art in gristmills, the two large grist stones powered by a store-bought turbine rather than a hand-built wheel. You can watch the miller make cornmeal, and even buy a pound of it. ✉ *U.S. 441, 2 mi north of Cherokee* ☎ *828/497 1901* ◷ *Mid-Mar.–late Nov.*

SCENIC STOPS

★ **Andrews Bald.** Getting to Andrews Bald isn't easy. You have to walk the rocky Forney Ridge trail some 1.8 mi one-way, with an elevation gain of almost 600 feet, the equivalent of a 60-story skyscraper. The payoff is several acres of grassy bald at over 5,800 feet, with stunning views of Lake Fontana and the southeastern Smokies. This is one of only two balds in the Smokies (the other is Gregory Bald on the Tennessee side) that the park service keeps clear. ✉ *1.8 mi from the Forney Ridge trailhead parking lot, at the end of Clingmans Dome Rd.*

★ **Clingmans Dome.** At an elevation of more than 6,600 feet, this is the third-highest peak east of the Rockies, only a few feet shorter than the tallest, Mt. Mitchell. Walk up a paved, but steep, ½-mi trail to an observation tower offering 360-degree views from the "top of Old Smoky." Temperatures here are usually 10°F lower than at the entrance to the park near Cherokee. Clingmans Dome Road is closed to vehicular traffic in winter (December–March), but if there's snow on the ground you can put on your snowshoes and hike up to the peak. ✉ *At end of Clingmans Dome Rd., 7 mi from U.S. 441.*

Heintooga Overlook. This is one of the best spots to watch the sunset, with a sweeping view westward of the crest of the Great Smokies. ✉ *Off Heintooga Ridge Rd., at the picnic area, 7 mi from the BRP—the entrance to Heintooga Ridge Rd. is at MM 458.2* ◷ *Closed mid-Oct.–early May.*

Oconaluftee Valley Overlook. From atop the Thomas Divide, just a little below the crest of the Smokies, you can look down and see the winding Newfound Gap Road. This is also a good spot to view sunrise in the Smokies. ✉ *U.S. 441 (Newfound Gap Rd.) at MM 15.4.*

SPORTS AND THE OUTDOORS

FISHING

The North Carolina side of the Smokies has one of the best wild trout fisheries in the East. Deep Creek, Little Cataloochee, and Hazel Creek are streams known to serious anglers all over the country. Often, the best fishing is in higher-elevation streams, in areas that are more difficult to reach. Streams that are easily accessible, such as the Pigeon River, have greater fishing pressure.

HIKING

Great Smoky Mountains National Park has more than 800 mi of hiking trails. Some of the more popular trails are listed in this chapter; more detailed information and maps can be obtained from park visitor centers.

Fishing Rules

To fish in the park you must possess a valid fishing license or permit from either Tennessee or North Carolina; either state license is valid throughout the park and no trout stamp is required. For non-residents, the North Carolina license is the cheaper of the two and can be purchased in nearby towns or online at ⊕ *www.ncwildlife. org.* Kids under 16 don't need a license.

Only artificial flies or lures with a single hook can be used—no live bait. Fishing is permitted from a half hour before official sunrise to a half hour after official sunset. The limit for the combined total of brook, rainbow, or brown trout, or smallmouth bass, must not exceed five fish each day. You may not have more than five fish in your possession, regardless of whether they are fresh, stored in an ice chest, or otherwise preserved. Twenty rock bass may be kept in addition to the above limit.

The size limit is 7 inches for brook, rainbow, brown trout, and smallmouth bass. For rock bass there is no minimum size.

Keep in mind that the park has significant elevation changes and that some summer days, especially at lower elevations, can be hot and humid. ■TIP➜ **Be realistic about your physical condition and abilities. Carry plenty of water and energy-rich foods, like GORP (good old raisins and peanuts), energy bars, and fruit.**

Weather in the park is subject to rapid change. ■TIP➜ **Dress in layers and be prepared for temperature changes, especially snow in winter. Carry rain gear and expect rain at any time.** Be sure to allow plenty of time to complete your hike before dark. As a rule of thumb, when hiking in the Smokies you'll travel only about 1½ mph, so a 10-mi hike will take almost seven hours.

EASY **Deep Creek Waterfalls.** For the effort of a 2.4-mi hike, this trail will reward you with three pretty waterfalls, Tom Branch, Indian Creek, and Juney Whank. Deep Creek also has a picnic area and campground. Tubing on Deep Creek is fun, too. ✉*Trailhead at end of Deep Creek Rd., near Bryson City entrance to park.*

MODERATE **Clingmans Dome Trail.** If you've been driving too long and want some exercise, along with unbeatable views of the Smokies and an ecological lesson, too, take the ½-mi (1-mi round-trip) from the Clingmans Dome parking lot to the observation tower at the top of Clingmans Dome, the highest peak in the Smokies. While short and paved, the trail is fairly steep, and at well over 6,000 feet elevation you'll probably be gasping for air. Most of the fir trees here are dead, killed by the balsam wooly adelgid. ✉*Trail begins at the Clingmans Dome parking lot* ☯*Clingmans Dome Rd. is closed in winter.*

Flat Creek. This is one of the hidden gems among Smokies trails. It's little known, but it's a delightful hike, especially in the summer when this higher-elevation means respite from stifling temperatures. The path stretches through a pretty woodland, with evergreens, birch,

8

rhododendron, and wildflowers. The elevation gain is about 570 feet. The trail is only 2.6 mi if you use a two-car shuttle, one at the trailhead at mile 5.4 of Heintooga Ridge Road, and the other at the Heintooga picnic area; if you don't do a two-car shuttle, you'll have to walk 3.6 mi along Heintooga Ridge Road to your car, but even this is pleasant, with spruce and fir lining the road and little traffic. ⊠ *Trail begins at Flat Creek trailhead at mile 5.4 of Heintooga Ridge Rd.; alternatively, you can begin at the trailhead at Heintooga picnic area, 3.6 mi away* ⊙ *Heintooga Ridge Rd. is closed in winter.*

★ **Little Cataloochee.** No other hike in the Smokies offers a cultural and historic experience like this one. In the early 20th century Cataloochee Cove had the largest population of any place in the Smokies, around 1,200 people. Most of the original structures have been torn down or succumbed to the elements, but a few historic frame buildings remain, such as a log cabin near Davidson Gap at mi 2.6, an apple house at mi 3.3, and a church at mi 4, preserved by park staff. You'll see several of these, along with rock walls and other artifacts, on the Little Cataloochee Trail. The trail is 5.9 mi (one-way) including about 0.8 mi at the beginning on Pretty Hollow Gap Trail. It is best hiked with a two-car shuttle, with one vehicle at the Pretty Hollow Gap trailhead in Cataloochee Valley and the other at the Little Cataloochee trailhead at Old Highway 284 (Cove Creek Road). Including the time it takes to explore the historic buildings and cemeteries, you should allow at least six hours for this hike. ⊠ *The Pretty Hollow Gap trailhead is near Beech Grove School in the Cataloochee Valley.*

> ## THE AT
>
> Each spring about 1,500 hikers set out to conquer the Appalachian Trail (AT), the 2,175-mi grand-daddy of all hikes. Most hike north from Springer Mountain, Georgia, toward Mt. Katahdin, Maine. By the time they get to the Great Smokies, 160 mi from the trailhead in Georgia, about one-half of the hikers will already have dropped out. Typically, only about 400 hikers per year complete the entire AT. Of course, you don't have to hike the whole thing to experience the wonders of the trail; you can get on it for a short hike from Newfound Gap Road on the North Carolina–Tennessee line.

HORSEBACK RIDING

Get back to nature and away from the crowds with a horseback ride through the forest. Guided horseback rides are offered by one park concessionaire stable at Smokemont near Cherokee. Rides are at a walking pace, so they are suitable for even inexperienced riders.

OUTFITTERS   **Smokemont Riding Stable.** The emphasis here is on a family-friendly horseback riding experience, suitable even for novice riders. Choose either the one-hour trail ride or a 2½-hour waterfall ride (departing daily at 9 and noon). Riders must be at least 5 years old and weigh no more than 225 pounds. Smokemont also occasionally offers wagon rides. Check with the stables for dates and times. ⊠ *135 Smokemont Riding Stable Rd. (near MM 27.2), Cherokee* ☎ *828/497–2373* ⊕ *www.smokemontridingstable.com* ⊜ *$20–$48* ⊙ *Late May–Oct., daily 9–5.*

TUBING

On a hot summer's day there's nothing like hitting the water. You can swim or go tubing on Deep Creek near Bryson City. The upper section is a little wild and woolly, with white water flowing from cold mountain springs. The put-in is at the convergence of Indian Creek and Deep Creek where the sign says NO TUBING BEYOND THIS POINT. The lower section of Deep Creek is more suitable for kids. Put-in for this section is at the swimming hole just above the first bridge on the Deep Creek trail.

OUTFIT-
TERS AND
EXPEDITIONS
You can rent an inner tube for tubing on Deep Creek for less than $5 a day at these outfitters, all located near the Deep Creek entrance to the park near Bryson City. **Deep Creek Store & Tubes** (✉ *1840 W. Deep Creek Rd., Bryson City* ☎ *828/488–9665* ⊕ *www.smokymtncampground.com*) rents tubes and sells camping supplies. **Deep Creek Tube Center** (✉ *1090 Deep Creek Rd., Bryson City* ☎ *882/488–6055* ⊕ *www.deepcreekcamping.com/tubing.html*) rents inner tubes and sells creek shoes and other tubing accessories in their camp store.

SPRING WILDFLOWER PILGRIMAGE

Each year in late April, the Great Smoky Mountains National Park hosts the **Spring Wildflower Pilgrimage** (⊕ *www.springwildflowerpilgrimage.org*), which attracts wildflower enthusiasts from all over the country for five days of wildflower and natural history walks, seminars, classes, photography tours, and other events. Instructors include National Park Service staff, along with outside experts. Most activities are at various locations in the park, both on the North Carolina and Tennessee sides, but some are in Gatlinburg or elsewhere outside the park.

8

EDUCATIONAL OFFERINGS

Discover the flora, fauna, and mountain culture of the Smokies with scheduled ranger programs and nature walks.

Interpretive Ranger Programs. The National Park Service sponsors all sorts of orientation activities, such as daily guided hikes and talks. The focus of the programs vary widely, from Earthcaching (like geocaching—a high-tech treasure hunt played with GPS devices—but with an education component), using GPS units loaned by the park, to talks on mountain culture to old-time fiddle and banjo music. Most are free, though a ranger-led hayride costs $8.50. Many of the programs are suitable for older children as well as for adults. For schedules, go to the Oconaluftee Visitor Center and pick up a free copy of *Smokies Guide* newspaper, or check online. ☎ *865/436–1200* ⊕ *www.nps.gov/grsm* 🎫 *Free, $8.50 hayride.*

Junior Ranger Program for Families. Children ages 5 to 12 can take part in these hands-on educational programs. Kids should pick up a Junior Ranger booklet ($3) at Oconaluftee or at other park visitor centers. After they've completed the activities in the booklet, they can stop by a visitor center to talk to a ranger and receive a Junior Ranger badge. Especially during the summer, the park offers many age-appropriate demonstrations, classes, and programs for Junior Rangers, such as

Blacksmithing, Stream Splashin', Geology, Critters and Crawlies, Cherokee Pottery for Kids, and—our favorite—Whose Poop's on Our Boots? ☎*865/436–1200* ⊕*www.nps.gov/grsm/forkids/index.htm* 🎫*$3.*

WHERE TO EAT

There are no restaurants within the park. Picnic areas, however, provide some amenities such as restrooms and pavilions.

PICNIC AREAS

★ **Deep Creek Picnic Area.** Deep Creek offers more than picnicking. You can go tubing (rent a tube for the day for under $5 at nearby tubing centers). Hike about 2 mi to three pretty waterfalls. Go trout fishing. You can even go mountain biking here, as this is one of the few park trails where bikes are allowed. The picnic area, open year-round, has 58 picnic tables, plus a pavilion that seats up to 70. ✉*1912 E. Deep Creek Rd., Bryson City, NC. From downtown Bryson City, follow signs for 3 mi to Deep Creek.*

Fodor's Choice **Heintooga Picnic Area.** This is our favorite developed picnic area in the
★ park. Located at more than a mile high, and set in a stand of spruce and fir, the picnic area has 41 tables. Nearby is Mile High Overlook, which offers one of the most scenic views of the Smokies and is a great place to enjoy the sunset. For birders, this is a good spot to see golden-crowned kinglets, red-breasted nuthatches, and other species that prefer higher elevations. You're almost certain to see the common raven here. Nearby are a campground and trailheads for several good hiking trails including Flat Creek. You can return to Cherokee via an unpaved backroad, Balsam Mountain Road, which is one-way, to Big Cove Road. ✉*Near end of Heintooga Ridge Rd. From Cherokee, take the Blue Ridge Parkway 11 mi to the turnoff for Heintooga Ridge Rd. Follow Heintooga Ridge Rd. about 9 mi to picnic area.*

WHERE TO CAMP

There is no lodging, other than camping, inside the park on the North Carolina side. Camping is permitted only in designated campsites, whether you're in the backcountry or frontcountry. There are five developed campgrounds in North Carolina. Developed campgrounds have restrooms with cold running water and flush toilets, but there are no showers or electrical or water hookups in the park.

$ ⛺ **Balsam Mountain Campground.** If you like a high, cool campground,
Fodor's Choice with a beautiful setting in evergreens, Balsam Mountain will be your
★ favorite campground in the park. It's the highest elevation in the park, at over 5,300 feet. By evening, you may want a campfire even in summer. The 46 campsites—first-come, first served—are best for tents, but small trailers or RVs up to 30 feet can fit in some sites. Most of the 10-x 10-foot tent pads and the picnics tables have been recently replaced, so they're in good shape. Restrooms are clean. For the Smokies' best sunset, go to the nearby Heintooga picnic area and hike a short way to Mile High Overlook. The campground has bear boxes and requires standard food protection policies, but bears are rarely a problem in this

area. Due to its somewhat remote location off the Blue Ridge Parkway, Balsam Mountain Campground is rarely full even on peak summer and fall weekends. Several good hiking trails are nearby, and you can drive or bike the unpaved Balsam Mountain Road, which is one-way from the campground, and Big Cove Road to Cherokee. **Pros:** appealing high-elevation campground, where it's cool even in summer; rarely busy; good hiking and great scenic vistas nearby. **Cons:** a little remote and a moderate drive for supplies and groceries; most campsites don't have views and are a little closer together than you'd like. ⊠*Near end of Heintooga Ridge Rd.* ⊹*From Cherokee, take the Blue Ridge Parkway 11 mi to the turnoff for Heintooga Ridge Rd. Follow Heintooga Ridge Rd. about 9 mi to campground, which is just beyond the picnic area.* ☎*877/444–6777* ⊕*www.recreation.gov* ⇥*46 sites for RVs/trailers up to 30 feet and tents* ♿*Flush toilets, drinking water, bear boxes, fire pits, grills, picnic tables* ⊘*Early May–Oct.*

$$ ⚠ **Deep Creek Campground.** Rollin', rollin', you're rollin' down the river—at least, you're floating on an inner tube down Deep Creek. This campground is near the most popular tubing spot in the Smokies. Officially, the park service doesn't recommend tubing in the streams of the Smokies, due mainly to the risk of injury from slips and slides, but thousands of kids and the young at heart do it at Deep Creek every summer. Commercial businesses near this campground rent tubes all day for $5 or less. There's also swimming in several swimming holes. (Don't confuse this park campground with a similarly named commercial campground just outside the Deep Creek entrance of the park.) Of the 92 first-come, first-served sites here, sites 1–42 are for tents only, and the other sites are for tents and small RVs/trailers up to 26 feet in length. Nearby are several easy to moderate hiking trails, including a short loop a little over 2 mi that takes you to three waterfalls. **Pros:** lots of family tubing and swimming fun on the creek; convenient to the pleasant small town of Bryson City. **Cons:** with several private campgrounds and tube rental businesses, the entrance to the park has a commercial feel. ⊠*1912 East Deep Creek Rd., Bryson City, NC* ⊹*From downtown Bryson City, follow signs for 3 mi to Deep Creek* ☎*877/444–6777* ⊕*www.recreation.gov* ⇥*92 sites for RVs/trailers up to 26 feet and tents* ♿*Flush toilets, drinking water, bear boxes, fire pits, grills, picnic tables, public telephone, swimming creek* ⊘*Early Apr.–Oct.*

$$–$$$ ⚠ **Smokemont Campground.** With 142 sites, Smokemont is the largest campground on the North Carolina side of the park. Some of the campsites are a little jammed up, but the individual sites themselves are spacious. Tent sites have a 13- x 13-foot tent pad, fire ring with cooking grill, and a picnic table with lantern pole. Sites in F loop, open to RVs only, are wooded and more private. Sites F2, 4, 6, 8, 34, 36, 38, 40, 42, 44, and 46 are on the river. In RV areas, generator use is restricted to 8 AM to 8 PM and prohibited altogether in loops A, B, and C from mid-May–October. The Bradley Fork River runs through the campground. There's fishing and tubing (bring your own tubes) in the river, and the campground allows access to the Bradley Fork Trail, located at the top of D loop, which leads to a number of other hiking trails. In summer and fall rangers offer interpretive talks at the campground, and there

8

are mountain music and storytelling programs. The nearby Smokemont Stable offers horseback rides and sells firewood and ice. This campground stays open most of the year, closing only in January, February, and the first few days of March. **Pros:** pleasant, large campground; lots for families and kids to do including tubing, fishing, horseback riding, and hiking; easy access to Cherokee and to sites such as Mingus Mill and Mountain Farm Museum. **Cons:** with so many RVs, you're not exactly in the wilderness. ⊠ *Off U.S. Hwy. 441 (Newfound Gap Rd.), 6 mi north of Cherokee* ☎ *877/444–6777* ⊕ *www.recreation.gov* ⟱ *142 sites for RVs up to 40 feet and trailers up to 35 feet, and tents* ⌂ *Flush toilets, drinking water, bear boxes, pit fires, grills, picnic tables, public telephone, swimming creek* ☉ *Early Mar.–Dec.*

TENNESSEE SIDE

Cades Cove is first among sightseeing spots on the Tennessee side of the park. This broad valley with its preserved old buildings—pioneer homesteads and churches and the Cable Mill—is the most popular destination in the park. It's also one of the best places to see wildlife, including black bears.

Roaring Fork Motor Nature Trail (closed in winter) is a drivable tour that delivers both nature and history.

SCENIC DRIVES

Fodor'sChoice **Cades Cove Loop Road.** This 11-mi loop through Cades Cove is the most
★ popular route in the park and arguably the most scenic part of the entire Smokies. The one-way, one-lane paved road starts 7.3 mi from the Townsend entrance. Stop at the orientation shelter at the start of the loop and pick up a Cades Cove Tour booklet ($1.50). The drive begins with views over wide pastures to the mountains at the crest of the Smokies. Few other places in the Appalachians offer such views across wide valley bottoms with hayfields and wildflower meadows, framed by split-rail fences and surrounded by tall mountains. Along the way, you'll pass three 19th-century churches and many restored houses, log cabins, and barns. All are open for exploration. A highlight of the loop road, about midway, is the Cable Mill area, with a visitor center, working water-powered grist mill, and a restored farmstead. The Cades Cove Loop Road is also an excellent place to see wildlife, including black bears (especially in the late summer and fall), white-tailed deer, and wild turkeys. The road, open year-round, is closed from sunset to sunrise. ■ TIP➜ On Wednesday and Saturday mornings until 10 AM the loop is open only to bicyclists and walkers. On almost any day, you can expect traffic delays, as passing points on the one-way road are few and far between, and if just one vehicle stops, scores of vehicles behind it also have to stop and wait. Allow at least two hours just to drive the loop, longer if you want to stop and explore the historic buildings.

★ **Roaring Fork Motor Nature Trail.** Roaring Fork offers a dramatic counterpoint to Cades Cove Loop Road. Where Cades Cove Loop meanders through a wide open valley, Roaring Fork closes in, with the forest sometimes literally just inches from your car's fender. The one-way, paved road is so narrow in places that RVs, trailers, and buses are not permitted. To get to Roaring Fork, from Parkway (U.S. 441) turn onto Historic Nature Trail at stop light number 8 in Gatlinburg and follow it to the Cherokee Orchard entrance of the park. The 6-mi Roaring Fork Motor Nature Trail starts just beyond the Noah "Bud" Ogle farmstead and the Rainbow Falls trailhead. Stop and pick up a Roaring Fork Auto Tour booklet ($1) at the information shelter. Numbered markers along the route are keyed to 16 stops highlighted in the booklet. Along the road are many opportunities to stop your car and get closer to nature. Among the sites are several old cabins and the Alfred Reagan place, which is painted in the original blue, yellow, and cream, "all three colors that Sears and Roebuck had," according to a story attributed to Mr. Reagan. At one point the roadside is littered with fallen and now decaying chestnut trees that were killed by the chestnut blight in the early part of the 20th century. There are several good hiking trails starting along the road, including Trillium Gap trail that leads to Mt. LeConte. The road follows Roaring Fork Creek a good part of the way, and the finale is a small waterfall called "The Place of a Thousand Drips," right beside the road. Roaring Fork Motor Nature Trail is closed in winter (usually December–March).

WHAT TO SEE

HISTORIC SIGHTS

Fodor'sChoice **Cades Cove.** The Cherokee name for this 6,800-acre valley is Tsiyahi,
★ place of otters. Its English name may have come from a Cherokee chief called Kade, or possibly from the name of the wife of another chief, Abraham of Chilhowee, whose wife was called Kate. Under the terms of the Calhoun Treaty of 1819, the Cherokee forfeited their rights to Cades Cove, and the first white settlers came in the early 1820s. By the middle of the 19th century, well over 100 families lived in the cove, growing corn, wheat, oats, cane, and vegetables. For a while, when government-licensed distilleries were allowed in Tennessee, corn whisky was the major product of the valley, and even after Tennessee went dry in 1876 illegal moonshine was still produced. After the establishment of the park in the 1930s, many of the nearly 200 buildings were torn down to allow the land to revert to its natural state. However, in 1940 the Park Service decided that the human history of the valley was worth preserving. Since then, the bottomlands in the cove have been maintained as open fields and the remaining farmsteads and other structures have been restored to depict life in Cades Cove as it was from around 1825 to 1900. Today, Cades Cove has more historic buildings than any other area in the park. Driving, hiking, or biking the 11-mi Cades Cove Loop Road, you can see three old churches (Methodist, Primitive Baptist, and Missionary Baptist), a working grist mill (Cable Mill), a number of log cabins and houses in a variety of styles, and many outbuildings, including cantilevered barns, which used balanced beams to support large overhangs. ⊠ *Cades Cove Loop Rd.* ☎ *865/436–1200.*

8

Roaring Fork. You can visit several preserved mountain cabins and other buildings in the Roaring Fork area near Gatlinburg. Roaring Fork was settled by Europeans in the 1830s and '40s. The land was rocky and steep and not particularly well suited to farming. At its height around the turn of the 20th century, there were about two dozen families in the area. Most lived a simple, even hardscrabble existence, trying to scrape out a living from the rough mountain land. The Noah "Bud" Ogle self-guided nature trail, on Orchard Road just before entering the one-way Roaring Fork Motor Nature Trail, offers a walking tour of an authentic mountain farmstead and surrounding hardwood forest. Highlights include a log cabin, barn, streamside tub mill, and a wooden flume system to bring water to the farm. Among historic structures on the Motor Nature Trail, all open for you to explore, are the Jim Bales cabin, the Ephraim Bales cabin, and the Alfred Reagan house, one of the more "upscale" residences at Roaring Fork. ⊠ *Orchard Rd. and Roaring Fork Motor Nature Trail* ☎ *865/436–1200.*

SCENIC STOPS

★ **Chimney Tops Overlook.** From any of the three overlooks grouped together on Newfound Gap Road, you'll have a good view of the Chimney Tops—twin peaks that cap 2,000-foot-high cliffs. You also see hundreds of dead fir and spruce trees, along with some dead hemlocks, victims of woolly adelgids and air pollution. ⊠ *MM 7.1, Newfound Gap Rd. (U.S. 441).*

★ **Dan Lawson Cabin.** From many points along the 11-mi, one-way Cades Cove Loop Road, you'll enjoy iconic views of the broad Cades Cove valley. The Park Service keeps hayfields and pastures cleared, so you can see how the valley may have looked in the late 19th century when it was farmed by more than 100 families. Typical is the view across the valley from the front porch of the Dan Lawson cabin, the original portion of which was built in 1856. ⊠ *6.6 mi from the beginning of Cades Cove Loop Rd.*

Gregory Bald. From almost 5,000 feet on Gregory Bald, you have a breathtaking view of Cades Cove and Rich Mountain to the north, and the Nantahala and Yellow Creek mountains to the south. You can also see Fontana Lake to the southeast. Many hybrid rhododendrons grow on and around the bald. Gregory Bald is one of only two balds in the Smokies that are being kept cleared of tree growth by the Park Service. This is a view that just a few thousand people a year will see, as it's reachable only by a hike of more than 5 mi. ⊹ *Hike the Gregory Ridge Trail (5.5 mi) from Cades Cove.*

SPORTS AND THE OUTDOORS

BIKING

★ **Cades Cove.** Arguably the best place to bike, the 11-mi loop road is mostly level and being on a bike allows you to get around traffic backups. However, traffic can be heavy, especially on weekends in summer and fall, and the road is narrow. ■ TIP➔ **The best time to bike the Cove is from mid-May to mid-September on Wednesday and Saturday mornings until 10 AM when it is closed to motor vehicles.** Bicycles and helmets can be rented ($20 per day) in summer and fall at an annex behind Cades Cove Campground Store (⊠ *Cades Cove Campground* ☎ *865/448–9034*).

Gatlinburg Trail. This is the only hiking trail on the Tennessee side where bikes are permitted. The trail travels 1.9 mi (one-way) from the Sugarlands Visitor Center to the outskirts of Gatlinburg. Pets on leashes are also allowed on this trail.

FISHING

There are over 200 mi of wild trout streams on the Tennessee side of the park. Trout streams are open to fishing year-round. Among the best trout streams on the Tennessee side are Little River, Abrams Creek, and Little Pigeon River.

HIKING

EASY **Elkmont Nature Trail.** This 1-mi loop is good for families, especially if you're camping at Elkmont. Pick up a self-guided brochure (50¢) at the start of the trail. ⊠ *Near Elkmont campground.*

Laurel Falls. Mostly paved, this trail is easy except for the last .75 mi, which is moderate. It takes you past a series of cascades to a 60-foot waterfall and a stand of old-growth forest. The trail is extremely popular in summer and on weekends almost anytime (trolleys from Gatlinburg stop here), so don't expect solitude. ■ **TIP→ The 1.3-mi paved trail to the falls is wheelchair accessible.** Wooden posts mark every tenth of a mile and the total round-trip hike is 4.1 mi. ⊠ *Trailhead is on the west side of Little River Rd. between Sugarlands Visitor Center and Elkmont campground, about 3.9 mi west of Sugarlands.*

Noah "Bud" Ogle Nature Trail. Settlers Noah "Bud" Ogle and his wife, ★ Cindy, built a cabin and started farming here in 1879. Although this is more of a nature walk than a hike, it offers a lot in a .75-mi loop. You'll see the Ogle Tub Mill on LeConte Creek, lots of wildflowers, and the Ogle cabin and barn, which you can explore. It's a fine trail for families with kids. ⊠ *Cherokee Orchard Rd., just before entering the Roaring Fork Motor Nature Trail.*

MODERATE **Abrams Falls.** This 5-mi round-trip trail is one of the most popular in ★ the Smokies, in part due to the trailhead location at Cades Cove, which gets more than 2 million visitors a year. Beginning at the wooden bridge over Abrams Creek, the trail first goes along a pleasant course through rhododendron. It becomes somewhat steep at a couple of points, especially near Arbutus Ridge. The path then leads above Abrams Falls and down to Wilson Creek. Though only about 20 feet high, the falls are beautiful, with a good volume of water and a broad pool below. ⊠ *For trailhead, park in the large parking lot on an unpaved side road between signposts 10 and 11 on Cades Cove Loop Rd.*

Fodor's Choice **Alum Cave Bluffs.** One of the best and most popular hikes, the fairly short ★ 2.3-mi one-way hike (4.6 mi round-trip) to Alum Cave Bluffs contains some of the most interesting geological formations in the Smokies. Arch Rock, about 1.3 mi in, is a natural arch created by millions of years of freezing and thawing. At the end of the trail, at mi 2.3, are a steep set of stairs which lead to Alum Cave Bluffs, a large overhanging rock ledge, or bluff. The name comes from deposits of alum, a chemical compound formerly used in a variety of industrial processes including dyeing. This very well-known trail does not offer much solitude, especially on weekends. From the bluffs you can continue on another 2.8 mi and reach Mt. LeConte, passing awe-inspiring mountain vistas. This additional section of the trail is difficult and steep. Alum Cave Bluffs is the shortest of five trail routes to LeConte Lodge, but it is the steepest, with an elevation gain of over 2,700 feet. The elevation gain to Alum Cave is only about 1,125 feet. ⊠ *Trailhead is well-marked, with a large parking lot on the east side of Newfound Gap Rd. at MM 10.4.*

★ **Appalachian Trail at Newfound Gap.** For those who want to say they hiked part of the AT, this section is a great place to start; it's easy to get to and not too steep. From Newfound Gap to Indian Gap the trail goes 1.7 mi through spruce-fir high-elevation forest, and in late spring and summer there are quite a few wildflowers along the trail. The total round-trip distance is 3.4 mi. *Park at Newfound Gap parking lot and cross Newfound Gap Rd. (U.S. 441) to the AT trailhead.*

Trillium Gap Trail to Grotto Falls. Grotto Falls is the only waterfall in the park that you can walk behind. The Trillium Gap trail, off of the Roaring Fork Motor Nature Trail, which leads to Grotto Falls, is primarily through a hemlock forest. With an easy slope and only 1.3 mi long, this trail is suitable for novice hikers. The total round-trip distance is 2.6 mi. The Motor Nature Trail is closed in winter. ⊠ *Take the Roaring Fork Motor Nature Trail to stop number 5 on the auto tour and the trailhead for Trillium Gap trail.*

HORSEBACK RIDING

Three park concession stables located on the Tennessee side—Cades Cove, Sugarlands, and Smoky Mountain Riding Stables near Gatlinburg—offer guided horseback rides at $20 to $25 an hour. Weight limit for riders is generally 225 pounds and reservations are not available except for large groups.

OUTFITTERS **Cades Cove Riding Stables** (⊠ *Cades Cove Campground* ☎ *865/448–6286* ☾ *Mar.–Oct.*) offers carriage rides and hayrides in addition to horseback riding.

Smoky Mountain Riding Stables (⊠ *U.S. 321, Gatlinburg, TN* ☎ *865/436–5634* ⊕ *www.smokymountainridingstables.com* ☾ *Mid-Mar.–late Nov.*) has been in business for 20 years and has 40 trained horses.

A mile from the park's Gatlinburg entrance, near Sugarlands Visitor Center, **Sugarlands Riding Stables** (⊠ *Sugarlands Visitor Center* ☎ *865/436–3535 Mar.–Oct.*) offers horseback rides through the park.

TUBING

☾ Little River is the most popular tubing river on the west side of the Smokies with mostly flat water (Class I), and a few mild Class II rapids.

OUTFITTERS **River Rage** (⊠ *8303 Hwy. 73, Townsend, TN* ☎ *865/448–8000* ⊕ *www.river-ragetubing.com*) has inner tubes available for rent on the Little River, a go-kart track, and a barbecue restaurant next door.

The **River Rat** (⊠ *205 Wears Valley Rd., Townsend, TN* ☎ *865/448–8888* ⊕ *www.smokymtnriverrat.com*) offers tubing and kayaking on the Little River and white-water rafting on the Pigeon River.

WHERE TO EAT

¢ **✗Cades Cove Camp Store Snack Bar.** The only eating establishment in the
AMERICAN park is a little snack bar inside the Cades Cove camp store. Here, you
can buy hot dogs, pizza, sandwiches, soup, soft serve ice cream, and
other snacks. Breakfast items include coffee and bagels. The camp store,
about the size of a small convenience store, also sells canned pork 'n
beans, s'more fixings, soft drinks, chips, and other junk food. Firewood
is also sold here and you can rent bicycles. ⊠*Cades Cove Campground*
☎*865/436–1200* ⊕*www.nps.gov/grsm* ⊟*MC, V.*

PICNIC AREAS

Fodor'sChoice **Chimneys Picnic Area.** Chimneys, just off Newfound Gap Road and a little
★ over 6 mi from the Sugarlands Visitor Center, may be the most popular
picnic area in the park. Along both sides of a well-shaded loop road
through the area are 89 picnic tables with grills. Some are wheelchair
accessible. The prime spots along the stream that runs through the site
fill up first. Huge boulders in the stream make for a striking view from
your table. Potable water and flush toilets are available. ⊠*Newfound
Gap Rd. (U.S 441), MM 6.2* ☉*Sept.–Apr., daily dawn–dusk; May–
Aug., daily dawn–8.*

Metcalf Bottoms Picnic Area. This large, 165-table picnic area is midway
between Sugarlands Visitor Center and Cades Cove. The Little River
is nearby, where you can fish or take a cooling dip. Metcalf Bottoms
has restrooms with flush toilets, potable water, and a 70-seat pavilion
(open March–October) that can be reserved in advance for $20. Two
easy hiking trails, Metcalf Bottoms and Little Brier, begin at the picnic
area. ⊠*Off Little River Rd. about 11 mi west of Gatlinburg.*

WHERE TO STAY

Fodor'sChoice ⌁**LeConte Lodge.** Set at 6,360 feet near the summit of Mt. LeConte, this
★ hike-in lodge is remote, rustic, and remarkable. It is not, however, luxurious. Seven small, rough-hewn wood cabins and three group sleeping
rooms have double bunk beds and propane heaters. There is no electricity; lighting is by kerosene lamps. There is also no running water;
you bathe in a washbasin or with a bucket (bring your own washcloth
and hand towel). Shared bathrooms do have flush toilets. The appeal of
LeConte Lodge is in the mountaintop setting, taking in the views from
your deck rocking chair and star gazing at night—you can see the Milky
Way, meteor showers, and, starting in the early fall, the northern lights.
At this elevation, the temperature has never reached 80°F, mornings can
be frosty even in June, and spring and fall snows are not uncommon. A
hearty breakfast and dinner are included in the $110 per person rate,
served family-style in a rustic dining room. Wine with dinner—a bot-
tomless glass—is available for $9 per person. There is no road access to
the lodge; the only way in is by foot, up one of five trails, none of which
is short or easy. The 6.5-mi Trillium Gap trail is probably the easiest
trail to the lodge as it is not as steep as the other trails. The Alum Cave
Bluffs trail is the shortest trail to the lodge, but it is fairly steep. If you're
in good condition, you may be able to do the Alum Cave Bluffs trail in

four hours. Other trails take up to six hours or longer, so get an early start. You can prove you've been to the lodge by purchasing a LeConte Lodge T-shirt, sold only at the lodge. Lodge supplies are brought in by llama, up the Trillium Gap trail, and once a year by helicopter. Pack your backpack lightly and remember a flashlight, rain gear, layered clothing, sturdy shoes, snacks, water for your hike, and personal items. ■ TIP→ Bring cash for purchases and tips, as credit cards are not accepted at the lodge itself (though they are accepted for room reservations). The lodge typically begins booking reservations for the following year's season (late March to late November) on October 1 of the year before. **Pros:** unique setting high on Mt. LeConte; a true escape from civilization; a special experience available only to a few. **Cons:** books up far in advance; hike-in access only; simplest of accommodations with few modern conveniences. ⊠ *Mt. LeConte* ⌖ *250 Apple Valley Rd., Sevierville, TN* ☎ *865/429–5704* 🖷 *865/774–0045* ⊕ *www.lecontelodge.com* ↪ *7 cabins, 3 group sleeping rooms, all with shared bath* ⚐ *In-room: no phone, no TV, no a/c. In-hotel: restaurant, no-smoking rooms* ⊟ *AE, D, MC, V* �’⦿❘ *MAP* ☉ *Open late Mar.–late Nov.*

WHERE TO CAMP

$$–$$$ ⛺ **Cades Cove Campground.** This is one of the largest campgrounds in
ⵠ the Smokies, the one with the most services on-site, and the only one in the park open year-round. It has a small general store with a snack bar, bike rentals, horse stables, hayrides, a small amphitheater, picnic area, and an RV dump station. Located near the entrance to the Cades Cove loop, the most visited destination in the park, this is a popular campground and often fills up in summer and fall. It is one of only three (the others are Smokemont and Elkmont) that offers wheelchair-accessible campsites and restrooms. **Pros:** convenient to beautiful Cades Cove; plenty of services and amenities on-site. **Cons:** overrun at peak times; you'll see (and perhaps hear) your neighbors; hot and humid in summer. ⊠ *10042 Campground Dr., approx. 9 mi from Townsend* ☎ *877/444–6777* ⊕ *www.recreation.gov* ↪ *159 tent or RV/trailer (up to 40 feet) sites* ⚏ *Reservations essential* ⚐ *Flush toilets, drinking water, bear boxes, fire pits, grills, picnic tables, food service, general store, public telephone, creek* ☉ *Year-round.*

$$–$$$ ⛺ **Elkmont Campground.** Elkmont is the best place to see the synchronous
ⵠ fireflies *(Photinus carolinus)* blink in unison in early June. Little River
★ trail is a good viewing spot, but you may not be alone as Gatlinburg runs shuttle trolleys to Elkmont during this time. Easy hiking trails and the ability to wade, tube (bring your own inner tubes), fish, and swim in Little River, which runs through the campground, make it ideal for kids. Also near the campground are a number of old summer cottages formerly owned by wealthy Tennessee families. This resort community was placed on the National Registry of Historic Places in 1994. The Park Service has been stabilizing and restoring several of these homes, but they currently are not open to visitors. ■ TIP→ The best campsites are along the stream, especially B2–10 and C1–3, D1, 3, 4, and 6, and E1, 3, 5, 7, and 9. Loops C, D, E, F, G, H, J, and K all have a lot of RV sites. The camp store sells ice, firewood, and a few camping supplies. Even though it is the

largest campground in the Smokies, it is often fully booked during peak summer, fall color, and firefly weekends. There are wheelchair-accessible campsites and restrooms. **Pros:** attractive riverside setting; nice spot for families; great place to see the fireflies. **Cons:** a large campground overrun with RVs at times; best spots by river book up early. ⊠*434 Elkmont Rd., 8 mi from Gatlinburg. From Gatlinburg, take Newfound Gap Rd. (U.S. 441) South into the park; turn right at Sugarlands Visitor Center; go 4½ mi to the Elkmont entrance and turn left at the Elkmont Campground sign; go 1.5 mi to the campground office* ☎*877/444–6777* ⌦*Reservations essential* ⊕*www.recreation.gov* ⟳*220 tent, RV (up to 35 feet), and trailer (up to 32 feet) sites* ♿*Flush toilets, drinking water, bear boxes, fire pits, grills, picnic tables, general store, public telephone, dump station, swimming (creek)* ♥*Early Mar.–Oct.*

WHAT'S NEARBY IN NORTH CAROLINA

Whether you're looking for a hot meal and a comfy bed after days of camping out or just want some "unnatural" diversion, these small towns have everything from big casinos to quaint potteries to keep you entertained.

CHEROKEE

178 mi east of Charlotte; 51 mi west of Asheville; 2 mi from entrance to Great Smoky Mountains National Park.

The 56,000-acre Cherokee reservation is known as the Qualla Boundary, and the town of Cherokee is its capital. Truth be told, there are two Cherokees. There's the Cherokee with the sometimes tacky pop culture, designed to appeal to the masses of tourists, many of whom are visiting nearby Great Smoky Mountains National Park or have come to gamble at the massive Harrah's casino (the largest private employer in the region). But there's another Cherokee that's a window onto the rich heritage of the tribe's Eastern Band. Although now relatively small in number—tribal enrollment is 12,500—these Cherokee and their ancestors have been responsible for keeping alive the Cherokee culture. They are the descendants of those who hid in the Great Smoky Mountains to avoid the Trail of Tears, the forced removal of the Cherokee Nation to Oklahoma in the 19th century. They are survivors, extremely attached to the hiking, swimming, trout fishing, and natural beauty of their ancestral homeland. The reservation is dry, with no alcohol sales anywhere, even at the casino. This also means that there are few upscale restaurants in the area (since they depend on wine and cocktail sales for much of their profits), just fast-food and mom-and-pop places.

GETTING HERE AND AROUND
The Blue Ridge Parkway's southern terminus is at Cherokee, and the Parkway is by far the most beautiful route to Cherokee and to Great Smoky Mountains National Park. A faster option is U.S. 23 and U.S. 74/U.S. 441 connecting Cherokee with I–40 from Asheville or from Franklin in the south. The least pleasant route is U.S. 19 from I–40, a mostly two-lane road pocked with touristy roadside shops.

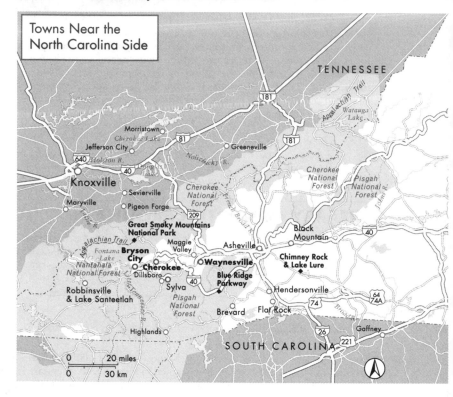

Towns Near the
North Carolina Side

ESSENTIALS

Visitor Information Cherokee Visitors Center (✉ *U.S. 441 Business* ☎ *828/497–9195 or 800/438–1601* ⊕ *www.cherokee-nc.com*).

EXPLORING

The **Museum of the Cherokee Indian,** with displays and artifacts that cover 12,000 years, is one of the best Native American museums in the United States. Computer-generated images, lasers, specialty lighting, and sound effects help re-create events in the history of the Cherokee: for example, you'll see children stop to play a butter-bean game while adults shiver along the snowy Trail of Tears. The museum has an art gallery, a gift shop, and an outdoor living exhibit of Cherokee life in the 15th century. ✉ *U.S. 441 at Drama Rd.* ⌂ *Box 1599* ☎ *828/497–3481* ⊕ *www. cherokeemuseum.org* ☞ *$9* ⊙ *June–Aug., Mon.–Sat. 9–8, Sun. 9–5; Sept.–May, daily 9–5.*

☾ At the historically accurate, re-created **Oconaluftee Indian Village** guides
★ in native costumes will lead you through a village of 225 years ago while others demonstrate traditional skills such as weaving, pottery, canoe construction, and hunting techniques. ✉ *U.S. 441 at Drama Rd.* ☎ *828/497–2315* ⊕ *www.oconalufteevillage.com* ☞ *$15* ⊙ *Mid-May– mid-Oct., daily 9:30–5:30.*

☺ Every mountain county has significant deposits of gems and minerals, and at the **Smoky Mountain Gold and Ruby Mine,** on the Qualla Boundary, you can search for gems such as aquamarines. Children love panning precisely because it can be wet and messy. Here they're guaranteed a find. Gem ore can be purchased, too, for $4–$10 per bag: gold ore costs $5 per bag. ✉*U.S. 441 N* ☎*828/497–6574* ☜*$4–$10, depending on gems* ☉*Mar.–Nov., daily 10–6.*

WHERE TO STAY

$–$$ 🖵**Fairfield Inn & Suites.** This three-story chain motel is directly across from Harrah's Casino, so you can walk to the casino without worrying about parking. Rooms here are typical of the Fairfield Inn chain—comfortable and clean but not deluxe. **Pros:** convenient to casino; usual chain motel amenities. **Cons:** like all Fairfield motels. ✉*568 Painttown Rd.* ☎*828/497–0400* 🖷*828/497–4242* ⊕*www.marriott.com* ➪*96 rooms, 4 suites* ⅄*In-room: refrigerator, Wi-Fi. In-hotel: pool, laundry facilities, laundry service, parking (free), no-smoking rooms* ⊟*AE, D, DC, MC, V* ⑩*CP.*

$$$–$$$$ 🖵**Harrah's Cherokee Casino Hotel.** The 15-story hotel, which opened in 2002 and doubled in size with an addition in 2005, towers over the mom-and-pop motels nearby and the casino next door, to which it is umbilically attached via a series of escalators and walkways. The lobby and other public areas incorporate traditional Cherokee art themes. Rooms are large, about 500 square feet, and have 32-inch TVs. For high-rollers, there are suites on the top floor. The Selu Garden Café in the hotel and the Seven Sisters restaurant in the casino are handy after a day of playing the slots. Restaurants and the casino do not offer alcoholic drinks, as the sale of alcohol is prohibited on the Cherokee reservation. A $650 million expansion that will bring the total of hotel rooms here to over 1,000 and also add new restaurants, shops, and a spa, and increase the number of video gaming machines to over 5,000 is expected to be completed by 2012. **Pros:** supersized hotel; convenient to casino. **Cons:** hotel often fully booked due to comps and deals for gamblers; no booze. ✉*U.S. 19 at U.S. 441 Business* ☎*800/427–7247 or 828/497–7777* ⊕*www.harrahs.com* ➪*576 rooms* ⅄*In-room: refrigerator (some), Wi-Fi. In-hotel: 5 restaurants, pool, gym, no-smoking rooms* ⊟*AE, D, DC, MC, V* ⑩*EP.*

SHOPPING

The **Qualla Arts and Crafts Mutual** (✉*U.S. 441 at Drama Rd.* ☎*828/497–3103*), across the street from the Museum of the Cherokee Indian, is a cooperative that displays and sells items created by 300 Cherokee craftspeople. The store has a large selection of high-quality baskets, masks, and wood carvings, which can cost hundreds of dollars.

BRYSON CITY

65 mi east of Asheville; 11 mi southwest of Cherokee.

Bryson City is a little mountain town on the Nantahala River, one of the lesser-known gateways to the Great Smokies. The town's most striking feature is a city hall with a four-sided clock. Since becoming the depot and headquarters of the Great Smoky Mountains Railroad, the downtown shopping area has been rejuvenated, mostly with gift shops and ice-cream stands.

GETTING HERE AND AROUND

Bryson City is a 15-minute drive from Cherokee on U.S. 19. Near Bryson City are two entrances to the Great Smokies.

EXPLORING

The popular train rides of the **Great Smoky Mountains Railroad** include excursions from Bryson City, and several special trips. Diesel-electric or steam locomotives go along the Nantahala Gorge. Open-sided cars or standard coaches are ideal for picture taking as the mountain scenery glides by. Some rides include a meal: on some Friday evenings there's a mystery theater train with dinner, and on Saturdays a gourmet dinner train. ✉ *225 Everett St., Stes. G & H, Bryson City* ☎ *800/872–4681* ⊕ *www.gsmr.com* 💲 *$34–$53 for standard seating; upgraded seating $12–$20 additional; rates plus $3 parking fee; most tickets include admission to the Smoky Mountain Model Railroad Museum.*

The most popular river in western North Carolina for rafting and kayaking is **Nantahala River,** which races through the scenic Nantahala Gorge, a 1,600-foot-deep gorge that begins about 13 mi west of Bryson City on U.S. 19. Class III and Class IV rapids (Class V are the most dangerous) make for a thrilling ride. Several outfitters run river trips or rent equipment. Happily, the severe drought that reduced water flow on many other rivers in the region doesn't affect the Nantahala, due to daily dam releases. ■TIP➔ **At several points along the river you can park your car and watch rafters run the rapids—on a summer day you'll see hundreds of rafts and kayaks going by.** ✉ *U.S. 19, beginning 13 mi west of Bryson City.*

WHERE TO EAT AND STAY

$

AMERICAN

✕ **River's End at Nantahala Outdoor Center.** The casual riverbank setting and high-energy atmosphere at NOC's eatery draws lots of hungry people just returned from an invigorating day of rafting. There are salads, soups, and sandwiches during the day and fancier fixin's in the evening. The chili's a winner—there are black- and white-bean versions ($5.25 for a bowl). For more upscale fare at NOC, try Relia's Garden, which specializes in steak and trout (closed Monday–Wednesday). ✉ *13077 Hwy. 19 W* ☎ *828/488–2176* ▭ *MC, V* ⊘ *Closed Nov.–Mar.*

$–$$

📷 **Fryemont Inn.** An institution in Bryson City for eight decades, the Fryemont Inn is on the National Register of Historic Places. The lodge exterior is bark, rooms in the main lodge are paneled in real chestnut, and the lobby has a fireplace big enough for 8-foot logs. If you need more luxury, choose one of the suites with fireplaces and air-conditioning. The restaurant ($$–$$$), serving Southern fare, is open to the public for breakfast and dinner. **Pros:** historic inn; comfortably rustic; charming restaurant with wholesome, simple food. **Cons:** rooms in main lodge are far from posh; can be warm on a summer day; no swimming pool. ✉ *Freymont St., Box 459, Bryson City* ☎ *828/488–2159 or 800/845–4879* ⊕ *www.fryemontinn.com* 🛏 *37 rooms, 3 suites, 1 cabin* 👪 *In-room: no a/c (some), no phone, no TV (some). In-hotel: restaurant, pool* ▭ *D, MC, V* ⊘ *No lunch* ⊠ *MAP.*

$–$$ ⊞**Hemlock Inn.** This folksy, friendly mountain inn on 50 acres above Bryson City is the kind of place where you can rock, doze, and play Scrabble. Even if you're not a guest at the inn, you can make a reservation for dinner Monday through Saturday and for lunch on Sunday. The all-you-can-eat meals (breakfast included in the rates, dinner packages available) are prepared with regional foods and served family-style on lazy Susans at big round tables. Fly-fishing and river rafting–kayaking and other packages are available. **Pros:** unpretentious, family-oriented inn; delicious Southern-style food; like a visit to grandma's. **Cons:** no modern conveniences like Wi-Fi, TVs, or in-room phones; family-style meals may not suit everyone; no alcohol served; no swimming pool. ⊠*Galbraith Creek Rd.* ⌂*Box 2350* ✛*1 mi north of U.S. 19* ☎*828/488–2885* ⊕*www.hemlockinn.com* ⇆*22 rooms, 3 cottages* ⚅*In-room: no a/c, no phone, no TV. In-hotel: restaurant* ▤*D, MC, V* ☯ ⑩*BP.*

SPORTS AND THE OUTDOORS

RAFTING AND KAYAKING **Nantahala Outdoor Center (NOC)** (⌂*13077 Hwy. 19 W* ☎*800/232–7238* ⊕*www.noc.com*) guides more than 30,000 rafters every year on the Nantahala and eight other rivers: the Chattooga, Cheoah, FrenchBroad, Nolichucky, Ocoee, Gauley, New, and Pigeon. Due to the severe regional drought in 2007–2008, the French Broad River was at its lowest flow level in more than 100 years, and as of this writing most rafting trips on the French Broad have been discontinued. ■**TIP➜ The Cheoah River has reopened for rafting and kayaking, after being dammed and closed for years, but only for about 17 days a year. Serious rafters and kayakers looking for a challenge on Class IV/IV+ river should consider the Cheoah.** NOC also rents kayaks, ducks, and other equipment. The NOC complex on the Nantahala River is virtually a tourist attraction itself, especially for young people, with three restaurants, cabin and campground rentals, an inn, a stop for the Great Smokies Railroad, and an outdoor store.

WAYNESVILLE

17 mi east of Cherokee on U.S. 19.

This is where the Blue Ridge Parkway meets the Great Smokies. Waynesville is the seat of Haywood County. About 40% of the county is occupied by Great Smoky Mountains National Park, Pisgah National Forest, and the Harmon Den Wildlife Refuge. The town of Waynesville is a rival of Blowing Rock and Highlands as a summer and vacation-home retreat for the well-to-do, though the atmosphere here is a bit more countrified. A Ramp Festival, celebrating the smelly local cousin of the onion, is held in Waynesville annually in early May. New B&Bs are springing up like wildflowers. Local restaurants celebrated in 2008, when the town voted to allow liquor by the drink. Ghost Town, a Wild West theme park popular with kids, is nearby, in Maggie Valley.

Cold Mountain, the vivid best-selling novel by Charles Frazier, has made a destination out of the real **Cold Mountain.** About 15 mi from Waynesville in the Shining Rock Wilderness Area of Pisgah National Forest, the 6,030-foot rise had long stood in relative anonymity. But with the success of Frazier's book, people want to see the region that Inman and Ada, the book's Civil War–era protagonists, called home.

8

For a view of the splendid mass stop at any of a number of overlooks off the Blue Ridge Parkway. Try the Cold Mountain Parking Overlook, just past mile marker 411.9; the Wagon Road Gap parking area, at mile marker 412.2; or the Water-rock Knob Interpretative Station, at mile marker 451.2. You can climb the mountain, but beware, as the hike to the summit is strenuous. No campfires are allowed in Shining Rock, so you'll need a stove if you wish to cook. Inform the ranger station (☎ 828/877–3350) if you plan to hike or camp.

WORD OF MOUTH

"Just returned from two nights at The Swag and feel we have found heaven in North Carolina. It is a wonderful, peaceful, soulful location. The physical setting is gorgeous on 250 acres adjacent to the Great Smoky Mountains National Park—wonderful hiking with trail maps and suggestions. The innkeepers are warm and welcoming—making an effort to meet each guest and ask about their stay. The rooms are very well equipped, with great attention to detail. You even get a take-home gift—a personalized walking stick. We will be returning." —RagtopGirl

☺ **Ghost Town in the Sky** is a Wild West theme park on top of a mountain. Originally opened in 1961, it closed in 2002 but came back to life in 2007 under new ownership. You ride up 3,300 feet in a chairlift or an inclined railway. At the top you're greeted by gunslingers who stage O.K. Corral–style gunfights. One cowhand says he's been in more than 50,000 gunfights at Ghost Town. There are 40 replica buildings meant to represent an 1880s Western town. Also at the park are thrill rides, including the new "Cliff Hanger" roller coaster. ⊠ *16 Fie Top Rd., Maggie Valley* ☎ *828/926–1140* ⊕ *www.ghosttowninthesky.com* ⬚ *$30 ($24 if purchased online)* ⊙ *Early May, Fri.–Sun. 10–6; mid-May–early Sept., daily 10–6; and early Sept.–early Nov., Fri.–Sun. 10–6.*

The **Museum of North Carolina Handicrafts,** in the Shelton House (circa 1875), has an exhibit of 19th-century heritage crafts. ⊠ *307 Shelton St.* ☎ *828/452–1551* ⬚ *$5* ⊙ *May–Oct., Tues.–Fri. 10–4.*

WHERE TO EAT AND STAY

$$$–$$$$

ARGENTINE

✕ **Lomo Grill.** Waynesville's best restaurant combines Mediterranean-style ingredients with the chef-owner's Argentine background. The grilled steaks are perfectly prepared and served with delicately cooked, fresh local vegetables. Many of the fruits and vegetables are grown in the chef's garden. In a 1920s downtown space with a high, crimson-red ceiling, Lomo Grill has superlative servers, efficient and friendly without being obsequious. Try the key lime pie—it's the best in the mountains. ⊠ *44 Church St.* ☎ *828/452–5222* ⊟ *AE, D, DC, MC, V* ⊙ *Closed Sun. and Mon. No lunch.*

$$$$

★

⬚ **The Swag Country Inn.** This rustic inn sits at 5,000 feet, high atop the Cataloochee Divide overlooking a deep depression in otherwise high ground. Its 250 wooded acres share a border with Great Smoky Mountains National Park. Guest rooms and cabins were assembled from six authentic log structures and transported here. All have exposed beams and wood floors and are furnished with early American crafts. New beds and other upgrades were added in 2008. Dinners here are social events, with hors d'oeuvres, conversation, and an option of family-style or individual seating. There's a two-night minimum stay; bring your own beverages, as the inn is in a dry county. **Pros:** small inn with personality; fabulous location on a nearly mile-high mountaintop; delicious meals included. **Cons:** remote; expensive; no TV. ⊠ *2300 Swag Rd.* ☎ *828/926–0430 or 800/789–7672* ⊕ *www.theswag.com* ⊅ *16 rooms, 3 cabins* ⅁ *In-room: no TV, no air-conditioning. In-hotel: restaurant, no-smoking rooms* ⊟ *AE, D, MC, V* ⊙ *Closed Nov.–Mar.* ⦿ *FAP.*

WHAT'S NEARBY IN TENNESSEE

PIGEON FORGE

2.5 mi southeast of Knoxville.

Pigeon Forge, is best known as the home of mountain native Dolly Parton's namesake theme park, Dollywood. In recent years, it has exploded with enough heavy-duty outlet shopping and kids' entertainment—from indoor skydiving simulators to laser tag—to keep families busy for a few days. But the intentionally cornpone image can become wearing, and it fails to reflect the quiet folksiness of the Appalachian communities scattered throughout these parts. Pigeon Forge has more than 200 outlet specialty stores, crafts shops, country hoedown emporiums, and kid-friendly attractions that line the main thoroughfare for several miles.

GETTING HERE AND AROUND

Pigeon Forge begins at the southern border of Sevierville and stretches for about 5 mi along U.S. 441, a five-lane parkway that is an endless row of tourist attractions, franchise restaurants, and motels before abruptly ending and narrowing back into a wooded road running alongside the Little Pigeon River. The entrance to Great Smoky Mountains National Park is about 8 mi south of the southern limits of Pigeon Forge.

ESSENTIALS

Visitor Information Pigeon Forge Information Center (⊠ *3107 Pkwy., Pigeon Forge, TN*). **Pigeon Forge Department of Tourism** (⊠ *2450 Pkwy., Pigeon Forge, TN*). **Pigeon Forge Welcome Center** (⊠ *1950 Pkwy., Pigeon Forge, TN* ☎ *865/453–8574 or 800/251–9100* ⊕ *www.mypigeonforge.com*).

EXPLORING

☺ **Dollywood,** singer Dolly Parton's popular theme park, embodies the
★ country superstar's own flamboyance—plenty of Hollywood flash mixed with simple country charm that you either love or hate. This endeavor brings to life the folklore, fun, food, and music of the Great Smokies, which inspired many of Parton's early songs. In a re-created 1880 mountain village, scores of talented and friendly craftspeople demonstrate their artistry. Museum exhibits trace Parton's rise to stardom from her backwoods upbringing. There are many rides including River Battle, a water adventure, and Thunderhead, a wooden roller coaster. Music, however, is the unifying theme of the park, with live shows on the park's many stages. Dolly occasionally makes a surprise appearance. Nearby is Dollywood's Splash Country, a water park that includes

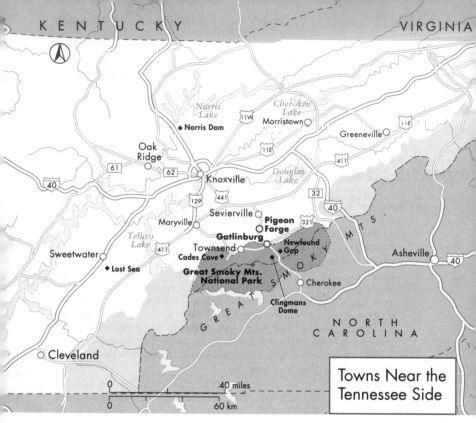

nearly 30 water slides, a 25,000-square-foot wave pool and children's play areas. ⊠*1020 Dollywood La.* ☎*865/428–9488 or 800/365–5996* ⊕*www.dollywood.com* ⊠*$53.50* ☉*Late Mar.–early Jan., days and hours vary.*

The 1830s-era **Old Mill,** beside the Little Pigeon River, still grinds corn, wheat, and rye on water-powered stone wheels. A 20-minute tour explains the process. Flour, meal, grits, and buckwheat are for sale as are other items in the numerous shops around the mill. ⊠*160 Old Mill Ave.* ☎*865/453–4628 or 888/453–6455* ⊕*www.old-mill.com* ⊠*$3 mill tours* ☉*Daily 9–8; mill tours weekdays 9–2.*

WHERE TO EAT AND STAY

$$
AMERICAN
✕**Bullfish Grill.** This popular spot on the main drag offers lots of hearty entrées including meatloaf, fish 'n chips, and chicken Florentine. There's a full selection of steaks and numerous grilled fresh fish, including salmon, swordfish, and Ahi tuna. Finish off your meal with a decadent dessert such as New York cheesecake or two-layer Key lime pie. ⊠*2441 Pkwy.* ☎*865/868–1000* ⊕*www.bullfishgrill.com* ⚠*Reservations not accepted* ▭*AE, D, MC, V.*

¢–$
AMERICAN
✕**The Old Mill.** This rambling, raucous family-friendly restaurant just east of the main drag dishes up all-American specialties like fried chicken, country ham, and pot roast. Lines start early and spill out the

door. Across the street, the less crowded Old Mill's café and grill serves sandwiches, salads, steaks, and seafood. The main restaurant is open seven days, including breakfast. The café and grill is open for lunch and dinner only. ⊠*164 Old Mill Ave.* ☎*865/429–3463* ⊕*www.old-mill. com* ⊟*AE, D, MC, V.*

¢ 🖪 **Best Western Plaza Inn.** Convenient to shops, restaurants, and attrac-
⊙ tions, the Best Western is a good choice for families. It has three swimming pools (one indoor and two outdoor) and some rooms overlook mountain scenery. **Pros:** adjacent to Dixieland Stampede show; good value; free Wi-Fi. **Cons:** rather standard rooms; sits right along main drag with heavy traffic. ⊠*3755 Pkwy.* ☎*865/453–5538 or 800/232– 5656* ⟲*198 rooms, 3 suites* ⬩*In-room: refrigerator, Wi-Fi. In-hotel: pools, Wi-Fi, parking (free), no-smoking rooms* ⊟*AE, D, MC, V* ⦿*CP.*

¢–$ 🖪 **Holiday Inn Pigeon Forge.** This hotel is in the middle of the action.
⊙ Its indoor pool includes a waterfall and adjacent game room, which is sure to please the kids. **Pros:** convenient location; nice pool; free Wi-Fi. **Cons:** uninspiring surroundings; lots of traffic on road outside. ⊠*3230 Pkwy.* ☎*865/428–2700 or 800/782–3119* ⊕*www.4lodging. com/PGFTN* ⟲*200 rooms, 6 suites* ⬩*In-room: refrigerator, Wi-Fi. In-hotel: restaurant, room service, pool, gym, laundry service, Wi-Fi, parking (free), some pets allowed, no-smoking rooms* ⊟*AE, D, DC, MC, V.*

WHERE TO CAMP

$$$–$$$$ △ **Waldens Creek Campground.** Pigeon Forge's newest campground is within the town limits and has 35 sites on concrete pads, with easy access to hiking and fishing. There's a supermarket within walking distance. It is located west of the main drag, just off Wears Valley Road. **Pros:** showers available; tents allowed along the creek. **Cons:** no swimming; sites are close together. ⊠*2485 Henderson Springs Rd.* ☎*865/908–2727 or 877/908–2727* ⊕*www.waldenscreekcampground.com* ⟲*35 sites* ⬩*Flush toilets, full hookups, drinking water, guest laundry, showers, fire pits, picnic tables, electricity, Wi-Fi* ⊟*AE, D, MC, V.*

NIGHTLIFE AND THE ARTS

Pigeon Forge has a host of theaters, with many concentrated around the 2000 block of Parkway. The **Comedy Barn** (⊠*2775 Pkwy.* ☎*865/428– 5222 or 800/295–2844* ⊕*www.comedybarn.com*) presents a family variety show. The **Country Tonite Theater** (⊠*129 Showplace Blvd.* ☎*865/453–2003 or 800/792–4308* ⊕*www.countrytonitepf.com*) has foot-stompin' country music. Hearty country dinners are accompanied by a colorful, Western-theme musical show and rodeo at Dolly Parton's **Dixie Stampede** (⊠*3849 Pkwy.* ☎*865/453–4400 or 800/356–1676* ⊕ *www.dixiestampede.com*), located at the south end of town.

SHOPPING

For mountain crafts, stop at **Old Mill Village** (⊠*175 Old Mill Ave., off Pkwy., turn east at traffic light No. 7*), whose shops include **Pigeon River Pottery** (☎*865/453–1104*) and **Old Mill General Store** (☎*865/453–4628*).

8

OUTLETS Every imaginable outlet store can be found somewhere in the maze of outlet centers at the heart of Pigeon Forge. The massive indoor **Belz Factory Outlet World** (⊠*2655 Teaster La.* ☎*865/453–7316*) has over 75 stores offering major brands of clothes, shoes, and accessories. The **Pigeon Forge Factory Outlet Mall** (⊠*2850 Pkwy.* ☎*865/428–2828*) has housewares as well as clothes and shoes. The **Shoppes of Pigeon Forge** (⊠*161 E. Wears Valley Rd.* ☎*865/428–7002*) has stores including Liz Claiborne, Tommy Hilfiger, and Nautica.

GATLINBURG

8 mi southeast of Pigeon Forge.

Gateway city to Great Smoky Mountains National Park, Gatlinburg, popular with honeymooners and families, has steadily expanded from a remote little town with a sprinkling of hotels, chalets, and mountain crafts shops to a tourist town packed with attractions, including an aquarium, ski resort, amusement park, and "shoppes" peddling souvenirs and fudge. During the summer, the town is clogged with tourists, complete with the annoyances of traffic jams and packed restaurants. Nevertheless, Gatlinburg is an enduringly popular mountain resort town, with more visitors than Great Smoky Mountains National Park.

GETTING HERE AND AROUND

Gatlinburg is directly outside the entrance to the national park, where U.S. 441 becomes Parkway. Heading out of town to the north, U.S. 321 splits to the northeast, and after a few miles, Glades Road branches off and swiftly leaves behind the commercialism of Gatlinburg for a winding journey past bucolic mountain landscapes and log cabins interspersed with the workshops of local artisans. Parkway is the main drag running through town.

ESSENTIALS

Visitor Information Gatlinburg Chamber of Commerce (⊠*811 E. Pkwy., Gatlinburg, TN* ☎*800/568–4748* ⊕*www.gatlinburg.com*).

EXPLORING

Arrowmont School of Arts & Crafts (⊠*556 Pkwy.* ☎*865/436–5860*) is a nationally known visual arts complex. The **Gatlinburg Sky Lift** (☎*865/436–4307* ⊕*www.gatlinburgskylift.com*), via which you can reach the top of Crockett Mountain, makes a fun outing for the family. The **Ober Gatlinburg Tramway** (☎*865/436–5423* ⊕*www.obergatlinburg. com*) whisks visitors to a mountaintop amusement park, ski center, and restaurants.

WHERE TO EAT

¢ ✕**Pancake Pantry.** This restaurant, with its century-old brick, polished-oak paneling, rustic copper accessories, and spacious windows, is a family favorite for breakfast and lunch. Austrian apple-walnut pancakes covered with apple cider compote, black walnuts, powdered sugar, and whipped cream are a house specialty. Other selections include omelets, sandwiches, and fresh salads. The line often stretches out the door. ⊠*628 Pkwy.* ☎*865/436–4724* ⌧*Reservations not accepted* ⊟*No credit cards* ⊘*No dinner.*

AMERICAN

$–$$ ✕**Smoky Mountain Trout House.** This restaurant is a throwback to tra-
SEAFOOD ditional mountain vacation eateries, with pine paneling, checkered
tablecloths, and stuffed fish mounted on the walls. Of the 15 distinctive trout preparations to choose from at this cozy restaurant, an old
favorite is trout Eisenhower: pan-fried, with cornmeal breading and
served with bacon-and-butter sauce. Steaks, country ham, and grilled
chicken are also on the menu. There is no designated parking for the
restaurant, but the attendant at the paid lot across the street should be
able to give you a ticket which the restaurant will reimburse. ⊠*410
Pkwy.* ☎*865/436–5416* ⌖*Reservations not accepted* ⊟*AE, D, DC,
MC, V* ⊘*No lunch.*

WHERE TO STAY

$ 🏨**Best Western Twin Islands Motel.** This chain motel is located in the
thick of the tourist strip, beside the Little Pigeon River and in between
Ripley's Aquarium of the Smokies and Gatlinburg's Hard Rock Cafe.
Rooms have balconies overlooking the river, and you can fish on the
motel property. **Pros:** comfortable rooms; an easy walk to all Gatlinburg
attractions; free Wi-Fi. **Cons:** in a high-traffic area with lots of noise; no
restaurant. ⊠*539 Pkwy.* ☎*865/436–5121 or 800/223–9299* ⊕*www.
bestwestern.com* ⇔*92 rooms, 20 suites* ⌖*In-room: refrigerator, Wi-Fi.
In-hotel: pool, no-smoking rooms* ⊟*AE, D, MC, V.*

$ 🏨**Buckhorn Inn.** This charming country inn is set on 40 acres of remote
Fodor'sChoice woodlands about 5 mi outside Gatlinburg. Guests—including seclu-
★ sion-seeking diplomats, government officials, and celebrities—have
been coming here since 1938. The views of Mt. LeConte and the Great
Smokies are spectacular, and the Great Smoky Arts and Crafts Community is nearby. A nature trail winds through the property, and guests may
spot ducks, birds, or bears nearby. Rooms are spread among the main
inn building, three guesthouses, and seven cottages. The inn has wicker
rockers, paintings by local artists, a huge stone fireplace, and French
doors that open onto a large stone porch. All rooms are spacious, and
some have balconies and gas fireplaces. Full breakfasts are included
in the rate. A four-course gourmet dinner ($35) is served nightly at 7.
Pros: peaceful setting; away from the bustle of Gatlinburg. **Cons:** Wi-Fi
not available throughout entire property; two-night minimum required
on weekends. ⊠*Off U.S. 321 and Buckhorn Rd., 2140 Tudor Mountain Rd.* ☎*865/436–4668 or 866/941–0460* ⊕*www.buckhorninn.com*
⇔*19 rooms, 4 suites* ⌖*In-room: no phone, kitchen (some), refrigerator (some), DVD. In-hotel: restaurant, gym, parking (free), no-smoking
rooms* ⊟*D, MC, V* ⍟*BP.*

¢ 🏨**Garden Plaza Hotel.** Two impressive indoor pools provide ample
☺ recreation opportunities for families. There's also a game room with
video games and Ping-Pong. The hotel is actually a multi-building
complex located a short distance from the main drag on a mountain
road. A breakfast buffet is included with room rates. **Pros:** concierge;
conveniently located near Gatlinburg attractions; free Wi-Fi. **Cons:** no
public Internet terminal; no restaurant. ⊠*520 Historic Nature Trail*
☎*865/436–9201 or 800/435–9201* ⊕*www.4lodging.com/gattn* ⇔*400
rooms* ⌖*In-room: refrigerator, Wi-Fi. In-hotel: bar, pools, gyms, coin*

8

laundry, public Wi-Fi, some pets allowed, no-smoking rooms ▤*AE, D, MC, V* ⦶⦵ *BP.*

WHERE TO CAMP

$$$$ ⛰ **Twin Creek RV Resort.** This RV resort offers large sites along a mountain stream. Located northeast of downtown, just past the turnoff for Glades Road, it is a short drive from beautiful mountain scenery and the workshops of the Great Smoky Arts and Crafts Community. Cabins are available for rent as well. **Pros:** lots of amenities and activities; good for RVs. **Cons:** no tents allowed; not within walking distance of Gatlinburg attractions. ✉*1202 E. Pkwy.* ☎*865/436–7081 or 800/252–8077* ⊕*www.twincreekrvresort.com* ⇆*72 RV sites* ⅋*Flush toilets, full hookups, drinking water, guest laundry, showers, fire pits, grills, picnic tables, electricity, general store, play area, swimming (pool), Wi-Fi* ▤*MC, V* ⊗*Closed Nov.–mid-Mar.*

SHOPPING

The mountain towns of East Tennessee are known for Appalachian folk crafts, especially wood carvings, cornhusk dolls, pottery, dulcimers, and beautiful handmade quilts. The **Great Smoky Arts and Crafts Community** is a collection of 80 shops and craftspeople's studios along 8 mi of rambling country road. Begun in 1937, the community includes workers in leather, pottery, weaving, hand-wrought pewter, stained glass, quilt making, hand carving, marquetry, and more. Everything sold here is made on the premises by the community members. Also here is the popular tearoom and lunch spot, **Wild Plum Tearoom,** on Buckhorn Road near the Buckhorn Inn. ✉*Off U.S. 321 on Glades Rd., 3 mi east of Gatlinburg* ⓓ*Box 807, Gatlinburg 37738* ☎*865/671–3600 or 800/565–7330* ⊕*www.gatlinburgcrafts.com.*

South Carolina

MYRTLE BEACH TO HILTON HEAD

WORD OF MOUTH

"I hope you plan to stay in the historic district [of Charleston]. A walking map is all you need. Go to the [Old City Market] for fun flea market shopping. Slip into an old church for a rest. Be cheesy . . . take a carriage ride. Eat shrimp and grits. Read some Pat Conroy before you go."

—twigsbuddy

Updated by
Mary Erskine
and Eileen
Robinson
Smith

South Carolina has three regions—its 200-mi coastline, its interior heart, and its hilly north country. Few places on the planet are as endowed with natural beauty as the South Carolina coast. The Low Country's miles of pristine beaches, subtropical vegetation, and stretches of golden marshlands with waist-high grasses are as evocative and poetic as the tendrils of silver Spanish moss that adorn its centuries-old live oaks. A warm primal sensuality seems to permeate everything.

Myrtle Beach is the glitzy jewel of the Grand Strand, a 60-mi stretch of white sand beaches and family friendly recreational activities. Towns south of Myrtle Beach offer small-town respite. The scenic Lowcountry shoreline is punctuated by the historic yet vibrant port city of Charleston, known for its elegant homes and fine museums. Anchoring the southern end of the shore is the tasteful, low-key resort town of Hilton Head, most famous for its plethora of golf courses. Nearby is the port city of Beaufort with lovely streets dotted with preserved 18th-century homes.

ORIENTATION AND PLANNING

GETTING ORIENTED

While most resort communities boast beaches and water activities, the Grand Strand is known for much more. Lush botanical gardens, elegant waterfronts, quirky art galleries, high-end and kitschy shopping, and tasty seafood are just some of the Strand's assets. South Carolina's other coastal communities, Charleston and Hilton Head Island cater to a wealthier lifestyle.

The Myrtle Beach Area. Myrtle Beach is the center of activity on the Grand Strand; its year-round population of 23,000 explodes to about 450,000 in summer. Here you'll find the amusement parks and other children's activities that make the area so popular with families, as well as most of the nightlife that keeps parents and teenagers alike entertained.

The Southern Grand Strand. Where the tourist traps and neon of Myrtle Beach end at the border of Horry and Georgetown counties, the South Strand begins. Georgetown County, featuring seafood-centric Murrells Inlet, "arrogantly shabby" Pawleys Island, and historic Georgetown, boasts a rustic elegance in its communities.

Charleston. Charleston is one of the nation's best preserved cities. The heart of the city is on a peninsula, called "downtown." The main part of the historic district is found "North of Broad" Street, a densely

TOP REASONS TO GO

Brookgreen Gardens: More than 500 works from American artists are set amid 250-year-old oaks, palm trees, and flowers in America's oldest sculpture garden in the Grand Strand. A restored plantation, nature trail, and animal sanctuary are also part of the 9,200-acre property.

Tours from the water: Paddle a kayak or ride a pontoon boat past the ruins of the rice plantations that line the shores around Georgetown. Look closely and you can often see the ancient wooden irrigation gates that were raised by hand to allow water into the paddies.

Spoleto Festival USA: If you're lucky enough to visit Charleston in late May and early June, you'll find a city under siege: Spoleto's flood of indoor and outdoor performances (opera, music, dance, and theater) is impossible to miss and almost as difficult not to enjoy.

Historic homes: Charleston's preserved 19th-century houses, including the Nathaniel Russell House, are highlights; outside the city, plantations like Boone Hall, with its extensive garden and grounds, make scenic excursions.

Challenging golf: Hilton Head's nickname is "Golf Island," and its many challenging courses have an international reputation.

packed area with the lion's share of the historic district's homes, B&Bs, and restaurants. King Street, Charleston's main shopping street, is here as well.

Hilton Head and the Lowcountry. One of the southeast coast's most popular tourist destinations, Hilton Head is known for its golf courses and tennis courts. It's a magnet for timeshare owners and retirees. Beaufort is a charming town just inland from Hilton Head and is a destination in its own right, with a lively dining scene and cute B&Bs.

PLANNING

WHEN TO GO

South Carolina is loveliest in spring, when azaleas and dogwood bloom. Between mid-March and mid-April you can catch tours of private mansions in Charleston, and the city is alive with Spoleto events in May and June. For price breaks on the coast, consider visiting in the off-season, October through February, but remember that some restaurants and a few attractions close around that time and the water may be cool.

GETTING HERE AND AROUND

AIR TRAVEL

The best way to reach the Grand Strand is through Myrtle Beach International Airport (MYR). Charleston International Airport is about 12 mi west of downtown. To reach Hilton Head, most travelers use the Savannah/Hilton Head International Airport, which is less than an hour from Hilton Head.

Air Contacts Charleston International Airport (⊠ *5500 International Blvd., North Charleston* ☎ *843/767–1100*). **Myrtle Beach International Airport** (*MYR*

✉ *1100 Jetport Rd.* ☎ *843/448–1580).* **Savannah/Hilton Head International Airport** (✉ *400 Airways Ave., Savannah, GA* ☎ *912/964–0514* ⊕ *www.savannahairport.com).*

CAR TRAVEL

Midway between New York and Miami, the Grand Strand isn't connected directly by any interstate highways but is within an hour's drive of Interstate 95, Interstate 20, Interstate 26, and Interstate 40. U.S. 17 Bypass and Business are the major north–south coastal routes through the Strand.

Interstate 26 traverses the state from northwest to southeast and terminates at Charleston. U.S. 17, the coastal road, also passes through Charleston. Interstate 526, also called the Mark Clark Expressway, runs primarily east–west, connecting the West Ashley area, North Charleston, Daniel Island, and Mount Pleasant.

RESTAURANTS

With the sand at your feet, seafood will most likely be on your mind. Restaurants on the Grand Strand boast all types of seafood, whether you're seeking a buffet or a more intimate dining spot, there are nearly 2,000 spots to whet your whistle. Eating is a serious pastime in Charleston. Local chefs have earned reputations for preparing Lowcountry cuisine with a contemporary flair, and there is plenty of incredible young talent in the city's kitchens. Reservations are a good idea for dinner year-round, especially on weekends, as there is almost no off-season for tourism. Although hard to fathom, relatively few restaurants on Hilton Head are on the water or even have a water view. Although you will find more high-end options, there are still holes-in-the-wall that serve good-tasting fare and are frequented by locals.

HOTELS

High-rise and kitschy beach hotels line the Grand Strand, but a variety of other accommodations is also available. Beachside camping, luxury resorts, and weekly beach-house rentals are popular choices. Charleston is known for lovingly restored mansions that are now atmospheric bed-and-breakfasts, as well as deluxe inns, all found in the residential blocks of the historic district. Hilton Head is awash in regular hotels and resorts that are called plantations, not to mention beachfront or golf-course-view villas, cottages, and mansions. Here and on private islands you can expect the most modern conveniences and world-class service at the priciest places.

WHAT IT COSTS				
¢	$	$$	$$$	$$$$
Restaurant	under $10	$10–$14	$15–$19	$20–$24	over $24
Hotel	under $100	$100–$150	$151–$200	$201–$250	over $250

Restaurant prices are for a main course at dinner. Hotel prices are for two people in a standard double room in high season.

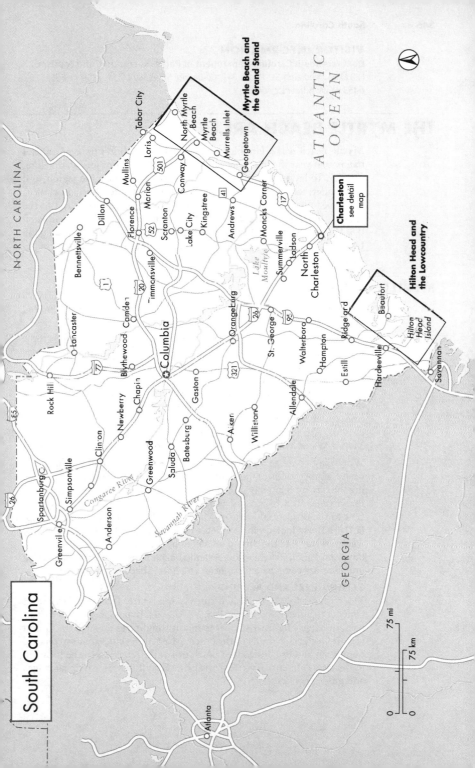

South Carolina

NORTH CAROLINA

GEORGIA

ATLANTIC OCEAN

Myrtle Beach and the Grand Stand

Charleston see detail map

Hilton Head and the Lowcountry

Tabor City
North Myrtle Beach
Myrtle Beach
Murrells Inlet
Georgetown
Loris
Mullins
Marion
Conway
501
Scranton
Florence
Dillon
Bennettsville
Kingstree
Lake City
41
Andrews
Moncks Corner
52
Summerville
Ladson
North Charleston
17
Timmonsville
1
20
Camden
Blythewood
Columbia
Orangeburg
26
St. George
95
Walterboro
Hampton
Ridgeland
Hardeeville
Beaufort
Hilton Head Island
Savannah
Estill
Allendale
Williston
321
Gaston
Aiken
Batesburg
Saluda
Chapin
Newberry
Greenwood
Clinton
Simpsonville
Spartanburg
Greenville
Anderson
Rock Hill
Lancaster
77
85
Atlanta

Congaree River
Savannah River
Lake Moultrie

75 mi
75 km
0
0

N

VISITOR INFORMATION
Contacts **South Carolina Department of Parks, Recreation, and Tourism**
(✉ *1205 Pendleton St., Room 248, Columbia, SC* ☎ *803/734–1700 or 888/727–6453* ⊕ *www.travelsc.com*).

THE MYRTLE BEACH AREA

Myrtle Beach was a late bloomer. Until 1901 it didn't have an official name; that year the first hotel went up, and oceanfront lots were selling for $25. Today, more than 13 million people a year visit the region, and no wonder: lodging, restaurants, shopping, and entertainment choices are varied and plentiful. The many golf courses in the area add to the appeal. ■TIP➔ Be sure to take note of whether an establishment is on U.S. 17 Business or U.S. 17 Bypass when getting directions—confusing the two could lead to hours of frustration. U.S. 17 Business is also referred to as Kings Highway.

MYRTLE BEACH

94 mi northeast of Charleston via U.S. 17; 138 mi east of Columbia via U.S. 76 to U.S. 378 to U.S. 501.

Myrtle Beach has a reputation as a frenzied strip of all-you-can-eat buffets, T-shirt shops, and bars. That reputation isn't completely unwarranted, but this side of Myrtle Beach's character is generally limited to parts of Ocean Boulevard (the "strip"), Kings Highway, and Restaurant Row (sometimes called the Galleria area). Some blocks may be a bit seedy, but the pedestrian-friendly strip is generally safe and clean (though at night the sidewalks can be crowded with the young bar crowd). Attractions such as Family Kingdom Amusement Park and Myrtle Waves Water Park can add a dose of fun to your afternoon.

What may come as a surprise is that it's also not terribly difficult to spend a quiet vacation here, dining in sophisticated spots after spending the day on relatively uncrowded beaches. Myrtle Beach State Park, for instance, is a bastion of peace and quiet, as are the beaches adjacent to the residential areas of Myrtle Beach at either end of the strip. ■TIP➔ Those looking for a quieter time take note: The third and fourth weeks of May find the Strand inhabited by bikers in town for the Harley-Davidson Spring Rally and the Atlantic Beach Bike Fest. Traffic and noise problems are common occurrences, and hotel space is scarce.

GETTING HERE AND AROUND

Most routes to Myrtle Beach run via interstate, I–95 and I–40, and connect to either U.S. 501 or U.S. 17. U.S. 17 Bypass and U.S. 17 Business, or Kings Highway, are the main thoroughfares through the Grand Strand. Both run parallel to the beach. Most of the city's main streets are numbered and are designated north or south, referring to the location in the city. Palmetto Tour & Travel and Gray Line offer tour packages and guide services.

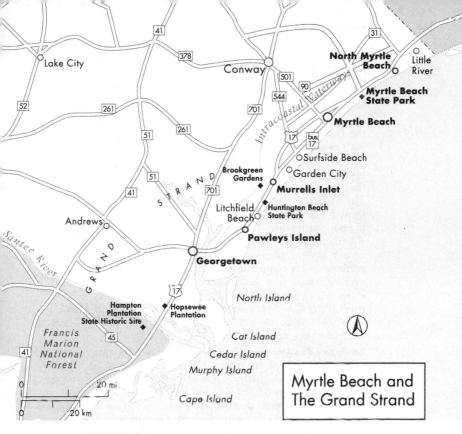

Myrtle Beach and
The Grand Strand

ESSENTIALS

Tour Contacts Gray Line Myrtle Beach (☎ 800/261-5991). **Palmetto Tour & Travel** (☎ 843/626-2431).

Visitor Information Myrtle Beach Area Chamber of Commerce and Information Center (✉ 1200 N. Oak St., Box 2115, Myrtle Beach ☎ 843/626-7444 or 800/356-3016 ⊕ www.myrtlebeachinfo.com ⊗ April–Labor Day, weekdays 8:30-5, Sat. 9-5, Sun. 10-2; post-Labor Day–Mar., weekdays 8:30-5, Sat. 10-2, closed Sun.).

EXPLORING

Carolina Safari Jeep Tours. You'll visit everything from a plantation house to an alligator-laden salt marsh to an 18th-century church on these jeep tours. Along the way you'll learn fun facts and scary ghost stories, told from a script that keeps even history-phobes entertained. The 3½-hour tour, which includes some walking, provides a surprisingly complete overview of the region and beautiful views of the Grand Strand's varied ecosystem. Call to make a reservation; you'll be picked up at your hotel in a Jeep that seats about a dozen people. ✉ 725 Seaboard St., Unit E ☎ 843/497-5330 or 843/272-1177 ⊕ www.carolinasafari.com ☞ $40 ⊗ Arrange tour times when making reservations.

☺ **Freestyle Music Park.** This music-themed park is divided into five themed sections—the VIP Plaza, Country USA, Across the Pond, Myrtle's Beach, and Kids in America. The park's signature ride is the Time Machine, a roller coaster with twists, turns, and inversions with five different audio tracks that take you back in musical time to the '60s, '70s, '80s, '90s or 2000s. There are also four 25-minute live shows, like CSI: Live!, based on the popular forensic TV show and Adrenaline Rush, where the audience roots for their team in an extreme sports competition. Each evening ends with a fireworks show. ✉ *211 George Bishop Parkway* ✛ *Off U.S. 501, beside Medieval Times, Central Myrtle Beach* ☎ *843/236–7625* ⊕ *freestylemusicpark.com* ✍ *$42.95* ☺ *11* AM *to 10* PM, *hours vary, call to confirm.*

☺ **Family Kingdom Amusement Park.** Dominated by a gigantic white wooden roller coaster called the Swamp Fox, this amusement park is set right on the ocean. There are thrill and children's rides, a log flume, go-cart track, old-fashioned carousel, and the Slingshot Drop Zone, which rockets riders straight down a 110-foot tower. It's a bit like going to a state fair that runs all summer long. Operating hours can vary, so it's worthwhile to call before visiting, especially on Saturday when the park is often rented by groups. ■ TIP➜ **Money-saving bundled tickets and multiday passes for water parks and other recreational venues are readily available, check out Web sites for more information.** ✉ *300 S. Ocean Blvd., The Strip* ☎ *843/626–3447* ⊕ *www.family-kingdom.com* ✍ *Fees vary for individual attractions; 1-day unlimited access to most rides $22.75* ☺ *June–mid-Aug., weekdays 4* PM*–midnight, Sat. 1–midnight, Sun. 4–midnight; mid-Apr.–May and late Aug.–Sept., weekdays 6* PM*–close, Sat. 1–close, Sun. 1–6.*

☺ **Mt. Atlanticus Minotaur Golf.** Climb up and over several levels to experience the fun of this multilevel mini-golf attraction. Mount Atlanticus features two different courses and is challenging enough to suit picky mini-golfers, while kids have plenty to look at with mythical creatures, caves, and lagoons throughout the courses. If you get a hole-in-one on the nearly impossible final hole, you can play free for life. ✉ *707 N. Kings Hwy.* ✛ *Off 7th Ave. N, near U.S. 501, Central Myrtle Beach* ☎ *843/444–1008* ✍ *$8* ☺ *Daily 9* AM*–midnight.*

☺ **Myrtle Waves.** You can shoot through twisty chutes, swim in the Ocean in Motion Wave Pool, float the day away on an inner tube on the LayZee River, or ride a boogie board on the Racer River at South Carolina's largest water park. There's beach volleyball, too, for when you've had enough water. Shaded areas with lounge chairs offer respite from the sun. Free soft drinks and sunscreen are available with the price of admission. Lockers are available to keep money and valuables safe. ■ TIP→ **Admission discounts are available after 2 PM daily. Wear a well-secured swimsuit if you're going on the big slides, or else you may reach the end of the slide before your suit does.** ⊠ *U.S. 17 Bypass and 10th Ave. N, Central Myrtle Beach* ☎ *843/913–9260* ⊕ *www.myrtlewaves. com* ⊠ *$28 for full day, $18 after 2* ⊙ *June–Aug., daily 10–6; early May and early Sept., daily 10–5.*

☾ **NASCAR SpeedPark.** You can drive on seven different NASCAR-replica tracks here. The cars vary in their sophistication and speed; to use the most advanced track you need to be a licensed driver. The 26-acre facility also has racing memorabilia, an arcade, and miniature golf. NASCAR drivers often make scheduled appearances, so call ahead. ■ TIP→ **Lines at attractions are shortest on Monday.** ⊠ *1820 21st Ave. N, corner of U.S. 17 Bypass and 21st Ave. N, Central Myrtle Beach* ☎ *843/918–8725* ⊕ *www.nascarspeedpark.com* ⊠ *$32 unlimited day pass or $3 individual tickets* ⊙ *Open daily 10* AM, *closing hrs. vary, call to confirm.*

☾ **Ripley's Aquarium.** An underwater tunnel exhibit longer than a football field and exotic marine creatures on display, from poisonous lionfish to moray eels to an octopus, are the main draws. Children can examine horseshoe crabs and eels in touch tanks. Special exhibits are often included in the price of aquarium admission. ■ TIP→ **Admission discounts are available when combined with price of Ripley's Ocean Boulevard attractions.** ⊠ *Broadway at the Beach, U.S. 17 Bypass between 21st Ave. N and 29th Ave. N, Central Myrtle Beach* ☎ *843/916–0888 or 800/734–8888* ⊕ *www.ripleysaquarium.com* ⊠ *$18.99* ⊙ *Daily 9* AM–*10* PM.

☾ **Wild Water & Wheels.** About 9 mi south of Myrtle Beach in Surfside Beach, this water park has 25 water-oriented rides and activities, along with go-carts and mini-golf. If your children are old enough to navigate the park on their own, spend a few minutes at the adults-only lounge pool, where you can sit immersed in Jacuzzi-like bubbles. ⊠ *910 U.S. 17 S, Surfside Beach* ☎ *843/238–3787* ⊕ *www.wild-water.com* ⊠ *$24.98, $14.98 after 3* ⊙ *Late May–early Aug., daily 10–6.*

9

WHERE TO EAT

$$$$

ECLECTIC

★

✗ **Collectors Café.** A successful restaurant, art gallery, and coffeehouse rolled into one, this unpretentiously arty spot has bright, funky paintings and tile work covering its walls and tabletops. The cuisine is among the most inventive in the area. Try the grilled tuna with Indian spices, served with Cuban black-bean sauce and mango salsa—it's a far cry from standard Myrtle Beach fish-house fare. They don't serve lunch, but you can stop in for dessert or coffee beginning at noon. ⊠ *7726 N. Kings Hwy., North End* ☎ *843/449–9370* ⊕ *www.collectorscafeand-gallery.com* ▤ *AE, D, MC, V* ⊙ *Closed Sun. No lunch.*

¢

AMERICAN

✗ **Dagwood's Deli.** Comic-strip characters Dagwood and Blondie could split one of the masterful sandwiches at Dagwood's Deli. There are the usual suspects—ham, turkey, and the like—but you won't regret trying one of the more distinctive creations, such as blackened mahimahi with homemade pineapple salsa, or the grilled chicken breast with bacon, provolone, and ranch dressing. Salads and burgers round out the menu, and they deliver (for $1) to most of Myrtle Beach, ✉ *400 Mr. Joe White Ave.* ☎ *843/448–0100* ⊕ *www.dagwoodsdeli.com* ⚐ *Reservations not accepted* ☰ *AE, MC, V* ⊘ *Closed Sun. No dinner.*

> **WORD OF MOUTH**
>
> "[E. Noodles] is a great inexpensive noodle/dim sum restaurant. Very creative, lots of choices, much, much better than your typical strip shopping center 'China City.'"
> —beach_dweller

¢–$
CHINESE
✗ **E. Noodles & Co.** The dramatic lighting, sleek furnishings, and top-notch Asian specialties transport diners out of the beach and straight to the city. The menu pulls from Chinese, Thai, and Japanese flavors. Double panfried noodles promise to foil all but the most die-hard Atkins follower. Grouper tempura is a terrific local take on the classic. ✉ *400 20th. Ave. S* ☎ *843/916–8808* ⊕ *www.enoodlesmb.com* ⚐ *Reservations not accepted* ☰ *MC, D, V* ⊘ *Closed Sun.*

$$$–$$$$
AMERICAN
✗ **Thoroughbreds Chophouse & Seafood Grille.** For a special night out, or to fulfill a red-meat craving, Thoroughbreds, with its dark wood, leather banquettes, and top-notch meat, is a romantic escape from the whirlwind of Myrtle Beach. Fish selections are fresh and well prepared, but steaks, pork chops, and rack of lamb steal the show. There's a great wine list, too. ✉ *9706 N. Kings Hwy.* ☎ *843/497–2636* ⊕ *www.thoroughbredsrestaurant.com* ⚐ *Reservations essential* ☰ *AE, D, MC, V* ⊘ *No lunch.*

$–$$
ITALIAN
★
✗ **Villa Romana.** It's all about family at Villa Romana, where owners Rinaldo and Franca come in early to make the gnocchi and stick around to greet customers. It's hard to resist filling up on the stracciatella soup, bruschetta, salad, and rolls (perhaps the best on the Strand) that accompany every meal, but try. The gnocchi is a perfect foil for any of the homemade sauces, and the veal Absolut (sautéed veal in a sauce of cream, mushrooms, and vodka) is a specialty. ■ **TIP→ Michael the accordion player can entertain diners with songs that range from "Mack the Knife" to "Stairway to Heaven."** ✉ *707 S. Kings Hwy.* ☎ *843/448–4990* ⊕ *www.villaromanamyrtlebeach.com* ⚐ *Reservations essential* ☰ *AE, D, MC, V* ⊘ *No lunch.*

WHERE TO STAY

¢–$
☺
🛏 **Affordable Family Resort.** With suites and cottages large enough to house three generations of family members, this spot is both budget conscious and family-friendly. The water play area is sure to get smiles from the kids. The resort features waterslides, pools, and even a duck pond. The Honeymoon Suite boasts a heart-shaped hot tub. **Pros:** pets are welcome; arcade for the kids. **Cons:** rooms are not rented to anyone under 25. ✉ *2300 S. Ocean Blvd., South End* ☎ *888/839–4330* ⊕ *www.affordablefamilyresort.com* ↻ *13 suites, 6 cottages* ⚑ *In hotel: pools, laundry facilities, Wi-Fi* ☰ *AE, D, MC, V.*

$$–$$$
🛏 **Grande Shores.** Like many of the newer properties in Myrtle Beach—this one was built in 2001—Grande Shores is a combination of rentable condos with full kitchens and standard hotel rooms outfitted with refrigerators, coffeemakers, and, in a few cases, kitchenettes. Whichever

you choose, all of the airy rooms at Grande Shores have balconies with a view of the ocean and free high-speed Internet. Pools abound: there's an indoor pool, an outdoor pool with a meandering stream that gently propels swimmers, and a rooftop garden with a pool and four hot tubs. **Pros:** there are water features for all age groups. **Cons:** only a select group of rooms actually face the ocean, most either face north or south, offering glimpses, rather than views. ✉*201 77th Ave. N* ☎*843/692–2397 or 877/798–4074* ⊕*www.grandeshores.com* ↯*136 rooms* ⚵*In-hotel: restaurant, bar, pools, gym, parking (free)* ▤*AE, D, DC, MC, V.*

$$$-$$$$
★ ⛱**Hampton Inn and Suites Oceanfront.** This property combines the reliability of an established hotel chain with the joys of a beach resort. Rooms have balconies and a cheerful style; all have ocean views. There's a lazy river—a pool with a moving current—that carries swimmers along its course. **Pros:** crisp white bed linens offer a tropical, beachy feel to the rooms. **Cons:** construction projects in the area are noisy and disruptive. ✉*1803 S. Ocean Blvd., South End* ☎*843/946–6400 or 877/946–6400* ⊕*www.hamptoninnoceanfront.com* ↯*80 rooms, 36 suites* ⚵*In-room: refrigerator. In-hotel: pools, gym* ▤*AE, D, DC, MC, V* ⦿*CP.*

$$$-$$$$
★ ⛱**Myrtle Beach Marriott Resort & Spa.** Entering this plantation-chic highrise resort, with its airy wicker furniture, giant palms, and mahogany details will take you away from the hubbub of Myrtle Beach and straight to a tropical locale. Green-and-gold guest rooms have plush carpet that makes them quiet and serene, perfect for watching the waves break on the beach. The spa, which offers a full range of treatments, is top-notch, and the health club has well maintained, state-of-the-art machines. The golf and tennis clubs are both on-site, as is a marina with charters and personal watercraft, boat, and kayak rentals. **Pros:** striped hammocks swing near the dunes with views of the ocean; several pools and water features are available. **Cons:** the hotel is located near a construction site; some rooms have a view of either the parking lot or bare earth and bulldozers. ✉*8400 Costa Verde Dr.* ☎*843/449–8880* ⊕*www.myrtlebeachmarriott.com* ↯*400 rooms* ⚵*In-room: refrigerator. In-hotel: restaurant, room service, tennis court, pools* ▤*AE, D, MC, V* ⦿*BP.*

¢-$
★ ⛱**Serendipity Inn.** This cozy Spanish-villa-style inn is about 300 yards from the beach. Though the layout is much like a hotel, each guest room is decorated in a different way, most with four-poster beds and antique chests in pine or mahogany. Included in each room is a copy of the movie *Serendipity*, starring John Cusack, for your viewing pleasure. There's also a colorful pool area dotted with hanging flowers and a trickling fountain. A breakfast of homemade coffee cake, hardboiled eggs, yogurt, cereal, and fruit is served in the wicker-appointed garden room. **Pros:** the tranquil setting helps you forget the hustle and bustle of busy Myrtle Beach. **Cons:** some amenities are dated, but still pleasant; don't expect brand-new lounge chairs or an architecturally designed pool. ✉*407 71st Ave. N, North End* ☎*843/449–5268 or 800/762–3229* ⊕*www.serendipityinn.com* ↯*12 rooms, 2 suites* ⚵*In-room: no phone, kitchen (some), refrigerator, DVD, Wi-Fi. In-hotel: pool, Wi-Fi* ▤*MC, V* ⦿*BP.*

9

¢ ⊞ **Waikiki Village Motel.** If you're looking for something beyond high-rises and luxury rooms with steep price tags, try this mom-and-pop motel. The rooms, in aqua and white, are centered around a pool, and the beach is an easy stroll across Ocean Boulevard. The budget-friendly room rate doesn't increase during Bike Week or the summer months. **Pros:** friendly, helpful staff; affordable. **Cons:** no hot breakfast; couples and families are preferred. ⊠ *1500 S. Ocean Blvd., South End* ☎ *843/448–8431* ↩ *46 rooms* ♿ *In-hotel: pool* ⊟ *D, MC, V.*

NIGHTLIFE AND THE ARTS

CLUBS AND
LOUNGES

South Carolina's only Hard Rock Cafe, daiquiri bar Fat Tuesday, and karaoke haven Broadway Louie's are just a few of the hot spots at **Broadway at the Beach** (⊠ *U.S. 17 Bypass between 21st and 29th Aves. N, Central Myrtle Beach* ☎ *843/444–3200*), which also has shopping. In the evening, dueling piano players compete to perform the most outlandish versions of audience requests at **Crocodile Rocks** (⊠ *Broadway at the Beach, U.S. 17 Bypass between 21st and 29th Aves. N, Central Myrtle Beach* ☎ *843/444–2096*); singing along is part of the fun. The shag (South Carolina's state dance) is popular at **Studebaker's** (⊠ *2000 N. Kings Hwy., Central Myrtle Beach* ☎ *843/448–9747*).

FILM

IMAX 3D Theatre (⊠ *Broadway at the Beach, U.S. 17 Bypass between 21st and 29th Aves. N, Central Myrtle Beach* ☎ *843/448–4629*) shows educational films on a six-story-high screen.

MUSIC AND
LIVE SHOWS

Carolina Opry (⊠ *8901A U.S. 17 Business N, North End* ☎ *800/843–6779*) is a family-oriented variety show featuring country, light rock, show tunes, and gospel. At **Dolly Parton's Dixie Stampede** (⊠ *8901B U.S. 17 Business N, North End* ☎ *843/497–9700 or 800/433–4401*) dinner theater, dozens of actors on horseback re-create Civil War cavalry battles. **Legends in Concert** (⊠ *301 U.S. 17 Business S, Surfside Beach* ☎ *843/238–7827 or 800/960–7469*) has high-energy shows by impersonators of Elvis, Garth Brooks, and the Blues Brothers.

The elegant **Palace Theatre** (⊠ *Broadway at the Beach, U.S. 17 Bypass between 21st and 29th Aves. N, Central Myrtle Beach* ☎ *843/448–0588 or 800/905–4228*) hosts the acrobatic feats of Le Grande Cirque, as well as solo performances by acts such as Larry the Cable Guy. Watch knights on horseback battle for their kingdom, followed by a real jousting tournament, at **Medieval Times Dinner & Tournament** (⊠ *2904 Fantasy Way* ☎ *843/236–4635 or 888/935–6878*).

SPORTS AND THE OUTDOORS

BEACHES

Since much of Myrtle Beach's coastline is dominated by high-rise hotels, there are plenty of places to get lunch or a cool drink without having to get back in your car. Many of these hotels also rent beach chairs, umbrellas, and boogie boards. Some also have nets set up for games of beach volleyball. ■**TIP→ For a quieter beach experience, look for beach accesses away from the high-rise hotels. Spots between 30th and 48th avenues North are good bets.**

For a more out-of-the-way experience, head south of Myrtle Beach to **Myrtle Beach State Park.** There you can swim in the ocean, hike on a nature trail, and fish in the surf or from a pier. You can also camp, but you need to book in advance. ⊠*U.S. 17, 3 mi south of Myrtle Beach* ☎*843/238–5325* ☜*$4.50 to fish off pier, no license required.*

FISHING The Gulf Stream makes for good fishing from early spring through December. Anglers can fish from 10 piers and jetties for amberjack, sea trout, and king mackerel. Surfcasters may snare bluefish, whiting, flounder, pompano, and channel bass. In the South Strand, salt marshes, inlets, and tidal creeks yield flounder, blues, croakers, spots, shrimp, clams, oysters, and blue crabs.

GOLF Many of the Grand Strand's more than 100 courses are championship layouts; most are public. **Tee Times Central** (☎*843/347–4653 or 800/344–5590)* makes it easy to book tee times at nearly all the Strand's courses. ⚠ **Alligators have taken up residence in many of the Strand's golf courses. If you see one, don't investigate: they're faster than they look.**

Two of Myrtle Beach's courses are particularly notable. Built in the 1920s, **Pine Lakes** (⊠*5603 Woodside Ave.* ☎*843/315–7700)* is considered the granddaddy of Strand courses. In spring you can get mimosas on the 10th tee; in winter they serve clam chowder. Pine Lakes is a terrific walking course. The course is currently undergoing renovations, including upgrades to cart paths, new grass, and more. All changes will either maintain or enhance the course's Scottish style, and the course is slated to reopen in March 2009. Former home to the Senior PGA Tour, the Tom Fazio–designed **Tournament Players Club at Myrtle Beach** (⊠*1189 TPC Blvd., Murrells Inlet* ☎*888/742–8721 or 843/357–3399* ⊕*www. tpcmyrtlebeach.com)* boasts narrow fairways amid water hazards and wetlands.

A bit less demanding, but still interesting, thanks to surprising changes in elevation, **The Witch** (⊠*1900 S.C. 544, East Conway* ☎*843/448– 1300* ⊕*www.witchgolf.com)* is built on wetlands and contains nearly 4,000 feet of bridges. Known for its top-notch condition, regardless of the season, **Arrowhead** (⊠*1201 Burcale Rd.* ☎*800/236–3243* ⊕*www. arrowheadcc.com)* is the only Raymond Floyd–designed course in the region. Several of the 27 holes run along the Intracoastal Waterway and you might spot dolphins cavorting in the smooth water.

There are a few bargains on the Myrtle Beach golfing scene. One is **Indigo Creek** (⊠*9480 Indigo Club Dr., Murrells Inlet* ☎*800/718–1830 or 843/650–1809* ⊕*www.indigocreekgolfclub.com)*, which is cut through forests of huge oaks and pines. Built on the site of an old airbase, **Whispering Pines** (⊠*U.S. 17 Business and 22nd Ave. S* ☎*843/918–2305* ⊕*www.wpinesgolf.com)* is recognized as an Audubon Cooperative Sanctuary.

SCUBA DIVING You don't have to go far off the coast of the Grand Strand to explore the underwater world. Man-made reefs boast an array of fish including sea fans, sponges, reef fish, anemones, urchins, and crabs. A number of shipwrecks are also worth exploring under the waves. Paddle-wheelers, freighters, and cargo ships lie in ruins off the coast, and are popular scuba spots. ■**TIP→ Always wanted to dive but never learned how? Most dive shops can have you PADI-certified in a weekend.**

9

Instruction and equipment rentals, as well as an indoor dive tank, are available in the Sports Corner shopping center from **Nu Horizons Dive and Travel** (✉ *515 U.S. 501, Ste. A* ☎ *843/839–1932 or 800/505–2080*)

TENNIS **Prestwick Country Club** (✉ *1001 Links Rd.* ☎ *843/293–4100, 888/250–1767*) offers court time, instruction, and tournament opportunities; clay and hard courts are lighted for nighttime play. **Grande Dunes Tennis** (✉ *U.S. 17 Bypass at Grande Dunes Blvd.* ☎ *843/449–4486*) is a full fitness facility with 10 lighted Har-Tru courts; the club also offers lessons, clinics, camps, and match opportunities.

WATER Hobie Cats, personal watercraft, ocean kayaks, and sailboats are avail-
SPORTS able for rent at **Downwind Sails** (✉ *2915 South Ocean Blvd. at 29th Ave. S, South End* ☎ *843/448–7245*); they also have banana-boat rides (where you're towed in a long, yellow inflatable raft) and parasailing. ■ **TIP→ Don't forget to bring your own towels and sunscreen when you head out. Ocean Watersports** (✉ *3rd Ave. S and beach, between Family Kingdom amusement park and Westgate Resort, The Strip* ☎ *843/445–7777*) rents water-sports equipment.

SHOPPING

For recreational shopping, Myrtle Beach's main attraction is **Broadway at the Beach** (✉ *U.S. 17 Bypass between 21st Ave. N and 29th Ave. N*). More than 100 shops include everything from high-end apparel to Harley-Davidson–theme gifts. A new endeavor that combines high-end shopping with upscale living and dining spaces, **The Market Common** (✉ *4017 Deville Street* ✛ *Off Farrow Parkway, between U.S. 17 Business and U.S. 17 Bypass, South End* ☎ *843/839–3500* ⊕ *www.mar-ketcommonmb.com* ⊙ *Mon.–Sat. 10 AM–9 PM, Sun. noon–6*) features stores like Banana Republic, Anthropologie, and Tommy Bahama.

DISCOUNT The **Tanger Factory Outlet Center** (✉ *U.S. 501* ☎ *843/236–5100*) is a
OUTLETS large outlet center with Nike, Polo, Brooks Brothers, and J. Crew. **Tanger Factory Outlet Center** (✉ *10785 Kings Rd., at U.S. 17, North End* ☎ *843/449–0491*) has 75 factory outlet stores, including Gap, Banana Republic, and Old Navy.

NORTH MYRTLE BEACH

5 mi north of Myrtle Beach via U.S. 17.

North Myrtle Beach, best known as the site where the shag, South Carolina's state dance, originated, is made up of the beach towns Cherry Grove, Crescent Beach, Windy Hill, and Ocean Drive. Entering North Myrtle Beach from the south on U.S. 17, you'll see Barefoot Landing, a huge shopping and entertainment complex that sits on the Intracoastal Waterway. As you make your way east toward the ocean, then north on Ocean Boulevard South, high-rises give way to small motels, then to single beach houses, many of which are available for rent. This end of the strand marks the tip of a large peninsula, and there are lots of little islands, creeks, and marshes between the ocean and the Intracoastal to explore by kayak or canoe. ■ **TIP→ Mosquitoes can be a problem on the marsh, especially in the early evening. Be sure to pack repellent.**

GETTING HERE AND AROUND

North Myrtle Beach is an easy jaunt up U.S. 17 from Myrtle Beach or just south of Little River. Once inside the city limits, the numbered cross streets connect to Ocean Drive, the beachfront road.

ESSENTIALS

Visitor Information North Myrtle Beach Chamber of Commerce Convention and Visitor's Bureau (⊠ *270 U.S. 17 N, North Myrtle Beach* ☎ *843/281-2662 or 877/332-2662* ⊕ *www.northmyrtlebeachchamber.com* ⊙ *Weekdays 8:30 AM–5 PM, weekends 10–4).*

EXPLORING

Alligator Adventure has interactive reptile shows, including an alligator-feeding demonstration. Boardwalks lead through marshes and swamps on the 15-acre property, where you'll see wildlife of the wetlands, including a pair of rare white albino alligators; Utan, the largest known crocodile in captivity; giant Galápagos tortoises; river otters; and all manner of reptiles, including boas, pythons, and anacondas. Unusual plants and exotic birds also thrive here. ⊠ *U.S. 17, at Barefoot Landing* ☎ *843/361-0789* ⊕ *www.alligatoradventure.com* ▨ *$16.95* ⊙ *Daily 9 AM–11 PM.*

Hawaiian Rumble is the crown jewel of Myrtle Beach miniature golf. The course hosts championship tournaments, and is best known for its smoking volcano, which rumbles and belches fire at timed intervals. ⊠ *3210 33rd Ave. S, at U.S. 17* ☎ *843/272-7812* ▨ *$8 for one round, $12 for two rounds until 5 PM* ⊙ *Daily 8 AM–1 AM.*

La Belle Amie Vineyard. This shady vineyard is off U.S. 17 just outside of North Myrtle Beach. The wines sold here are created from the sweet muscadine grapes grown on the property. Tastings and tours are available during operating hours. Saturdays are typically festival days and usually feature live music, food, and free tours of the grounds. The gift shop features everything from wine to savory dips and fun grape-themed items. ⊠ *1120 St. Joseph Rd., on the corner of St. Joseph Rd. and S.C. 90, Little River* ☎ *843/839-WINE* ⊕ *www.labelleamie.com* ▨ *$8 on festival days. Call for group tour pricing* ⊙ *Mon.–Sat. 10–6.*

WHERE TO EAT AND STAY

$$$-$$$$
ECLECTIC
★ ✕**Greg Norman's Australian Grille.** Overlooking the Intracoastal Waterway, this large restaurant in Barefoot Landing has leather booths, Australian aboriginal art on the walls, an extensive wine list, and a classy bar area. The menu features grilled meats, and many of the selections have an Asian flair. (The Australian theme comes through more strongly in the decor, and the Greg Norman merchandise for sale, than in the food.) Highlights are the lobster dumplings, miso-marinated sea bass, and habanero-rubbed tenderloin. ⊠ *4930 U.S. 17S* ☎ *843/361-0000* ⌆ *Reservations essential* ⊟ *AE, D, MC, V.*

$$-$$$
SEAFOOD
✕**Rockefellers Raw Bar.** Yes it's a raw bar—and a good one, with a bounty of fresh seafood—but don't sell the cooked items short at this small, casual locals' joint. The oysters Rockefeller, with their splash of Pernod and fresh spinach, are the real deal, and the iron pot of steamed mussels, clams, scallops, and other goodies is a terrific version of a Lowcountry

9

staple. ⊠*3613 U.S. 17S* ☎*843/361–9677* ⚲*Reservations not accepted* ⊟*AE, D, MC, V.*

$–$$ 🏨 **Barefoot Resort.** This luxury golf resort includes more than 325 one- to four-bedroom condominium units along fairways as well as in the 62-unit, 14-story North Tower, which overlooks the Intracoastal Waterway. Furnishings in each unit vary, but all have been tastefully decorated and have all the amenities of a hotel, including daily maid service. The waterfront pool covers an acre of land and is said to be one of the largest on the east coast. The Barefoot Landing shopping and entertainment center is just across the inlet. **Pros:** pretty views of the Intracoastal Waterway surround the resort. **Cons:** getting to the beach and the ocean requires driving across a busy highway. ⊠*2200 Premier Resorts Blvd., North Myrtle Beach* ☎*877/237–3767* ⊕*www. barefootgolfresort.com* ↪*387 condos* ⟲*In-hotel: 3 restaurants, bar, golf courses, pools* ⊟*AE, D, MC, V.*

$–$$ 🏨 **Best Western Ocean Sands.** One of the few fairly small, family-owned
ⓒ properties left in North Myrtle Beach, the Ocean Sands has some nice touches that make it a good choice for families, including full kitchens in every room and large suites with true separate bedrooms. Although it's not luxurious, it's clean and breezy, and all rooms have balconies. ■**TIP→ The exercise room is very small, with just a treadmill and stair climber. Pros:** friendly, available staff. **Cons:** annex building is down the street away from the central hotel. ⊠*1525 S. Ocean Blvd.* ☎*843/272–6101 or 800/588–3570* ⊕*www.oceansands.com* ↪*80 rooms, 36 suites* ⟲*In-room: kitchen. In-hotel: pools, no-smoking rooms* ⊟*AE, D, MC, V.*

NIGHTLIFE AND THE ARTS

CLUBS AND
LOUNGES
Sassy and saucy, but with live music that ranges from R&B to classic rock to beach favorites, **Dick's Last Resort** (⊠*Barefoot Landing, 4700 U.S. 17S* ☎*843/272–7794*) is big and loud, and the beer is cold.

You can dance the shag at **Duck's** (⊠*229 Main St.* ☎*843/249–3858*), and take lessons from the pros. The club often hosts shag events throughout the year for dedicated and novice dancers.

MUSIC AND
LIVE SHOWS
Live acts, and country-and-western shows in particular, are a big draw on the Grand Strand. Music lovers have many family-oriented shows to choose from. The 2,250-seat **Alabama Theatre** (⊠*Barefoot Landing, 4750 U.S. 17S* ☎*843/272–1111*) has a regular variety show with a wonderful patriotic closing; the theater also hosts different guest music and comedy artists during the year. The **House of Blues** (⊠*Barefoot Landing, 4640 U.S. 17S* ☎*843/272–3000 for tickets*) showcases big names and up-and-coming talent in blues, rock, jazz, country, and R&B on stages in its Southern-style restaurant and patio as well as in its 2,000-seat concert hall. The gospel brunch is a great deal.

SPORTS AND THE OUTDOORS

FISHING
The **Cherry Grove Fishing Pier** (⊠*3500 N. Ocean Blvd.* ☎*843/249–1625*) has a two-story observation deck and reaches 985 feet into the ocean, making it the place to catch pompano, bluefish, and mackerel. You can rent tackle and buy bait at the pier. ■**TIP→ Early morning and late afternoon are the best time to catch fish. Little River Fishing Fleet** (⊠*1901*

U.S. 17 ☎843/361–3323 or 800/249–9388) offers half- and full-day excursions, including night fishing.

GOLF   In Cherry Grove Beach you'll find the much-touted 18-hole, par-72 **Tidewater Golf Club and Plantation** (✉1400 Tidewater Dr. ☎843/913-2424 ⊕www.tidewatergolf.com), one of only two courses in the area with ocean views. The challenging fairways and high bluffs are reminiscent of Pebble Beach.

The four 18-hole championship courses at **Barefoot Resort and Golf** (✉4980 Barefoot Resort Bridge Rd. ☎843/390–3200 or 800/320–6536) were designed by Tom Fazio, Davis Love III, Pete Dye, and Greg Norman and have proven to be new favorites of Grand Strand golfers. Notable details include a replica of plantation ruins on the Love course and only 60 acres of mowable grass on the Norman course. ■ TIP→ An online Web special features an offer to play three courses and get the fourth free.

WATER   You can rent your own pontoon boats or Jet Skis at **Myrtle Beach Water**
SPORTS **Sports, Inc.** (✉4495 Mineola Ave., Little River on the docks ☎843/280–7777), or try parasailing or a ride on *Sea Screamer,* touted as the World's Largest Speed Boat. Learn to scuba dive, take a dive trip, or just rent equipment at **Coastal Scuba** (✉1501 U.S. 17S ☎843/361–3323 or 800/249–9388 ⊕www.coastalscuba.com), which is PADI-certified.

SHOPPING

MALLS   **Barefoot Landing** (✉4898 U.S. 17S ☎843/272–8349) has more than 100 specialty shops, along with numerous entertainment activities. During the summer, check out fireworks displays here every Monday night.

SPECIALTY   Beach-music lovers have been finding their long-lost favorites at **Judy's**
STORES   **House of Oldies** (✉300 Main St. ☎843/249–8649), for years. Find classics on cassette and CD at this small but packed-to-the-gills music emporium.

9

THE SOUTHERN GRAND STRAND

Unlike the more developed area to the north, the southern end of the Grand Strand—Murrells Inlet, Pawleys Island, and Georgetown—has a barefoot, laid-back vibe that suits its small restaurants, shops, galleries, and outdoor outfitters. And what this part of the Strand lacks in glitz, it more than makes up for in natural beauty.

MURRELLS INLET

15 mi south of Myrtle Beach on U.S. 17.

Murrells Inlet, a fishing village with some popular seafood restaurants, is a perfect place to rent a fishing boat or join an excursion. A notable garden and state park provide other diversions from the beach.

GETTING HERE AND AROUND

Driving south on U.S. 17 takes you through Murrells Inlet. If you stay on U.S. 17 Bypass, though, you'll miss some of the town's character. Try taking U.S. 17 Business to get a taste of the real Murrells Inlet. Most cross streets connect to the bypass if you get turned around.

EXPLORING

Fodor's Choice ★ Just beyond *The Fighting Stallions,* the Anna Hyatt Huntington sculpture alongside U.S. 17, lies **Brookgreen Gardens,** one of the Grand Strand's most magnificent hidden treasures. Here, in the oldest and largest sculpture garden in the United States, are more than 550 examples of figurative American sculpture by such artists as Frederic Remington and Daniel Chester French. Each is carefully set within garden rooms and outdoor galleries graced by sprawling live oak trees, colorful flowers, and peaceful ponds. The gardens are lush and full in spring and summer, and in winter splashes of color from winter-blooming shrubs are set off against the stark surroundings.

The 9,000-acre property was originally a winter home for industrialist Archer Huntington and his wife Anna Hyatt Huntington, but they quickly decided to open it to the public as a sculpture garden and wildlife sanctuary. Today, more than 70 years later, their legacy endures as a center for not only American art but Lowcountry culture and nature preservation. You'll find a wildlife park, an aviary, a cypress swamp, nature trails, and an education center. Several tours, including a boat tour of tidal creeks and a Jeep excursion into the preserve, leave from Brookgreen. ■TIP→ **Outdoor concerts under the stars are a tradition, check the Web site for dates.** ⊠ *West of U.S. 17, 3 mi south of Murrells Inlet* ☎*843/235–6000 or 800/849–1931* ⊕*www.brookgreen.org* ⌨*$12, good for 7 days* ☉*June–Sept., Wed.–Fri. 9:30–9, Sat.–Tues. 9:30–5; Oct.–May, daily 9:30–5.*

Huntington Beach State Park, the 2,500-acre former estate of Archer and Anna Huntington, lies east of U.S. 17, across from Brookgreen Gardens. The park's focal point is **Atalaya** (circa 1933), their Moorish-style 30-room home. There are nature trails, fishing, an education center with aquariums and a loggerhead sea turtle nesting habitat, picnic areas, a playground, concessions, and a campground. ⊠*East of U.S. 17, 3 mi south of Murrells Inlet* ☎*843/237–4440* ⊕*www.huntingtonbeachsc. org* ⌨*$5* ☉*6 AM–10 PM daily.*

WHERE TO EAT

$$$–$$$$
AMERICAN
★
✕ **Bovine's Wood-Fired Specialties.** What started as a meat-lovers-only restaurant has quietly morphed into a local favorite not just for delicious mesquite-grilled beef, lamb, pork, and fish, but also for superb crisp-crusted pizzas, baked in an imported brick oven and topped with a creative assortment of toppings. Add to that a terrific view of Murrells Inlet and Surfside Beach in the distance and a sleek, modern decor, and Bovine's is a nice change from the usual waterfront establishment. ⊠*3979 U.S. 17 Business* ☎*843/651–2888* ⌂*Reservations essential* ▭*AE, D, MC, V* ☉*No lunch.*

$$$–$$$$
SEAFOOD
✕ **The Crab Cake Lady.** A weathered yellow shack with a hand-lettered sign heralds this unassuming spot in Murrells Inlet. Although you can't

sit down and eat, you can order the famous creations of An, known as the Crab Cake Lady, who fishes daily for crab to go into her handmade cakes. Creek Rolls, a twist on the classic egg roll, feature baby shrimp caught daily in the inlet. ⊠ *4525 Wesley Rd., off U.S. 17* ☎*843/651–0708* ▤*AE, D, MC, V* ⊗*Closed Sun.*

$$$–$$$$ ✕**Lee's Inlet Kitchen.** They're closed at lunchtime, on Sunday, and in win-
SEAFOOD   ter; they don't take reservations or have a view, but nobody fries up a
★   mess of seafood like Lee's. Even the biggest eaters will get their fill when they order the Shore Dinner: fried or broiled flounder, shrimp, oysters, scallops, deviled crab, and lobster, along with a shrimp cocktail, clam chowder, hush puppies, fries, and coleslaw. Sure, you can get your fish broiled or grilled, but why mess with deep-fried perfection? ⊠*4660 U.S. 17 Business* ☎*843/651–2881* ⚠*Reservations not accepted* ▤*AE, MC, V* ⊗*Closed Sun., Dec., and Jan. No lunch.*

$$–$$$ ✕**Nance's Creekfront Restaurant.** You can smell the brine and Old Bay
SEAFOOD   seasoning the minute you leave your car and head toward the front door of Nance's. There's not much atmosphere, but that's okay. Oysters, the small local ones that taste of saltwater and seaweed, are the specialty, available raw or steamed in an iron pot and served with butter. There are other selections on the menu, but it's really all about the oysters—and the 10-layer chocolate cake, made specially for Nance's by a local baker. ⊠*4883 U.S. 17 Business* ☎*843/651–2696* ⚠*Reservations not accepted* ▤*D, MC, V* ⊗*No lunch.*

NIGHTLIFE

You can have a drink, watch boats come back from a day of fishing, and enjoy the evening breeze on the deck at **Captain Dave's Dockside** (⊠*4037 U.S. 17 Business* ☎*843/651–5850*), where there's live music most nights in summer. Strewn with party lights and offering live bands every night, the **Hot Fish Club** (⊠*4911 U.S. 17 Business* ☎*843/357–9175*) is a happening spot with a great view.

SPORTS AND THE OUTDOORS

BOATING   **Capt. Dick's** (⊠ *4123 U.S. 17 Business* ☎*843/651–3676*) runs half- and full-day fishing and sightseeing trips. You can also rent boats and kayaks and go parasailing. The evening ghost-story cruise is scary fun.

PAWLEYS ISLAND

10 mi south of Murrells Inlet via U.S. 17.

About 4 mi long and ½ mi wide, this island, sometimes referred to as "arrogantly shabby," began as a resort before the Civil War, when wealthy planters and their families summered here. It's mostly made up of weathered old summer cottages nestled in groves of oleander and oak trees. You can watch the famous Pawleys Island hammocks being made and bicycle around admiring the beach houses, many dating to the early 1800s. Golf and tennis are nearby. ■TIP➜ **Parking is limited on Pawleys and facilities are nil, so arrive early and bring what you need.**

GETTING HERE AND AROUND

Pawleys Island is located south of Murrells Inlet on U.S. 17. Take North Causeway Drive off the main highway to experience the natural beauty of the island. A 2-mi long historic district is home to rustic beach cottages, historic buildings, and even a church.

WHERE TO EAT

$$$–$$$$
AMERICAN
★

✕ **Frank's.** This local favorite serves dishes that give traditional cooking methods and ingredients a new twist. In a former 1930s grocery store with wood floors, framed French posters, and cozy fireside seating, diners indulge in large portions of fish, seafood, beef, and lamb cooked over an oak-burning grill. The local grouper with mustard-bacon butter, served with a side of stone-ground grits, is a star. Behind Frank's is the casual (but still pricey) Outback, a lush candlelit garden with a huge stone fireplace. ■TIP→ **Enjoy a before- or after-dinner drink at Outback's bar. Heaters will keep you warm in winter.** ⊠*10434 U.S. 17* ☎*843/237-3030* ☐*AE, D, MC, V* ☉*Closed Sun. No lunch.*

¢–$
BARBECUE
Fodor'sChoice
★

✕ **Hog Heaven.** Part barbecue joint, part raw bar (after 5), Hog Heaven's wonderful smoky aroma perfumes U.S. 17 for miles. Pulled-pork barbecue has the tang of vinegar and the taste of long hours in the pit. Although sandwiches are available, the buffet, which includes fried chicken, greens, and sweet-potato casserole, is the main event. In the evening try the seafood tray, an assortment of shellfish steamed to order and served piping hot. ⊠*7147 U.S. 17* ☎*843/237-7444* ♤*Reservations not accepted* ☐*MC, V.*

¢
CAFÉ

✕ **Landolfi's.** This Italian pastry shop and restaurant, fourth-generation-owned, has excellent coffee, hearty hoagies, pizzas, homemade sorbet, and delicious and authentic pastries, including cannoli and *pasticciotti* (a rich cookielike pastry filled with jam). Both counter and table service is available. ⊠*9305 Ocean Hwy.* ☎*843/237-7900* ☐*MC, V* ☉*Closed Sun. and Mon. Open until 5 PM Tues. and Wed., and until 9 Thurs.–Sat.*

$–$$
AMERICAN

✕ **Pawleys Island Tavern.** This little eatery has terrific crab cakes, hickory-smoked barbecue, roasted chicken, and pizza. On summer weekend nights tiki torches outside blaze and live music rocks the place. ⊠*The Island Shops, U.S. 17* ☎*843/237-8465* ☐*AE, MC, V* ☉*Closed Mon.*

WHERE TO STAY

$–$$
Fodor'sChoice
★

▥ **Litchfield Beach and Golf Resort.** This beautifully landscaped 4,500-acre resort runs along both sides of U.S. 17. The almost 2-mi stretch of oceanfront accommodations ranges from condos to the 160-room Litchfield Inn, which has motel rooms; other options, such as high-rise condos, duplexes, and even Charleston-style beach houses, overlook fairways, lakes, or the marsh. All accommodations are grouped into miniresorts, each with its own pool and tennis courts. A bike trail connects them all to the large lake, which has a small fishing dock and a couple of resident alligators. There's a one-week minimum for oceanfront rentals during June, July, and August, except at the Inn, where the minimum is three nights. ■TIP→ **Resort guests have access to Litchfield's oceanfront cabana, where there's parking, bathrooms, and a water fountain. Pros:** geared to all kinds of travelers. **Cons:** some properties are as much as a 15-minute walk to the beach. ⊠*U.S. 17, 2 mi north* of Pawleys Island, Litchfield Beach ☎ 843/237–3000 or 800/845–1897 ⊕ www.litchfieldbeach.com ➘ 140 rooms, 216 suites, 200 condominiums, cottages, and villas ♿ In-hotel: 2 restaurants, golf courses, tennis courts, pools, gym, bicycles ⊟ AE, D, MC, V

$$$–$$$$ 🛏 **Litchfield Plantation.** Period furnishings adorn suites of this impeccably restored 1750 rice-plantation manor house–turned–country inn. All of the rooms are lovely, with rich fabrics and views of lakes, woods, or creeks. Use of a beachhouse club a short drive away is part of the package, as is a full breakfast at the elegant Carriage House Club; guests also have golf privileges at eight nearby courses. The resort is approximately 2 mi south of Brookgreen Gardens on U.S. 17 (turn right at the Litchfield Country Club entrance and follow signs). **Pros:** shared condos are ideal for a group of friends getting together. **Cons:** shared condos can be awkward if staying with people you don't know. ✉ Kings River Rd. ☎ 843/237–9121 or 800/869–1410 ⊕ www.litchfieldplantation.com ➘ 35 rooms, 3 suites, 9 two- and three-bedroom cottages ♿ In-hotel: restaurant, tennis courts, pool ⊟ AE, D, DC, MC, V ⃝ BP.

$$$–$$$$ 🛏 **Sea View Inn.** A "barefoot paradise," Sea View is a no-frills beach-side boardinghouse (there are no TVs or in-room phones) with long porches. Rooms in the main inn, with views of the ocean or marsh, have half baths; showers are down the hall and outside. Cottage rooms are marshside and have air-conditioning. Three meals, served family style—with grits, gumbo, crab salad, pecan pie, and oyster pie—make this an unbeatable deal. There's a two-night minimum stay during May and September and a one-week minimum from June through August. **Pros:** live oak trees and a nearby nature preserve keep you insulated from resort hustle and bustle. **Cons:** no handicapped access; only six of the 14 rooms have air-conditioning; some showers are outside of room. ✉ 414 Myrtle Ave. ☎ 843/237–4253 ⊕ www.seaviewinn.com ➘ 20 rooms, 1 cottage ♿ In-room: no a/c (some), no phone, no TV. In-hotel: restaurant ⊟ No credit cards ⃝ Closed Dec.–Mar. ⃝ FAP.

SPORTS AND THE OUTDOORS

GOLF The live-oak alley and wonderful greens help make the **Heritage Club** (✉ 478 Heritage Dr. ☎ 800/552–2660 ⊕ www.legendsgolf.com) one of the South Strand's top courses, and its fees are lower than courses of similar difficulty and condition. **Litchfield Country Club** (✉ 619 Country Club Dr. off U.S. 17S ☎ 843/235–4653) is a mature, old-style course with tight fairways and moss-laden oaks.

HANGIN' AROUND

Created nearly 100 years ago by a riverboat captain tired of sleeping on his grain-filled mattress, the original Pawleys Island rope hammock is handcrafted in Pawleys Island exactly as it was by Captain Ward. More than 1,000 feet of rope are knitted by hand, pulled between oak stretcher bars, and tied with bowline knots to the body. In the 1930s Captain Ward's brother-in-law began selling the hammocks at a general store called the Hammock Shop. Still standing at the same location on U.S. Highway 17, the shop's weaving room is open to visitors most Saturdays.

9

Pawleys Plantation Golf & Country Club (⊠70 *Tanglewood Dr. off U.S. 17S* ☎843/237–6100 *or* 800/367–9959) is a Jack Nicklaus–designed course; several holes play along saltwater marshes.
Willbrook (⊠379 *Country Club Dr,. off U.S. 17S* ☎843/237–4900) is on a former rice plantation and winds past historical markers, a slave cemetery, and a tobacco shack.

TENNIS   You can get court time, rental equipment, and instruction at **Litchfield Country Club** (⊠*U.S. 17S* ☎843/235–4653).

SHOPPING
The **Hammock Shops at Pawleys Island** (⊠10880 *Ocean Hwy.* ☎843/237–8448) is a complex of two dozen boutiques, gift shops, and restaurants built with old beams, timber, and ballast brick. Outside the Original Hammock Shop, in the Hammock Weavers' Pavilion, craftspeople demonstrate the 19th-century art of weaving the famous cotton-rope Pawleys Island hammocks. Also look for jewelry, toys, antiques, and designer fashions.

GEORGETOWN

13 mi south of Pawleys Island via U.S. 17.

Founded on Winyah Bay in 1729, Georgetown became the center of America's colonial rice empire. A rich plantation culture developed on a scale comparable to Charleston's, and the historic district is among the prettiest in the state. Today oceangoing vessels still come to Georgetown's busy port, and the **Harborwalk**, the restored waterfront, hums with activity. ■**TIP**➔ **Many of the restaurants along the riverside of Front Street have back decks overlooking the water that come alive in the early evening for happy hour.**

GETTING HERE AND AROUND
Georgetown is accessible from U.S. 17, as well as S.C. 701. The heart of the town is located near the waterfront—an easy trip off the highway down any side street is worth it. Take Cannon Street to Front Street to see the harbor.

ESSENTIALS
Visitor Information Georgetown County Chamber of Commerce (⑤531 *Front St., Box 1776, Georgetown 29442* ☎843/546–8436 ⊕ *www.georgetown-chamber.com*).

EXPLORING
Hampton Plantation State Historic Site preserves the home of Archibald Rutledge, poet laureate of South Carolina for 39 years until his death in 1973. The 18th-century plantation house is a fine example of a Lowcountry mansion. The exterior has been restored; cutaway sections in the finely crafted interior show the changes made through the centuries. The grounds are landscaped, and there are picnic areas. ⊠*Off U.S. 17, at edge of Francis Marion National Forest, 16 mi south of Georgetown* ☎843/546–9361 ▧*Mansion $4, grounds free* ☉*Mansion Mar.–Oct., Tues.–Sun. noon–4; Nov.–Feb., Thurs.–Sun. noon–4. Grounds daily 9–6.*

Hopsewee Plantation, surrounded by moss-draped live oaks, magnolias, and tree-size camellias, overlooks the North Santee River. The circa-1740 mansion has a fine Georgian staircase and hand-carved lighted-candle moldings. ☒*U.S. 17, 12 mi south of Georgetown* ☎*843/546–7891* ⊕*www.hopsewee.com* ☒*Mansion $15; grounds only $5 per car; parking fees apply toward tour* ☉*Mansion and grounds Feb.–Nov., weekdays 10–4; Dec.–Jan. by appointment.*

Overlooking the Sampit River from a bluff is the **Kaminski House Museum** (circa 1769). It's especially notable for its collections of regional antiques and furnishings, its Chippendale and Duncan Phyfe furniture, Royal Doulton vases, and silver. ☒*1003 Front St.* ☎*843/546–7706* ☒*$7* ☉*Mon.–Sat. 9–5, Sun. 1–5.*

The graceful market and meeting building in the heart of Georgetown, topped by an 1842 clock and tower, has been converted into the **Rice Museum,** with maps, tools, and dioramas. At the museum's Prevost Gallery next door is the Brown's Ferry river freighter, the oldest American-built water-going vessel in existence. The museum gift shop has local pine needle baskets, African dolls, and art (including baskets made from whole cloves), and carries South Carolina rice and honey. ☒*Front and Screven Sts.* ☎*843/546–7423* ☒*$7* ☉*Mon.–Sat. 10–4:30.*

WHERE TO EAT

¢–$
CAFÉ
FodorsChoice
★

✕**Kudzu Bakery.** Come here for the justifiably famous key lime pie and red velvet cake, both of which are available whole or by the slice, and can be eaten in the garden. Kudzu is also a great source for ready-to-cook specialties such as cheese biscuits, macaroni and cheese, and quiche. In addition, you'll find fresh bread, deli items, and a terrific selection of wines. ☒*120 King St.* ☎*843/546–1847* ▤*MC, V* ☉*Closed Sun. No dinner.*

$$$–$$$$
AMERICAN
★

✕**Rice Paddy.** At lunch, locals flock to this Lowcountry restaurant for the shrimp and bacon quesadilla and the creative salads and sandwiches. Dinner in the Victorian building, with windows overlooking Front Street, is more relaxed. Grilled local tuna with a ginger-soy glaze is a winner, as are the crab cakes, which you can get uncooked to go. ☒*732 Front St.* ☎*843/546–2021* ☒*Reservations essential* ▤*AE, MC, V* ☉*Closed Sun.*

$–$$
SEAFOOD

✕**River Room.** This restaurant on the Sampit River specializes in char-grilled fish, Cajun fried oysters, seafood pastas, and steaks. For lunch you can have shrimp and grits or your choice of sandwiches and salads. The dining room has river views from most tables. It's especially romantic at night, when the oil lamps and brass fixtures cast a warm glow on the dark wood and brick interior of the early-20th-century building. ☒*801 Front St.* ☎*843/527–4110* ☒*Reservations not accepted* ▤*AE, MC, V* ☉*Closed Sun.*

WHERE TO STAY

$–$$

▥**Harbor House Bed and Breakfast.** Watch the shrimp boats come into the harbor from the front porch of Georgetown's only waterfront B&B; if you're lucky, innkeeper Meg Tarbox will turn some of the catch into shrimp and grits for breakfast. All four rooms (named for ships that have docked at Georgetown) have water views, as well as decades-old heart-

9

pine floors and family antiques. Refreshments in the afternoon include more of those shrimp, this time in the family's locally famous dip. Pros: great views of Winyah Bay. Cons: guests typically socialize, so those who prefer to keep to themselves might be turned off. ⊠*15 Cannon St.* ☎*843/546–6532 or 877/511–0101* ⊕*www.harborhousebb.com* ⊅*4 rooms* ⚿*In-hotel: bicycles* ⊟*MC, V* ⊘*Closed mid-Dec.–mid-Feb.* ⦿*BP.*

SPORTS AND THE OUTDOORS

BOATING Cruise past abandoned rice plantations and hear stories about the belles who lived there with Cap'n Rod of **Lowcountry Plantation Tours**

(⊠*Front St., on the harbor* ☎*843/477–0287*); other tours include a lighthouse expedition and a ghost-stories cruise. Feel the spray on your face as you explore Winyah Bay aboard a 40-foot yacht with Captain Dave of **Wallace Sailing Charters** (⊠*Front St., on the harbor* ☎*843/902–6999*). Each trip is limited to six passengers, so it feels like you're touring on a private yacht.

★ **Black River Outdoor Center and Expeditions** (⊠*21 Garden Ave., U.S. 701* ☎*843/546–4840* ⊕*www.blackriveroutdoors.com*) offers naturalist-guided canoe and kayak day and evening tours (including moonlight tours) of the tidelands of Georgetown. Guides are well versed not just in the wildlife, but in local lore. Tours take kayakers past settings such as Drunken Jack's (the island that supposedly holds Blackbeard's booty), and Chicora Wood plantation, where dikes and trunk gates mark canals dug by slaves to facilitate rice growing in the area. It's said that digging the canals required as much manual labor as Egypt's pyramids. Black River also rents and sells equipment. ■TIP➔ Wildlife tends to be more active during the early morning or late afternoon; there's a good chance you'll hear owls hooting on the evening tours, especially during the fall.

GOLF The premier course in the Georgetown area, and the only one with a ghost story, is the 18-hole, par-73 **Wedgefield Plantation** (⊠*129 Club House La., off U.S. 701* ☎*843/448–2124 or 843/546–8587*). People have reported sightings of the ghost of a Revolutionary War–era British soldier, who lost his head to Francis Marion while guarding valuable prisoners in the plantation house. The spirit's appearance near the plantation house is accompanied by the sound of horses' hooves.

CHARLESTON

94 mi southwest of Myrtle Beach via U.S. 17.

Wandering through the city's historic district, you would swear it was a movie set. The spires and steeples of more than 180 churches punctuate the low skyline, and the horse-drawn carriages pass centuries-old mansions and carefully tended gardens overflowing with heirloom plants. It's known for its quiet charm, and has been called the most mannerly city in the country.

Immigrants settled here in 1670. They flocked here initially for religious freedom and later for prosperity (compliments of the rice, indigo, and cotton plantations). Preserved through the poverty following the Civil War, and natural disasters like fires, earthquakes, and hurricanes, many of Charleston's earliest public and private buildings still stand. And thanks to a rigorous preservation movement and strict Board of Architectural Review, the city's new structures blend with the old ones. In many cases, recycling is the name of the game—antique handmade bricks literally lay the foundation for new homes. But although locals do live—on some literal levels—in the past, the city is very much a town of today.

The heart of the city is on a peninsula, sometimes just called "downtown" by the nearly 60,000 residents who populate the area. Walking Charleston's peninsula is the best way to get to know the city. Nearly 2,000 historic homes and buildings occupy this fairly compact area divided into South of Broad (Street) and North of Broad. King Street, the main shopping street in town, cuts through Broad Street, and the most trafficked tourist area ends a few blocks south of the Crosstown, where U.S. 17 cuts across Upper King.

Beyond downtown, the Ashley River hugs the west side of the peninsula, and the region on the far shore is called West Ashley. The Cooper River runs along the east side of the peninsula, with Mount Pleasant on the opposite side and the Charleston Harbor in between.

GETTING HERE AND AROUND

BUS TRAVEL The Charleston Area Regional Transportation Authority (CARTA), the city's public bus system, takes passengers around the city and to the suburbs. Bus 11, which goes to the airport, is convenient for travelers. CARTA operates DASH, which runs buses that look like vintage trolleys along three downtown routes; a single ride is $1.25 (exact change only), and a daylong pass is $4.

ESSENTIALS

Bus Contacts CARTA (✉ *3664 Leeds Ave., North Charleston* ☎ *843/747–0922* ⊕ *www.ridecarta.com*).

Visitor Information Charleston Visitor Center (✉ *375 Meeting St., Upper King* ✆ *423 King St., 29403* ☎ *843/853–8000 or 800/868–8118* ⊕ *www.charlestoncvb.com*). **Historic Charleston Foundation** (☎ *843/723–1623* ⊕ *www.historiccharleston.org*). **Preservation Society of Charleston** (☎ *843/722–4630* ⊕ *www.preservationsociety.org*).

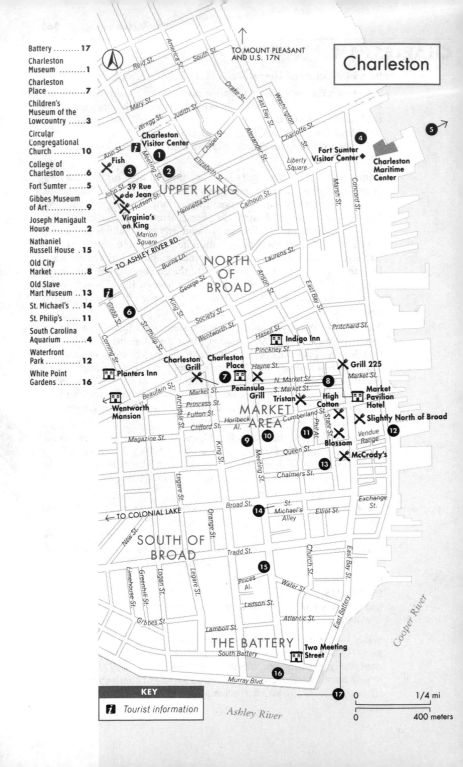

Charleston

TO MOUNT PLEASANT AND U.S. 17N

Reid St.
South St.
America St.
Drake St.
Mary St.
Hragg St.
Judith St.
East Fay St.
Washington St.
Charlotte St.
Alexander St.
Charleston Visitor Center
Fort Sumter Visitor Center
Charleston Maritime Center
Ann St.
Meeting St.
Chapel St.
Elizabeth St.
Liberty Square
Concord St.
Fish
John St.
39 Rue de Jean
Hutson St.
UPPER KING
Henrietta St.
Calhoun St.
Marsh St.
Virginia's on King
Marion Square
TO ASHLEY RIVER RD.
Burns Ln.
George St.
Laurens St.
NORTH OF BROAD
Anson St.
East Bay St.
King St.
Society St.
Wentworth St.
Hasell St.
Pritchard St.
St. Philip St.
Coming St.
Glebb St.
Indigo Inn
Pinckney St.
Planters Inn
Charleston Grill
Charleston Place
Hayne St.
Grill 225
Market St.
Beaufain St.
Market St.
Peninsula Grill
N. Market St.
S. Market St.
High Cotton
Market Pavilion Hotel
Archdale St.
Princess St.
Fulton St.
Tristan
Wentworth Mansion
Clifford St.
Horlbeck Al.
Cumberland St.
Slightly North of Broad
Magazine St.
MARKET AREA
Phil St.
State St.
Blossom
Vendue Range
Queen St.
McCrady's
Chalmers St.
Legare St.
Meeting St.
King St.
Orange St.
Exchange St.
TO COLONIAL LAKE
Broad St.
St. Michael's Alley
Elliot St.
New St.
SOUTH OF BROAD
Tradd St.
Church St.
East Bay St.
Prices Al.
Water St.
Limehouse St.
Greenhill St.
Logan St.
Legare St.
Grbbes St.
Ladson St.
Atlantic St.
East Battery
Lamboll St.
Cooper River
THE BATTERY
South Battery
Two Meeting Street
Murray Blvd.
Ashley River

0   1/4 mi
0   400 meters

EXPLORING

NORTH OF BROAD

Large tracts of available land made the area North of Broad ideal for suburban plantations during the early 1800s. A century later, the peninsula had been built out, and today the area is a vibrant mix of residential neighborhoods and commercial clusters, with verdant parks scattered throughout. This area is comprised of three primary neighborhoods: Upper King, the Market area, and the College of Charleston. Though there are a number of majestic homes and pre-Revolutionary buildings in this area, the main draw is the area's collection of stores, museums, restaurants, and historic churches.

① **Charleston Museum.** Founded in 1773, the country's oldest museum is
Ⓒ housed in a contemporary complex. (The original Greek Revival pillars
★ are all that remain standing at the museum's former home on Rutledge Avenue.) The museum's decorative-arts holdings and its permanent Civil War exhibit are extraordinary. There are more than 500,000 items in the collection, including silver, toys, snuffboxes, and Indian artifacts. There are also fascinating exhibits on natural history, archaeology, and ornithology. The suspended whale skeleton (the museum's mascot to many locals) is a must-see. ∎TIP➔**Combination tickets that give you admission to the Joseph Manigault House and the Heyward-Washington House are a bargain at $22.** ✉*360 Meeting St., Upper King* ☎*843/722-2996* ⊕*www.charlestonmuseum.org* 🎫*$10* ⊘*Mon.–Sat. 9–5, Sun. 1–5.*

② **Charleston Place.** The city's most renowned hotel is flanked by upscale
★ boutiques and specialty shops. Stop by for afternoon tea at the classy Thoroughbred Club. The city's finest public restrooms are downstairs by the shoe-shine station. Entrances for the garage and reception area are on Hasell Street between Meeting and King streets. ✉*130 Market St., Market area* ☎*843/722–4900.*

③ **Children's Museum of the Lowcountry.** Hands-on exhibits at this top-notch
Ⓒ museum keep kids up to 12 occupied for hours. They can climb on a
★ replica of a local shrimp boat, play in exhibits that show how water evaporates, and wander the inner workings of a medieval castle. ✉*25 Ann St., Upper King* ☎*843/853–8962* ⊕*www.explorecml.org* 🎫*$7* ⊘*Tues.–Sat. 10–5, Sun. 1–5.*

∎ **NEED A BREAK?** Take a break with an icy treat at **Paolo's Gelato Italiano** (✉*41 John St., Upper King* ☎*843/577-0099).* Flavors include various fruits and florals, as well as traditional flavors like pistachio. It also serves crepes covered with delicious sauces.

⑩ **Circular Congregational Church.** The first church building erected on this site in the 1680s gave bustling Meeting Street its name. The present-day Romanesque structure, dating from 1890, is configured on a Greek-cross plan and has a breathtaking vaulted ceiling. Explore the graveyard, the oldest in the city, with records dating to 1696. ✉*150 Meeting St., Market area* ☎*843/577–6400* ⊕*www.circularchurch.org.*

⑥ **College of Charleston.** Randolph Hall—an 1828 building with a majestic Greek Revival portico designed by Philadelphia architect William

9

HISTORY YOU CAN SEE

Charleston was founded in 1670, and it's the oldest city between Virginia and Florida. Immigrants, like the French Hugenots, flocked here initially for religious freedom.

The city has one of the country's most colorful histories. It played a pivotal role in the American Revolution, as depicted in Mel Gibson's feature film, *The Patriot.* Later, the first shots of the Civil War were fired here at Fort Sumter.

Charleston persevered through the poverty following the Civil War, and despite natural disasters like fires, earthquakes, and hurricanes, many of Charleston's earliest public and private buildings still stand. And thanks to a rigorous preservation movement and strict Board of Architectural Review, the city's new structures blend with the old ones.

Strickland—anchors the central Cistern area of the college. Draping oaks envelop the Cistern's lush green quad, where graduation ceremonies and concerts take place. The college was founded in 1770. Scenes from *Cold Mountain* were filmed here. ⊠*St. Philip and George Sts., College of Charleston Campus* ⊕*www.cofc.edu.*

❺ Fort Sumter National Monument. The first shot of the Civil War was fired at Fort Sumter on April 12, 1861. After a 34-hour battle, Union forces surrendered the fort, which became a symbol of Southern resistance. The Confederacy held it, despite almost continual bombardment, from August 1863 to February 1865. When it was finally evacuated, the fort was a heap of rubble. Today the National Park Service oversees it.

The **Fort Sumter Liberty Square Visitor Center,** next to the South Carolina Aquarium, contains exhibits on the Civil War. This is a departure point for ferries headed to the island where you find Fort Sumter itself. ⊠*340 Concord St., Upper King* ☎*843/577–0242* ⊠*Free* ⊙*Daily 8:30–5.*

Rangers conduct guided tours of the restored **Fort Sumter.** To reach the fort, you have to take a ferry; boats depart from Liberty Square Visitor Center and from Patriot's Point in Mount Pleasant. There are six crossings daily between mid-March and mid-August. The schedule is abbreviated the rest of the year, so call ahead for details. ⊠*Charleston Harbor* ☎*843/577–0242* ⊕*www.nps.gov/fosu* ⊠*Fort free; ferry $15, kids 9 and under $5* ⊙*Mid-Mar.–early Sept., daily 10–5:30; early Sept.– Mar., daily 10–4 (11:30–4 Jan.–Feb.).*

❾ Gibbes Museum of Art. Housed in a beautiful Beaux Arts building, this museum boasts a collection of 10,000 works, principally American with a local connection. Each year there are a dozen special exhibitions, often of contemporary art. The museum shop is exceptional, with artsy, Charlestonian gifts. ⊠*135 Meeting St., Market area* ☎*843/722–2706* ⊕*www.gibbesmuseum.org* ⊠*$9* ⊙*Tues.–Sat. 10–5, Sun. 1–5.*

❷ Joseph Manigault House. An outstanding example of federal architecture, this home was designed by Charleston architect Gabriel Manigault in 1803. It's noted for its carved-wood mantels, grand staircase, elaborate plasterwork, and garden "folly." The pieces of rare tricolor Wedgwood are noteworthy. ⊠ *350 Meeting St., Upper King* ☎ *843/722–2996* ⊕ *www.charlestonmuseum.org* ⊡ *$10* ⊘ *Mon.–Sat. 10–5, Sun. 1–5.*

8 Old City Market. This area is often ⓒ called the Slave Market because it's where house slaves once shopped for produce and fish. Today stalls are lined with restaurants and shops selling children's toys, leather goods, and regional souvenirs. Local "basket ladies" weave and sell sweetgrass, pine-straw, and palmetto-leaf baskets—a craft passed down through generations from their West African ancestors. ⊠ *North and South Market Sts. between Meeting and E. Bay Sts., Market area* ⊘ *Daily 9–dusk.*

> **BASKET LADIES**
>
> Drive along U.S. 17 N, through and beyond Mount Pleasant, to find the basket ladies set up at rickety roadside stands, weaving sweetgrass, pine-straw, and palmetto-leaf baskets. Baskets typically cost less on this stretch than in downtown Charleston. Each purchase supports the artisans, who are becoming fewer and fewer each year. Nevertheless, be braced for high prices.

13 Old Slave Mart Museum. This is likely the only building still in existence

Fodor'sChoice that was used for slave auctioning, which ended in 1863. It is part of a ★ complex called Ryan's Mart, which contains the slave jail, the kitchen, and the morgue. The history of Charleston's role in the slave trade is recounted here. ⊠ *6 Chalmers St., Market area* ☎ *843/958–6467* ⊕ *www.charlestoncity.info* ⊡ *$7* ⊘ *Mon.–Sat. 9–5.*

11 St. Philip's (Episcopal) Church. The namesake of Church Street, this graceful late-Georgian building is the second on its site: the congregation's first building burned down in 1835 and was rebuilt in 1838. During the Civil War the steeple was a target for shelling; one Sunday a shell exploded in the churchyard. The minister bravely continued his sermon. Afterward, the congregation gathered elsewhere for the duration of the war. Notable Charlestonians like John C. Calhoun are buried in the graveyard. ⊠ *146 Church St., Market area* ☎ *843/722–7734* ⊕ *www.stphilipschurchsc.org* ⊘ *Church weekdays 9–11 and 1–4; cemetery daily 9–4.*

4 South Carolina Aquarium. The 380,000-gallon Great Ocean Tank has ⓒ the tallest aquarium window in North America. Exhibits display more ★ than 10,000 creatures, representing more than 500 species. You travel through the five major regions of the Southeast Appalachian Watershed: the Blue Ridge Mountains, the Piedmont, the coastal plain, the coast, and the ocean. Little ones can pet stingrays at one touch tank and horseshoe crabs and conchs at another. ⊠ *100 Aquarium Wharf, Upper King* ☎ *843/720–1990 or 800/722–6455* ⊕ *www.scaquarium.org* ⊡ *$16* ⊘ *Mid-Apr.–mid-Aug., Mon.–Sat. 9–5, Sun. noon–5; mid-Aug.–mid-Apr., Mon.–Sat. 9–4, Sun. noon–4.*

12 Waterfront Park. Enjoy the fishing pier's porch-style swings, stroll along ★ the waterside path, or relax in the gardens overlooking Charleston Harbor. Home to two fountains, one known as the "Pineapple Fountain,"

9

the other a walk-in (or jump-in) fountain to refresh you on hot summer days. The park is at the foot of Vendue Range, along the east side of Charleston Harbor and Cooper River. ☒ *Prioleau St., Market area* ☎ *843/724–7321* ☒ *Free* ☉ *Daily 6* AM–*midnight.*

SOUTH OF BROAD

The heavily residential area south of Broad Street and west of the Battery brims with beautiful private homes, most of which bear plaques with a short description of the property's history. Mind your manners, but feel free to peek through iron gates and fences at the verdant displays in elaborate gardens.

⑰ Battery. From the intersection of Water Street and East Battery you can look east toward the city's most-photographed mansions; look west for views of Charleston Harbor and

LIKE A LOCAL

In centuries past, the Lowcountry was studded with some of the largest plantations in the south, which were worked by African slaves. The slaves developed a patois that became known as Gullah, as a means of communication. It was a mélange of African dialects and English, and had a lyrical rhythm. There are a number of African-Americans, particularly on the sea islands who strive to keep the Gullah language alive. In the Charleston area, Alphonso Brown is an expert on Gullah culture and conducts tours highlighting the Gullah culture and traditions (☎ *843/763-7551* ⊕ *www.gullahtours.com*).

Fort Sumter. Walk south along East Battery to White Point Gardens, where the street curves and becomes Murray Boulevard. ☒ *East Bay St. and Murray Blvd., South of Broad.*

⑮ Nathaniel Russell House. One of the nation's finest examples of Adam-style architecture, the Nathaniel Russell House was built in 1808. The interior is distinguished by its ornate detailing, its lavish period furnishings, and the "free flying" staircase that spirals three stories with no visible support. The garden is well worth a stroll. ☒ *51 Meeting St., South of Broad* ☎ *843/724–8481* ⊕ *www.historiccharleston.org* ☒ *$10; $16 with admission to Aiken-Rhett House* ☉ *Mon.–Sat. 10–5, Sun. 2–5.*

⑭ St. Michael's Episcopal Church. The cornerstone of St. Michael's was set in place in 1752, making it Charleston's oldest surviving church. Through the years other elements were added: the steeple clock and bells (1764); the organ (1768); the font (1771); and the altar (1892). The pulpit—original to the church—was designed to maximize natural acoustics. ☒ *14 St. Michael's Alley, South of Broad* ☎ *843/723–0603* ⊕ *www. stmichaelschurch.net* ☉ *Weekdays 9–4:30, Sat. 9–noon.*

⑯ White Point Gardens. Pirates once hung from gallows here; now it's a serene park with Charleston benches—small wood-slat benches with cast-iron sides—and views of the harbor and Fort Sumter. Children love to climb on the replica cannon and pile of cannonballs. ☒ *Murray Blvd. and E. Battery, South of Broad* ☎ *843/724-7327* ☉ *Weekdays 9–5, Sat. 9–noon.*

MOUNT PLEASANT

East of Charleston, across the Arthur Ravenel Jr. Bridge, the largest single-span bridge in North America, is the town of Mount Pleasant, named not for a mountain or a hill but for a plantation in England from which some of the area's settlers hailed.

★ **Boone Hall Plantation & Gardens.** A ½-mi drive through a live-oak alley draped in Spanish moss introduces you to the still-operating plantation, the oldest of its kind. Tours take you through the 1935 mansion, the butterfly pavilion, the heirloom rose garden, and nine antebellum-era brick slave cabins. Seasonal Gullah culture performances in the theater are laudable. Stroll along the winding river, tackle the fields to pick your own strawberries, pumpkins, or tomatoes. Across the highway are a farmers' market and gift shop. ✉ *1235 Long Point Rd., off U.S. 17N, Mount Pleasant* ☎ *843/884–4371* ⊕ *www.boonehallplantation.com* ✆ *$17.50* ☾ *Apr.–early Sept., Mon.–Sat. 8:30–6:30, Sun. 1–5; early Sept.–Mar., Mon.–Sat. 9–5, Sun. 1–4.*

WHERE TO EAT

NORTH OF BROAD

$$$
FRENCH
★
✗ **39 Rue de Jean.** In classic French-bistro style—gleaming wood, cozy booths, and white-papered tables—Charleston's trendy set wines and dines until the wee hours on such favorites as steamed mussels in a half-dozen preparations. Order them with *pomme frites,* as the French do. Each night of the week there's a special, such as the bouillabaisse on Sunday. Rabbit with a whole-grain mustard sauce was so popular it jumped to the nightly menu. The duck confit with lentils, braised endive, and blood orange velouté is the most popular new item. If you're seeking quiet, ask for a table in the dining room on the right. It's noisy—but so much fun—at the bar, especially since it has the city's best bartenders. ✉ *39 John St., Upper King* ☎ *843/722–8881* ⌕ *Reservations essential* ⊟ *AE, D, DC, MC, V.*

$$
SOUTHERN
✗ **Blossom.** Exposed white rafters and linenless tables make this place casual and yet upscale. The terrace with a view of St. Philip's majestic spire, the dining room, and the bar are heavily populated with young professionals. The open, exhibition kitchen adds to the high-energy atmosphere. Lowcountry seafood is a specialty, and the pastas are made on the premises. Special seasonal menus can be expected, and the new bar menu is available as late as 1 AM on Friday and Saturday nights. ✉ *171 E. Bay St., Market area* ☎ *843/722–9200* ⊟ *AE, DC, MC, V.*

$$$$
SOUTHERN
Fodor's Choice
★
✗ **Charleston Grill.** Bob Waggoner's groundbreaking New South cuisine is now served in a dining room highlighted by pale wood floors, flowing drapes, and elegant Queen Anne chairs. A jazz ensemble adds a hip, yet unobtrusive, element. As it was hoped, the Grill, which has been reborn in a more relaxed form, now attracts a younger and more vibrant clientele than its original incarnation. The affable and highly talented chef raised the culinary bar in this town and continues to provide what many think of as its highest gastronomic experience. He utilizes only the best produce, such as the organic vegetables used in the golden beet salad. The menu is now in four quadrants: simple, lush (foie gras and

HOW TO SNACK

Boiled peanuts are a big-time snack in the Lowcountry, and the official state snack food of South Carolina. The freshly harvested or "green" peanuts are boiled in salty water for hours until the nuts are soft. Sold with the shell on, you often have to use your teeth to remove the soggy shells before eating. Street vendors in downtown Charleston sell the snack (they're more visible during festivals). Just outside the city limits, farm stands selling produce cook up boiled peanuts as well. If you see men tending big, steaming vats near the side of the road, pull over and buy a brown bag full. Be aware, though, these soggy nuts are an acquired taste.

Benne wafers and pecan pralines are two other traditional Lowcountry treats. Benne is the African word for sesame seeds (considered good luck), which are scattered within these thin, sweet cookies.

other delicacies), cosmopolitan, and Southern. A nightly tasting menu offers a way to sample it all. The pastry chef sends out divine creations like chocolate caramel ganache. Sommelier Rick Rubel has 1,300 wines in his cellar, with many served by the glass. ✉ *Charleston Place Hotel, 224 King St.*, *Market area* ☎ *843/577–4522* ⚴ *Reservations essential* ⊟ *AE, D, DC, MC, V* ⊘ *No lunch.*

$$$
ECLECTIC
★

✕ **Fish.** Since its European chef, Nico Romo, raised it to a high culinary level, settling into the niche of French/Asian cuisine with the freshest of seafood, the popularity of Fish has soared. The dim sum appetizer is more beautiful than a flower arrangement. The sweet-chili calamari and other petite plates give the menu a new kick. The bouillabaisse with coconut-lemongrass broth and ginger croutons is one-of-a-kind. Increasing business has triggered a major redo of the spaces, which blend antiqued mirrors and stainless steel, and a new dining room has gone into the adjacent building. The original bar has tripled in size. Some "jazzy" contemporary musicians play on "Wine Wednesdays," when bottles of wine are half-price from 6 to 8. ✉ *440–442 King St., Upper King* ☎ *843/722–3474* ⚴ *Reservations essential* ⊟ *AE, MC, V* ⊘ *Closed Sun., no lunch Sat.*

$$$$
STEAK
Fodor's Choice
★

✕ **Grill 225.** This atmospheric establishment has been stockpiling accolades over the years and has never been better. Its popularity and status as a special-occasion restaurant makes it popular year-round as a superior dining experience, with a staggering array of excellent wines and professional, caring service. Dress up and add to the elegance created by wood floors, white linens, and red-velvet upholstery. It makes sense to opt for the USDA prime steaks; the fillet with foie gras with a fig demi-glace (hold the béarnaise) may be the best you will ever have anywhere. You will need to share a side or two, such as the mashed sweet potatoes with Boursin cheese. Presentation is at its best with the appetizers like the tuna tower tartare. Expect hefty portions, but save room for the pastry chef's shining creations, which include a contemporized version of baked Alaska, with a nutty crust, flambéed tableside. ✉ *Market*

Pavilion Hotel, 225 E. Bay St., Market area ☎*843/266–4222* ▤*AE, D, DC, MC, V.*

$$$–$$$$
SOUTHERN
★
✗**High Cotton.** Chef Anthony Gray, who has been with the restaurant since 1991, has taken over as chef, and so far the transition has gone smoothly. Lazily spinning paddle fans, palm trees, and brick walls still create a plantation ambience. As for the food, Gray combines wonderful flavors and flawless presentation for memorable meals. His Southern and Italian background translates to such specialties as homemade sausages and excellent sauces and marinades for meat. You can feast on bourbon-glazed pork and white-cheddar grits. The chocolate soufflé with blackberry sauce and the praline soufflé are both remarkable. Sunday brunch is accompanied by musicians who sweeten the scene. At night the bar is enlivened with jazz. ✉ *199 E. Bay St., Market area* ☎*843/724–3815* ⌕*Reservations essential* ▤*AE, D, DC, MC, V* ⊘*No lunch weekdays.*

$$$$
AMERICAN
★
✗**McCrady's.** Young chef Sean Brock has come of age, turning McCrady's into a superb culinary venture. Passionate about his profession, he spends his nights coming up with innovative pairings that are now working, although he favors meat on the rare side for some tastes. For your appetizer, try the slow-cooked lobster tail with parsnips, leeks, almond puree, and citrus; follow with a main course such as spice-roasted rack of lamb with eggplant, pine nuts, and golden raisins. The bar area has a centuries-old tavern feel and is frequented by well-heeled downtown residents. The encyclopedia-size wine list is matched by some wonderful wines by the glass. The cold soft chocolate with a mascarpone filling is one of the impressive desserts; the sorbet is easily shared: nine tiny cones filled with vivid flavors. ✉ *2 Unity Alley, Market area* ☎*843/577–0025* ⌕*Reservations essential* ▤*AE, MC, V* ⊘*No lunch.*

$$$$
SOUTHERN
★
✗**Peninsula Grill.** Eighteenth century–style portraits hang on walls covered in olive-green velvet in this dining room. You sit beneath black-iron chandeliers feasting on longtime executive chef Robert Carter's imaginative entrées, including rack of lamb with a sesame-seed crust and a coconut-mint pesto. If you start with the foie gras with a duck barbecue biscuit and peach jam—superb—you might want to go simple. Carter prepares fresh, thick fillets, such as the black grouper, perfectly; all you have to do is chose your sauce, say a ginger-lime butter. Palate cleanse with the homemade sorbet or the signature dessert, a three-way chocolate dessert that comes with a shot of ice-cold milk. The servers, who work in tandem, are pros; the personable sommelier makes wine selections that truly complement your meal, anything from bubbly to clarets and dessert wines. The atmosphere is animated and convivial. ✉ *Planters Inn, 112 N. Market St., Market area* ☎*843/723–0700* ⌕*Reservations essential* ▤*AE, D, DC, MC, V* ⊘*No lunch.*

$$$–$$$$
SOUTHERN
★
✗**Slightly North of Broad.** This former warehouse with brick-and-stucco walls has a chef's table that looks directly into the open kitchen. It's a great place to perch if you can "take the heat," as chef Frank Lee, who wears a baseball cap instead of a toque, is one of the city's culinary characters. Known for his talent in preparing game, his venison is exceptional. Many of the items come as small plates, which make them perfect for sharing. The braised lamb shank with a ragout of white

9

beans, arugula, and a red demi-glace is divine. Lunch can be as inexpensive as $9.95 for something as memorable as mussels with spinach, grape tomatoes, and smoked bacon. ⊠*192 E. Bay St., Market area* ☎*843/723–3424* ⊟*AE, D, DC, MC, V* ⊙*No lunch weekends.*

$$$–$$$$
SOUTHERN
Fodor'sChoice
★

✕**Tristan.** Within the French Quarter Inn, this fine dining room has a sleek, contemporary style with lots of metal, glass, contemporary art, and fresh flowers. The menu has been purposely tailored to complement the decor: it's ultrachic, innovative, and always evolving. The banquettes that line the wall are sought after, so ask for one when you reserve. The young talent who has moved up to executive chef, Aaron Deal, has expanded the prix-fixe lunch, consisting of three courses from the dinner menu, for a mere $20—less than that chicken wings place down the block. Imagine sitting down to a lunch of baby beet salad, then lamb ribs with a chocolate barbecue sauce, and moving on to violet crème brûlée. After dark the prices escalate—it's a status place with a sophisticated bar scene. On Sunday there's a fab brunch with a jazz trio and residents of the Holy City reserve for after church. ⊠*French Quarter Inn, 55 S. Market St., Market area* ☎*843/534–2155* ⊟*AE, D, MC, V.*

$$
SOUTHERN

✕**Virginia's on King.** This Charleston newcomer is a tribute to an old Southern tradition, mom's home-cooked Southern family meals. In this case, the mother is Ms. Virginia Bennett, and she has shared her recipes for traditional fare that she still prepares for her extended family. Ms. Virginia makes sure prices here are affordable. Starters are such classics as tomato pie, fried green tomatoes, she-crab soup, okra soup, oyster stew, tomato aspic, and Waldorf salad. Supper might be a creamy chicken and dumplings or country-fried steak with red-eye gravy. And sides? Oh yes—collard greens, grits, sweet-potato fries, and more. ⊠ *412 King St., Upper King* ☎*843/735–5800* ⊟*AE, D, DC, MC, V* ⊙*No lunch Sat. No dinner Sun.*

WHERE TO STAY

Downtown residents rent out a room or two through the reservation service, **Historic Charleston Bed & Breakfast Association** (☎*843/722–6606* ⊕*www.historiccharlestonbedandbreakfast.com*). Handsomely furnished, these rooms can be less expensive than commercial operations. However, since the owners or families are usually on-site, they may not offer the same level of privacy as more traditional B&Bs or small inns.

DOWNTOWN CHARLESTON

$$$$
★

▦**Charleston Place.** Even casual passersby enjoy gazing up at the hand-blown Murano glass chandelier in the hotel's open lobby, clicking across the Italian marble floors, and admiring the antiques from Sotheby's. A gallery of upscale shops completes the ground-floor offerings. Rooms are furnished with period reproductions. The impeccable service is what you would expect from an Orient-Express property, particularly on the Club Level, where rooms carry a $100 surcharge that gets you a breakfast spread, afternoon tea, and cocktails and pastries in the evening. A truly deluxe day spa, with an adjacent fitness room, has an inviting indoor salt- and mineral-water pool with a retractable roof and illuminated skylight for night swimming. **Pros:** two great restaurants; located in the historic district on the best shopping street; pet-friendly. **Cons:** no Wi-Fi; rooms aren't as big as one would expect for the price; much of the business is conference groups in shoulder seasons. ⊠ *130 Market St., Market area* ☎*843/722–4900 or 800/611–5545* ⊕*www.charlestonplacehotel.com* ⟿*400 rooms, 42 suites* ⌂*In-room: safe, refrigerator, Internet. In-hotel: 2 restaurants, bars, pool, gym, spa, Internet terminal, parking (paid), some pets allowed, no-smoking rooms* ⊟*AE, D, DC, MC, V.*

$$–$$$ 🖼 **Indigo Inn.** A former indigo warehouse in Charleston's colonial times is painted an appealing smoky green. The location is convenient to King Street and to the Market, yet it is solidly quiet, with a parklike, inner courtyard. There you can take your complimentary Hunt Breakfast or the wine and hors d'oeuvres that are set out nightly. All-day beverages, from lemonade to coffee, are available in the petite lobby, which is the meeting ground for guests. The front desk and long-term management of this family-owned hotel are particularly welcoming and helpful; repeat guests are the norm. Rooms are comfy, done in period reproductions, some with four-posters; a couple have desks. The free in-room Wi-Fi is a plus, as is the adjacent parking lot, but there is a $10 fee. **Pros:** location, location; mini-bottles of liquor and good bottles of wine can be purchased from front desk; free local calls. **Cons:** rooms are not large and some are dark; opened in 1981, and rooms are a little dated. ⊠ *1 Maiden La., Lower King* ☎*843/577–5900* ⊕*www.indigoinn.com* ⟿*40 rooms* ⌂*In-room: Wi-Fi. In-hotel: Internet terminal, Wi-Fi, parking (paid), some pets allowed, no-smoking rooms* ⊟*AE, D, MC, V* ⦿*BP.*

$$$$ 🖼 **Market Pavilion Hotel.** The melee of one of the busiest corners in the
Fodor's Choice city vanishes as soon as the uniformed bellman opens the lobby door
★ to dark, wood-paneled walls, antique furniture, and chandeliers hung from high ceilings. It resembles a European grand hotel from the 19th century, and you feel like visiting royalty. Get used to being pampered—smartly attired bellmen and butlers are quick at hand. Rooms are decadent with French-style chaises and magnificent marble baths. One of Charleston's most prestigious fine-dining spots, Grill 225, is here. All guests enjoy delectable refreshments in their respective lounge, with those on the executive fourth floor getting a hot breakfast, afternoon tea, and (good) wine service. **Pros:** opulent furnishings; architecturally impressive, especially the tray ceilings; conveniently located for everything. **Cons:** the building was constructed to withstand hurricane-force winds, which thus far has prohibited Wi-Fi and can limit cell phone reception; those preferring a minimalist decor may find the opulent interior too elaborate. ■ **TIP→ Join sophisticated Charlestonians who come for cocktails and appetizers at the rooftop Pavilion Bar.** ⊠ *225 E. Bay St., Market area* ☎*843/723–0500 or 877/440–2250* ⊕*www.marketpavilion.com* ⟿*61 rooms, 9 suites* ⌂*In-room: Internet. In-hotel: restaurant, bar, pool, Internet terminal, no-smoking rooms* ⊟*AE, D, DC, MC, V.*

$$$$ 🖼 **Planters Inn.** Part of the Relais & Châteaux group, this boutique
★ property is a stately sanctuary amid the bustle of Charleston's Market. Light streams into a front parlor with its velvets and Oriental antiques.

9

It serves as the lobby for this exclusive inn that has both an historic side and a new building wrapped around a two-story piazza and overlooking a tranquil garden courtyard. Rooms all look similar and are beautifully maintained, but the main building has more atmosphere and a more residential feel. Service is genteel and unobtrusive but not stuffy, and the hospitality feels genuine. The best rooms have fireplaces, verandas, and four-poster canopy beds; the "piazza" suites with whirlpool baths and top-tier suites are suitably over the top in terms of comfort. Packages that include either breakfast or dinner at the on-site Peninsula Grill are a good value. **Pros:** triple-pane windows render the rooms soundproof; the same front desk people take your initial reservation and know your name upon arrival; the Continental and full breakfasts are exceptional. **Cons:** no pool; no fitness center; views are not outstanding. ⊠*112 N. Market St., Market area* ☎*843/722–2345 or 800/845–7082* ⊕*www.plantersinn.com* ⊅*56 rooms, 6 suites* ⚲*In-room: safe, Wi-Fi. In-hotel: restaurant, Wi-Fi, parking (paid), no-smoking rooms* ▤*AE, D, DC, MC, V.*

$$$–$$$$ ⭐   🖼 **Two Meeting Street.** As pretty as a wedding cake, this Queen Anne mansion has overhanging bays, colonnades, balustrades, and a turret. While rocking on the front porch you can look through soaring arches to White Point Gardens and the Ashley River. Tiffany windows, carved-oak paneling, and a crystal chandelier dress up the public spaces. Some guest rooms have a veranda and working fireplace. Expect to be treated to afternoon high tea as well as a delightful, creative Southern breakfast. **Pros:** 24-hour free on-street parking; community refrigerator on each floor; ringside seat for a Battery view and horse-drawn carriages clipping by. **Cons:** not wheelchair-accessible, some rooms have thick walls and make Wi-Fi spotty; small TVs only get local stations (no cable at all). ⊠*2 Meeting St., South of Broad* ☎*843/723–7322* ⊕*www.twomeetingstreet.com* ⊅*9 rooms* ⚲*In-room: no phone, safe, Wi-Fi. In-hotel: no kids under 12, parking (free), no-smoking rooms* ▤*No credit cards* ⦿*BP.*

$$$$ **Fodor's**Choice   ⭐   🖼 **Wentworth Mansion.** Charlestonian Francis Silas Rodgers made his money in cotton; in 1886 he commissioned this four-story mansion with such luxuries as Austrian crystal chandeliers and hand-carved marble mantles. Now guests admire the Second Empire antiques and reproductions, the rich fabrics, inset wood paneling, and original stained-glass windows. In the colder months, the baronial, high-ceilinged guest rooms have the velvet drapes drawn and the gas fireplaces lighted. The complimentary evening wine and delectable hors d'oeuvres are now served in the sunny, glass-enclosed porch. Breakfast, with a new expanded hot menu, has been moved to Circa 1886, the inn's laudable restaurant, which shares the former carriage house with the spa. **Pros:** luxury bedding, including custom-made mattresses, down pillows, and Italian linens; new carpet and furnishings lend a fresh look. **Cons:** not child-friendly; Second Empire style can strike some people as foreboding; the building has some of the woes of an old building, including loudly creaking staircases. ⊠*149 Wentworth St., College of Charleston Campus* ☎*843/853–1886 or 888/466–1886* ⊕*www.wentworthman-*

CLOSE UP

Spoleto Festival USA

For 17 glorious days in late May and early June, Charleston gets a dose of culture from the **Spoleto Festival USA** (☎ *843/722–2764* ⊕ *www. spoletousa.org*). This internationally acclaimed performing-arts festival features a mix of distinguished artists and emerging talent from around the world. Performances take place in magical settings, such as beneath a canopy of ancient oaks or inside a centuries-old cathedral. Everywhere you turn, the city's music halls, auditoriums, theaters, and outdoor spaces (including the Cistern at the College of Charleston) are filled with the world's best in opera, music, dance, and theater.

Because events sell out quickly, insiders say you should buy your Spoleto tickets several months in advance. (Tickets to mid-week performances are a bit easier to secure.) Hotels definitely fill up quickly, so book a room at the same time and reserve your tables for our trendy downtown restaurants. You may not be able to get in if you wait until the last minute.

---

sion.com ⇴*21 rooms* ⑤*In-room: Internet. In-hotel: restaurant, spa, no-smoking rooms* ▤*AE, D, DC, MC, V* ⑩*BP.*

KIAWAH ISLAND

$$$–$$$$
Fodor's Choice
★

🖰 **Kiawah Island Golf Resort.** Choose from one- to four-bedroom villas and three- to seven-bedroom private homes in two upscale resort villages on 10,000 wooded and oceanfront acres. The decades-old inn complex is no longer open, but a number of the smaller two-bedroom condo-villas are still fairly affordable. Or you can opt to stay at the Sanctuary at Kiawah Island, an amazing 255-room luxury waterfront hotel and spa. Its vast lobby is stunning, with walnut floors covered with hand-woven rugs and a wonderful collection of artworks. When a pianist plays in the lobby lounge it is dreamlike. The West Indies theme is evident in the guest rooms; bedposts are carved with impressionistic pineapple patterns, and plantation-style ceilings with exposed planks are painted white. The Ocean Room has incredible architectural details—wrought-iron gates and sculptures and a stained-glass dome. Its contemporary cuisine is of an international caliber. Along with the 10 mi of island beaches, recreational options include kayak and surfboard rental, nature tours, and arts-and-crafts classes. **Pros:** one of the most prestigious resorts in the country, it is still kid-friendly; the Ocean Room is an ideal venue for an anniversary or a proposal. **Cons:** not all hotel rooms have even an angular view of the ocean; it is pricey and a substantial drive from town. ⊠*12 Kiawah Beach Dr., Kiawah Island* ☎*843/768–2121 or 800/654–2924* ⊕*www.kiawahresort.com* ⇴*255 rooms, 600 villas and homes* ⑤*In-room: safe (some), refrigerator, Internet, Wi-Fi. In-hotel: 10 restaurants, golf courses, tennis courts, pools, gym, spa, beachfront, water sports, children's programs (ages 3–12), Internet terminal, Wi-Fi, parking (free), no-smoking rooms* ▤*AE, D, DC, MC, V.*

9

NIGHTLIFE AND THE ARTS

THE ARTS

CONCERTS The **Charleston Symphony Orchestra** (☎ *843/723–7528* ⊕ *www.charlestonsymphony.com*) season runs from October through April, with pops series, chamber series, family-oriented series, and holiday concerts. This symphony is nationally and even internationally renown, as it is also the Spoleto Festival Orchestra.

VENUES Bluegrass, blues, and country musicians step onto the historic stage of **Charleston Music Hall** (✉ *37 John St., Upper King* ☎ *843/853–2252* ⊕ *www.charlestonmusichall.com*) especially for Piccolo Spoleto performances. **Gaillard Municipal Auditorium** (✉ *77 Calhoun St., Upper King* ☎ *843/577–7400*) hosts symphony and ballet companies, as well as numerous festival events. The box office is open weekdays from 10 to 6. Dance, symphony, and theater productions are among those staged at the **North Charleston Performing Art Center** (✉ *5001 Coliseum Dr., North Charleston* ☎ *843/529–5050* ⊕ *www.coliseumpac.com*). Performances by the College of Charleston's theater department and music recitals are presented during the school year at the **Simons Center for the Arts** (✉ *54 St. Phillips St., College of Charleston Campus* ☎ *843/953–5604*).

NIGHTLIFE

BARS AND BREWERIES Atop the Market Pavilion Hotel, the outdoor **Pavilion Bar** (✉ *225 E. Bay St., Market area* ☎ *843/266–4218*) offers panoramic views of the city and harbor. Sit at the east overlook to appreciate the grand architecture of the Customs House. Enjoy appetizers, delicacies created with lobster and duck and such, with a signature martini. **Social Restaurant & Wine Bar** (✉ *188 E. Bay St., Market area* ☎ *843/577–5665*) offers 60 wines by the glass, as well as bottles and flights (to better compare and contrast several wines in smaller portions). Light menu choices are available, and there are pizzas and flavorful microbrews, too. **Southend Brewery** (✉ *161 E. Bay St., Market area* ☎ *843/853–4677*) has a lively bar serving beer brewed on the premises; try the wood-oven pizzas and the smokehouse barbecue. Thursday is salsa night, Friday showcases a bluegrass band, and Saturday night a guitarist. You can dance if the music moves you. In fact, it is encouraged.

JAZZ CLUBS The elegant **Charleston Grill** (✉ *Charleston Place Hotel, 224 King St.,*
★ *Market area* ☎ *843/577–4522*) has live jazz nightly and draws a mature, upscale clientele, hotel guests, and more recently an urbane thirtysomething crowd. At **Mistral** (✉ *99 S. Market St., Market area* ☎ *843/722–5709*) live blues and jazz make patrons feel good on Monday, Tuesday, Thursday, and Saturday nights. On Wednesday two French musicians sing their renditions of pop and folk songs. On Friday a Dixieland band really animates those who grew up with this music.

LIVE MUSIC **Mercato** (✉ *102 N. Market St., Market area* ☎ *843/722–6393*) is a popular restaurant that has become almost as well known for its entertainment, which begins on Wednesday nights (from 7 to 10), when there is customarily a jazz vocalist. The music usually cranks up from Thursday to Saturday at 8 and goes until 11. **The Thoroughbred Club** (✉ *Charleston Place Hotel, 130 Market St., Market area* ☎ *843/722–4900*) is both fun and classy, with a horse-racing theme and excellent appetizer menu. Go for the impressive afternoon tea (even with alcoholic libations), or sip a cocktail and enjoy the soothing piano being played Monday through Saturday after 1 PM (or Sunday after 5). Listen to authentic Irish music at **Tommy Condon's** (✉*15 Beaufain St., Market area* ☎*843/577–3818*).

SPORTS AND THE OUTDOORS

BEACHES

Trees, palmettos, and other natural foliage cover the interior, and there's a river that winds through **Folly Beach County Park** (✉*1100 W. Ashley Ave., off U.S. 17, Folly Island* ☎*843/588–2426* 🌐*www.ccprc.com* *$10 per car* ⏲*Apr., Sept., and Oct., daily 10–6; May–Aug., daily 9–7; Nov.–Mar., daily 10–5*) . The beach, 12 mi southwest of Charleston, is more than six football fields long. Play beach volleyball or rent a raft at the 600-foot-long beach in the **Isle of Palms County Park** (✉*1 14th Ave., Isle of Palms, Mount Pleasant* ☎*843/886–3863 or 843/768–4386* 🌐*www.ccprc.com* *$10 per car* ⏲*May–Aug., daily 9–7; Apr., Sept., and Oct., daily 10–6; Nov.–Mar., daily 10–5*). The public **Kiawah Beachwalker Park** (✉*Beachwalker Dr., Kiawah Island* ☎*843/768–2395* 🌐*www.ccprc.com* *$10 per car* ⏲*Mar., weekends 10–5; Apr. and Oct., weekends 10–6; May–Aug., daily 10–7; Sept., daily 10–6*), about 28 mi southwest of Charleston, has 500 feet of deep beach.

BOATING

If you want a sailing or motor yacht charter, perhaps a beach barbecue, or ecotour, or just to go offshore fishing, contact **AquaSafaris** (✉*Patriots Point Marina, Mount Pleasant* ☎*843/886–8133* 🌐*www.aqua-safaris.com*). Outings for individuals, families, and groups are provided by **Coastal Expeditions** (✉*514B Mill St., Mount Pleasant* ☎*843/884–7684*). **Island Bike & Surf Shop** (✉*3665 Bohicket Rd., John's Island* ☎*843/768–1158*) rents surfboards and kayaks and will deliver to the resort islands. Boards cost $15 a day. You can rent kayaks from **Middleton Place Plantation** (✉*4300 Ashley River Rd., West Ashley* ☎*843/556–6020* 🌐*www.theinnatmiddletonplace.com*) and glide along the Ashley River. Do make advance reservations. Take your family sailing, be at the helm, and learn how to command your own 26-foot sailboat on Charleston's beautiful harbor with the guidance of an instructor at **Ocean Sailing Academy** (✉*24 Patriots Point Rd., Mount Pleasant* ☎*843/971–0700* 🌐*osasailing.com*).

9

FISHING

Bohicket Marina (✉*1880 Andell Bluff Blvd., John's Island* ☎*843/768–1280* 🌐*www.bohicket.com*) has half- and full-day charters on 24- to 48-foot boats. For inshore fishing, expect to pay about $395 for 3 hours minimum (4 to 6 people), including bait, tackle, and licenses. Saltwater fly-fishers looking for an Orvis-endorsed guide do best by calling **Captain Richard Stuhr** (✉*547 Sanders Farm La., North Charleston* ☎*843/881–3179* 🌐*www.captstuhr.com*), who has been fishing the waters of Charleston, Kiawah, and Isle of Palms since 1991; he'll haul his boat, a 19-foot Action Craft, to you. **Palmetto Charters** (✉*224 Patriots Point Rd., Mount Pleasant* ☎*843/849–6004*) has guided trips that take you out in the ocean or stay close to shore. They also handle power yacht charters, crewed sailboat charters, and bareboats, both locally and in the Caribbean.

GOLF

With fewer golfers than in Hilton Head, the courses around Charleston have more choice starting times available. Nonguests can play at private island resorts, such as Kiawah Island, Seabrook Island, and Wild Dunes. There you will find breathtaking ocean views within a pristine setting. The public **Charleston Municipal Golf Course** (⊠*2110 Maybank Hwy., James Island* ☎*843/795–6517*) is a walker-friendly course. Green fees run $29 to $37. The **Dunes West Golf Club** (⊠*3535 Wando Plantation Way, Mount Pleasant* ☎*843/856–9000*) has great marshland views and lots of modulation on the greens. Green fees are $45 to $92. There are three championship courses at **Kiawah Island Resort** (⊠*12 Kiawah Beach Dr., Kiawah Island* ☎*800/576–1570*): Gary Player–designed Marsh Point; Tom Fazio–designed Osprey Point; and Jack Nicklaus–designed Turtle Point. All three charge the same green fees: $175 for resort guests, $219 for nonguests. **Links at Stono Ferry** (⊠*4812 Stono Links Dr., Hollywood* ☎*843/763–1817*) is a popular public course with reasonable rates. Green fees are $45 to $86. The prestigious **Ocean Course** (⊠*1000 Ocean Course Dr., Kiawah Island* ☎*843/266-4670*), designed by Pete Dye, was the site of the 1991 Ryder Cup. Unfortunately, its fame translates to green fees of $298 for resort guests, $350 for nonguests. (It is a walking-only facility until noon.) **Seabrook Island Resort** (⊠*Seabrook Island Rd., Seabrook Island* ☎*843/768–2529*) has two championship courses: Crooked Oaks, by Robert Trent Jones Sr., and Ocean Winds, by Willard Byrd. Green fees are $95 to $150. **Shadowmoss Golf Club** (⊠*20 Dunvegan Dr., West Ashley* ☎*843/556–8251*) is a well-marked, forgiving course with one of the best finishing holes in the area. Green fees are $28 to $52. Tom Fazio designed the Links and the Harbor courses at **Wild Dunes Resort** (⊠*10001 Back Bay Dr., Isle of Palms* ☎*843/886–2180* ⊠*5881 Palmetto Dr., Isle of Palms* ☎*843/886–2301*). Green fees are $140 to $165.

SPAS

Charleston Place Spa (⊠*130 Market St., Market area* ☎*843/722–4900* ⊕*www.charlestonplacespa.com*), a truly deluxe day spa, has nine treatment rooms and a wet room where seaweed body wraps and other treatments are administered. Four-handed massages for couples are a popular option. Locker rooms for men and women have showers and saunas; men also have a steam room. Adjacent is a fitness room, an indoor pool with skylights, and a spacious hot tub. In a historic Charleston "single house," **Stella Nova** (⊠*78 Society St., Lower King* ☎*843/723–0909* ⊕*www.stella-nova.com*) is just off King Street. It's serious about all of its treatments, from waxing to salt scrubs. For couples, there are aromatherapy massages and men's services, too. You enjoy refreshments on the breezy verandas and it is open daily, even on Sunday, when street parking is easier to find.

WATER SPORTS

Island Bike and Surf Shop (⊠ *3665 Bohicket Rd., John's Island* ☎ *843/768–1158*) rents surfboards, shredders, and kayaks and will deliver to the resort islands. Boards cost $15 a day. The pros at **McKevlin's Surf Shop** (⊠ *8 Center St., Folly Beach* ☎ *843/588–2247*) can teach you what you need to know about surfing at Folly Beach County Park. Surfboard rentals and instruction can be arranged. **Sun & Ski** (⊠ *1 Cedar St., Folly Beach* ☎ *843/588–0033*) rents Jet Skis off the beach, just to the left of the fishing pier. You can also rent a chair and umbrella here for five hours for $20.

SHOPPING

SHOPPING DISTRICTS

Fodor'sChoice ★ The Market area is a cluster of shops and restaurants centered around the **Old City Market** (⊠ *E. Bay and Market Sts., Market area*). Sweetgrass basket weavers work here and you can buy the resulting wares, although these artisan crafts have become expensive. The shops run the gamut, from inexpensive stores selling T-shirts and souvenirs to upscale boutiques catering to the sophisticated tourist. In the covered, open-air market vendors have stalls with everything from jewelry to dresses and purses. **King Street** is the major shopping street in town. Lower King (from Broad to Market streets) is lined with high-end antiques dealers. Middle King (from Market to Calhoun streets) is a mix of national chains like Banana Republic and Pottery Barn. Upper King (from Calhoun Street to Cannon Street) is the up-and-coming area where fashionistas like the alternative shops such as Putumayo. That area has been dubbed the Design District as well, for the furniture and interior-design stores selling home fashion. Some are minimalist contemporary, others carry Euro-antiques, and they all will ship.

SPECIALTY STORES

ANTIQUES **Birlant & Co**. (⊠ *191 King St., Lower King* ☎ *843/722–3842*) mostly carries 18th- and 19th-century English antiques, but keep your eye out for a Charleston Battery bench, for which they are famous. **English Rose Antiques** (⊠ *436 King St., Upper King* ☎ *843/722–7939*) has country-style accessories at some of the best prices on the Peninsula. **Haute Design** (⊠ *489 King St., Upper King* ☎ *843/577–9886*) sells antiques, chandeliers, and French and Italian furniture, as well as custom-designed pieces like tables and mirrors. Belgian linen and hand-screen-printed fabrics are a specialty, and available accessories include Vinnini blown glass and "antique" pillows. Interior design services are available. If you don't live locally, they will ship your treasures. The **King Street Antique Mall** (⊠ *495 King St., Upper King* ☎ *843/723–2211*) is part flea market, part antiques store.

ART GALLERIES ★ The **Eva Carter Gallery** (⊠ *132 E. Bay St., Market area* ☎ *843/722–0506*) displays the most recognized abstract paintings in the area of owner Eva Carter, and abstract works by the late William Halsey. **Horton Hayes Fine Art** (⊠ *30 State St., Market area* ☎ *843/958–0014*) carries the sought-after Lowcountry paintings depicting coastal life by Mark Kelvin Horton, who paints architectural and figurative works as well. Shannon

9

Rundquist is among the other Lowcountry artists shown; she has a fun, whimsical way of painting local life and is known for her blue crab art.

Fodor'sChoice ★   The **Martin Gallery** (✉ *18 Broad St., South of Broad* ☎843/723–7378), in a former bank building, is the city's most impressive gallery, selling art by nationally and internationally acclaimed artists, sculptors, and photographers. The gallery is known especially for its bronzes and large wooden sculptures, as well as glass sculpture and custom-designed jewelry.

CLOTHING   **Christian Michi** (✉ *220 King St., Market area* ☎843/723–0575) carries chichi women's clothing and accessories. Designers from Italy, such as Piazza Sempione and Bella Harari, are represented. High-end fragrances add to the luxurious air. Shop **Copper Penny** (✉ *311 King St., Market area* ☎843/723–2999) for trendy dresses and names like Trina Turk and Nanette Lepore. Boutique favorite **Finicky Filly** (✉ *303 King St., Lower King* ☎843/534–0203) carries exceptional women's apparel and accessories by such designers as Lela Rose, Molly B., and Etro. **The Trunk Show** (✉ *281 Meeting St., Market area* ☎843/722–0442) is an upscale consignment shop selling designer dresses, handbags and shoes, and vintage apparel. The back room is all about interior design. The shop has become known for its estate jewelry and also custom-made jewelry from semiprecious stones. It has an excellent selection of gowns and evening wear. Many items now come in new from other shops.

FOOD   **Charleston Candy Kitchen** (✉ *32A N. Market St., Market area* ☎843/723–4626) sells freshly made fudge, Charleston chews, and sesame-seed wafers. Make time to stop at **Market Street Sweets** (✉ *100 N. Market St., Market area* ☎843/722–1397) for the melt-in-your-mouth pralines and fudge.

FURNITURE   **Carolina Lanterns** (✉ *917 Houston Northcutt Blvd., Mount Pleasant* ☎843/881–4170 ⊕*www.carolinalanterns.com*) sells gas lanterns based on designs from downtown's historic district. **Historic Charleston Reproductions** (✉ *105 Broad St., South of Broad* ☎843/723–8292) has superb replicas of Charleston furniture and accessories, all authorized by the Historic Charleston Foundation. Royalties from sales contribute to restoration projects.

GIFTS   **Charleston Cooks/Maverick Kitchen Store** (✉ *194 E. Bay St., Market area* ☎843/722–1212) carries just about any gourmet kitchen tool or accessory you can think of. Regional food, cookbooks, and culinary gifts abound. And you can also enjoy cooking classes and demonstrations. If you want to learn to cook, the store focuses on Lowcountry cuisine by day and has a litany of other classes in the evening. You get to taste what is prepared, with wine as a complement. Gift certificates are offered, too.

JEWELRY   **Dixie Dunbar Jewelry** (✉ *192 King St., Lower King* ☎843/722–0006) deals in artisitic, unique jewelry. The hand-made pieces here can be delightfully unpredictable.

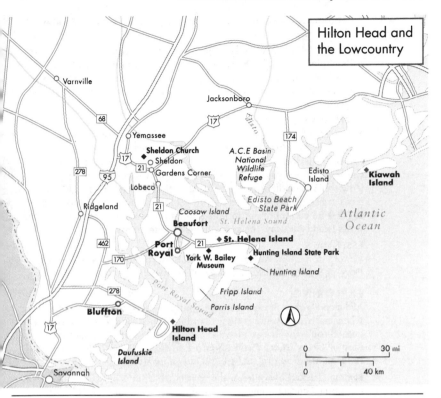

Hilton Head and the Lowcountry

HILTON HEAD AND THE LOWCOUNTRY

The action-packed island of Hilton Head anchors the southern tip of South Carolina's coastline and attracts 2.5 million visitors each year. Although it historically has drawn an upscale clientele, and it still does, you'll find that the crowd here is much more diverse than you might think. Although it has more than its fair share of millionaires (you might run into director Ron Howard at the Starbucks, for instance), it also attracts families in search of a good beach.

North of Hilton Head, the coastal landscape is peppered with quiet small towns and flanked by rural sea islands. Beaufort is a cultural treasure, a graceful antebellum town with a compact historic district and waterfront promenade. Several of the 18th- and 19th-century mansions have been converted to bed-and-breakfasts.

HILTON HEAD

112 mi southwest of Charleston via U.S. 17.

This half-tame, half-wild island is home to more than 25 world-class golf courses and even more resorts, hotels, and top restaurants. No matter how many golf courses pepper its landscape, however, Hilton Head will always be a semitropical barrier island. That means the 12 mi of beaches are lined with towering pines, palmetto trees, and wind-sculpted live oaks.

Since the 1950s, resorts sprung up all over. Although gated resorts, called "plantations," are private residential communities, all have public restaurants, marinas, shopping areas, and recreational facilities. All are secured, and cannot be toured unless arrangements are made at the visitor office

GETTING HERE AND AROUND

Hilton Head Island is 19 mi east of I–95. Take Exit 8 off I–95 South and then Hwy. 278 directly to the bridge. If you're heading to the southern end of the island, your best bet to save time and avoid traffic is to take the Toll Expressway. The cost is $1 each way. Know that U.S. 278 can slow to a standstill at rush hour and during holiday weekends, and the signs are so discreet that it's easy to get lost without explicit directions. ■ TIP➔ Be careful of putting the pedal to the metal, particularly on the Cross Island Parkway. The speed limits change dramatically.

ESSENTIALS

Visitor Information **Welcome Center of Hilton Head** (⊠ *100 William Hilton Pkwy.* ☎ *843/689–6302 or 800/523–3373* ⊕ *www.hiltonheadisland.org*).

EXPLORING

Audubon-Newhall Preserve, in the south, is 50 acres of pristine forest, where native plant life is tagged and identified. There are trails, a self-guided tour, and seasonal walks. ⊠ *Palmetto Bay Rd., near southern base of Cross Island Pkwy., South End* ☎ *843/842–9246* ⊕ *www.hiltonheadaudubon.org* ⊠ *Free* ⊙ *Daily dawn–dusk.*

★ **Bluffton.** Tucked away from the resorts, charming Bluffton has several old homes and churches, a growing artists' colony, several good restaurants (including Truffles Cafe), and oak-lined streets dripping with Spanish moss. You could grab Southern-style picnic food and head to the boat dock at the end of Pritchard Street for great views. There are interesting little shops and galleries and some limited-service B&Bs that provide a nearby alternative to Hilton Head's higher prices. This town and surrounding area are experiencing some rapid growth, since Hilton Head has little remaining undeveloped land. Much of the area's work force, especially its young, Latin, and international employees, live here. ⊠ *Route 46, 8 mi northwest on U.S. 278.*

★ **Coastal Discovery Museum.** The museum has relocated to what was the Horn Plantation, and it's an all-new and wonderful Lowcountry learning experience, especially for visitors and children. Although a small museum, its interpretive panels and exhibits are presented with a contemporary mind-set. Kids, for example, can dress up in the clothing of centuries past. The museum's mission is to develop an understanding of and appreciation for the cultural heritage and natural history of the Lowcountry. Visitors will learn about the early development of Hilton Head as an island resort from the Civil War to the 1930s. Admission is free, and its menu of lectures and tours on subjects both historical and natural range from $3 and up. The terrace and grounds are such that it is simply a comfortable, stress-free green landscape just off the Cross Island Parkway entrance ramp, though it feels a century away.

The gift shop remains in its original location, within the Visitors Center at 100 William Hilton Pkwy. ⊠ *Hwy. 278 at Gumtree Rd., North End* ☎ *843/689–6767* ⊕ *www.coastaldiscovery.org* ☜ *Free* ☺ *Mon.–Sat. 9–5, Sun. 10–3.*

Sea Pines Forest Preserve. At this 605-acre public wilderness tract, walking trails take you past a stocked fishing pond, waterfowl pond, and a 3,400-year-old Indian shell ring. Pick up the extensive activity guide at the Sea Pines Welcome Center to take advantage of goings-on—moonlight hayrides, storytelling around campfires, and alligator- and bird-watching boat tours. The preserve is part of the grounds at Sea Pines Resort. ⊠ *Off U.S. 278, Sea Pines Resort, South End* ☎ *843/363–4530* ⊕ *www.seapines.com* ☜ *$5 per car* ☺ *Daily dawn–dusk.*

WHERE TO EAT

$$$
SEAFOOD

✕**Boathouse 11.** Boathouse 11 is an actual waterfront restaurant; although hard to fathom, waterfront dining is difficult to find on this island. To soak in the salty atmosphere, reserve an outdoor table on its partially covered patio, where the bar looks out on the charter fishing pier. Fish and shellfish are the best choices here; for lunch you can order a perfect oyster po'boy. Yes, there are a few landlubber main courses, too. Want chicken instead? Ask for the teriyaki sandwich named after a local DJ. Distinguished by quality, fresh produce, this casual place also has a surprisingly admirable wine list with reasonably priced glasses and a number of bottles under $40. Brunch is a Sunday happening and quite popular. ⊠ *397 Squire Pope Rd., North End* ☎ *843/681–3663* ▭ *AE, D, MC, V*

$$$$
FRENCH

✕**Charlie's L'Etoile Verte.** This family-owned culinary landmark has oozed personality for a quarter-century. Originally one tiny room, its popularity with locals and repeat visitors sparked the move to these new spacious digs. At your first step into the door, you'll be wowed by the eclectic, country French decor and the homey ambience. Unusual for Hilton Head, the blackboard menu is handwritten daily according to market availability. The menu is just as homespun and cozy, primarily French classics. Certain items are constants, like the perfect curried shrimp salad at lunch. Come nightfall, out come the pâté maison and veal tenderloin with wild mushroom sauce. The wine list is distinguished. ⊠ *8 Orleans Rd., Mid-Island* ☎ *843/785–9277* ☜ *Reservations essential* ▭ *AE, MC, V* ☺ *Closed Sun. No lunch Mon.*

$$$$
ECLECTIC
Fodor's Choice
★

✕**CQs.** If you heard that all island restaurants are in shopping centers and lack atmosphere, then you need to experience CQs. Its rustic ambience—heart-pine floors, sepia-toned island photos, and a lovely second-story dining room—coupled with stellar cuisine, a personable staff, live piano music, and a feel-good spirit put most of the island's other restaurants to shame. Chef Eric Sayer's imaginative, original creations are divine. Imagine a lobster triumvirate as an appetizer, with an incredible lobster cheesecake the standout. Imagine a golden-brown Alaskan halibut afloat in a crab cream sauce. Manager Drew can pair your wine perfectly from an impeccable list. The gate pass for Sea Pines ($5) will be reimbursed with purchase of one main course or more. ⊠ *Harbour Town, 140 Lighthouse La., South End* ☎ *843/671–2779* ☜ *Reservations essential* ▭ *AE, MC, V* ☺ *No lunch.*

9

$$$–$$$$

ITALIAN

Fodor'sChoice

★

✕**Michael Anthony's.** This throwback goes back to the days when the most exotic, ethnic restaurant in most towns was a family-owned Italian spot. This is that kind of place, but contemporized and more upscale, with fresh, top-quality ingredients, simple yet elegant sauces, and waiters who know and care about the food they serve. Owned by a talented, charismatic Philadelphia family, the restaurant has a convivial spirit, and its innovative pairings and plate presentations are au courant. Locals file in for the early-dining menu, which includes three courses and a glass of wine; this is a superior value for about $20. But you can order off the à la carte menu, and after homemade gnocchi or a succulent veal chop with wild mushroom sauce, you can finish happily with a Sambuca and panna cotta. ✉*Orleans Plaza, 37 New Orleans Rd., Ste. L, South End* ☎843/785–6272 ⌕*Reservations essential* ⊟*AE, D, MC, V* ☾*Closed Sun. No lunch.*

$$$–$$$$

CONTINENTAL

★

✕**Old Fort Pub.** Overlooking the sweeping marshlands of Skull Creek, this romantic restaurant has almost panoramic views. It offers one of the island's best overall dining experiences: the building is old enough to have some personality, and the professional waiters do their duty. More important, the kitchen serves flavorful food, including a great appetizer of roasted calamari with sun-dried tomatoes and olives. Entrées like duck confit in rhubarb sauce and filet mignon with shiitake mushrooms hit the spot. The wine list is extensive, and there's outdoor seating plus a third-floor porch for toasting the sunset. Sunday brunch is celebratory and includes a mimosa. ✉*65 Skull Creek Dr., North End* ☎843/681–2386 ⊟*AE, D, DC, MC, V* ☾*No lunch.*

¢

AMERICAN

✕**Signe's Heaven Bound Bakery & Café.** Every morning locals roll in for the deep-dish French toast, crispy polenta, and whole-wheat waffles. Since 1974, European-born Signe has been feeding islanders her delicious soups (the chilled cucumber has pureed watermelon, green apples, and mint), curried chicken salad, and loaded hot and cold sandwiches. The beach bag ($10 for a cold sandwich, pasta or fresh fruit, chips, a beverage, and cookie) is a great deal. The key-lime bread pudding is amazing, as are the melt-in-your mouth cakes and the rave-worthy breads, especially the Italian ciabatta. If you want to become part of the Hilton Head scene, you need to know Signe. ✉*93 Arrow Rd., South End* ☎843/785–9118 ⊟*AE, D, MC, V* ☾*Closed Sun. No dinner.*

WHERE TO STAY

$

🏨**Hampton Inn on Hilton Head Island.** Tree-shaded, this hotel, which is sheltered from the noise and traffic, is a good choice if you have kids. The two-bedroom family suites are surprisingly upscale; the parents' rooms are tastefully appointed, and the kids' rooms are cool enough to have foosball tables. King-size studios with sleeper sofas are another alternative for families. Breakfast is as Southern as country gravy and biscuits or as European as Belgian waffles. Major renovations throughout the buildings included the replacement of carpets, bedspreads, and other fabrics. **Pros:** good customer service; clean; eight different breakfast menus. **Cons:** not on a beach (the closest is Folly Field, 2 mi away); grounds are not memorable, and your view is often the parking lot. ✉*1 Dillon Rd., Mid-Island* ☎843/681–7900 ⊕*www.hampton-inn.*

com ↪*115 rooms, 7 suites* ♿ *In-room: Internet. In-hotel: pool, Wi-Fi, parking (free), no-smoking rooms* ⊟*AE, D, DC, MC, V* ⦿*BP.*

$$$$ ⊡**Hilton Head Marriott Resort & Spa.** Marriott's standard rooms get a
☾ tropical twist at this palm-enveloped resort: sunny yellow-and-green
★ floral fabrics and cheery furnishings are part of the peppy decor. All
guest rooms have private balconies (spring for an oceanfront room),
writing desks, and down comforters. The tallest granddaddy of the
island's resorts, it's looking good after a major renovation in 2008 that
includes revamped pool areas and restaurants, notably Conroy's. To
take in the sea views, you can lounge by the pool or lunch at the fun,
outdoor snack bar. On rainy days and at dusk, the indoor pool under
a glass dome is a great alternative. Kids love Dive-in Theater nights
and the real sand castle in the lobby. Hammocks have been added to
the sandy knoll adjacent to the pool area. A new spa is also a must-do.
Pros: the multicultural staff has a great spirit; a full-service Marriott,
it is one of the best-run operations on the island. **Cons:** rooms could
be larger; in summer kids are everywhere; in-room Wi-Fi costs $9.95 a
day. ⊠*1 Hotel Circle, Palmetto Dunes, Mid-Island* ☎*843/686–8400
or 888/511–5086* 🖷*843/686–8450* ⊕*www.hiltonheadmarriott.com*
↪*476 rooms, 36 suites* ♿*In-room: safe, kitchen (some), Wi-Fi. In-
hotel: restaurant, bar, golf courses, tennis courts, pools, gym, spa,
beachfront, water sports, bicycles, Wi-Fi, children's programs (ages
3–12), no-smoking rooms* ⊟*AE, D, DC, MC, V.*

$$–$$$ ⊡**Hilton Oceanfront Resort.** There's a Caribbean sensibility to this five-
story chain hotel; the grounds are beautifully landscaped with decidu-
ous and evergreen bushes, and palms run along the beach. This resort
is far more casual, laid-back, and more family- than business-friendly.
The smallest accommodations are large, commodious studios with a
kitchenette; they go on up to two-bedroom suites. Many rooms face
the ocean, and all are decorated with elegant wood furnishings, such
as hand-carved armoires. A new, urbane lounge called the XO is a hap
pening nightspot. HH Prime is the steak house, and the excellent deli/
breakfast restaurant is being expanded at this writing. The resort has
three pools, one strictly for little children, another for families, and
an adults-only pool overlooking the ocean. Prices span a long range;
online deals can be the best, with outdoor cabana massages, breakfast,
and a bottle of wine included in some packages. **Pros:** competes more
with condos than hotels because of the size of its accommodations;
lots of outdoor dining options. **Cons:** boisterous wedding parties can
be too noisy; problems with cell reception; minimum stay is two nights
during summer. ⊠*23 Ocean La., Palmetto Dunes, Mid-Island* ✉*Box
6165, 29938* ☎*843/842–8000 or 800/845–8001* ⊕*www.hiltonhea-
dhilton.com* ↪*303 studios, 20 suites* ♿*In-room: kitchen, Internet.
In-hotel: restaurants, golf courses, pools, gym, water sports, bicycles,
Wi-Fi, children's programs (ages 5–12), no-smoking rooms* ⊟*AE, D,
DC, MC, V.*

$$$ ⊡**The Inn at Harbour Town.** The most buzz-worthy of Hilton Head's
properties is this European-style boutique hotel. A proper staff, clad in
kilts, pampers you with British service and a dose of Southern charm.
Butlers are on hand any time of the day or night, and the kitchen

9

delivers around the clock. The spacious guest rooms, decorated with neutral palettes, have luxurious touches like Frette bed linens, which are turned down for you each night. The back patio with its upscale furnishings, landscaping, and brickwork is enviable and runs right up to the greens of the fairways of the Harbour Town course. The lobby isn't a lobby per se; it just has a concierge desk for check-in. The Harbour Town Grill serves some of the best steaks on the island. Parking is free and easy, and valet service only costs $10. **Pros:** a service-oriented property, it is a centrally located Sea Pines address; unique, it is one of the finest hotel operations on island; complimentary parking. **Cons:** some concierges give you too much information to digest; no water views; golf-view rooms are $20 extra. ⊠*Lighthouse La., off U.S. 278, Sea Pines South End* ☎*843/363–8100 or 888/807–6873* ⊕*www.seapines. com* ⟱*60 rooms* ⚴*In-room: refrigerator, Wi-Fi. In-hotel: restaurant, golf courses, tennis courts, bicycles, laundry service, Wi-Fi, parking (free), no-smoking rooms* ⊟*AE, D, DC, MC, V.*

$$$$ ★ 🏨 **The Inn at Palmetto Bluff.** Fifteen minutes from Hilton Head, this is the Lowcountry's most luxurious resort. This 22,000-acre property has been transformed into a perfect replica of a small island town, complete with its own clapboard church. As a chauffeured golf cart takes you to your cottages, you'll pass the clubhouse, which resembles a mighty antebellum great house. All of the cottages are generously sized—even the one-bedrooms have more than 1,100 square feet of space. The decor is coastal chic, with sumptuous bedding, gas fireplaces, surround-sound home theaters, and marvelous bathroom suites with steam showers. Your screened-in porch puts you immediately in touch with nature. New is the Canoe Club with its restaurant, family pool, and bar. The spa puts you close to heaven with its pampering treatments. Dinner at its River House Restaurant is definitely worth an excursion from Hilton Head even if you do not stay here. **Pros:** the tennis/boccie/croquet complex has an atmospheric, impressive retail shop; the river adds both ambience and boat excursions; pillared ruins dotting the grounds are like sculpture. **Cons:** the mock Southern town is not the real thing; not that close to the amenities of Hilton Head. ⊠*476 Mount Pelia Rd., Bluffton* ☎*843/706–6500 or 866/706–6565* ⊕*www.palmettobluffresort.com* ⟱*50 cottages* ⚴*In-room: safe, refrigerator, Wi-Fi. In-hotel: 4 restaurants, bars, golf course, pools, water sports, bicycles, Internet terminal, Wi-Fi, no-smoking rooms* ⊟*AE, MC, V.*

$$-$$$ Fodor'sChoice ★ 🏨 **Main Street Inn & Spa.** This Italianate villa has stucco facades ornamented with lions' heads, elaborate ironwork, and shuttered doors. Staying here is like being a guest at a rich friend's estate. Guest rooms have velvet and silk brocade linens, feather duvets, and porcelain and brass sinks. An ample breakfast buffet is served in a petite, sunny dining room. In the afternoon there's complimentary wine at cocktail hour; before that, you can get gourmet coffee and homemade cookies which can be taken into the formal garden. Wi-Fi is free. The spa offers treatments ranging from traditional Swedish massages to Indian Kyria massages. Four king-size junior suites overlook the pool and gardens and are the inn's largest. Some rooms have balconies and fireplaces. **Pros:** when someone plays the piano while you are having your wine, it's

super-atmospheric; the lion's head fountains and other Euro-architectural details. Cons: weddings can overwhelm the resort, especially on weekends and throughout June; regular rooms are small. ☒*2200 Main St., North End* ☎*843/681–3001 or 800/471–3001* ⊕*www.mainstreetinn.com* ⤵*29 rooms, 4 jr. suites* ⚐*In-room: refrigerator, Wi-Fi. In-hotel: pool, spa, Internet terminal, Wi-Fi, no-smoking rooms* ▤*AE, D, MC, V* �○⦚*BP.*

$$$$
Ⓒ
Fodor'sChoice
★

⊞**Westin Hilton Head Island Resort & Spa.** A circular drive winds around a metal sculpture of long-legged marsh birds as you approach this luxury resort. The lush landscape lies on the island's quietest, least inhabited stretch of sand. Guest rooms, most with ocean views from the balconies, have homey touches, crown molding, and contemporary furnishings. If you need space to spread out, there are two- and three-bedroom villas. The service is generally efficient and caring. A new spa opened in 2007 and has become the big buzz on the island. This continues to be one of the top resorts on Hilton Head, particularly for honeymooners. Pros: the number and diversity of children's activities is amazing; a good destination wedding hotel, ceremonies are performed on the beach and at other atmospheric outdoor venues; the beach here is absolutely gorgeous. Cons: in the off-seasons, the majority of its clientele are large groups; the hotel's phone service can bog down; difficult to get cell-phone reception indoors. ☒*2 Grass Lawn Ave., North End* ☎*843/681–4000 or 800/228–3000* ⊕*www.westin.com* ⤵*412 rooms, 29 suites* ⚐*In-room: Internet, Wi-Fi. In-hotel: 3 restaurants, golf courses, tennis courts, pools, gym, beachfront, bicycles, children's programs (ages 4–12), no-smoking rooms* ▤*AE, D, DC, MC, V.*

PRIVATE VILLA
RENTALS

ResortQuest (☎*843/686–8144 or 800/448–3408* ⊕*www.resortquesthiltonhead.com*) boasts that it has the most comprehensive selection of accommodations (500-plus) on Hilton Head, from oceanfront to golf views, all in premier locations including the plantations.

Resort Rentals of Hilton Head Island (☎*843/686–6008 or 800/845–7017* ⊕*www.hhivacations.com*) represents some 300 homes and villas island-wide from the gated communities to some of the older non-gated areas that have the newest homes. In addition to the rental fee, you'll pay 11% tax, a $60 reservation fee, and a 4% administration fee.

Sea Pines Resort (☎*843/842–1496* ⊕*www.seapines.com*) operates in its own little world on the far south end of the island. The vast majority of the overnight guests rent one of the 500 suites, villas, and beach houses. In addition to quoted rates, expect to pay an additional 19.5% to cover the combined taxes and resort fees.

NIGHTLIFE

Reggae bands play at **Big Bamboo** (☒*Coligny Plaza, N. Forest Beach Dr., South End* ☎*843/686–3443*), a bar with a South Pacific theme. The **Hilton Head Brewing Co.** (☒*Hilton Head Plaza, Greenwood Dr., South End* ☎*843/785–2739*) lets you shake your groove thing to 1970s-era disco on Wednesday. There's live music on Friday and karaoke on Saturday. **Jazz Corner** (☒*The Village at Wexford, C-1, South End* ☎*843/842–8620*) will always be known and remembered for its live music and fun, New Orleans–style atmosphere. The restaurant has

9

a newly updated menu, so to assure yourself of a seat on busy nights, make reservations for dinner. **Jump & Phil's Bar & Grill** (⊠*3 Hilton Head Plaza, South End* ☎*843/785–9070*) is a happening scene, especially for locals, and you could pass this nondescript building by if you didn't know. "Jump," whose real name is John Griffin, is an author of thriller novels under the pen name John R. Maxim, and this place is a magnet for area writers and football fans during the season. **The Metropolitan Lounge** (⊠*Park Plaza, Greenwood Dr., South End* ☎*813/785–8466*) is the most sophisticated of several fun places on Park Plaza. With a Euro-style that appeals to all ages, it is known for its martini menu. On weekends there is dancing in an anteroom separated by a wrought-iron gate. Here you will see all ages, from golf guys to the island's sassy, young, beautiful people. **Monkey Business** (⊠*Park Plaza, Greenwood Dr., South End* ☎*843/686–3545*) is a dance club popular with young professionals. On Friday there's live beach music. One of the island's latest hot spots, **Santa Fe Cafe** (⊠*Plantation Center in Palmetto Dunes, 700 Plantation Center, North End* ☎*843/785–3838*) is where you can lounge about in front of the adobe fireplace or sip top-shelf margaritas on the rooftop. The restaurant's clientele is predominately local residents and tends to be older than those who frequent the Boathouse because of its Southwestern atmosphere, unique on the island, and its guitarist(s). **Turtle's** (⊠*The Westin Hilton Head Resort & Spa, 2 Grass Lawn Ave., North End* ☎*843/681–4000*) appeals to those who still like to hold their partner when they dance.

SPORTS AND THE OUTDOORS

BEACHES   Although resort beach access is reserved for guests and residents, there are four public entrances to Hilton Head's 12 mi of ocean beach. The two main parking spots are off U.S. 278 at Coligny Circle in the South End, near the Holiday Inn, and on Folly Field Road, Mid-Island. Both have changing facilities. South of Folly Field Road, Mid-Island along U.S. 278, Bradley Beach Road and Singleton Road lead to beaches where parking space is limited. ■**TIP➜ A delightful stroll on the beach can end with an unpleasant surprise if you don't put your towels, shoes, and other earthly possessions way up on the sand. Tides here can fluctuate as much as 7 feet. Check the tide chart at your hotel.**

BIKING   There are more than 40 mi of public paths that crisscross Hilton Head Island, and pedaling is popular along the firmly packed beach. The island keeps adding more to the "boardwalk" network as visitors are utilizing it and it is such a safe alternative for kids. Keep in mind when crossing streets that in South Carolina, vehicles have the right-of-way. ■**TIP➜ Bikes with wide tires are a must if you want to ride on the beach. They can save you a spill should you hit loose sand on the trails.**

Bicycles can be rented at most hotels and resorts. You can also rent bicycles from the **Hilton Head Bicycle Company** (⊠*112 Arrow Rd., South End* ☎*843/686–6888* ⊕*www.hiltonheadbicycle.com*) and **Pedals Bicycles** (⊠*71 Pope Ave., South End* ☎*843/842–5522*). **South Beach Cycles** (⊠*Sea Pines Resort, off U.S. 278, South End* ☎*843/671–2453* ⊕*www.southbeachracquetclub.com*) rents bikes, helmets, tandems, and adult tricycles.

BOATING This is one of the most delightful ways to commune with nature on this commercial but physically beautiful island. You paddle through the creeks and estuaries and try to keep up with the dolphins!

Outside Hilton Head (⊠ *Sea Pines Resort, off U.S. 278, South End* ⊠ *Shelter Cove Lane at U.S. 278, Mid-Island* ☎ *843/686–6996 or 800/686–6996* ⊕ *www.outsidehiltonhead.com*) is an ecologically sensitive company that rents canoes and kayaks; it also runs nature tours and dolphin-watching excursions.

FISHING Captain Jim of **The Stray Cat** (⊠ *The Docks at Charlie's Crab, 3 Hudson La., North End* ☎ *843/683–5427* ⊕ *www.straycatcharter.com*) will help you decide whether you want to fish "in-shore" or go offshore into the deep blue. You can go for four, six, or eight hours, and the price is $120 an hour; bait and tackle are provided, but you must bring your own lunch.

GOLF
COURSES
Arthur Hills at Palmetto Hall (⊠ *Palmetto Hall, 108 Fort Howell Dr., North End* ☎ *843/689–9205* ⊕ *www.palmettohallgolf.com* ⅄ *18 holes. 6918 yds. Par 72. Green Fee: $60–$104*) is a player favorite from the renowned designer Arthur Hills; this course has his trademark: undulating fairways. The course, punctuated with lakes, gently flows across the island's rolling hills, winding around moss-draped oaks and towering pines. Although it's part of a country club, the course at **Country Club of Hilton Head** (⊠ *70 Skull Creek Dr., North End* ☎ *843/681–4653 or 888/465–3475* ⊕ *www.golfisland.com* ⚞ *Reservations essential* ⅄ *18 holes. 6919 yds. Par 72. Green Fee: $50–$119*) is open for public play. A well kept secret, it's never overcrowded. This 18 hole Rees Jones designed course is a more casual environment than many of the others. Jack Nicklaus created **Golden Bear Golf Club at Indigo Run** (⊠ *Indigo Run, 72 Golden Bear Way, North End* ☎ *843/689–2200* ⊕ *www.goldenbear-indigorun.com* ⅄ *18 holes. 6643 yds. Par 72. Green Fee $85 $109*). Located in the upscale Indigo Run community, it's in a natural woodlands setting and offers easy-going rounds. It is a course that requires more thought than muscle, yet you will have to earn every par you make. And there are the fine points—the color GPS monitor on every cart and women-friendly tees. After an honest, traditional test of golf, most golfers finish up at the plush clubhouse and with some food and drink at Just Jack's Grille.

FodorsChoice
★
Harbour Town Golf Links (⊠ *Sea Pines Resort, 11 Lighthouse La., South End* ☎ *843/842–8484 or 800/955–8337* ⊕ *www.golfisland.com* ⅄ *18 holes. 6973 yds. Par 71. Green Fee: $153–$295*) is considered by many golfers to be one of those must-play courses. Designed by Pete Dye, the layout is reminiscent of Scottish courses of old. The Golf Academy is ranked among the top 10 in the country. **The May River Golf Club** (⊠ *Palmetto Bluffs, 476 Mt. Pelia Rd., Bluffton* ☎ *843/706–6500* ⊕ *www.palmettobluffresort.com/golf* ⅄ *18 holes. 7171 yds. Par 72. Green Fee: $90–$260*), an 18-hole Jack Nicklaus course, has several holes along the banks of the scenic May River and will challenge all skill levels. The greens are covered by Paspalum, the latest eco-friendly turf. Caddy service is always required, even if you chose to rent a golf cart, and then no carts are allowed earlier than 9 AM. **Old South Golf**

9

Links (✉ *50 Buckingham Plant Dr., Bluffton* ☎*843/785–5353* ⊕*www.golfisland.com* ⚑*18 holes. 6772 yds. Par 72. Green Fee: $75–$85*) has scenic holes with marshland and views of the Intracoastal Waterway. A recent Internet poll had golfers preferring it over the famous Harbour Town Golf Links and **Robert Trent Jones at Palmetto Dunes** (✉*7 Robert Trent Jones Way, North End* ☎*843/785–1138* ⊕*www.palmettodunes.com* ⚑*18 holes. 7005 yds. Par 72. Green Fee: $125–$165*), which is one of the island's most popular layouts. Its beauty and character are accentuated by the par-5, 10th hole, which offers a panoramic view of the ocean. It's one of only two oceanfront holes on Hilton Head.

GOLF SCHOOLS **The Academy at Robert Trent Jones** (✉*Palmetto Dunes Resort, 7 Trent Jones La., Mid-Island* ☎*843/785–1138* ⊕*www.palmettodunes.com*) offers one-hour lessons, daily clinics, one- to three-day schools, and clinics by Doug Weaver, former PGA tour pro. **The TOUR Academy of Palmetto Hall Plantation** (✉ *Palmetto Hall Plantation, 108 Fort Hollow Dr., North End* ☎*843/681–1516* ⊕*www.palmettohallgolf.com*) is the only golf school on island affiliated with the PGA. This academy is known for its teaching technologies that include video analysis. Students can chose from a one-hour private lesson to up to five days of golf instruction to include a round of golf with an instructor.

SPAS The low-key **Faces** (✉*The Village at Wexford, 1000 William Hilton Pkwy., North End* ☎*843/785–3075* ⊕*www.facesdayspa.com*) has been pampering loyal clients for 20 years, with body therapists and cosmetologists who do what they do well. It has a fine line of cosmetics and does makeovers or evening makeups. Open seven days a week, Monday Fodor'sChoice night is for the guys. **Heavenly Spa by Westin** (✉ *Westin Resort Hilton ★ Head Island, Port Royal Plantation, 2 Grasslawn Ave., North End* ☎*843/681–4000, Ext. 7519*) is a new facility at the Westin resort offering the quintessential sensorial spa experience. Unique is a collection of treatments based on the energy from the color indigo, once a cash crop in the Lowcountry. The full-service salon, the relax room with its teas and healthy snacks, and the adjacent retail area with products like sweet-grass scents are heavenly, too. The **Spa at Main Street Inn** (✉*2200 Main St., North End* ☎*843/681–3001* ⊕*www.mainstreetinn.com*) has holistic massages that will put you in another zone. A petite facility, it offers deep muscle therapy, couples massage, hydrotherapy soaks, and outdoor courtyard massages. Jack Barakatis instructs both his students and his own clients in the art of de-stressing, with a significant dose of spirituality. The **Spa at Palmetto Bluffs** (✉*476 Mount Pelia Rd., Bluffton* ☎*843/706–6500* ⊕*www.palmettobluffresort.com*) has been dubbed the "celebrity spa" by locals, for this two-story facility is the ultimate pamper palace. It is as creative in its names that often have a Southern accent, as it is in its treatments. There are Amazing Grace and High Cotton bodyworks and massages, sensual soaks and couples massage, special treatments for gentlemen/golfers and Belles and Brides packages as this is a premier wedding destination. Nonguests are welcome. **Spa Soleil** (✉*Marriott Hilton Head Resort & Spa, Palmetto Dunes, 1 Hotel Circle, Mid-Island* ☎*843/686–8400* ⊕*www.csspagroup.com*) is one of the newest spas on island; this $7 million facility has the atmosphere and professionalism, the therapies, and litany of massages found in the country's finest spas. Since the facility is all new, everything is still quite pristine. The colors, aromas, teas, and snacks make your treatment a soothing, therapeutic experience.

TENNIS There are more than 300 courts on Hilton Head. Tennis comes in at a close second as the island's premier sport after golf. It is recognized as one of the nation's best tennis destinations. Hilton Head has a large international organization of coaches. Spring and Fall are the peak seasons for cooler play with numerous tennis packages available at the resorts and through the schools.

Palmetto Dunes Tennis Center (⊠*6 Trent Jones La., Mid-Island* ☎*843/ 785–1152* ⊕*www.palmettodunes.com*) welcomes nonguests. **Port Royal** (⊠*15 Wimbledon Ct., North End* ☎*843/686–8803* ⊕*www. heritagegolfgroup.com*) has 16 courts, including two grass. **Sea Pines Racquet Club** (⊠*Sea Pines Resort, off U.S. 278, 32 Greenwood Dr., South End* ☎*843/363–4495*) has 23 courts, instructional programs, and a pro shop. Highly rated **Van der Meer Tennis Center/Shipyard Racquet Club** (⊠*Shipyard Plantation, 19 de Allyon Rd., Mid-Island* ☎*843/686– 8804* ⊕*www.vandermeertennis.com*) is recognized for tennis instruction. Four of its 28 courts are covered.

SHOPPING

ART GALLERIES **Linda Hartough Gallery** (⊠*Harbour Town, 140 Lighthouse Rd., South End* ☎*843/671–6500*) is all about golf. There's everything from landscapes of courses to golden golf balls to pillows embroidered with sayings like "Queen of the Green." The **Red Piano Art Gallery** (⊠*220 Cordillo Pkwy., Mid-Island* ☎*843/785–2318*) showcases 19th- and 20th-century works by regional and national artists.

GIFTS The **Audubon Nature Store** (⊠*The Village at Wexford, U.S. 278, Mid-Island* ☎*843/785–4311*) has gifts with a wildlife theme. **Outside Hilton Head** (⊠*The Plaza at Shelter Cove, U.S. 278, Mid-Island* ☎*843/686– 6996 or 800/686–6996*) sells Pawleys Island hammocks (first made in the late 1800s) and other items that let you enjoy the great outdoors.

JEWELRY The **Bird's Nest** (⊠*Coligny Plaza, Coligny Circle and N. Forest Beach Dr., South End* ☎*843/785–3737*) sells locally made shell and sanddollar jewelry, as well as island-theme charms. The **Goldsmith Shop** (⊠*3 Lagoon Rd., Mid-Island* ☎*843/785–2538*) carries classic jewelry and island charms. **Forsythe Jewelers** (⊠*71 Lighthouse Rd., South End* ☎*843/342–3663*) is the island's leading jewelry store.

BEAUFORT

38 mi north of Hilton Head via U.S. 278 and Rte. 170; 70 mi southwest of Charleston via U.S. 17 and U.S. 21.

Charming homes and churches grace this old town on Port Royal Island. Come here on a day-trip from Hilton Head, Savannah, or Charleston, or to spend a quiet weekend at a B&B while you shop and stroll through the historic district. Tourists are drawn equally to the town's artsy scene (art walks are regularly scheduled) and the area's water-sports possibilities. Actually, more and more transplants have decided to spend the rest of their lives here, drawn to Beaufort's small-town charms, and the area

The World of Gullah

In the Lowcountry, Gullah refers to several things: a language, a people, and a culture. Gullah (the word itself is believed to be derived from Angola), an English-based dialect rooted in African languages, is the unique language of the African-Americans of the Sea Islands of South Carolina and Georgia, more than 300 years old. Most locally born African-Americans of the area can understand, if not speak, Gullah.

Descended from thousands of slaves who were imported by planters in the Carolinas during the 18th century, the Gullah people have maintained not only their dialect but also their heritage. Much of Gullah culture traces back to the African rice-coast culture and survives today in the art forms and skills, including sweetgrass basket-making, of Sea Islanders. During the colonial period, when rice was king, Africans from the West African rice kingdoms drew high premiums as slaves. Those with basket-making skills were extremely valuable because baskets were needed for agricultural and household use. Made by hand, sweetgrass baskets are intricate coils of a marsh grass with a sweet, haylike aroma.

Nowhere is Gullah culture more evident than in the foods of the region.

Rice appears at nearly every meal—Africans taught planters how to grow rice and how to cook and serve it as well. Lowcountry dishes use okra, peanuts, benne (the African word for sesame seeds), field peas, and hot peppers. Gullah food reflects the bounty of the islands: shrimp, crabs, oysters, fish, and such vegetables as greens, tomatoes, and corn. Many dishes are prepared in one pot, a method similar to the stew-pot cooking of West Africa.

On St. Helena Island, near Beaufort, Penn Center is the unofficial Gullah headquarters, preserving the culture and developing opportunities for Gullahs. In 1852 the first school for freed slaves was established at Penn Center. You can delve into the culture further at the York W. Bailey Museum.

On St. Helena, many Gullahs still go shrimping with hand-tied nets, harvest oysters, and grow their own vegetables. Nearby on Daufuskie Island, as well as on Edisto, Wadmalaw, and Johns islands near Charleston, you can find Gullah communities as well. A famous Gullah proverb says: *If oonuh ent kno weh oonuh dah gwine, oonuh should kno weh oonuh come f'um.* Translation: If you don't know where you're going, you should know where you come from.

is burgeoning. A truly Southern town, its picturesque backdrops have lured filmmakers here to film *The Big Chill*, *The Prince of Tides*, and *The Great Santini*, the last two being Hollywood adaptations of best-selling books by author Pat Conroy. Conroy has waxed poetic about the Lowcountry and calls the Beaufort area home. The city closest to the Marine base on Parris Island, Beaufort also has a naval hospital.

GETTING HERE AND AROUND
Beaufort is 25 mi east of I–95, on U.S. 21. The only way here is by private car.

Gullah Heritage Trail Tours give a wealth of history about slavery and the Union takeover of the island during the Civil War. Gullah 'n' Geechie Mahn Tours lead groups throughout Beaufort with a focus on African-American culture.

ESSENTIALS

Tour Contacts **Gullah 'n' Geechie Mahn Tours** (✉ *671 Sea Island Pkwy., Beaufort* ☎ *843/838–7516* ⊕ *www.gullahngeechietours.net*).

Visitor Information **Beaufort Visitors Center** (✉ *2001 Boundaray St., Beaufort* ☎ *843/525–8523*). **Regional Beaufort Chamber of Commerce** (✉ *1106 Carteret St., Box 910, Beaufort* ☎ *843/986–5400* ⊕ *www.beaufortsc.org*).

EXPLORING

Henry C. Chambers Waterfront Park, off Bay Street, is a great place to survey the scene. Trendy restaurants and bars overlook these 7 landscaped acres along the Beaufort River. There's a farmers' market here on Saturday, April through August, 8 to noon.

★ Secluded **Hunting Island State Park** has nature trails and about 3 mi of public beaches—some dramatically and beautifully eroding. Founded in 1993 to preserve and promote its natural existence, it harbors 5,000 acres of rare maritime forests. Nonetheless, the light sands decorated with driftwood and the raw, subtropical vegetation is breathtaking. Stroll the 1,300 foot long fishing pier, among the longest on the East Coast, or you can go fishing or crabbing. You will be at one with nature. The fit can climb the 181 steps of the **Hunting Island Lighthouse** (built in 1859 and abandoned in 1933) for sweeping views. The nature center has exhibits, an aquarium, and lots of turtles. The park is 18 mi southeast of Beaufort via U.S. 21; if you want to stay on the island, be sure to call for reservations. From April 1 to October 31 there is a one-week minimum stay, November 1 to March 31 the minimum is two nights. Cabins that sleep up to six or eight ($–$$) must be reserved far in advance for summer weekends (there are only 12). Expect to pay about $25 for campsites with electricity, $17 without. ✉ *1775 Sea Island Pkwy., off St. Helena Island, Hunting Island* ☎ *843/838–2011* ⊕ *www. southcarolinaparks.com* 💲 *$4* ☉ *Park: Apr.–Oct., daily 6 AM–9 PM; Nov.–Mar., daily 6–6. Lighthouse daily 11–4.*

John Mark Verdier House Museum, built in the Federal style, has been restored and furnished as it would have been between its construction in 1805 and the visit of Lafayette in 1825. It was the headquarters for Union forces during the Civil War. A combination ticket that gets you into the Beaufort Museum & Arsenal (under renovations until Spring 2009) and the John Mark Verdier House Museum saves you $1. ✉ *801 Bay St.* ☎ *843/379–6335* 💲 *$5* ☉ *Mon.–Sat. 10–3:30.*

St. Helena Island, 9 mi southeast of Beaufort via U.S. 21, is the site of the Penn Center Historic District. Established in the middle of the Civil War, Penn Center was the South's first school for freed slaves; now open to the public, the center provides community services, too. This island

9

is both residential and commercial, with nice beaches, cooling ocean breezes, and a great deal of natural beauty.

The **York W. Bailey Museum** has displays on the Penn Center, and on the heritage of Sea Island African-Americans; it also has pleasant grounds shaded by live oaks. The Penn Center (1862) was one of the first schools for the newly emancipated slaves. These islands are where Gullah, a musical language that combines English and African languages, developed. This is a major stop for anyone interested in the Gullah history and culture of the Lowcountry. ⊠ *16 Martin Luther King Jr. Blvd., St. Helena Island* ☎ *843/838–2432* ⊕ *www.penncenter.com* ⊟ *$5* ⊘ *Mon.–Sat. 11–4.*

WHERE TO EAT

$$$$
ECLECTIC
Fodor'sChoice
★
✕ **Bateaux.** This contemporary restaurant, which was formerly on Lady's Island, has a new home in a historic brick building in Port Royal, 6 mi southwest of Beaufort. The location affords waterfront views, which are best from the second story, although some downstairs tables also offer a glimpse of the blue. The move has brought major changes; lunch is no longer served, and "Chip" Ulbrich is no longer a partner. For now, owner Richard Wilson is in the kitchen. He continues creating imaginative Southern cuisine, and the menu keeps evolving. The food is fresh, elegant, and artistically presented. Foodies love that they can get foie gras in crepes and other dishes. Seafood is the obvious specialty; try the shrimp and scallops over red-pepper risotto with fried prosciutto and spinach. The staff is well-trained and knowledgeable. ⊠ *610 Paris Ave., Port Royal* ⊕ *Box 2179, Port Royal 29935* ☎ *843/379–0777* ⊟ *AE, MC, V* ⊘ *Closed Sun. No lunch.*

$–$$
AMERICAN
✕ **Plums.** Down the alley behind Shipman's Gallery is this homey frame house with plum-colored awnings shading the front porch. Plums still uses old family recipes for its crab-cake sandwiches and curried chicken salad, but now it also offers a blue cheese and portobello mushroom sandwich. Dinner has creative and affordable pasta and seafood dishes. The crowd is a mix of locals, particularly twenty- to thirtysomethings, and tourists, often with children. Its downtown riverfront location, fun atmosphere, and reasonable prices are the draw. There's live music on weekends, starting at around 10 PM and geared to the younger crowd. ⊠ *904½ Bay St.* ☎ *843/525–1946* ⊟ *AE, MC, V.*

$$$$
ECLECTIC
Fodor'sChoice
★
✕ **Saltus River Grill.** Owner Lantz Price has given this 19-century loft a classy sailing motif, with portals and oversize photos of sailboats. The hippest eatery in Beaufort wins over epicureans with its cool design (subdued lighting, mod booths, dark-wood bar), waterfront patio, and nouveau Southern menu. Come early (the kitchen opens at 4 PM) and sit outdoors on the river with your cocktails. There are separate menus for sushi and oysters. A flawless dinner might start off with the skillet crab cakes with corn relish and beurre blanc sauce, then segue to the skewered, grilled quail with Oriental glaze. The wine list is admirable, and the staff is adept at pairings. Desserts change nightly; if offered, the pineapple upside-down cake can be the perfect end to your meal. ⊠ *802 Bay St.* ☎ *843/379–3474* ⊟ *AE, D, MC, V.*

$–$$
SEAFOOD
✕ **Shrimp Shack.** On the way to Fripp and Hunting Islands, follow the cue of locals and stop at this endearing little place where Ms. Hilda,

the owner, will take good care of you. All seating is outdoors, and once seated, you can't see the water. The menu includes all the typical Lowcountry fried plates, as well as South Carolina crab cakes, boiled shrimp, and gumbo, but it is best known for its shrimp burgers, sweet-potato fries, and sweet tea. Dinner is served only until 8 PM. Doors open at 11 AM. ⊠*1929 Sea Island Pkwy., 18 mi southeast of Beaufort, St. Helena* ☎*843/838–2962* ▤*No credit cards* ⊗*Closed Sun.*

WHERE TO STAY

$$–$$$ 📺**Beaufort Inn.** This peach-painted 1890s Victorian inn charms you with its gables and wraparound porches. Pine-floor guest rooms have period reproductions, striped wallpaper, and comfy chairs. Several have fireplaces and four-poster beds. This is a homey place right in the heart of the historic district, and most rooms have views of the surrounding buildings. Room options in the main inn range from a standard queen-size room to suites, which are the most popular. Deluxe Suites have living rooms and are in separate cottages. There are also one two-bed-room, two-bathroom apartment in a separate, historic building over-looking Bay Street. Garden Cottages are modern buildings and don't have the same traditional feel, but they do have garden or courtyard views; decor here is more contemporary, with heavier, darker woods and replica claw-foot tubs. Regrettably, the restaurant has closed, which is a loss to Beaufort's culinary scene. **Pros:** located in the heart of the historic district; continental breakfast has a chef-attended omelet station; the evening social hour includes snacks, refreshments, and wine. **Cons:** atmosphere may feel too dated for those seeking a more contemporary hotel; no more restaurant; deluxe suites have the worst views of all—the parking lot. ⊠*809 Port Republic St.* ☎*843/521–9000* ⊕*www.beaufortinn.com* ⇨*28 rooms* &*In-room: DVD. In-hotel: bicycles, no kids under 8, parking (free), no-smoking rooms* ▤*AE, D, MC, V* ⊚*BP.*

$$$–$$$$ 📺**Cuthbert House Inn.** Named after the original Scottish owners, who
★ made their money in cotton and indigo, this 1790 home is filled with 18th- and 19th-century heirlooms. It retains the original Federal fire-places and crown and rope molding. When Beaufort was occupied by the Union army during the Civil War, this home was used as the gen-erals' headquarters. Guest rooms and oversize suites have endearing architectural details, comfortable with hand-knotted rugs on the pine floors and commanding beds piled high with quilts. Choose one that looks out on the bay and the glorious sunset. The Mariner's Suite has a veranda, too. Beautifully lighted at night, this antebellum house, with white pillars and dual verandas, typifies the Old South. Wedding parties can rent out the whole inn, and many couples spend their honeymoon nights here. But it appeals foremost to an older generation. A renova-tion of all rooms was in progress at this writing and was expected to be finished by mid-2009. **Pros:** owners are accommodating; other guests provide good company during the complimentary wine service. **Cons:** some furnishings are a bit busy; some artificial flower arrange-ments; stairs creak. ⊠*1203 Bay St.* ☎*843/521–1315 or 800/327–9275* ⊕*www.cuthberthouseinn.com* ⇨*6 rooms, 2 suites* &*In-room: refrig-erator, DVD, Wi-Fi. In-hotel: bicycles, no kids under 12, no-smoking rooms* ▤*AE, D, MC, V* ⊚*BP.*

9

$$$–$$$$
Fodor'sChoice
★

Rhett House Inn. Art and antiques abound in a circa-1820 home turned storybook inn. Look for the little luxuries—down pillows and duvets, a CD player in each room, and fresh flowers. The best rooms open out onto the veranda (No. 2) or the courtyard garden (No. 7). The interior decor is Beaufort traditional coupled with Manhattan panache. Breakfast, afternoon tea, evening hors d'oeuvres, and dessert are included in the rate. Visiting celebrities have included Barbra Streisand, Jeff Bridges, and Dennis Quaid. The remodeled (not so historic) house across the street has eight more rooms, each of which has a gas fireplace, a whirlpool bath, a private entrance, and a porch. **Pros:** all guests come together for breakfast and other social hours; more private in annex. **Cons:** annex does not have the charisma of the main inn; in the main house you can hear footsteps on stairs and in hallways. ⊠*1009 Craven St.* ☎*843/524–9030* ⊕*www.rhetthouseinn.com* ⇦*16 rooms, 1 suite* ⚐*In-hotel: restaurant, bicycles, no kids under 5, parking (free), no-smoking rooms* ▤*AE, D, MC, V* ⎅*BP.*

SPORTS AND THE OUTDOORS

KAYAK AND
BOAT TOURS

Beaufort is where the Ashepoo, Combahee, and Edisto rivers form the A.C.E. Basin, a vast wilderness of marshes and tidal estuaries loaded with history. For sea kayaking, tourists meet at the designated launching areas for fully guided, two-hour tours.

Adults pay $40 at **Beaufort Kayak Tours** (⊠*600 Linton La.* ☎*843/525–0810* ⊕*www.beaufortkayaktours.com*). **A.C.E. Basin Tours** (⊠*1 Coosaw River Dr., Coosaw Island* ☎*843/521–3099* ⊕*www.acebasintours.com*) might be the best bet for the very young, or anyone with limited mobility, as it operates a 38-foot pontoon boat tour. A tour costs $35.

GOLF

Most golf courses are about a 10- to 20-minute scenic drive from Beaufort.

Fripp Island Golf & Beach Resort (⊠*201 Tarpon Blvd., Fripp Island* ☎*843/838–2131 or 843/838–1576* ⊕*www.frippislandresort.com* ⚐*Ocean Creek: 18 holes. 6643 yds. Par 71. Ocean Point: 18 holes. 6,556 yds. Par 72. Green Fee: $89–$99*) has a pair of championship courses. Ocean Creek Golf Course, designed by Davis Love, has sweeping views of saltwater marshes. Designed by George Cobb, Ocean Point Golf Links runs along the ocean the entire way. This is a wildlife refuge, so you'll see plenty of it, particularly marsh deer. That coupled with the ocean or marsh views, you have to focus to keep your eyes on the ball. Nonguests should call the golf pro to make arrangements to play.

SHOPPING

ART GALLERIES

At **Bay Street Gallery** (⊠*719 Bay St.* ☎*843/525–1024 or 843/522–9210*) Laura Hefner's oils of coastal wetlands magically convey the mood of the Lowcountry. At **Four Winds Gallery** (⊠*709 Bay St.* ☎*843/838–3295*) Marianne Norton imports folk art, antiques, sculpture, photography, furniture, rugs, textiles, and weavings, connecting cultures and artists and artisans around the world. Southern art, both Gullah and New Orleans artwork, is new. The **Rhett Gallery** (⊠*901 Bay St.* ☎*843/524–3339*) sells Lowcountry art by four generations of the Rhett family, as well as antique maps and Audubon prints.

Tennessee

MEMPHIS, NASHVILLE, CHATTANOOGA, AND KNOXVILLE

WORD OF MOUTH

"I am not a fan [of Elvis] but found Graceland interesting—even moving (surprise!). We also loved the Civil Rights Museum (extremely moving, less of a surprise), the barbecue and staying at the Peabody upgraded to Club Level. We were there in March a number of years ago as part of a Nashville/Memphis jaunt. If you have an interest in American history and the history of American music, I'd say there's much to offer in that part of the country."

—Leely2

Updated by
Michael Ream

Historically, Tennessee embodies a courageous pioneer spirit, harkening back to the days when settlers fed up with colonial life in Virginia and North Carolina crossed the mountains and settled in what is now Knoxville.

The state flag has three stars, each representing one of the distinct regions of the state: East Tennessee, Middle Tennessee, and West Tennessee. These three areas differ not only in landscape—mountains and heavily forested hillsides in the east, rolling hills in the middle, and flat, fertile land in the west—but also in the attitudes of the residents and the ambience of the cities and towns found there.

Memphis is tucked into the southwest corner of Tennessee on the banks of the Mississippi River. The colorful history of the Delta region, flavorful barbecue, and soulful music give Memphis a unique atmosphere. Nashville, in the middle of the state, is the center of state government, a hub of the nation's health-care industry, home to several universities and colleges, and the heart of the country music industry. Natural beauty abounds in the eastern part of the state, where the Great Smoky Mountains straddle the border between Tennessee and North Carolina.

ORIENTATION AND PLANNING

GETTING ORIENTED

Mountains and music—Tennessee has these gifts in abundance and shares them generously with millions of visitors each year. From Memphis in the west to Knoxville in the east, with Nashville, Chattanooga, and the Great Smoky Mountains in between, Tennessee is a playground for music lovers and nature seekers.

Memphis. Memphis, home of the blues, rises out of the flat, cotton-kissed southwest corner of the state, on the banks of the Mississippi River. South of the city's downtown, Beale Street nurtured some of America's most celebrated musicians, from blues artists W. C. Handy and B. B. King to rockers Elvis Presley and Jerry Lee Lewis. Today, with live music in Handy Park and echoing out of the clubs lining both sides of Beale Street, Memphis still vibrates with American sounds.

Nashville. Nashville, Tennessee's state capital, is also the country-music capital of the world. Music City, U.S.A., as Nashville is known, sits in the heart of Tennessee's rolling hills, and is home to powerhouse music publishers on Music Row, struggling singers and songwriters with dreams of making it big, raucous honky tonks where music pours out onto the sidewalk, and the venerable Grand Ole Opry, which continues to pack devotees into its pew-lined auditorium for performances by country legends and up-and-coming stars.

TOP REASONS TO GO

Live music: Whether your taste leans toward blues, rock 'n' roll, or soul, Memphis is not to be missed. Nashville, aka Music City, U.S.A., is the heart of country music, with both small clubs and the spectacle of the Grand Ole Opry, as well as a thriving music publishing industry. Country isn't the only game in town; Nashville also has everything from small rock clubs to a new and impressive symphony hall.

American history: Tennessee has played a key role in U.S. history, from trailblazing pioneers to Civil War battles to Works Progress Administration (WPA) projects (such as the Tennessee Valley Authority) to civil rights events. The state is peppered with battlefields, dams, national parks, and other sites that are testaments to this rich legacy.

Local culture: The state is chock-full of galleries and craft workshops, performing arts companies, and museums displaying historical artifacts and great works of art.

Nature: The Great Smoky Mountains form Tennessee's eastern border and the Mississippi River the western border. In between are lakes, rivers, waterfalls, and limestone bluffs galore for outdoor enthusiasts.

Barbeque and Southern food: Memphis is the barbecue capital of the state, though you can find excellent 'cue all over Tennessee. You can also find distinctly Southern "meat-and-three" (where you pick a meat and three vegetable sides) restaurants throughout the state.

Chattanooga. Chattanooga sits cradled in a ring of mountains facing the Tennessee River. Once a less than appealing industrial city, it now offers many railroad-themed attractions and activities.

Knoxville. Knoxville, set in the foothills of the Great Smoky Mountains, one to two hours from the western entrances to the park, is a college town with numerous museums and a thriving dining scene and nightlife district.

PLANNING

WHEN TO GO

During the height of summer, Tennessee is mostly hot and humid, especially in July and August (though it's cooler in the mountains). The best times to visit Tennessee are early spring, when temperatures are pleasantly mild and everything seems to be in bloom, and during the long autumn, which begins in late September and lasts well into November. Winter in the mountains, particularly from January through February, can be rather cold.

FESTIVALS Festivals are held throughout the year, mostly during the warmer months. Major events include Awesome April in Nashville, a month packed with events such as the Country Music Marathon, Tin Pan South Songwriters Festival, Gospel Music Association Gospel Week and the Dove Awards, the Nashville Film Festival, and the CMT Music Awards. The Memphis International Film Festival also takes place in

10

April; in May, the city hosts the World Championship Barbecue Cooking Contest and the Beale Street Music Festival.

In June country music fans descend on Nashville for the CMA Music Festival, while rock fans gather on a farm in Manchester (about 60 mi southeast of Nashville) for four days of the Bonnaroo Music and Arts Festival. Elvis fans head to Memphis in droves to pay tribute to the king during Elvis Week in August.

GETTING HERE AND AROUND

AIR TRAVEL

With its central location a few hours' drive from both Memphis and Chattanooga, Nashville is probably the most convenient spot to touch down in Tennessee. Memphis International Airport, 9 mi south of downtown Memphis, has quite a few connecting flights throughout the United States.

Airport Contacts **Chattanooga Metropolitan Airport** (✉ *1001 Airport Rd.* ☎ *423/855-2200* ⊕ *www.chattairport.com*). **Memphis International Airport** (✉ *2491 Winchester Rd.* ☎ *901/922-8000* ⊕ *www.mscaa.com*).**Nashville International Airport** (✉ *1 Terminal Dr.* ☎ *615/275-1675* ⊕ *www.nashintl.com*).

CAR TRAVEL

Tennessee is bordered by eight states (Kentucky, Virginia, North Carolina, Georgia, Alabama, Mississippi, Arkansas, and Missouri), making it incredibly accessible by car. I–40 traverses the state, connecting it to North Carolina in the east and Arkansas in the west. I–65 runs north and south through Tennessee, leading to Indiana to the north and Alabama to the south. Georgia lies to the southeast via I–24.

RESTAURANTS

While the culinary roots of Tennessee are purely Southern, with lots of fried chicken and catfish, barbecue, and rich desserts, finer dining has arrived in the state, particularly in Nashville. Ethnic food isn't as prevalent as in other major U.S. cities, but you can still find ethnic staples like Mexican, Indian, and Vietnamese. Most restaurants have a casual atmosphere.

HOTELS

Pretty much every type of lodging is available, including luxury hotels, renovated historic hotels, intimate bed-and-breakfasts, and newer boutique hotels. All the major chains, both high- and middle-end, are clustered in Nashville, Memphis, and Chattanooga.

WHAT IT COSTS				
	¢	$	$$	$$$	$$$$
Restaurant	under $7	$7–$11	$12–$16	$17–$22	over $22
Hotel	under $70	$70–$110	$111–$160	$161–$220	over $220

Restaurant prices are per person for a main course at dinner. Hotel prices are for a standard double room, excluding state and local taxes.

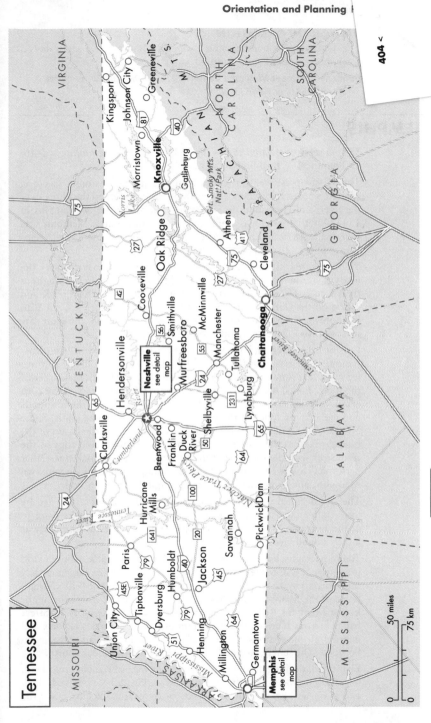

Tennessee

10

VISITOR INFORMATION

The Tennessee Welcome Center is open 24 hours a day, seven days a week, and is staffed daily from 9 to 6.

Contacts Tennessee Welcome Center (✉ *119 N. Riverside Dr., Memphis* ☎ *901/543-5333 or 888/633-9099*).

MEMPHIS

382 mi west of Atlanta via I–78; 213 mi west of Nashville via I–40; 190 mi north of Birmingham via I–65.

The Mississippi River, on whose banks Memphis was built, has long exerted a powerful influence. Chickasaw Indians settled the bluffs over the river, and Hernando de Soto crossed it at the site of Memphis in 1541. After the area was claimed by the United States, Memphis was founded in 1819 and named after the city in Egypt, due to the resemblance of the Mississippi to the Nile.

The river drew steamboats throughout the 19th century to carry the loads of cotton that poured into Memphis from plantations throughout the Mississippi Delta. The city was a major center of the slave trade and a stop on the Underground Railroad. Occupied during the Civil War, Memphis suffered some decline during Reconstruction but soon saw its cotton-based economy up and running again.

Cotton made Memphis great, and new arrivals poured in from Mississippi, Arkansas, and the rest of Tennessee. The melding of cultures led to a great American art form: the blues. W. C. Handy, the Father of the Blues, honed his craft on Beale Street in the early years of the 20th century, laying down the songs that popularized the rhythmic sounds and melancholy lyrics of the cotton fields and delta juke joints. Some 50 years later, another Memphian, Elvis Presley, took the basics of the blues, mixed in the gospel on which he was raised, and topped the results off with the moves that made him the first big rock star. Other performers followed Elvis's lead at Sam Phillips's Sun Studio in midtown Memphis, and soon Memphis was the capital of rock 'n' roll.

The city declined economically in the mid-20th century, hastened by unrest after the assassination in 1968 of Dr. Martin Luther King Jr. at the Lorraine Motel, south of Beale Street, and its downtown was largely abandoned.

Today, Memphis has rebounded, thanks largely to FedEx, whose world headquarters is near Memphis Airport, which moves more cargo than any other airport in the world. Downtown is now home to the FedExForum, home of the Memphis Grizzlies, and AutoZone Park, where the minor league Memphis Redbirds take to the diamond. Nearby Beale Street has numerous blues clubs and restaurants, as it did in its heyday, and impromptu jam sessions start up at Handy Park, in the heart of the neighborhood. The stately, storied Peabody Hotel is a few blocks north.

Elvis is still the king in Memphis. His legacy burns bright at Graceland, his estate on the far southern end of Memphis, where he lived, died, and is buried. Every year, hundreds of thousands of fans make the pilgrimage to pay homage to the man and his music. Elvis Week, held annually in mid-August at Graceland and throughout Memphis, has grown to match the myth.

GETTING HERE AND AROUND

BOAT AND FERRY TRAVEL
The paddle-wheel steamers of the Majestic America Line and barge hotels of RiverBarge Excursion Lines stop at Memphis. Memphis Riverboats has 1½-hour sightseeing and 2-hour dinner cruises—contact them for their schedule. Blues City Tours offers riverboat rides.

BUS AND TROLLEY TRAVEL
Memphis Area Transit Authority buses run throughout the city and some suburbs. Adult fare is $1.20, transfers 10¢.

The Memphis Area Transit Authority also operates the 2½-mi Main Street Trolley, fare $1, in downtown Memphis. The Riverfront Loop extension, adjacent to Riverside Drive, connects with the Main Street Trolley.

CAR TRAVEL
Memphis is best explored by car, although the trolley line along Main Street is useful for getting from downtown hotels to Beale Street for a night out, and another trolley line goes south of downtown to the National Civil Rights Museum. Many attractions are outside downtown in midtown and East Memphis, though, and Graceland, is on the far south side of the city.

TAXIS AND SHUTTLES
The taxi fare from the airport to downtown Memphis runs $25–$30; try Yellow Cab and Checker Cab; they run 24 hours a day, 7 days a week.

The taxi fare in Memphis is $3.80 for the first mile, $1.80 for each additional mile, and stands are at the airport and bus station. Call to order a taxi.

TOURS
Blues City Tours offers motor-coach tours to Memphis sites, including Graceland, Mud Island, and Beale Street, plus nightly tours that include dinner and a show.

The Center for Southern Folklore gives tours focusing on music and folk art. Carriage Tours of Memphis offers horse-drawn carriage rides and tours, as does the Carriage Company. Heritage Tours explores the area's rich African-American culture, including slavery, the blues, and the civil rights movement.

10

ESSENTIALS

Boat and Ferry Contacts Majestic America Line (⊠ 2101 4th Ave., Suite 1150, *Seattle, WA* ☎ 800/343–1232). **Memphis Riverboats** (☎ 901/527–2628 or 800/221–6197 ⊕ www.memphisriverboats.net). **RiverBarge Excursion Lines, Inc.** (⊠ 201 Opelousas Ave., *New Orleans, LA* ☎ 888/462–2743).

Bus Contacts Memphis Area Transit Authority (☎ 901/274–6282 ⊕ www.matatransit.com).

Taxi and Shuttle Contacts Yellow Cab and Checker Cab (☎ 901/577–7777 or 800/796–7750 ⊕ www.premierofmemphis.com).

Tour Contacts Blues City Tours (☎ 901/522–9229 ⊕ www.bluescitytours. com). **Carriage Tours of Memphis** (☎ 901/527–7542 ⊕ www.carriagetoursofmemphis.com). **Carriage Company** (☎ 901/507–2587 or 877/589–1812 ⊕ www.carriagecomemphis.com). **Center for Southern Folklore** (⊠ 119 S.

Main St., Downtown ☎ *901/525–3655*
⊕ *www.southernfolklore.com).* **Heritage**
Tours (☎ *901/527–3427* ⊕ *www.heri-*
tagetoursmemphis.com).

Visitor Contacts Memphis Conven-
tion & Visitors Bureau (✉ *47 Union*
Ave. ☎ *901/543–5300 or 800/873–*
6282 ⊕ *www.memphistravel.com).*

PLANNING YOUR TIME

Spend a morning strolling down-
town and Beale Street, perhaps popping into the Peabody Hotel to
admire its impressive lobby and see the signature Peabody ducks splashing in the grand marble fountain. Check out the W. C. Handy Home &
Museum or the Memphis Rock 'n' Soul Museum, both on Beale Street
in the shadow of FedExForum. Head over to Sun Studio, a short ride
from downtown and virtually unchanged since Elvis and other rock
'n' roll pioneers recorded there. For lunch, stop in at one of Memphis's
famous barbecue restaurants throughout the city.

EXPLORING

DOWNTOWN MEMPHIS

TOP ATTRACTIONS

❸ **National Civil Rights Museum.** The Lorraine Motel, where Dr. Martin
★ Luther King Jr. was assassinated on April 4, 1968, has been transformed
into a museum that documents the struggle of African-Americans and
the civil rights movement. Exhibits include a Montgomery, Alabama,
bus, like the one on which Rosa Parks refused to give up her seat,
sparking an uprising against segregation; scenes of lunch-counter sit-ins;
and audiovisual displays. King's room at the motel has been re-created
as it was at the time of his death, an additional exhibit space across
the street delves at length into his assassination. ✉ *450 Mulberry St.,*
South Main ☎ *901/521–9699* ⊕ *www.civilrightsmuseum.org* 💲 *$12;*
free Mon. after 3 ⊙ *Sept.–May, Mon. and Wed.–Sat. 9–5, Sun. 1–5;*
June and Aug., Mon. and Wed.–Sat. 9–6, Sun. 1–6.

❻ **Sun Studio.** Sun Studio is still housed in the original, cramped building where Elvis wandered in one day and recorded two songs—one in
honor of his beloved mother—for producer Sam Phillips. Pictures of the
King and other well-loved musicians who launched their careers at Sun,
including B. B. King, Jerry Lee Lewis, Johnny Cash, and Carl Perkins,
adorn the walls, and their hits play in the background during tours.
There's also a small gift shop with well-chosen paraphernalia (guitar
picks, drinking glasses) and a hall-of-fame gallery. ✉ *706 Union Ave.,*
The Edge ☎ *901/521–0664 or 800/441–6249* ⊕ *www.sunstudio.com*
💲 *$9.50* ⊙ *Daily 10–6, tours every hr on the ½ hr, last tour at 5:30.*

❺ **W. C. Handy Memphis Home & Museum.** Handy, who wrote some of his
most famous blues pieces in this small wood-frame house, is recalled
here through photographs, sheet music, and memorabilia. Visitors get
an inside look at the humble beginnings of the Father of the Blues, who

HISTORY YOU CAN SEE

The Civil War ravaged Tennessee like no other state except Virginia; brother literally fought brother, and neighbor fought neighbor. Geography and politics dictated that the state would be a major battlefield. Military campaigns consisted mainly of Federal thrusts southward and Confederate attempts to stop them, and major battles included Fort Donelson (near Dover), Shiloh (near Savannah, at the Tennessee River, near the Mississippi border), Stones River (Murfreesboro), Chickamauga (Georgia), and Chattanooga.

The **Tennessee Antebellum Trail** (☎ *800/381–1865 for a map and admission prices*), which has more than 54 historic sites, plantations, and Civil War battlefields, is a 90-mi loop tour that begins in Nashville and continues through historic Maury and Williamson Counties. Nine sites are open to the public daily.

You can explore many battlefields in Tennessee. In 1863 Union and Confederate forces fought for control of Chattanooga, the gateway to the deep South, at what is now

Chickamauga and Chattanooga National Military Park (⊠ *Lookout Mountain/Point Park, 110 Point Park Rd., Lookout Mountain* ☎ *423/821– 7786* ⊕ *www.nps.gov/chch*). The unconditional surrender at **Fort Donelson National Battlefield** (⊠ *Off Hwy. 79, Dover* ☎ *931/232– 5706 www.nps.gov/fodo*) was the North's first major victory in the Civil War and led Union troops deeper into Dixie. **Franklin's Carnton Plantation** (⊠ *1345 Carnton La., Franklin* ☎ *615/794–0903* ⊕ *www.carnton. org*) served as a Confederate field hospital during the bloody Battle of Franklin. **Shiloh National Military Park** (⊠ *1055 Pittsburg Landing Rd., Shiloh* ☎ *731/689–5696* ⊕ *www. nps.gov/shil*) preserves the site of the intense April 1862 battle as well as the subsequent siege, battle, and occupation at nearby Corinth, Mississippi. **Stones River National Battlefield** (⊠ *3501 Old Nashville Hwy., Murfreesboro* ☎ *615/794–0903* ⊕ *www.nps.gov/stri*) in Murfreesboro was the site of one of the bloodiest battles of the Civil War.

lived in this two-room house with his wife and six children. ⊠ *352 Beale St., Beale Street* ☎ *901/527–3427* 🎟 *$3* ⊙ *May–Sept., Tues.–Sat. 10–5; Oct.–Apr., Tues.–Sat. 11–4.*

WORTH NOTING

❶ ★ **Center for Southern Folklore.** These must-see exhibits on the people, music, food, crafts, and traditions of the South, particularly of the Mississippi Delta region, pay tribute to one of America's most interesting cultural identities. Perhaps more than any other Memphis institution, the center has its finger on the pulse of local culture, and a visit here is both edifying and entertaining. The space includes a restaurant with Southern food such as barbecue, greens, and corn bread; a bar and performance area; and videos about Memphis and Beale Street. Weekend concerts feature blues, gospel, jazz, rockabilly, and folk music. Each year the center sponsors one of Memphis's finest music festivals, the three-day **Memphis Music & Heritage Festival,** held Labor Day weekend. The gift shop carries regional folk art and handiwork, plus cassettes, videos, and books

10

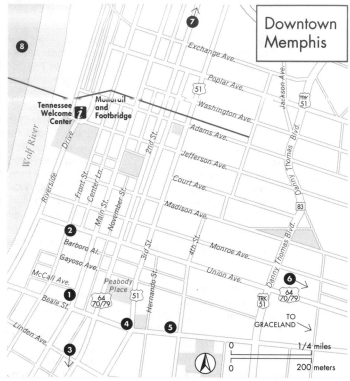

Downtown Memphis

pertaining to the South. ⊠*119 S. Main St., Downtown* ☎*901/525–3655* ⊕*www.southernfolklore.com* ⊠*Free* ⊙*Mon.–Sat. 11–5.*

② **Cotton Museum at the Memphis Cotton Exchange.** Relive the days of "King Cotton" in the architectural splendor of the city's cotton trading floor, re-created as it appeared in 1939, when Memphis did a booming business in the crop. Numerous cotton-related artifacts are on display. ⊠*65 Union Ave., Downtown* ☎*901/531–7826* ⊕*www.memphiscottonmuseum.org* ⊠*$5* ⊙*Tues.–Sat. 10–5, Sun. noon–5.*

④ **Memphis Rock 'n' Soul Museum.** In the plaza of the FedExForum on Beale Street, this museum showcases Memphis as musical mecca, tracing the history of legendary performers who made lasting contributions to blues, rock 'n' roll, and other musical forms. Jukeboxes give visitors the opportunity to listen to hits that originated in Memphis. ⊠*191 Beale St., at 3rd St. Beale Street Historic District* ☎*901/205–2533* ⊕*www.memphisrocknsoul.org* ⊠*$10* ⊙*Daily 10–7.*

⑧ **Mud Island.** Accessible by car, monorail, or pedestrian walkway, this 52-acre park on an island opposite downtown explores Memphis's intimate relationship with the Mississippi. At the **Mississippi River Museum,** galleries bring the history of the Mississippi to life with exhibits ranging from scale-model boats to life-size, animatronic river characters (Mark Twain spins his tales anew) and the Theater of River Disasters.

The most extraordinary exhibit is outside: **River Walk,** a five-block-long scale model of the Mississippi that replicates its every twist, turn, and sandbar from Cairo, Illinois, to New Orleans, ending in a huge swimming pool bordered by a man-made, sandy beach. Canoe, kayak, pedal boat, and bicycle rentals are available. There's even an opportunity to camp out on the island—call for dates and information. ⊠ *125 N. Front St. (footbridge and mono-rail), Downtown* ☎ *901/576–7241 or 800/507–6507* ⊕ *www.mudis-land.com* ⊠ *River park free, Mis-sissippi River Museum $8* ⊙ *Apr. 11–May 23 and Sept. 2–Oct. 31, Tues.–Sun. 10–5; May 24–Sept. 1, daily 10–8; closed Nov.–Apr. 10.*

❼ Slave Haven Underground Railroad Museum/Burkle Estate. This pre–Civil War era house was a stop on the Underground Railroad. A German immigrant built the modest middle-class home circa 1850, when Memphis was a slave trade center. Ads and artifacts depict the history of slavery, and secret cellars and trapdoors reveal the escape route of runaway slaves; the basement sheltered run-aways for weeks at a time. Heritage Tours operates the museum and provides guided tours. ⊠ *826 N. 2nd St., Downtown* ☎ *901/527–3427* ⊠ *$6* ⊙ *Mon.–Sat. 10–4; closed Mon. and Tues. Nov.–Mar.*

GREATER MEMPHIS

★ Graceland. The tour of the colonial-style mansion once owned by Elvis Presley reveals the spoils of stardom—from gold records to glittering show costumes—and a circuit of the grounds (shuttle service is available) leads to the Meditation Garden, where Elvis is buried. Separate tours are available for additional fees. Among them is the **Elvis Presley Automobile Museum,** where a continuous film montage of Elvis on the road is shown drive-in style as viewers sit in seats pulled from 1957 Chevys. Elvis's jet, the *Lisa Marie* (named for his daughter), complete with 24-karat-gold-plated seat-belt buckles and a queen-size bed covered in light blue ultrasuede, stars in the **Airplanes Tour. Sincerely Elvis** is a small museum with personal items such as home movies, photos, and clothes. There are several restaurants and, of course, shops on the premises, along with a post office—few can resist the lure of a Grace-land postmark. ⊠ *3734 Elvis Presley Blvd. (off I-55), 12 mi south-east of downtown, Whitehaven* ☎ *901/332–3322 or 800/238–2000* ⊕ *www.elvis.com* ⊠ *Home tour $28, all attractions $33, parking $7* ⌚ *Reservations essential* ⊙ *Mon.–Sat. 9–5, Sun. 10–4. Hrs may vary with season. Mansion closed Tues. Dec.–Feb.*

Memphis Brooks Museum of Art. The collections of this museum in Over-ton Park span eight centuries and 7,000 pieces, including a notable

10

collection of Italian Renaissance works, English portraiture, Impressionist and American modernist paintings, decorative arts, prints, and photographs. A popular exhibit upstairs gives a global survey of ancient art from Greece and the Mediterranean, the Americas, and Africa. ⊠ *1934 Poplar Ave., Overton Park/Midtown* ☎ *901/544–6200* ⊕ *www.brooksmuseum.org* ☐ *$7, free Wed. Fees vary for major exhibits* ☉ *Tues.–Fri. 10–4, Sat. 10–5, Sun. 11:30–5; first Wed. of month 10–8.*

NEED A BREAK?

At the **Brushmark Restaurant** (☎ *901/544–6200* ⊕ *www.brooksmuseum. org*), an elegant but casual eatery on the Memphis Brooks Museum of Art's first floor, art lovers can rest their feet while enjoying lunch, wine, and serene views of Overton Park. It's open Tuesday–Sunday 11:30–2:30.

🄲 **Memphis Pink Palace Museum and Mansion and Sharpe Planetarium.** Clarence Saunders, founder of the Piggly Wiggly self-service stores that are the predecessors of today's supermarkets, built this rambling pink marble mansion in the 1920s. Exhibits are eclectic, including natural and cultural history displays, a hand-carved miniature three-ring circus, and a replica of the original Piggly Wiggly. The Sharpe Planetarium explores the most current cosmic discoveries. The museum also has an IMAX theater. ⊠ *3050 Central Ave., Midtown* ☎ *901/320–6362* ⊕ *www. memphismuseums.org* ☐ *Museum $8.75, museum and planetarium $11.25, museum and IMAX $13.50, museum, planetarium, and IMAX $18* ☉ *Mon.–Sat. 9–5, Sun. noon–5.*

★ **Stax Museum of American Soul Music.** Look for the marquee reading SOULS-VILLE U.S.A., and listen for the sounds of musical icons like Otis Redding, Isaac Hayes, and Aretha Franklin as you approach the former home of Stax Records, rebuilt from the ground up to look as it did during the label's heyday in the 1960s and early '70s. Inside, it's wall-to-wall music, along with a history of Stax, from its beginnings as a home base for local musicians to its status as an international sensation. An on-site record shop gives visitors the opportunity to purchase some soul classics. ⊠ *926 E. McLemore Ave., Soulsville* ☎ *901/946–2535* ⊕ *www.staxmuseum.com* ☐ *$10* ☉ *Apr.–Oct., Mon.–Sat. 10–5, Sun. 1–5; Nov.–Mar., Tues.–Sat. 10–5, Sun. 1–5, closed Mon.*

OFF THE BEATEN PATH

Shiloh National Military Park. The site of one of the Civil War's grimmest and most pivotal battles, Shiloh National Military Park is the resting place of almost 4,000 soldiers, many unidentified. A self-guided automobile tour (about 2½ hours) leads you past markers explaining monuments and battle sites. The visitor center runs a 25-minute film explaining the battle's strategy and has a display of Civil War artifacts. To get to Shiloh from Memphis, head east on U.S. 64, then 10 mi south on TN 22; it's about 100 mi east of Memphis and 165 mi southwest of Nashville. ⊠ *TN 22, 1055 Pittsburgh Landing Rd., Shiloh* ☎ *731/689–5275* ⊕ *www.nps.gov/shil* ☐ *$3 per person or $5 per family* ☉ *Visitor center daily 8–5.*

WHERE TO EAT

Hidden among Memphis's many delicious but calorie-laden barbecue joints, soul food restaurants, and meat-and-threes are some true gems. Of course, you must sample barbecue at least once on a visit to Memphis—this is one of the capitals of the sweet and smoky treasure.

BEALE STREET

$$–$$$ ✕ **Alfred's on Beale.** Not surprisingly, music is the theme at this busy restaurant on Beale Street, in the city's bluesy entertainment district. Up to 500 people can be accommodated inside and on the two-story outdoor patio. Southern plate lunches, burgers, pork chops, pasta, catfish, and barbecued ribs make up the comforting menu. The kitchen is open until 3 AM; the bar serves until 5 AM on weekends. ✉*197 Beale St., Beale Street* ☎*901/525–3711* ⊕*www.alfredsonbeale.com* 🖃*AE, D, DC, MC, V.*

AMERICAN

$$–$$$ ✕ **Blues City Café.** This downtown diner specializes in huge steaks and ribs, hamburgers, and hot tamales. An adjoining retail shop sells a plethora of music-related merchandise, including Elvis and blues items. ✉*138 Beale St., Beale Street* ☎*901/526–3637* ⊕*www.bluescitycafe. com* 🖃*AE, MC, V.*

SOUTHERN

DOWNTOWN

$$$–$$$$ ✕ **Automatic Slim's Tonga Club.** This funky restaurant is downtown near the Peabody Hotel. Hungry diners crowd into the split-level room for Southwestern and Caribbean fare served in thick, spicy sauces; signature dishes include deep-fried red snapper with tomato and jalapeño relish and Jamaican jerk duck. ✉*83 S. 2nd St., Downtown* ☎*901/525–7948* 🖃*AE, MC, V* ⊘*No lunch weekends.*

ECLECTIC

$$$–$$$$ ✕ **Bluefin.** This is a *very* hip room on Main Street's restaurant row, with sunken tables, curving lines, mood lighting, and a simulated waterfall by the sushi bar. The restaurant serves a full selection of sushi, plus entrées like pan-roasted sea bass, Moroccan lamb shank, and butter-poached lobster. The cocktail menu is almost as lengthy as the food listings. ✉*135 S. Main St., Downtown* ☎*901/528–1010* ⊕*www.bluefinmemphis.com* 🖃*AE, D, MC, V* ⊘*No lunch Sat.–Mon.*

JAPANESE

Fodor'sChoice
★

$$–$$$ ✕ **Charles Vergo's Rendezvous.** In an alley just north of the Peabody Hotel's main entrance sits another Memphis landmark. Since 1948, the Vergos family has created their unique charcoal-smoked ribs basted with vinegar and dusted with savory spices derived from their Greek heritage. The often crowded basement dining room is festooned with memorabilia and surrounds a central bar. White-shirted waiters bring forth platters of ribs, pork shoulder sandwiches, chicken, and other dishes. ✉*52*

SOUTHERN

Fodor'sChoice
★

10

S. 2nd St., Downtown ☎*901/523–2746* ⊕*www.hogsfly.com* ⊟*AE, D, MC, V* ☉*Closed Sun. and Mon. No lunch Tues.–Thurs.*

$$$$
CONTINENTAL
Fodor's Choice
★
✕**Chez Philippe.** This Memphis institution in the Peabody Hotel serves sophisticated dishes in an ornately decorated dining room. Nightly creations might include Scottish salmon with black mustard tomato coulis, snapper in sour orange–saffron–garlic broth, and lamb porterhouse with Niçoise olive risotto cake and sundried tomato–caper relish. Desserts include baked Alaska (sponge cake topped with ice cream and meringue, then baked) and crème brûlée. A lovely afternoon tea is served Tuesday through Saturday from 2 to 3, but you'll need to make a reservation 24 hours in advance. ⊠*Peabody Hotel, 149 Union Ave., Downtown* ☎*901/529–4188* ⊕*www.peabodymemphis. com* ⌖*Reservations essential* ⊟*AE, D, DC, MC, V* ☉*Closed Sun. and Mon. No lunch.*

$$–$$$
AMERICAN
✕**Encore.** Upscale comfort food in an intimate space from Chef Jose Gutierrez, a veteran of 20 years next door at Chez Phillipe. Crispy chicken paillard (pounded thin and grilled) is garnished with Parmesan and baked macaroni gratin, while the pork chop is paired with gnocchi. The burger topped with roasted red pepper aioli and a choice of blue, Gruyère, or aged cheddar cheese is a bargain at $12, while the key lime pie is rumored to be the best in town. ⊠*150 Peabody Pl., Suite 111* ⌖*Street entrance is on S. 2nd St. between Linden and Peabody Pl., Downtown* ☎*901/528–1415* ⊕*www.encore-memphis.com* ⊟*AE, D, MC, V* ☉*No lunch.*

¢–$
SOUTHERN
✕**Gus's Fried Chicken.** This family-owned joint serves up some of the region's best fried chicken, with coleslaw and baked beans on the side. It's not for the timid—the seasoning includes spicy red pepper. Seating is in booths, and blues plays in the background. Credit cards aren't accepted for orders under $10. This location is just south of downtown. ⊠*310 S. Front St., Downtown* ☎*901/527–4877* ⊟*MC, V.*

$$$–$$$$
MODERN
SOUTHERN
★
✕**McEwen's on Monroe.** Upscale regional food described as "contemporary Southern" is served at this popular downtown restaurant where the menu changes every two months and everything uses farm-fresh local ingredients. Appetizers such as duck confit enchiladas and buttermilk-fried oysters are the perfect start to a meal of sweet-potato-crusted catfish and seared rib eye with a habanero-mango glaze. ⊠*122 Monroe St., Downtown* ☎*901/527–7085* ⊕*www.mcewensonmonroe.com* ⊟*AE, D, MC, V* ☉*Closed Sun. No lunch Sat.*

PINCH DISTRICT

$
SOUTHERN
✕**Alcenia's.** The food at this hole-in-the-wall lunch spot just north of downtown is as down-home and funky as the decor—walls lined with eclectic artwork and a jukebox stocked with Memphis hits. The kitchen turns out its own versions of "meat and two," including fried chicken and pork chops served alongside sweet-potato fries, fried green tomatoes, and other vegetables. Desserts, including pecan pie and sweet potato pie, bread pudding, and pound cake, are as sinfully rich as the sweet tea Alcenia's serves up in tall glasses. ⊠*317 N. Main St., Pinch District* ☎*901/523–0200* ⊟*AE, MC, V* ☉*Closed Sun. and Mon. No dinner (except Fri.).*

$–$$ ✕**Westy's.** This unpretentious bar and grill in the Pinch District dishes
AMERICAN out large portions of steak and seafood, excellent burgers, and a selection of wild rice–based dishes, including several vegetarian options. A weekday meat-and-two lunch special includes entrées like country-fried steak and catfish accompanied by sides like macaroni and cheese, turnip greens, and other vegetables. The kitchen stays open until 3 AM every night. ⊠*346 N. Main St., Pinch District* ☎*901/543–3278* ⊕ *www. eatatwestys.com* ⊟*AE, D, MC, V.*

MIDTOWN

$$$$ ✕**Café Society.** At this European-style bistro, complete with sidewalk
FRENCH tables shaded by umbrellas, the simple menu includes dishes like roasted sea bass, roasted chicken, and filet of dry-aged beef. The best dessert is the crème brûlée, and the wine list is extensive. ⊠*212 N. Evergreen St., Midtown* ☎*901/722–2177* ⊟*AE, MC, V* ⊘*No lunch weekends.*

$–$$ ✕**The Cupboard.** Home style Southern cooking is served with enthusiasm
SOUTHERN at this no-frills midtown favorite with vinyl booths, Formica tables, and mix-and-match meat-and-three plates. Choose from daily offerings like fried chicken, hamburger steak, and smothered pork chops, with mac 'n' cheese, black-eyed peas, and butter beans among the sides. Daily deserts include a fresh fruit cobbler or banana pudding as well as homemade sweet potato or lemon icebox pie. ⊠*1400 Union Ave., Midtown* ☎*901/276–8015* ⊟*AE, D, DC, MC, V.*

$$$–$$$$ ✕**Paulette's.** This Overton Square classic in a half-timbered house with
AMERICAN an elegantly appointed dining room, serves all-American classics like
★ grilled pork tenderloin, Louisiana crab cakes, and filet mignon with either salmon, grilled jumbo shrimp, or lobster tail. Try the hot chocolate crepe for dessert. The restaurant also has a popular Sunday brunch. ⊠*2110 Madison Ave., Midtown/Overton Square* ☎*901/726–5128* ⊕*www.paulettes.net* ⊟*AE, D, DC, MC, V.*

$$$$ ✕**Restaurant Iris.** Kelly English, who earned his cooking chops in New
AMERICAN Orleans, is creating some of Memphis's most innovative and exciting
★ new cooking in a tidy, handsome midtown house by Overton Square, formerly occupied by the restaurant La Tourelle. The vibe is upscale yet casual, with tables arranged close together in the front rooms. English's take on surf and turf combines a New York strip steak with fried oysters and blue cheese, and he updates the Southern classic shrimp and grits by adding andouille sausage. Diver scallops with potato gnocchi is another standout. The five-course prix-fixe menu runs $55, $75 with a selection of wines by the house sommelier. The restaurant also serves Sunday brunch. ⊠ *2146 Monroe Ave., Midtown/Overton Square* ☎*901/590–2828* ⊕*www.restaurantiris.com* ⌁*Reservations essential* ⊟*AE, D, MC, V* ⊘*Closed Mon.*

$$$–$$$$ ✕**Ronnie Grisanti and Sons.** This classy spot on the eastern edge of mid-
ITALIAN town serves upscale Tuscan fare in a busy dining room decorated with paintings of Italy and tiny white lights. Steaks and veal dishes are standouts, and daily specials are creative. ⊠*2855 Poplar Ave., Midtown* ☎*901/323–0007* ⊕*www.ronniegrisantiandsons.com* ⊟*AE, MC, V* ⊘*Closed Sun. No lunch.*

10

Memphis Barbeque

Aficionados of North Carolina, Texas, and Kansas City barbecue can be very passionate and vocal about each of those states being king of the smoked Southern treasure, but there's no doubt Memphis has a strong case for the barbecue crown. The city is packed with barbecue joints, ranging from sit-down restaurants to ramshackle take-out spots. Just look for the telltale cloud from a smoker and follow your nose toward the sweet smell of meat slowly reaching perfection.

Barbecue fans gather every spring for the city's **World Championship Barbecue Cooking Contest,** part of the **Memphis in May** festival at Tom Lee Park in downtown. Contact the Memphis Convention and Visitors Bureau for more information.

Asking locals about the best barbecue in Memphis is sure to lead to a lengthy debate, but it's hard to go wrong with so many worthy spots in town. Here are some favorite Memphis barbecue joints. **A & R Bar-B-Que** (⊠ *1802 Elvis Presley Blvd., South Memphis* ☎ *901/774-7444* ⊕ *www. aandrbbq.com*) is a no-frills storefront on a gritty stretch of road a few miles north of Graceland. **Bar-B-Q Shop** (⊠ *1782 Madison Ave., Midtown* ☎ *901/272-1277* ⊕ *dancingpigs.*

com) is ideally located for a pit stop while hitting midtown music clubs. **Central BBQ** (⊠ *2249 Central Ave., Midtown* ☎ *901/272-9377* ⊕ *www. cbqmemphis.com*) has a nice dining room and features pork with extra "bark," or crispy crust. **Charles Vergos' Rendezvous** (⊠ *52 S. 2nd St., Downtown* ☎ *901/523-2746* ⊕ *www. hogsfly.com*) has a unique, succulent blend of spices that make its dry-rubbed ribs especially tasty. **Cozy Corner** (⊠ *745 North Pkwy., Uptown* ☎ *901/527-9158* ⊕ *www.cozy-cornerbbq.com*), near a large medical complex north of downtown, has plump and juicy barbecued Cornish hen, as well as barbeque spaghetti and widely praised rib tips. **Interstate Bar-B-Que** (⊠ *2265 S. 3rd St., South Memphis* ☎ *901/775-2304* ⊕ *www. interstatebarbecue.com*) a block north of I-55, is an old warhorse of Memphis barbecue—there's even a branch at the Memphis Airport. **Payne's Bar-B-Que** (⊠ *1762 Lamar Ave., Midtown* ☎ *901/272-1523*) is praised by locals for its pork sandwich. **Tops Bar-B-Q** (⊠ *1286 Union Ave., Midtown* ☎ *901/725-7527* ⊕ *www. topsbarbq.com*) is a local chain that's been around for more than 50 years, with numerous other locations in the Memphis area.

EAST MEMPHIS

$$$$ ✕**Erling Jensen.** In a cozy cottage on a quiet corner a short distance
FRENCH from Poplar Avenue and I–240 is some of Memphis's most sophisti-
Fodor'sChoice cated cuisine. Chef Erling Jensen turns out a frequently changing menu,
★ utilizing seasonal fresh ingredients to create dishes like seared ahi tuna with cassoulet and sautéed mero bass in soy truffle butter, as well as grilled bison rib eye and rack of lamb. Dessert may include a tempting chocolate soufflé with milk chocolate and Maker's Mark crème anglaise or spiced peach cobbler with vanilla ice cream. ⊠ *1044 S. Yates Rd., East Memphis* ☎ *901/763-3700* ⊕ *www.ejensen.com* ⚃ *Reservations essential* ⊟ *AE, DC, MC, V* ⊗ *No lunch.*

$$$$ ✕**Folk's Folly Prime Steak House.**
STEAK   Folk's has been a favorite Memphis
steakhouse for more than 30 years,
with clubby rooms paneled in dark
wood and white tablecloths. Specials change every Wednesday, but
the old standbys are always there,
including filet mignon and cowboy
rib eye, as well as a 28-ounce porterhouse for $59.95. Duck breast,
lobster ravioli, and wasabi-encrust-
ed sea bass are good choices as well,
as is Maine lobster. The restaurant
has a piano bar and a retail shop
if you want to take some steaks
home. ☒*551 S. Mendenhall Rd.,
East Memphis* ☏*901/762–8200
or 800/467–0245* ⓦ*www.folks-
folly.com* ⌕*Reservations essential*
▭*AE, D, MC, V* ☉*No lunch.*

WORD OF MOUTH
"I lived in Memphis for a year and you cannot miss Cozy Corner. They have the best BBQ I've ever had. Ribs, Cornish game hens, BBQ spaghetti (you have to taste it to believe it). The original owner Mr. Robinson died a few years ago. He was a great person and took me under his wing since I was a Yankee who knew nothing. People lined up at Thanksgiving for his turkeys, game hens, etc. Plus, the grandmother used to make this amazing lemon pound cake, not that I usually had room for it."   —SharonG

SOULSVILLE

¢   ✕**The Four Way.** A soul food restaurant patronized by Dr. Martin Luther
SOUTHERN   King Jr., this longtime favorite near the Stax Museum of American
★   Soul Music offers a set meat and two every day, with meats such as
roasted turkey and dressing, meatloaf, smothered pork chops, and salmon croquettes. Black-eyed peas and buttered corn are among the side
dishes. ☒*998 Mississippi Blvd., Soulsville* ☏*901/507–1519* ▭*MC,
V* ☉*Closed Mon.*

WHERE TO STAY

Memphis hotels are especially busy during the month-long Memphis-
in-May International Festival and in mid-August, during Elvis Tribute
Week. Book well ahead at these times.

DOWNTOWN

$$$–$$$$ 🖵**Doubletree Downtown.** Next door to the Peabody, this hotel has glass
elevators that whisk you to rooms arranged around a stunning 10-story
atrium with exposed brick walls. Renovated in October 2008, with
rooms now featuring 32-inch flatscreen TVs, it's across the street
from AutoZone Park (you can see the field from some rooms). **Pros:**
good value for a downtown hotel; newly renovated rooms; free Wi-Fi.
Cons: no airport shuttle; no concierge. ☒*185 Union Ave., Downtown*
☏*901/528–1800* ⊕*www.doubletree.com* ⮐*274 rooms, 6 suites* ⌂*In-
room: refrigerator (some), Internet, Wi-Fi. In-hotel: restaurant, room
service, pool, gym, laundry service, Wi-Fi, parking (paid), no-smoking
rooms* ▭*AE, D, MC, V.*

$$$–$$$$ 🖵**Hampton Inn and Suites at Beale Street.** Some of the rooms in this com-
★   fortable, functional hotel just steps from the nightlife have views of
Beale Street, and the suites come with full kitchens. Hampton Inn has
several other locations in the Memphis area, mainly in East Memphis.

10

Pros: good location for walking downtown; complimentary breakfast; free Wi-Fi. **Cons:** no airport shuttle; no concierge. ⊠*175 Peabody Pl., Downtown* ☏*901/260–4000* ⊕*www.hampton-inn.com* ⋑*108 rooms, 36 suites* ♿*In-room: kitchen (some), refrigerator (some), Wi-Fi. In-hotel: pool, gym, laundry facilities, laundry service, Wi-Fi, parking (paid), no-smoking rooms* ⊟*AE, MC, V* ⓞ*CP.*

$$$–$$$$ 🖳**The Inn at Hunt Phelan.** This columned redbrick mansion with a view of downtown's skyline from the front porch served as Ulysses Grant's headquarters while he planned the siege of Vicksburg. Today, it's a B&B with four rooms and a suite, plus an adjacent building with five condo suites that include full kitchen and laundry facilities. **Pros:** quiet rooms; spacious suites; free Wi-Fi; Continental breakfast included. **Cons:** no elevator in main house; on an isolated stretch of Beale Street several long blocks from the entertainment district. ⊠*533 Beale St., Beale Street* ☏*901/525–8225* ⊕*www.huntphelan.com* ⋑*4 rooms, 6 suites* ♿*In-room: no phone, kitchen (some), refrigerator (some), no TV (some), Wi-Fi. In-hotel: 2 restaurants, laundry facilities, Wi-Fi, parking (free), no-smoking rooms* ⊟*AE, D, MC, V* ⓞ*CP.*

$$$$
Fodor'sChoice
★
🖳**Madison Hotel.** This downtown luxury hotel is giving the Peabody a run for its money as the top place to stay in Memphis. A former bank (you can see the vault door in the basement fitness room), it features a gorgeous, music-themed lobby with modern touches, two-story windows, and a rooftop observation deck with spectacular views of the Mississippi River. High tea is served in the afternoon. **Pros:** complimentary Continental breakfast; concierge; free Wi-Fi. **Cons:** no airport shuttle; service can be a little slow. ⊠*79 Madison Ave., Downtown* ☏*901/333–1200 or 866/446–3674* ⊕*www.madisonhotelmemphis. com* ⋑*274 rooms, 36 suites* ♿*In-room: refrigerator (some), Wi-Fi. In-hotel: restaurant, room service, bar, pool, gym, laundry service, Wi-Fi, parking (paid), no-smoking rooms* ⊟*AE, D, MC, V.*

$–$$ 🖳**Memphis Marriott Downtown.** Memphis's largest hotel sits across the street from the city's convention center, with a trolley stop outside the front door for easy access to downtown restaurants farther south. A glass elevator shoots up 19 stories into downtown's skyline. **Pros:** executive floor; concierge; free laundry machines. **Cons:** no airport shuttle; charge for Internet terminal; no Wi-Fi in guest rooms. ⊠*250 N. Main St., Downtown* ☏*901/527–7300* ⊕*www.marriott.com* ⋑*590 rooms, 10 suites* ♿*In-room: Internet. In-hotel: restaurant, room service, bar, pool, gym, laundry service, Wi-Fi, parking (paid), no-smoking rooms* ⊟*AE, D, DC, MC, V.*

$$$$
Fodor'sChoice
★
🖳**Peabody Hotel.** Even if you're not staying here, it's worth a stop to see this 12-story downtown landmark, built in 1925. The lobby has the original stained-glass skylights and the travertine marble fountain that is home to the hotel's resident ducks, which emerge from the elevator at 11 and go back up to their penthouse at 5 every day. ∎**TIP➔Get there early if you want a good view; there tends to be a crush of people around the fountain.** Gloved bellboys carry luggage to the rooms, which are decorated in a variety of period styles. The Presidential Suite goes for $2,200 a night. **Pros:** beautiful rooms; historic lodging; entertaining ducks; Memphis landmark; free Wi-Fi. **Cons:** no airport shuttle;

charge for Internet terminal; pricey. ✉ *149 Union Ave., Downtown* ☎ *901/529–4000 or 800/732–2639 reservations only* ⊕ *www.peabodymemphis.com* ⌁*447 rooms, 17 suites* ⭑ *In-room: kitchen (some), refrigerator (some), Wi-Fi. In-hotel: 2 restaurants, room service, bars, pool, gym, spa, laundry service, Wi-Fi, parking (paid), no-smoking rooms* ▤ *AE, D, DC, MC, V* ⏢|*BP.*

$$–$$$ 🛏 **Sleep Inn at Court Square.** Renovated in October 2008, this chain hotel is conveniently located near two highways and within walking distance of Mud Island; Beale Street is a short walk or trolley ride away (there's a stop right outside on Main Street). **Pros:** free Continental breakfast; good value for downtown; free Wi-Fi. **Cons:** no airport shuttle; no pool; rooms facing Main Street may be bothered by street noise. ✉ *40 N. Front St., Downtown* ☎ *901/522–9700* ⊕ *www.sleepinn.com* ⌁*114 rooms, 10 suites* ⭑ *In-room: refrigerator, Wi-Fi. In-hotel: gym, laundry service, Wi-Fi, parking (paid), no-smoking rooms* ▤ *AE, D, MC, V* ⏢|*CP.*

$$–$$$ 🛏 **Talbot Heirs Guesthouse.** This unique place to stay in the heart of
★ downtown Memphis has spacious studios and suites with overstuffed couches and wicker chairs atop floors made of hardwood or pink Tennessee marble. All rooms are equipped with kitchens; if you call ahead with a grocery list staff will stock the cupboards and refrigerator for no extra charge (you pay the cost of the groceries). Some rooms have small outdoor areas. **Pros:** great location; fully equipped kitchens; free washer and dryer. **Cons:** no elevator; no airport shuttle. ✉ *99 S. 2nd St., Downtown* ☎ *901/527–9772 or 800/955–3956* ⊕ *www.talbothouse.com* ⌁*7 rooms* ⭑ *In-room: kitchen, refrigerator, DVD, Wi-Fi. In-hotel: laundry facilities, Wi-Fi, parking (paid), no-smoking rooms* ▤ *AE, D, MC, V.*

GREATER MEMPHIS

$ 🛏 **Days Inn Graceland.** Virtually next door to Graceland, this modest hotel with external corridors plays the Elvis theme to the hilt, including a guitar-shaped swimming pool. **Pros:** airport shuttle; close to Graceland. **Cons:** no concierge; rather noisy due to Elvis songs played constantly over the outdoor sound system. ✉ *3839 Elvis Presley Blvd., Whitehaven* ☎ *901/346–5500* ⊕ *www.daysinn.com* ⌁*59 rooms, 1 suite* ⭑ *In-room: safe, refrigerator, Internet. In-hotel: pool, Wi-Fi, parking (free), some pets allowed, no-smoking rooms* ▤ *AE, D, MC, V.*

$–$$ 🛏 **Elvis Presley's Heartbreak Hotel.** Next door to Graceland, this hotel has a profusion of leopard print and gold as well as a heart-shaped

10

swimming pool, jungle room bar, and a channel playing Elvis movies 24 hours a day. Themed suites include the Graceland and Burning Love suites. A free downtown shuttle runs at night. **Pros:** airport shuttle; free Continental breakfast; free Wi-Fi. **Cons:** no concierge; can get a little hectic with all the Graceland visitors. ✉ *3677 Elvis Presley Blvd., Whitehaven* ☎ *901/332–1000* ⊕ *www.elvis.com/epheartbreakhotel* ↘ *118 rooms, 48 suites* ♿ *In-room: refrigerator, Wi-Fi. In-hotel: restaurant, bar, pool, gym, laundry facilities, Wi-Fi, parking (free), no-smoking rooms* ⊟ *AE, D, MC, V* ❢❢ *CP.*

$$–$$$ ⌗**Embassy Suites.** A simulated stream flows through the atrium lobby of this East Memphis all-suites hotel. The hotel restaurant is Frank Grisanti, run by the famous Memphis Italian restaurant family. **Pros:** complimentary breakfast and evening reception; airport shuttle. **Cons:** no concierge; at a busy intersection. ✉ *1022 S. Shady Grove Rd., East Memphis* ☎ *901/684–1777* ⊕ *www.memphis.embassysuites.com* ↘ *220 suites* ♿ *In-room: refrigerator, Wi-Fi. In-hotel: restaurant, room service, bar, pool, gym, laundry facilities, laundry service, Wi-Fi, parking (free), no-smoking rooms* ⊟ *AE, D, MC, V* ❢❢ *CP.*

$–$$ ⌗**Hilton Memphis.** Rising alongside I–240 is a 27-story mirrored cylinder of a hotel with a bright, multicolored lobby and a conference center. **Pros:** airport shuttle; concierge. **Cons:** hidden away in a corporate campus; rather uninspiring surroundings overlooking an interstate highway. ✉ *939 Ridge Lake Blvd., East Memphis* ☎ *901/684–6664 or 800/444–2326* ⊕ *www.hilton.com* ↘ *399 rooms, 6 suites* ♿ *In-room: DVD, Wi-Fi. In-hotel: restaurant, room service, pool, gym, laundry service, Wi-Fi, parking (free and paid), no-smoking rooms* ⊟ *AE, D, MC, V.*

$–$$ ⌗**Radisson Inn Memphis Airport.** Right at the entrance to Memphis International Airport, this hotel is a standard chain with several free amenities. **Pros:** airport shuttle; free Internet terminal. **Cons:** right next to airport; no concierge. ✉ *2411 Winchester Rd., Airport* ☎ *901/332–2370* ⊕ *www.radisson.com* ↘ *211 rooms, 4 suites* ♿ *In-room: Wi-Fi. In-hotel: restaurant, room service, bar, pool, gym, laundry service, Wi-Fi, parking (free), no-smoking rooms* ⊟ *AE, D, DC, MC, V.*

NIGHTLIFE AND THE ARTS

THE ARTS

For a complete listing of weekly events, check *Go Memphis*, the weekend section in the Friday *Memphis Commercial Appeal* (⊕ *www.gomemphis.com*), or the *Memphis Flyer* (⊕ *www.memphisflyer.com*), distributed free at newsstands around the city.

The **Memphis Symphony Orchestra** (☎ *901/537–2525* ⊕ *www.memphissymphony.org*) performs at various locations.

The **Orpheum Theatre** (✉ *203 S. Main St., Downtown* ☎ *901/525–3000 or 901/525–7800* ⊕ *www.orpheum-memphis.com*) is a restored 1920s movie house that hosts touring Broadway shows as well as performances by Opera Memphis and Ballet Memphis.

NIGHTLIFE

A handful of areas make for good stepping out downtown, but **Beale Street,** however touristy, tops the list, with more venues per square foot than any other place in town.

BEALE STREET **Alfred's on Beale** (⊠ *197 Beale St., Beale Street* ☎*901/525–3711* ⊕*www. alfreds-on-beale.com*), one of the city's hottest dance clubs, also serves great food. Rock bands perform at the club, and a DJ—sometimes the legendary George Klein, Elvis's good friend—spins popular dance tunes. For quality blues, **B. B. King's Blues Club** (⊠*143 Beale St., Beale Street* ☎*901/524–5464* ⊕*www.bbkingsclub.com*) sets the standard among Memphis's high-profile clubs, with infrequent appearances by the legendary blues artist for whom the club is named. You're more likely to see local legends such as Ruby Wilson than King. The food focuses on Southern specialties, naturally, and the place can be packed; it's a favorite among locals and visitors alike. At the **New Daisy Theatre** (⊠*330 Beale St., Beale Street* ☎*901/525–8981* ⊕*www.newdaisy.com*)—the 900-seat venue where B. B. King got his start—blues, jazz, and (predominantly) rock bands perform. As an old stage theater turned music hall, the New Daisy has excellent acoustics, and it regularly hosts martial arts contests. The **Rum Boogie Cafe** (⊠*182 Beale St., Beale Street* ☎*901/528–0150* ⊕*www.rumboogie.com*) stages live blues nightly, accompanied by Cajun cuisine and barbecue, and has live jam sessions with local blues artists.

MUD ISLAND Big-name entertainers from Willie Nelson to Norah Jones to Fall Out Boy appear at the 5,000-seat **Mud Island Amphitheatre** (☎*901/576–7222*) from April through October. With the downtown skyline as a backdrop, this outdoor theater is scenic, but on a breezeless summer night the heat is not for the faint of heart.

PINCH DISTRICT The historic **Pinch District,** north of downtown between N. Front and N. 3rd streets, in the shadow of the Pyramid, was a working-class neighborhood back in the 1920s and '30s, but now is famous for bars and restaurants. The Main Street Trolley travels here from downtown hotels. **High Point Pinch** (⊠*111 Jackson Ave., Pinch District* ☎*901/525–4444*), near the Main Street Trolley, has live music and is a good spot for lunch. The **North End** (⊠*346 N. Main St., Pinch District* ☎*901/527–3663*) is a popular bar and restaurant that hosts bands.

MIDTOWN Midtown is the center of Memphis's grittier music scene—lots of home grown and out-of-town bands play the neighborhood bars and rock clubs.

Buccaneer Lounge (⊠*1368 Monroe Ave., Midtown* ☎*901/278–0909*), a funky dive in an old house, is a regular gigging spot for several local bands. **Hi-Tone Cafe** (⊠*1913 Poplar Ave., Midtown* ☎*901/278–8663*) has become a music mecca showcasing everything from rap to rockabilly. Elvis Costello played several shows here in 2004, which were recorded and later released on DVD. Fuel up while clubbing in midtown at **Huey's** (⊠*1915 Madison Ave., Midtown* ☎*901/726–4372*), a Memphis institution with big, thick cheeseburgers. There's also a location downtown on the same corner as the Peabody Hotel. **Lamplighter Lounge** (⊠*1702 Madison Ave., Midtown* ☎*901/726–1101*) is an authentically grungy

10

CLOSE UP

If Beale Street Could Talk

Hailed as the birthplace of the blues, the Delta's most famous street rises from the bluffs of the river and meanders for miles into Memphis's flat downtown. Among its brightly lit bar fronts and barren lots lies a history of race and music, prosperity and decline, and, ultimately, renewal.

In the 1840s Beale Street was a thriving suburb, home to scores of Irish and Italian immigrants and at least 300 free African-Americans. During the Civil War Ulysses S. Grant came to town and, with his keen eye for Southern properties, chose the Hunt-Phelan home on Beale as his headquarters, where he mapped out his Vicksburg campaign.

Bloodshed and disease marred the street during Reconstruction. When an African-American boy was accused of killing an Irish boy, mob riots and fires ravaged the street for days. In the 1870s the entire city was besieged—and eventually bankrupted—by cholera and yellow fever epidemics. African-Americans, with a higher degree of immunity to these diseases, were able to remain in the Beale area and helped rebuild the community. Soon Beale became "Main Street" for Southern African-American life, with dentists, clothiers, dry goods and grocery stores, saloons, furniture stores, restaurants, loan offices, newspapers, photography studios, pawn shops, and tailors. The South's first black millionaire, Robert Church, known as the Boss of Beale Street, owned land, stores, saloons, and more. In 1905 he founded Memphis's first African-American bank, the Solvent Savings Bank and Trust, at 392 Beale. Next door, at 391 Beale, he built a 6-acre park and concert hall, where peacocks roamed and children played among the planted trees; Church's Park became a social center.

Onto this street at the turn of the century stepped the young W. C. Handy, credited with writing the first blues song here, in 1909: "The Memphis Blues." Beale was a natural destination, home during the Civil War era to the Young Man's Brass Band, the first known all-African-American musical group. During Reconstruction several bands rose to prominence here playing violins and banjos without written scores in the honky tonks and juke joints. The Handy era was the street's heyday, when many distinguished musicians got their start, including Muddy Waters, Furry Lewis, Albert King, Alberta Hunter, Bobby "Blue" Bland, Memphis Minnie McCoy, and Riley "Blues Boy" King, who became known as B. B. King.

After the Depression took its toll, the bustling neighborhood fell into decline, and in the late 1960s a ghostly version of Beale was named to the National Register of Historic Places. In the 1980s community and government revitalization efforts breathed life into the deserted blocks, and soon clubs, theaters, shops, and restaurants returned to the area, leading to today's somewhat self-conscious entertainment district and tourist playground. Despite the tourism, Beale remains an excellent place to pay respects, catch a show, people-watch, and chow down. Venues such as the New Daisy Theatre and B. B. King's Blues Club and festivals such as the Memphis Music Heritage Festival and Handy Awards Music Festival keep the history alive and continue to make Beale Street worth talking about.

bar adjacent to another live music venue, the Full Moon Club. **Nocturnal** (⊠*1588 Madison Ave., Midtown* ☏*901/726–1548*) has all types of live bands, with an emphasis on younger, unsigned acts. Feed your music-buying habit at **Shangri-La Records** (⊠*1916 Madison Ave., Midtown* ☏*901/274–1916*), a record fan's heaven. They even have 45s!

SOUTH MAIN   The atmospheric blocks surrounding **South Main,** though often eerily quiet, house a handful of Memphis's most authentic clubs. **Earnestine & Hazel's** (⊠*531 S. Main St., South Main* ☏*901/523–9754*), an old-time juke joint, is cherished for its well-stocked jukebox. **Marmalade's Restaurant and Lounge** (⊠*153 G E Patterson Ave., South Main* ☏*901/522–8800*) serves up soul food along with occasional live performances by local jazz, blues, and R&B artists. **Raiford's Hollywood Disco** (⊠*115 Vance Ave., South Main* ☏*901/525–9210*), an on-again, off-again club, attracts patrons from all walks of life to its DJ-driven dance floor. If you end up partying all night, you can grab a classic short-order breakfast at **Arcade** (⊠*540 S. Main St., South Main* ☏*901/526–5757*); the classic greasy spoon and Memphis institution showed up in the movie *Mystery Train,* which featured Screamin' Jay Hawkins playing a hotel night clerk.

SPORTS AND THE OUTDOORS

BASEBALL

The **Memphis Redbirds** (⊠*175 Toyota Plaza, Downtown* ☏*901/721–6000* ⊕*www.memphisredbirds.com*), a St. Louis Cardinals AAA farm team, play at AutoZone Park.

BASKETBALL

The NBA's **Memphis Grizzlies** (⊠*191 Beale St., Downtown* ☏*901/888–HOOP or 866/648–4667* ⊕*www.grizzlies.com*), play at FedExForum on Beale Street.

BOATING, BIKING, AND HIKING

Get back to nature at **Meeman-Shelby Forest State Park,** a 13,500-acre tract bordering the Mississippi, with boat rentals, hiking, and biking. ⊠*910 Riddick Rd.* ✛*10 mi north of Memphis, off U.S. 51, Millington* ☏*901/876–5215 or 800/471–5293* ⊕*www.tennessee.gov/environment/parks/MeemanShelby* ⊡*Free* ☉*Daily 7* AM*–10* PM.

The 4,500-acre **Shelby Farms Park** (⊠*500 North Pine Lake Dr.* ☏*901/382–0235* ⊕*www.shelbyfarmspark.org/sfpc*) has hiking and biking trails and horseback riding. The **Lichterman Nature Center** (⊠*5992 Quince Rd.* ☏*901/767–7322* ⊡*$6* ☉*Tues.–Thurs. 9–4, Fri. and Sat. 9–5*) offers 65 acres of wildlife in East Memphis, along with 3 mi of trails alongside a lake.

GOLF

In June the Tournament Players Club at Southwind Country Club hosts the **Stanford Jude Championship** (⊠*3325 Club at Southwind* ☏*901/748–0534*), featuring top pros.

If you prefer playing to watching, the **Memphis Park Commission** (☏*901/523–7888 or 901/576–4260*) operates five 18-hole and three 9-hole public golf courses. A good choice is **The Links at Galloway**

10

($\boxtimes$*3815 Walnut Grove Rd., East Memphis* ☎*901/685–7805*), 18 holes, par 71; or try **T.O. Fuller State Park** ($\boxtimes$*1500 Mitchell Rd. W* ☎*901/543–7771*), 18 holes, par 72.

SHOPPING

SHOPPING DISTRICTS

Two antiques districts bracket Mid America Mall: **South Main Historic District,** on Main Street between Linden and St. Paul Avenues; and the **Pinch District,** north of downtown, in the shadow of the Pyramid, between Front and 3rd streets, also known for its bars and restaurants. For more local color, midtown's **Cooper-Young District,** at the intersection of Cooper Street and Young Avenue, offers a handful of funky shops, vintage clothing stores, and cafés.

MALLS

Oak Court Mall ($\boxtimes$*4465 Poplar Ave., East Memphis* ☎*901/682–8928*), in the busy Poplar/Perkins area of East Memphis, has 70 specialty stores and two department stores. **Overton Square** ($\boxtimes$*24 S. Cooper St., Midtown* ☎*901/278–6300*) in midtown—a three-block shopping, restaurant, and entertainment complex in vintage buildings and newer structures—has upscale boutiques and specialty shops. At **Wolfchase Galleria** ($\boxtimes$*2760 N. Germantown Pkwy., at I–40, about 18 mi east of downtown Memphis, Cordova* ☎*901/381–2769*), the four anchor stores are Dillard's, Macy's, Sears, and JCPenney. A large carousel attracts scores of children, and there is a multiplex cinema.

SPECIALTY SHOPS

A. Schwab Dry Goods Store ($\boxtimes$*163 Beale St., Beale Street* ☎*901/523–9782*) is an old-fashioned store whose motto is "If you can't find it at A. Schwab's, you're better off without it!" Elvis shopped here, and you can, too—for top hats, spats, tambourines, and bow ties. **Davis-Kidd Booksellers** ($\boxtimes$*387 Perkins Ext., East Memphis* ☎*901/683–9801*) is a Tennessee-based chain with an expansive collection of titles as well as in-store cafés. The **Woman's Exchange** ($\boxtimes$*88 Racine St., Midtown* ☎*901/327–5681*) specializes in children's wear and handcrafted items and has a tearoom for weekday luncheons.

NASHVILLE

213 mi northeast of Memphis via I-40.

Heralded as Music City, U.S.A., Tennessee's fast-growing capital city is a dynamic business center with a vibrant cultural life. A consistent influx of new residents, two recently added professional sports teams, and significant new construction downtown have moved Nashville into the major leagues of American cities.

Nashville is best known for music, and venues—for country, of course, but rock, blues, jazz, and classical as well—dot the city. At the south end of downtown, you can't walk a block without hearing the familiar chords of a country song pouring out the doors of Broadway's honky tonks or from the lone guitars of sidewalk musicians. The Country

Tennessee Facts

■ During the War of 1812 so many Tennesseans answered native son General Andrew Jackson's call to serve that the state acquired the sobriquet "The Volunteer State." The sentiment lives on in the nickname of the University of Tennessee's athletic teams.

■ Tennessee has several official state songs, including a bicentennial rap song. One of them is "The Tennessee Waltz" by Redd Stewart and Pee Wee King. Another—perhaps to the chagrin of non-UT fans—is "Rocky Top" by Boudleaux and Felice Bryant.

■ **Lowest Point:** The Mississippi River, at 175 feet.

■ **Highest Point:** Clingmans Dome in Great Smoky Mountains National Park, at 6,643 feet.

■ **Famous Tennesseans:** Davy Crockett, Andrew Jackson, Andrew Johnson, James K. Polk, Aretha Franklin, Amy Grant, Dolly Parton, Justin Timberlake, Minnie Pearl, Sequoyah, Lester Flatt.

Music Hall of Fame and the Ryman Auditorium, the "Mother Church of Country Music," are just a short walk away. Nearby Music Row, home to record labels and music publishers, beckons aspiring singers and songwriters.

Nashville's *Grand Ole Opry* radio program planted the seeds of the town as an American music mecca and thrived through the Great Depression all the way to country's ascendancy into mainstream success in the 1990s. Today, fans flock to Opry performances by artists ranging from country legends to up-and-coming stars in the sleek $15 million Opry House, in an outlying part of northeast Nashville known as "Music Valley."

Outside downtown, several older neighborhoods have been transformed into hip, urban places to live and play. A short drive north of the State Capitol is Germantown, a tight cluster of streets lined with old redbrick buildings recently reclaimed by young families and urban professionals. The Gulch, site of a former rail yard just southwest of downtown, now hosts some of Nashville's most talked-about eateries.

Also known as the "Athens of the South," Nashville is home to 16 institutions of higher learning, including consistently high-ranked Vanderbilt University, which stands just down the street from a full-size replica of the Parthenon. Tennessee State University and Fisk University, both north of downtown, are historically black institutions, with the latter home to the renowned Fisk Jubilee Singers.

With a past marked by both the Civil War and the civil rights movement, Nashville offers fans of history plenty to see throughout the city and surrounding area, including the Hermitage, home of Tennessee's most celebrated historical figure, Andrew Jackson, as well as historic homes Belle Meade Plantation and Travellers' Rest.

10

DISCOUNTS AND DEALS

If you're feeling ambitious, you may want to pick up a Music City Total Access pass for $45, which gives entry to any four popular attractions, including the Adventure Science Center, Country Music Hall of Fame, The Hermitage, Nashville Shores, and Ryman Auditorium. The pass is available for purchase at downtown's two visitor information centers, at the corner of 5th Avenue and Broadway (in the glass tower of the Sommet Center) and at the corner of 4th Avenue N and Commerce Street (on the ground floor of the U.S. Bank Building), by phone at ☎800/657–6910, or online at ⊕ www.visitmusiccity.com.

GETTING HERE AND AROUND

BUS TRAVEL   Metropolitan Transit Authority (MTA) buses serve the entire county; the fare is $1.60 (exact change).

CAR TRAVEL   From Nashville I–65 leads north into Kentucky and south into Alabama, and I–24 leads northwest into Kentucky and Illinois and southeast into Chattanooga and Georgia. Interstate 40 traverses the state east–west, connecting Knoxville with Nashville and Memphis. Interstate 440 connects I–40, I–65, and I–24, and helps circumvent clogged major arteries during Nashville's rush hour.

TAXI TRAVEL   Try Allied Taxi, Music City Taxi, or Yellow Cab.

TOURS   The *General Jackson*, Opryland's four-deck paddle wheeler, has a wide variety of cruises along the Cumberland River daily, including lunch and dinner cruises, with a music review in the Victorian Theater.

Gray Line Bus Tours has sightseeing tours that include drives past stars' homes and visits to the Grand Ole Opry, Music Row, and the District, as well as tours to outlying areas including Civil War sites and the Jack Daniel's distillery.

Johnny Walker Tours has two-night package tours that include stars' homes, the Grand Ole Opry, and riverboat cruises.

ESSENTIALS

Bus Contacts Metropolitan Transit Authority (☎615/862–5950 ⊕www. nashvillemta.org).

Taxi Contacts Allied Taxi (☎615/883–2323). **Music City Taxi** (☎615/742–3030). **Yellow Cab** (☎615/256–0101).

Tour Contacts Gray Line (☎888/883–5555 ⊕www.graylinenashville.com). *General Jackson* (☎866/567–5225 ⊕www.generaljackson.com). **Johnny Walker Tours** (☎615/834–8585 or 800/722–1524 ⊕www.johnnywalkertours.com).

Visitor Contacts Nashville Visitor Center (✉ 150 4th Avenue N, Suite G-250, Downtown ☎800/657–6910 ⊕www.visitmusiccity.com).

EXPLORING

DOWNTOWN NASHVILLE

Downtown Nashville has much to offer in the way of history, music, entertainment, dining, and specialty shopping. It's fairly easy to get around downtown by foot, although most hotels are clustered at the north end while many attractions—including the Country Music Hall

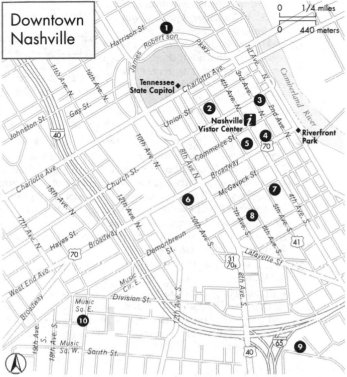

of Fame and Broadway's famous honky tonks—lie at the south end,
at the bottom of a hill. The Cumberland River horizontally bisects
Nashville's downtown. Numbered avenues, running north–south, are
west of and parallel to the river; numbered streets are east of the river
but also parallel to it.

TOP ATTRACTIONS

7 **★** **Country Music Hall of Fame and Museum.** This tribute to country music's
finest, among them Hank Williams Sr., Loretta Lynn, Patsy Cline, and
Johnny Cash, reopened in 2001 in a new $37 million facility just south
of the Sommet Center. A block long, with an exterior that evokes a
piano, a Cadillac fin, and a radio tower, the museum contains plaques
honoring country greats, a two-story wall with every gold and platinum
country record ever made, a theater that screens a digital film on the
industry, and daily live entertainment, not to mention Elvis Presley's
solid-gold 1960 Cadillac limo. ■TIP➔**Buses depart regularly from the
museum for tours of Historic RCA Studio B.** ✉222 5th Ave. S, at Demon-
breun St., Downtown ☎615/416–2001 ⊕www.countrymusichallof-
fame.com ✉$17.95 ⊙Daily 9–5.

6 **☺** **★** **Frist Center for the Visual Arts.** This art gallery boasts 24,000 feet of exhibit
space and hosts first-class exhibitions of paintings, sculpture, and other
visual art. The historic building, with its original art deco exterior, was

formerly Nashville's downtown post office. In its current incarnation, the building houses art galleries, a children's discovery gallery, a 250-seat auditorium, a gift shop, a café, art workshops, and an art resource center. ⊠ *209 10th Ave. S, Downtown* ☏ *615/244-3340* ⊕ *www.fristcenter.org* ☞ *$8.50* ⊗ *Mon.-Wed. 10–5:30, Thur. and Fri. 10–9, Sat. 10–5:30, Sun. 1–5:30.*

WORD OF MOUTH

"Hatch Show Print on Broadway is fun to spend a little time in—you can see the printing press in the back and all the posters they've done over the years."   —jent103

❹ **Hatch Show Print.** One of the nation's oldest letterpress poster print shops, Hatch Show Print, now owned by the Country Music Hall of Fame and Museum, has been in business since 1879 and has printed posters for vaudeville shows, circuses, sporting events, and, most notably, Grand Ole Opry stars. The store now makes posters and prints for contemporary artists and events. There's no formal tour, but this place is a slice of history that you can explore on your own. ⊠ *316 Broadway, Downtown* ☏ *615/256-2805* ⊕ *www.countrymusichalloffame.com* ⊗ *Weekdays 9–5, Sat. 10–5.*

❿ **Historic RCA Studio B.** In the first big Nashville hit factory, where Chet Atkins helped create the "Nashville sound," visitors can step through the same spaces where stars including Elvis, Roy Orbison, Dolly Parton, and the Everly Brothers laid down some of their greatest hits. Audio and video displays tell the history of the studio. Tickets are sold in conjunction with the Country Music Hall of Fame and Museum and shuttle buses from the Hall of Fame run here. ⊠ *1611 Roy Acuff Pl., Music Row* ☏ *615/416-2001* ⊕ *www.countrymusichalloffame.com* ☞ *$12.95* ⊗ *Daily 9–5*

❺ **Ryman Auditorium and Museum.** The the Ryman's pew-filled auditorium,
★ known as the "Mother Church of Country Music," was home to the Grand Ole Opry from 1943 to 1974 and is listed on the National Register of Historic Places. The former Union Gospel Tabernacle has acoustics that are said to rival Carnegie Hall's and seats more than 2,000 for live performances of classical, jazz, pop, gospel, and, of course, country. The Opry stages its popular live country show at the Ryman from November through January. Self-guided tours include photo-ops on the legendary stage and the museum, with its photographs and memorabilia of past performances. Backstage tours are also available. ⊠ *116 5th Ave. N, Downtown* ☏ *615/889-3060 tickets* ⊕ *www.ryman.com* ☞ *Tours $12.50, backstage tour $16.25* ⊗ *Daily 9–4; call for show schedules and ticket prices.*

WORTH NOTING

❾ **Adventure Science Center.** Science is an adventure in this museum packed
☺ with hands-on activities, including the new 15,000-square-foot Space Chase exhibit with a moon walk and weightlessness simulator, planetarium, and flight simulator. The museum's location at the top of a hill means it has wonderful views of Nashville, making it an ideal spot to watch the city's Fourth of July fireworks. ⊠ *800 Fort Negley Blvd., Fort Negley Park* ☏ *615/862-5160* ⊕ *www.adventuresci.com* ☞ *$11* ⊗ *Mon.-Sat. 10–5, Sun. 12:30–5:30.*

1 Bicentennial Capitol Mall State Park. Completed in 1996 to celebrate Tennessee's bicentennial, this beautifully landscaped 19-acre park just north of the Tennessee State Capitol includes a 2,000-seat amphitheater, a scale map of the state in granite, a World War II memorial, a wall etched with a timeline of state events, and fountains representing each of Tennessee's rivers (you'll see both kids and adults splashing in them April–October). The nearby farmers' market has several dining options. ⊠ *600 James Robertson Pkwy., Downtown* 🕾 *615/741–5280* 🎫 *Free* ☼ *Daily 7 AM–10 PM.*

3 The District. Thanks to an extensive preservation program begun in the early 1980s, this 16-square-block area between Church Street and Broadway is packed with handsomely restored 19th-century redbrick warehouses and storefronts. Revelers flock to the Wildhorse Saloon, a huge country music dance hall, and to popular restaurants and clubs.

8 Musicians Hall of Fame & Museum. Not as well-known as the nearby Country Music Hall of Fame, this museum still has an impressive collection of musical mementos. It focuses on the often overlooked Nashville studio musicians of the 1950s and '60s, including Jimi Hendrix, who helped lay down what became known as the "Nashville sound." ⊠ *301 6th Ave. S, Downtown* 🕾 *615/244–3263* ⊕ *www.musicianshalloffame.com* 🎫 *$14.95* ☼ *Mon.–Thurs. 10–6, Fri. and Sat. 10–5.*

Tennessee State Capitol. The state capitol is largely the same as when it was completed in 1859. It was designed by noted Philadelphia architect William Strickland (1788–1854), who was so impressed with his Greek revival creation that he requested—and received—entombment behind one of the building's walls. On the grounds you'll also find the graves of the 11th U.S. president, James K. Polk, and his wife. ⊠ *600 Charlotte Ave., between 6th and 7th Aves., Downtown* 🕾 *615/741–1621* 🎫 *Free* ☼ *Tours weekdays on the hour 9–11 and 1–3.*

2 Tennessee Performing Arts Center. Part of the state capitol complex, TPAC, as it's known, comprises Jackson Hall, Johnson Hall, and Polk Theater—named for the three U.S. presidents Tennessee has produced. **TPAC Friends** (🕾 *615/298–3877*) offers backstage tours of the center by appointment. ⊠ *505 Deaderick St., Downtown* 🕾 *615/782–4000* ⊕ *www.tpac.org* 🎫 *Free* ☼ *Tues.–Sat. 10–5, Sun. 1–5.*

GREATER NASHVILLE

To get a more complete feeling for the city, you'll want to explore the area beyond downtown, which includes historic plantations, museums covering everything from history to science, and some great places for kids, including the Nashville Zoo—not to mention the Grand Ole Opry, in "Music Valley," in northeast Nashville, which features the nearly 200-store Opry Mills shopping and entertainment complex and the massive Gaylord Opryland Resort and Convention Center, with nearly 3,000 hotel rooms, numerous restaurants, and boat rides on an indoor artificial river.

TOP ATTRACTIONS

12 ★ Belle Meade Plantation. Known as the "Queen of Tennessee Plantations," this stunning Greek revival house is recognizable by the Civil War bullet holes that riddle its columns. Guides in period costumes lead you

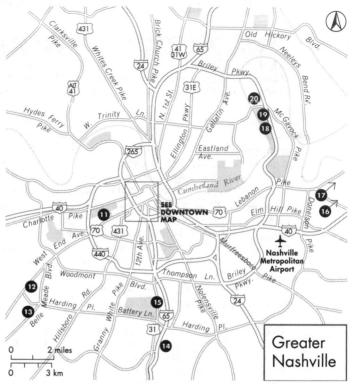

Greater
Nashville

through the mansion, which is furnished in the antebellum style and is the centerpiece of a 5,300-acre estate that was one of the nation's first and finest Thoroughbred breeding farms. It was also the site of the famous Iroquois Steeplechase, the oldest amateur steeplechase in America, a society event now run each May in nearby Percy Warner Park. A Victorian carriage museum with an impressive collection continues the equine theme. A two-story visitor center is modeled after a traditional Southern paddock. The last tour of the day starts at 4, and the excellent restaurant here is called Martha's at the Plantation. ✉ *5025 Harding Rd., Belle Meade* ☎ *615/356–0501* ⊕ *www.bellemeadeplantation.com* 💲 *$15* ⊙ *Mon.–Sat. 9–5, Sun. 11–5.*

18 **Grand Ole Opry.** The longest running radio show in the United States, cur-
★ rently performed in the Grand Ole Opry House, has been broadcasting country music from Nashville since 1925. You may see superstars, legends, and up-and-coming stars on the Opry's stage. The auditorium seats about 4,400 people in deep wooden pews, and there's not a bad seat in the house. Performances (Broadcast live on WSM AM 650) are every Tuesday (7, March–mid-December only), Friday (8), and Saturday (6:30 and 9:30). Buy tickets ($34.50–$47.50) well in advance, particularly during CMA Music Festival week in June. The Opry also has a winter run at the Ryman Auditorium in downtown Nashville from November

through January. ⊠*2804 Opryland Dr., Music Valley* ☎*615/871–6779 or 800/733–6779 ticket information* ⊕*www.opry.com.*

🔟 **Hermitage.** The life and times of
★ Andrew Jackson, known as "Old Hickory," are reflected with great care at this house and museum. Jackson built the mansion on 600 acres for his wife, Rachel, for whose honor he fought and won a duel. Both are buried in the family graveyard. The Andrew Jackson Center, a 28,000-square-foot museum, visitor center, and education center, contains many Jackson artifacts. By the 1840s, more than 140 African-American slaves lived and worked on the Hermitage Plantation, and archaeological digs have uncovered the remains of many slave dwell

WORD OF MOUTH

"I concur about NOT staying at the Opryland Hotel...we stayed one night there on our recent trip because we had tickets to the Grand Ole Opry and because we got a good deal, but I wouldn't stay there again. It is cool to see the public areas though so allow some time when you go to the Opry and wander around. Stay downtown (there are lots of good choices) and visit all the music clubs on Lower Broadway... no cover charges and live music everywhere, even during the daytime at some of them!"

—musicfan

ings—yard cabins, Alfred's Cabin, and field quarters. Mansion tours are led by costumed guides, while tours of the grounds are self-guided. Wagon tours are offered April through October. The Garden Gate Café, a museum store, and the Hermitage Garden Shop are also on the grounds. The Hermitage is 12 mi east of Nashville; take I–40E to the Old Hickory Boulevard exit. ⊠*4580 Rachel's La., Hermitage* ☎*615/889–2941* ⊕*www.thehermitage.com* 🎫*$14* ⊙*Apr. 1–Oct. 15, daily 8:30–5; Oct. 16–Mar. 31, daily 9–4:30, closed third week in Jan.*

WORTH NOTING

🔟 **Cheekwood Botanical Garden and Museum of Art.** Thirty acres of gardens
★ showcase annuals, perennials, and seasonal wildflowers, and a carefully restored neo-Georgian mansion holds the museum. The permanent exhibition shows American art to 1945, while the Temporary Contemporary gallery presents local and national artists. A collection of Fabergé pieces—including three Imperial Easter eggs—from the Matilda Geddings Gray Foundation is also on display. ⊠*1200 Forrest Park Dr., Belle Meade* ☎*615/356–8000* ⊕*www.cheekwood.org* 🎫*$10* ⊙*Tues.–Sat. 9:30–4:30, Sun. 11–4:30.*

🔟 **Gaylord Opryland Resort and Convention Center.** Famous for its imaginative public spaces and displays of artwork, this immense hotel (it has close to 3,000 rooms), dining, and entertainment complex is Nashville at its biggest and most spectacular. Three separate atriums hold indoor gardens, presenting landscapes including the Caribbean and the Mississippi Delta, the latter of which has boat tours along an indoor river. A full slate of restaurants offers everything from international flavors to casual fare. Numerous nightlife options abound as well. ⊠*2800 Opryland Dr., Music Valley* ☎*615/889–1000* ⊕*www.gaylordhotels.com.*

10

⓴ Music Valley Wax Museum. The lure of lifelike wax figures is as strong as ever, and Nashville's country music stars make ripe material. Here fans can stroll among 50 of country's brightest dressed in authentic costumes and view video displays of stars' performances. A walk down the Sidewalk of the Stars yields the rewards of 280 entertainers' footprints, handprints, and signatures in concrete. ⊠ *2515 McGavock Pike, Music Valley* ☎ *615/883–3612* 🖳 *$3.50* 🕙 *Apr.–mid-Sept., daily 9–8; mid Sept. Mon., daily 9 5.*

⓰ Nashville Shores. If you want to go to the beach while visiting Nashville, 🆑 head to this water park on Percy Priest Lake for slides, pools, and lake cruises on the *Nashville Shoreliner.* ⊠ *4001 Bell Rd., Hermitage* ☎ *615/889–7050* ⊕ *www.nashvilleshores.com* 🖳 *$23.95* 🕙 *May 24–Aug. 10, Mon.–Sat. 10–6, Sun. 11–6; Aug. 11–15, Mon.–Fri. 10–3; May 17–May 18 and Aug. 16–Sept. 7, Sat. 10–6, Sun. 11–6, closed weekdays.*

⓯ Nashville Zoo at Grassmere. More than 600 exotic animals are on display 🆑 in naturalistic environments here, including clouded leopards, lions, white tigers, ring-tailed lemurs, giraffes, and red pandas. The Unseen New World exhibit has red-eyed tree frogs, rhino iguanas, leaf-nosed bats, and about 75 other species of reptiles, amphibians, insects, mammals, and birds. At the **Jungle Gym Playground,** children can enjoy 66,000 square feet of play area, including a pond, cargo netting, slides, and climbers. The **Grassmere Historic Home and Farm** brings to life an 1880s-era working farm, with a barn, livestock, hands-on demonstrations, and period gardens illustrating a typical variety of uses—culinary, medicinal, and decorative. The Italianate-style home, built in 1810, is the second-oldest residence in Davidson County open to the public. ⊠ *3777 Nolensville Rd., South Nashville* ☎ *615/833–1534* ⊕ *www. nashvillezoo.org* 🖳 *$13* 🕙 *Mar. 15–Oct. 15, daily 9–6; Oct. 16–Mar. 14, daily 9–4.*

⓫ Parthenon. An exact copy of the Athenian original, Nashville's Parthe-★ non was constructed for Tennessee's 1897 centennial exposition. Across the street from Vanderbilt University's campus, in Centennial Park, it's a magnificent sight, perched on a gentle green slope beside a duck pond. Inside are the 63-piece Cowan Collection of American art, traveling exhibits, and the 42-foot *Athena Parthenos,* the tallest indoor sculpture in the Western world. ⊠ *West End and 25th Aves., West End/ Vanderbilt* ☎ *615/862–8431* ⊕ *www.nashville.gov/parthenon* 🖳 *$5* 🕙 *Sept.–May, Tues.–Sat. 9–4:30; June and Aug., Tues.–Sat. 9–4:30, Sun. 12:30–4:30.*

⓮ Travellers' Rest. Following the fortunes of pioneer landowner and judge John Overton—the law partner, mentor, campaign manager, and lifelong friend of Andrew Jackson, whose own home is nearby—this early-19th-century clapboard home metamorphosed from a four-room cottage to a 12-room mansion with Federal-influenced and Greek revival additions. The interior has been restored to its mid-19th-century state with period furnishings, and the grounds contain a restored smokehouse, kitchen house, and formal gardens. Travellers' Rest is off I–65 S at the first of two Harding Place exits. ⊠ *636 Farrell Pkwy., Oak Mills*

☎615/832–8197 ⊕www.travellersrestplantation.org ✉$10 ⊙Tues.–Sat. 10–4, Sun. 1–4.

OFF THE BEATEN PATH

Jack Daniel's Distillery. Lynchburg has become known worldwide for its best-known product: whiskey. The quaint town, about 75 mi southeast of Nashville, is home to the Jack Daniel's Distillery, the oldest registered distillery in the country. The distillery offers free tours, where you can observe every step of the art of making sour-mash whiskey. *✉182 Lynchburg Hwy., Lynchburg ☎931/759–4221 ⊕www.jackdaniels. com ✉Free ⊙Guided tours daily 9–4:30.*

WHERE TO EAT

Nashville's dining scene has gone upscale. It's now possible to find inventive menus and creative combinations of ingredients in restaurants in revitalized neighborhoods like the Gulch and East Nashville, both a short hop from downtown. Many restaurants are also clustered in the neighborhoods around Vanderbilt University: Midtown, Elliston Place, and Hillsboro Village.

Despite Nashville's culinary revolution, diners are still often casually dressed and enjoy lingering over meals. Those craving old Southern favorites like catfish, barbecue, and the ever-popular, no-frills "meat and three" can find plenty of options alongside the city's trendier eateries.

DOWNTOWN

¢ SOUTHERN ★ ✕**Arnold's Country Kitchen.** Grab a tray and join the workaday lunchtime crowd at Formica tables tucking into Southern feasts inside this archetypal meat-and-three diner. A cheerful staff dishes out heaping helpings of carved ham, pork brisket, fried chicken, meatloaf, and other comfort foods from stainless-steel steam tables. Sides include turnip greens cooked with bacon and creamy coleslaw. A full slate of pies including peach, strawberry, and chocolate tempts already full diners. Arnold's is only open for lunch, but you may not need dinner if you chow down here! ✉605 8th Ave. S, 8th Avenue South ☎615/256–4455 ▤MC, V ⊙No dinner. Closed Sat. and Sun.

$$$$ AMERICAN ★ ✕**Capitol Grille and Oak Bar.** This charming restaurant in downtown's historic Hermitage Hotel serves cuisine with a regional flair, including seafood and Black Angus beef, and is consistently ranked as one of Nashville's top restaurants. As a testament to its opulence, a 14-ounce, 21-day-dry-aged strip loin goes for $65. Breakfast, lunch, and dinner are served, as well as brunch on Sunday. ✉231 6th Ave. N, Downtown ☎615/345–7116 ⊕www.thehermitagehotel.com ⌔Reservations essential ▤AE, D, DC, MC, V.

$–$$ BARBEQUE ✕**Jack's Bar-B-Que.** This hole-in-the-wall barbecue joint is perfectly located to grab a bite before hitting the honky tonks on Broadway. The no-frills menu dips into several barbecue regions, with plates and sandwiches of Tennessee pork shoulder, Texas beef brisket, and St. Louis pork ribs and side dishes including coleslaw, baked beans, and potato salad. ✉416 Broadway, Downtown ☎615/254–5715 ⊕www. jacksbarbque.com ▤AE, D, MC, V.

$$–$$$ AMERICAN ✕**Merchants Restaurant.** This restaurant is housed in the former Merchants Hotel, built in 1892. The first-floor dining room offers a casual

10

bar-and-grill atmosphere and menu, while the second floor has formal dining in a room with hardwood floors, brick walls, and ceiling fans. Many of the old hotel's original elements have been incorporated into the decor, including fireplaces, wainscoting, and custom sconces. ⊠ *401 Broadway, Downtown* ☎ *615/254–1892* ⊕ *www.merchantsrestaurant. com* ⌔ *Reservations essential* ▤ *AE, D, DC, MC, V* ⊗ *No lunch Sun.*

$–$$ ✕ **Old Spaghetti Factory.** Brick walls, hardwood floors, and booths made
ITALIAN from converted antique beds create a comfortable, rustic ambience in this converted tobacco warehouse in downtown. There are stained-glass windows, antique light fixtures, and an authentic Nashville trolley car in the dining room, plus an extensive collection of photographs and prints of historic Nashville. Guests pass through the doorway arch of the old Bank of London on their way from the vestibule into the main room. The mostly spaghetti menu is perfect for kids. Chicken parmigiana and spaghetti with meatballs are popular. ⊠ *160 2nd Ave. N, Downtown* ☎ *615/254–9010* ⊕ *www.osf.com* ▤ *AE, D, MC, V.*

$$$$ ✕ **Radius 10.** This former warehouse sits in the shadow of the Union
ECLECTIC Station Hotel in the Gulch, one of Nashville's most happening dining
★ destinations. The creative and frequently changing menu has featured ahi tuna and coconut chicken as well as updated versions of Southern favorites like crawfish with dirty rice. Desserts are on the rich side. ⊠ *101 McGavock St., The Gulch* ☎ *615/259–5105* ⊕ *www.radius10. com* ▤ *AE, MC, V* ⊗ *Closed Sun.*

$$$$ ✕ **The Standard at the Smith House.** This restaurant is in a historic 24-room
AMERICAN downtown mansion, built in the 1840s, and it retains much of the home's original decor, including fireplaces, oak floors, antiques, and paintings. Specialties include homemade crab bisque, crab cakes, and sweet potato fries. ⊠ *167 8th Ave. N, Downtown* ☎ *615/254–1277* ⊕ *www.thestandardnashville.com* ⌔ *Reservations essential* ▤ *AE, D, MC, V* ⊗ *No dinner Sun. and Mon. No lunch.*

AROUND VANDERBILT UNIVERSITY

$$$–$$$$ ✕ **The Bound'ry.** This large, lavishly appointed space west of downtown
AMERICAN near the Vanderbilt campus is festooned with murals and sculptures. Curved booths are nestled in gleaming polished-wood settings, and two fireplaces warm the dining room. A wood-fired oven turns out manly portions of steak and seafood as well as dishes like rack of lamb and smoked ostrich. When you're finished eating you can adjourn to the balcony for cigars and martinis. There is open-air dining in front, with a tree in the center of the patio. Sunday brunch is served 11 to 3. ⊠ *911 20th Ave. S, Midtown* ☎ *615/321–3043* ⊕ *www.pansouth.net* ⌔ *Reservations essential* ▤ *AE, D, DC, MC, V* ⊗ *No lunch.*

¢ ✕ **Elliston Place Soda Shop.** Come to this old-fashioned soda shop for great
AMERICAN burgers, frothy ice cream sodas, and delicious chocolate shakes. ⊠ *2111 Elliston Pl., Elliston Place* ☎ *615/327–1090* ▤ *MC, V* ⊗ *Closed Sun.*

$–$$ ✕ **Mafiaoza's Pizzeria & Neighborhood Pub.** Locals flock to the outdoor
PIZZA terrace of this stone-oven pizzeria in the newly trendy 12 South neighborhood. Toppings include portobello mushrooms, shrimp, scallops, and eggplant, as well as standard meats and vegetables. A spicy vodka cream sauce is a highlight among the pasta offerings, and the menu has several sandwiches and salads. It can get noisy in and around the

bar, especially during happy hour. ✉ *2400 12th Ave. S, 12 South* ☎*615/269–4646* ⊕*www.mafiaozas.com* ⊟*AE, D, MC, V* ⊘*Closed Mon. No lunch weekdays.*

¢–$ ✕**Pancake Pantry.** This Nashville
SOUTHERN institution is the place to go for
Fodor's Choice breakfast. It's a favorite haunt of
★ celebrities like Garth Brooks and Alan Jackson and also popular with local politicos. Breakfast is the specialty, with 20 kinds of pancakes and homemade syrups. The menu also has soups and sandwiches for lunch. ■**TIP**➡**Get there by 8:15 weekdays to avoid lines, but be prepared to wait on weekends.** ✉*1796 21st Ave. S, Hillsboro Village* ☎*615/383–9333* ♙*Reservations not accepted* ⊟*AE, D, DC, MC, V* ⊘*No dinner.*

> **WORD OF MOUTH**
>
> "If you are free for breakfast, near [the] Vandy campus, visit Pancake Pantry. Long lines on weekends but worth the wait. Visit Belle Meade plantation, and go to Loveless Motel for fried chicken served homestyle."   —aliska

$–$$ ✕**Rotier's.** Vinyl booths, cheap wood paneling, and sports on the tele-
AMERICAN vision are responsible for the lack of ambience at this classic Vandy diner, which specializes in burgers on French bread. The milkshakes are also popular, and the steak and chicken dinners aren't bad. ✉ *2413 Elliston Pl., Elliston Place* ☎*615/327–9892* ⊕*rotiers.com* ⊟*MC, V* ⊘*Closed Sun.*

$–$$ ✕**Sitar.** The attentive staff and relaxed atmosphere make this comfort-
INDIAN able Indian eatery near the Vanderbilt campus a standout. The dining room is decorated with traditional Indian artwork, and there's a very affordable hot buffet lunch with favorites like chicken tikka masala (baked chicken in a spiced tomato sauce) and *sag paneer* (spinach, cheese, and spices) as well as an extensive menu of meat, seafood, and tandoori specialties. ✉*116 21st Ave. N, Midtown* ☎*615/321–8889* ⊕*www.sitarnashville.com* ⊟*AE, D, MC, V.*

$$$–$$$$ ✕**Sunset Grill.** Seafood, pastas, steaks, and vegetarian specials highlight
AMERICAN the menu of this restaurant that displays the work of local artist Paul
Fodor's Choice Harmon. A good entrée choice is voodoo pasta, with andouille sausage,
★ chicken, and pork roast slow braised in milk over roasted potato-shallot ravioli and cider-glazed parsnips, carrots, and onions. Sublime homemade sorbet can finish your meal, and the restaurant serves 70 wines by the glass. A special late-night menu is available from 10 PM to midnight Monday through Thursday and midnight to 1:30 AM Friday and Saturday. ✉*2001 Belcourt Ave., Hillsboro Village* ☎*615/386–3663 or 866/496–3663* ⊕*www.sunsetgrill.com* ⊟*AE, D, MC, V* ⊘*No lunch Sat.–Mon.*

EAST NASHVILLE

¢–$ ✕**Bolton's Spicy Chicken and Fish.** It may not look like much inside or out,
FAST FOOD but this low-slung cinderblock shack on a gritty commercial strip just east of the Victory Memorial Bridge is one of a handful of purveyors of a dearly beloved Nashville consumable: hot chicken. The crackly, bright orange skin of the legs, breasts, and wings gives more than a hint of the scorching to be delivered to the lips, tongues, and palates of adventurous diners who make the trek to this largely take-out joint. A mixture of spices provides the punch—be sure to have plenty of iced tea

10

or lemonade on hand! The chicken comes with side dishes like french fries and coleslaw. If you can't take the heat, ribs and fried fish are also on the menu. ⊠ *624 Main St., East Nashville* ☎*615/254–8015* ▭*D, MC, V* ⊘ *Closed Mon.*

$$ ✕**Marché Artisan Foods.** A mixture of Mediterranean and American
AMERICAN Southern flavors predominate at this airy, well-lit casual spot in East Nashville. A changing menu features entrées such as braised Kurobuta pork belly with black-eyed peas and cabbage, marinated skirt steak with bacon polenta, and braised kale and chicken breast with tabouleh. The restaurant is very popular for lunch and all-day weekend brunches. ⊠ *1000 Main St., East Nashville* ☎*615/262–1111* ⊕*www.marcheartisanfoods.com* ▭*AE, D, MC, V* ⊘ *Closed Mon.*

$$$–$$$$ ✕**Margot Café and Bar.** The worn brick exterior shoehorned onto an
FRENCH East Nashville street belies the wizardry that goes on in the kitchen.
★ With the emphasis on French and Italian flavors, the changing menu may include braised mackerel with roasted red pepper sauce, hanger steak with fingerling potatoes, and grilled cobia with preserved lemon and caper pesto. ⊠ *1017 Woodland St., East Nashville* ☎*615/227–4668* ⊕*www.margotcafe.com* ▭*D, MC, V* ⊘ *No lunch. Closed Mon. Brunch only on Sun.*

$$–$$$ ✕**Rosepepper Cantina & Mexican Grille.** Housed in a former neighborhood
MEXICAN grocery on a stretch of backstreet in up-and-coming East Nashville, this restaurant serves innovative, Sonoran-influenced Mexican cooking. Enchiladas, tacos, and burritos are available, but so are dishes like tempura-battered sweet peppers on a bed of sunflower seeds with chipotle relish. Margarita fans can choose from six handcrafted varieties. The funky decor adds to the ambience. ⊠ *1907 Eastland Ave., East Nashville* ☎*615/227–4777* ⊕*www.rosepepper.com* ⌕*Reservations not accepted* ▭*AE, D, MC, V* ⊘ *No lunch Sun.*

GREATER NASHVILLE

$$$$ ✕**F. Scott's.** This Green Hills spot offers innovative dishes on a season-
AMERICAN ally changing menu that may include pan-seared scallops or cornmeal-dusted trout as well as steaks and pasta. The wine list is extensive. ⊠*2210 Crestmoor Rd., Green Hills* ☎*615/269–5861* ⊕*www.fscotts.com* ▭*AE, D, DC, MC, V* ⊘ *No lunch. Closed Sun.*

$$–$$$ ✕**Germantown Café.** The interior is dimly lit and stylish, with blond
AMERICAN wood, exposed ducts, and modern art on the walls, but this is actually
★ a relaxing neighborhood hangout. Try the flatiron steak, the coconut curry salmon with risotto, or the fried green tomatoes. Crab cakes are available as an entrée or an appetizer. The Germantown strudel appetizer is a sample of fillings in phyllo pastry, including artichoke hearts, spinach and cheese, and spicy beef. ⊠ *1200 5th Ave. N, Germantown* ☎*615/242–3226* ⊕*www.germantowncafe.com* ▭*AE, D, MC, V* ⊘ *No lunch Sat.*

$–$$ ✕**Loveless Cafe.** This is an experience in true down-home Southern
SOUTHERN cooking, off I–40 west of Nashville, near the northern terminus of the
★ Natchez Trace. Don't come for the decor—decidedly lax, with red-and-white-checked tablecloths—but for the feather-light homemade biscuits and preserves, country ham and red-eye gravy, and fried chicken. The restaurant offers great country breakfasts, too. ⊠*8400 Hwy. 100,*

Pasquo Community ☎615/646–9700 ⊕*www.lovelesscafe.com* ☰*AE, D, MC, V.*

$$$–$$$$ ✕**Mad Platter.** This local favorite is housed in a cozy redbrick store-
AMERICAN front on a quiet corner in Germantown, just north of downtown. The
menu blends traditional gourmet with California cuisine, using locally
available ingredients from the nearby farmers' market. The pan-seared
salmon with okra and sweet corn, rack of lamb, and bananas Foster are
favorites. ✉*1239 6th Ave. N, Germantown* ☎615/242–2563 ⌔*Res-
ervations essential* ☰*AE, D, DC, MC, V* ⊗*No dinner Mon. and Tues.
No lunch weekends.*

$$ ✕**Monell's.** One set price gets you a Southern smorgasbord at this
SOUTHERN casual family-style restaurant in a mansion built in 1880. Diners sit
at large tables and pass around heaping platters of main courses that
might include chicken, lasagna, pulled pork, and pot roast and sides
like green beans, black-eyed peas, turnip greens, and mashed potatoes.
Desserts are suitably rich. Pitchers of sweetened iced tea help wash it
all down. Country breakfast is served Saturday and Sunday until 1
and Sunday supper is from 11 to 4. ✉*1235 6th Ave. N, Germantown*
☎615/248–4747 ⊕*monellsdining.ypguides.net* ⌔*Reservations not
accepted* ☰*MC, V* ⊗*No dinner Sun. or Mon. No lunch Sat.*

$$$–$$$$ ✕**New Orleans Manor.** Old-fashioned gas lamps illuminate the driveway
AMERICAN as you approach this restaurant in a classic house with white columns
near the airport. The steak and seafood menu includes Maine lobster
and king crab legs. ✉*1400 Murfreesboro Rd., Airport* ☎615/367–
2777 ⊕*www.neworleansmanor.com* ☰*AE, D, MC, V* ⊗*No lunch.*

$$$–$$$$ ✕**Sperry's.** A reconstructed English Tudor–style building near Belle
STEAK Meade and Cheekwood is home to this longtime elegant steak and
seafood house. This is steeplechase country, and the framed paintings
hanging in the dining room show equestrian themes. A double fireplace
separates the bar/lounge area from the columns, wood paneling, and wall
hangings in the banquet room. Choose from several fresh fish entrées
nightly, including Alaskan king crab and jumbo lobster tail, plus steaks
and chops galore. ✉*5109 Harding Rd., Belle Meade* ☎615/353–0809
⊕*www.sperrys.com* ☰*AE, D, DC, MC, V* ⊗*No lunch.*

10

WHERE TO STAY

Nashville has an impressive selection of accommodations in all price
categories and at all levels of luxury. Some establishments increase rates
slightly during the peak summer travel season, especially CMA Music
Festival week in mid-June, and some downtown luxury hotels offer
lower rates on weekends, when the legislators and business travelers
have gone home. For a good selection of B&Bs throughout Nashville,
check out ⊕*www.bedandbreakfast.com/nashville-tennessee.html.*

DOWNTOWN

$$$–$$$$ ▦**Courtyard Nashville Downtown.** In a former bank opposite Printer's
Alley, this hotel is conveniently near the center of downtown Nash-
ville. Rooms have ergonomic desk chairs and luxurious bedding, and
the hotel has a breakfast restaurant. **Pros:** good location for exploring
downtown; comfortable beds. **Cons:** no free parking; no pool. ✉*170*

4th Ave. N, Downtown ☎*615/256–0900 or 888/687–9377* ⊕*www.
marriott.com* ➪*181 rooms, 11 suites* ⚒*In-room: refrigerator (some),
Wi-Fi. In-hotel: gym, laundry facilities, Wi-Fi, parking (paid)* ⊟*AE,
D, DC, MC, V.*

$$–$$$ 🏨**Doubletree Hotel Nashville.** Newly remodeled in late 2008, this hotel
★ is just a short hike to the State Capitol, Ryman Auditorium, and the
Country Music Hall of Fame. Rooms are fitted out with large plasma-
screen televisions and coffeemakers with gourmet coffee. **Pros:** airport
shuttle; executive floor. **Cons:** charge for in-room Internet; Wi-Fi available only in lobby. ✉*315 4th Ave. N, Downtown* ☎*615/244–8200*
⊕*www.doubletree.com* ➪*331 rooms, 6 suites* ⚒*In-room: Internet.
In-hotel: 2 restaurants, room service, bar, pool, gym, laundry service,
Wi-Fi, parking (paid), no-smoking rooms* ⊟*AE, D, MC, V.*

$$$–$$$$ 🏨**Hampton Inn & Suites Downtown Nashville.** This hotel, opened in 2007 in
★ the rapidly developing area south of downtown, is just a stone's throw
from the Country Music Hall of Fame. **Pros:** short walk to museums
and honky tonks; good value for downtown; complimentary breakfast.
Cons: no airport shuttle; no restaurant. ✉*310 4th Ave. S, Downtown*
☎*615/277–5000* ⊕*www.hamptoninn.com* ➪*100 rooms, 54 suites*
⚒*In-room: kitchen (some), refrigerator, Wi-Fi. In-hotel: pool, gym,
laundry services, Wi-Fi, parking (free), no-smoking rooms* ⊟*AE, D,
MC, V* ⓘ○ⓒ*CP.*

$$$$ 🏨**The Hermitage Hotel.** Nashville's grandest hotel, the Hermitage is a
Fodor's Choice downtown institution where everything is luxurious, from the large
★ rooms to the plush robes to the marble bathrooms. A pampering pack-
age for pets includes a special room-service pet menu and custom pet
beds. The concierge is well-equipped to address *any* request, and the
hotel restaurant is the much-heralded Capitol Grille. Afternoon tea
is available in the main lobby. The presidential suite overlooks the
Tennessee State Capitol and has its own kitchen and dining room for
$2,500 a night. **Pros:** sumptuous rooms; 24-hour fitness center and
room service; a short walk to the Tennessee State Capitol and other
downtown attractions. **Cons:** no pool; parking is not free. ✉*231 6th
Ave. N, Downtown* ☎*615/244–3121 or 888/888–9414* ⊕*www.the-
hermitagehotel.com* ➪*112 rooms, 10 suites* ⚒*In-room: refrigerator
(some), DVD, Wi-Fi. In-hotel: restaurant, room service, bar, gym, spa,
laundry service, Wi-Fi, parking (paid), some pets allowed, no-smoking
rooms* ⊟*AE, D, DC, MC, V.*

$$$–$$$$ 🏨**Hilton Nashville Downtown.** An all-suites hotel in the center of Nash-
★ ville's new cultural heart, the Hilton is within walking distance of the
Sommet Center, Schermerhorn Symphony Center, the Country Music
Hall of Fame, the Ryman Auditorium, the downtown convention cen-
ter, and Broadway's honky tonks. The soaring lobby is bright and airy.
Pros: comfortable rooms; close to many downtown attractions. **Cons:**
concierge could be a little more knowledgeable; main entrance is a bit
crowded with a notable walk to check-in desk; limited public Wi-Fi.
✉*121 4th Ave. S, Downtown* ☎*615/620–1000* ⊕*www.nashvillehil-
ton.com* ➪*330 suites* ⚒*In-room: refrigerator, Wi-Fi. In-hotel: 2 res-
taurants, room service, bars, pool, gym, laundry service, parking (paid),
no-smoking rooms* ⊟*AE, D, DC, MC, V.*

$$–$$$ 🏨**Renaissance Nashville Hotel.** This modern glass high-rise hotel adjoins the Nashville Convention Center and features a bright, colorful lobby with floor-to-ceiling televisions blaring music videos. Club-level rooms offer access to a private lounge. **Pros:** a short walk to downtown attractions; very hip bar. **Cons:** no on-site parking; no airport shuttle. ✉*611 Commerce St., Downtown* ☎*615/255–8400 or 800/327–6618* ⊕*www.marriott.com* ⇆*649 rooms* ♿*In-room: Wi-Fi. In-hotel: restaurant, bars, pool, gym, laundry service, Wi-Fi, no-smoking rooms* ▭*AE, D, MC, V.*

$$–$$$ 🏨**Sheraton Nashville Downtown.** Downtown, near the State Capitol, this 28-story tower has a vast, skylit atrium awash with greenery and overseen by glassed-in elevators. Rooms are spacious, with contemporary designs, and have great views of the growing Nashville skyline. **Pros:** incredible downtown views from higher floors; nice pool. **Cons:** rooms are rather standard; rooms on east side of building can get too hot in the summer. ✉*623 Union St., Downtown* ☎*615/259–2000 or 800/447–9825* ⊕*www.sheraton.com* ⇆*465 rooms, 9 suites* ♿*In-room: Wi-Fi. In-hotel: restaurant, bar, pool, gym, laundry service, Wi-Fi, parking (paid), some pets allowed, no-smoking rooms* ▭*AE, D, DC, MC, V.*

$$–$$$ 🏨**Union Station Hotel.** After a two-year, $10 million renovation ending
Fodor's Choice in 2008, this imposing hotel occupying Nashville's majestic, century-old
★ train station stands out with its impressive limestone exterior accented by a soaring clock tower and its grand atrium lobby with stained-glass ceiling. Rooms are good-sized with tasteful accents and include plasma-screen televisions. **Pros:** very comfortable rooms; close to all downtown attractions and lively restaurant scene in the Gulch. **Cons:** some rooms have no tubs, just showers; no pool. ✉*1001 Broadway, Downtown* ☎*615/726-1001 or 877/999–3223* ⊕*www.unionstationhotelnashville.com* ⇆*125 rooms, 12 suites* ♿*In-room: Wi-Fi. In-hotel: restaurant, room service, bar, gym, laundry service, Wi-Fi, parking (paid), no-smoking rooms* ▭*AE, D, DC, MC, V.*

MIDTOWN AND EAST NASHVILLE

$$$ 🏨**East Park Inn.** The chandelier in the dining room and the Salvador Dalí prints are just a few of the nice touches in this Queen Anne–style B&B dating from the 1880s. The two suites have exposed hardwood floors, canopied beds, and wicker furniture, and one has a Jacuzzi tub. Additional small rooms are available for two people for up to $50. Dial-up Internet access is available in rooms. **Pros:** quiet and hospitable rooms; pleasant grounds outside. **Cons:** not within walking distance of downtown sights; no telephones in rooms. ✉*822 Boscobel St., East Nashville* ☎*615/226–8691 or 800/484–1195* ⊕*www.bbonline.com/ tn/eastpark* ⇆*2 suites* ♿*In-room: no phone, no TV, Internet. In-hotel: no-smoking rooms* ▭*AE, D, DC, MC, V* ⏏*BP.*

$$$–$$$$ 🏨**Loews Vanderbilt Plaza.** This beautiful hotel towers over West End Avenue near Vanderbilt University and has a well-deserved reputation for attentive service. Room levels include designer and executive suites. **Pros:** three concierge floors; near Centennial Park and the Parthenon. **Cons:** not within walking distance of downtown attractions; some rooms are a little small. ✉*2100 West End Ave., Midtown* ☎*615/320–1700 or 800/336–3335* ⊕ *www.loewshotels.com/en/Hotels/Nashville-Hotel*

10

326 rooms, 14 suites ⚐*In-room: Internet. In-hotel: 2 restaurants, room service, bar, gym, spa, laundry service, Wi-Fi, parking (paid), some pets allowed, no-smoking rooms* ▤*AE, D, DC, MC, V.*

GREATER NASHVILLE

$ 🏨**Alexis Inn & Suites.** Three miles from the Grand Ole Opry, this five-story hotel is also conveniently near Nashville's airport. **Pros:** free Wi-Fi and Continental breakfast; airport shuttle. **Cons:** rather charmless location and surrounding scenery; no pool. ✉*600 Ermac Dr. (Elm Hill Pike exit from Briley Pkwy.), Airport* ☎*615/889–4466* ⊕*www. alexisinn.com* *73 rooms, 35 suites* ⚐*In-room: refrigerator, Wi-Fi. In-hotel: gym, parking (free), Wi-Fi, no-smoking rooms* ▤*AE, D, MC, V* ⏏*CP.*

$–$$ 🏨**Embassy Suites Nashville–Airport.** This hotel is set among office buildings in a business district 8 mi east of downtown and 2 mi south of the airport. The interior atrium has waterfalls and flowering plants. **Pros:** airport shuttle; complimentary breakfast buffet. **Cons:** inconveniently located in the depths of an office park; jets fly overhead from nearby airport. ✉*10 Century Blvd., Airport* ☎*615/871–0033 or 800/362–2779* ⊕*www.nashvilleairport.embassysuites.com* *293 suites* ⚐*In-room: refrigerator, Wi-Fi. In-hotel: restaurant, room service, bar, pool, laundry facilities, laundry service, Wi-Fi, parking (free), no-smoking rooms* ▤*AE, D, DC, MC, V* ⏏*CP.*

¢–$ 🏨**Fiddler's Inn.** This Music Valley motel consists of three separate buildings just down the road from the Grand Ole Opry. **Pros:** low rates; free Wi-Fi. **Cons:** rooms a little spartan; wedged among the bustle of Music Valley tourist sights. ✉*2410 Music Valley Dr., Music Valley* ☎*615/885–1440 or 877/223–7621* ⊕*www.fiddlers-inn.com* *202 rooms, 2 suites* ⚐*In-room: Wi-Fi. In-hotel: pool, Wi-Fi, parking (free), no-smoking rooms* ▤*AE, D, MC, V.*

$$$–$$$$ 🏨**Gaylord Opryland Resort and Convention Center.** This massive hotel, din-
★ ing, and entertainment complex adjacent to the Grand Ole Opry and Opry Mills shopping mall has a 2-acre glass-walled conservatory filled with 10,000 tropical plants and a skylit indoor area with water features and a half-acre lake. More than 700 of the resort's hotel rooms have private balconies overlooking the spectacular atrium. Seven restaurants, three pools, an on-site spa, and a nearby golf course provide plenty to do. **Pros:** no shortage of activities; conveniently located for Opry performances. **Cons:** a little overwhelming—more a destination in and of itself rather than a convenient spot from which to see the city. ✉*2800 Opryland Dr., Music Valley* ☎*615/889–1000* ⊕*www.gaylordhotels. com/gaylord-opryland* *2,881 rooms, 165 suites* ⚐*In-room: kitchen (some), refrigerator, Wi-Fi. In-hotel: 7 restaurants, room service, bars, golf course, pools, gym, spa, children's programs, laundry service, parking (paid), no-smoking rooms* ▤*AE, D, MC, V.*

NIGHTLIFE AND THE ARTS

Musicians throughout Nashville will tell you it all starts with a song, which is good news for fans of live music: Nashville is absolutely cluttered with music venues, spread throughout the city's neighborhoods.

Plenty of other entertainment options are available as well. To get an idea of what's going on in town, check out weekly newspapers *All the Rage* or *Nashville Scene,* available for free throughout downtown and in many hotels. Both have extensive music and nightlife listings. You can also check with the Nashville Visitor Center.

THE ARTS

Vanderbilt University stages music, dance, and theater productions (many free) at its **Blair School of Music** (⊠ *2400 Blakemore Ave., Vanderbilt University* ☎ *615/322–7651* ⊕ *www.vanderbilt.edu/Blair*). The **Schermerhorn Symphony Center** (⊠ *1 Symphony Pl., at 4th Ave. S, Downtown* ☎ *615/687–6400* ⊕ *www.nashvillesymphony.org*) opened in late 2006 as the new home of the Nashville Symphony; touring artists perform here as well. The Nashville Symphony puts on free summer outdoor concerts in city parks. Rock and country touring events are held at the **Sommet Center** (⊠ *501 Broadway, Downtown* ☎ *615/770–2000*). The **Tennessee Performing Arts Center** (⊠ *505 Deaderick St., Downtown* ☎ *615/782–4000* ⊕ *www.tpac.org*) is the venue for performances by the **Nashville Ballet** (☎ *615/297–2966* ⊕ *www.nashvilleballet.com*), **Nashville Opera** (☎ *615/832–5242* ⊕ *www.nashvilleopera.org*), and **Tennessee Repertory Theatre** (☎ *615/244–1878* ⊕ *www.tnrep.org*). The center also offers Family Field Trips, Saturday afternoon shows that feature a variety of child-friendly performances. The center's Andrew Jackson Hall hosts touring Broadway shows.

THEATER

Chaffin's Barn (⊠ *8204 Hwy. 100, Pasquo/Bellvue* ☎ *615/646–9977 or 800/282–2276* ⊕ *www.dinnertheatre.com*) is a dinner theater that offers Southern buffet-style eating and Broadway plays year-round. **Circle Players** (⊕ *www.circleplayers.net*), in operation for more than 50 seasons, is Nashville's oldest volunteer-run theatrical organization. The community troupe presents several shows per year in various local theaters. For more experimental fare, the **Darkhorse Theater** (⊠ *4610 Charlotte Ave., Sylvan Park* ☎ *615/297–7113* ⊕ *www.darkhorsetheater.com*) puts on original works and alternative theater and dance.

☾ The **Nashville Children's Theatre** (⊠ *724 2nd Ave. S, Downtown* ☎ *615/254–9103* ⊕ *www.nashvillechildrenstheatre.org*) is home to a professional children's theater troupe that performs October through June.

NIGHTLIFE
BARS

Musicians and Nashville hipsters wet their whistles at the **3 Crow Bar** (⊠ *1022–24 W. Woodland St., East Nashville* ☎ *615/262–3345*). **Big River Grille & Brewery Works** (⊠ *111 Broadway, Downtown* ☎ *615/251–4677* ⊕ *www.bigrivergrille.com*) is one of Nashville's hottest brewpubs. The Nashville brewpub **Boscos Nashville Brewing Company** (⊠ *1805 21st Ave. S, Hillsboro Village* ☎ *615/385–0050* ⊕ *www.boscosbeer.com*), in the heart of Hillsboro Village, serves Famous Flaming Stone Beer, a steinbier brewed using hot granite (a method beloved among beer connoisseurs for the slightly caramel tone and taste it produces in the brew). Every weekday at 5:30 a customer is chosen to be a "Cellarman" and tap the cask of Cask Conditioned Ale; pub food is cooked in wood-

10

fired ovens. The local branch of the **Hard Rock Cafe** (⊠*100 Broadway, Downtown* ☎*615/742–9900* ⊕*www.hardrock.com*) is packed with rock memorabilia from around Nashville and the world. The **Red Door Saloon** (⊠*1010 Forrest Ave., East Nashville* ☎*615/226–7660*) is a popular East Nashville bar.

COUNTRY AND BLUEGRASS MUSIC

BROADWAY'S HONKY TONKS
The scene on Broadway, with its strip of honky tonks and souvenir and record shops, perhaps best captures the stripped-down essence of country music: friendly and welcoming, yet a little wild and not averse to getting down in the gutter.

Robert's Western World (⊠*416 Broadway, Downtown* ☎*615/244–9552*) was originally a clothing store; cowboy boots adorn the walls, but today country music is what makes it famous. For many years local legends BR5-49 (named after a long-running bit on *Hee Haw*) were the popular house band. Perhaps the most famous honky tonk on Broadway is **Tootsie's Orchid Lounge** (⊠*422 Broadway, Downtown* ☎*615/726–0463*), where the music pours out the front door and onto the street.

Fodor'sChoice
★
The **Grand Ole Opry** (⊠*2802 Opryland Dr., Music Valley* ☎*615/889–6611 or 800/733–6779 ticket information* ⊕*www.opry.com*) has drawn country fans since 1925. You never know who will turn up on the Opry's down-home stage. Show times are Friday at 8, Saturday at 7 and 9:30 (Saturday late shows are select dates only), and Tuesday at 7 (March–December only for Tuesday shows). **Nashville Nightlife Dinner Theater** (⊠*2620 Music Valley Dr., Music Valley* ☎*615/885–4747 or 800/308–5779* ⊕*www.nashvillenightlife.com*) presents a 1½-hour country music show accompanied by all the trimmings of a full Southern country dinner. The **Texas Troubadour Theatre** (⊠*2416 Music Valley Dr., Music Valley* ☎*615/889–2474*) has several regular shows, including the Midnite Jamboree, a free late-night Saturday jam session (show up before midnight to guarantee a seat) featuring Opry acts who come over after they finish there, and the **Cowboy Church** show, which features artists singing hymns every Sunday at 10 AM.

SMALLER MUSIC VENUES
For a change of pace, check out some of Nashville's smaller music clubs.

Fodor'sChoice
★
At the famous **Bluebird Cafe** (⊠*4104 Hillsboro Rd., Green Hills* ☎*615/383–1461* ⊕*www.bluebirdcafe.com*), in a strip mall among gas stations and fast-food joints in an outlying neighborhood (look for the red neon lights), singers and songwriters try out their latest material as well as some old favorites. There's no stage—musicians sit in the middle of the intimate space, within elbow room of the tables. A strict no-talking rule gives guests the chance to hear fully the tales of heartache and, occasionally, happiness, pouring out of guitars and microphones. The kitchen turns out yummy snacks, and there's a full bar. **Douglas Corner Cafe** (⊠*2106A 8th Ave. S, 8th Avenue South* ☎*615/298–1688* ⊕*www.douglascorner.com*) is well known for everything from blues to country. For rock bands, check out the **Exit/In** (⊠*2208 Elliston Pl., Elliston Place* ☎*615/321–3340* ⊕*www.exitin.com*), which is popular with Vandy students. The **Station Inn** (⊠*402 12th Ave. S, The Gulch* ☎*615/255–3307* ⊕*www.stationinn.com*) hosts a longtime bluegrass jam Sunday nights

and a full slate of bluegrass artists the rest of the week.

MUSIC VENUES AROUND TOWN For cutting-edge music by unknown performers, cross the Victory Memorial Bridge over the Cumberland River to **East Nashville**. The **Family Wash** (⊠ *2038 Greenwood Ave., East Nashville* ☎ *615/226–6070* ⊕ *www.familywash.com*) is a nondescript bar and restaurant on a quiet residential street where unknown singer-songwriters take to the small stage. The **5 Spot** (⊠ *1006 Forrest Ave., East Nashville* ☎ *615/650–9333*) has a weekly jam session with local musicians.

NEED A BREAK?

Locals swear by **I Dream of Weenie** (⊠ *1108 West Woodland St., East Nashville*), a hot dog stand housed in a converted Volkswagen bus. You can try some Tennessee chowchow (sweet and hot cabbage-based relish) on your dog, but it's something of an acquired taste.

In the **District**, along 2nd Avenue downtown, check out the **Wild Horse Saloon** (⊠ *120 2nd Ave. N, District* ☎ *615/902–8200* ⊕ *www.wildhorsesaloon.com*), which offers daily dance lessons and live performances in a huge three-story space that includes five bars and a 2,500-square-foot dance floor. A full menu is available.

FESTIVALS

In the second week of June, the **CMA Music Festival** brings country music stars and their fans face to face with concerts and events at Riverfront Park and at LP Field (Nashville's coliseum).

SPORTS AND THE OUTDOORS

PARTICIPANT SPORTS

BOATING AND FISHING Boating is popular at scenic **J. Percy Priest Lake** (⊠ *3737 Bell Rd., 11 mi east of Nashville, off I–40* ☎ *615/889–1975*). Boats can be rented from Memorial Day to Labor Day at **Nashville Shores** (⊠ *4001 Bell Rd., Hermitage* ☎ *615/889–7050*).

GOLF Public courses open year-round include the 18-hole, par-72 **Harpeth Hills** (⊠ *2424 Old Hickory Blvd., Belle Meade* ☎ *615/862–8493*). The **Hermitage Golf Course** (⊠ *3939 Old Hickory Blvd., Old Hickory City* ☎ *615/847–4001*) has two 18-hole, par-72 links. In northern Nashville is the 18-hole, par-72 **Rhodes Golf Course** (⊠ *1901 Ed Temple Blvd., North Nashville* ☎ *615/862–8463*).

JOGGING Centennial Park, the Vanderbilt University track, J. Percy Priest Lake, and Percy Warner Park are great for jogging. The Music City Marathon takes place in late April. The 1,000-member running club **Nashville Striders** (☎ *615/870–3330*) can recommend choice running spots and will provide information on many summer races.

10

SPECTACTOR SPORTS

AUTO RACING NASCAR Winston Racing Series weekly stock-car racing takes place March through September at **Music City Motorplex** (⌨ *Tennessee State Fairgrounds* ☎615/726–1818).

BASEBALL The **Nashville Sounds**, a AAA affiliate of the Milwaukee Brewers, play home games from mid-April through mid-September at **Hershel Greer Stadium** (☎615/242–4371).

FOOTBALL Nashville's **LP Field** (⌨*1 Titans Way* ☎615/565–4000 or 888/313–8326) is home to the NFL's **Tennessee Titans**. The 69,000-seat natural-grass stadium sits on the banks of the Cumberland River across from downtown Nashville.

HOCKEY The National Hockey League's **Nashville Predators** (⌨*501 Broadway, Downtown* ☎615/770–2355), play at the Sommet Center downtown.

HORSE SHOW For 10 days, from late August to early September, Shelbyville, 50 mi southeast of Nashville, holds the **Tennessee Walking Horse National Celebration** (⌨*Box 1010, 37162* ☎931/684–5915), the world's greatest walking-horse show.

SHOPPING

Nashville abounds in antiques stores, boutiques for fashionable Western wear, and souvenir shops hawking country-and-western memorabilia. For shopping, downtown is a good place to start, but you'll find plenty of interesting shops along the city's edges, too.

ANTIQUES

The shops along **8th Avenue South** make a good browsing ground for lovers of antiques and mid-century modern. **The Factory at Franklin** (⌨*230 Franklin Rd., Franklin* ☎615/791–1777 ⊕*www.factoryatfranklin. com*) houses boutiques, antiques, restaurants, a guitar shop, and a theater in this airy brick complex of late-1920s-era buildings. Once home to a stoveworks, it's now listed on the National Register of Historic Places. **Goodlettsville Antique Mall** (⌨*213 N. Main St., Goodlettsville* ☎615/859–7002) and **Tennessee Antique Mall** (⌨*654 Wedgewood Ave., 8th Avenue South* ☎615/259–4077) are good places for antiques browsing. At **Hermitage Antique Mall** (⌨*4144-B Lebanon Rd., Hermitage* ☎615/883–5789), you can shop for antiques at Andrew Jackson's stomping grounds.

BOOKS

BookMan/BookWoman (⌨*1713 21st Ave. S, Hillsboro Village* ☎615/383–6555 ⊕*www.bookmanbookwoman.com* ☉*Sun. and Mon. 11–5, Tues.–Sat. 10–6*) is the quintessential used bookstore. Its two halves feature books collected by a husband-and-wife team, the female side of which highlights women's studies and female authors. **Davis-Kidd Booksellers and Cafe** (⌨*The Mall at Green Hills, 2121 Green Hills Village Dr., Green Hills* ☎615/385–2645 ⊕*www.daviskidd.com*) has two floors of books covering all interests, including an extensive section on local history and local novelists.

MALLS

Cool Springs Galleria (✉*1800 Galleria Blvd., Exit 69 [Moore's La.] off I–65 South, Franklin* ☎*615/771–2128* ⊕*www.coolspringsgalleria. com*) offers Belk, Macy's, and Dillard's department stores, as well as Eddie Bauer, Fossil, Aeropostale, and many others. Numerous smaller shopping centers and many restaurants can be found in the area around the mall. **The Mall at Green Hills** (✉*2126 Abbot Martin Rd., Green Hills* ☎*615/298–5478* ⊕*www.mallatgreenhills.com*) has Macy's and Dillard's department stores, J. Crew, Restoration Hardware, Pottery Barn, and luxury purveyors like Louis Vuitton and Tiffany & Co. **Opry Mills** (✉*433 Opry Mills Dr., Music Valley* ☎*615/514–1100* ⊕*www.oprymills.com*) offers more than a million square feet of stores, restaurants, and entertainment spots. In addition to mall perennials such as Ann Taylor, Bass Pro Shops, and Barnes & Noble, this supercomplex also houses multiple movie screens and an IMAX theater. Twenty-five miles east of Nashville, the **Prime Outlets of Lebanon** (✉*Exit 238 off I–40 East, Lebanon* ☎*615/444–0433* ⊕*www.primeoutlets.com*) is a favorite of locals looking for deals on Aeropostale, Ann Taylor, Brooks Brothers, Ralph Lauren, and more.

CHATTANOOGA

137 mi southeast of Nashville via I–24.

An industrial city on the Tennessee River reborn as a tourist destination, Chattanooga offers numerous family-friendly attractions and activities for outdoor enthusiasts. An important site for the Tennessee Valley Authority, the city sits cradled in the Appalachian Mountains on the banks of the Tennessee River.

Sweeping views of the river and city can be enjoyed from the car-free Walnut Street Bridge, just a few blocks from the Tennessee Aquarium, one of the largest in the world. A walk across the bridge brings you to the North Shore, where the streets are lined with trendy shops and restaurants.

South of downtown lies Main Street and the city's old railroad terminal, made famous in song by Glenn Miller and now a hotel with numerous dining options. The surrounding streets once were home to warehouses and factories and are now seeing an influx of artists and restaurants. Farther out is Lookout Mountain, which stretches over the state line into Georgia and is home to two of America's most enduring tourist stops: Rock City Gardens and Ruby Falls. Nearby is Chickamauga and Chattanooga National Military Park, which commemorates two intense and pivotal Civil War battles.

10

GETTING HERE AND AROUND

BUS TRAVEL A free shuttle on electric buses runs between the Chattanooga Choo-Choo Hotel and the downtown riverfront, stopping near the Tennessee Aquarium and Creative Discovery Museum. Another shuttle line runs across the Tennessee River to the North Shore neighborhood.

CAR TRAVEL I–75, I–24, and I–59 all have exits in Chattanooga.

ESSENTIALS

Bus Contacts Chattanooga Regional Transportation Authority
(☎ *423/629–1473 or 423/629–1411* ⊕ *www.gocarta.org*).

Visitor Information Chattanooga Area Convention and Visitors Bureau (⊠ *2 Broad St.* ☎ *423/756–8687 or 800/322–3344* ⊕ *www.chattanoogafun.com*).

EXPLORING

DOWNTOWN CHATTANOOGA

A good place to start exploring downtown is the Chattanooga Visitors Center, next to the Tennessee Aquarium. It has brochures for sights and self-guided walking tours of historic districts, as well as combination tickets to many attractions.

TOP ATTRACTIONS

☾ **Chattanooga Choo-Choo.** Chattanooga's turn-of-the-century terminal station, immortalized in song by Glen Miller in the 1940s, is now a Holiday Inn, but it's still one of the area's best-loved attractions. Stop by, if only to see the elegant lobby under the original 85-foot freestanding dome, which appears much as it did before trains stopped chugging in in 1970. Explore the area around the renovated train cars (now used for lodging), the hotel's gardens, and a model railroad museum. ⊠ *1400 Market St., Main Street* ☎ *423/266–5000* ⊕ *www.choochoo.com.*

☾ **Tennessee Aquarium.** Chattanooga is home to the world's second-largest
★ freshwater aquarium, housed in two buildings that total nearly 200,000 square feet. The River Journey building's exhibit areas include an appalachian cove forest and the Mississippi Delta, while the Ocean Journey building has a tropical cove and an undersea cavern. A separate building holds an IMAX 3-D theater, and the *River Gorge Explorer* takes visitors on tours of Tennessee's Grand Canyon aboard a high-speed catamaran, running up to four tours a day. ⊠ *1 Broad St., Downtown* ☎ *800/262–0695* ⊕ *www.tnaqua.org* ⊠ *$19.95, $25.95 for joint ticket with IMAX 3-D theater, River Gorge Explorer $29, ticket packages also available with Creative Discovery Museum* ⊙ *Daily 10–6.*

Walnut Street Bridge. The Tennessee Riverwalk promenade connects Ross's Landing Park and Plaza to the Walnut Street Bridge, which some claim is the longest pedestrian bridge in the world. Built in 1891 and listed in the National Register of Historic Places, this 2,370-foot truss bridge spans the Tennessee River and has lovely views of the city and surrounding mountains. The bridge is popular for strolling and also as a site for special events and festivals.

WORTH NOTING

☾ **Chattanooga Zoo.** This small but interesting zoo with habitats, including a Himalayan passage with snow leopards, rare red pandas, a Gombe forest with chimpanzees, and a Corcovado jungle with jaguars, macaws, and spider monkeys, also has a restored vintage carousel, with rides for $1. ⊠ *1254 E. 3rd St., East Chattanooga* ☎ *423/697–1322* ⊕ *www. zoo.chattanooga.org* ⊠ *$6* ⊙ *Daily 9–5.*

☾ **Creative Discovery Museum.** This museum has abundant, inventive hands-on activities and displays in several exhibit areas, including art and music studios, an inventor's clubhouse, and a river area. Children may build a robot, dig for dinosaur bones, or pilot a simulated riverboat. The Little Yellow House has activities for toddlers. ⊠ *321 Chestnut St., Downtown* ☎*423/756–2738* ⊕*www.cdmfun.org* ☜*$8.95; parking $4* ☉*Mar. 1–June 20, Mon.–Sat. 10–5, Sun. noon–5; June 21–Aug., daily 9:30–5:30; Sept.–Feb., daily 10–5, closed Wed.*

Hunter Museum of Art. Housed partially in a restored classical revival mansion, the riverside Hunter Museum, in the Bluff View Art District, houses an eclectic collection of mostly American paintings (from early portraits and Hudson River School works to Impressionist paintings and abstract pieces by artists such as Helen Frankenthaler), photography, and sculpture. ⊠ *10 Bluff View, Bluff View* ☎*423/267–0968* ⊕*www.huntermuseum.org* ☜*$8* ☉*Mon., Tues., Fri., and Sat. 10–5, Wed. and Sun. noon–5, Thur. 10–8.*

Houston Museum of Decorative Art. This small Victorian home, in the Bluff View Art District, is packed literally to the rafters with mainly American decorative arts collected by the eccentric Anna Safley Houston (who eventually owned 15,000 pitchers). The emphasis is on antique art glass and American pressed glass; also of note are the pieces of blue Staffordshire and English lusterware china. ⊠ *201 High St., Bluff View* ☎*423/267–7176* ⊕*www.thehoustonmuseum.com* ☜*$9* ☉*Mon.–Fri. 9:30–4.*

☺ **International Towing and Recovery Museum.** The first tow truck was created in Chattanooga, and this beguiling collection of shiny vehicles from the past and present grabs the attention of both adults and kids. ⊠ *401 Broad St., Southside* ☎*423/267–3132* ⊕*www.internationaltowingmuseum.org* ☜*$8* ☉*Mar. 1–Oct. 31, Mon.–Sat. 9–5, Sun. 11–5; Nov. 1–Feb. 28, Mon.–Sat. 10–4:30, Sun. 11–5.*

Ross's Landing Park and Plaza. This area includes the **Tennessee Aquarium** and **Tennessee Aquarium 3-D IMAX Theater**. World-class architects, artists, and landscape designers have provided an open-air retrospective of Chattanooga's history as the starting point for the infamous Trail of Tears (the forced march of the Cherokee from their home territories), the site of key Civil War battles, and a major railroad town. The Chattanooga Visitors Center is also here.

GREATER CHATTANOOGA

Beyond downtown are a number of the area's longtime attractions, including some musts for Civil War buffs.

Battles for Chattanooga Museum. Music, narration, and lights on an electric-map rendering of critical battles help you visualize key events in Chattanooga's Civil War history. The museum also has small displays of war artifacts and a good bookstore and is near the entrance to **Point Park** on Lookout Mountain. ⊠ *1110 E. Brow Rd., Lookout Mountain* ☎*423/821–2812* ⊕*www.battlesforchattanooga.com* ☜*$6.95* ☉*Daily 10–5.*

FodorśChoice **Chickamauga and Chattanooga National Military Park.** The 1863 battles for
★   Chattanooga were some of the most violent ever fought and a major turning point in the Civil War. The Union hoped to gain control of the area and the city, a rail center and a gateway to the Confederacy, but

10

was defeated at nearby Chickamauga by General Braxton Bragg. Southern troops surrounded Union ones in Chattanooga before Generals George Thomas and Ulysses Grant launched assaults that led to Union control of most of the state. In 1864, General William Sherman started from Chattanooga on his march to Atlanta and the sea. The battlefield, which became the first national military park, in 1895, includes Lookout Mountain Battlefield and Point Park in Tennessee and Chickamauga Battlefield just over the Georgia state line. Both sites have visitor centers with displays and are about 13 mi apart. The Chickamauga site shows a movie about the battles. ⊠ *Lookout Mountain/Point Park, 110 Point Park Rd., TN* ☎ *423/821–7786* ⊕ *www.nps.gov/chch* ⊠ *Visitor center free; Point Park $3* ⊙ *Daily 8:30–5* ⊠ *Chickamauga, U.S. 27, Fort Oglethorpe, GA* ☎ *706/866–9241* ⊕ *www.nps.gov/chch* ⊠ *Free* ⊙ *Daily 8:30–5.*

OFF THE BEATEN PATH

Dayton. A 36-mi drive north along U.S. 27 from Chattanooga, this small town was the site of the famous "Scopes Monkey Trial" in 1925. The room where the trial took place has been preserved at the **Rhea County Courthouse.** A small museum has displays about it. ⊠ *1475 Market St., Dayton* ☎ *423/775–7801 or 423/775–7892* ⊠ *Free* ⊙ *Mon.–Fri. 9–4:30.*

Incline Railway. The steepest passenger railway in the world, at a grade of 72.7 degrees, the Incline Railway seems to defy gravity as its tracks cut a swath straight up Lookout Mountain. The view is spectacular. ⊠ *827 E. Brow Rd., Lookout Mountain* ☎ *423/821–4224* ⊕ *lookoutmtn-attractions.com* ⊠ *$14* ⊙ *Mar. 9–Oct. 31: weekdays 9–6, weekends 9–7; Nov. 1–Mar. 8, daily 10–6; trains run every 15–20 mins.*

★ **Lookout Mountain.** Chattanooga's poshest homes sit atop Lookout Mountain, which extends into Georgia. Plan to visit Point Park and Rock City Gardens. Alhough Lookout Mountain can be reached by car, the Incline Railway is a thrilling alternative.

Point Park. Part of Chickamauga/Chattanooga National Military Park, this breezy, wooded promontory atop Lookout Mountain has sweeping views of the outlying region. Markers remind you of the Union soldiers who scrambled up the craggy mountainside in a mad effort to escape Confederate bullets during the 1863 Battle Above the Clouds, part of the eventual Union victory. A visitor center has information; from June through August, rangers give tours and talks on the site. ⊠ *E. Brow Rd.* ☎ *423/821–7786* ⊕ *www.nps.gov/chch* ⊠ *$3* ⊙ *Visitor center daily 8:30–5.*

Ⓒ **Rock City Gardens.** This craggy tribute to fairy tales and geology, just over the state line in Georgia, began in 1932 as a network of paths through rock formations with such names as Fat Man's Squeeze. The project grew as exhibits depicting the tales of Mother Goose and Little Red Riding Hood were added. Walt Disney even consulted with Rock City's founders before designing his own magical kingdom. The garden's position atop Lookout Mountain provides views for hundreds of miles (a sign point out the direction of seven states). Winter holiday displays of lights are popular. ⊠ *1400 Patten Rd., Lookout Mountain, GA* ☎ *706/820–2531 or 800/854–0675* ⊕ *www.seerockcity.com*

⬛$15.95; combo tickets available with Ruby Falls and Incline Railway ⊙ May 24–Sept. 7, daily 8:30–8; Sept. 8–Oct. 31 and Mar. 8–May 23, daily 8:30–6; Nov. 1–Nov. 19 and Jan. 4–Mar. 7, daily 8:30–5; Nov. 20–Jan. 3, daily 8:30–4.

Ruby Falls. Aboveground are a restaurant, souvenir shops, lookout tower, and children's playground, all contained within one castlelike structure, but inside is the real draw: an elevator whisks groups of visitors several hundred feet below to a natural cave. A ½-mi path leads past formations such as stalagmites and stalactites to the deepest and highest underground waterfall (145 feet) in the United States. ✉ 1720 Lookout Mountain Scenic Hwy., Lookout Mountain ☎ 423/821–2544 ⊕ www. rubyfalls.com ⬛$14.95 ⊙ Daily 8–8.

Ⓒ **Tennessee Valley Railroad.** Ride the rails of the largest historic railroad still operating in the South. Steam and diesel locomotives take visitors on one-hour, 6-mi rides, and you can explore antique trains at the station. ✉ 4119 Cromwell Rd., Missionary Ridge ☎ 423/894–8028 ⊕ www. tvrail.com ⬛$14 ⊙ Mar. 1–Oct. 1, Tues.–Sun. 10–5; Oct. 2–Nov. 28, Tues.–Thurs. 10–1, Fri. and Sat. 10–5; Nov. 29–Dec. 22, Sat. 10–5; closed Dec. 22–Mar. 1.

WHERE TO EAT

$$–$$$ ✕ **212 Market.** This restaurant near the Tennessee Aquarium serves
AMERICAN New American cuisine, with an emphasis on healthy yet tasty fare. Try
★ the grilled salmon or the Taylor River enchilada with fresh spinach, black beans, cheese, and salsa. The contemporary dining room is bright and unpretentious. ✉ 212 Market St., Downtown ☎ 423/265–1212 ⊕ www.212market.com ⊟ AE, D, DC, MC, V ⊙ No lunch Sun.

$–$$ ✕ **Big River Grille & Brewing Works.** You can watch the brewing process
AMERICAN through a soaring glass wall beside the bar of this restored trolley warehouse, handsomely designed with high ceilings, exposed brick walls, and hardwood floors. Order the sampler for a taste of this microbrewery's four different concoctions. The sandwiches and salads are generous and tasty. ✉ 222 Broad St., Downtown ☎ 423/267–2739 ⊕ www. bigrivergrille.com ⬚ Reservations not accepted ⊟ AE, D, MC, V.

$$–$$$ ✕ **Blue Orleans.** Operated by native New Orleanians who relocated to
CAJUN Chattanooga in the wake of Hurricane Katrina, this narrow, well-lit restaurant dishes up the cuisine of the Big Easy. Old favorites red beans and rice and crawfish étouffée are on the menu along with steaks and pasta. The requisite jazz plays on the sound system and Mardi Gras masks hang on the walls. ✉ 1463 Market St., Main Street ☎ 423/757–0088 ⊕ www.blueorleansdowntown.com ⊟ AE, D, MC, V ⊙ Closed Sun. No dinner Mon. No lunch Sat.

$$–$$$ ✕ **Niko's Southside Grill.** This handsome restaurant south of downtown,
AMERICAN a short stroll from the Choo-Choo, reinterprets the food of the region
★ with a gourmet touch. Hardwood floors offset the dark paneled walls, which are hung with fine art. Pan-seared sesame grouper and grilled herbed boneless lamb loin are just two choices on the seasonally changing menu. ✉ 1400 Cowart St., Main Street ☎ 423/266–6511 ⊕ www. NikosSouthside.com ⊟ AE, D, MC, V ⊙ Closed Sun.

10

WHERE TO STAY

$$–$$$ ★   ☆ **Bluff View Inn.** Painstakingly restored and tastefully decorated with 18th-century English antiques and art, this colonial revival mansion was built in 1928 on a bluff overlooking the river. The River Gallery Sculpture Garden is beside the inn, near the Riverwalk, and the Tennessee Aquarium is within walking distance. Two other early-20th-century mansions have rooms as well, and a complimentary breakfast is made to order. The inn is part of the Bluff View Art District area of shops and restaurants. **Pros:** good choice of restaurants in adjoining art district; lushly landscaped grounds; free Wi-Fi. **Cons:** not a good place for kids (lots of antiques around); no elevator. ⊠ *411 E. 2nd St., Bluff View Art District* ☎ *423/265–5033 or 800/725–8338* ⊕ *www.bluffviewartdistrict.com* ⌁ *13 rooms, 3 suites* ☝ *In-room: kitchen (some), refrigerator (some), DVD, Wi-Fi. In-hotel: 2 restaurants, Wi-Fi, parking (free), no-smoking rooms* ☰ *AE, D, MC, V* ❚◯❚ *BP.*

$–$$ ☆ **Chattanooga Choo-Choo Holiday Inn.** The Beaux-Arts lobby of this hotel in Chattanooga's famous train station hints at past grandeur. The vast complex of buildings, including numerous shops and restaurants, is topped by an impressive dome crowned with a neon locomotive and stretches back into the former rail yards, including several rooms in converted train cars. The hotel is showing its age and is a little worn around the edges, but the gas torches along the tracks add an opulent air. **Pros:** free airport shuttle; variety of restaurants and activities on-site. **Cons:** a long walk to the pool or lobby from more remote rooms; train car rooms can be a little noisy. ⊠ *1400 Market St., Main Street* ☎ *423/266–5000 or 800/872–2529* ⊕ *www.choochoo.com* ⌁ *303 rooms, 10 suites, 48 railcars* ☝ *In-room: Wi-Fi. In-hotel: 5 restaurants, bar, tennis courts, pools, gym, laundry service, Wi-Fi, parking (free), some pets allowed, no-smoking rooms* ☰ *AE, D, MC, V.*

$$$ ☆ **Doubletree Hotel Chattanooga.** This hotel reopened in October 2008 after a two-year overhaul and is just a few blocks from the aquarium and other downtown attractions. A simulated fire pit welcomes guests on arrival, and there are several waterfalls throughout the hotel. The saltwater pool is a hip touch. Rooms are comfortable and well-appointed. **Pros:** quiet rooms; convenient location to downtown. **Cons:** no concierge; no airport shuttle. ⊠ *407 Chestnut St., Downtown* ☎ *423/756–5150* ⊕ *www.chattanooga.doubletree.com* ⌁ *168 rooms, 18 suites* ☝ *In-room: kitchen (some), refrigerator, Wi-Fi. In-hotel: restaurant, room service, bar, pool, gym, laundry service, Wi-Fi, parking (paid), no-smoking rooms* ☰ *AE, D, DC, MC, V.*

$$–$$$ ☆ **Stone Fort Inn.** The neighborhood outside this B&B on the outskirts of downtown is a little sketchy, but the old redbrick structure has a lot of character, and a stroll around the corner will take you past the historic U.S. Courthouse and classical-style municipal building. A billiards room and several sitting rooms fill out the first floor. Room televisions are equipped with VCRs, and there's a free library of VHS movies. Warehouse Row mall is also a short stroll away. **Pros:** wine and cheese reception on Saturdays; antique-bedecked halls and rooms. **Cons:** no airport shuttle; not within walking distance of downtown sights. ⊠ *120 East 10th St., City Hall* ☎ *423/267–7866 or 888/945–7866* ⊕ *www.*

stonefortinn.com ⇨*12 rooms, 4 suites* *In-room: Wi-Fi. In-hotel: Wi-Fi, parking (free), no kids under 12, no-smoking rooms* ▭*AE, DC, MC, V.*

NIGHTLIFE AND THE ARTS

THE ARTS

The **Chattanooga Theatre Center** (✉*400 River St., North Chattanooga* ☎*423/267–8534*) stages 20 productions a year. The **Memorial Auditorium** (✉*399 McCallie Ave., Downtown* ☎*423/757–5042*) is a venue for concerts and operas. Throughout the summer free concerts in musical styles from blues to Celtic play on **Miller Plaza** (✉*850 Market St., Downtown* ☎*423/265–0771*). A city highlight, the mid-June **Riverbend Festival** (☎*423/265–4112* *$30 at the gate, $23 at the outlet stores*) brings live rock, country, blues, jazz, and folk music to five stages over nine days and nights. The single admission is good for all 100 or so acts.

NIGHTLIFE

Pick up a copy of *The Pulse* or *FYI Weekend,* part of the Friday edition of the *Chattanooga Times Free Press*, for weekend nightlife listings.

Chattanooga has several live music venues. **JJ's Bohemia** (✉*231 E. Martin Luther King Blvd., University* ☎*423/266–1400*) is a popular spot to see local bands. **The Local Performance Hall** (✉*306 Cherokee Blvd., North Chattanooga* ☎*423/698–4849*) on the hipper side of the river, features more of an underground vibe, with some cutting-edge sounds. Every Friday night **Mountain Opry** (✉*Walden Ridge Civic Center, 2501 Fairmount Pike, Signal Mountain* ☎*423/886–3252*) showcases a free program of traditional bluegrass and mountain music. **Rhythm & Brews** (✉*221 Market St., Downtown* ☎*423/267–4644*) is a laid-back spot that has everything from rock to soul to jazz.

SPORTS AND THE OUTDOORS

Chattanooga is chock-full of outdoor activities; check the visitors center downtown for brochures listing the numerous outfitters for kayaking, canoeing, hang gliding, and other activities, including golf.

Chattanooga is perhaps the largest center for hang gliding in the United States; if you've ever wanted to soar through the sky, this is the place to do it. Hang gliding centers offer tandem rides, in which a seasoned instructor pilots the glider while you hold on and enjoy the ride.

CANOEING AND RAFTING

The Sequatchie River, gentler than the nearby Ocoee, is suitable for year-round floating; try **Canoe the Sequatchie** (☎*423/949–4400* 🌐*www.sequatchie.com/canoe.htm*) for canoe trips. **Hiwassee Outfitters** (☎*423/338–8115 or 800/338–8133* 🌐*www.hiwasseeoutfitters.com*), on the Hiwassee River in Reliance, has kayaks and rafts for beginners and intermediates; the nearby Hiwassee has occasional rapids. The Ocoee River, site of international kayaking competitions, has powerful Class III and IV rapids. **Outdoor Adventure Rafting** (☎*423/338–5746 or 800/627–7636* 🌐*www.raft.com*) can take you for a ride on the Ocoee.

HANG GLIDING

At **Lookout Mountain Flight Park and Training Center** (⊠ *7201 Scenic Hwy., Rising Fawn, GA* ☎ *706/398–3541 or 800/688–5637* ⊕ *www.hanglide. com*), you can soar tandem (with an instructor); lessons and packages are available.

SHOPPING

Hamilton Place (⊠ *2100 Hamilton Place Blvd., North Chattanooga* ☎ *423/894–7177*) is Tennessee's largest mall, with four department stores, more than 200 other stores, and 30-plus eateries. **River Gallery** (⊠ *400 E. 2nd St., Bluff View* ☎ *423/267–7353*), in the Bluff View Art District, carries lovely crafts, from pottery to wood and metal pieces, as well as paintings and sculpture. An outlet center, **Warehouse Row** (⊠ *1110 Market St., Downtown* ☎ *423/267–1111*) yields some of the region's best (and most chic) buys, in several attractive, restored red-brick railroad warehouses.

KNOXVILLE

108 mi northeast of Chattanooga via I–75; 45 mi northwest of the Gatlinburg entrance to the Great Smoky Mountains National Park.

In 1786 General James White and a few pioneer settlers built a fort beside the Tennessee River. A few years later, territorial governor William Blount selected White's fort as capital of the newly formed Territory of the United States South of the River Ohio and renamed the settlement Knoxville after his longtime friend Secretary of War Henry Knox. It flourished from its beginning as the gateway to the frontier and became the state capital when Tennessee was admitted to the Union in 1796.

Throughout the 20th century and into the 21st Knoxville has been synonymous with energy: the headquarters of the Tennessee Valley Authority (TVA), with its hydroelectric dams and recreational lakes, is here, and during World War II, atomic energy was secretly developed at nearby Oak Ridge. Today the University of Tennessee adds its own energy—both intellectual and cultural—to this dynamic city. Along the Tennessee River, Volunteer Landing is a series of concrete walkways that includes restaurants and residential town houses. Downtown, Market Square has several restaurants, and the nearby Old City district is a neighborhood of former warehouses converted to hip nightlife spots.

Knoxville is surrounded by three national parks—Great Smoky Mountains National Park, Cumberland Gap National Historic Park (nearby in Kentucky), and Big South Fork National River and Recreation Area.

GETTING HERE AND AROUND

Knoxville sits at the intersection of I–40, which runs east–west through miles of franchised commercial development on the west side of the city, and I–75, which runs north–south. To get to Great Smoky Mountains National Park and the adjacent tourist towns, take exit 407 off I–40, by the Tennessee Smokies baseball stadium, where there are tourist information centers.

ESSENTIALS

Visitor Information **Knoxville Visitor Center** (⊠ *301 S. Gay St., Knoxville* ☎ *865/523-7263 or 800/727-8045* ⊕ *www.knoxville.org*).

EXPLORING

Downtown Knoxville is fairly easy to explore on foot, with Gay Street stretching downhill from the visitor center, passing by restaurant-rich Market Square before ending at the Tennessee River and Volunteer Landing. The Old City, an industrial neighborhood reborn as a hip nightlife spot, lies just north of downtown. The sprawling campus of the University of Tennessee is immediately west of downtown, off Cumberland Avenue. The free Knoxville Trolley runs several lines through downtown, stopping at hotels there.

James White's Fort. Different eras of Knoxville history are celebrated at James White's Fort, a series of seven log cabins with authentic furnishings and pioneer artifacts that was once part of the 1,000-acre estate bequeathed to White after his service as a captain in the American Revolutionary War. ⊠ *205 E. Hill Ave., Downtown* ☎ *865/525-6514* ⊕ *www.jameswhitesfort.org* ☚ *$5* ⊗ *Apr.–Dec., weekdays 9:30–4:30, Sat. 9:30–3:30; Jan.–Mar., weekdays 9–4. Closed during home university football games.*

Knoxville Museum of Art. Designed by renowned museum architect Edward Larrabee Barnes, the four-level concrete-and-steel building is faced in Tennessee pink marble. It devotes plenty of space to regional artists and includes four exhibition galleries, an exploratory gallery for children, a great hall, an auditorium, a museum store, and outdoor sculpture and educational program gardens. ⊠ *1050 World's Fair Park Dr., World's Fair Park* ☎ *865/525-6101* ⊕ *www.knoxart.org* ☚ *$5* ⊗ *Tues.–Thurs. and Sat. 10–5, Fri. 10–8, Sun. 1–5.*

⟳ **Knoxville Zoological Park.** You can spend a full day at the zoo famous for breeding big cats and African elephants. Among the 1,100 animals are rare red pandas, wild creatures native to the African plains, polar bears, seals, and penguins. The working miniature steam train, elephant rides, and petting zoo will keep kids occupied for hours. Gorilla Valley, Cheetah Savanna, and Chimpanzee Ridge are among the best exhibits, and the zoo also offers bird shows and camel rides. ⊠ *3500 Knoxville Zoo Park, in Chilhowee Park on Rutledge Pike S, 4½ mi east of I–40 Exit 392, Chilhowee Park* ☎ *865/637-5331* ⊕ *www.knoxville-zoo.org* ☚ *$16.95* ⊗ *Memorial Day–Labor Day, daily 9:30–6; Labor Day–Memorial Day, daily 10–4:30.*

Mabry-Hazen House. The house served as headquarters for both Confederate and Union forces during the Civil War. It was built by prominent Knoxvillian Joseph A. Mabry Jr. in 1858 and is now on the National Register of Historic Places. ⊠ *1711 Dandridge Ave., Morningside* ☎ *865/522-8661* ⊕ *www.mabryhazen.com* ☚ *$5* ⊗ *Wed.–Fri. 11–5, Sat. 10–3.*

10

WHERE TO EAT

$-$$ ✕**Calhoun's on the River.** Delicious barbecued ribs are served riverside at
BARBECUE this sprawling restaurant with an outdoor patio and its own boat dock.
Calhoun's ribs are famous throughout the South. ✉*400 Neyland Dr.,*
Volunteer Landing ☎*865/673–3335* ⊕*www.calhouns.com* ☜*Reservations not accepted* ⊟*AE, D, DC, MC, V.*

$$$ ✕**Copper Cellar.** This intimate restaurant is a favorite with the college
AMERICAN crowd and young professionals. Entrées such as pan-blackened Florida grouper, chicken Oscar (with crabmeat, asparagus, and béarnaise
sauce), steamed lobster tails, and a full slate of steaks are available. The
wine list is impressive and microbrews are available on tap. ✉*1807
Cumberland Ave., University* ☎*865/673–3411* ⊕*www.coppercellar.
com* ⊟*AE, D, DC, MC, V.*

$$ ✕**Cumberland Grill.** In the same building as the Copper Cellar, this brass
AMERICAN rail bar and grill has a laid-back feel. The pub grub includes burgers and
famous chicken wings, as well as steaks and salads. Several microbrews
are on tap. ✉*1807 Cumberland Ave., University* ☎*865/673–3411*
⊕*www.cumberlandgrill.com* ⊟*AE, D, MC, V.*

$$-$$$ ✕**Regas Restaurant.** This cozy, old-world-style Knoxville classic, with
AMERICAN fireplaces and original art, has been around since 1919. The specialty,
★ prime rib, is baked very slowly all day, then sliced to order and served
with creamy horseradish sauce. The selection of steaks and seafood
is good, and, if you're there for lunch, look for hostess Hazel Smith,
who's been working at the restaurant since 1954. ✉*318 N. Gay St.,
Old City* ☎*865/637–3427* ⊕*www.thechophouse.com* ⊟*AE, D, DC,
MC, V* ⊗*Closed Sun. No lunch Sat.*

$-$$ ✕**Sunspot.** This low-key off-campus hangout has a healthy mix of
AMERICAN salads, sandwiches, and entrées like chili-crusted salmon, portobello
empanadas, blackened crab quesadillas, and several tasty pasta dishes.
It's also a popular brunch spot. ✉*1909 Cumberland Ave., University*
☎*865/637–4663* ⊕*www.aubreysrestaurant.com* ⊟*D, DC, MC, V.*

¢-$ ✕**Tomato Head.** This perennially popular and affordable spot on restaurant-lined Market Square features organic comfort food with a vegetarian
VEGETARIAN twist. The extensive menu of pizzas (with an option of soy cheese)
and sandwiches has selections like goat cheese, pesto, and herbed tomato as well as meat choices like Tuscan chicken and lamb sausage. There
are good burritos and quesadillas here too, but it gets noisy during the
lunch and dinner rush. ✉*12 Market Sq., Market Square* ☎*865/637–
4067* ⊕*www.thetomatohead.com* ⊟*AE, MC, V.*

WHERE TO STAY

$-$$ ▦**Crowne Plaza Knoxville.** Just north of downtown, this standard business hotel has comfortable rooms and a well-lit lobby. **Pros:** executive
floor; convenient for walking to downtown restaurants and Old City
nightlife; free Wi-Fi. **Cons:** rather standard rooms; no airport shuttle.
✉*401 W. Summit Hill Dr., Downtown* ☎*865/522–2600* ⊕*www.
crowneplaza.com* ⇴*195 rooms, 2 suites* ⌕*In-room: Wi-Fi. In-hotel:
restaurant, room service, bar, pool, gym, laundry service, Wi-Fi, parking
(paid), some pets allowed, no-smoking rooms* ⊟*AE, D, DC, MC, V.*

$$ ⛺**Hilton Knoxville.** Originally built for the 1982 World's Fair, this highrise hotel has since gone through several renovations and is now modern and upscale. Some rooms have views of the mountains and Neyland Stadium. **Pros:** good restaurant; convenient for strolling downtown; free Wi-Fi. **Cons:** no on-site parking; outdoor pool is seasonal only; no airport shuttle. ✉*501 W. Church Ave., Downtown* ☎*865/523–2300* ⊕*www.hilton.com* ⤳*312 rooms, 5 suites* ♿*In-room: Wi-Fi. In-hotel: restaurant, room service, bar, pool, gym, laundry service, Wi-Fi, some pets allowed, no-smoking rooms* ▭*AE, D, MC, V.*

$–$$ ⛺**Knoxville Marriott.** Adjacent to the Women's Basketball Hall of Fame, this white ziggurat sits atop a hill overlooking the Tennessee River and Knoxville's downtown. The eight-story skylit atrium lobby has modern furnishings and art. Glass elevators take guests to rooms that look out on the surrounding mountains. **Pros:** some rooms a bit larger; lots of amenities on-site. **Cons:** outdoor pool is seasonal only; no airport shuttle; you pay for Wi-Fi. ✉*500 Hill Ave. SE, Downtown* ☎*865/637– 1234 or 800/228–9290* ⊕*www.marriott.com* ⤳*354 rooms, 24 suites* ♿*In-room: refrigerator (some), Wi-Fi. In-hotel: restaurant, room service, bar, pool, laundry service, Wi-Fi, parking (free), no-smoking rooms* ▭*AE, D, DC, MC, V.*

NIGHTLIFE AND THE ARTS

The **Knoxville Opera Company** (☎*865/524–0795* ⊕*www.knoxvilleopera.com*) presents operatic performances as well as other musical events. The **Knoxville Symphony Orchestra** (☎*865/523–1178* ⊕*www.knoxvillesymphony.com*) offers many concerts throughout the Knoxville area, often with esteemed guest artists. Both both perform at the **Bijou Theatre** (✉*803 S. Gay St.* ☎*865/522–0832*), which also hosts a variety of touring pop music acts. The **Tennessee Theatre** (✉*803 S. Gay St., Downtown* ☎*865/522–0832* ⊕*www.tennesseetheatre.com*), an ornate former movie house, serves as the city's performing arts center.

The Old City, a historic warehouse district a few blocks north of downtown, is the site of Knoxville's most varied nightlife, with several restaurants and clubs.

Barley's Taproom (✉*200 E. Jackson Ave., Old City* ☎*865/521–0092*) has a restaurant, patio, pool tables, darts, and 40 brews on tap. The **Crown and Goose** (✉*100 N. Central St., Old City* ☎*865/637–4255*) is an authentic English pub. **Patrick Sullivan's Steakhouse** (✉*100 N. Central Ave., Old City* ☎*865/637–4255*) is popular both for dining and for its bar.

10

Virginia

SHENANDOAH NATIONAL PARK
TO VIRGINIA BEACH

WORD OF MOUTH

"Welcome in advance to Virginia . . . I live in Williamsburg, so hopefully I can help you with some details. First of all, while you're in this area be sure to include Jamestown. It is definitely worth a day. There is plenty to keep you busy here for 5 days. When you go to Charlottesville, try to get out in the countryside for a few hours. A good way to see some pretty country is to follow the winery trail, even if you don't visit the wineries . . . Weekends in particular are full of farmers markets and festivals in the Fall."

—bobbysue

Updated by
Amy McK-
eever, Donna
M. Owens,
Alice Lec-
cese Powers,
and Ginger
Warder

Opportunities to step back in time abound in Virginia: the legacy of America's earliest permanent settlement remains at Jamestown; one can experience living history at Colonial Williamsburg; and there are pivotal Civil War sites such as Appomattox Courthouse and Fredericksburg. While some very prominent attractions reveal the ethic, spirit, and personality of the nation, even the smallest communities typically have historical societies, house-museums, and centuries-old inns and taverns brimming with character.

The diverse scenery of Virginia lends itself to all types of outdoor activities. Along the eastern shore, animal lovers can spot wildlife and surfers can catch a ride on the swells at Virginia Beach. The mountainous west delights ardent outdoors enthusiasts: you can canoe, kayak, and hike through Shenandoah National Park.

Some of the fiercest and most pivotal battles ever staged on American soil took place in Virginia during the American Revolution and the Civil War. The National Park Service operates many of these battlefield sites as living-history museums, with carefully preserved or reconstructed fortifications; interpretive centers that show dramatic films and exhibits; and a wide range of narrated walking and driving tours.

If leisure and relaxation are what you seek, head to one of Virginia's abundant country inns. Many of these princely retreats boast talented chefs turning out innovative, regionally driven cuisine. And it's not uncommon to find great fly-fishing, hiking, golfing, wine tasting, and posh spas on-site or nearby.

ORIENTATION AND PLANNING

GETTING ORIENTED

The fourth-largest of the South Atlantic states, Virginia stretches 470 mi from the Easern shore to its western extremities. Towns in the eastern part of the state have been shaped by their close proximity to water—the James and York rivers, the Cheseapeake Bay, and the Atlantic Ocean. Moving inland, Tidewater Virginia eases into the Piedmont, the central section of rolling plains that reaches toward the mountain barrier in the western part of the state. The dramatic Blue Ridge and Appalachian mountain ranges in the west are havens for outdoor sports and scenic drives.

Alexandria. Among the northernmost cities in Virginia, Alexandria was once part of the District of Columbia and now shares its border. Buildings in Alexandria's old downtown, referred to often as "Old Town,"

TOP REASONS TO GO

Presidential history: Get up close and personal with Thomas Jefferson, James Monroe, and George Washington at their restored homes and estates.

Scenic drives: Perhaps the best-known element of the treasured Shenandoah National Park is the picturesque 105-mi long Skyline Drive.

Civil War battlefields: After Virginia seceded from the Union in 1861, it became a major battleground in the War Between the States. You can experience the Civil War history from Richmond's White House of the Confederacy to Fredericksburg's battlefields.

Quaint inns: Small, tranquil, and increasingly sophisticated, the mountain towns and bay-side villages of Virginia are home to some of the most sumptuous country inns and bed-and-breakfasts in America.

Colonial Williamsburg: Part of Virginia's "Historic Triangle," this restored 18th-century Colonial city features some 300 acres that include homes, shops, and public buildings where patriots laid the groundwork for the nation's founding.

are reminiscent of the Federal period (1780–1830). Alexandria was a thriving Colonial port, and these days Old Town is also a bustling nightspot with a variety of ethnic restaurants and dozens of pubs.

Mount Vernon, Woodlawn, and Gunston Hall. Three splendid examples of plantation architecture remain on the Virginia side of the Potomac, 16 mi south of D.C. Mount Vernon, the most-visited historic house in America, was the home of George Washington; Woodlawn was the estate of Washington's step-granddaughter; and Gunston Hall was the residence of George Mason, a patriot and author of the document on which the Bill of Rights was based.

Charlottesville and Shenandoah National Park. Charlottesville, just east of the Blue Ridge, centers around Thomas Jefferson's architectural genius—Monticello and the University of Virginia. Skyline Drive in Shenandoah National Park and the Blue Ridge Parkway ride the spine of the Blue Ridge.

Richmond and Fredericksburg. Richmond is within a day's drive of half of the U.S. population. Serving as Virginia's capital since 1780, it is also the former capital of the Confederacy. Besides numerous Revolutionary War and Civil War sites, the city also contains a vibrant shopping district, and a wealth of restaurants and nightclubs. Less than an hour north of Richmond sits the appealing city of Fredericksburg, a quaint historic city full of both Colonial and Civil War history, with hundreds of impressive 18th- and 19th-century homes and a treasure trove of art and antiques stores.

The Historic Triangle and Virginia Beach. There is probably no better place in America to study this country's prerevolutionary war history than the Historic Triangle. Between Williamsburg, Jamestown, and Yorktown visitors get a full picture of life in Colonial times. The lessons are multisensory: museums, battlefields, restorations, and reenactments appeal to history buffs of every age. On the Atlantic shore, Virginia Beach, which in the 1950s claimed to have the world's longest public beach, has a showy boardwalk.

PLANNING

WHEN TO GO

Spring brings horse racing to Virginia, with many point-to-points and steeplechases that are interesting to watch and visit. Public gardens are in full bloom; garden clubs conduct tours of private properties throughout both states. In Shenandoah National Park, Skyline Drive overlooks a blooming panorama.

Summer draws the largest numbers of visitors, particularly at Virginia Beach and other resorts on the bay and the ocean. Keep in mind that some parts of the state can get quite humid in the summer.

Autumn brings spectacular colors in the foliage of the rolling Piedmont region; the temperatures become more comfortable for hiking and biking. Equestrian events resume in the fall as well.

Winter temperatures may make it too cold to swim, yet the major resorts continue to draw vacationers with seasonal peace and quiet at much lower off-season rates. Other travelers come for romantic seclusion at a B&B. Virginia was the first Southern state to develop skiing commercially, and now both downhill and cross-country skiing are popular activities at resorts in the Shenandoah Valley.

GETTING HERE AND AROUND
AIR TRAVEL

Many travelers to Virginia prefer to fly into international airports in the Washington-Baltimore area (Dulles, Reagan National, Baltimore-Washington International), then commute by rental car; all three areas are within two hours' drive of western Virginia destinations. Alexandria is only a few miles from Ronald Reagan Washington National Airport.

The three largest airports in Central and Western Virginia—Charlottesville-Albermarle, Lynchburg, and Roanoke—are small and relatively hassle-free.

To reach Eastern Virginia, it is often much less expensive to fly to and from Norfolk International Airport and Newport News/Williamsburg International Airport than nearby Richmond.

Air Contacts Baltimore/Washington International-Thurgood Marshall Airport (☎ *410/859–7100* ⊕ *www.bwiairport.com*). **Charlottesville-Albemarle Airport** (✛ *8 mi north of Charlottesville at intersection of Rtes. 606 and 649 off Rte. 29* ☎ *434/973–8342* ⊕ *www.gocho.com*). **Dulles International Airport** (☎ *703/572–2700* ⊕ *www.metwashairports.com/Dulles*). **Lynchburg Regional Airport** (⊠ *Rte. 29S* ☎ *434/455–6090*). **Newport News/Williamsburg International Airport** (PHF ⊠ *12525 Jefferson Ave., at I-64, Newport News* ☎ *757/877–0221* ⊕ *www.nnwairport.com*). **Norfolk International Airport** (ORF ⊠ *2200 Norview Ave., Norfolk* ☎ *757/857–3351* ⊕ *norfolkairport.com*). **Richmond International Airport** (⊠ *Airport Dr.* ☎ *804/226–3000* ⊕ *www.flyrichmond.com*). **Roanoke Regional Airport** (⊠ *Off I–581* ☎ *540/362–1999* ⊕ *www.roanokeairport.com*). **Ronald Reagan Washington National Airport** (☎ *703/417–8000* ⊕ *www.metwashairports.com/National*).

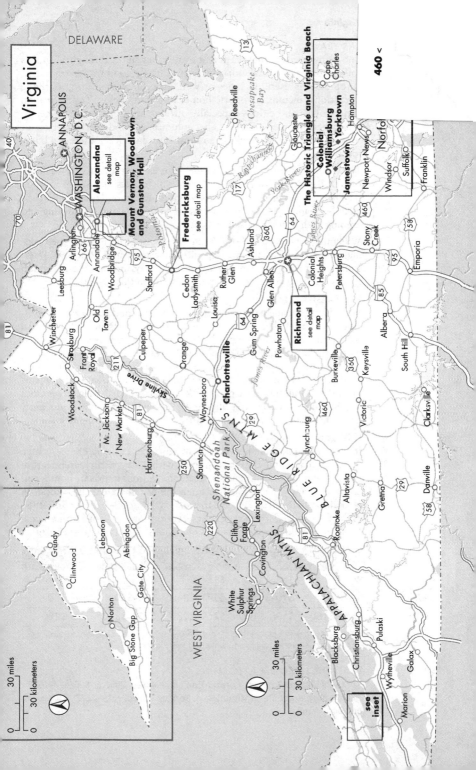

CAR TRAVEL

The many pleasant highways and routes that snake through Virginia's rolling countryside make driving a particularly good way to travel. An automobile is useful in cities as well, especially for touring outlying attractions, including historic homes and battlefields. Traffic around major towns and cities—especially during rush hours—can be heavy. Bumper-to-bumper jams are also common around the University of Virginia and Virginia Tech on autumn Saturdays when there is a home football game.

The Custis Memorial Parkway, I–66, runs east–west between Washington, DC, and I–81 near Front Royal, which takes you south through the Shenandoah or north to West Virginia. Richmond is easily reached from I–95 and I–64, but avoid these major roads during morning and evening rush hours if possible.

Williamsburg is west of I–64, 51 mi southeast of Richmond; the Colonial Parkway joins Williamsburg with Jamestown and Yorktown. Interstate 664 forms the eastern part of a beltway through the Hampton Roads area and connects Newport News with Portsmouth.

RESTAURANTS

From haute cuisine to down-home diners, the food of Virginia is deliciously diverse. Alexandria has a wide variety of ethnic and American restaurants at reasonable prices. In central Virginia, peanut soup and ham biscuits are among the traditional dishes, as is this region's version of barbecue: pork shoulder smoked tender and served in a savory sauce. In western Virginia home-style cooking rules. Small towns with generations-old restaurants serve good stick-to-your-ribs dishes. In larger cities like Richmond, Charlottesville, and Fredericksburg, innovative chefs are emphasizing fresh, local ingredients in exquisite nouveau cuisine.

HOTELS

It's best to book your hotel room in advance. Lodging choices range from familiar hotel chains to homes with 18th-century architecture blended with modern amenities. Accommodations in private homes and converted inns are available through the **Bed and Breakfast Association of Virginia** (⊠ *Box 1077, Standardsville* ☎ *888/660–2228 or 800/296–1246* ⊕ *www.innvirginia.org*). Reservations at inns can also be made through **Virginia is for Lovers** (☎ *800/847–4882* ⊕ *www.virginia.org*).

WHAT IT COSTS				
¢	$	$$	$$$	$$$$
Restaurant	under $10	$10–$16	$17–$23	$24–$30	over $30
Hotel	under $100	$100–$160	$161–$230	$231–$300	over $300

Restaurant prices are per person for a main course at dinner. Hotel prices are for a standard double room, excluding state and local taxes.

VISITOR INFORMATION

Contacts Virginia Tourism Corporation (☎ *804/786–2051 or 800/847–4882* ⊕ *www.virginia.org*). The **National Park Service** (☎ *202/619–7222* ⊕ *www.nps.gov/parks.html*).

CLOSE UP

Virginia Facts

11

- **State Nickname:** Old Dominion
- **State Song:** "Carry Me Back to Old Virginia"
- **State Capital:** Richmond (which was also the capital of the Confederacy)
- Eight U.S. Presidents hailed from Virginia—George Washington, Thomas Jefferson, James Madison, James Monroe, William Henry Harrison, John Tyler, Zachary Taylor, and Woodrow Wilson—more than any other state.

- Both the American Revolution and the Civil War ended in Virginia, with the surrenders at Yorktown and Appomattox, respectively.

- Virginia was named for Queen Elizabeth I of England, who was known as the Virgin Queen.

ALEXANDRIA

A lively mix of historic homes, taverns, restaurants, and shops, Alexandria seems to exist in two or three centuries at once. Founded in 1749 by Scottish merchants eager to capitalize on the booming tobacco trade, Alexandria first emerged as one of the most important ports in Colonial America. The city is linked to many significant events and personages of the Colonial, Revolutionary, and Civil War periods. Members of the Lee family of Revolutionary and Civil War fame lived here, and George Washington had a town house and attended church here, though he lived a few miles south in Mount Vernon.

For many African-Americans fleeing slavery, part of their journey on the Underground Railroad included a stop in Alexandria. Harriett Beecher Stowe modeled her account of the slave trade in *Uncle Tom's Cabin* on the city's Bruin's Slave Jail.

This vibrant past remains alive in the historic district of **Old Town Alexandria**—an area of cobbled streets, restored 18th- and 19th-century homes, churches, and taverns close to the water. The main arteries of this district are Washington Street (the G. W. Parkway as it passes through town) and King Street.

DISCOUNTS AND DEALS

Purchase either the Market Square or Tricorn pass from the Alexandria Visitors Center for discounted admission to three museums in the historic Old Town ($9).

GETTING HERE AND AROUND

Alexandria is only a few miles from Ronald Reagan Washington National Airport. It's easy to get there by Metrorail (on the blue or yellow lines), taxi, water taxi, or Metrobus. Visit the Old Town sights on foot if you're prepared to walk 20 blocks or so; parking is usually scarce, especially close to the river, and the parking police seem to catch every violation (especially in alleys). ■TIP➔The visitor center at Ramsay House will give you a 24-hour permit for free parking at any two-hour metered spot.

TOURS   Old Town Experience runs walking tours that leave from the Ramsay House Visitors Center 10:30 AM Monday through Saturday and 2 PM Sunday; tickets are $15. Another tour operator, Footsteps to the Past, also leads tours from the visitor center at 11:30 AM and 1:30 PM Monday through Saturday and 10:30 AM on Sunday; tickets are $10. Alexandria Colonial Tours leads guided walking tours of historic Alexandria by reservation. Ghost-and-graveyard tours (reservations not required) are conducted Friday, Saturday, and Sunday nights, although in summer you can also take a tour on Wednesday and Thursday nights.

ESSENTIALS

Tours **Alexandria Colonial Tours** (☎ *703/519–1749*). **Footsteps to the Past** (☎ *703/683–3451*). **The Old Town Experience** (☎ *703/836–0694*).

Visitor Information Alexandria Convention and Visitors Association (✉ *Ramsay House, 221 King St., Alexandria* ☎ *703/838–4200 or 800/388–9119* ⊕ *www.visitalexandria.com*).

EXPLORING

③ Carlyle House. Alexandria forefather and Scottish merchant John Carlyle built a grand house here, completed in 1753 and modeled on a country manor house in the old country. Students of the French and Indian War will want to know that the dwelling served as General Braddock's headquarters. The house retains its original 18th-century woodwork and is furnished with Chippendale furniture and Chinese porcelain. An architectural exhibit on the second floor explains how the house was built; outside there's an attractive garden of Colonial-era plants. ✉ *121 N. Fairfax St., Old Town* ☎ *703/549–2997* ⊕ *www.carlylehouse.org* 🎫 *$4* ☉ *Tues.–Sat. 10–4, Sun. noon–4, guided tour every ½ hr.*

④ Gadsby's Tavern Museum. The two buildings that now comprise this muse-
☾ um—a circa-1785 tavern and the 1792 City Hotel—were centers of polit-
★ ical and social life. George Washington celebrated his birthdays in the ballroom. Other noted patrons included Thomas Jefferson, John Adams, and the Marquis de Lafayette. The taproom, dining room, assembly room, ballroom, and communal bedrooms have been restored to their original appearance. The tours on Friday evenings are led by a costumed guide carrying a lantern. ✉ *134 N. Royal St., Old Town* ☎ *703/838–4242* ⊕ *www.gadsbystavern.org* 🎫 *$4, lantern tour $5* ☉ *Nov.–Mar., Wed.–Sat. 11–4, Sun. 1–4, last tour at 3:45; Apr.–Oct., Tues.–Sat. 10–5, Sun. and Mon. 1–5, last tour at 4:45; tours 15 mins before and after the hour. Half-hour lantern tours Mar.–Nov., Fri. 7–9:30.*

⑦ George Washington Masonic National Memorial. Because Alexandria, like
★ Washington, DC, has no really tall buildings, the spire of this memorial dominates the surroundings and is visible for miles. It's a respectable uphill climb from the King St. Metrorail and bus stations. From the ninth-floor observation deck (reached by elevator) you get a spectacular view of Alexandria and Washington, DC, but access above the first and mezzanine floors is by guided tour only. The building contains furnishings from the first Masonic lodge in Alexandria. George Washington became a Mason in 1752 in Fredericksburg, and became Charter Master of the Alexandria lodge when it was chartered in 1788, remaining active in Masonic affairs during his tenure as president, 1789–97.

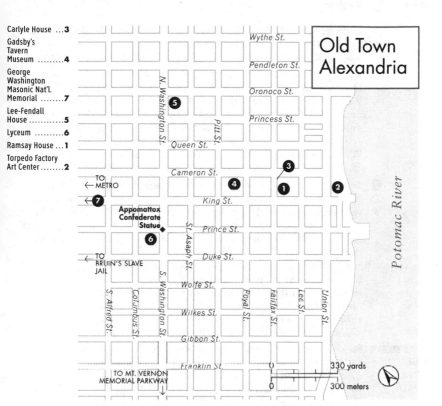

Old Town Alexandria

Wythe St.

Pendleton St.

N. Washington St.

Oronoco St.

❺

Princess St.

Pitt St.

Queen St.

Cameron St.

❸

TO
← METRO

❹

❶

❷

←❼

King St.

**Appomattox
Confederate
Statue**◆

Prince St.

St. Asaph St.

❻

TO
← BRUIN'S SLAVE
JAIL

Duke St.

S. Washington St.

Wolfe St.

S. Alfred St.

Columbus St.

Wilkes St.

Royal St.

Fairfax St.

Lee St.

Union St.

Gibbon St.

Franklin St.

TO MT. VERNON
MEMORIAL PARKWAY
↓

0   330 yards
0   300 meters

Potomac River

✉ *101 Callahan Dr., Old Town* ☎ *703/683-2007* ⊕ *www.gwmemorial.org* ☞ *Free* ⊙ *Daily 9–4; 1-hr guided tour of building and observation deck daily at 10, 11:30, 1:30, and 3.*

❺ **Lee-Fendall House.** At historic Lee Corner at North Washington and Oronoco streets, the Lee-Fendall House was built in 1785; over the course of the next 118 years it was home to 37 members of the Lee family and served as a Union hospital. The house and its furnishings, of the 1850–70 period, present an intimate study of 19th-century family life. Highlights include a splendid collection of Lee heirlooms, period pieces produced by Alexandria manufacturers, and the beautifully restored, award-winning garden. ✉ *614 Oronoco St., Old Town* ☎ *703/548–1789* ☞ *$4* ⊙ *Feb.–mid-Dec., Tues., Thurs., Fri., and Sat. 10–4; Wed. and Sun. 1–4; sometimes closed weekends, closed Dec. 15–Feb. 1.*

❻ **Lyceum.** Built in 1839 and one of Alexandria's best examples of Greek Revival design, the Lyceum is also the city's official history museum. Over the years the building has served as the Alexandria Library, a Civil War hospital, a residence, and offices. Restored in the 1970s for the Bicentennial, it has an impressive collection including examples of 18th- and 19th-century silver, tools, stoneware, and Civil War photographs taken by Mathew Brady. ✉ *201 S. Washington St., Old*

Town ☎ *703/838–4994* ⊕ *www.alexandriahistory.org* 💲 *$2 donation suggested* ⊙ *Mon.–Sat. 10–5, Sun. 1–5.*

❶ **Ramsay House.** The best place to start a tour of Alexandria's Old Town is at the **Alexandria Convention and Visitors Association,** in Ramsay House, the home of the town's first postmaster and lord mayor, William Ramsay. The structure is the site of the first house in Alexandria. The unusually helpful staff hands out brochures, maps for self-guided walking tours, and 24-hour permits for free parking at any two-hour metered spot. ✉ *221 King St., Old Town* ☎ *703/838–4200, 800/388–9119, 703/838–6494 TDD* ⊕ *www.funside.com* 💲 *Guided tours $10–$15* ⊙ *Daily 9–5; tours Mon.–Sat. 10:30 and 11:30, Sun. 10:30 and 2.*

❷ **Torpedo Factory Art Center.** Torpedoes were manufactured here by the U.S. Navy during World War II. Now the building, housing the studios and workshops of about 160 artists and artisans, has become one of Alexandria's most popular attractions. You can observe printmakers, jewelry makers, sculptors, painters, and potters as they create original work in their studios. The Torpedo Factory also houses the Alexandria Archaeology Museum, which displays artifacts such as plates, cups, pipes, and coins from an early tavern, and Civil War soldiers' equipment. If digging interests you, call to sign up for the well-attended public digs (offered once a month from June to October ☎ *703/838–4399* 💲 *$5* ♿ *Reservations are required*). ✉ *105 N. Union St., Old Town* ☎ *703/838–4565* ⊕ *www.torpedofactory.org* 💲 *Free* ⊙ *Daily 10–5.*

OFF THE
BEATEN
PATH

Fodor's Choice ★ **Arlington National Cemetery.** More than 250,000 American war dead, as well as many notable Americans (among them presidents William Howard Taft and John F. Kennedy), are interred in these 624 acres across the Potomac River from Washington, established as the nation's cemetery in 1864. While you're at Arlington there's a good chance you'll hear a bugler playing taps, or the sharp reports of a gun salute. Approximately 28 funerals are held daily. If you arrive at Reagan National Airport, Arlington is an easy drive west along the George Washington Parkway. You can also take the Metrorail to either the Rosslyn or Arlington Cemetary station and then walk about ½ mi to the large paid parking lot at the skylighted Visitor Center on Memorial Drive. You can pick up a free brochure with a detailed map at the Visitor Center. ✉ *West end of Memorial Bridge* ☎ *703/607–8000 to locate a grave* ⊕ *www.arlingtoncemetery.org* 💲 *Free* ⊙ *Apr.–Sept., daily 8–7; Oct.–Mar., daily 8–5.*

Fodor's Choice ★ **Manassas National Battlefield Park.** The Confederacy won two important victories—in July 1861 and August 1862—at Manassas National Battlefield Park, or Bull Run. General Thomas Jonathan Jackson earned his nickname Stonewall here, when he and his brigade "stood like a stone wall." When the second battle ended, the Confederacy was at the zenith of its power. Originally farmland, the battlefield bore witness to casualties of nearly 30,000 troops. The Stone House, used as an aid station during the war, still stands. President Taft led a peaceful reunion of thousands of veterans here in 1911—50 years after the first battle. A self-guided walking or driving tour of the park begins at the visitor center, whose exhibits and audiovisual presentations greatly enhance a visit. From Arlington and Fairfax take I–66 west (use I–495 to get to I–66 from Alexandria) to Exit 47B (Sudley Road/Route 234 North). Don't be fooled by the earlier Manassas exit for Route 28. The visitor center is ½ mi north on the right. ✉*6511 Sudley Rd.* ☎*703/361–1339* ⊕*www.nps.gov/mana* ▣*$3 for 3 days* ⊙*Park daily dawn–dusk, visitor center daily 8:30–5.*

WHERE TO EAT

$$$ ✕**Gadsby's Tavern.** In the heart of the historic district, this circa-1792
AMERICAN tavern provides a taste of the interior decoration, cuisine, and entertainment of the early Republic. A strolling balladeer usually makes the rounds on Friday and Saturday nights. The tavern was a favorite of Thomas Jefferson and George Washington, who is commemorated on the menu: George Washington's Favorite Duck is half a duck roasted with peach-apricot dressing and served with Madeira sauce. Other period offerings are Gentlemen's Pye (made with game), Sally Lunn bread, and a rich English trifle. Brunch is served on Sunday. ✉*138 N. Royal St.* ☎*703/548–1288* ⊕*www.gadsbystavernrestaurant.com* ▭*AE, D, DC, MC, V.*

$$–$$$ ✕**La Porta's.** At the west end of Old Town and about two blocks from
AMERICAN the King Street Metrorail station, La Porta's combines great food with
★ a variety of gentle, good music nightly in an intimate setting. Fresh seafood is the strong suit here, especially the crab cakes. Monday and Tuesday you can choose two entrée specials plus a bottle of wine for $28 per couple—a great deal. Park free in their enclosed lot beside the restaurant. Brunch is served Sunday 11–3:30. ✉*1600 Duke St.* ☎*703/837–9117* ⊕*www.laportas.net* ▭*AE, D, DC, MC, V* ⊙*No lunch Sat.* Ⓜ*King St.*

$$$ ✕**Le Refuge.** This petite French restaurant one block from Alexandria's
FRENCH busiest intersection has been a local favorite for 25 years. It is Alexandria's oldest French restaurant with its original owners, Jean François and his wife Françoise. Enjoy lovingly prepared, authentic French country fare with beaucoup flavor; popular selections include trout, bouillabaisse, garlicky leg of lamb, frogs' legs, and beef Wellington. Polish it all off with an order of profiteroles or crème brûlée. Personal service (they don't like to keep you waiting between courses) makes this cozy restaurant popular. ✉*127 N. Washington St.* ☎*703/548–4661* ⊕*www.lerefugealexandria.com* ▭*AE, DC, MC, V* ⊙*Closed Sun.*

¢–$ ✕**Rocklands.** This homegrown barbecue stop is known for its flavorful
BARBECUE pork ribs smoked over hickory and red oak. Sides like silky corn pud-
☺ ding, rich mac 'n' cheese, and crunchy slaw are as good as the meats, which cover everything from beef brisket and chopped pork barbecue to chicken and fish. The family crowd comes for dinner, but they also do popular take-out. There is another branch in Arlington at 3471 Washington Blvd. ✉*25 S. Quaker La., Alexandria, VA* ☎*703/778–9663* ⊕*www.rocklands.com* ▭*AE, MC, V.*

WHERE TO STAY

Alexandria & Arlington Bed and Breakfast Network (✉ *4938 Hampden La., Suite 164, Bethesda* ☎ *703/549–3415 or 888/549–3415* ⊕ *www.aabbn. com*) can arrange accommodations in Northern Virginia.

$$–$$$ 🖃**Embassy Suites Old Town Alexandria.** The relaxing sound of rushing
Ⓒ   water from the atrium fountain adjacent to the restaurant greets you inside this modern all-suites hotel three blocks from Alexandria's landmark George Washington Masonic Temple. Train buffs should request a suite facing the Amtrak and Metrorail stations across the street. Each suite has a living room with overstuffed sofa and chairs and a work desk; beds have an abundance of fluffy pillows. A free shuttle is available to transport you to the scenic Alexandria riverfront, which has shops and restaurants. **Pros:** the cooked-to-order breakfast is complimentary; kids can romp in the playroom. **Cons:** train station across the street can be noisy; Wi-Fi use costs $9.95 a day. ✉ *1900 Diagonal Rd.* ☎ *703/684–5900 or 800/362–2779* ⊕ *www.embassysuites.com* ⬅ *268 suites ♿ In-room: kitchen, refrigerator, Ethernet. In-hotel: restaurant, pool, gym, laundry facilities, laundry service, public Wi-Fi (fee), parking (fee)* ⊟ *AE, D, DC, MC, V* ⃝BP Ⓜ *King St.*

$$–$$$ 🖃**Morrison House.** The architecture, parquet floors, crystal chandeliers,
★   decorative fireplaces, and furnishings here are so faithful to the Federal period (1790–1820) that it's often mistaken for a renovation rather than what it is: a structure built from scratch in 1985. The hotel blends Early American charm with modern conveniences. Some rooms have fireplaces, and all have four-poster beds, hair dryers, and bathrobes. The highly regarded Grille restaurant serves American contemporary cuisine. **Pros:** in the heart of Old Town, about a 15-minute walk from the train and Metrorail stations; modern building with historic charm. **Cons:** can be a little pricey; fireplaces are decorative only. ✉ *116 S. Alfred St.* ☎ *703/838–8000 or 800/367–0800* ⊕ *www.morrisonhouse.com* ⬅ *42 rooms, 3 suites ♿ In-room: DVD. In-hotel: 2 restaurants, room service, bars, public Wi-Fi, parking (fee)* ⊟ *AE, DC, MC, V* Ⓜ *King St.*

NIGHTLIFE

BARS AND PUBS

Aficionados praise Alexandria's **Shenandoah Brewing Company** (✉ *652 S. Pickett St.* ☎ *703/823–9508*) for its stouts and ales, especially the Bourbon Stoney Stout, aged in oak casks previously used to make premium bourbon. Inside, the atmosphere is slightly industrial and the menu is limited to foods grown or made in Virginia: peanuts, potato chips, chili, and a delicious beer-queso dip. **Union Street Public House** (✉ *121 S. Union St., Old Town* ☎ *703/548–1785* ⊕ *www.usphalexandria.com*) has three dining rooms and two bars that twist through this 200-year-old building. Although it's also a restaurant, come late for a beer in the busy main bar or chat with friends in the cozy OysterBar area.

LIVE MUSIC

The **Birchmere** (✉ *3701 Mt. Vernon Ave.* ☎ *703/549–7500* ⊕ *www. birchmere.com*) is one of the best places outside the Blue Ridge Mountains to hear acoustic folk and bluegrass. Tickets are on the expensive side, with big names fetching up to $95.

SPORTS AND THE OUTDOORS

BIKING

Rent a bike at the idyllic **Washington Sailing Marina**, on the Mount Vernon Bike Trail. A 12-mi ride south will take you to the front doors of Mount Vernon, and a 6-mi ride north across the Memorial Bridge will put you at the foot of the Washington Monument. All-terrain bikes rent for $6 per hour or $22 per day; cruisers cost $4 per hour or $16.50 per day. The marina is open 9–5 daily.

BOATING

The **Washington Sailing Marina** (✉ *1 Marina Dr.* ☎ *703/548–9027* ⊕ *www.washingtonsailingmarina.com*), on the George Washington Memorial Parkway just south of the airport, rents sailboats from around mid-May to mid-October. Aqua Fins are $10 per hour, the larger Flying Scots are $19 per hour. There's a two-hour minimum, and reservations are required (along with certification from a sailing school or passing a written test). Phone early; boats are limited.

HIKING

Huntley Meadows Park (✉ *3701 Lockheed Blvd.* ☎ *703/768–2525* ☞ *Free* ☉ *Park daily dawn–dusk; visitor center Mon. and Wed.–Fri. 9–5; call for weekend hrs*), a 1,460-acre refuge, is made for birders. You can spot more than 200 species—from ospreys to owls, egrets, and ibis. Much of the park is wetlands, home to a variety of aquatic species. A boardwalk circles through a marsh, enabling you to spot beaver lodges, and 4 mi of trails wind through the park, making it possible that you'll see deer, muskrats, and river otters as well.

The **Mount Vernon Trail,** an asphalt bike path, is a favorite with Washington runners and bikers. You can access it from the north just short of Key Bridge in Rosslyn, beside the I–66 off-ramp. It then passes Ronald Reagan National Airport, and goes through the Alexandria waterfront. This stretch is approximately 9.5 mi one-way. The southern section of the trail (approximately 9 mi) takes you along the banks of the Potomac from Alexandria all the way to Mount Vernon, George Washington's estate.

SHOPPING

Old Town Alexandria is dense with antiques shops—many of them quite expensive—that are particularly strong in the Federal and Victorian periods. The Alexandria Convention and Visitors Association has maps and lists of the dozens of stores (available at Ramsay House).

Dating to 1753, the **Saturday Morning Market at Market Square** (✉ *City Hall, 301 King St.*) may be the country's oldest operating farmers' market. Vendors sell baked goods, fresh produce, plants, flowers, and

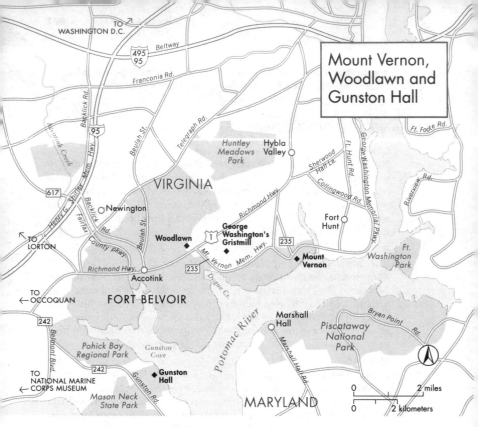

Mount Vernon,
Woodlawn and
Gunston Hall

high-quality crafts. Come early; the market opens at 6 AM, and by 10 AM it's all over.

MOUNT VERNON, WOODLAWN, AND GUNSTON HALL

Several splendid examples of plantation architecture remain on the Virginia side of the Potomac, 15 mi or so south of Washington, D.C. On hillsides overlooking the river, three estates offer magnificent vistas and make a bygone era vivid: Mount Vernon, the home of George Washington and one of the most popular sites in the area; Woodlawn, the estate of Washington's step-granddaughter; and Gunston Hall, the home of George Mason, author of the document that inspired the Bill of Rights.

MOUNT VERNON

⏱ *8 mi south of Alexandria.*

Fodor'sChoice ★ Mount Vernon and the surrounding lands had been in the Washington family for nearly 90 years by the time George inherited it all in 1761. Before taking command of the Continental Army, Washington was a

Martha Washington: Hot or Not?

11

As hard as it may be to believe from the portraits of her in your U.S. history book, Martha Washington was a hottie. Far from the frumpy, heavy-set woman we know as the first first lady, Martha wore sequined purple high heels on her wedding day, read Gothic romance novels, and had many admirers, not to mention a previous husband. A team of forensic anthropologists used a 1796 portrait of Mrs. Washington to digitally create an image of what she might have looked like in her 20s. The image inspired Michael Deas to create a portrait of the young first lady which now hangs in the Education building at Mount Vernon.

yeoman farmer managing the 8,000-acre plantation, of which more than 3,000 acres were under cultivation. He also oversaw the transformation of the main house from an ordinary farm dwelling into what was, for the time, a grand mansion.

EXPLORING

Mount Vernon's state-of-the-art Orientation Center and Museum and Education Center is not to be missed. George Washington comes to life through interactive displays, life-size models, action-adventure movies, short educational videos, and more than 500 artifacts on display for the first time. Perhaps the most awe-inspiring artifact is the terra-cotta bust of Washington that is believed to be the most accurate depiction of this great leader. And, since it was installed at his actual height, it almost seems to come to life. Other artifacts of note: Washington's sword, shoe and knee buckles, and his last will and testament. The 20-minute mini-epic film shown in the Orientation Center reenacts the pivotal moment in our country's history when Washington crossed the Delaware River. There's also a scale replica of the mansion and an incredible stained-glass window that depicts momentous times in Washington's life.

The red-roof house is elegant though understated, with a yellow pine exterior that's been painted and coated with layers of sand to resemble white-stone blocks. The first-floor rooms are quite ornate, especially the large formal dining room, with a molded ceiling decorated with agricultural motifs. Throughout the house are other smaller symbols of the owner's eminence, such as a key to the main portal of the Bastille—presented to Washington by the Marquis de Lafayette—and Washington's presidential chair. When you step into Washington's private sanctuary, the first-floor study, you can't help but imagine him sitting at his desk, reading overseer's reports, making entries in his diary, or referencing one of his 884 books that are displayed in the glass-enclosed bookshelves. As you tour the mansion, guides are stationed throughout the house to describe the furnishings and answer questions.

You can stroll around 45 of the estate's 500 acres. In addition to the mansion, highlights include four gardens with heirloom plants dating to the 1700s and 13 trees that were planted by George Washington, slave quarters, smokehouse, kitchen, carriage house, greenhouse, and, down the hill toward the boat landing, the tomb of George and Martha Washington. There's also a pioneer farmer site: a 4-acre hands-on exhibit with a reconstruction of George Washington's 16-sided treading barn as its centerpiece. ■ TIP→ Among the souvenirs sold at the plantation are stripling boxwoods that began life as clippings from bushes planted in 1798, the year before Washington died. A tour of the house and grounds takes about four hours. Private evening candlelight tours of the mansion with staff dressed in 18th-century costumes can be arranged. Throughout the year special events are held at the estate including festivals, holiday celebrations, walking tours, craft fairs, and children's storytelling sessions. Check the Web site when planning your visit.

George Washington's Distillery & Gristmill, located 3 mi from Mount Vernon on Route 235, is open daily April–October. During the guided tours, led by historic interpreters, you can meet an 18th-century miller, watch the water-powered wheel grind grain into flour just as it did 220 years ago, and learn techniques of distilling using five of the original copper stills. Tickets can be purchased either at the distillery and gristmill itself or at Mount Vernon's Main Gate. ⊠*Southern end of George Washington Pkwy., Mount Vernon, VA* ☎*703/780-2000* ⊕*www.mountvernon.org* ⊠*$13, gristmill $4, combination ticket $15* ☉*Mar., Sept., and Oct., daily 9–5; Apr.–Aug., daily 8–5; Nov.–Feb., daily 9–4.*

WOODLAWN

3 mi west of Mount Vernon.

Woodlawn was once part of the Mount Vernon estate. From here you can still see traces of the bowling green that fronted Washington's home. The house was built for Washington's step-granddaughter, Nelly Custis, who married his favorite nephew, Lawrence Lewis. (Lewis had come to Mount Vernon from Fredericksburg to help Uncle George manage his five farms.)

GETTING HERE AND AROUND

To drive to Woodlawn, travel southwest on Route 1 to the second Route 235 intersection (the first leads to Mount Vernon). The entrance to Woodlawn is on the right at the traffic light. From Mount Vernon, travel northwest on Route 235 to the Route 1 intersection; Woodlawn is straight ahead through the intersection.

EXPLORING

The Lewises' home, completed in 1805, was designed by Dr. William Thornton, a physician and amateur architect from the West Indies who drew up the original plans for the U.S. Capitol. Like Mount Vernon, the Woodlawn house is constructed of native materials, including the clay for its bricks and the yellow pine used throughout its interior. ■ TIP→ Built on a site selected by George Washington, the house has commanding views of the surrounding countryside and the Potomac River

beyond. In the tradition of Southern riverfront mansions, Woodlawn has a central hallway that provides a cool refuge in summer. At one corner of the passage is a bust of George Washington set on a pedestal so the crown of the head is at 6 feet, 2 inches—Washington's actual height.

Woodlawn was once a plantation where more than 100 people, most of them slaves, lived and worked. As plantation owners, the Lewises lived in luxury. Docents talk about how the family entertained and how the slaves grew produce and prepared these lavish meals as well as their own. As intimates of the Washingtons' household, the Lewises displayed a collection of objects in honor of their illustrious benefactor. Many Washington family items are on display today. In 1957 the property was acquired by the National Trust for Historic Preservation, which had been operating it as a museum since 1951.

Also on the grounds of Woodlawn is the **Pope-Leighey House** (⊕ *www. popeleighey1940.org*). Frank Lloyd Wright designed his Usonian houses like this one as a means of providing affordable housing for people of modest means. It was built in 1940 and moved here from Falls Church, Virginia, in 1964. ⊠ *9000 Richmond Hwy., Mount Vernon, VA* ☎ *703/780–4000* ⊕ *www.woodlawn1805.org* ☉ *$7.50 for either Woodlawn or Pope-Leighey House, combination ticket $13* ☉ *Mar.– Dec., Tues.–Sun. 10–4; limited guided tours in Mar. because of annual needlework show; tours leave every ½ hr; last tour at 3:30.*

GUNSTON HALL

12 mi south of Woodlawn.

Gunston Hall Plantation, down the Potomac from Mount Vernon, was the home of another important George. Gentleman farmer George Mason was a colonel of the Fairfax militia and author of the Virginia Declaration of Rights, the model for the U.S. Bill of Rights, which called for freedom of the press, tolerance of religion, and other fundamental democratic principles. Mason was a framer of the Constitution but refused to sign the final document because it didn't stop the importation of slaves, adequately restrain the powers of the federal government, or include a bill of rights. Mason's objections spurred the movement for the inclusion of the Bill of Rights into the Constitution.

GETTING HERE AND AROUND

Travel south on Route 1, 9 mi past Woodlawn to Route 242; turn left there and go 3½ mi to the plantation entrance.

EXPLORING

Mason's home was built circa 1755. ■**TIP→ The Georgian-style mansion has some of the finest hand-carved ornamented interiors in the country. It's the handiwork of the 18th-century's foremost architect, William Buckland, who also designed the Hammond-Harwood and Chase-Lloyd houses in Annapolis.** Gunston Hall is built of brick, black walnut, and yellow pine. The style of the time demanded symmetry in all structures, which explains the false door set into one side of the center hallway. The house's interior, which has carved woodwork in styles from Chinese to Gothic, has been meticulously restored, with paints made from the original formulas and carefully carved replacements for the intricate mahogany medallions in the moldings. Restored outbuildings include a kitchen, dairy, laundry, and smokehouse. A schoolhouse has also been reconstructed.

The formal gardens, under excavation by a team of archaeologists, are famous for their boxwoods—some now 12 feet high—thought to have been planted during George Mason's time, making them among the oldest in the country. The Potomac is visible past the expansive deer park. Also on the grounds is an active farmyard with livestock and crop species; special programs, such as history lectures and hearth-cooking demonstrations, are offered throughout the year. ■ TIP→A tour of Gunston Hall takes at least 45 minutes; tours begin at the visitor center, which includes a museum and gift shop. ✉ *10709 Gunston Rd., Mason Neck, VA* ☎ *703/550–9220* ⊕ *www.gunstonhall.org* ✆ *$8* ⊙ *Daily 9:30–5; first tour at 10, last tour at 4:30.*

CHARLOTTESVILLE AND SHENANDOAH NATIONAL PARK

Surrounded by a lush countryside, Charlottesville is the most prominent city in the foothills of the Blue Ridge Mountains. Thomas Jefferson's hilltop home and the University of Virginia, the enterprise of his last years, draw appreciators of architecture. On the Blue Ridge itself are popular Shenandoah National Park and the park's spectacular Skyline Drive.

CHARLOTTESVILLE

Charlottesville is 71 mi northwest of Richmond via I–64.

Charlottesville is still Jefferson's city, focused on Monticello and the University of Virginia. The downtown pedestrian mall, a brick-paved street of restored buildings that stretches along six blocks of Main Street, is frequented by humans and canines. Outdoor restaurants and cafés, concerts, street vendors, and impromptu theatrical events keep things lively.

DISCOUNTS AND DEALS

A Presidential Pass, purchased for $29 at Monticello, Ash Lawn-Highland, or Michie Tavern, grants access to these three sites with a $5 combined savings.

GETTING HERE AND AROUND

Charlottesville is off of I–64, just an hour from Richmond or two hours from Washington, D.C. Although the pedestrian mall in downtown Charlottesville is walkable, you'll need a car to see the historic presidential homes, wineries, and attractions in the region. CTS offers a free trolley service daily between downtown and the university.

ESSENTIALS

Trolley Information **Charlottesville Transit Service** (CTS ✉ *315 4th St. NW* ☎ *434/296-7433*).

Visitor Information **Charlottesville/ Albemarle Convention and Visitors Bureau** (✉ *Rte. 20 S, Box 178, Charlottesville* ☎ *434/293–6789 or 877/386–1102* ⊕ *www.charlottesvilletourism.org*).

EXPLORING

Standing in contrast to the grandiose Monticello is the modest **Ash Lawn–Highland.** James Monroe, who held more major political offices than any other U.S. president, intentionally kept it a simple farmhouse,

WORD OF MOUTH

"Charlottesville is lovely. Monticello and UVA have wonderful history. There is cute shopping and dining on the downtown pedestrian mall and you are only a short drive from some beautiful hiking or scenic driving"
—Schlegal1

building the home in 1799, 2 mi from his friend Jefferson's estate. A later owner added on a more prominent two-story section where two original Monroe rooms burned down. Though it definitely has a more common feel than Monticello, the small rooms in Ash Lawn–Highland are similarly crowded with gifts from notables and souvenirs from Monroe's time as envoy to France. Allow a couple of hours to visit Monroe's estate, a perfect way to complete a day that begins at Monticello. The outdoor Ash Lawn Opera Festival draws music aficionados in July and August. ✉ *1000 James Monroe Pkwy., Rte. 795 southwest of Monticello* ☎ *434/293–9539* ⊕ *www.ashlawnhighland.org* ✎ *$9* ⏲ *Apr.–Oct., daily 9–6; Nov.–Mar., daily 11–5.*

Fodor'sChoice
★ **Monticello,** long featured on the back of the U.S. nickel, is well worth the admission and the almost inevitable wait. Arrive early, ideally on a weekday, and allow at least three hours to explore the nuances of Jefferson's life as exemplified by the architecture, inventions, and layout throughout his grand, hilltop estate. Monticello (which means "little mountain") is the most famous of Jefferson's homes, constructed from 1769 to 1809. Note the narrow staircases—hidden because he considered them unsightly and a waste of space—and his inventions, such as a seven-day clock and a two-pen contraption that allowed him to make a copy of his correspondence as he wrote it without having to show it to a copyist. On-site are re-created gardens, the plantation street where his slaves lived, and a gift shop. ✉ *Rte. 53* ☎ *434/984–9822* ⊕ *www.monticello.org* ✎ *$15* ⏲ *Mar.–Oct., daily 8–5; Nov.–Feb., daily 9–4:30.*

★ The **University of Virginia** is simply called "The University" by many associated with it, annoying its rivals. Unquestionably, though, it is one of the nation's most notable public universities, founded and designed by 76-year-old Thomas Jefferson, who called himself its "father" in his own epitaph. Even if you're not an architecture or history buff, the green terraced expanse called the Lawn, surrounded by redbrick, columned buildings, is inviting. The Rotunda is a half-scale replica of Rome's Pantheon, suggesting Jefferson's Monticello and the U.S. Capitol. Behind the Pavilions, where senior faculty live, serpentine walls surround small, flowering gardens. Edgar Allan Poe's room—where he spent one year as a student until debt forced him to leave—is preserved on the West Range at No. 13. Campus tours (daily at 10, 11, 2, 3, and 4) begin indoors in the Rotunda, whose entrance is on the Lawn side, lower level. The **University of Virginia Art Museum** (⊠*Bayly Bldg., 155 Rugby Rd.* ☎*434/924–7458* ⊠*Free* ☉*Tues.–Sun. noon–5*), one block north of the Rotunda, exhibits art from around the world from ancient times to the present day. ⊠*University* ☎*434/924–3239* ⊕*www.virginia.edu* ⊠*Free* ☉*Rotunda daily 9–4:45. University closed during winter break in Dec. and Jan. and spring exams 1st 3 wks of May.*

♨ At the **Virginia Discovery Museum** children can step inside a giant kaleidoscope, explore a reconstructed log cabin, or watch bees in action in a working hive. The hands-on exhibits are meant to interest children (and their parents) in science, the arts, history, and the humanities. The museum is at the east end of the downtown mall. ⊠*524 E. Main St., Downtown* ☎*434/977–1025* ⊕*www.vadm.org* ⊠*$4* ☉*Tues.–Sat. 10–5, Sun. 1–5.*

WHERE TO EAT

¢   ✗**Bodo's Bagels.** You may have to wait in line at one the three locally
AMERICAN   owned locations, especially at breakfast, but locals swear these are the
★   best bagels south of the Big Apple. In true New York style, bagels are boiled before being baked, and all 10 varieties are true water bagels made with no fats or preservatives. Lunchtime is also popular, and the low prices appeal to both students and visitors. There are also locations at 505 Preston Avenue and 1609 University Avenue. ⊠*1418 Emmet St., Downtown* ☎*434/293–6021* ⊕*www.bodosbagels.com* ⊠*Reservations not accepted* ☱ *MC, V* ☉*No dinner Sunday.*

$$–$$$ ✗**C&O Restaurant.** Don't let the exterior fool you: behind the boarded-up
ECLECTIC   storefront hung with an illuminated Pepsi sign is an exemplary restau-
★   rant. The formal dining room upstairs, the lively bistro downstairs, and the cozy mezzanine in between share a French-influenced menu that has Pacific Rim and American Southwest touches. The heated patio and urban terrace are also lovely dining spaces in fall and spring. For a starter try the panfried sweetbread medallions; the entrées include steak *chinoise* with fresh ginger, tamari, and scallion cream sauce. The chefs source their products from local markets and farms, so the menu changes seasonally. The wine list is 300 strong. ⊠*515 E. Water St., Downtown* ☎*434/971–7044* ⊕*www.candorestaurant.com* ☱*AE, MC, V.*

▌MEALS
ON
WHEELS
While you're strolling the downtown pedestrian mall, pick up a gourmet nosh from Hamdinger's Food Cart (⊕*www.hamdingerscart.com*). This one-man show makes global cuisine from local ingredients. Try the Moroccan chicken or masala curry. He's open weekdays from 11:30 until 2.

$–$$ ✗**Crozet Pizza.** It may look like a shack, but this red clapboard restau-
PIZZA   rant 12 mi west of Charlottesville has been serving up what is renowned
★   as some of Virginia's best pizza since 1977. You have about three dozen toppings to choose from, including seasonal items such as snow peas and asparagus spears. Like its outside, the interior is rustic, with portraits of the owners' forebears and one wall covered with business cards from around the world. On weekends, takeout must be ordered hours in advance. ⊠*5794 3 Notched Rd. at Rte. 240, Crozet* ☎*434/823–2132* ☱*No credit cards.*

$$$
AMERICAN
✕ **Duner's.** This former motel diner 5 mi west of Charlottesville fills up early, and since they don't accept reservations, be prepared to wait up to 30 minutes. The fanciful menu, which changes daily, emphasizes fresh, seasonal fare in its seafood and pasta dishes. Appetizers may include lamb and green peppercorn pâté with grilled bread. Several fish selections appear daily on the menu, along with specialties like veal sweetbreads or duck breast, continental style. Although there isn't a kids' menu, the chef will make a burger or kid-friendly meal, as well as special vegetarian or dietary requests. ⊠ *Rte. 250 W, Ivy* ☎ *434/293–8352* ⊕ *www.dunersrestaurant.com* ⌁ *Reservations not accepted* ⊟ *AE, MC, V* ⊘ *No lunch.*

WHERE TO STAY

Various accommodations in and near Charlottesville can be found through **Guesthouses** (✉ *Box 5737, Charlottesville 22905* ☎ *434/979– 7264* ⊕ *www.va-guesthouses.com*).

$$$–$$$$
⌂ **Boar's Head Inn.** Set on 55 acres in west Charlottesville, this local landmark resembles an English country inn, with flower gardens, ponds, and a gristmill from 1834. The rooms have king-size four-poster beds and Italian Anichini linens; many have balconies. Some suites have fireplaces. There are lots of activities here, from cooking classes and wine tastings to hot-air ballooning. The Old Mill Room restaurant is open for a lunch buffet and dinner and there are two other restaurants on-site. **Pros:** true luxury; tons of amenities; sumptuous lunch buffet. **Cons:** add-on activities can make this a pricey stay; compared to other inns, this larger property can feel impersonal. ⊠ *U.S. 250 W, Ednam Dr.* ☎ *434/296–2181* ⊕ *www.boarsheadinn.com* ⌁ *160 rooms, 11 suites* ⌂ *In-room: Ethernet. In-hotel: 3 restaurants, golf course, tennis courts, pools, gym, spa* ⊟ *AE, D, DC, MC, V.*

$$$$
★
⌂ **Clifton Country Inn.** This small inn is a member of the Relais & Châteaux group, the ultimate in luxury. Top shelf amenities include Mascioni linens and robes and Molton Brown toiletries in the 18 uniquely appointed rooms and suites, situated on 100 acres with spectacular views of the Blue Ridge Mountains. Many of the rooms are named to reflect the property's ties to the Jefferson family. About 350 acres passed to Thomas Jefferson's daughter and her husband, Thomas Mann Randolph, who established their home Edgehill on the property. The foundations of the main building are thought to be the original foundations of one of Mann's warehouses. **Pros:** great food; luxury in a small setting; massive private lake. **Cons:** far from downtown Charlottesville; expensive. ⊠ *1296 Clifton Inn Dr.* ☎ *434/971/1800* ⊕ *www.cliftoninn. net* ⌁ *18 rooms* ⌂ *In-room: Ethernet. In-hotel: 2 restaurants, pool, tennis court* ⊟ *AE, D, MC, V*

$$$$
Fodor'sChoice
★
⌂ **Keswick Hall at Monticello.** If you've got the money for it, this 1912 Tuscan villa on 600 lush acres 5 mi east of Charlottesville is a luxurious, cosmopolitan retreat. Since it is now owned by the Orient-Express, you can expect the ultimate in luxury amenities and service. The 48 guest rooms and suites contain all the modern amenities like high-speed Internet and flat screens, which exist in harmony with English and American antiques and claw-foot tubs. Some rooms have whirlpool baths and balconies. The 18-hole golf course, designed by Arnold

CLOSE UP

Virginia's Wineries

Jamestown's Colonial settlers are believed to have made the first wine in Virginia, but only in the past 30 years has the Commonwealth's wine industry truly come into its own. The number of wineries here has grown from fewer than 10 in the 1970s to more than 130 wineries in the Charlottesville area alone. As you drive through the state, keep an eye out for grape-cluster signs on the highway, which identify nearby wineries. Virginia Tourism offers a free wine trail map. The Monticello Wine Trail connects 22 area vineyards, including the **Jefferson Vineyards** (⊕ *www. jeffersonvineyards.com*), located on land where Thomas Jefferson himself grew grapes. Virginia is becoming well known on the national oenophile radar for its viogniers, and for vintages from vintners like Kluge.

For more information on Virginia vineyards and wineries, contact the **Virginia Wineries Association** (☎ *800/828–4637* ⊕ *www.virginiawine.org*) or the **Jeffersonian Wine Grape Growers Society** (☎ *434/296–4188* ⊕ *www.monticellowinetrail.org*), sponsor of the Monticello Wine Trail.

Among central and western Virginia's more popular wineries are Barboursville Vineyards, near Charlottesville, and Château Morrisette Winery, on the Blue Ridge Parkway in the southern part of the state.

Barboursville Vineyards. This vineyard between Charlottesville and Orange was the first in the state to grow only vinifera (old-world) grapes. The grapes were planted in 1976 on the former plantation of James Barbour, governor from 1812 to 1814. His house, designed by Thomas Jefferson,

was gutted by fire in 1884; the ruins remain. ⊠ *17655 Winery Rd., near intersection of Rtes. 20 and 23, Barboursville* ☎ *540/832–3824* ⊕ *www. barboursvillewine.com* ☑ *Tours free; tastings $4* ⊙ *Tastings Mon.–Sat. 10–5, Sun. 11–5.*

Château Morrisette Winery. With the Rock Castle Gorge nearby, this winery has spectacular surroundings. Tastings allow you to sample the dozen different wines produced here. ⊠ *Winery Rd. off Rte. 726, west of Blue Ridge Pkwy. at milepost 171.5, Meadows of Dan* ☎ *540/593–2865* ⊕ *www.thedogs.com* ☑ *Tour and tasting $5* ⊙ *Mon.–Thurs. 10–5, Fri. and Sat. 10–6, Sun. 11–5.*

Kluge Estate. Established in 1999 just 9 mi from the birthplace of Virginia viticulture at Monticello, Kluge is making world-class whites, reds, and rosé in its 2,000-acre vineyard on Carter's Mountain. Grapes are harvested by hand and most of the wines are made in *methode traditionelle.* Taste one of the chardonnays, a blanc de blanc, or a Bordeaux blend at the estate's Farm Shop, which also offers food and wine pairings. ⊠ *100 Grand Cru Dr., Charlottesville* ☎ *434/977–3895 or 434/984–4855* ⊕ *www.klugeestateonline.com* ⊙ *11 AM–5:30 PM.*

Palmer, spreads across the rear of the estate. There's no check-in desk here; you are welcomed inside as if you are entering someone's home. The facilities of the private Keswick Club are open to those staying overnight. **Pros:** two restaurants and pub on-site; top-shelf toiletries. **Cons:** expensive for the area; lacking Colonial history of many inns. ⊠*701 Club Dr., Keswick* ☎*434/979–3440 or 888/778/2565* ⊕*www. keswick.com* ⚲*40 rooms, 8 suites* ⟁*In-room: Ethernet, safe. In-hotel: 2 restaurants, golf course, tennis courts, pools, gym, spa, bicycles, some pets allowed* ⊟*AE, D, DC, MC, V.*

$$
★ 🏠 **Silver Thatch Inn.** Four-poster beds and period antiques are just part of the charm of this 1780 white-clapboard Colonial farmhouse 8 mi north of town. The friendly hosts help their guests arrange outdoor activities at nearby locations. The original structure was built to house Hessian soldiers captured during the Revolutionary War and still remains as the Hessian Room. **Pros:** fascinating Colonial history; romantic fireplaces; canopy beds; pub and restaurant on-site. **Cons:** small size means few amenities, particularly in the rooms. ⊠*3001 Hollymead Dr.* ☎*434/978–4686 or 800/261–0720* ⊕*www.silverthatch.com* ⚲*7 rooms* ⟁*In-room: Wi-Fi, no phone, no TV. In-hotel: restaurant, pool, no kids under 14, no-smoking rooms* ⊟*AE, DC, MC, V* ⊚|*BP.*

A SIP OF A SIDE-TRIP **The Starr Hill Brewery** (⊠*5391 Three Notched Rd., Crozet* ☎*434/823– 5671*) is one of the most well-respected breweries on the East Coast, featuring four house brews including Amber Ale, Pale Ale, Jomo Lager, and Dark Starr Stout and open for tastings on Saturdays from noon to 5. If apple cider is more to your taste, visit **Carter's Mountain Orchard** (⊠*1435 Carters Mountain Trail, Charlottesville* ☎*434/977–1833*) for stunning views of Charlottesville and some of the best apples in the state.

NIGHTLIFE AND THE ARTS

For listings of cultural events, music, and movies, and a guide to restaurants, pick up a free copy of the *C-Ville Weekly* (⊕*www.c-ville.com*), an arts-and-entertainment newspaper available in restaurants and hotels throughout the city. If you're near the University of Virginia campus, grab a free copy of the student newspaper, the *Cavalier Daily* (⊕*www. cavalierdaily.com*), for the latest on college sports and events.

FESTIVALS In March, **Virginia Festival of the Book** (☎*434/924–6890* ⊕*www.vabook. org*) draws authors that have included Garrison Keillor and Michael Ondaatje. Thousands attend the festival, which is open to the public and promotes literacy while celebrating the book. Every autumn, Charlottesville hosts the **Virginia Film Festival** (☎*800/882–3378* ⊕*www.vafilm. com*), with screenings of important new movies, panel discussions, and appearances by stars of the cinema. The movies are shown at four sites around the university and downtown.

SPORTS AND THE OUTDOORS

James River Runners Inc (⊠*10082 Hatton Ferry Rd., Scottsville* ☎*434/286–2338*), about 35 minutes south of Charlottesville, offers canoe, kayak, tubing, and rafting trips down the James.

SHOPPING

Charlottesville, at heart an academic community, supports a large
number of independent bookstores,
especially specialists in used and
antiquarian books. Whether it's a
rare first edition you are seeking or
just some unique bargains, try **Blue
Whale Books** (⊠*115 W. Main St., Downtown* ☎*434/296–4646*). Run
by an antiquarian book dealer, the shop has thousands of books in all
categories and price ranges, from one dollar to several hundred. **Dae-
dalus Bookshop** (⊠*123 4th St. NE, Downtown* ☎*434/293–7595*) has
three floors of books crammed into every nook and cranny. **Heartwood
Books** (⊠*5 Elliewood Ave., University* ☎*434/295–7083*), close to the
university campus, stocks scholarly works, including a good collection
of theology and philosophy. Legal-thriller master John Grisham kicks
off book tours at **New Dominion Bookshop** (⊠*404 E. Main St., Downtown* ☎*434/295–2552*).

★ The **Downtown Mall** (⊠*Main St., Downtown* ⊕*www.downtowncharlot-
tesville.net*) is a six-block brick pedestrian mall with specialty stores,
cinemas, art galleries, restaurants, and coffeehouses in restored 19th-
and early-20th-century buildings.

SHENANDOAH NATIONAL PARK

*Southern entrance is 18 mi west of Charlottesville via I–81; northern
entrance is at Front Royal.*

Though Shenandoah National Park is only a narrow ribbon on the
map, stretching 80 mi along the Blue Ridge but rarely more than 5 mi
wide, it is easy to imagine being much deeper in the wilderness as you
travel through it or spend a night camping here. Steep, wooded ridges
with rocky slopes stand out in the foreground of vistas taking in the
Shenandoah Valley to the west and the Piedmont to the east. Skyline
Drive traverses the park end to end, from Waynesboro to Front Royal,
and is the most common way to see the park. But hikers can find beautiful terrain just yards from the drive on some of the park's 500 mi of
trails, trout fishers may wade into more than 25 streams, and riders can
rent horses for wilderness trail rides. Those who want to know more
about the area's flora and fauna may want to take a guided hike, which
naturalists lead daily throughout the summer. The seasonal activities of
the park are outlined in the *Shenandoah Overlook,* a free newspaper
you can pick up on entering the park.

ESSENTIALS

Visitor Information **Shenandoah Visitor Center** (🖉 *Park Superintendent, Box
348, Rte. 4, Luray 22835* ☎*540/999–3500* ⊕*www.nps.gov/shen* 🖃*Park and
Skyline Dr. $15 car [$10 car Dec.–Feb.], $10 motorcycle, $8 bicycle or pedestrian;
tickets are valid 7 days*).

11

EXPLORING

Fodor's Choice ★ **Skyline Drive** runs 105 mi, alternating between open vistas and forest-hemmed stretches and offering easily accessible wilderness. Designated as a National Historic Landmark, the two-lane highway runs from Rockfish Gap at Afton, Virginia, to Front Royal. During weekends and holidays it can seem a little too much like city driving—a 35-mph speed limit, rubber-necking leaf-lookers, narrow overlook turnouts, and the occasional black bear sighting can back traffic up uncomfortably. It's best to choose a weekday and allow the entire day; you may want to spend an hour or two resting on one roadside boulder.

■ **TIP→** Continue south on Skyline Drive past the park gates and over Interstate 64, and the road becomes the **Blue Ridge Parkway, which continues 471 mi** south to Cherokee, North Carolina. Unlike Skyline Drive, the parkway is free, and the speed limit is 45 mph.

Luray Caverns, 9 mi west of Skyline Drive on U.S. 211, are the largest caverns in the state. The world's only "stalacpipe organ" is composed of stalactites (calcite formations hanging from the ceilings of the caverns) that have been tuned to concert pitch and are tapped by rubber-tip plungers. The organ is played electronically for every tour and may be played manually on special occasions. A one-hour tour begins every 20 minutes. ⊠ *U.S. 211, 101 Cave Hill Rd., Luray* ☎ *540/743–6551* ⊕ *www.luraycaverns.com* ⊠ *$19* ⊗ *Mid-Mar.–mid-June, daily 9–6; mid-June–Labor Day, daily 9–7; Labor Day–Oct., daily 9–6; Nov.–mid-Mar., weekdays 9–4, weekends 9–5.*

WHERE TO STAY

$–$$ ⊠ **Jordan Hollow Farm.** The oldest of the four buildings here is a 1790 farmhouse, now a restaurant serving American regional cuisine. The youngest structure, built of hand hewn logs almost 200 years later, contains four of the inn's most luxurious rooms, which include a fireplace, whirlpool, and TV. The 150-acre horse farm is near the tiny town of Stanley, 6 mi from Luray and 15 mi from Shenandoah National Park. From here you can gaze out over pastures full of horses and playful llamas toward a backdrop of the Blue Ridge Mountains. The only "pets" allowed are horses, which can be boarded for a fee. Nearby trails are good for hiking and mountain biking. **Pros:** equestrian friendly; rustic luxury. **Cons:** a 20-minute drive from the park; limited availability. ⊠ *326 Hawksbill Park Rd., Stanley* ☎ *540/778–2285 or 888/418–7000* ⊕ *www.jordanhollow.com* ⟋ *8 rooms, 7 suites* 🛇 *In-room: refrigerator, DVD. In-hotel: restaurant, bar, bicycles, no-smoking rooms, no kids under 18* ☐ *AE, D, DC, MC, V* ⟊ *BP.*

¢–$ ⊠ **Skyland Resort.** At the highest point on Skyline Drive (3,680 feet), with views across the Shenandoah Valley, this facility has lodging that ranges from rustic cabins and motel-style rooms to suites. This resort is one of three different properties within the park: **Big Meadows Lodge,** originally built by the Civilian Conservation Corps, is in a spectacular setting surrounding by grassy meadows full of deer and wildlife. **Lewis Cabins** are the real and very rustic thing for an authentic outdoor adventure. Since these three properties in the park are in sought-after locations, you'll need to book up to a year in advance. There's no air-conditioning, but days above 80°F are rare at this altitude. **Pros:** stunning scenery;

alternative to in-park camping. Cons: must plan far in advance; no phones or TVs in many rooms; closed in winter. ⊠*Milepost 41.7 on Skyline Dr.* ☏*800/778–2851* ⊕*www.visitshenandoah.com* ↻*177 rooms* ♿*In-room: no a/c, no phone, no TV (some). In-hotel: restaurant, bar* ▤*AE, D, DC, MC, V* ☉*Closed Dec.–mid-Mar.*

SPORTS AND THE OUTDOORS

CANOEING At **Downriver Canoe** (⊠ *884 Indian Hollow Rd. Rte. 613 near Front Royal, Bentonville* ☏*540/635–5526* ⊕*www.downriver.com*), day and overnight trips start at $49 per canoe (or $32 per kayak, $16 per tube, and $79 per raft). **Front Royal Canoe** (⊠ *8567 Stonewall Jackson Hwy., U.S. 340, near Front Royal* ☏*540/635–5440 or 800/270–8808* ⊕*www.frontroyalcanoe.com*) offers a $16 tube trip as well as canoe, kayak, and raft trips of from one hour up to three days for $40–$130. The company also rents boats and sells fishing accessories. **Shenandoah River Outfitters** (⊠*6502 S. Page Valley Rd., Rte. 684, Luray* ☏*540/743–4159* ⊕*www.Shenandoah-river.com*) rents canoes and kayaks for $20 to $84, and tubes from $18.

HIKING The **Appalachian Trail** is more than 2,000 mi long, but you don't have to go that far, or even 2,000 feet, along it to see glorious foliage, rock formations, and wildlife. The trail zigzags across Skyline Drive through the park, offering easy access by car, variable hike lengths from a few feet to many miles, and connections with the more than 500 mi of the park's own trail network.

RICHMOND AND FREDERICKSBURG

Richmond, 100 mi south of Washington, D.C, on the James River, is the state's historic capital. It's easy to get here on I–95. Midway between Washington and Richmond on I–95, Fredericksburg is a lovely place to relax and retrace 18th- and 19th-century history in homes and museums and on nearby battlefields.

RICHMOND

100 mi south of Washington, D.C.

Centered on the fall line of the James River, about 75 mi upriver from the Chesapeake Bay, Richmond completes the transition from Tidewater Virginia into the Piedmont. Not only is Richmond the capital of the Commonwealth, but it was also the capital of the Confederacy. As a result, the city is studded with historic sites. At the start of the Civil War, Richmond was the most industrialized city in the South, and it remains an important city for national industries. After years of urban decay, Richmond transformed itself into a lively and sophisticated modern town, adding high technology to traditional economic bases that include shipping and banking.

GETTING HERE AND AROUND

By car, I–95 and I–64 come directly to Richmond, and state routes 1, 5, and 301 are scenic alternatives. Cabs are metered in Richmond; they charge $2.50 for the first mile and $1.50 for each additional mile.

Greater Richmond Transit operates bus service in Richmond. Buses run daily, 5 AM–1 AM; fares are $1.25 (exact change required). ■TIP➔ A free lunch express shuttles throughout the downtown area weekdays from 11:30 to 2:30. Three 22-passenger vans loop around downtown, stopping at nine restaurants every 10 minutes. This is a great way to get around the downtown area during midday. See ⊕*www.ridegrtc.com* for the lunch express route map.

FESTIVALS

Spring here is spectacular, especially during **Virginia's Annual Garden Week** in April (⊕*www.vagardenweek.org*). In September the **Virginia State Fair** (☎*804/228–3200* ⊕*www.statefair.com*), in Richmond, is a classic conglomeration of carnival rides, livestock shows, displays of farm equipment, and lots of food for sale. The **Richmond Folk Festival** (⊕*www.richmondfolkfestival.org*) takes place in October downtown, and Lewis Ginter Botanical Garden is ablaze with 450,000 lights during December's **Garden Festival of Lights** (⊕*www.lewisginter.org*).

TOURS

Historic Richmond Tours, a service of the Valentine Richmond History Center, offers guided tours that cover such topics as the historic Hollywood Cemetery and the River District and Jackson Ward. You can take either a walking tour or one of the thematic bus tours with topics that change monthly. Richmond Discoveries' excursions include tours that highlight Civil War history and customized trips for large groups or small families. Segway Tours offers a 2½-hour tour by Segway of the historic sites of the city and includes a training lesson before departing. Tours meet at the Richmond Visitors Center on 3rd Street.

ESSENTIALS

Taxi Companies Groome Transportation (▢ *Richmond Airport* ☎*804/222–6464*). **Metro Taxicab Service** (✉*2405 Westwood Ave.* ☎*804/353–5000*). Yellow Cab Service Inc (✉*3203 Williamsburg Rd.* ☎*804/222–7300*).

Tour Information Historic Richmond Tours (☎*804/649–0711* ⊕ *www.richmondhistorycenter.com*). **Richmond Discoveries** (☎*804/222–8595* ⊕*www.richmonddiscoveries.com*). **Segway Tours** (✉*405 N. 3rd St.* ☎*800/979–3370* ⊕ *www.segwayofrichmond.com* 🖾*$65* ⊗ *Daily tours at 10 AM and 2 PM*).

Visitor Information Richmond Regional Visitor Center (✉*401 N. 3rd St.* ☎*800/370–9004* ⊕ *www.visit.richmond.com*).

EXPLORING
DOWNTOWN

Richmond is divided into four quadrants: Northside (north of the James River), Southside (south of the James River), West End, and East Richmond. The main attractions, sites, hotels, restaurants, and shopping are spread out between several popular neighborhoods. Starting with Church Hill at the east end of downtown, heading west you'll come to Shockoe Bottom and Shockoe Slip, downtown, the Fan District which is home to Virginia Commonwealth University, the Museum District, the popular shopping area Carytown, and finally to the West End, a major residential and business area.

Richmond's historic attractions lie in the Northside quadrant. The heart of Old Richmond is the Court End district downtown. This area, close to the Capitol, contains seven National Historic Landmarks, three museums, and 11 additional buildings on the National Register of Historic Places—all within eight blocks.

7 American Civil War Center. This museum weaves the stories of the Union, Confederate, and African-American experiences during the Civil War into a national context. The permanent exhibit *In the Cause of Liberty* is housed in the old Gun Foundry, where more than 1,100 Confederate cannons were made. ⊠*500 Tredegar St.* ☎*804/780–1865* ⊕*www.tredegar.org* 🖻*$8* ⊙*Daily 9–5*

6 Black History Museum & Cultural Center of Virginia. The goal of this museum in the Jackson Ward is to gather visual, oral, and written records and artifacts that commemorate the lives and accomplishments of blacks in Virginia. On display are 5,000 documents, fine art objects, traditional African artifacts, textiles from ethnic groups throughout Africa, and artwork by Sam Gilllam, John Biggers, and P.H. Polk. ⊠*3 Clay St., at Foushee St.* ☎*804/780–9093* ⊕*www.blackhistorymuseum.org* 🖻*$5* ⊙*Tues.–Sat. 10–5.*

OFF THE BEATEN PATH

Citie of Henricus. Visit the home of Pocahontas and the second successful English settlement in the New World. Costumed interpreters reenact the lives of Virginia's Native Americans and English settlers who helped create the nation we know today. ⊠*251 Henricus Park Rd., Chester* ☎*804/706–1340* ⊕*www.henricus.org* 🖻*$7* ⊙*Tues.–Sun. 10–5.*

2 Edgar Allan Poe Museum. Richmond's oldest residence, the Old Stone House in Shockoe Bottom, just west of Church Hill Historic District, now holds a museum honoring the famous writer. Poe grew up in Richmond, and although he never lived in this early- to mid-18th-century structure, his disciples have made it a monument with some of the writer's possessions on display. ⊠*1914 E. Main St.* ☎*804/648–5523* or *888/213–2703* ⊕*www.poemuseum.org* 🖻*$6* ⊙*Tues.–Sat. 10–5, Sun. 11–5. Guided tours on the hr; last tour departs at 4.*

Fodor's Choice
★

4 Museum and White House of the Confederacy. These two buildings provide a look at a crucial period in the nation's history. The museum (a good place to start) has elaborate permanent exhibitions on the Civil War era. The "world's largest collection of Confederate memorabilia" includes such artifacts as the sword Robert E. Lee wore to the surrender at Appomattox. Next door, the "White House" has in fact always been painted gray. Made of brick in 1818, the building was stuccoed to give the appearance of large stone blocks. Preservationists have painstakingly re-created the interior as it was during the Civil War, when Jefferson Davis lived in the house. During the 45-minute guided tour, you see the entry hall's period 9-foot-tall French rococo mirrors and its floor cloth, painted to resemble ceramic tiles. You can park free in the adjacent hospital parking garage; the museum will validate tickets. ⊠*1201 E. Clay St.* ☎*804/649–1861* ⊕*www.moc.org* 🖻*Combination ticket $11; museum only, $8; White House only, $8* ⊙*Mon.–Sat. 10–5, Sun. noon–5.*

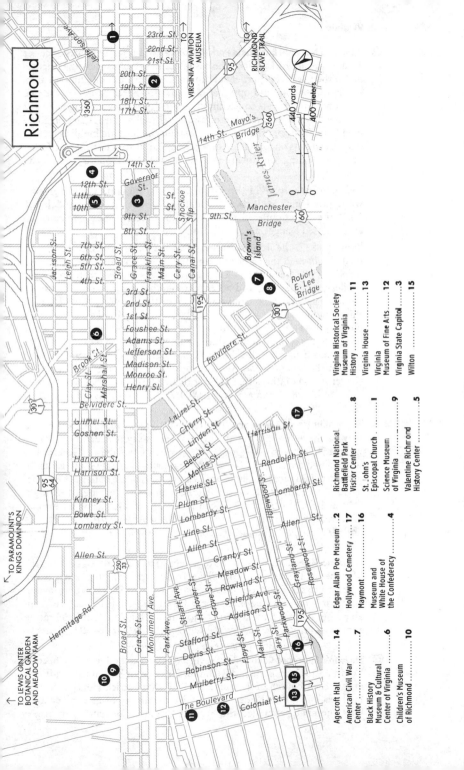

Richmond

23rd. St.
22nd St.
21st St.
20th St.
19th St.
18th St.
17th St.

TO VIRGINIA AVIATION MUSEUM

TO RICHMOND SLAVE TRAIL

14th St.
Mayo's Bridge

James River

Manchester Bridge

Brown's Island

Robert E. Lee Bridge

14th St.
Governor St.
12th St.
11th St.
10th St.
9th St.
8th St.
Shockoe Slip

7th St.
6th St.
5th St.
4th St.

3rd St.
2nd St.
1st St.
Foushee St.
Adams St.
Jefferson St.
Madison St.
Monroe St.
Henry St.

Belvidere St.
Gilmer St.
Goshen St.

Hancock St.
Harrison St.

Kinney St.
Bowe St.
Lombardy St.

Allen St.

Laurel St.
Cherry St.
Linden St.
Beech St.
Mottis St.
Harvie St.
Plum St.
Lombardy St.
Vine St.
Allen St.
Granby St.
Meadow St.
Rowland St.
Shields Ave.
Addison St.

Harrison St.
Randolph St.
Lombardy St.
Allen St.

TO PARAMOUNT'S KINGS DOMINION

TO LEWIS GINTER BOTANICAL GARDEN AND MEADOW FARM

Hermitage Rd.

Broad St.
Grace St.
Monument Ave.
Park Ave.
Stuart Ave.
Hanover St.
Grove St.
Granby St.
Stafford St.
Davis St.
Robinson St.
Mulberry St.
The Boulevard
Colonial St.

Floyd St.
Main St.
Cary St.
Parkwood St.
Grayland St.
Roselwood St.

Agecroft Hall **14**
American Civil War Center **7**
Black History Museum & Cultural Center of Virginia **6**
Children's Museum of Richmond **10**
Edgar Allan Poe Museum .. **2**
Hollywood Cemetery **17**
Maymont **16**
Museum and White House of the Confederacy **4**
Richmond National Battlefield Park Visitor Center **8**
St. ohn's Episcopal Church **1**
Science Museum of Virginia **9**
Valentine Richmond History Center **5**
Virginia Historical Society Museum of Virginia History **11**
Virginia House **13**
Virginia Museum of Fine Arts **12**
Virginia State Capitol **3**
Wilton **15**

440 yards
400 meters

⑧ Richmond National Battlefield Park Visitor Center. Inside what was once the Tredegar Iron Works, this is the best place to get maps and other materials on the Civil War battlefields and attractions in the Richmond area. A self-guided tour and optional tape tour for purchase covers the two major military threats to Richmond—the Peninsula Campaign of 1862 and the Overland Campaign of 1864—as well as the impact on Richmond's home front. Three floors of exhibits in the main building include unique artifacts on loan from other Civil War history institutions. Other original buildings on-site are a carpentry shop, gun foundry, office, and company store.

Kids can participate in the Junior Ranger program. They're given a workbook which leads them through the exhibits in search of "clues." Once they've completed their book, they receive their choice of an embroidered Ranger patch or a Ranger pin.

Built in 1837, the ironworks, along with smaller area iron foundries, made Richmond the center of iron manufacturing in the South. When the Civil War began in 1861, the ironworks geared up to make the artillery, ammunition, and other material that sustained the Confederate war machine. Its rolling mills provided the armor plating for warships, including the ironclad CSS *Virginia*. The works—saved from burning in 1865—went on to play an important role in rebuilding the devastated South; it also produced munitions in both world wars. The center has a pay parking lot ($3), but free parking is available next door at the Belle Isle lot. Also, be aware that the American Civil War Center is also on this site, but is a private museum that charges admission. ⊠ *5th and Tredegar Sts.* ☎ *804/771–2145* ⊕ *www.nps.gov/rich* ☲ *Free* ⊘ *Daily 9–5.*

OFF THE BEATEN PATH

Fodor's Choice ★ Appomattox Court House. To many in Virginia, the Civil War has never ended, but the history books say it ended here, 95 mi west of Richmond, on April 9, 1865, when Confederate General Lee surrendered the Army of Northern Virginia to General Grant, leader of pursuing Union forces. There are 27 structures in the national historical park, restored to its 1865 appearance; most can be entered. A highlight is the reconstructed McLean House, in whose parlor the articles of surrender were signed. ⊠ *3 mi north of Appomattox, on Rte. 24* ☎ *434/352–8987* ⊕ *www.nps.gov/apco/* ☲ *June–Aug. $4; Sept.–May $3* ⊘ *Daily 8:30–5.*

Richmond Slave Trail. Walk in the footsteps of Richmond's slaves from the Manchester Docks, down the Slave Trade path along the James River, past former slave auction houses in cobblestoned Shockoe Bottom and Lumpkin's Jail. Free booklets for a 1.3-mi self-guided walk are available from the city park system, or join in the big Freedom Celebration annually on June 19. ⊠ *Manchester Docks* ☎ *804/646–8911* ⊕ *www. ci.richmond.va.us/departments/parks/james.aspx* ☲ *Free.*

① St. John's Episcopal Church. For security reasons, the rebellious Second Virginia Convention met in Richmond instead of Williamsburg; it was in this 1741 church on March 23, 1775, that Patrick Henry delivered the speech in which he declared, "Give me liberty or give me death!" His argument persuaded the Second Virginia Convention to arm a

Fodor's Choice ★

Virginia militia. The speech is reenacted Memorial Day to Labor Day on Sunday at 2 PM. The cemetery includes the graves of Edgar Allan Poe's mother, Elizabeth Arnold Poe, and many famous early Virginians, notably George Wythe, a signer of the Declaration of Independence. The visitor center, in a restored redbrick schoolhouse, has Colonial crafts and other items for sale. Guided tours are led on the half-hour. ✉ *2401 E. Broad St., at 24th St.* ☎ *804/648–5015* ⊕ *www. historicstjohnschurch.org* ✏ *$6* ⊙ *Mon.–Sat. 10–3:30, Sun. 1–4.*

> **RICHMOND ART SCENE**
>
> Richmond is one of the South's preeminent art cities, flourishing with avant-garde painting and sculpture in addition to artifacts and magnificent traditional works, such as the Fabergé eggs in the Virginia Museum of Fine Arts. Throughout the year (except July and August), a free First Friday Art Walk in the heart of downtown features local galleries and artists in a festival atmosphere on the first Friday of the month.

⑤ Valentine Richmond History Center. For more than 100 years the Valentine Richmond History Center, established in 1898, has celebrated one of America's most historic cities. It has collected more than a million objects—one of the nation's largest collections focusing on a single city—including preserved photographs, textiles, and artifacts, and interprets 400 years of Richmond's history through items of everyday life. The large collection is kept in the History Center Archives, and is available for study and research by appointment. **Wickham House** (1812), a part of the Valentine, is more rightly a mansion; it was designed by architect Alexander Parris, the creator of Boston's Faneuil Hall. ✉ *1015 E. Clay St.* ☎ *804/649–0711* ⊕ *www. richmondhistorycenter.com* ✏ *$10, includes John Marshall House and Wickham House* ⊙ *Tues.–Sat. 10–5, Sun. noon–5; guided Wickham House tours Tues.–Sat. 11–4 and Sun. 1–4.*

❻ Virginia State Capitol. Thomas Jefferson designed this grand edifice in
★ 1785, modeling it on a Roman temple— the Maison Carrée—in Nîmes, France. After an extensive renovation, the Capitol has a new handicapped-accessible entrance on Bank Street. A visitor center is in the adjacent Bell Tower, and the expanded Capitol features an exhibit gallery, gift shop, and Meriwether's Capitol Café. Indoor guided tours last one hour and include the Old House and Senate chambers, the Rotunda, and two rooms restored in 2007. A map for self-guided tours is also available. ✉ *1000 Bank St.* ☎ *804/698–1788* ⊕ *www.virginiacapitol. gov* ✏ *Free* ⊙ *Mon.–Sat. 8:30–5, Sun. 1–4.*

GREATER RICHMOND

❿ Children's Museum of Richmond. A welcoming, hands-on complex for chil-
☺ dren and families, the museum is a place to climb, explore, experiment,
★ and play until every surface area is smudged with fingerprints. Bright, colorful, and crowded, the museum's different sections focus on educational fun. How It Works lets children experiment with tools, materials, and their own endless energy. Our Great Outdoors houses the museum's most popular attraction, the Cave, where children explore a 40-foot replica of a limestone cave and are introduced to earth science, ocean-

HISTORY YOU CAN SEE: A CIVIL WAR TOUR

When Virginia seceded from the Union in 1861, it would become a major battleground. Civil War sites are among the most compelling reasons to visit the state, and the itinerary below covers the standout attractions. One of the most compelling times to visit a Civil War battlefield is when volunteers are staging a battle reenactment. Thousands of Civil War history enthusiasts participate in these events, which often last for several days. For more information, log on to ⊕ www.civilwarnews.com.

DAY 1: RICHMOND

Begin your tour at Richmond's Museum and White House of the Confederacy and the National Battlefield Park Visitor Center. Also see the Virginia Historical Society Museum of Virginia History, which has some 800 pieces of Confederate weaponry, although only a few are on display. Take a trip out to Appomattox Court House, where Lee formally surrendered to Grant, thus officially ending the Civil War. The park here consists of some 27 original structures, and the self-guided tour is exceptionally good. From Richmond it's a leisurely

and scenic drive southwest on U.S. 360 and west on U.S. 460.

DAYS 2 AND 3: FREDERICKS-BURG

For days 2 and 3, proceed north from Richmond up I–95 to Fredericksburg, which has blocks of historic Civil War–era homes and a Confederate Cemetery with the remains of more than 2,000 soldiers. Detour to see the four battlefields at Fredericksburg/Spotsylvania National Military Park.

DAYS 4 AND 5: NORTHERN VIRGINIA

For days 4 and 5, base yourself around Alexandria or Arlington, which puts you close to the key attractions in this area—from Fredericksburg, you reach the area by heading north up I–95. Spend one day touring Manassas National Battlefield Park (aka "Bull Run"), site of two important Confederate victories—it's here that General Thomas Jonathan Jackson earned the nickname "Stonewall," when he and his brigade "stood like a stone wall." On your second day, head to Arlington National Cemetery.

---

ography, and rock collecting. ⊠ 2626 W. Broad St. ☎ 804/474–2667 ⊕ www.c-mor.org ☜ $7 ☉ Tues.–Sat. 9:30–5, Sun. noon–5.

OFF THE BEATEN PATH

Lewis Ginter Botanical Garden. You'll find year-round beauty on this historic property with more than 40 acres of spectacular gardens, dining, and shopping. The classical domed conservatory is the only one of its kind in the Mid-Atlantic, and houses ever-changing displays, tropical plants, and more than 200 orchids in bloom. The rose garden features 80 varieties, with more than 1,800 roses, and a pavilion for special events including wine tastings and evening jazz concerts. A Children's Garden offers a wheelchair-accessible tree house—fun for kids and adults—an Adventure Pathway, sand- and water-play areas, as well as an international village. More than a dozen theme gardens include a Healing Garden, Sunken Garden, Asian Valley, and Victorian Garden. The marvelous display of Christmas lights has become a Richmond tradition. Dining options include the Garden Café and the Tea House, and the shop offers an interesting selection of attractive gifts. ✉ *1800 Lakeside Ave.* ☎ *804/262–9887* ⊕ *www.lewisginter.org* 🎟 *$9* ⊙ *Daily 9–5.*

☪ **Meadow Farm** This living-history complex has programs, exhibits, and
★ interpretive demonstrations of the life and culture on a working farm in 1860. On weekends, costumed interpreters work in the fields, the barns, the doctor's office, the blacksmith forge, and the farmhouse, offering a glimpse into the daily activities of original owner Dr. John Mosby Sheppard and his family. The grounds are open year-round from dawn to dusk, and there are special activities for children. Other scheduled events include storytelling days, Civil War lantern tours, and harvest-picking parties, and best of all, these programs are free. ✉ *3400 Mountain Rd., Glen Allen* ☎ *804/501–5520* ⊕ *www.co.Henrico.va.us/ rec* 🎟 *Free* ⊙ *Tues.–Sun. noon–4; closed 1st 2 wks Jan.*

⑨ **Science Museum of Virginia.** Aerospace, astronomy, electricity, physical sci-
☪ ences, computers, crystals, telecommunications, and the Foucault pen-
★ dulum are among the subjects covered in exhibits here, many of which strongly appeal to children. The biggest spectacle is the Ethyl IMAX Dome and Planetarium, which draws the audience into the movie or astronomy show. The Virginia Tech Solar Decathlon House is a working model of a green home of the future. The museum is in a former train station with a massive dome. ✉ *2500 W. Broad St. 23220* ☎ *804/864– 1400* ⊕ *www.smv.org* 🎟 *Museum $10; IMAX $8.50; IMAX and planetarium $17.50* ⊙ *Mon.–Sat. 9:30–5, Sun. 11:30–5.*

⑪ **Virginia Historical Society Museum of Virginia History.** With 7 million manuscripts and 200,000 books, the library here is a key stop for researchers and genealogists. The visitor-friendly museum mounts regularly changing exhibits and has permanent exhibitions that include an 800-piece collection of Confederate weapons and equipment and "The Story of Virginia, an American Experience," which covers 16,000 years of history and has galleries on topics such as Becoming Confederates and Becoming Equal Virginians. The Society also operates the Virginia House (⇨ *see below*) and sells combination admission tickets for just one dollar more. ✉ *428 North Blvd., at Kensington Ave.* ☎ *804/358–4901* ⊕ *www.vahistorical.org* 🎟 *$5, free on Sun.* ⊙ *Mon.–Sat. 10–5, Sun., galleries only, 1–5. Research library closed Sun.*

⑫ **Virginia Museum of Fine Arts.** The panorama of world art here, spanning
Fodor'sChoice the ages from ancient times to the present, features such important
★ works as the Mellon collections of British Sporting Art and French impressionist and postimpressionist art—including nine original wax sculptures and seven bronzes by Edgar Degas; works by Goya, Renoir, and Monet; classical and Egyptian art; Roman marble statues; and one of the world's leading collections of Indian, Nepalese, and Tibetan art. The museum's most beloved pieces are its five Fabergé eggs. At this writing, the museum is undergoing a major expansion until early 2010, which will double existing gallery space, create a sculpture garden, and enlarge parking. During this time some galleries and collections will be off view: call ahead for specific information. ✉ *200 North Blvd.* ☎ *804/340–1400* ⊕ *www.vmfa.state.va.us* 🎟 *Free, $5 suggested donation* ⊙ *Wed.–Sun. 11–5.*

RICHMOND'S PARKS AND ESTATES

Not far from downtown are mansions and country estates, two with buildings transported from England. Presidents and Confederate leaders are buried in Hollywood Cemetery.

⑭ Agecroft Hall. Built in Lancashire, England, in the 15th century during the reign of King Henry VIII, Agecroft Hall was transported here in 1926. It's one of the finest Tudor manor houses in the United States. Set amid gardens planted with specimens typical of 1580–1640, the house contains an extensive assortment of Tudor and early Stuart art and furniture (1485–1660) as well as collector's items from England and elsewhere in Europe. A Tudor kitchen lets visitors learn about the culinary tools of that age. ⊠ *4305 Sulgrave Rd.* ☎ *804/353–4241* ⊕ *www. agecrofthall.com* 🖵 *$8* ☉ *Tues.–Sat. 10–4, Sun. 12:30–5.*

⑰ Hollywood Cemetery. Designed in a garden style along the banks of the James River, the cemetery requires at least an hour to stroll through the grounds. Many noted Virginians are buried here, including presidents John Tyler and James Monroe; Confederate president Jefferson Davis; generals Fitzhugh Lee, J. E. B. Stuart, and George E. Pickett; the statesman John Randolph; and Matthew Fontaine Maury, a naval scientist. See the pyramid memorial to Confederate soldiers. ⊠ *412 S. Cherry St. Albemarle* ☎ *804/648–8501* 🖵 *Free* ☉ *Mon.–Sat. 7–5, Sun. 8–5.*

⑯ Maymont. On this 100-acre Victorian estate are the lavish Maymont
☾ House museum, a carriage collection, and elaborate Italian and Japa-
★ nese gardens. A true family attraction, Maymont's complex includes the Nature Visitor Center, native wildlife exhibits, and a children's farm. Kids love the pair of playful otters in the aquarium and the waterfall above the Japanese garden. A Bald Eagle Habitat and Raptor Valley are popular additions to the wildlife areas of the park. Take the hop-on, hop-off tram for $3 to see this huge park and its exhibits. Guided mansion tours are on the hour and half hour until 4:30 PM. A café is open for lunch. Carriage rides are also available for $3. ⊠ *2201 Shields Lake Dr.* ☎ *804/358–7166* ⊕ *www.maymont.org* 🖵 *Donation welcome* ☉ *Grounds Apr.–Oct., daily 10–7; Nov.–Mar., daily 10–5. Mansion, nature center, and barn Tues.–Sun. noon–5.*

⑬ Virginia House. Alexander and Virginia Weddell had this 16th-century manor house, originally built on the site of a 12th-century English monastery, shipped across the Atlantic and up the James River in the 1920s. After three years of reconstruction and the planting of lush year-round gardens, the couple realized their dream of a re-created European estate. Alexander Weddell spent a lifetime in the diplomatic service in Mexico, Argentina, and Spain, and the house contains an extensive collection of Spanish and Latin American antiques. The estate (named after Mrs. Weddell, and not the state) passed to the Virginia Historical Society when the Weddells died in a New Year's Day train accident in 1948. Combination tickets including the Virginia Historical Society are only one dollar more. ⊠ *4301 Sulgrave Rd.* ☎ *804/353–4251* ⊕ *www. vahistorical.org* 🖵 *$5* ☉ *Fri. and Sat. 10–4, Sun. 12:30–5; last tour begins 1 hr before closing.*

15 **Wilton.** William Randolph III built this elegant Georgian house in 1753 on what is now the only James River plantation in Richmond. Once 14 mi downriver, the home was moved brick by brick to its current site when industry encroached upon its former location. Wilton is the only house in Virginia with complete floor-to-ceiling panels in every room, and the pastel-painted panels and sunlit alcoves are a large part of its beauty. The home's 1815 period furnishings include the family's original desk bookcase and an original map of Virginia drawn by Thomas Jefferson's father. The Garden Club of Virginia landscaped the terraced lawns that overlook the James River. ✉ *215 S. Wilton Rd.* ☎ *804/282–5936* ⊕ *www.wiltonhousemuseum.org* ✍ *$10* ☉ *Mar.– Jan., Tues.–Fri. 1–4:30, Sat. 10–4:30, Sun. 1:30–4:30.*

WHERE TO EAT

$–$$

EUROPEAN

★

✕ **Café Rustica.** Chef-owner Andy Howell is a star on the Richmond culinary scene. Opened in 2008, his latest success is a European bistro in the heart of downtown. Howell sources his ingredients regionally and whips up European comfort food for breakfast, lunch, and dinner. The roast chicken with vegetables will transport you to the south of France, while the schnitzel is pure Heidelberg. A wine bar and daily cheese plate specials make Café Rustica a great pre- and postevent stop as well. Seating is limited, but they don't take reservations. ✉ *14 E. Main St.* ☎ *804/225–8811* ✍ *Reservations not accepted* ▭ *AE, D, MC, V* ☉ *Closed Mon.*

$–$$

MEDITERRANEAN

✕ **Chez Foushee.** This hip bistro just off Broad Street near Virginia Commonwealth University is a popular lunch and brunch spot, and also has a take-out operation. It's a regular stop on the free GRTC lunch express, with a wide variety of seasonal soups, salads, wraps, and hot entrées. The wine list features French vintages to complement the simple Continental fare. ■ **TIP →** **The restaurant opens for special dinners once a month for the First Friday Art Walk; reservations for these nights are a must.** ✉ *203 N. Foushee St.* ☎ *804/648–3225* ⊕ *www.chezfoushee. com* ▭ *AE, D, MC, V* ☉ *Closed weekends. No dinner except for Art Walk nights.*

$$–$$$

SOUTHERN

✕ **Comfort.** This local favorite is always packed, partly because of its proximity to the National Theater, a popular concert venue. Specializing in Southern comfort food from fried catfish to macaroni and cheese, each entrée is marked with two prices so you can choose either two or three of the seasonal sides like squash casserole and fried okra. If you're looking for small-batch bourbon, Comfort's whiskey bar stocks more than 40 of the best. ✉ *200 W. Broad St.* ☎ *804/780–0004* ⊕ *www. comfortrestaurant.com* ✍ *Reservations not accepted* ▭ *AE, D, MC, V* ☉ *Closed Sun. No lunch Sat.*

¢–$

BARBEQUE

☉

✕ **Halligan Bar & Grill.** This hole-in-the-wall barbecue joint has taken off like a house on fire . . . literally. Owned by a 17-year fire service veteran, and staffed by Henrico County's finest, Halligan is a tribute to firefighters with a 1973 Seagrave fire truck that serves as a backdrop to the bar, authentic helmets doubling as pendant lights, and walls covered with memorabilia. Meat is smoked in-house for hearty Southern favorites like the Carolina-style pulled-pork sandwich, classic chicken, and Texas-style beef brisket. Don't be surprised to hear sirens and see lights set off periodically to salute the customers. ⊠ *3 N. 17th St.* ☎ *804/447–7981* ▭ *AE, D, MC, V.*

$$–$$$ ✕ **The Hard Shell.** This fun and unpretentious restaurant has many fresh
SEAFOOD and local seafood dishes, and those with other tastes can choose from such options as filet mignon and prime rib; even vegetarians are well cared for. Raw bar enthusiasts will be enticed, too, with the option of getting a half pound of steamed shrimp, Dungeness crab legs, snow crab legs, or littleneck clams. From live Maine lobsters to blue-point oysters, this is the place for any kind of seafood you crave. Although the interior is romantic, with exposed brick and dark wood, if the weather's nice, dine alfresco on one of the city's favorite patios. The Sunday brunch is especially attractive, as are the specialty drinks, particularly the martinis. ⊠ *1411 E. Cary St.* ☎ *804/643–2333* ⊕ *www.thehardshell.com* ▭ *AE, D, DC, MC, V* ⊘ *No lunch weekends.*

$$–$$$ ✕ **Julep's.** In the River District, and in the city's oldest commercial build-
AMERICAN ing (1817), Julep's has a spiral staircase joining the upper and lower dining areas. The specialty here is New Southern cuisine, with seasonal lunch and dinner menus that include tempting dishes such as roasted game hen stuffed with a risotto of country ham, green peas, and mushrooms. The wine list is one to linger over. Try not to leave without sampling one of the restaurant's namesakes. ⊠ *1719–21 E. Franklin St.* ☎ *804/377–3968* ⊕ *www.juleps.net* ▭ *AE, MC, V* ⊘ *Closed Sun. No lunch Sat., no dinner Mon.*

$$$$ ✕ **Lemaire.** Named after Etienne Lemaire, Maître d'Hôtel to Thomas
AMERICAN Jefferson from 1794 until the end of his presidency, this is the grandest restaurant in Richmond. Jefferson's tastes included adding light sauces and fresh herbs to dishes prepared with the region's more than abundant supply of ingredients. Today the menu follows the same theme with updated regional Southern cuisine that includes dashes of European classical and American contemporary influences. Typical dishes might include rack of venison, or crispy-skin Chesapeake Bay rockfish, and a tasting menu with wine pairings is available in addition to the regular offerings. ⊠ *Jefferson Hotel, 101 W. Franklin St.* ☎ *804/788–8000* ⊕ *www.jeffersonhotel.com* ▭ *AE, D, DC, MC, V.*

¢–$ ✕ **Millie's Diner.** Be prepared to wait in line to check out Richmond's
AMERICAN favorite diner. Locals often bring lawn chairs and games to pass the time while waiting for their chance to try the upscale, contemporary selections at this quirky eatery. This is the place for brunch for everything from huevos rancheros to the signature Devil's Mess kitchen-sink omelet. Although the vibe is straight out of the '50s, with personal jukeboxes in every booth, the food is strictly 21st century, with contemporary takes on Southern classics, as well as global offerings like Thai spicy shrimp. Try the mac 'n cheese with oyster mushrooms, asparagus, and foie gras butter or the pan-seared venison with black grapes and Yorkshire pudding. The dinner menu changes every three weeks, although the most popular lunch and breakfast offerings are always available. ⊠ *2603 E. Main St.* ☎ *804/643–5512* ⚠ *Reservations not accepted* ▭ *AE, D, MC, V* ⊘ *Closed Mon.*

WHERE TO STAY

$$–$$$ ★ 🏨 **Berkeley Hotel.** Although built in the style of the century-old warehouses and buildings that surround it, this boutique hotel dates from 1988. Those seeking extra space and luxury should opt for the Governor's Suite, which has a luxurious king bed, a private terrace, and a living room with panoramic views over the historic Shockoe Slip area. Norman guest rooms have four-poster beds and traditional furnishings. Guests staying here get free entry to the YMCA health and fitness facilities. **Pros:** complimentary car service; steps from several restaurants and shops. **Cons:** extremely busy street; limited parking. ✉ *1200 E. Cary St.* ☎ *804/780–1300 or 888/780–4422* ⊕ *www.berkeleyhotel.com* 🛏 *54 rooms, 1 suite* ♿ *In-room: Wi-Fi. In-hotel: restaurant, bar, gym, concierge, laundry service, parking (fee), no-smoking rooms* ▭ *AE, D, DC, MC, V.*

$–$$ ★ 🏨 **Commonwealth Park Suites Hotel.** When it was the Rueger back in 1846, this hotel was a bootlegging saloon with rooms for its clientele. After a fire during the Civil War it fell into disrepair for 50 years. It was rebuilt in 1912, and after several renovations it now has 59 luxurious rooms and suites. Because the Commonwealth is across from the Capitol, some senators and representatives make this their home when the state legislature is in session. Maxine's Café is open for breakfast, lunch, and dinner. **Pros:** across the street from Capitol and visitor center; large suites for extended stays. **Cons:** limited food service on-site. ✉ *901 Bank St.* ☎ *804/343–7300 or 888/343–7301* 🖷 *804/343–1025* 🛏 *10 rooms, 49 suites* ♿ *In-room: Ethernet. In-hotel: restaurant, laundry service, no-smoking rooms* ▭ *AE, D, DC, MC, V.*

$$$ Fodor's Choice ★ 🏨 **Jefferson Hotel.** A 70-foot-high ceiling with a stained-glass skylight and 10 of the original Louis Comfort Tiffany stained-glass windows, rich tapestries, and replicas of traditional Victorian furniture make this the most elegant hotel in Richmond. The Palm Court Lobby is home to Edward Valentine's full-size statue of the president and to a magnificent sweeping staircase reminiscent of the one in *Gone With the Wind*. The rooms are done in a total of 57 different styles, and the 1,550-square-foot Presidential Suite has its own private balcony. Since the hotel is older, the rooms are somewhat small, but exquisitely appointed with period furnishings and top-of-the-line amenities including Frette linens and robes. **Pros:** luxury lodging; pet-friendly; excellent concierge service. **Cons:** standard rooms are small; some older amenities. ✉ *101 W. Franklin St., at Adams St.* ☎ *804/788–8000 or 800/424–8014* ⊕ *www. jeffersonhotel.com* 🛏 *228 rooms, 36 suites* ♿ *In-hotel: 2 restaurants, room service, bar, pool, gym* ▭ *AE, D, DC, MC, V.*

$–$$ 🏨 **Omni Richmond.** Part of the historic Shockoe Slip area, this hotel looks classically Southern. The rooms on the club level come with private concierge service and access to a club lounge; Get Fit rooms come with a portable treadmill. Many restaurants and stores are in the James Center itself, and just outside is Shockoe Slip. If you stay here, you have access to the nearby Capital Club health and fitness facilities. **Pros:** close to restaurants and shopping. **Cons:** limited parking. ✉ *James Center, 100 S. 12th St.* ☎ *804/344–7000* ⊕ *www.omnihotels.com* 🛏 *353 rooms, 8 suites* ♿ *In-room: Wi-Fi. In-hotel: 2 restaurants, room service, bar, pool, gym, parking (fee), no-smoking rooms* ▭ *AE, D, DC, MC, V.*

NIGHTLIFE AND THE ARTS

ART VENUES **The National Theater** (✉*708 E. Broad St.* ☎*804/612–1900* ⊕*www.nationalva.com*), a locally owned venue, hosts everything from the Richmond Symphony to the Black Crowes, with a full schedule throughout the year.

The **Richmond Coliseum** (✉*601 E. Leigh St.* ☎*804/780–4956* ⊕*www.richmondcoliseum.net*) has been a Richmond institution since the early 1970s. With 11,330 permanent seats, and nearly 2,000 more for concerts, it hosts top entertainers and artists, the Ringling Brothers circus, Richmond Riverdogs hockey team, wrestling, and other large events.

THEATER **Carpenter Center** (✉*600 E. Grace St.* ☎*804/225–9000* ⊕*www.carpentercenter.org*), a restored 1928 motion-picture palace, is now a performing-arts center that mounts opera, traveling shows, symphonic music, and ballet. **Landmark Theatre** (✉*6 N. Laurel St.* ☎*804/646–4213*) was built in an extremely elaborate style with towering minarets and desert murals. Just west of downtown, the Landmark is known for its excellent acoustics and has the largest permanent proscenium stage on the East Coast. It hosts road versions of Broadway shows, symphony performances, ballet, children's theater, concerts, and fashion shows.

BARS From the college bars in the Fan District to upscale martini and wine bars, Richmond has a vibrant nightlife. One local favorite is **Havana 59** (✉*16 N. 7th St.* ☎*804/780–2822* ⊕*www.havana59.net*) in Shockoe Bottom. Styled after the Cuban clubs that gave Havana the nickname "the Paris of the '50s," this multilevel club is decked out in palm trees and twinkling white lights. Latin music, traditional mojitos, and a cigar-friendly atmosphere keep Havana hopping into the wee hours.

SPORTS AND THE OUTDOORS

GOLF In Richmond aficionados tee off most of the year. The area has 24 golf courses open to the public—the **Virginia State Golf Association** (⊕*www.vsga.org*) has a good handle on them all; its Web site even allows you to book tee times online.

RAFTING Richmond is the only city within the United States that has rafting within its city limits. **Richmond Raft** (☎*804/222–7238 or 800/222–7238* ⊕ *www.richmondraft.com*) conducts white-water rafting trips through the city on the James River (Class III and IV rapids), as well as float trips from March through November.

SHOPPING

Carytown is a nine-block shopping-and-entertainment district (✉*West end of Cary St. from the Powhite Pkwy. to Boulevard* ⊕*www.carytown.org*). More than 300 shops and more than 25 restaurants are packed into this district. Parking is scarce on weekends. The 17th Street **Farmers' Market** (✉*100 N. 17th St., at Main St.* ⊕*www.17thstreetfarmersmarket.com*), beside the old Main Street Station, has been a public gathering place since 1737. Market days are Thursday, Saturday, and Sunday. **Shockoe Slip** (✉*E. Cary St. between 12th and 15th Sts.*), a neighborhood of tobacco warehouses during the 18th and 19th centuries, has boutiques, antiques stores, and international furniture stores like the multilevel, supermodern La Difference.

FREDERICKSBURG

57 mi north of Richmond via I–95; 54 mi southwest of Washington, D.C., via I–95.

Halfway between Richmond and Washington, near the falls of the Rappahannock River, Fredericksburg is a popular destination for history buffs.

Although its site was visited by explorer Captain John Smith as early as 1608, Fredericksburg wasn't founded until 1728. Established as a frontier port to serve nearby tobacco farmers and iron miners, Fredericksburg was at one point the 10th largest port in the colonies.

George Washington knew Fredericksburg well, having grown up just across the Rappahannock on Ferry Farm. The myths about chopping down a cherry tree and throwing a coin (actually a rock) across the Rappahannock (later confused with the Potomac) refer to this period of his life.

Fredericksburg prospered in the decades after independence. When the Civil War broke out, it became the linchpin of the Confederate defense of Richmond and therefore the target of Union assaults. In December 1862, Union forces attacked the town in what was to be the first of four major battles fought in and around Fredericksburg. In the battle of Sunken Road, Confederate defenders sheltered by a stone wall at the base of Marye's Heights mowed down thousands of Union soldiers who charged across the fields.

At Chancellorsville in April 1863, General Robert E. Lee led 60,000 troops to a brilliant victory over a much larger Union force of 134,000, and this resulted in Lee's invasion of Pennsylvania. The following year, Grant's troops battled Lee's Confederates through the Wilderness, a region of dense thickets and overgrowth south of the Rapidan River, then fought them again at Spotsylvania. Although neither side was victorious, Grant continued heading his troops toward the Confederate capital of Richmond.

Fredericksburg's cemeteries hold the remains of 17,000 soldiers from both sides. Miraculously, despite heavy bombardment and house-to-house fighting, much of the city remained intact.

Today, the charming, historic town appeals to commuters fleeing the Washington, D.C., area for kinder, less-expensive environs. Tourists aren't scarce either, and not just to visit the historical sights. These days Fredericksburg has reinvented itself as a cute small town chock-a-block with boutiques and antiques and specialty stores, as well as a lively selection of small cafés and restaurants.

GETTING HERE AND AROUND

By car, Fredericksburg is easily accessible from Interstate 95 or Route 1, about an hour north of Richmond or south of Washington, D.C. The unmanned Fredericksburg train station is two blocks from the historic district.

TOURS

Trolley Tours of Fredericksburg runs a 75-minute narrated tour of Fredericksburg's most important sights. Tours cost $17 and leave from the visitor center.

The tour coordinator at the Fredericksburg Visitor Center can arrange a group walking tour of the city as well as of battlefields and other historic sites to which you can drive. Reservations are required. The Fredericksburg Department of Tourism (in the visitor center) publishes a booklet that includes a short history of Fredericksburg and a self-guided tour covering 29 sights.

ESSENTIALS

Tours Trolley Tours of Fredericksburg (☎ *540/898–0737* ⊕ *www.fredericksburgtrolley.com).*

EXPLORING
DOWNTOWN

Fredericksburg, a modern commercial town, includes a 40-block National Historic District with more than 350 original 18th- and 19th-century buildings. No play-acting here—residents live in the historic homes and work in the stores, many of which sell antiques. A walking tour through the town proper takes three to four hours; battlefield tours will take at least that long.

6 Confederate Cemetery. This cemetery contains the remains of more than 2,000 soldiers (most of them unknown) as well as the graves of generals Dabney Maury, Seth Barton, Carter Stevenson, Daniel Ruggles, Henry Sibley, and Abner Perrin. ⊠ *1100 Washington Ave., near Amelia St., Historic District* ⊙ *Daily dawn–dusk.*

1 Fredericksburg Visitor Center. Beyond the usual booklets, pamphlets, and maps, this visitor center offers a money-saving pass to city attractions ($32 for entry to nine sights including Washington's boyhood home, a better than 40% discount over individual admission prices). Before your tour, you may want to see the center's 10-minute orientation slide show. The center building itself was constructed in 1824 as a residence and confectionery; during the Civil War it was used as a prison. ⊠ *706 Caroline St., Historic District* ☎ *540/373–1776 or 800/678–4748* ⊕ *www.visitfred.com* ⊙ *Daily 9–5; hrs extended in summer.*

7 Gari Melchers Home and Studio. The last owner of this 1790s Georgian-style house was American artist Gari Melchers, who chaired the Smithsonian Commission to establish the National Gallery of Art in Washington. His wife, Corinne, deeded the 27-acre estate and its collections to Virginia. The home is now a public museum and a Virginia National Historic Landmark administered by the University of Mary Washington. You can take a one-hour tour of the spacious house, which is furnished with a rich collection of the owners' antiques. Galleries in the stone studio, built by the Melchers in 1924, house the largest repository of the artist's work. An orientation movie is shown in the reception area, which was once the carriage house. ⊠ *224 Washington St.* ☎ *540/654–1015* ⊕ *www.garimelchers.org* ⊠ *$10* ⊙ *Mon.–Sun. 10–5.*

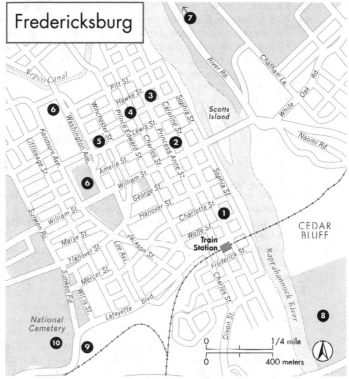

11

NEED A BREAK?

Goolrick's Pharmacy (⊠ *901 Caroline St., Historic District* ☎ *540/373-9878*) opened in 1869 and has been in its present location since the late 1890s. In 1912 the soda fountain was installed, and it is now the oldest operating in the United States. In addition to malts and egg creams (made of seltzer, milk, and syrup, but not egg or cream), Goolrick's serves light meals weekdays 8:30–7 and Saturday 8:30–6.

2 **Hugh Mercer Apothecary Shop.** Offering a close-up view of 18th- and 19th-century medical instruments and procedures, the apothecary was established in 1761, and demonstrates the work of Dr. Mercer, a Scotsman who served as a brigadier general of the Continental Army (he was killed at the Battle of Princeton). Dr. Mercer may have been more careful than other Colonial physicians, but his methods might still make you cringe. A costumed hostess explicitly describes amputations and cataract operations before the discovery of anesthetics. You can also hear about therapeutic bleeding, see the gruesome devices used in Colonial dentistry, and watch a demonstration of leeching. ⊠ *1020 Caroline St., at Amelia St., Historic District* ☎ *540/373-3362* ☞ *$5* ☉ *Mar.–Nov., Mon.–Sat. 9–5, Sun. 11–5; Dec.–Feb., Mon.–Sat. 10–4, Sun. noon–4.*

⑤ Kenmore. Named Kenmore by a later owner, this house was built in 1775
Fodor's Choice on a 1,300-acre plantation owned by Colonel Fielding Lewis, a patriot,
★ merchant, and brother-in-law of George Washington. Lewis sacrificed
his fortune to operate a gun factory and otherwise supply General
Washington's forces during the Revolutionary War. As a result, his debts
forced his widow to sell the home following his death. The outstanding plaster moldings in the ceilings and over the fireplace in the dining
room are even more ornate than those at Mount Vernon. It's believed
that the artisan responsible for them worked frequently in both homes,
though his name is unknown, possibly because he was an indentured
servant. A recent multiyear renovation has returned the grand house to
its original state. It is interesting to note that the walls vary in thickness:
36 inches in the basement, 24 inches on the ground floor, and 18 inches
upstairs. Guided 45-minute architectural tours of the home are conducted by docents; the subterranean Crowningshield Museum on the
grounds displays Kenmore's collection of fine Virginia-made furniture
and family portraits as well as changing exhibits on Fredericksburg life.
✉ *1201 Washington Ave., Historic District* ☎ *540/373–3381* ⊕ *www.
kenmore.org* 🖾 *$8* ☉ *Jan.–July, daily 10–5; Aug.–Dec, daily 10–4; last
tour begins at 4:15.*

④ Mary Washington House. George purchased a three-room cottage for his
★ mother in 1772 for £225, renovated it, and more than doubled its size
with additions. She spent the last 17 years of her life here, tending the
garden where her original boxwoods still flourish today, and where
many a bride and groom now exchange their vows. The home has
been a museum since 1930. Inside, displays include Mrs. Washington's
"best dressing glass," a silver-over-tin mirror in a Chippendale frame;
her teapot; Washington family dinnerware; and period furniture. The
kitchen, in a rather lopsided wooden house in the pretty gardens, and
its spit are original. Tours begin on the back porch with a history of the
house. ✉ *1200 Charles St., Historic District* ☎ *540/373–1569* ⊕ *www.
apva.org/marywashingtonhouse* 🖾 *$5* ☉ *Mar.–Nov., Mon.–Sat. 9–5,
Sun. 11–5; Dec.–Feb., Mon.–Sat. 10–4, Sun. noon–4.*

③ Rising Sun Tavern. In 1760 George Washington's brother Charles built
as his home what later became the Rising Sun Tavern, a watering hole
for such patriots as the Lee brothers (the only siblings to sign the Declaration of Independence); Patrick Henry, the five-term governor of
Virginia who said, "Give me liberty or give me death"; and future
presidents Washington and Jefferson. Two male indentured servants
and a "wench" in period costume lead a tour without stepping out
of character. From them, you hear how travelers slept and what they
ate and drank at this busy institution. ✉ *1304 Caroline St., Historic District* ☎ *540/371–1494* ⊕ *www.apva.org/risingsuntavern* 🖾 *$5*
☉ *Mar.–Nov., Mon.–Sat. 9–5, Sun. 11–5; Dec.–Feb., Mon.–Sat. 10–4,
Sun. noon–4.*

AROUND FREDERICKSBURG

Surrounding the town of Fredericksburg are historic sites and gorgeous
vistas where, in 1862, Union forces once stood. Today you see only
the lively Rappahannock and beautiful homes on a lovely drive across
the river.

11

⑨ **Fredericksburg/Spotsylvania National Military Park.** The 9,000-acre park
Fodor's Choice actually includes four battlefields and four historic buildings. At the
★ Fredericksburg and Chancellorsville visitor centers you can learn about
the area's role in the Civil War by watching a 22-minute film ($2) and
viewing displays of soldiers' art and battlefield relics. In season, park
rangers lead walking tours. The centers offer recorded tours ($4.95 rent-
al, $7.50 purchase) and maps that show how to reach the battlefields,
Chancellorsville (where General Stonewall Jackson was mistakenly shot
by his own troops), and Spotsylvania Court House battlefields—all
within 15 mi of Fredericksburg.

Just outside the Fredericksburg Battlefield Visitor Center is Sunken
Road, where on December 13, 1862, the Confederates achieved a
resounding victory over Union forces attacking across the Rappahannock (there were 18,000 casualties on both sides). Much of the stone
wall that protected Lee's infantrymen is now a re-creation, but 100
yards from the visitor center part of the original wall overlooks the
statue *The Angel of Marye's Heights,* by Felix de Weldon (sculptor of
the famous *Marine Corps War Memorial* statue in Arlington). This
memorial honors Sergeant Richard Kirkland, a South Carolinian who
risked his life to bring water to wounded foes; he later died at the
Battle of Chickamauga. ⊠*Fredericksburg Battlefield Visitor Center,
1013 Lafayette Blvd. at Sunken Rd., Historic District* ☎*540/373–
6122* ⊠*Chancellorsville Battlefield Visitor Center, Rte. 3 W, Plank
Rd., Chancellorsville* ☎*540/786–2880* ⊕*www.nps.gov/frsp* ☜*Free*
⊗ *Visitor centers daily 9–5 with extended hrs in summer; walking tours
on a seasonal basis dawn–dusk.*

⑧ **George Washington's Ferry Farm.** If it hadn't been for the outcries of his-
ⓒ torians and citizens, a Wal-Mart would have been built on this site, the
★ boyhood home of our first president. The land was saved by the George
Washington's Fredericksburg Foundation, and the discount store found
a location farther out on the same road. Recently, archaeologists have
uncovered the original fireplaces and four cellars from the house where
Washington was raised, as well as thousands of new artifacts. Ferry
Farm, which once consisted of 600 acres, is across the Rappahannock
River from downtown Fredericksburg and was the site of a ferry crossing. Living here from age 6 to 19, Washington received his formal edu-
cation and taught himself surveying while *not* chopping a cherry tree
or throwing a coin across the Rappahannock—legends concocted by
Parson Weems. The mainly archaeological site also has an exhibit on
"George Washington: Boy Before Legend." The ongoing excavations
include a summer program for children and adults, "Digging for Young
George." Ferry Farm became a major artillery base and river-crossing
site for Union forces during the Battle of Fredericksburg. ⊠*Rte. 3
E, 268 Kings Hwy., at Ferry Rd., Fredericksburg* ☎*540/370–0732*
⊕*www.kenmore.org* ☜*$5* ⊗ *Daily 10–5; last tour begins at 4:15.*

⑩ **National Cemetery.** The National Cemetery is the final resting place of
15,000 Union dead, most of whom have not been identified. ⊠*Lafayette Blvd. at Sunken Rd., Historic District* ☎*540/373–6122* ⊗*Daily
dawn–dusk.*

WHERE TO EAT

$$$–$$$$ ✗**Augustine's at Fredericksburg Square.** Named after Augustine Washing-
AMERICAN ton, George's father, who owned most of the property along Caroline
Street, the 1837 mansion is the place to go in Fredericksburg for formal
dining. The well-spaced tables are set in the traditional European style,
including the use of gold charger plates and service by white-gloved
waiters. The creative and attractively presented dishes, prepared in a
New American style, might include saffron-braised angler fish and Vir-
ginia pheasant. A five-course prix-fixe dinner is offered for $87. The
wine list is not only extensive in its selections but also creatively pre-
sented. ✉ *525 Caroline St.* ☎ *540/310–0063* ⊕ *www.augustinesrest.
com* ▭ *AE, D, MC, V* ⊘ *Closed Sun. and Mon. No lunch.*

$$–$$$ ✗**Claiborne's.** On the walls of this swank eatery in the 1910-era Fred-
SOUTHERN ericksburg train station are historic train photographs. The restaurant,
decorated in dark green and navy with mahogany-and-brass bars,
specializes in Low Country Southern dishes, including crawfish, grits,
and collard greens. Accompanying the steaks, chops, and seafood are
ample vegetable side dishes served family style. ✉ *200 Lafayette Blvd.,
Historic District* ☎ *540/371–7080* ⊕ *www.clairbornesrestaurant.com*
▭ *AE, MC, V.*

$–$$ ✗**La Petite Auberge.** Housed in a pre–Civil War brick general store, this
FRENCH white-tablecloth restaurant actually has three dining rooms decorated
like a French garden, with numerous paintings by local artists for sale.
For over two decades, this has been a Fredericksburg favorite for its
consistently good food and service. The interesting menu changes with
the seasons, and the chef sources his products locally. Specialties like
house-cut beef, French onion soup, and seafood are all served with a
Continental accent. A fixed-price ($17) four-course dinner is served
from 5:30 to 7 Monday through Thursday. ✉ *311 William St., Historic
District* ☎ *540/371–2727* ▭ *AE, D, MC, V* ⊘ *Closed Sun.*

¢–$ ✗**Sammy T's.** Vegetarian dishes, healthful foods, and homemade soups
AMERICAN and breads share the menu with hamburgers, oyster and crab-cake sandwiches, and dinner platters at this unpretentious place. Eclectic vegetarian and vegan offerings from tzatziki and tabbouleh to black-bean cakes
and veggie chili make this the go-to place for noncarnivores, but it's the
list of more than 20 sandwiches and wraps that make Sammy T's a hot
spot for the in-town lunch crowd. The bar is stocked with nearly 50
brands of beer. There's a separate no-smoking section around the corner,
but a tin ceiling, high wooden booths, and wooden ceiling fans make
the main dining room much chummier. ✉ *801 Caroline St., Historic
District* ☎ *540/371–2008* ⊕ *www.sammyts.com* ▭ *AE, D, MC, V.*

$–$$ ✗**Smythe's Cottage & Tavern.** Entering this cozy dining room in a black-
AMERICAN smith's house built in the early 1800s is like taking a step back in time,
and may remind you of the Colonial taverns in Williamsburg. The lunch
and dinner menus are classic Virginia: seafood pie, quail, stuffed flounder, peanut soup, and Smithfield ham biscuits. The wine list features
Virginia vintages as well. Smythe's is in the heart of the historic district,
making it a convenient stop for lunch. ✉ *303 Fauquier St., Historic
District* ☎ *540/373–1645* ▭ *MC, V* ⊘ *Closed Tues.*

The Historic Triangle and Virginia Beach > **499**

11

WHERE TO STAY

$$ 🏨**Homewood Suites.** In a newly developed area locals call the "campus," this new all-suites hotel is a sister property to the Hampton Inn, and in addition to one-bedroom suites, features the only two-bedroom suites in Fredericksburg. A sumptuous complimentary breakfast in the lobby lounge is included in the rate, as is an afternoon happy hour. The spacious suites are like having your own well-appointed apartment making them perfect for families or extended stays since they have full kitchens that include dishes and dishwashers. **Pros:** largest suites in town; free breakfast and happy hour included. **Cons:** not close to historic attractions; 10-minute drive to town. ✉*1040 Hospitality La.* ☎*540/786–9700* ⊕*www.homewoodsuites.com* ↩*124 suites* ☐*Inhotel: pool, gym, public Wi-Fi* ▭*AE, D, DC, MC, V.*

$–$$ 🏨**Kenmore Inn.** This 18th-century historic home is easily recognizable by its magnificent and inviting front porch. There are two types of rooms. The deluxe ones, in the original part of the house, have working fireplaces and canopy beds; the slightly smaller standard rooms have Colonial furnishings. The English pub, with its Mahogany Horseshoe Bar, serves lighter dishes and imported draft beer; it's open Tuesday to Sunday evenings. **Pros:** charming decor; restaurant on-site; high-speed Internet. **Cons:** limited availability; some rooms are small. ✉*1200 Princess Anne St., Historic District* ☎*540/371–7622* ⊕*www.kenmoreinn. com* ↩*9 rooms* ☐*In-room: no TV (some), Wi-Fi. In-hotel: restaurant, bar* ▭*AE, D, DC, MC, V* ⓘⒸⓅ.

$$ 🏨**Richard Johnston Inn.** This elegant B&B was constructed in 1793 and
★ served as the home of Richard Johnston, mayor of Fredericksburg from March 1809 to March 1810. Guest rooms are decorated with period antiques and reproductions, and have working fireplaces, along with high-speed wireless and the purely Southern amenity of complimentary cream sherry. The aroma of freshly baked breads and muffins entices you to breakfast in the large Federal-style dining room, where the table is set with fine china, silver, and linens. The inn is just across from the visitor center and two blocks from the train station. Ample private parking is behind the inn. **Pros:** Wi-Fi in a historic setting; massage therapy; true Southern experience. **Cons:** advance deposit required; expensive. ✉*711 Caroline St., Historic District* ☎*540/899–7606 or 877/557–0770* ⊕*www.therichardjohnstoninn.com* ↩*7 rooms, 2 suites* ☐*In-room: VCR, Wi-Fi. In-hotel: parking (no fee), no-smoking rooms* ▭*AE, MC, V* ⓘⒸⓅ.

THE HISTORIC TRIANGLE AND VIRGINIA BEACH

Virginia's number one tourist attraction has you pinching yourself to make sure you haven't entered a time machine. You'll believe you're in another century, and you really are. Colonial Williamsburg, a careful, on-the-spot restoration of the former Virginia capital, gives you the chance to walk into the 18th century and see how earlier Americans lived. A ticket or pass (price is based on the number of attractions and the duration of visit) admits the holder to sites in the restored area,

but it costs nothing just to walk around and absorb the atmosphere.
■TIP→Although admission is free to amble around the historic district, you will miss some of the most interesting aspects of Williamsburg by not entering the buildings or seeing the excellent programs staged by skilled reenactors. It is well worth the price of admission.

Williamsburg anchors three elements of Colonial National Historical Park. To keep the chronology straight, visit Virginia's "Historic Triangle," in the order of Jamestown, Williamsburg, and then Yorktown. Historic Jamestowne was the location of the first permanent English settlement in North America. Yorktown was the site of the final major battle in the American Revolutionary War. Close by are Jamestown Settlement and the excellent Yorktown Victory Center, both run by the Jamestown-Yorktown Foundation. Like Colonial Williamsburg, these two sites re-create the buildings and activities of the 18th century, using interpreters in period dress.

To see another waterfront area of Virginia, head to the Eastern shore. The Virginia Beach resort area attracts families and sun-seekers coming to enjoy the long boardwalk and miles of Atlantic beaches.

JAMESTOWN

9 mi southwest of Colonial Williamsburg via Colonial Pkwy.

The desperate strivings of Englishmen to stay alive and establish a foothold in the New World become evident when visiting Jamestown, the beginning of English settlement in this country. Its two major sights are places to explore the early relationship between the English and Native Virginia Indians.

GETTING HERE AND AROUND

From April to October, the Jamestown Area Shuttle provides loop service around the Jamestown area every 30 minutes between Historic Jamestowne, the Jamestown Settlement, and the Jamestown Glasshouse (part of Historic Jamestowne).

FERRY TRAVEL   The Jamestown–Scotland Ferry began providing service across the James River in 1925. This is the best free ride in Virginia; it takes you back 400 years to when the colonists first spied the site where they founded Jamestown. The ferry leaves the Jamestown dock about every hour on the half hour, leaving the opposite port, Scotland, on the hour 24 hours a day. Wait times vary from 15 to 30 minutes (sometimes longer in summer). Cars, campers, trucks, and motorcycles are allowed on the ferry. Foot passengers may ride, but there's nowhere to park at the ferry landing.

ESSENTIALS

Ferry Information Jamestown–Scotland Ferry (✉ *2317 Jamestown Rd., Rte. 31* ☎ *757/222–6100* ⊕ *www.virginiadot.org/comtravel/ferry-jamestown.asp*).

Visitor Information Jamestown Settlement and Yorktown Victory Center (☎ *757/253–4838 or 888/593–4682* ⊕ *www.historyisfun.org*).

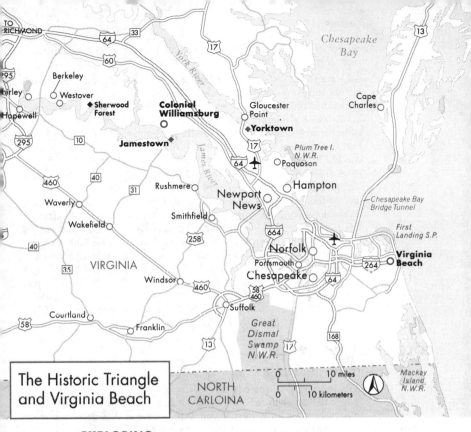

The Historic Triangle
and Virginia Beach

EXPLORING

Ⓒ **Historic Jamestowne,** an island originally separated from the mainland

Fodor's Choice by a narrow isthmus, was the site of the first permanent English settle-

★ ment in North America (1607) and the capital of Virginia until 1699. May 13, 2007, marked the 400th anniversary of its founding. The only standing structure is the ruin of a church tower from the 1640s, now part of the Memorial Church built in 1907; the markers within indicate the original church's foundations.

Near the entrance to the park, you can stop at the reconstructed Glass-house to observe a demonstration of glassblowing, an unsuccessful business venture of the early colonists. The products of today are for sale in a gift shop. Archaeological discoveries from the site are showcased at the Archaearium, and you can also observe digs on-site.

A visitor center near the main parking lot tells the history of Jamestown and the Virginia Indians, Europeans, and African peoples who lived here. Ranger-guided tours, held daily, explore many different events in Jamestown's history. Living-history programs are presented daily in summer and on weekends in spring and autumn.

A 5-mi or 8-mi nature drive that rings the island is posted with informative signs and paintings. ✉ *Off Colonial Pkwy.* ☎ 757/898–2410 🖅 $8;

combined entry to both Jamestowne and Yorktown, $10 ⊙ *Daily 9–5; gates close at 4:30.*

Ⓒ Adjacent to but distinct from Historic Jamestowne is a mainland living-
FodorsChoice history museum called **Jamestown Settlement.** The site marries 40,000
★ square feet of indoor facilities (completed in 2006) with outdoor replicas of the early James Fort, the three ships that brought the founding
colonists from England, and a Powhatan Indian village. Within James
Fort, interpreters in costume cook, forge metal, and describe what life
was like living under thatch roofs and between walls of wattle and daub
(stick framework covered with mud plaster). In the Powhatan Indian
Village you can enter a *yehakin* (house) and see buckskin-costumed
interpreters cultivate a garden and make tools. At the pier are full-scale
reproductions of the ships in which the settlers arrived: *Godspeed,
Discovery,* and *Susan Constant.* The new *Godspeed,* commissioned
in 2006, sails to commemorative events along the East Coast; all the
vessels are seaworthy. You may climb aboard the *Susan Constant* and
find out more from the sailor-interpreters. Spring and fall bring lots of
school groups, so it's best to arrive after 2 PM. ⊠ *Rte. 31 off Colonial
Pkwy.* ☎ *757/253–4838 or 888/593–4682* ⊕ *www.historyisfun.org*
🎟 *$13.50; combination ticket with Yorktown Victory Center $19.25*
⊙ *June 15–Aug. 15, daily 9–6; Aug. 16–June 14, daily 9–5.*

COLONIAL WILLIAMSBURG

51 mi southeast of Richmond via I–64.

Williamsburg was the capital of Virginia from 1699 to 1780, after
Jamestown and before Richmond. Williamsburg hasn't been politically
Ⓒ important for a long time, but now that **Colonial Williamsburg** is there
FodorsChoice to represent it in its era of glory, it's a jewel of the commonwealth.
★ Outside the restored area is a modern city with plenty of dining and
lodging options and attractions, including outlet shops and a large
water park.

Colonial Williamsburg sells a number of all-inclusive tickets that cost
more than a $34 one-day pass. The Freedom Pass ($59) allows you to
visit for one full year. The Independence Pass ($72), also valid for a
year, includes all the benefits of the Freedom Pass as well as admission
to all special events and special discounts.

DISCOUNTS AND DEALS

The America's Historic Triangle Vacation Package includes unlimited
visits to all five attractions—Colonial Williamsburg, Jamestown Settlement and Historic Jamestowne, Yorktown Victory Center and Yorktown Battlefield—in the Historic Triangle. There is also an America's
Historic Triangle Ticket that does not include lodging. For information
on the vacation package, visit ⊕ *www.AmericasHistoricTriangle.com* or
call ☎ *800/495–8804.* For information about America's Historic Triangle Ticket visit ⊕ *www.historyisfun.org/Vacation-Packages.htm.*

GETTING HERE AND AROUND

CAR TRAVEL Parking near the Colonial Williamsburg historic area can be difficult during summer months and special events. It's best to park at the visitor center and ride the shuttle to the park. The parking lot behind the Merchants Square shopping area is a good bet if you're planning a short visit or going out to eat around the area.

All vehicular traffic is prohibited within Colonial Williamsburg to preserve the illusion. Shuttle buses run continuously from 9 AM to 10 PM to and from the visitor center.

BIKE TRAVEL Biking around Colonial Williamsburg is a wonderful way to explore its 301 acres. Rental bikes are available for those staying at the Williamsburg Inn, Williamsburg Lodge, or Colonial Houses. Bikesmith, in Williamsburg, rents bikes and has especially reasonable multiday rental prices. Bikes Unlimited, close to the Williamsburg Transportation Center, also rents bikes.

TOURS

Hour-long guided walking tours of the historic area depart from the Greenhow Lumber House daily from 9 to 5. Reservations should be made on the day of the tour at the Lumber House and can be made only by those with tickets to Colonial Williamsburg. "The Original Ghosts of Williamsburg" Candlelight Tour is based on the book of the same name by L. B. Taylor Jr. The tour is offered every evening at 8 (there's also an 8:45 tour June–August). The 1¼-hour, lantern-lighted guided tour through historic Williamsburg costs $8.50. Interpreters well versed in Williamsburg and Colonial history are available to lead groups on tours of the historic area. Carriage and wagon rides are available daily, weather permitting. General ticket holders may purchase tickets on the day of the ride at the Lumber House. ■TIP➔For walking tours, be sure to park at the visitor center, as cars are not permitted on Duke of Gloucester Street.

Lanthorn Tours take you on an evening walking tour of trade shops where jewelry and other products are made in 18th-century style. The separate ticket required for this program may be purchased at the visitor center or from the Greenhow Lumber House.

Three self-guided audio tours of Colonial Williamsburg can be rented at the Colonial Williamsburg Visitor Center: "Highlights of the Historic Area," "Reading the Restoration Architecture," and "Voices of the Revolution." Wander at your own pace; when you stop in front of a numbered location, enter the number into the player and hear all about it. Each tape is about 45 minutes and costs $6 for ticketed guests or $15 for those without tickets.

ESSENTIALS

Bike Rentals Bikesmith (✉ 515 York St. ☎ 757/229–9858). **Bikes Unlimited** (✉ 141 Monticello Ave. in the Williamsburg shopping area ☎ 757/229–4620).

Walking Tours Greenhow Lumber House (✉ Duke of Gloucester St. ☎ 757/220–7645 or 800/447–8679). **Interpreters** (☎ 800/228–8878). **"The Original Ghosts of Williamsburg" Candlelight Tour** (☎ 757/253–1058).

Visitor Information Colonial Williamsburg Dining and Lodging Reservations (☎ *800/447-8679*). Colonial Williamsburg Visitor Center (⌂ *102 Visitor Center Dr., Williamsburg* ☎ *800/246-2099* or *757/229-1000* ⊕ *www. history.org* or *www.colonialwilliamsburg.org*). Greater Williamsburg Chamber and Tourism Alliance (⊠ *421 N. Boundary St., Box 3495* ☎ *757/229-6511* or *800/368-6511* ⊕ *www.williamsburgcc.com*).

EXPLORING

TOP ATTRACTIONS

The lovely brick Episcopal **Bruton Parish Church** has served continuously as a house of worship since it was built in 1715. One of its 20th-century pastors, W. A. R. Goodwin, provided the impetus for Williamsburg's restoration. The church tower, topped by a beige wooden steeple, was added in 1769; during the Revolution its bell served as the local "liberty bell," rung to summon people for announcements. The stone baptismal font is believed to have come from an older Jamestown church. Many local eminences, including one royal governor, are interred in the graveyard. The fully operational church is open to the public; contributions are accepted. ⊠ *Duke of Gloucester St. west of Palace St.* ∎ TIP➔Check **Williamsburg's weekly program listing for free candlelight recitals in the evening at Bruton Parish Church.**

The **Capitol** is the building that made this town so important. It was here that the prerevolutionary House of Burgesses (dominated by the ascendant gentry) challenged the royally appointed council (an almost medieval body made up of the bigger landowners). In 1765 the House eventually arrived at the resolutions, known as Henry's Resolves (after Patrick Henry), that amounted to rebellion. An informative tour explains the development, stage by stage, of American democracy from its English parliamentary roots. Occasional reenactments, including witch trials, dramatize the evolution of American jurisprudence.

What stands on the site today is a reproduction of the 1705 structure that burned down in 1747. Dark-wood wainscoting, pewter chandeliers, and towering ceilings contribute to a handsome impression. That an official building would have so ornate an interior was characteristic of aristocratic 18th-century Virginia. ∎ TIP➔The stirring Fifes and Drums March leaves from the Capitol to the Palace Green. Don't miss the spectacle of dozens of young men dressed in period costume marching through Williamsburg's streets. Check the program guide for dates and times. ⊠ *East end of Duke of Gloucester St.*

His Majesty's Governor Alexander Spotswood built the original **Governor's Palace** in 1720, and seven British viceroys, the last of them Lord Dunmore in 1775, lived in this appropriately showy mansion. The 540 weapons, including 230 muskets and pistols, arrayed on the walls of several rooms herald the power of the Crown. Some of the furnishings are original, and the rest are matched to an extraordinary inventory of 16,000 items. Lavishly appointed as it is, the palace is furnished to the time just before the Revolution. During the Revolution, it housed the commonwealth's first two governors, Patrick Henry and Thomas Jefferson. The original residence burned down in 1781, and today's reconstruction stands on the original foundation.

CLOSE UP

Colonial Williamsburg Basics

11

The restoration project that gave birth to Colonial Williamsburg began in 1926, inspired by a local pastor, W. A. R. Goodwin, and financed by John D. Rockefeller Jr. The work of the archaeologists and historians of the not-for-profit Colonial Williamsburg Foundation continues to this day. A total of 88 original 18th-century and early-19th-century structures have been meticulously restored, and another 500 have been reconstructed on their original sites. In all, approximately 225 period rooms have been re-created with the foundation's collection of more than 60,000 pieces of furniture, ceramics, glass, silver, pewter, textiles, tools, paintings, prints, maps, firearms, and carpets. Period authenticity also governs the landscaping of the 301 acres of gardens and public greens. The restored area is surrounded by a greenbelt controlled by the foundation, which guards against development that could mar the illusion of the Colonial city.

Despite its huge scale, Colonial Williamsburg can seem almost cozy. Nearly 1 million people come here annually, and all year hundreds of costumed interpreters, wearing bonnets or three-corner hats, rove and ride through the streets (you can even rent outfits for your children). Dozens of skilled craftspeople, also in costume, demonstrate and explain their trades inside their workshops. They include the shoemaker, the cooper (he makes barrels), the gunsmith, the blacksmith, the musical instrument maker, the silversmith, and the wig maker. Their wares are for sale nearby at the Prentis Store. Four taverns serve food and drink that approximate the fare of more than 220 years ago.

Colonial Williamsburg makes an effort to represent not just the lives of a privileged few, and not to gloss over disturbing aspects of history. Slavery, religious freedom, family life, commerce and trade, land acquisition, and the Revolution are portrayed in living-history demonstrations. In the two-hour "Revolutionary City Program" you can become an active citizen in everyday life against the backdrop of momentous, world-changing events. The vignettes that are staged throughout the day take place in the streets and in public buildings. These may include dramatic afternoon court trials or fascinating estate appraisals. Depending on the days you visit, you may see the House of Burgesses dissolve, its members charging out to make revolutionary plans at the Raleigh Tavern.

Because of the size of Colonial Williamsburg and the large crowds (especially in the warmer months), it's best to begin a tour early in the day, so it's a good idea to spend the night before in the area. The foundation suggests allowing three or four days to do Colonial Williamsburg justice, but that will depend on your own interest in the period—and that interest often increases on arrival. Museums, exhibits, and stores close at 5 PM, but walks and events take place in the evening, usually ending by 10 PM. Some sites close in winter on a rotating basis.

A costumed guide greets you at the door for a tour through the building, offering commentary and answering questions. Social events are described on the walk through the great formal ballroom, where you might even hear the sounds of an 18th-century harp, clavichord, or piano. The supper room leads to the formal garden and the planted terraces beyond. ⊠ *Northern end of Palace Green.*

Raleigh Tavern was the scene of prerevolutionary revels and rallies that were often joined by Washington, Jefferson, Patrick Henry, and other major figures. The spare but elegant blue-and-white Apollo Room is said to have been the first meeting place of Phi Beta Kappa, the scholastic honorary society founded in 1776. The French general Marquis de Lafayette was fêted here in 1824. In 1859 the original structure burned, and today's building is a reconstruction based on archaeological evidence and period descriptions and sketches of the building. ⊠ *Duke of Gloucester St., west of Capitol.*

The **visitor center** is the logical first stop at Colonial Williamsburg. Here you can park free; buy tickets; see a 35-minute introductory movie, *Williamsburg—the Story of a Patriot*; and pick up *This Week*, which has a list of regular events and special programs and a map of the historic area. Tickets are also sold at the Lumber House in the historic area. ⊠ *102 Information Center Dr., off U.S. 60* ☎ *757/ 229–1000 or 800/447–8679* ⊕ *www.colonialwilliamsburg.com* ⊡ *$34–$72* ⊙ *Daily 9–5.*

WORTH NOTING

The **Abby Aldrich Rockefeller Folk Art Museum,** within the DeWitt Wallace Decorative Arts Museum, showcases American "decorative usefulware"—toys, furniture, weather vanes, coffeepots, and quilts—within typical 19th-century domestic interiors. There are also folk paintings, rustic sculptures, and needlepoint pictures. Since the 1920s, the 2,000-piece collection has grown from the original 400 pieces acquired by the wife of Colonial Williamsburg's first and principal benefactor. ⊠ *Francis St.*

The **Brush-Everard House** was built in 1717 by John Brush, a gunsmith, and later owned by Thomas Everard, who was twice mayor of Williamsburg. The wood-frame house contains remarkable, ornate carving work but is open only for special-focus tours. Temporary exhibits and vignettes on slaves' lives are held here in summer. ⊠ *Scotland St. at Palace Green.*

The original **Courthouse** of 1770 was used by municipal and county courts until 1932. Civil and minor criminal matters and cases involving slaves were adjudicated here; other trials were conducted at the Capitol. The stocks once used to punish misdemeanors are outside the building: they can make for a humorous photo opportunity. The courthouse's exterior has been restored to its original appearance. Visitors often participate in scheduled reenactments of court sessions. ⊠ *North side of Duke of Gloucester St., west of Queen St.*

The spine of Colonial Williamsburg's restored area is the broad 1-mi-long **Duke of Gloucester Street.** On Saturday at 1 PM from March to October, the Fifes and Drums Corps marches the length of the street and performs a stirring drill. Along this artery alone, or just off it, are two-dozen attractions. Walking west on Duke of Gloucester Street from the Capitol, you can find a dozen 18th-century shops—including those of the apothecary, the wig maker, the silversmith, and the milliner.

The **Guardhouse** once served in the defense of the Magazine's lethal inventory. Special interpretive programs about the military are scheduled here. ⊠*Duke of Gloucester St. near Queen St.*

At **James Anderson's Blacksmith Shop,** smiths forge the nails, tools, and other iron hardware used in construction throughout the town. The shop itself was reconstructed by carpenters using 18th-century tools and techniques. ⊠*Between Botetourt and Colonial Sts., on south side of Duke of Gloucester St.*

The original **Magazine** (1715), an octagonal brick warehouse, was used for storing arms and ammunition—at one time 60,000 pounds of gunpowder and 3,000 muskets. It was used for this purpose by the British, then by the Continental army, and again by the Confederates during the Civil War. Today 18th-century firearms are on display within the arsenal. This is the largest collection of Colonial muskets in the country. Every able-bodied man in Colonial times was expected to have and maintain a musket in his home. Between the ages of 16 and 55 men were expected to be a part of the militia, the civilian army that could be called to arms in defense of hearth and home. ⊠*West of Queen St. on south side of Duke of Gloucester St.*

In **Market Square,** an open green between Queen and Palace streets along Duke of Gloucester, cattle, seafood, dairy products, fruit, and vegetables were all sold—as were slaves. Both the market and slave auctions are sometimes reenacted.

NEED A BREAK?

At the west end of Duke of Gloucester Street, for a block on both sides, **Merchants Square** has more than 40 shops and restaurants, including an ice-cream parlor, coffee shop, cheese shop, chocolatier, movie theater, peanut shop, and gourmet food store. Services also include three banks and a drugstore. The William and Mary College bookstore is operated by Barnes and Noble and has a wealth of information on Williamsburg and Virginia history. The Kimball Theatre on Merchants Square shows movies daily and has live family entertainment on weekends. For the schedule, go to ⊕ *www.kimballtheatre.com.*

The handsome **Palace Green** runs north from Duke of Gloucester Street up the center of Palace Street, with the Governor's Palace at the far end and notable historic houses on either side.

The **Public Hospital,** a reconstruction of a 1773 insane asylum, provides an informative, shocking look at the treatment of the mentally ill in the 18th and 19th centuries. It also serves as cover for a modern edifice that houses very different exhibitions; entrance to the DeWitt Wallace Decorative Arts Museum is through the hospital lobby. ⊠*Francis St.*

On the outskirts of the historic area is **Robertson's Windmill,** a Colonial mill for grinding grains. It's currently closed to the public for repairs. ⊠*N. England St.*

Wetherburn's Tavern, which offered refreshment, entertainment, and lodging beginning in 1743, may be the most accurately furnished building in Colonial Williamsburg, with contents that conform to a room-by-room inventory taken in 1760. Excavations at this site have yielded more than 200,000 artifacts. The outbuildings include the original dairy and a reconstructed kitchen. Vegetables are still grown in the small garden. ⌧ *Duke of Gloucester St. across from Raleigh Tavern.*

WHERE TO EAT

$$ ✕ **Aberdeen Barn.** Saws, pitchforks, oxen yokes, and the like hang on the
AMERICAN barn walls, but the wood tables are lacquered, and the napkins are linen. Specialties include slow-roasted prime rib; baby-back Danish pork ribs barbecued with a sauce of peach preserves and Southern Comfort; and shrimp Dijon. An ample wine list offers a wide variety of domestic and imported choices. ⌧ *1601 Richmond Rd.* ☎ *757/229–6661* ⊕ *www. aberdeen-barn.com* ▤ *AE, D, MC, V* ⊗ *No lunch.*

¢–$ ✕ **College Delly.** It's easy to forget that this is a college town, but this
DELI cheerful dive keeps up the school spirit. The white-brick eatery with forest-green canvas awnings is dark and scruffy inside. Walls are hung with fraternity and sorority pictures, graduation snapshots, and sports-team photos. Booths and tables are in the William and Mary colors of green and gold. Deli sandwiches, subs, specialty pizzas, pasta, stromboli, and Greek dishes are all prepared with fresh ingredients and are all delicious, and there's a wide selection of beers on tap. The Delly delivers free to nearby hotels from 6 PM to 1 AM. ⌧ *336 Richmond Rd.* ☎ *757/229–6627* ▤ *MC, V.*

$$$ ✕ **Le Yaca.** A mall of small boutiques is the unlikely location for this
FRENCH French-country restaurant. The dining room has soft pastel colors,
★ hardwood floors, candlelight, and a central open fireplace. The menu is arranged in the French manner, with four prix-fixe menus and 10 entrées, including whole duck breast with peach and pepper sauce, leg of lamb with rosemary garlic sauce, bouillabaisse, and fresh scallops and shrimp with champagne sauce. Le Yaca is on U.S. 60 East, near Busch Gardens. ⌧ *Village Shops at Kingsmill, 1915 Pocahontas Trail* ☎ *757/220–3616* ⊕ *www.leyacawilliamsburg.com* ▤ *AE, D, DC, MC, V* ⊗ *Closed Sun. No lunch Sat.*

¢ ✕ **Old Chickahominy House.** Reminiscent of old-fashioned Virginia tea-
SOUTHERN rooms, this Colonial-style restaurant has delectable goodies served in
☾ an 18th-century dining room. For breakfast there's Virginia ham and eggs, made-from-scratch biscuits, country bacon, sausage, homemade pancakes, and grits. Lunch brings Brunswick stew, Virginia ham biscuits, chicken and dumplings, fruit salad, and homemade pie. There's a gift shop adjacent to the restaurant. It's a great, inexpensive, and filling place for families on a budget. ⌧ *1211 Jamestown Rd.* ☎ *757/229–4689* ⊕ *www.oldchickahominy.com* ▤ *MC, V* ⊗ *No dinner.*

$$$$ ✕ **Regency Room.** This hotel restaurant is known for its elegance, atten-
CONTINENTAL tive service, and quality cuisine. Among crystal chandeliers, Asian
★ silk-screen prints, and full silver service, you can sample chateaubriand carved tableside, as well as rack of lamb, Dover sole, lobster bisque, and house-smoked and -cured salmon. It may almost seem as if you're treated like royalty. A jacket and tie are required at dinner and

optional at Sunday brunch. ✉ *Williamsburg Inn, 136 E. Francis St.* ☎*757/229–1000* ✍*Reservations essential* ☞*Jacket required for dinner* ▭*AE, D, DC, MC, V.*

¢–$ ✗**Sal's Restaurant by Victor.** Locals
ITALIAN love this family Italian restaurant and pizzeria. Victor Minichiello and his staff serve up pasta, fish, chicken, and veal dinners as well as subs and pizzas. It's a good choice for families who want to please the kids: parents can get quality "adult food" while their children graze on pizza and subs. An interesting side note: Chef Victor was on the International Olympics Committee. The restaurant delivers free to nearby hotels. ✉*1242 Richmond Rd.* ☎*757/220–2641* ⊕*www.salsbyvictor.com* ▭*AE, D, MC, V.*

WORD OF MOUTH

"It is amazing what they are doing at Colonial Williamsburg to teach not only kids, but adults, what it is like to live in the 17th century. A tavern meal (Kings Arms and Christiana Campbell are my favorites) an evening tour such as the Palace Concert or To Go A Pirating would be a wonderful way to end a busy day. The outdoor performance of Revolutionary City is not to be missed." —girlwilltravel

COLONIAL TAVERNS

For an authentic dining experience to match the historic setting, it's nearly a requirement to dine in one of the reconstructed "taverns" in Colonial Williamsburg—essentially casual restaurants with beer and wine available. Colonial-style and modern American fare is served at lunch, dinner, and Sunday brunch. Although the food can be uneven, a meal at any tavern is a good way to get into the spirit of the era.

No reservations are taken for lunch (or anytime at Chowning's Tavern), but make dinner reservations up to two or three weeks in advance. Hours also change according to season, so check by calling the reservations number (☎*800/447–8679*). Smoking is not permitted in any of the taverns. To see tavern menus, go to: ⊕*www.history.org/visit/diningExperience.*

$ ✗**Chowning's Tavern.** A reconstructed 18th-century alehouse, Chowning's
AMERICAN serves casual quick fare for lunch, including traditional pit-style BBQ, beef brisket sandwiches, and Smithfield ham and Gloucester cheese on a pretzel roll. You can eat either inside the tavern or under a grape arbor behind the tavern. After 5 PM, Chownings becomes a true Colonial tavern where Gambols (18th-century entertainment), a program presented for 25 years, operates throughout the evening. Costumed balladeers lead family sing-alongs, and costumed servers play popular games of the day. From 8 PM until closing, Chowning's caters to a more mature audience. ✉*Duke of Gloucester St.* ▭*AE, D, DC, MC, V.*

$$$ ✗**Kings Arms.** This 18th century–style chop house is where the finest
AMERICAN gentry dined in Colonial days, and is still the best of the historic area's four Colonial taverns. The genteel surroundings imitate those experienced by Thomas Jefferson and Patrick Henry. Don't miss favorites such as peanut soup or Game Pye, made of venison, rabbit, duck, vegetables, and bacon in a wine sauce. Roast Prime Rib of Beef, tender pork, and lamb are on offer. Weather permitting, you can eat in the garden behind the tavern. ✉*Duke of Gloucester St.* ▭*AE, D, DC, MC, V.*

WHERE TO STAY

There are more than 200 hotel properties in Williamsburg, including many bed-and-breakfasts. For a complete list, contact the **Williamsburg Area Convention and Visitors Bureau** (⊠ *421 N. Boundary St., Box 3495, Williamsburg* ☎ *757/253–0192 or 800/368–6511*). **Williamsburg Vacation Reservations** (☎ *800/446–9244*), representing more than 70 hostelries, provides free lodging reservation services

$ ⊡ **Colonial Houses.** A stay here seems particularly moving at night, when
★   the town's historic area is quiet and you have Williamsburg pretty much to yourself. Five of the 25 homes and three lodging taverns are 18th-century structures; the others have been rebuilt on their original foundations. Antiques and period reproductions furnish the rooms, and the costumed staff reinforces the historical air. Modern amenities include hair dryers, irons, ironing boards, coffeemakers, and a complimentary fruit basket and bottle of wine. The Colonial Houses share the facilities of the adjacent Williamsburg Inn and the Lodge. **Pros:** you can't beat the accommodations for the total Colonial experience. **Cons:** children might rather escape the summer's heat with a dip in a motel pool. ⊠ *136 E. Francis St., Box 1776* ☎ *757/229–1000 or 800/447–8679* ⊕ *www. colonialwilliamsburg.com* ↪ *77 rooms* ⊘ *In-hotel: room service, laundry service, no smoking rooms* ⊟ *AE, D, DC, MC, V.*

$$ ⊡ **Kingsmill Resort and Spa.** This manicured 2,900-acre resort on the
★   James River owned by Anheuser-Busch is home to the largest golf resort in Virginia: it hosts the LPGA's Michelob ULTRA Open each May. You can play year-round on three championship courses, including the River Course, renovated in 2005. The 9-hole course is free if you stay here, and so is a shuttle bus to Busch Gardens, Water Country USA, and Colonial Williamsburg. The guest rooms have fireplaces and Colonial-style furniture. The inventive menu at the expensive Bray Bistro emphasizes seafood. **Pros:** lots of space to roam around the resort and away from the hustle and bustle of Colonial Williamsburg. **Cons:** away from the hustle and bustle of Williamsburg. ⊠ *1010 Kingsmill Rd.* ☎ *757/253–1703 or 800/832–5665* ⊕ *www.kingsmill.com* ↪ *235 rooms, 175 suites* ⊘ *In-room: dial-up. In-hotel: 6 restaurants, golf courses, tennis courts, pools, gym, spa, beachfront, concierge, laundry service* ⊟ *AE, D, DC, MC, V.*

$–$$ ⊡ **War Hill Inn.** This inn was designed by a Colonial Williamsburg architect to resemble a period structure: the two-story redbrick building at the center has a wood-frame wing. Appropriate antiques and reproductions decorate the interior. The War Hill is inside a 32-acre operating cattle farm, 4 mi from the Colonial Williamsburg information center. Those in search of privacy may want one of the cottages or the first-floor suite (other rooms open onto a common hallway). **Pros:** children are welcome and may enjoy the farm experience. **Cons:** breakfast, but no restaurant; no handicapped accessibility. ⊠ *4560 Longhill Rd.* ☎ *757/565–0248 or 800/743–0248* ⊕ *www.warhillinn.com* ↪ *4 rooms, 2 cottages* ⊘ *In-hotel: no elevator, public Wi-Fi* ⊟ *MC, V* ⊚ *BP.*

¢–$ ⊡ **Williamsburg Hospitality House.** Across the street from the College of William and Mary and two blocks from the historic area, this hotel is a prime site for conferences and reunions, so you won't be the only one standing under the crystal chandelier in the lobby. Guest rooms are furnished in styles ranging from 18th century to art deco; all have hair dryers, irons, ironing boards, and in-room coffeemakers. The large poolside patio is very inviting after a day exploring the Historic Triangle. **Pros:** two blocks from the historic district; handicapped accessible with elevator. **Cons:** can be busy as the site of conferences and conventions. ✉*415 Richmond Rd.* ☎*757/229–4020 or 800/932–9192* ⊕*www.williamsburghosphouse.com* ⇗*296 rooms, 11 suites* ♿*In-room: Wi-Fi. In-hotel: 2 restaurants, room service, bar, pool, concierge, executive floor, laundry facilities, laundry service, parking (no fee), no-smoking rooms* ▤*AE, D, DC, MC, V* ⎆*CP.*

$$$$ 🏨**Williamsburg Inn.** This grand hotel from 1937 is owned and operated
★ by Colonial Williamsburg. Rooms are beautifully and individually furnished with reproductions and antiques in the English Regency style, and genteel service and tradition reign. Rooms come with such perks as morning coffee and afternoon tea, a daily newspaper, turndown service, and bathrobes. The Providence Wings, adjacent to the inn, are less formal; rooms are in a contemporary style with Asian accents and overlook the tennis courts, a private pond, and a wooded area. **Pros:** this is the most elegant property operated by Colonial Williamsburg. **Cons:** may be pricey for families on a budget. ✉*136 E. Francis St., Box 1776* ☎*757/229–1000* ⊕*www.colonialwilliamsburg.com* ⇗*62 rooms, 14 suites* ♿*In-room: VCR, Wi-Fi. In-hotel: 3 restaurants, room service, bar, golf courses, tennis court, pool, gym, spa, concierge, laundry service, no-smoking rooms* ▤*AE, D, MC, V.*

$ 🏨**Woodlands Hotel and Suites.** An official Colonial Williamsburg property with contemporary furnishings, this 300-room hotel is adjacent to the HUZZAH! restaurant and the visitor center complex. You can enjoy the extensive free continental breakfast indoors or on the large patio—kids and adults enjoy making their own homemade waffles. There's gated free parking so you can abandon your car and walk to the free shuttle buses. **Pros:** good choice for families; suites are available; some double rooms have futons for children. **Cons:** if you want luxurious lodgings you might want to book elsewhere. ✉*102 Visitor Center Dr.* ☎*757/229–1000 or 800/447–8679* ⊕*www.colonialwilliamsburg.com* ⇗*204 rooms, 96 suites* ♿*In-room: refrigerator, Ethernet. In-hotel: restaurant, bar, pool, laundry service, public Internet, no-smoking rooms* ▤*AE, D, DC, MC, V* ⎆*CP.*

NIGHTLIFE AND THE ARTS

Busch Gardens Williamsburg (✉*U.S. 60* ☎*757/253–3350*) hosts popular song-and-dance shows (country, gospel, opera, German folk) in several theaters; in the largest, the 5,000-seat Royal Palace, pop stars often perform. Well-known artists on tour play at the 10,000-seat **Phi Beta Kappa Hall** (✉*601 Jamestown Rd. entrance to campus* ☎*757/21–2674 Box office*) at the College of William and Mary.

SPORTS AND THE OUTDOORS

☼ **Busch Gardens Europe,** a 100-acre amusement park that has been voted the world's most beautiful theme park for 15 years, has more than 40 rides and six beautifully landscaped "countries" with re-creations of French, German, English, Scottish, Irish, and Italian areas. In addition to roller coasters, bumper cars, and water rides, the park has eight main stage shows and a magical children's area. Costumed actors add character to the theme areas while cable-car gondolas pass overhead. ⊠ *U.S. 60, 3 mi east of Williamsburg* ☎ *800/343–7946* ✉ *$56.95, child $49; parking $10* ☉ *Late Mar.–mid-May, weekends 10–8; mid-May–Labor Day, weekdays 10–9, weekends 10–10; early Sept.–Oct., Fri.–Sun. 10–10; call for exact hrs.*

THEME PARKING

What they don't tell you: even as expensive as they are, tickets don't include parking at either Busch Gardens or Water Country You must pay $10 per car to enter and park ($15 for premium parking that's closer to the entrance). To avoid having to pay for parking, stay at a motel or hotel that offers free shuttle service to the parks.

☉ At **Water Country USA,** the more than 30 water rides and attractions, live entertainment, shops, and restaurants have a colorful 1950s and '60s surf theme. The Meltdown is a four-person toboggan with 180-degree turns and a 76-foot drop. The Nitro Racer is a superspeed slide down a 382-foot drop into a big splash. The largest attraction is a 4,500-square-foot heated pool. ⊠ *Rte. 199, 3 mi off I–64, Exit 242B* ☎ *757/253–3350 or 800/343–7946* ✉ *$39.95 for anyone 10 and older, child $32.90; parking $10* ☉ *Mid-May, weekends 10–6; early–mid-June, daily 10–6; mid-June–mid-Aug., daily 10–8; mid–late Aug., daily 10–7; early Sept., daily 10–6; mid-Sept., weekends 10–6.*

SHOPPING

Merchants Square, on the west end of Duke of Gloucester Street, has both licensed Willliamsburg shops and non-Colonial, upscale shops that include Laura Ashley, the Porcelain Collector of Williamsburg, and the J. Fenton Gallery. There's also Quilts Unlimited and the Campus Shop, which carries William and Mary gifts and clothing.

Three Colonial Williamsburg stores have individual offerings. **Williamsburg at Home** (☎*757/220–7749*) features the full line of Willliamsburg furniture, bedding, rugs, fixtures, and wallpapers. **Williamsburg Celebrations** (☎*757/565–8642*) displays seasonal decorations and accessories. The **Williamsburg Craft House** (☎*757/220–7747*) sells a full line of Willliamsburg dinnerware, flatware, glassware, pewter, giftware, and jewelry.

YORKTOWN

14 mi northeast of Colonial Williamsburg via Colonial Pkwy.

It was at Yorktown that the combined American and French forces surrounded Lord Cornwallis's British troops in 1781; this was the end to the Revolutionary War and the beginning of our nation. In Yorktown today, as at Jamestown, two major attractions complement each other. Yorktown Battlefield, the historical site, is operated by the National Park Service; and Yorktown Victory Center, which has re-creations and informative exhibits, is operated by the state's Jamestown–Yorktown Foundation. As well, a stately Watermen's Museum educates visitors about those who earn their living from the nearby waters.

GETTING HERE AND AROUND

From mid-March through the end of October, the County operates the Yorktown Trolley, providing free service between the Yorktown Battlefield Visitor Center and the Yorktown Victory Center, as well as seven stops between in the historic village. The trolley runs approximately every half hour.

ESSENTIALS

Visitor Information Colonial National Historical Park (🖂 *Box 210, Yorktown 23690* ☎ *757/898–3400* 🌐 *www.apva.org*). **York County Tourism** (☎ *757/890–3300* 🌐 *www.yorkcounty.gov/tourism*).

EXPLORING

Riverwalk Landing is a group of specialty shops, an upscale restaurant, and an outdoor performance venue on the shores of the York River. Two piers for medium-size cruise ships and personal watercraft are also along the waterfront. Yet Yorktown remains a small community of year-round residents. Route 238 leads into town, where along Main Street are preserved 18th-century buildings on a bluff overlooking the York River.

The **Watermen's Museum** is sited in a Colonial Revival manor house on Yorktown's waterfront that was floated across the York River on a barge in 1987. In it you can learn more about the generations of men who have wrested a living from the Chesapeake Bay and nearby waters. The five galleries house ship models, dioramas, and artifacts themed on Chesapeake watermen, bay boats, harvesting fish, aquaculture, tools, and treasures. Outdoor exhibits include an original three-log canoe, dredges, engines, and other equipment used by working watermen past and present. 🖂 *309 Water St.* ☎ *757/887–2641* 🌐 *www.watermens.org* 🎟 *$4* 🕐 *Apr.–Thanksgiving, Tues.–Sat. 10–5, Sun. 1–5; Thanksgiving–Mar., Sat. 10–5, Sun. 1–5.*

Yorktown Battlefield preserves the land where the British surrendered to American and French forces in 1781. The museum in the visitor center has on exhibit part of General George Washington's original field tent. Dioramas, illuminated maps, and a film about the battle make the sobering point that Washington's victory was hardly inevitable. A look around from the roof's observation deck can help you visualize the events of the campaign. Guided by an audio tour purchased from the gift shop, you may explore the battlefield by car, stopping at the site of Washington's headquarters, a couple of crucial redoubts (breastworks dug into the ground), the field where surrender took place, and the Moore House, where the surrender terms were negotiated. 🖂 *Rte. 238*

Ⓒ
Fodor's Choice
★

COLONIAL PARKWAY

For a beautiful drive along countryside that's nearly the same as land the Jamestown settlers trod, take the 23-mi scenic Colonial Parkway between Jamestown and Yorktown, a 40-minute drive one-way. The road between Yorktown and Williamsburg, which was aligned along the York River, was completed in 1937, but it wasn't until 1955, for the 350th anniversary of Jamestown, that the road was completed to America's first permanent English settlement. The limited-access highway has broad sweeping curves, is meticulously landscaped, and is devoid of commercial development.

off Colonial Pkwy. ☎757/898–2410 ᎒*$5; combined entry fee to both Jamestowne and Yorktown, $10* ⊙ *Visitor center daily 9–5.*

♨ On the western edge of Yorktown Battlefield, the **Yorktown Victory Center** Fodor'sChoice has wonderful exhibits and demonstrations that bring to life the Ameri-★ can Revolution. Textual and graphic displays along the open-air Road to Revolution walkway cover the principal events and personalities. A renovated *Declaration of Independence* entrance gallery and long-term exhibition, *The Legacy of Yorktown: Virginia Beckons*, debuted in 2006. Life-size tableaux show 10 "witnesses," including an African-American patriot, a loyalist, a Native American leader, two Continental Army soldiers, and the wife of a Virginia plantation owner. ■ TIP→**The "witnesses" testimony is very dramatic and makes the American Revolution real for children. This presentation brings the personal trials of the colonists to life more effectively than the artifacts of the war.**

The exhibit galleries contain more than 500 period artifacts, including many recovered during underwater excavations of "Yorktown's Sunken Fleet" (British ships lost during the siege of 1781). Outdoors, visitors may participate in a Continental Army drill at an encampment with interpreters costumed as soldiers and female auxiliaries, who reenact and discuss daily camp life. In another outdoor area, a re-created 1780s farm includes a dwelling, kitchen, tobacco barn, crop fields, and kitchen garden, which show how many Americans lived in the decade following the end of the Revolution. ⊠*Rte. 238 off Colonial Pkwy.* ☎757/253–4838 or 888/593–4682 ⊕*www.historyisfun.org* ᎒*$9.25; combination ticket for Yorktown Victory Center and Jamestown Settlement $19.95* ⊙*June 15–Aug. 15, daily 9–6; Aug. 16–June 14, daily 9–5.*

WHERE TO EAT AND STAY

$$ ✕**Nick's Riverwalk Restaurant.** Whether you dine indoors or out, enjoy SEAFOOD the view of the York River, the Coleman Bridge, and Gloucester on the opposite shore. Nick's Riverwalk offers casual meals of soups, salads, and sandwiches at the Rivah Café and outdoor courtyard; the River-walk Dining Room is more formal, with a menu featuring baked crab-meat imperial, sautéed fillets, and local oysters. Right outside of the café are a boardwalk and a sandy beach. Parking is available across the street. There are many shops just outside the Riverwalk's door. ⊠*323 Water St.* ☎757/875–1522 ▤*MC, V.*

¢   ▥**Duke of York Motel.** All rooms in this classic 1960s motel face the water and are only a few steps from a sandy public beach on the York River. The furnishings include quilted bedspreads and Queen Anne–style reproduction wood furniture. The motel also has a swimming pool and a restaurant that serves breakfast and lunch daily and dinner Wednesday–Sunday. It is an easy walk to the riverfront and its shops and restaurants. The free Yorktown Trolley stops right outside the hotel. **Pros:** some rooms have kitchenettes; modestly priced. **Cons:** the decor is half a century old. ⊠*508 Water St.* ☎757/898–3232 ⊕*www.duke-ofyorkmotel.com* ⇆*57 rooms* ⚙*In-room: Ethernet, dial-up. In-hotel: restaurant, pool, beachfront, no elevator* ▤*AE, D, DC, MC, V.*

VIRGINIA BEACH

18 mi east of Norfolk via I–64 to Rte. 44.

The heart of Virginia Beach—a stretch of the Atlantic shore from Cape Henry south to Rudee Inlet—has been a popular summertime destination for years. With 6 mi of public beach, high-rises, amusements, and a busy 40-block boardwalk, Virginia's most populated city is now a place for communion with nature. The boardwalk and Atlantic Avenue have an oceanfront park; an old-fashioned fishing pier ($7.50) with shops, a restaurant, and a bar; and a 3-mi bike trail. The farther north you go, the more beach you find in proportion to bars, T-shirt parlors, and video arcades. Most activities and events in town are oriented to families.

GETTING HERE AND AROUND

CAR TRAVEL   Virginia Beach has no shortage of parking lots and spaces. The cost for a day of parking is about $5 to $7 at the central beach lots and $4 or $5 for the remote beach areas. Municipal lots/decks are at 4th Street (metered only), 9th Street and Pacific Avenue, 19th Street and Pacific Avenue, 25th Street and Pacific Avenue, 31st Street and Atlantic Avenue, and Croatan and Sandbridge beaches. Metered spaces have a three-hour limit.

BIKE TRAVEL   Bikes (two- or four-wheel) can be rented at several shops and hotels along the beach for $4 to $20 per hour. In Virginia Beach there are numerous locations along the boardwalk where you can rent bikes. Rental shops away from the boardwalk are more reasonable and have better bikes. Seashore Bikes & Fitness is near First Landing Park. Back Bay Getaways is on the other side of Virginia Beach in the Sandbridge area. They offer bikes and guided biking tours.

Hampton Roads Transit buses have bike racks, and their paddle-wheel ferries across the Elizabeth River allow bikes, so cyclists can cover a lot of territory from Newport News through Norfolk and on to Virginia Beach.

ESSENTIALS

Bike Rental Back Bay Getaways (✉ *3713 S. Sandpiper Rd.* ☎ *757/721–4484*). **Seashore Bikes & Fitness** (✉ *2268 Seashore Shops* ☎ *757/481–5191*).

Bus Contacts Hampton Roads Transit (☎ *757/222–6100* ⊕ *www.hrtransit.org*).

Visitor Information Virginia Beach Visitor Information Center (✉ *2100 Parks Ave.* ☎ *800/822–3224* ⊕ *www.vbfun.com*).

TIMING

Virginia Beach is one of the prime destinations for college students on spring break. Thousands of them descend on the community in April and may constitute a rowdy crowd. Avoid Virginia Beach during that time—unless you are a college student.

EXPLORING

☺ The **Naval Air Station, Oceana,** on the northern edge of the city, is an impressive sight, home to more than 200 navy aircraft, including the F/A-18 Tomcat (the type of plane flown by the Blue Angels) and other planes assigned to the aircraft carriers of the Atlantic Fleet. From an observation park on Oceana Boulevard at the POW/MIA Flame of Hope

Memorial Park, near the runways, you can watch aircraft take off and land. Non–Defense Department visitors can access the base only on the Hampton Roads Transit summer-only tours (photo ID required) or during the annual air show in September. Tours depart at 9:30 AM and 11:30 AM from the 24th Street

WORD OF MOUTH

"In Virginia Beach there is the Aquarium and Marine Science Center which is lots of fun for little ones and great for a rainy day." —fourfortravel

transit kiosk on Atlantic Avenue in Virginia Beach and stop at an aviation historical park with 13 aircraft. ✉*Tomcat Blvd.* ☎*757/433–3131* ⊕*www.nasoceana.navy.mil/Visitors.htm* ✆*Tour $7.50.*

At the northeastern tip of Virginia Beach, on the cape where the mouth of the bay meets the ocean, the historic **Old Cape Henry Lighthouse** is near the site where the English landed on their way to Jamestown in 1607. This lighthouse, however, didn't light anyone's way until 1792. Across the street to seaward is the replacement to the old lighthouse, but it isn't open to visitors. Be prepared to show a photo ID at the military checkpoint at the Fort Story base entrance. ✉*U.S. 60* ☎*757/422–9421* ✆*$4* ⊙*Mid-Mar.–Oct., daily 10–5; Nov.–mid-Mar., daily 10–4.*

Along the oceanfront, the **Old Coast Guard Station,** a 1903 Lifesaving Station, contains photographic exhibits, examples of lifesaving equipment, and a gallery that depicts German U-boat activity off the coast during World War II. ✉*24th St. at Atlantic Ave.* ☎*757/422–1587* ✆*$3* ⊙*Tues.–Sat. 10–5, Sun. noon–5.*

Ⓒ
★ The sea is the subject at the popular **Virginia Aquarium and Marine Science Center,** a massive facility with more than 200 exhibits. This is no place for passive museumgoers; many exhibits require participation. You can use computers to predict the weather and solve the pollution crisis, watch the birds in the salt marsh through telescopes on a deck, handle horseshoe crabs, take a simulated journey to the bottom of the sea in a submarine, and study fish up close in tanks that re-create underwater environments. The museum is almost 2 mi inland from Rudee Inlet at the southern end of Virginia Beach. The Virginia Aquarium and Marine Science Center has a nature trail—well worth it, but be sure to wear comfortable shoes. ✉*717 General Booth Blvd.* ☎*757/485–3474* ⊕*www.virginiaacquarium.com* ✆*Aquarium $11.95; combination ticket for aquarium and IMAX $16.95* ⊙*Memorial Day–Labor Day, daily 9–7; Labor Day–Memorial Day, daily 9–5.*

WHERE TO EAT

$–$$
AMERICAN
✕**Five 01 City Grill.** More than a grill in name only, this restaurant has an open-grill kitchen in the dining room. It can be noisy on the bar side when live bands play in the evening. Locals get comfortable in padded chairs and some booths as they quaff the $2 beer of the month or order from the extensive wine vault. The California-inspired fusion menu offers a variety of price ranges: excellent homemade pizza from wood-burning ovens, sandwiches, pasta, chicken, steaks, and seafood followed by sinful desserts such as Homemade Bourbon Chocolate Chip Pecan Pie. ✉*501 N. Birdneck Rd.* ☎*757/425–7195* ⊕*www.goodfood-gooddrink.com* ▤*AE, MC, V.*

$–$$ ✕**Rockafeller's.** The Down East architecture of this local favorite with
AMERICAN double-deck porches hints at the seafood that's available. The restaurant has a bar, a raw bar, and alfresco dining in good weather (in cool weather, the large window wall still gives you a water view). Seafood, pasta, chicken, and beef share the menu with salads and sandwiches. Rockafeller's (and several others) are on Rudee Inlet. To get here, go south on Pacific Avenue and turn right on Winston-Salem immediately before the Rudee Inlet bridge. The street ends at Mediterranean Avenue. ✉*308 Mediterranean Ave.* ☎*757/422–5654* ⊕*www.rockafellers.com* ☰*AE, D, DC, MC, V.*

$–$$ ✕**Waterman's Beachwood Grill.** The last freestanding restaurant on the
SEAFOOD beach not inside a hotel, this aqua-painted clapboard building houses a
★ family-owned seafood grill. Inside, the ocher walls heighten the sun rays penetrating the ceiling-to-floor windows. Awnings shade the outdoor patio where live musicians perform in season. A local menu favorite is the Crab Ripper, a crab-cake sandwich topped with mozzarella and crisp bacon. A fried seafood sampler, fish and steak platters, steamed fish, appetizers, salads, burgers, and other sandwiches fill out the menu. Banquet facilities are available, and the Beach Nut Gift Shop is also on the premises. ✉*1423 N. Great Neck Rd.* ☎*757/496–3333* ⊕*www.watermans.com* ☰*AE, D, MC, V.*

WHERE TO STAY

Apartment and house rentals are quite the thing to do at Virginia Beach. Rentals vary greatly in size, cost, and degree of luxury, so research possibilities thoroughly. Local agents include **Long and Foster Real Estate** (✉*317 30th St., Virginia Beach* ☎*757/428–4600 or 800/941–3333*) and **Siebert Realty** (✉*601 Sandbridge Rd., Virginia Beach* ☎*757/426–6200 or 877/422–2200* ⊕*www.siebert-realty.com*). **Virginia Beach Reservations** (☎*800/822–3224*) can make a reservation in your choice of about 75 hotels.

$ ⌂**Cavalier Hotels.** In the quieter north end of town, this 18-acre resort
★ complex combines the original Cavalier Hotel of 1927, a seven-story redbrick building on a hill, with an oceanfront high-rise built across the street in 1973. The clientele is about evenly divided between conventioneers and families. F. Scott and Zelda Fitzgerald stayed regularly in the original hotel. If you stay in the hilltop building you can see the water—and get to it easily by shuttle van or a short walk. The newer building overlooks 600 feet of private beach. There's a fee for tennis, but the other athletic facilities are free. **Pros:** great choice of people who appreciate historic properties. **Cons:** might be too staid for spring-break students. ✉*Atlantic Ave. at 42nd St.* ☎*757/425–8555 or 888/746–2327* ⊕*www.cavalierhotel.com* ⇆*400 rooms* ⌂*In-room: Ethernet, dial-up. In-hotel: 5 restaurants, tennis courts, pools, gym, beachfront, no-smoking rooms* ☰*AE, D, DC, MC, V.*

$$$$ ⌂**Hilton Virginia Beach Oceanfront.** This Hilton opened in 2005 and is the only four-star hotel in Virginia Beach. Towering 21 stories over the oceanfront, it has shops, three restaurants, and a rooftop bar and infinity pool. The seafood restaurant Catch 31 has gotten good reviews, and there is great outdoor seating overlooking the boardwalk. At night the bar is a happening scene for thirtysomethings. Most rooms have

balconies with panoramic views. **Pro:** a luxury hotel with all the amenities. **Con:** the priciest choice in Virginia Beach. ✉*3001 Atlantic Ave.* ☎*757/213–3000* ⊕*www.hiltonvb.com* ↪*290 rooms* ⚘*In-room: Wi-Fi. In-hotel: 3 restaurants, pool, gym, public Wi-Fi* ☰*AE, D, MC, V.*

$–$$ 🖥**Wyndham Virginia Beach Oceanfront.** With its 17-story tower, the for-
★   mer Ramada Plaza Resort Oceanfront, has been sold to private owners who promise a renovation of the 1960s-era high-rise. Rooms that
do not face the ocean directly have either a partial view or overlook
the swimming pool. The modern lobby has a skylighted atrium. The
Surf Club Ocean Grill, serves—predictably—seafood. The hotel offers
a children's program. **Pros:** the Wyndham Virginia Beach accepts pets
(additional fee), but only if the reservation is made directly through the
hotel. **Cons:** the hotel is north of the main action on the boardwalk.
✉*57th St. at oceanfront* ☎*757/428–7025 or 800/365–3032* ⊕*wynd-ham.com* ↪*243 rooms* ⚘*In-room: safe, refrigerator. In-hotel: restau-rant, bar, pool, gym, children's programs (ages 5–13), laundry service, no-smoking rooms* ☰*AE, D, DC, MC, V.*

NIGHTLIFE

Harpoon Larry's (✉*24th St. at Pacific Ave.* ☎*757/422–6000*) is a local
watering hole with true character, not a tourist trap. Don't be surprised
to see a great white shark staring back at you as you eat a juicy piece
of that shark's cousin (mahimahi) stuffed with fresh Chesapeake Bay
crabmeat, or enjoy raw oysters and a cold Corona. There's free nightly entertainment from April through Labor Day weekend at the 24th
Street stage or 24th Street Park on the boardwalk. **Murphy's Grand Irish
Pub and Restaurant** (✉*2914 Pacific Ave.* ☎*757/417–7701*) has entertainment every night in summer and Tuesday–Saturday during winter—
there's typically an Irish musician or two.

SPORTS AND THE OUTDOORS

GOLF   There are several public golf courses in Virginia Beach, some with moderate fees. All charge more for nonresidents and have varying fees,
depending upon the day of the week and start time. **Honey Bee Golf Club**
(✉*2500 S. Independence Blvd.* ☎*757/471–2768*) has green fees of
$30–$60 weekdays and $44–$69 weekends. **Kempsville Greens Municipal
Golf Course** (✉*4840 Princess Anne Rd.* ☎*757/474–8441*) is a municipal
course and the least expensive: weekdays $18–$23, weekends $24–$28,
not including cart.

WATER   **Back Bay Getaways** (✉*Sandbridge* ☎*757/721–4484*) has a variety of
SPORTS   kayak rentals and tours, pontoon boats, surfboards, and Jet Skis in the
Sandbridge area. **Lynnhaven Dive Center** (☎*757/481–7949*) leads dives
and gives lessons. Their boats are at Rudee Inlet. **Wild River Outfitters**
(☎*757/431–8566 or 877/431–8566*) has guided kayak tours, moonlight paddles, river tours, dolphin tours, and more.

Travel Smart
Essential South

WORD OF MOUTH

"We used to drive from Louisiana to Boston each summer. A good route would be to first head west from New Orleans to Cajun Country. . . . Then head on up to I-10 and take it east to the MS Gulf Coast. . . . Then, travel east to the Destin/Ft. Walton Beach area. Spend a day or two at some of the best beaches in America. From there, I'd head north up to Atlanta. Go to a Braves game, tour the aquarium, [and] visit the CNN Center. . . . Spend the next two nights in Asheville, NC, and hike in the Smoky Mountains. . . . Then, I'd head on down to Charleston, SC. . . . Spend two nights there, touring the historic city. From there, I'd make my way to the Outer Banks of NC, and stay a night there. This allows you to visit the key Southern cities [and] sample the coast and the mountains."

— bkluvsNola

GETTING HERE AND AROUND

If you don't have a specific goal in mind—seeing a particular city or national park, or spending time at one coastal resort—the easiest way to explore the South is to confine your trip to two or three states and follow a somewhat linear route through them by car, making stops along the way. Another option is to take the hub-and-spoke approach, flying into one of the major cities like Charlotte, Atlanta, or New Orleans and spending a few days in that city and its surrounding area before heading to a different city.

If you're planning to spend more than several days and visit more than a couple of cities, you might consider driving your own car rather than flying in and renting one—especially if you live anywhere within 500 mi of the region (i.e., the mid-Atlantic states, the Midwest, the lower Plains states, and Texas) and you're traveling with three or more in your group. Even if you have to spend a night at a motel on your way there and back, you'll save a considerable amount of money on airfare and car rentals.

If coming by plane, plan to fly into one of the South's major airports, where fares tend to be considerably lower than at smaller, regional facilities. For example, the sheer competition and wealth of connections at Atlanta's busy Hartsfield-Jackson Atlanta International Airport makes it an excellent choice—Atlanta is less than 500 mi from virtually every town in the South and within 300 mi of Savannah, Charleston, Charlotte, Asheville, Knoxville, Nashville, Birmingham, and Montgomery. Charlotte Douglas International Airport, in North Carolina, is probably the second-most central airport geographically. Less central but also with a wide range of connections and generally reasonable fares are the airports in New Orleans, Memphis, and Nashville.

TRAVEL TIMES	BY AIR	BY CAR
Atlanta to New Orleans	1½ hours	6½–7 hours
Nashville to Memphis	1 hour	3 hours
Memphis to New Orleans	1¼ hours	6 hours
Atlanta to Charleston	1 hour	5 hours
Charlotte to Atlanta	1 hour	4 hours
Charlotte to Nashville	1½ hours	6½–7 hours
Richmond to Atlanta	1½ hours	8½ hours

▮ AIR TRAVEL

Flying time to Atlanta is 2½ hours from New York, 2 hours from Chicago, 4½ hours from Los Angeles, 2 hours from Dallas, and 9 hours from London.

AIRPORTS

Atlanta's Hartsfield-Jackson Atlanta International Airport (ATL) is by far the biggest hub in the South, with the most national and international connections. Many travelers flying into the Carolinas are likely to pass through here, and most indirect flights within the region make their connections here.

North Carolina's Charlotte Douglas International Airport (CLT), near the border of North Carolina and South Carolina, is the closest major airport to the Great Smoky Mountains National Park. In the center of North Carolina is Raleigh-Durham International Airport (RDU), a prime gateway into central and eastern part of the state. South Carolina's busiest airports are Columbia Metropolitan Airport (CAE), which is mid-state, and Charleston International Airport (CHS), which serves the coast.

Virginia, is, of course, very well connected to the world thanks to its proximity to Washington D.C., which has several international airports and is only an hour or so by car from Fredericksburg and the towns ringing Shenandoah National Park. Richmond International Airport (RIC), however, is much more central to the state's many attractions, including Colonial Williamsburg and the coast. That said, depending on where you're flying from, fares into Richmond International are sometimes more expensive than those to one of D.C.'s major airports.

In Tennessee, Nashville International Airport (BNA) sees a lot of traffic and has some of the region's only nonstop connections to the West Coast and Canada; however, Memphis International Airport (MEM) is something of a hub within the South, offering more nonstop connections to East Coast, Southern, and Midwestern cities.

Florida has several major international airports, but it's Orlando International Airport (MCO), mid-state, that is the best gateway to the Daytona Beach area and the Kennedy Space Center. Orlando is four hours from Tallahassee—the eastern entry point to the panhandle—so to visit that area you're better off flying into Jacksonville International Airport (JAX), which is two hours west of Tallahassee, or one of the small regional airports in Tallahassee or Pensacola.

Airport Information Birmingham-Shuttlesworth International Airport (BHM) (☎ 205/595-0533 ⊕ www.bhamintl-airport.com). Blue Grass Airport (LEX) (☎ 859/425-3114 ⊕ www.bluegrassairport. com). Charleston International Airport (CHS) (☎ 843/767-1100 ⊕ www.chs-airport. com). Charlotte Douglas International Airport (CLT) (☎ 704/359-4000 ⊕ www. charlotteairport.com). Columbia Metropolitan Airport (CAE) (☎ 803/822-5000 ⊕ www.columbiaairport.com). Hartsfield-Jackson Atlanta International Airport (ATL) (☎ 404/530-7300 ⊕ www.atlanta-airport. com). Jackson-Evers International Airport (JAN) (☎ 601/939-5631 ⊕ www.jmaa.com). Jacksonville International Airport (JAX) (☎ 904/741-4902 ⊕ www.jia.aero). Louis Armstrong New Orleans International Airport (MSY) (☎ 504/464-0831 ⊕ www.flymsy. com). Louisville International-Standiford Airport (SDF) (☎ 502/367-4636 ⊕ www. flylouisville.com). Memphis International Airport (MEM) (☎ 901/922-8000 ⊕ www. mscaa.com). Nashville International Airport (BNA) (☎ 615/275-1675 ⊕ www.nashintl. com). Orlando International Airport (MCO) (☎ 407/825-2001 ⊕ www.orlandoairports. net). Raleigh-Durham International Airport (RDU) (☎ 919/840-7700 ⊕ www.rdu. com). Richmond International Airport (RIC) (☎ 804/226-3000 ⊕ www.flyrichmond.com).

FLIGHTS

Hartsfield-Jackson Atlanta International Airport is the primary hub of Delta Airlines and AirTran Airways—both airlines connect Atlanta to all major U.S. cities. US Airways has a hub at North Carolina's Charlotte Douglas International Airport. Memphis is a regional hub for Northwest Airlines, which also offers a good number of connections from Atlanta, Charlotte, and Orlando to the Midwest and West Coast.

Airline Contacts AirTran (☎ 770/994-8258 or 800/247-8726 ⊕ www.airtran. com). American Airlines/American Eagle (☎ 800/433-7300 ⊕ www.aa.com). Delta Airlines (☎ 800/221-1212 ⊕ www.delta.com). JetBlue (☎ 800/538-2583 ⊕ www.jetblue. com). Northwest Airlines (☎ 800/225-2525 ⊕ www.nwa.com). US Airways/US Airways Express (☎ 800/428-4322 for U.S. and Canada reservations, 800/622-1015 for international reservations ⊕ www.usairways.com).

■ BUS TRAVEL

Within most large Southern cities, it's possible to use municipal bus service to get around town, but relatively few nonlocals go this route—bus schedules and routes take a bit of learning, and many Southern cities sprawl to a degree that sightseeing this way is impractical.

▌ CAR TRAVEL

A car is your most practical means of traveling around the South, especially if you plan to cover more than two states, explore areas outside major cities, or visit National Parks or wilderness areas (a car is essential for seeing the Great Smoky Mountains). The only exception is a trip centered primarily in New Orleans, where you can get by with a combination of public transportation and cabs. Atlanta, Savannah, Charleston, Myrtle Beach, Nashville, Memphis, and Asheville can be explored fairly easily on foot or by using public transit and cabs, but a car is helpful to reach many of the most intriguing museums, parks, restaurants, and lodgings nearby.

INTERSTATE TRAVEL

If you want to make good time, there are three major interstates serving the region. I–95, which begins in Maine, runs south through the Mid-Atlantic states and enters Florida just north of Jacksonville. It continues south past Daytona Beach and the Space Coast ending in Miami. I–75 begins in Michigan at the Canadian border and runs south through Ohio, Kentucky, Tennessee, and Georgia, then moves south through the center of the state before veering west into Tampa. California and most southern states are connected to the Gulf Coast and Florida's panhandle by I–10, which moves east from Los Angeles through Arizona, New Mexico, Texas, Louisiana, Mississippi, and Alabama; it enters Florida at Pensacola and runs straight across the northern part of the state, ending in Jacksonville.

RENTAL CARS

Rates vary from city to city, generally being lowest in major cities, where there's the greatest competition. Note that airport rentals can be nearly twice as much as mid-city rentals thanks to concession fees, additional taxes, and higher demand:

To get the best deal, check online, starting with sites like Expedia and comparing prices to those offered on individual rental agency sites. When pricing cars, ask about the location of the rental lot. Some off-airport locations offer lower rates, and their lots are only minutes from the terminal via complimentary shuttle. Also ask whether certain frequent-flyer, AAA, corporate, or other such promotions are accepted and whether the rates might be lower the day before or after you had originally intended to travel. Remember to ask about required deposits, cancellation penalties, and drop-off charges if you're planning to pick up the car in one city and leave it in another, and reserve the car well in advance of your expected arrival.

Major Agencies Alamo (☎ *800/462–5266* ⊕ *www.alamo.com*). **Avis** (☎ *800/331–1212* ⊕ *www.avis.com*). **Budget** (☎ *800/527–0700* ⊕ *www.budget.com*). **Hertz** (☎ *800/654–3131* ⊕ *www.hertz.com*). **National Car Rental** (☎ *800/227–7368* ⊕ *www.nationalcar.com*).

ROAD CONDITIONS

Most roads in the mountains are well maintained, and warning signs alert you to dangerous curves and steep grades, but driving in wilderness areas—even on main national park roads—poses some challenges. You probably won't need a four-wheel-drive or high-clearance vehicle for basic exploration, but if you plan to do a lot of mountain driving, make sure your car is up to the challenge. In winter double-check road conditions in mountainous areas—the Newfound Gap Road through the Great Smoky Mountains National Park and higher elevation sections of the Blue Ridge Parkway are often closed in winter due to snow and ice.

RULES OF THE ROAD

Speed limits vary from state to state and from rural to urban areas, so check posted speeds frequently. The South is laced with busy interstate highways; limits on urban interstates are 55–70 mph while limits on rural interstates are 65–70 mph. Speed limits on main roads through national park areas are typically 35–45 mph, though speed limits on secondary park roads or Forest Service roads may be as low as 10 or 15 mph.

On weekdays between 6 and 10 AM and again between 4 and 7 PM expect heavy traffic, especially in big cities such as Atlanta, New Orleans, and Charlotte. To encourage carpooling, some freeways have special lanes for so-called high-occupancy vehicles (HOV)—cars carrying more than one passenger.

Drivers over the age of 18 are allowed to use cell phones while driving in all states in the South. In North Carolina drivers must have wireless headsets to use a cell phone on the road.

Motorcyclists are required to wear helmets in Alabama, Georgia, Louisiana, Mississippi, North Carolina, Virginia, and Tennessee. Florida, Kentucky, and South Carolina have partial helmet laws, requiring them only for riders under the age of 21.

Unless signs prohibiting the practice are posted at an intersection, you may make right turns on red in all states. Always strap children under age 3 into approved child-safety seats.

SCENIC HIGHWAYS

Although you'll make the best time traveling along the South's extensive network of interstate highways, keep in mind that U.S. and state highways offer some delightful scenery and the opportunity to stumble upon funky roadside diners, leafy state parks, and historic town squares. Although the South is rural, it's still densely populated, so you'll rarely drive for more than 20 or 30 mi—even on local roads—without passing roadside services, such as gas stations, restaurants, and ATMs.

Among the most scenic highways in the South, consider the following: the **Natchez Trace,** from Natchez, Mississippi, to just south of Nashville, Tennessee; **U.S. 78** from Memphis, Tennessee, across northern Mississippi and Alabama to near Augusta, Georgia; the **Great River Road** through southern Louisiana's Cajun Country; **U.S. 61** from New Orleans north through the Mississippi Delta to Memphis; **U.S. 441, 321, 25, 19, 74,** and 64 through the Smoky Mountains of eastern Tennessee and western North Carolina; **U.S. 17** from Brunswick, Georgia, along the coast through South Carolina and North Carolina; and the **Blue Ridge Parkway** from the eastern fringes of the Smoky Mountains through western North Carolina into Virginia.

■ TRAIN TRAVEL

Amtrak has a number of routes that pass through the South; several lines run from the northeast throughout Virginia, the Carolinas, and Georgia—the *Silver Meteor* and *Silver Star* lines run all the way from New York City to Miami. From New York, the *Crescent* arches inland to hit Atlanta and Birmingham before connecting with New Orleans. The *Sunset Limited,* which spans the country from Los Angeles to Orlando, connects New Orleans with the Gulf Coast and Florida's panhandle.

Amtrak offers a USA Rail Pass, available for 15-, 30-, or 45-day periods for $389–$749. Amtrak also has senior citizen, children's, disability, and student discounts, as well as occasional deals that allow a second or third accompanying passenger to travel for half price or even free. The Amtrak Vacations program customizes entire vacations, including hotels, car rentals, and tours.

Train Information Amtrak (☎ *800/872-7245* ⊕ *www.amtrak.com).*

ESSENTIALS

∎ ACCOMMODATIONS

With the exception of Atlanta, New Orleans, Savannah, and Charleston, most lodging rates in the South fall below the national average. All major chains are well represented in this part of the country, both in cities and suburbs, and interstates are lined with inexpensive to moderate chains. It's not uncommon to find clean but extremely basic discount chains offering double rooms for as little as $50 to $60 nightly along the busiest highways.

In cities and some large towns you might want to forgo the usual cookie-cutter modern hotel in favor of a historic property—there are dozens of fine old hotels throughout the South, many of them fully restored and quite a few offering better rates than chain properties that may have comparable amenities but nowhere near the ambience.

Rates can vary a great deal seasonally. Gulf and Atlantic Coastal regions as well as the Smoky Mountains tend to have significantly higher rates in summer, and New Orleans peaks in fall and spring (especially during Mardi Gras). Many Southern cities, including New Orleans, drop their rates a bit during the extremely hot summer months, when vacationers are more likely to flock to the mountains or the sea.

BED-AND-BREAKFASTS AND INNS

Historic bed-and-breakfasts and inns are found in just about every region in the South, including quite a few former plantation houses and lavish Southern estates. In many rural or less touristy areas, B&Bs offer an affordable and homey alternative to chain properties, but in tourism-dependent destinations you can expect to pay about the same or more for a historic inn as for a full-service hotel. Many of the South's finest restaurants

are also found in country inns. Although many B&Bs and smaller establishments offer a low-key, homey experience without TVs or numerous amenities, the scene has changed greatly in recent years, especially in cities and upscale resort areas, where many such properties now attempt to cater to business and luxury leisure travelers with in-room data ports, voice mail, whirlpool tubs, and DVD players. In keeping with the South's fondness for filling meals, quite a few inns and B&Bs serve substantial full breakfasts—the kind that may keep your appetite in check for the better part of the day.

Reservation Services Bed & Breakfast.com (☎ 512/322–2710 or 800/462–2632 ⊕ www. bedandbreakfast.com). **Bed & Breakfast Inns Online** (☎ 615/868–1946 or 800/215–7365 ⊕ www.bbonline.com). **BnB Finder.com** (☎ 212/432–7693 or 888/547–8226 ⊕ www. bnbfinder.com).

CABINS AND CAMPGROUNDS

With the Great Smoky, Shenandoah, and Blue Ridge Mountain ranges, the South has no shortage of great campsites. Good beach camping, often in secluded, primitive sites, can be found along Georgia's Atlantic Coast, Florida's panhandle, and on the Gulf Coast islands. Not all campsites take reservations (most are first-come, first-served), but for those that do, book as far in advance as possible, especially in the summer high season.

The National Park Service (⊕ www.recreation.gov) handles reservations for sites within national parks and monuments, including the Great Smoky Mountains National Park. (Note that the very popular Elkmont, Smokemont, Cades Cove, and Cosby sites within the Great Smokies require reservations from May 15 to October 31, and fill up quickly.) Some of the best tent camping in the region, particularly in the Carolinas and Georgia, is in state parks. For detailed information and to reserve spots, visit the state parks' Web sites.

Mountain cabins, from deluxe private homes to simple bunkhouses, are available through federal and state reservation sites, as well as through individual owners; park-run cabins can often be rented on a nightly basis, privately owned cabins may require weeklong stays. Vacation Rentals by Owner (⊕ *www.vrbo.com*) is a good resource for private rentals.

Contacts Alabama State Parks (☎ *800/252–7275* ⊕ *www.alapark.com/camping*). **Georgia State Parks** (☎ *800/864–7275* ⊕ *gastateparks.org*). **Great Smoky Mountains National Park** (☎ *877/444–6777* ⊕ *www.nps.gov/grsm*). **Gulf Islands National Seashore Camping** (☎ *877/444–6777* ⊕ *www.nps.gov/guis/planyourvisit/camping-on-the-islands.htm*). **Kentucky State Parks** (☎ *800/255–7275* ⊕ *parks.ky.gov*). **Mississippi State Parks** (☎ *800/467–2757* ⊕ *mississippistateparks.reserveamerica.com*). **North Carolina State Parks** (☎ *919/ 733–4181* ⊕ *www.ncparks.gov*). **South Carolina State Parks** (☎ *866/345–7275* ⊕ *www.southcarolinaparks.com*). **Tennessee State Parks** (☎ *888/867–2757* ⊕ *www.state.tn.us/environment/parks*). **Virginia Department of Conservation and Recreation** (☎ *800/933–7275* ⊕ *www.dcr.virginia.gov/state_parks/cabgen.shtml*).

▌CHILDREN IN THE SOUTH

Most of the South is ideal for travel with kids. It's an enjoyable part of the country for family road trips, and it's also relatively affordable—you'll have no problem finding inexpensive kid-friendly hotels and family-style restaurants. Just keep in mind that a number of fine, antique-filled bed-and-breakfasts and inns punctuate the landscape, and these places are less suitable for kids—many flat-out refuse to accommodate children. Also, some of the quieter and more rural parts of the region—although exuding history—lack child-oriented attractions.

Favorite destinations for family vacations in the South include Cajun Country around Lafayette, the Gulf Coast from Mississippi to Alabama, the Atlantic seaboard from Georgia through the Carolinas (especially Myrtle Beach and the Outer Banks), Opryland and the country-music sites in Nashville, the outstanding aquarium in Atlanta, the space and rocket center in Huntsville, Mud Island and the Civil Rights Museum in Memphis, and the many lively attractions strung throughout the Smoky Mountains from Chattanooga and Knoxville east to Asheville. You might guess that upscale historic cities such as Charleston and Savannah cater primarily to adults, but these towns also have plenty of museums and attractions geared toward children, as does New Orleans, although parts of the French Quarter are inappropriate—especially at night—for youth.

Places that are especially appealing to children are indicated by a rubber-duckie icon (🦆) in the margin.

▌DISCOUNTS AND DEALS

Most airlines, and consolidators like Travelocity, offer fly-drive packages, which may save you some money on rental cars. In big cities, look for discount visitor passes on public transit and stop at visitor centers for free maps, brochures, and discount coupons.

If you plan on visiting several national parks and federal historic sites—particularly ones with per person fees—you might want to purchase a National Parks America the Beautiful pass, valid for admission to any park for one year. Seniors especially should look into this option, as a lifetime pass costs only $10.

▌EATING OUT

Although certain ingredients and preparations are common in Southern cooking, the genre as a whole varies greatly not only from state to state but also from county to county. Nevertheless, in the South you'll often find restaurants serving black-eyed peas, catfish, chitterlings (fried intestines), corn on the cob, crab claws, coleslaw, crawfish, fried chicken, hush puppies, fried green tomatoes, grits, collard greens, chicken-fried steak, raw and fried shellfish (especially oysters and shrimp), and desserts infused with pecans, peaches, peanuts, caramelized bananas, or sweet potatoes.

More specific regional influences include similar but distinct Creole and Cajun cuisines of southern Louisiana, the soul food served in many African-American households, the coastal recipes of the Lowcountry in the Carolinas, and, of course, barbecue. The preparation of this latter delicacy differs tremendously, depending on whether you're in the Mississippi Delta, central Tennessee, the pine flats of North Carolina, or some other part of the South. Depending on where you are, you might find it prepared with shredded pork in a tomato-vinegar-based sauce, or perhaps with a mustard-based sauce and chicken or beef. The South's myriad culinary disciplines intermingle and influence one another, but Southern foodies are quite careful to recognize and preserve the localized distinctions among them.

You're also likely to encounter hearty and filling, if at times greasy, cuisine at most of the affordable luncheonettes, diners, and family-style eateries that proliferate in rural, suburban, and urban areas. Over the past couple of decades, most Southern cities—especially boomtowns such as Atlanta, Charleston, New Orleans, Savannah, and Charlotte—have partaken of the nation's culinary revolution. In these parts you'll discover regional ingredients and time-honored recipes alongside inventive twists and foods and styles borrowed from myriad faraway places, from Latin America to the Mediterranean. Chefs who dabble in such creative practices often dub their fare "New" or "Modern" Southern. It's no gimmick. Some of America's finest culinary talents operate restaurants in the South, in big cities, of course, but also in a

WORD OF MOUTH

Was the service stellar or not up to snuff? Did the food give you shivers of delight or leave you cold? Did the prices and portions make you happy or sad? Rate restaurants and write your own reviews or start a discussion about your favorite places in the Forums on ⊕ www.fodors.com. Your comments might even appear in our books. Yes, you, too, can be a correspondent!

surprising number of tiny, off-the-beaten-path hamlets.

■ TIP→ Always remember when you order an iced tea in the South to specify if you want it unsweetened.

■ GAY AND LESBIAN TRAVEL

Attitudes about gays and lesbians tend toward disapproving or intolerant in parts of the South, especially outside urban areas. On the whole, however, despite a reputation for conservative-minded residents, this part of the country is not any more hostile or dangerous for lesbians and gays—traveling solo or together—than the rest of the United States. It's prudent, however, to show an awareness of your surroundings and exercise a degree of discretion whenever you're venturing into unfamiliar territory.

As for lesbian and gay resources, there are several major newspapers serving the community throughout the South, including *Southern Voice* (⊕ www.southern-voice.com), in Atlanta, *Ambush* (⊕www.ambushmag.com), in New Orleans, and a host of smaller local papers in Memphis, Nashville, Birmingham, and the Carolinas. The gay nightlife and social scenes in New Orleans and Atlanta rival those of virtually any comparably sized cities in North America, and you'll also find thriving gay communities of varying sizes in Savannah, Charlotte, Charleston, Raleigh/Durham, Nashville, Memphis, Birmingham, and Columbia. With a much lower profile than most cities with gay populations, Asheville is something of a well-kept secret, with sizable women's and gay communities and a high number of gay-friendly businesses and accommodations.

▌HEALTH

There are relatively few health issues specific to the South. Hospitals are as common and medical care as proficient as elsewhere in the United States.

In coastal regions, especially along the Atlantic seaboard, swimmers and boaters should be respectful of the at-times powerful surf. Adhere to posted riptide warnings, and, to be perfectly safe, stick with areas that have lifeguards. Summers can be exceptionally hot and humid throughout much of the South—wear light-colored, loose-fitting, practical clothing during the summer months, drink plenty of fluids (and bring along bottled water on hikes, boat trips, and bike rides), and stay indoors during the hottest times of the day.

Mosquitoes, seasonal blackflies, and just about every other flitting and annoying insect known to North America proliferates in the humid and often lush Southern states. Exercise common precautions and wear lotions or sprays that keep away such pests.

Although you might associate Lyme disease with New England, where it was first well documented, this relatively common and potentially dangerous disease strikes frequently in the South, too. Lyme disease is spread by bites from infinitesimal deer ticks. Symptoms, unfortunately, vary considerably from victim to victim, and one common problem is delayed diagnosis—the longer you go without treating this problem, the more severe its effects.

Most victims show a red-ring-shaped rash around the bite from the deer tick, somewhat resembling a little bull's-eye and appearing from a week to many weeks after the incident. Flulike symptoms often follow—fever, achy joints, and swelling—and, if left untreated for more than a couple of months, chronic arthritis may set in.

When spending time in areas where tick infestation is a problem, wear long-sleeved clothing and slacks, tuck your pants legs into your boots and/or socks, apply tick and insect repellent generously, and check yourself carefully for signs of ticks or bites. It's a good idea to don light-colored clothing, as you'll have an easier time sighting ticks, which are dark. Remember that the more commonly found wood ticks do not carry the disease, and that deer ticks are extremely small—about the size of a pinhead.

▌HOURS OF OPERATION

Hours differ little in the South from other parts of the United States. Banks are usually open weekdays from 9 to 3 and some Saturday mornings, the post office from 8 to 5 weekdays and often on Saturday morning. Shops in urban and suburban areas, particularly in indoor and strip malls, typically open at 9 or 10 daily and stay open until anywhere from 6 PM to 10 PM on weekdays and Saturday, and until 5 or 6 on Sunday. It's a good idea to confirm Sunday hours, especially in smaller towns and for boutiques or specialty shops, even in large cities. Hours vary greatly, so call ahead when in doubt.

On major highways and in densely populated areas you'll usually find at least one or two supermarkets, drugstores, and gas stations open 24 hours, and in a few big cities and also some college towns you'll find a smattering of all-night fast-food restaurants (Waffle House is especially popular in the South among the 24/7 chain eateries), diners, and coffeehouses. In Atlanta a handful of nightclubs are open 24 hours on weekends, and in New Orleans bars are permitted to remain open and serve booze around the clock.

Most major museums and attractions in big cities are open daily or six days a week (with Monday being the most likely day of closing). Hours are often shorter on Saturdays and Sundays. The South also has scads of smaller museums—historical societies, small art galleries, highly specialized collections—that open only a few days a week and sometimes by appointment only during the winter or slow season.

∎ MEDIA

There's no major regional newspaper that serves the South, but the *Atlanta Journal-Constitution* (⊕*www.ajc.com*) and New Orleans's *Times-Picayune* (⊕*www.timespicayune.com*) rank among the most influential dailies in the region; just about every city with a population of greater than 40,000 or 50,000 also publishes its own daily paper.

Most major cities have very good alternative newsweeklies with useful Web sites and copious information on area dining, arts, and sightseeing—these are usually free and found in restaurants, coffeehouses, bookstores, tourism offices, hotel lobbies, and some nightclubs. Of particular note is Atlanta's *Creative Loafing* (⊕*atlanta.creativeloafing.com*), which has a separate edition for Charlotte, North Carolina (⊕*charlotte.creativeloafing.com*). Also check out the *Birmingham Weekly* (⊕*www.bhamweekly.com*); the *Louisville Eccentric Observer* (⊕*www.leoweekly.com*); New Orleans's *Gambit Weekly* (⊕*www.bestofneworleans.com*); Jackson, Mississippi's *Jackson Free Press* (⊕*www.jacksonfreepess.com*); Durham, North Carolina's *Independent Weekly* (⊕*www.indyweek.com*); Music City's *Nashville Scene* (⊕*www.nashvillescene.com*); Charlottesville, Virginia's *C-ville* (⊕*www.c-ville.com*); and Richmond's *Style Weekly* (⊕*www.styleweekly.com*).

Monthly *Southern Living* magazine (⊕*www.southernliving.com*) gives a nice sense of travel, food, and lifestyle issues relevant to the region. And local lifestyle magazines—including *Atlanta* (⊕*www.atlantamagazine.com*), *Louisiana Life* (⊕*www.louisianalife.com*), *New Orleans* (⊕*www.neworleansmagazine.com*), *Charleston Magazine* (⊕*www.charlestonmag.com*), *Louisville* (⊕*www.loumag.com*), and *Memphis* (⊕*www.memphismagazine.com*)—offer colorful stories and dining and entertainment coverage.

∎ MONEY

As with most of the United States, credit and debit cards are accepted at the vast majority of shops, restaurants, and accommodations in the South. Common exceptions include a handful of small, independent stores and also B&Bs in more rural areas. Banks—as well as convenience stores, groceries, and even nightclubs—with ATMs are easy to find in just about every community.

ITEM	AVERAGE COST
Mid-range chain hotel in Nashville	$80–$144 per night
Daily visitor pass on public transportation	$5–$12
National parks admission	Free–$10
Sandwich	$5–$8
One-mile taxi ride in New Orleans	$2.60 plus $1.60 per mile
Museum admission in Atlanta	$15–$25
Half-day Gulf Coast fishing trip	$450

The cost of living and traveling throughout most of the South is either slightly lower or comparable to that of most of the United States and is significantly cheaper than in many urban areas such as metropolitan San Francisco, New York, and Chicago. Although the cost of living remains fairly low in most parts of the South, travel-related costs (such as dining, lodging, museums, and transportation) have become increasingly steep in

Nashville, New Orleans, and Atlanta over the years and can also be high in coastal communities throughout Virgina, Georgia, the Carolinas, and Florida.

Prices throughout this guide are given for adults. Substantially reduced fees are almost always available for children, students, and senior citizens.

CREDIT CARDS

Throughout this guide, the following abbreviations are used: **AE**, American Express; **D**, Discover; **DC**, Diners Club; **MC**, MasterCard; and **V**, Visa.

∎ NATIONAL PARKS

The South yields many well-visited national parks, monuments, seashores, and forests. Probably the most famous is the swath of the Appalachians that comprises the 800-acre Great Smoky Mountains National Park—the park straddles the eastern Tennessee and western North Carolina borders and contains some 16 peaks higher than 6,000 feet. Hiking, camping, and boating are among park visitors' favorite activities. Shenandoah National Park in Virginia features more than 100 mi of the Appalachian Trail, as well as a long scenic drive with views of the Blue Ridge Mountains.

At the other extreme, at least vertically speaking, are the several national parks that lie along the Atlantic coastline, as well as the Gulf Islands National Seashore, a 150-mi-long chain of islands that stretches from the coast of Mississippi to Pensacola, Florida. In coastal Alabama bird-watchers flock to Bon Secour National Wildlife Refuge. The top Atlantic shore parks are Pea Island National Wildlife Refuge and Cape Hatteras and Cape Lookout national seashores, in North Carolina; Cumberland Island National Seashore and Okefenokee National Wildlife Refuge, in Georgia; and Fort Sumter National Monument, in South Carolina.

Information **National Park Service** (⊕ *www. nps.gov*).

∎ PACKING

There was a time, not too long ago, when any traveler planning to enjoy fine dining or the cushy confines of a luxury hotel in the South had to pack semiformal attire. As with the rest of the country, however, restaurants or hotel lobbies that require or even appreciate men dressed in jackets and ties and women in dresses have nearly disappeared. With a few formal exceptions, most of them in New Orleans and Atlanta, smart but casual attire works fine wherever you go.

Much of the South has hot, humid summers and sunny, mild winters. For colder months, pack a lightweight coat, slacks, and sweaters; you'll need heavier clothing in the more northerly states, where cold, damp weather prevails and snow is not unusual. Keeping summer's humidity in mind, pack absorbent natural fabrics that breathe; bring an umbrella, but leave the plastic raincoat at home. You'll want a jacket or sweater for summer evenings and for too-cool air-conditioning. And don't forget insect repellent and sun screen.

∎ TAXES

Sales taxes in the South are as follows: Alabama, Georgia, and Louisiana, 4%; North Carolina, 4.5%; Mississippi, 7%; South Carolina, 6%; and Florida, Kentucky, and Tennessee, 6%. Most municipalities also levy a lodging tax (from which small inns with only a few rooms are usually exempt, but rules vary regionally), and in some cases a restaurant tax. The hotel taxes in the South can be rather steep, greater than 10% in Georgia, Tennessee, and many counties in North Carolina.

∎ TIME

Georgia, the Carolinas, and eastern Tennessee fall in the Eastern Standard time zone (EST), three hours ahead of California, the same as New York and Florida. Western Tennessee, Alabama, Mississippi,

and Louisiana fall in the Central Standard time zone (CST), the same as Chicago and Dallas. The Florida Panhandle is split between the two time zones.
Time Zones Timeanddate.com (⊕ *www.time-anddate.com/worldclock*)

▌ VISITOR INFORMATION

For general information and brochures before you go, contact the state tourism bureaus.

Visitor Information Alabama Bureau of Tourism and Travel (☏ *334/242-4169 or 800/252-2262* ⊕ *www.touralabama. org*). **Florida Commission on Tourism** (☏ *850/488-5607* ⊕ *www.visitflorida.com*). **Georgia Department of Industry, Trade and Tourism** ☏ *800/847-4842* ⊕ *www.georgia. org/travel*). **Kentucky Department of Tourism** (☏ *502/564-4930 or 800/225-8747* ⊕ *www. kentuckytourism.com*). **Louisiana Office of Tourism** (☏ *225/342-8119 or 800/677-4082* ⊕ *www.louisianatravel.com*). **Mississippi Division of Tourism** (☏ *601/359-3297 or 866/733-6477* ⊕ *www.visitmississippi.org*). **North Carolina Travel and Tourism Division** (☏ *919/733-8372 or 800/847-4862* ⊕ *www.visitnc.com*). **South Carolina Department of Parks, Recreation, and Tourism** (☏ *803/734-1700 or 866/224-9339* ⊕ *www.discoversouthcarolina.com*). **Tennessee Department of Tourist Development** ☏ *615/741-2159 or 800/836-6200* ⊕ *www. tnvacation.com*). **Virginia Tourism Corporation** (☏ *804/786-2051 or 800/847-4882* ⊕ *www.virginia.org*).

FODORS.COM CONNECTION

Before your trip, be sure to check out what other travelers are saying in the Forums on ⊕ *www.fodors.com*

ONLINE TRAVEL TOOLS
HISTORY AND CULTURE
Civil War Traveler (⊕ *www.civilwartraveler. com*) has information about Civil War sites in the Carolinas and Georgia, as well as in other states. **Doc South** (⊕ *docsouth.unc.edu*) is a vast collection of historical documents and archives on Southern history, culture, and literature. The online edition of **Southern Living** (⊕ *www.southernliving.com*) has many articles on travel, attractions, gardens, and people in the region.

PARKS AND NATIONAL FORESTS
The **Appalachian Trail Conservancy** (⊕ *www.appalachiantrail.org*) is dedicated to preserving the nation's longest footpath, which runs from Georgia all the way to Maine. The **Blue Ridge Parkway Association Guide** (⊕ *www.blueridgeparkway.org*) has detailed information on one of the most beautiful roads in the United States. The **National Park Service** (⊕ *www.nps.gov*) has information on all of the national parks in the region, including the Great Smoky Mountains, the country's most popular national park.

INDEX

Photo credits:
8, Jason A. Wright/Shutterstock. 9 (left), J C Hix/Shutterstock. 9 (right), James Stuart Griffith/Shutterstock. 10, Jason Gobble. 11 (left), Stephen VanHorn/Shutterstock. 11 (right), Andrew F. Kazmierski/Shutterstock. 12, Jeff Kinsey/Shutterstock. 13, iofoto/Shutterstock. 14, Joao Virissimo/Shutterstock. 15 (left), Chet Mitchell/Shutterstock. 15 (right), SSS Photos Inc./Shutterstock. 16, Justin Leedy/wikipedia.org. 17 (left), U.S. Army Corps of Engineers/wikipedia.org. 17 (right), Monmouth Plantation. 18, JustASC/Shutterstock. 19 (left), Monmouth Plantation. 19 (right), Anne Hornyak/wikipedia. org. 20, David Jones/wikipedia.org. 21 (left), Lori Monahan Borden/Shutterstock. 21 (right), Niels Gerhardt/Shutterstock. 22, Colonial Williamsburg Foundation. 24, Samot/Shutterstock. 25, Melinda Fawver/Shutterstock. 26, William Struhs/Spoleto Festival USA. 27 (left), Terry Poche/Shutterstock. 27 (right), Ryankindelan/wikipedia.org. 28, Marie C. Fields/Shutterstock.

ABOUT OUR WRITERS

A journalist for 25 years, Liz Biro has covered everything from local fisheries to capital politics. Today Liz writes about food and dining for various publications, including the *Star-News* in Wilmington, N.C., and the statewide *North Carolina Signature* magazine. She updated the North Carolina coast.

Former Fodor's editor Carissa Bluestone has contributed to numerous guidebooks—most recently *Fodor's Mexico* and *Fodor's Pacific Northwest*—and has written for *Concierge.com* and *TravelandLeisure.com*. She updated the Travel Smart Essential South chapter of this book.

Michelle Delio, who updated the sights for New Orleans, splits her time living in Miami, New York City, and the Big Easy. A freelance editor, Michelle also contributes to *Fodor's New York City, Essential USA,* and *Florida.*

Born and raised in the Shenandoah Valley of Virginia, Mary Erskine left the mountains for the beaches of South Carolina in 2000. Her work has been featured along the South Carolina coast as a writer, designer, and editor. For this guide, she focused on the Grand Strand region, including Myrtle Beach.

Paul A. Greenberg, who updated New Orleans' dining and lodging, is a New Orleans-based writer and the Program Director for Journalism and Media Arts at Tulane University.

Rena Havner Philips loves to travel. So when the opportunity arose to write about her home state of Alabama, she jumped at it. Philips, a reporter for the *Press-Register* in Mobile, had her son, Logan, between edits of this book. She and her husband are now looking forward to a new type of travel, with their son in tow.

Molly Jahncke updated sights in New Orleans. Back in her hometown New Orleans and doing public affairs work for Delgado Community College, Molly still has a passion for freelance travel writing and globetrotting.

Alice Leccese Powers edits literary anthologies for Random House and writes guidebooks and innumerable articles for national magazines and newspapers. She lives in Washington, D.C., and updated the Historic Triangle and Virginia Beach sections of Virginia.

Snowbird Susan MacCallum-Whitcomb spends as much time as possible in the South. Little wonder: winters in her Nova Scotian hometown can be *looong*. Having already contributed to more than a dozen Fodor's guide books, she jumped at the chance to write the Front Matter for *Fodor's Essential South*'s first edition.

Gary McKechnie, who reported on the Panhandle, knows a lot about his native Florida, having worked as a Walt Disney World ferryboat pilot, Jungle Cruise skipper, steam-train conductor and double-decker bus driver. A two-time Lowell Thomas Travel Journalism Award winner, he writes for Harley-Davidson and is the author of *Great American Motorcycle Tours* and *National Geographic's USA 101.*

Amy McKeever spent most of her youth in Northern Virginia, when she wasn't traveling Europe as a Foreign Service brat. She has worked for the *Northern Virginia Journal, National Geographic Traveler* magazine and is now a D.C.-based freelance travel and culture writer. She updated the Northern Virginia sections.

Amber Nimocks is a North Carolina native who lives in downtown Raleigh with her husband, son, and two dogs. She writes a wine column for *The News & Observer* and is a contributing editor for *Edible Piedmont* magazine. She updated Charlotte and the Triangle sections of North Carolina.

Donna M. Owens is an award-winning free-lance journalist who happily juggles roles as a multimedia reporter, producer, and editor. Her byline has appeared in such outlets as NPR, the *Chicago Tribune*, *Baltimore Sun*, *O, the Oprah Magazine*, *Essence*, and AOL. A frequent globetrotter, she's based in Baltimore and worked on the Virginia chapter.

David Parker Jr., who updated the Nightlife section of New Orleans, is a fiction writer and journalist who contributes regularly to NOLAFugees.com.

As Managing Editor at *Gambit Weekly* newspaper in New Orleans, **Kandace Power Graves** keeps her finger on the pulse of the city's ever-changing retail and business landscape. With her passion for local shops and boutiques, Kandace was the perfect person to update the shopping section of New Orleans.

Michael Ream is a travel writer who has filed stories from three continents. His work has appeared in publications including *Southern Traveler*, *Saveur*, *Forbes* and *Travel Thru History.com*. Previously, he contributed to *Fodor's Texas* and *Fodor's Essential USA*, where he wrote about the Ozarks. He updated the Tennessee and Mississippi chapters.

Susan Reigler is a former travel writer and restaurant critic at the Louisville *Courier-Journal* and is the author of *Compass American Guides: Kentucky*, *Adventures in Dining: Kentucky Bourbon Country* and *The Complete Guide to Kentucky State Parks*. She lives in Louisville and updated the Kentucky chapter.

Asheville native and former New Orleans newspaper editor **Lan Sluder** has written a half-dozen books, including travel guides to Belize and the coast of the Carolinas and Georgia. He has also contributed to other Fodor's guides, including *Fodor's Belize* and *In Focus Great Smoky Mountains National Park*. Lan updated the Great Smoky Mountains and Asheville sections of this book.

Her family's move from Connecticut to South Carolina earned **Eileen Robinson Smith** the distinction of being Yankee-born and Southern-raised. A former editor of *Charleston* magazine, she has written for local, regional, and national publications such as *Latitudes* and *Sky*. For this guide she returned to her beloved Lowcountry, updating Charleston, Savannah, and Hilton Head.

A Yankee by birth, Northeast writer **Kerry Speckman** moved to Jacksonville, Florida in the early 1980s and has been basking in the sun and Southern hospitality ever since. She's a freelance travel writer who has written for *Zagat* and *AAA Going Places* and is a contributing writer to *Jacksonville Magazine*. She updated Daytona Beach and the Space Coast sections.

Sue Strachan is a freelance writer, as well as the public relations director for the Ogden Museum of Southern Art in New Orleans. She loves to travel, and she journeyed to Louisiana's Cajun and Plantation regions to revise those sections in the Louisiana chapter.

Christine Van Dusen may be a Yankee by birth, but she's a Southerner at heart, living in Atlanta for almost eight years with her husband and two dogs. The founder of Linchpin Media, she's an award-winning journalist whose work has appeared in numerous publications, including the *Atlanta Journal-Constitution*, *Atlanta Magazine*, *Creative Loafing Atlanta*, *Charlotte Magazine*, *US Weekly*, *Paste*, and *The Progressive*. She updated the Atlanta and Coastal Isles and the Okefenokee sections.

Ginger Warder grew up in Virginia horse country, and when she wasn't riding, she was on a boat or skiing behind one in the Potomac River. An active member of the Society of American Travel Writers, she updated Charlottesville, Shenandoah National Park, Richmond, and Fredericksburg, Virginia.